Cape Cod
Martha's Vineyard & Nantucket
AN EXPLORER'S GUIDE

Cape Cod
Martha's Vineyard & Nantucket
AN EXPLORER'S GUIDE

KIM GRANT

with photographs by
the author

Fourth Edition

The Countryman Press
Woodstock, Vermont

Dedication

For Lisa M. Otero,
to whom I'm deeply grateful

ISBN 0-88150-491-2
ISSN 1533-6875

Cover design by Bodenweber Design
Cover photograph and all interior photographs
   by Kim Grant
Text design by Glenn Suokko
Maps by Paul Woodward, © 2001 The
   Countryman Press

Published by The Countryman Press,
   P.O. Box 748, Woodstock, Vermont 05091

Distributed by W. W. Norton & Company, Inc.,
   500 Fifth Avenue, New York, NY 10110

Printed in the United States of America

10 9 8 7 6 5 4 3 2 1

Explore With Us!

Welcome to the fourth edition of the most comprehensive guide to Cape Cod, Martha's Vineyard, and Nantucket. I have been highly selective but broadly inclusive, based on years of repeated visits, cumulative research, and ongoing conversations with locals. All entries—attractions, inns, and restaurants—are chosen on the basis of personal experience, not paid advertising.

I hope you find the organization of this guide easy to read and use. The layout has been kept simple; the following pointers will help you get started.

WHAT'S WHERE

In the beginning of the book you'll find an alphabetical listing of special highlights and important information that you can reference quickly. You'll find advice on everything from where to find the best art galleries, to where to hop onto bicycle trails, to where to take a whale-watching excursion.

LODGING

Prices: Please don't hold us or the respective innkeepers responsible for the rates listed as of press time in 2001. Changes are inevitable. At the time of this writing, the state and local room tax was 9.7 percent. Please also see *Lodging* under "What's Where on Cape Cod, Martha's Vineyard, and Nantucket."

RESTAURANTS

In most sections, note the distinction between Dining Out and Eating Out. Restaurants listed under *Eating Out* are generally inexpensive and more casual; reservations are often suggested for restaurants in *Dining Out*. A range of prices for à la carte menu items is included with each entry.

GREEN SPACE

In addition to trails and walks, "green space" also includes white and blue spaces, that is, beaches and ponds.

KEY TO SYMBOLS

❋ The "off-season" icon appears next to appealing off-season or year-round lodging or attractions.

❦ The "special-value" icon appears next to lodging entries, restaurants, and activities that combine exceptional quality with moderate prices.

❀ The "child and family interest" icon appears next to lodging entries, restaurants, activities, and shops of special appeal to youngsters and families.

❀ The "pet-friendly" icon appears next to lodging where pets are welcome.

☂ The "rainy-day" icon appears next to things to do and places of interest that are appropriate for foul-weather days.

& The "handicap" symbol indicates establishments that are truly wheelchair accessible.

Author's Choice: I have indicated my recommendations for don't-miss attractions, lodging, and dining by highlighting entries with a gray box.

I appreciate comments and corrections about places you discover or know well. You may e-mail me at kgrantfoto@aol.com or address your correspondence to Explorer's Guide Editor, The Countryman Press, P.O. Box 748, Woodstock, VT 05091.

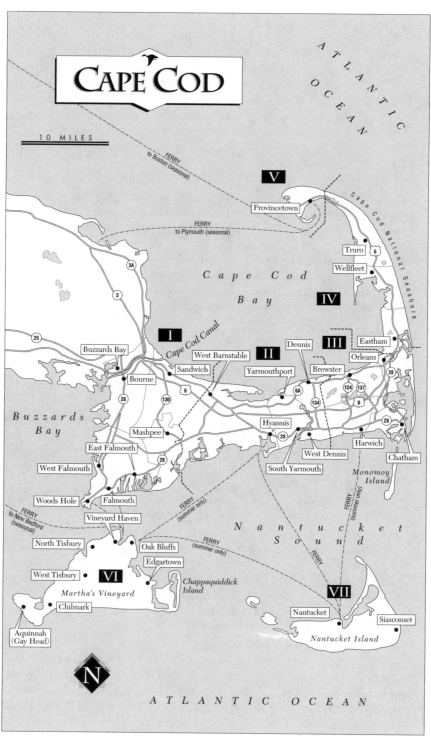

Contents

List of Maps

Introduction

Welcome to the fourth edition of *Cape Cod, Martha's Vineyard, and Nantucket: An Explorer's Guide.*

Developments in the dissemination of travel information are occurring at lightning speed. Thanks to the Internet, consumers have never had so much information at their fingertips. The access is unprecedented, and that's great. But with it, my job has changed from describing places to providing "decision assistance," as my colleague Tom Brosnahan likes to say. I have personally visited every place in this guide and hope it helps you determine where best to spend your hard-earned dollars and precious vacation time.

During the course of researching this edition, I began to detect a troubling trend. When I was seeking information from establishments, too many, in my opinion, were too quick to say, "Look at my web site." Too many wouldn't answer questions because they thought they didn't need my help "promoting" their businesses. Their web sites bring them all the business they need, they reasoned. Visitors can get all the information they need without a travel writer as intermediary, they reason. Perhaps. But my responsibility is not to promote their businesses and is greater than simply collecting information. I am in a position to ferret out the great from the good, to assess those intangible qualities that make a vacation memorable. What I am looking for when I research a place to stay, for instance, is how personable and friendly the innkeepers are; how service-oriented the staff are; how clean the rooms are. Those factors can't be measured by looking at a web page. Proprietors are constantly surprised when I tell them that I don't consult web sites. I'd rather visit a place. And thankfully, you appreciate the difference, since sales of this guide have increased about 20 percent with each edition. We can tell that you value independent assessment. And we're grateful.

The publishers and I take reader feedback seriously (to comment, please use the postcard included in this book). Some of you have mentioned that you want even more restaurant reviews. So I have provided more. But there are dozens and dozens of eateries along Route 28, for instance, that I don't review. You can trust that I've investigated every single one of them, and have chosen the best in each range, from budget to expensive, from family-friendly establishments to places for a romantic rendezvous.

Businesses do not pay to be included in this guide. In fact, I am often asked by restaurateurs and lodging owners, "How much does it cost to take out an ad in your book?" The answer, of course, is: "Nothing. If you do your job well and there is a market for it, I include you." Inevitably they follow up with, "Well, how do you make any money? Other guidebooks charge us for inclusion." The answer is simple. To paraphrase an old Smith-Barney advertisement, "We make money the old-fashioned way: We earn it"—by doing thorough research, and by our readers, in turn, valuing our advice enough to spend 19 bucks on it.

One other significant way this guide differs from the competition is that I alone have researched and written it since 1994. What that means to you, the reader, is that when I say a place is the best clam shack on the Cape, you know that I have visited them all. Many other guidebooks dispatch a team of researchers to various parts of the Cape; when these authors write that a place is the best clam shack on the Cape, what they really mean is, "This is the best clam shack in the territory I was assigned for this edition." Furthermore, because I have written every edition of this book since its inception, you will benefit from insights I have gained over the course of many years of research.

By most accounts and calculations, almost 120,000 cars cross the Cape Cod Canal every day in July and August, and the ferries to Martha's Vineyard and Nantucket transport more than 2.4 million people each summer. So it would be a stretch of the imagination to say that these fragile parcels of prized real estate are undiscovered or unexplored. In fact, sometimes it seems there isn't a grain of sand that hasn't been written about.

But just when I think I've seen it all, a ray of bright, clear sunlight will hit the Provincetown dune shacks in such a way as to make them seem new again. I'll strike up a conversation with a historical society curator, and she'll regale me with stories about town affairs at the turn of the century. I'll walk down a trail in October that I previously walked in May and hear different birds and see different plants. Or I'll take a walking tour with Dirk Roggeveen in Nantucket, and he'll find just the right anecdote to make history jump off a ship captain's logbook.

There is certainly no lack of information about Cape Cod, Martha's Vineyard, and Nantucket. But the way I see it, there are a few big problems with the material. Some stem from its abundance, and many of the compilations are overwhelming and undiscriminating. (You could fill file cabinets with the stuff—trust me, I have!) Much of what passes for editorial recommendation is actually just paid advertising copy written by the establishments themselves. Catchall web sites are certainly the same. Who do you suppose pays for the site to be put together and maintained? And finally, many of the special-interest brochures—for antiquing or kids' activities, for instance—cover the entire area. So if you're just visiting one town or concentrating on one region, you must wade through a lot of extraneous information.

This guidebook is intended to be many things to many people. The publishers and I have set our sights to include a wide audience. This book is written for people who live close enough, or are fortunate enough, to be able to make many short trips to the Cape throughout the year—people who know that the region takes on a whole different character from Labor Day weekend to Memorial Day weekend. (It is a common misconception that the region closes down from mid-October to mid-May.) It will prove valuable, as well, to year-rounders who must give advice to a steady stream of summer guests. It's for Cape residents who may live on the Upper Cape, but don't know much about the Lower Cape. It's for people whose only trip to the Cape or the islands is their annual summer holiday—people who have always vacationed in Wellfleet, let's say, but are ready to explore other places. My highest hope, though, is to introduce the "other Cape and islands" to that segment of the traveling public that assumes traffic jams, crowded beaches, and tacky souvenir shops define the region.

This book is the result of years of research, conversation, observation, pleasure reading, and personal exploration. I am a Bostonian who spent youthful summer vacations on Cape Cod, bicycling at the Cape Cod National Seashore, eating saltwater taffy in Provincetown, and camping on Martha's Vineyard. My introduction to Nantucket came later, in the mid-1980s; by then I was old enough to appreciate the island's sophisticated culinary treats and rich history all the more.

Since I am also a professional photographer, I am pleased to supplement my written observations and recommendations with a visual portrait. I have intentionally emphasized the region's tranquility; conventional wisdom already associates the Cape with masses of humanity. But the photos are proof, really, that there are beaches where you can walk alone on a sunny September day.

Traveling, and writing about it, is a nice lifestyle; there's no doubt about that, and I'm grateful for the opportunity to do it. But it is work (as my friends and family, temporarily abandoned in favor of my laptop computer, will attest). The book wouldn't have been possible without the encouragement, guidance, and firsthand experience of many people who appreciate the Cape and the islands from many different perspectives.

As much as I love both four-star dining and a bucket of fried clams from a shack on the pier, I just can't eat every dish on every menu. I have called upon my innkeeper friends, who benefit from the collective opinions of dozens of guests who eat in dozens of places night after night and then discuss their experiences the next morning over breakfast. Likewise, it is impossible to sleep in every room in every B&B, but I can assure you that I have personally visited and inspected every establishment in this guide.

The folks at The Countryman Press (a division of W. W. Norton) epitomize everything that's good about the publishing industry. I appreciate their responsiveness to and respect for writers, as well as their commitment to providing a quality guidebook to the book-buying public. My special appreciation goes out to managing editor Ann Kraybill, who is both a friend and a pleasure to work with; to Jennifer Goneau, who worked so hard to put this book together; and to Emily Webb, the publicity maven who makes sure the books reach you, my readers. And thanks to Norton, for its decision to allow these *Explorer's Guides* to carry on in their great tradition.

As with all editions, this one benefits from the accumulated knowledge that fellow explorers have shared with me, through letters and over breakfast at B&Bs.

For their local expertise and willingness to share it with me, thanks go out to Lynette Molnar and Frank Schaefer in Provincetown; Sue and Dan Hamar in Wellfleet; Nan Aitchison in Eastham; the Vessellas and Johnsons in Orleans; Jan McMaster in Chatham; Carol and Tom Edmondson in Brewster; Joyce Roth in Harwich; Marie Brophy in Dennis; Gerrie and Milt Graham, Valerie Butler, and Nancy Hamilton in Yarmouth; Bill Putman in Hyannis; Ken Traugot in West Barnstable; Caroline and Jim Lloyd in Falmouth; Elaine Dickson in Sandwich; Bob and Caroline Taylor and Sandy Knox-Johnston on Nantucket; Carl Buder on Martha's Vineyard. I also cannot underestimate the enthusiasm and fact checking provided by most towns' chamber of commerce staffs.

I welcome readers' thoughtful comments, criticisms, and suggestions for the next edition of *Cape Cod, Martha's Vineyard, and Nantucket: An Explorer's Guide*. Feel free to contact me at kgrantfoto@aol.com.

Suggested Itineraries

IF YOU HAVE 3 DAYS
 Thanks, in particular, for buying this book. It contains much more information than you'll ever be able to use. We hope you pass this book along to a friend after it serves you well.

IF YOU HAVE 5 DAYS
 You'll need to be efficient. Visit the village of Sandwich, poke around antiques and artisan shops on Route 6A, and drive down scenic bayside roads north of Route 6A, spending two nights mid-Cape. On the third morning, pop down to Main Street and the lighthouse in Chatham, and then head to the Outer Cape and the famed Cape Cod National Seashore beaches, stopping at the Salt Pond Visitor Center in Eastham. Spend two nights on the Outer Cape (or in Orleans): visit galleries in Wellfleet, walk the Atlantic beaches and short nature trails, and take a day trip to Provincetown.

IF YOU HAVE 7 DAYS
 You'll end up with a very enjoyable trip. Spend three nights mid-Cape and three on the Outer Cape. Do all of the above, plus linger longer in Sandwich, visiting the Glass Museum and/or Heritage Plantation. Add a beach walk at Barnstable's Sandy Neck Beach and/or Nauset Beach in Orleans. Visit the Cape Cod Museum of Natural History in Brewster and/or the Wellfleet Bay Wildlife Sanctuary. Spend a day and a half in Provincetown—watching people, walking Commercial Street, ducking into art museums and the informative Provincetown Museum, taking in a sunset from Race Point or Herring Cove, boarding a whale watch excursion.

IF YOU HAVE 10 DAYS
 You'll be very happy. Allot the entire three additional days (from the above plan) to Martha's Vineyard. (Trying to see the Vineyard in one day borders on silliness.) Or add a night or two in the diverse Falmouth/ Woods Hole area and a night in bustling Hyannis, the staging ground for a day trip to Nantucket. Back on the Cape, get out on the water with a trip to Monomoy Island in Chatham or some other boat tour. Add a couple of whistle stops at the Cape's small, sweet historic museums.

IF YOU HAVE TWO WEEKS
 You're really lucky. Allot three days to one of the islands. Add a quiet

canoe or kayak paddle somewhere. Take a leisurely bike ride or an aerial sightseeing flight. Get tickets to summer stock and cheer on the home team at a free baseball game. Slip into a parking space at Wellfleet's Drive-In. Investigate an old cemetery. Take an art class. Visit Mashpee's Indian sites and South Cape Beach State Park.

IF YOU LIVE ON THE CAPE & ISLANDS

You're the luckiest of all. Scribble comments in the margins of this book and loan it to visiting friends so you don't have to keep repeating yourself. Explore something new at least once a week. Isn't that one reason you live here?

What's Where on Cape Cod, Martha's Vineyard, and Nantucket

AREA CODE
The area code for the region of Cape Cod, Martha's Vineyard, and Nantucket is **508.**

AIRPORTS AND AIRLINES
There is regularly scheduled air service from Boston to Provincetown. Hyannis (Barnstable County Municipal Airport) is reached by air from Boston, Providence, and New York. Nantucket and Martha's Vineyard enjoy regularly scheduled year-round service; **Cape Air** (1-800-352-0714; www.flycapeair.com) offers the most flights. Sight-seeing by air is best done in Chatham, Barnstable, and Provincetown.

ANTIQUARIAN BOOKS
Among the many shops on Route 6A, four are great: **Titcomb's Book Shop** in Sandwich; **Punkhorn Bookshop** and **Kings Way Books and Antiques** in Brewster; and **Parnassus Book Service** in Yarmouthport. I also recommend **Isaiah Thomas Books & Prints** in Cotuit.

ANTIQUES
Antiques shops are located all along Route 6A, on the 32-mile stretch from Sandwich to Orleans, but there is an especially dense concentration in Brewster, often called Antique Alley. You'll also find fine antiques shops in

Sandwich Center, Barnstable, Chatham, and Nantucket. Look for the complete supplement "Arts & Antiques" in the *Cape Cod Times* or the free directory published by the **Cape Cod Antique Dealers Association,** available at on-Cape antiques stores.

AQUARIUMS
The **Woods Hole Science Aquarium** is small but it is an excellent introduction to marine life. There is also the small **Maria Mitchell Association Aquarium** on Nantucket.

ART GALLERIES
Wellfleet and Provincetown are the centers of fine art on the Cape. Both established and emerging artists are well represented in dozens of diverse galleries. Artists began flocking to Provincetown at the turn of the 20th century, and the vibrant community continues to nurture creativity. The islands also

attract large numbers of artists, some of whom stay to open their own studios and galleries. Chatham, Nantucket, and Martha's Vineyard also have many fine galleries.

On-Cape, pick up a copy of "Arts & Antiques," a very complete supplement published by the *Cape Cod Times*.

ATTIRE

The Cape and the islands are casual for the most part; a jacket and tie are rarely required. At the other end of the spectrum, you'll always need shoes and shirts at beachfront restaurants.

AUCTIONS

Estate auctions are held throughout the year; check the newspapers. Among the venues are: **Sandwich Auction House; Eldred's Auctions** in East Dennis; and **Rafael Osona** in Nantucket. Just a few of the benefit auctions include: the **Fine Arts Work Center Annual Benefit Silent Auction** and the **AIDS Support Group Auction** in Provincetown; an auction held by the **Truro Center for the Arts at Castle Hill;** and the celebrity-studded **Possible Dreams Auction** on Martha's Vineyard.

BASEBALL

The 10-team **Cape Cod Baseball League** was established in 1946. Only players with at least one year of collegiate experience are allowed to participate. Wooden bats are supplied by the major leagues. In exchange for the opportunity to play, team members work part time in the community, live with a community host, and pay rent. Carlton Fisk and the late Thurman Munson are just two alumni of the Cape Cod League who succeeded in the majors. Currently, about 100 major league players are former league players. Games are free and played from mid-June to mid-August; it's great fun. Baseball is listed under *Entertainment*.

KIM GRANT

BEACHES

Cape Cod National Seashore (CCNS) beaches are the stuff of dreams: long expanses of dune-backed sand. In fact, you could walk with only a few natural interruptions (breaks in the beach), as Henry David Thoreau did, from Chatham to the tip of Provincetown. My favorites on the Cape include **Sandy Neck Beach** in West Barnstable; **Nauset Beach** in Orleans; **Old Silver Beach** in North Falmouth; **Chapin Memorial Beach** in Dennis; **West Dennis Beach; Craigville Beach** near Hyannis; and all the **Outer Cape** ocean beaches. Practically all of Nantucket's beaches are public, and although the same cannot be said for Martha's Vineyard, there are plenty of places to lay your towel.

A daily parking fee is enforced from mid-June to early September; many of the smaller beaches are open only to residents and weekly cottage renters. CCNS offers a seasonal parking pass for its beaches. There is no overnight parking at beaches. Four-wheel-drive vehicles require a permit and their use is limited. Open beach fires require a permit. Greenhead biting flies plague non–Outer Cape beaches in mid- to late July; they disappear with the first high tide at the new or full moon in August, when the water level rises, killing the eggs.

Generally, beaches on Nantucket Sound have warmer waters than the Outer

Cape Atlantic Ocean beaches, which are also pounded by surf. Cape Cod Bay beaches are shallower and the water a bit cooler than Nantucket Sound beaches. Because of the proximity of the warm Gulf Stream, you can swim in Nantucket Sound waters well into September.

BICYCLING

The Cape is generally flat and there are many paved, off-road bike trails. The 26-mile **Cape Cod Rail Trail** runs along the bed of the Old Colony Railroad from Route 134 in Dennis to Wellfleet; bike trails can be found along both sides of the **Cape Cod Canal;** the **Shining Sea Trail** runs from Falmouth to Woods Hole; and bike trails can be found within the **Cape Cod National Seashore (CCNS)** in Provincetown and Truro. Nantucket is ideal for cycling, with six routes emanating from the center of town and then circling the island. Bicycling is also great on the Vineyard, but stamina is required for a trip up-island to Aquinnah. For more information, consult *Backroad Bicycling on Cape Cod, Martha's Vineyard, and Nantucket* by Susan Milton and Kevin and Nan Jeffrey (Backcountry Guides).

 Rubel Bike Maps (www.bikemaps. com) are simply the best, most detailed maps available for the Cape and islands. Rubel produces a combination Nantucket and Vineyard map ($1.95), as well as another that includes the islands, Cape Cod, and the North Shore ($4.25).

KIM GRANT

BIRD-WATCHING

The **Bird Watcher's General Store** in Orleans is on every birder's list of stops. Natural areas that are known for bird-watching include: **Monomoy National Wildlife Refuge** off the coast of Chatham; **Wellfleet Bay Wildlife Sanctuary; Felix Neck Wildlife Sanctuary** in Vineyard Haven; **Ashumet Holly and Wildlife Sanctuary** in East Falmouth; and on Nantucket, **Coatue–Coskata–Great Point.** The **Maria Mitchell Association** and **Eco Guides,** both in Nantucket, offer bird-watching expeditions, as do **Wellfleet Bay Wildlife Sanctuary** and **Monomoy National Wildlife Refuge.** Scheduled bird walks are also offered from both Cape Cod National Seashore (CCNS) visitors centers: **Salt Pond Visitor Center** in Eastham and **Province Lands Visitor Center** in Provincetown. The **Cape Cod Museum of Natural History** in Brewster is always an excellent source of information for all creatures within the animal kingdom residing on the Cape.

BUS SERVICE

The **Plymouth & Brockton** bus line (508-778-9767; www.p-b.com) serves some points along Route 6A and the Outer Cape from Boston; **Bonanza** (1-800-751-8800; www. bonanzabus.com) serves Bourne, Falmouth, Woods Hole, and Hyannis from Boston, Providence, and New York City.

CAMPING

There is no camping permitted on Nantucket, but there is still one campground on Martha's Vineyard. The Cape offers dozens of private campgrounds, but only those in natural areas are listed; the best camping is in **Nickerson State Park** in Brewster and in Truro.

KIM GRANT

CANOEING & KAYAKING

For guided naturalist trips there is no better outfitter than **Cape Cod Coastal Canoe & Kayak** in Brewster (508-564-4051; www.paddlecapecod.com; the knowledgeable owners have also written a guidebook, *Paddling Cape Cod: A Coastal Explorer's Guide* (Backcountry Guides). If you want lessons in basic paddling or to rent your own canoe, head to the **Goose Hummock Outdoor Center** in Orleans. There are also very good venues and outfitters on Martha's Vineyard and Nantucket.

CAPE COD NATIONAL SEASHORE

Established on August 7, 1961, through the efforts of President John F. Kennedy, the Cape Cod National Seashore (CCNS) stretches over 40 miles through Eastham, Wellfleet, Truro, and Provincetown. It encompasses more than 43,500 acres of land and seashore. Sites within the CCNS have been identified with "CCNS" at the beginning of the entry. The **Salt Pond Visitor Center** in Eastham and **Province Lands**

Visitor Center in Provincetown are excellent resources and offer a variety of exhibits, films, and ranger-led walks and talks. The CCNS is accessible every day of the year, although you must pay to park at the beaches in summer.

✎ CHILDREN, ESPECIALLY FOR

Within this guide a number of activities and sites that have special "child appeal" are identified by the crayon symbol "✎." When you're on the Cape, look for the free *Kids on the Cape* booklet, which gives a great overview of things to do.

KIM GRANT

CLASSES AND WORKSHOPS

Want to "improve" yourself on vacation, or brush up on some long-lost creative artistic urges? There are more programs in **Provincetown,** the **Vineyard,** and **Nantucket** than I can list here; see *To Do—Special Programs* under each town or region. As for the rest of the Cape, look into the excellent **Cooking School at the Captain Freeman Inn** in Brewster; the hands-on **Cape Cod Photo Workshops** in Eastham (where I teach); the **Wellfleet Bay Wildlife Sanctuary Adult Field School;** and myriad offerings at the **Truro Center for the Arts at Castle Hill.**

COUNTRY STORES

Old-fashioned country stores still exist on Cape Cod and the islands. Aficionados can seek out **Bournedale Country Store** in Bournedale; **The Brewster Store** in Brewster; and **Alley's General Store** in West Tisbury on the Vineyard.

CRAFTS

Craftspeople have made a living on the Cape and the islands since they began making baskets, ships, and furniture 300 years ago. The tradition continues with artists emphasizing the aesthetic as well as the functional. Today's craftspeople are potters, jewelers (particularly in Dennis), scrimshaw and bird carvers, weavers, glassblowers, clothing designers, and barrel makers. Look for the highly coveted (and pricey) lightship baskets in Nantucket, glass objects in Sandwich, Bourne, and Brewster, and barrels (yes, barrels) in Chatham. A partial list of the particularly noteworthy shops include **Woods Hole Handworks; Signature Gallery** in Mashpee; **The Spectrum** in Hyannis and Brewster; **West Barnstable Tables** and **Blacks Handweaving Shop,** both in Barnstable; **Always & Forever** in Harwichport; **Pewter Crafters** in Yarmouthport; and the **Orleans Carpenters**. There are too many artisans in Provincetown, Chatham, Nantucket, and Martha's Vineyard to detail here. The **Cape Cod Potters** publishes a small pamphlet that you can pick up in on-Cape shops and studios.

CRANBERRIES

The cranberry is one of only three native North American fruits (the other two are Concord grapes and blueberries). Harvesting began in Dennis in 1816 and evolved into a lucrative industry in Harwichport. Harvesting generally runs from mid-September to mid-October, when the bogs are flooded and ripe red berries float to the water's surface. Before the berries are ripe, the bogs look like a dense green carpet, separated by 2- to 3-foot dikes. Nantucket has

more than 200 acres of bogs, and Harwich, which lays claim to having the first commercial cranberry bog, celebrate with a **Cranberry Harvest Festival** in October. Most on-Cape bogs are located on the Mid- and lower Cape. Off-Cape, the **Cranberry World Visitors' Center** in Plymouth (508-747-2350), operated by Ocean Spray, offers tours and demonstrations about the history of cranberry cultivation and modern processing techniques.

KIM GRANT

DINING

Many fine restaurants stay open through the winter. During the off-season, many chefs experiment with creative new dishes and offer them at moderate prices. With the exception of July and August (when practically all places are open nightly), restaurants are rarely open every night of the week. The major problem for a travel writer (and a reader relying on the book) is that restaurants close depending on such unpredictable factors as weather and how many people are around. To avoid disappointment, it's best to phone ahead before setting out for a much-anticipated meal.

Expect to wait for a table in July and August, and make reservations whenever possible. Remember that many restaurants are staffed by college students who are just learning the ropes in June and who may depart before Labor Day weekend, leaving the owners shorthanded. Smaller seasonal establishments don't take credit cards.

ECOSYSTEM

This narrow peninsula and these isolated islands have a delicate ecosystem. Remember that dunes are fragile, and beaches serve as nesting grounds for the endangered piping plover; avoid the nesting areas when you see signs directing you to do so. Residents conserve water and recycle, and they hope you will do likewise.

EMERGENCIES

Call **911** from anywhere on Cape Cod.

EVENTS

The largest annual events are listed within each chapter of this book. Otherwise, invest 50¢ in the *Cape Cod Times,* which features a special section about the day's events, and on Friday a calendar supplement for the following week.

Two Cape-wide events are worth noting here. **Cape Cod Heritage Week** (508-862-0700; www.capecodcommission.org) in mid-June celebrates the cultural, historical, and environmental heritage of Cape Cod with over 100 scheduled events. The weeklong **Cape Cod Maritime Days** (mid-May; 508-862-0700; 1-888-332-2732) focuses on the region's commercial and cultural association with the sea.

The Massachusetts Office of Travel and Tourism operates a toll-free events line, **Great Dates in the Bay State,** updated every 2 weeks. Call 1-800-227-6277.

KIM GRANT

FERRIES

There are fast and slow ferries to Province-town from Boston and a day-tripper from Plymouth. To reach Martha's Vineyard, the car ferry departs from Woods Hole and passenger ferries depart from Woods Hole, Falmouth, Hyannis, New London, Connecticut, and Long Island, New York. There is a seasonal inter-island ferry. There are high-speed and slow ferries to Nantucket from Hyannis (car and passenger) and Harwich (passenger). See the appropriate chapter for details on schedules.

FISHING

You don't need a license for saltwater fishing, but you do for freshwater. Get a state license at any of the various Town Halls.

Charter boats generally take up to six people on 4- or 8-hour trips. Boats leave from the following harbors on Cape Cod Bay: Barnstable Harbor in West Barnstable; Sesuit Harbor in Dennis; Rock Harbor in Orleans; Wellfleet Harbor; and Provincetown. On Nantucket Sound, head to Hyannis Harbor, Saquatucket Harbor in Harwichport, and Chatham. You can also fish from the banks of the Cape Cod Canal and surf-fish on the Outer Cape. There are also plenty of opportunities for fishing off the shores of Nantucket and the Vineyard.

FLEA MARKETS

The two biggies are the **Wellfleet Drive-**

In Flea Market and Dick & Ellie's Flea Market in Mashpee.

GOLF
There are about 50 courses on the Cape and the islands, and because of relatively mild winters, many stay open all year (although perhaps not every day). **Highland Golf Links** in Truro is the Cape's oldest course; it's also very dramatic.

HANDICAP ACCESS
Look for the ♿ icon in the margin to find establishments that are truly wheelchair accessible.

HIGHWAYS
Route 6, also called the Mid-Cape Highway, is a speedy, four-lane, divided highway until exit 9½, when it becomes an undivided two-laner. After the Orleans rotary (exit 13), it becomes an undivided four-lane highway most of the way to Provincetown.

Scenic Route 6A, also known as Old King's Highway and Main Street, runs from the Sagamore Bridge to Orleans. It is lined with sea captains' houses, antiques shops, bed & breakfasts, and huge old trees. Development along Route 6A is strictly regulated by the Historical Commission. Route 6A links up with Route 6 in Orleans. Without stopping, it takes an extra 30 minutes or so to take Route 6A instead of Route 6 from Sandwich to Orleans.

Route 28 can be confusing. It is an elongated, U-shaped highway that runs from the Bourne Bridge south to Falmouth, then east to Hyannis and Chatham, then north to Orleans. The problem lies with the Route 28 directional signs. Although you're actually heading north when you travel from Chatham to Orleans, the signs will say: ROUTE 28 SOUTH. When you drive from Hyannis to Falmouth, you're actually heading west, but the signs will say: ROUTE 28 NORTH. Ignore

KIM GRANT

the north and south indicators, and look for towns that are in the direction you want to go.

HIGH SEASON
Memorial Day weekend in late May kicks things off, then there is a slight lull until school lets out in late June. From then on, the Cape is in full swing through Labor Day (early September). There is one exception to this, though, and it's one of the best-kept secrets for planning a Cape Cod vacation: The Cape is relatively quiet during the week following the July 4 weekend. You will find B&B vacancies and no lines at your favorite restaurant. As a rule, traveling to the Cape or the islands without reservations in high season is not recommended. Accommodations—especially cottages, efficiencies, and apartments—are often booked by January for the upcoming summer. The Cape and Islands are also quite busy from Labor Day through Columbus Day (mid-October). It's fairly common for B&Bs to be booked solid on every autumn weekend.

HISTORIC HOUSES
Every town has its own historical museum/house, but some are more interesting than others. Among the best are **Hoxie House** in Sandwich; **Centerville Historical Society Museum** and **Osterville Historical Society Museum,** both in Barnstable; **Winslow Crocker House** in Yarmouthport, operated by the Society for the Preservation of New England Antiquities

(SPNEA); **Truro Historical Museum;** and the **Provincetown Heritage Museum.** The center of Nantucket has been designated a historic district, so there are notable houses everywhere you turn; the oldest is the **Jethro Coffin House.** The **Nantucket Historical Association** publishes a walking guide to its 14 properties. Don't miss the **Martha's Vineyard Historical Society** on Martha's Vineyard.

HORSEBACK RIDING

There are a surprising number of riding facilities and trails on the Cape. Look for them in Bourne, Falmouth, Brewster, and on Martha's Vineyard.

INFORMATION

For those coming from the Boston area, Cape-wide information can be obtained at the tourist office on Route 3 (exit 5) in Plymouth (508-746-1150). It is open daily year-round (late May to mid-October 9–5, with shorter off-season hours). If you're coming from the south or west, stop at the information and rest area on Route 25 (508-759-3814), 3 miles east of the Bourne Bridge. It is open, at a minimum, daily 9–5 year-round.

There is also a year-round **Cape Cod Chamber of Commerce** information booth at exit 6 off Route 6 (508-862-0700; 1-888-332-2732; www.capecodchamber. com). In advance of your visit, write to them at P.O. Box 790, Hyannis 02601. In addition, there is a satellite booth located at a Mid-Cape rest area on Route 6 that is open 9–5 daily (at a minimum) from May through October.

LIBRARIES

The Cape and the islands boast a few libraries with world-class maritime collections and works pertaining to the history of the area: **Sturgis Library** in Barnstable; **William Brewster Nickerson Memorial Room** at Cape Cod Community College in West Barnstable; the **Atheneum** and the **Edouard A. Stackpole Library and Research Center** (a.k.a. Fair Street Research Library), both in Nantucket; and the **Martha's Vineyard Historical Society** in Edgartown on Martha's Vineyard. I have also included all town and village libraries, many of which provide Internet access. In addition to being great community resources, libraries also make great rainy-day destinations.

LIGHTHOUSES

It's a toss-up as to whether the most picturesque lighthouse is **Nobska Light** in Woods Hole or **Great Point Light** in Nantucket. (Nobska is certainly more accessible.) But there are also working lighthouses in Chatham, Eastham, Truro, and Provincetown. Nantucket and Martha's Vineyard, too, have their share of working lighthouses. For a really unusual trip, the lighthouses at Race Point in Provincetown and Monomoy Island off Chatham are available for overnights by advance reservation; see *Lodging* under each town.

KIM GRANT

LODGING

There are many choices—from inns and bed & breakfasts to cottages, apartments, and efficiencies. Rates quoted are for two people sharing one room. Cottages are rented from Saturday to Saturday. Most inns and bed & breakfasts don't accept children under 10 or 12 years of age. All accept credit cards unless otherwise noted. Pets are not accepted unless otherwise noted by our "🐾" icon in the margin. Many smaller establishments restrict smoking to outdoors. Many places require a 2-night minimum stay during the high season; holiday weekends often require a 3-night minimum stay.

LYME DISEASE

Ticks carry this disease, which has flu-like symptoms and may result in death if left untreated. Immediately and carefully remove any ticks that may have migrated from dune grasses to your body. Better yet, wear long pants, tuck pants into socks, and wear long-sleeved shirts whenever possible when hiking. Avoid hiking in grassy and overgrown areas of dense brush.

MOVIES

The **Cape Cinema** in Dennis is a special venue, but you can also find art films at the **Gaslight Theatre** in Nantucket. In addition to the standard multiplex cinemas located across the Cape, the **Wellfleet Drive-In** remains a much-loved institution. The **Nantucket Film Festival** in mid-June is a relatively new "must-see" event for independent-film buffs. Because movie-going is a popular vacation activity, I have also listed mainstream movie theaters under *Entertainment*.

MUSEUMS

People who have never uttered the words "museum" and "Cape Cod" in the same breath don't know what they're missing.

KIM GRANT

Don't skip the **Sandwich Glass Museum** and **Heritage Plantation of Sandwich,** both in Sandwich; **Museums on the Green** in Falmouth; **Aptucxet Trading Post and Museum** in Bourne Village; **Cahoon Museum of American Art** in Cotuit; **John F. Kennedy Hyannis Museum; Cape Museum of Fine Arts** in Dennis; **Cape Cod Museum of Natural History** in Brewster; **Provincetown Art Association & Museum,** the **Pilgrim Monument & Provincetown Museum,** and the **Old Harbor Lifesaving Station,** all in Provincetown; **Martha's Vineyard Historical Society** in Edgartown on Martha's Vineyard; and the **Nantucket Whaling Museum** and **Lifesaving Museum** on Nantucket.

Children will particularly enjoy the **Railroad Museum** in Chatham and the **Thornton W. Burgess Museum** in Sandwich.

MUSIC

Outdoor summertime band concerts are now offered by most towns, but the biggest and oldest is held in Chatham at **Kate Gould Park.** Sandwich offers a variety of outdoor summer concerts at **Heritage Plantation.**

Cape & Islands Chamber Music Festival (508-945-8060; 1-800-229-5739) presents fine classical and contemporary classical music at various venues across the Cape year-round. Founded by a New York City pianist in 1980, the festival includes

KIM GRANT

master classes and top-notch performances. Write or call for a schedule. The **Provincetown Playhouse Mews Series,** the **Nantucket Musical Arts Society,** and the Vineyard's **Chamber Music Society** are also excellent, albeit with much shorter seasons.

The 90-member **Cape Symphony Orchestra** (508-362-1111), based in Yarmouth, performs classical, children's, and pops concerts year-round.

There are a couple of regular venues for folk music, including the **Woods Hole Folk Music Society** and the **First Encounter Coffee House** in Eastham. Check out **Hot Tin Roof** on the Vineyard for live contemporary acts.

NATURE PRESERVES
There are walking trails—around salt marshes, across beaches, through ancient swamps and hardwood stands—in every town on the Cape and the islands, but some traverse larger areas and are more "developed" than others. For a complete guide, look for the excellent *Walks & Rambles on Cape Cod and the Islands* by Ned Friary and Glenda Bendure (Backcountry Guides). Watch for poison ivy and deer ticks; the latter carry Lyme disease.

To find some Upper Cape green space, head to: **Green Briar Nature Center & Jam Kitchen** in Sandwich; **Lowell Holly Reservation** in Mashpee; and **Ashumet**

Holly and Wildlife Sanctuary and **Waquoit Bay National Estuarine Research Reserve,** both in East Falmouth. In the Mid-Cape area, you'll find **Sandy Neck Great Salt Marsh Conservation Area** in West Barnstable. The Lower Cape offers **Nickerson State Park** in Brewster and **Monomoy National Wildlife Refuge** off the coast of Chatham. The **Cape Cod National Seashore** (CCNS) has a number of short interpretive trails on the Outer Cape, while Wellfleet has the **Wellfleet Bay Wildlife Sanctuary** and **Great Island Trail.**

On Martha's Vineyard you can escape the crowds at **Felix Neck Wildlife Sanctuary** in Vineyard Haven; **Cedar Tree Neck Sanctuary** and **Long Point Wildlife Refuge,** both in West Tisbury; and **Cape Pogue Wildlife Refuge** and **Wasque Reservation** on Chappaquiddick.

Nantucket boasts conservation initiatives that have protected one-third of the land from development, including the areas of **Coatue–Coskata–Great Point, Eel Point, Sanford Farm, Ram Pasture,** and **the Woods.**

NEWSPAPERS AND PERIODICALS
The *Cape Cod Times,* with Cape- and islandwide coverage, is published daily. The *Cape Codder* is published Tuesday and Friday and focuses on the Lower and Outer Cape. Their "What's on Cape" section is published on Tuesday and the "Weekend" section on Friday. Provincetown's weekly *Advocate* is noteworthy, as are the *Vineyard Gazette* (508-627-4311) and Nantucket's *Inquirer and Mirror* (508-228-0001).

In addition to its bimonthly magazine, *Cape Cod Life* (508-564-4466) publishes an annual guide and a "Best of the Cape & Islands" within its July edition.

❄ OFF-SEASON

In an attempt to get people thinking about visiting the Cape and the islands off-season, I have put the "❄" symbol next to activities, lodging, and restaurants that are open and appealing in the off-season.

🐾 PETS

Look for the "🐾" icon in the margin to find lodgings where your pet is welcome.

PONDS

Supposedly there are 365 freshwater ponds on Cape Cod, one for every day of the year. As glaciers retreated 15,000 years ago and left huge chunks of ice behind, depressions in the earth were created. When the ice melted, "kettle ponds" were born. The ponds are a refreshing treat, especially in August when salty winds kick up beach sand.

POPULATION

More than 200,000 people live year-round on the Cape and the islands. No one really has an accurate idea of how many people visit in summer, but it's in the millions.

RADIO

WOMR (92.1 FM) in Provincetown has diverse and great programming. Tune in to National Public Radio with WCCT (90.3 FM), WKKL (90.7 FM), or WSDH (91.5 FM). On the Vineyard tune to WMVY (92.7 FM), and on the Cape, try

KIM GRANT

WCOD (106.1 FM), WFCC (107.5 FM), and WQRC (99.9 FM).

☂ RAINY-DAY ACTIVITIES

Chances are, if it were sunny every day we would start taking the sunshine for granted. So when the clouds move in and the rain drops start falling on your head, be appreciative of the sun and look for the "☂" icon in this book, which tells you where to head indoors.

RECOMMENDED READING ABOUT CAPE COD

Henry Beston's classic *The Outermost House: A Year of Life on the Great Beach of Cape Cod* recounts his solitary year in a cabin on the ocean's edge. Cynthia Huntington's marvelous *The Salt House* updates it with a woman's perspective in the late 20th century. Also look for *The House on Nauset Marsh* by Wyman Richardson. Henry David Thoreau's naturalist classic *Cape Cod* meticulously details his mid-1800s walking tours. Josef Berger's 1937 Works Progress Administration (WPA) guide, *Cape Cod Pilot,* is filled with good stories and still-useful information. Pick up anything by modern-day naturalists Robert Finch and John Hay. Finch also edited a volume of writings by others about the Cape, *A Place Apart.* Another collection of writings about Cape Cod is *Sand in Their Shoes,* compiled by Frank

KIM GRANT

and Edith Shay. Look for *Cape Cod, Its People & Their History* by Henry Kittredge (alias Jeremiah Digges) and *The Wampanoags of Mashpee* by Russell Peters. Mary Heaton Vorse, a founder of the Provincetown Players, describes life in Provincetown from the 1900s to the 1950s in *Time and the Town: A Provincetown Chronicle*. And for children, Brian Shortsleeve has written an illustrated history book, *The Story of Cape Cod*. Look for Admont Clark's *Lighthouses of Cape Cod, Martha's Vineyard, and Nantucket: Their History and Lore* and photographer Joel Meyerowitz's *A Summer's Day* and *Cape Light*.

RECOMMENDED READING ABOUT MARTHA'S VINEYARD

Start with the *Vineyard Gazette Reader*, a marvelous "best-of" collection edited by Richard Reston and Tom Dunlop; it will give you an immediate sense of the island. *On the Vineyard II* contains essays by celebrity island residents, including Walter Cronkite, William Styron, and Carly Simon, and photographs by Peter Simon (Carly's brother). *Martha's Vineyard* and *Martha's Vineyard, Summer Resort* are both by Henry Beetle Hough, Pulitzer Prize–winning editor of the *Vineyard Gazette*. Photographer Alfred Eisenstadt, a longtime summer resident of the Vineyard, photographed the island for years. Contemporary *Vineyard Gazette* photographer Alison Shaw has two Vineyard

KIM GRANT

books to her credit: the black-and-white *Remembrance and Light* and the color collection *Vineyard Summer*.

RECOMMENDED READING ABOUT NANTUCKET

Edwin P. Hoyt's *Nantucket: The Life of an Island* is a popular history, and Robert Gambee's *Nantucket* is just plain popular. Architecture buffs will want to take a gander at *Nantucket Style* by Leslie Linsley and Jon Aron and the classic *Early Nantucket and Its Whale Houses* by Henry Chandler Forman.

ROTARIES

When you're approaching a rotary, cars already within the rotary have the right-of-way.

SEAL CRUISES

A colony of seals lounges around Monomoy, and there is no shortage of outfits willing to take you out to see them. See listings under Chatham and Wellfleet for detailed information. Chief among the operators is the **Wellfleet Bay Wildlife Sanctuary.**

SHELLFISHING

Permits, obtained from local Town Halls, are required for the taking of shellfish. Sometimes certain areas are closed to shellfishing due to contamination; it's always best to ask.

SHOPPING

Main Streets in Chatham, Falmouth, and Hyannis are well suited to walking and shopping. Commercial Street in Provincetown has the trendiest shops. Mashpee Commons features a very dense and increasingly fine selection of shops. Shopping on the Vineyard and Nantucket is a prime activity.

SUMMER CAMPS

Since the 1930s, programs all over the Cape give children opportunities to enjoy the

Cape's natural environment. Contact the **Cape Cod Association for Children's Camps,** P.O. Box 38, Brewster 02631.

SURFING AND WINDSURFING

Surfers should head to **Nauset Beach** in Orleans, **Coast Guard** and **Nauset Light Beaches** in Eastham, and **Marconi Beach** in Wellfleet. Windsurfers flock to Falmouth. The Vineyard beaches are also good for windsurfing.

SWIMMING POOLS

For a small fee, you can swim at the **Norseman Athletic Club** in Eastham and the **Nantucket Community Pool.** Swimming at the **Provincetown Inn** is free.

THEATER

Among the summer-stock and performing arts venues are **Cape Playhouse** in Dennis; **Cape Repertory Theatre** in Brewster; **Monomoy Theatre** in Chatham; **Academy Playhouse** in Orleans; **Wellfleet Harbor Actors Theater; Provincetown Repertory Theatre** and **Provincetown Theatre Company; College Light Opera Company** in Falmouth; **Barnstable Comedy Club; Harwich Junior Theatre;** the **Actors Theatre of Nantucket** and **Theatre Workshop of Nantucket;** and the **Vineyard Playhouse** on Martha's Vineyard.

TIDES

Tides come in and out twice daily; times differ from day to day and from town to town. At low tide the sandy shore is hard and easier to walk on; at high tide, what little sand is visible is more difficult to walk on. Since tides vary considerably from one spot to another, it's best to stop in at a local bait-and-tackle shop for a tide chart. For Cape Cod Canal tide information, call 508-759-5991.

KIM GRANT

TRAFFIC

It's bad in July and August no matter how you cut it. It's bumper to bumper on Friday afternoon and evening when cars arrive for the weekend. It's grueling on Sunday afternoon and evening when they return home. And there's no respite on Saturday when all the weekly cottage renters have to vacate their units and a new set of renters arrives to take their places. Call **Smart Traveler** (617-374-1234, *1 on your cellular phone) for up-to-the-minute information on traffic. This service uses remote cameras and airplanes to report current traffic conditions.

TRAINS

The **Cape Cod Scenic Railroad** runs between Sandwich and Hyannis, alongside cranberry bogs and the Sandy Neck Great Salt Marsh.

✿ VALUE

The "✿" symbol appears next to entries that represent an exceptional value.

WALKING

Cape Cod Pathways (508-362-3828), a growing network of trails linking open space in all 15 Cape Cod towns from Falmouth to Provincetown, is coordinated by the Cape Cod Commission, 3225 Route 6A, Barnstable 02630. They produce quite a comprehensive map that should be stored in the glove compartment of all explorers's cars.

Also see *Walks & Rambles on Cape Cod and the Islands* by Ned Friary and Glenda Bendure (Backcountry Guides).

WEATHER
You really can't trust Boston weather reports to provide accurate forecasts for all the microclimates between Route 28 and 6A, from the canal to Provincetown. If you really want to go to the Cape, just go. There'll be plenty to do even if it's cloudy or rainy. When in doubt, or when it really matters, call the radio station WQRC, 99.9 FM (508-771-5522).

WEB SITES
Web addresses for individual chambers of commerce, places to stay, and things to see and do are listed throughout. For general information you can look at www.capecod visit.net.

WHALE-WATCHING
Whale-watching trips leave from Provincetown Harbor, including the excellent **Dolphin Fleet Whale Watch** (508-349-1900; 1-800-826-9300), but you can also catch the **Hyannis Whale Watcher Cruises** (508-362-6088; 1-888-942-5392) out of Barnstable Harbor and the **Nantucket Whalewatch** (978-283-0313; 1-800-322-0013 within Massachusetts) from Nantucket.

WINERIES
The Cape and Islands are not Napa Valley, but you could drop in for tastings at **Truro Vineyards of Cape Cod** in Truro, **Chicama Vineyards** on Martha's Vineyard, and the **Cape Cod Winery** in East Falmouth. The **Nantucket Vineyard** (are you confused?) imports grapes to make wine.

YOUTH HOSTELS
Youth hostels are located on Martha's Vineyard, Nantucket, Eastham, and Truro. The unofficial hostel in Provincetown is dismal.

I. THE UPPER CAPE

Bourne
Sandwich
Falmouth and Woods Hole
Mashpee

KIM GRANT

Nobska Lighthouse, Woods Hole

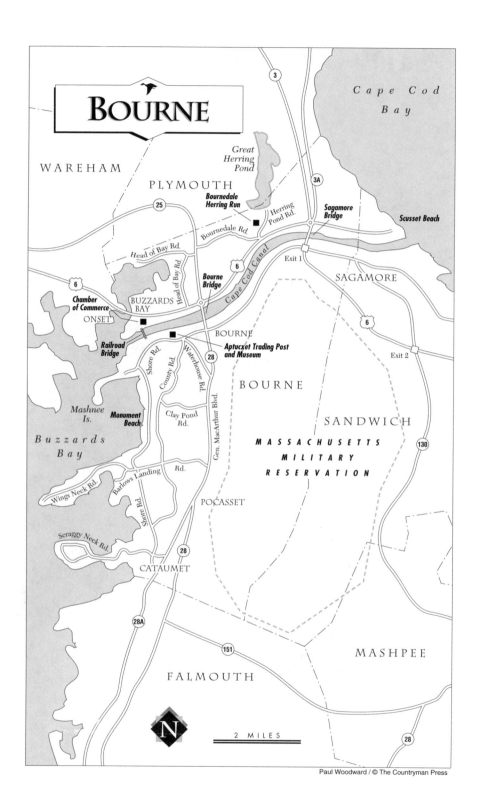

BOURNE

Cape Cod Bay

Great Herring Pond

WAREHAM

PLYMOUTH

Bournedale Herring Run

25

Herring Pond Rd.

3A

Sagamore Bridge

Scusset Beach

Bournedale Rd.

Head of Bay Rd.

6

Cape Cod Canal

Exit 1

SAGAMORE

6

Chamber of Commerce

BUZZARDS BAY

Bourne Bridge

6

ONSET

Railroad Bridge

BOURNE

28

Aptucxet Trading Post and Museum

Shore Rd.

County Rd.

Waterhouse Rd.

BOURNE

Exit 2

6

Mashnee Is.

Monument Beach

Clay Pond Rd.

Gen. MacArthur Blvd.

SANDWICH

130

Buzzards Bay

MASSACHUSETTS MILITARY RESERVATION

Barlows Landing Rd.

Wings Neck Rd.

Shore Rd.

POCASSET

Scraggy Neck Rd.

28

CATAUMET

28A

151

MASHPEE

FALMOUTH

N

2 MILES

28

Bourne

Despite summertime traffic tie-ups as you approach the Sagamore and Bourne Bridges, there's something magical about the first glimpse of them, a sure sign that you're entering a place separate from where you've been. All travelers, except those arriving by plane or boat, must pass through Bourne, over the bridges and the Cape Cod Canal.

Bourne straddles the canal, nips at the heels of Sandwich on the Cape Cod Bay side, and follows the coastline south toward Falmouth along Route 28. (All the land to the immediate east of Route 28 belongs to the Massachusetts Military Reservation.) Bourne is often completely bypassed as travelers head south to catch the Vineyard ferry from Falmouth or Woods Hole. Indeed, there is some justification for not spending a monthlong holiday here. Bourne is predominantly inhabited by year-rounders, who enjoy a quiet, rural, unhurried existence tending their gardens and their lives. But perhaps of the entire Cape, Bourne remains the most unexplored. The back roads off County and Shore Roads are lovely for bicycling, as are the peninsulas reached by Scraggy Neck Road and Wings Neck Road. Fishing, walking, and bicycling are prime activities along the Cape Cod Canal.

When Sandwich refused to grant Bourne its independence, an act of the state legislature incorporated it in 1884. Originally known for its fishing wharves, shipbuilding, and factories, Bourne quickly attracted prominent vacationers to its sandy shores. Named for an affluent resident who made his fortune during the whaling heyday, Bourne encompasses 40 square miles and consists of nine tiny villages.

Sagamore, on both sides of the canal and on Cape Cod Bay, has more in common with Sandwich; it even has a renowned glassmaking factory. Bournedale, on the "mainland" wedged between the two bridges, has a handsome country store, a diminutive old red schoolhouse, and a picturesque herring pond. And although Buzzards Bay, north and west of the Bourne Bridge, is the region's commercial center, it also offers some lovely glimpses of Buttermilk Bay. Buzzards Bay, by the way, was misnamed by inexperienced birders. If the original settlers had gotten it right, it would be called Osprey Bay today. On the western end of the canal, the Massachusetts Maritime Academy affords nice views of the canal as well as of handsome summer homes on the other side.

Across the 2,384-foot Bourne Bridge (almost twice as long as the Sagamore Bridge), the Cape villages of Monument Beach, Bourne Village, Gray Gables, Pocasset, and Cataumet are tranquil in summer and downright sleepy in winter, although many people live there year-round. The first Summer White House was in Gray Gables, where President Grover Cleveland spent the season fishing during the 1890s. Monument Beach, Cataumet, and Pocasset are pleasant, residential, seaside towns with old houses, just west of Route 28. Residents don't take much notice of visitors; they just go about their business, fishing, shopping, raising kids, and commuting to work. Cataumet Pier was the site of the nation's first labor strike, when dockworkers demanded a 100 percent pay raise in 1864, from 15¢ per hour to 30¢.

GUIDANCE

❋ **Cape Cod Canal Region Chamber of Commerce** (508-759-6000; www.capecodcanalchamber.org), 70 Main Street, Buzzards Bay 02532. At press time the chamber was unable to provide details about opening hours. Sadly, I have found this chamber to be the least helpful and knowledgeable on the Cape. I hope you have better luck. There is also a small booth at the Sagamore rotary.

❋ **U.S. Army Corps of Engineers** (USACE) Field Office (508-759-4431), Academy Drive off Main Street, Buzzards Bay 02532. Open 9–4 weekdays. Staffed by USACE personnel, the office dispenses information about boating, fishing, camping, and other canal activities. Many walks and talks are offered from early July to mid-October; see Green Space—Walks. There are also campfire programs at the Midway Recreational Area.

Herring Run Visitors Center (no phone), Route 6 on the mainland side of the canal, about a mile south of the Sagamore Bridge rotary. Open 8–dusk, year-round; staffed 9–4 in summer. Although this is the USACE's administrative building, the staff can also provide canal-related information.

The **Cape Cod Canal Recreation Hotline** (508-759-5991) is a 24-hour number with up-to-date tide, weather, and recreation information provided by the USACE.

PUBLIC REST ROOMS

You'll find them in the main chamber of commerce booth when the office is open.

GETTING THERE

By car: To reach Sagamore, take exit 1 onto Route 6A from the Sagamore Bridge. For Bournedale and Buzzards Bay, take Route 6 west at the Sagamore Bridge rotary. To reach the other villages, take the Bourne Bridge across the canal, and at the rotary take Shore Road. You can also whiz down Route 28 and head west to Pocasset, Cataumet, and Monument Beach.

By bus: **Bonanza** (1-888-751-8800; www.bonanzabus.com) operates buses from Bourne to Boston as well as Providence, New York City, and other points south and west of the Cape. The bus stops at the Tedeschi Food Shop at the Bourne Bridge rotary.

GETTING AROUND

Bourne is quite spread out, so you'll need a car to get around. The Cape Cod Canal has a great bicycle trail (see Outdoor Activities—Bicycling/Rentals).

PUBLIC LIBRARY

✸❆✞**Jonathan Bourne Public Library** (508-759-0644), 19 Sandwich Road, Bourne, is open Tuesday through Thursday 9–8, Friday and Saturday 9–5:30. Inquire about story hour and children's programs.

MEDICAL EMERGENCY

Call **911.**

TO SEE

Cape Cod Canal, 7.5 miles long, separates the mainland from Cape Cod. The canal, between 480 and 700 feet wide at various points, is the world's widest ocean-level canal. In 1623 Capt. Myles Standish, eager to facilitate trade between New Amsterdam (New York City) and the Plymouth colonies, was the first to consider creating a canal, which also would eliminate the treacherous 135-nautical-mile voyage around the tip of the Cape. George Washington brought up the idea again in the late 18th century as a means to protect naval ships and commercial vessels during war, but the first serious effort at digging a canal was not attempted until 1880, by the Cape Cod Canal Company.

For a few months, the company's crew of 500 immigrants dug with hand shovels and carted away the dirt in wheelbarrows. Then, in 1899, New York financier Augustus Belmont's Boston, Cape Cod, and New York Canal Company took over the project with more resolve. They began digging in 1909, and the canal opened to shipping five years later, on July 30, 1914. (It beat the Panama Canal opening by a scant 17 days.) On hand at the opening was then Assistant Secretary of the Navy Franklin D. Roosevelt. But the enterprise wasn't a financial success, because the canal was too narrow (it could handle only one-way traffic) and early drawbridges caused too many accidents. In 1928 the federal government purchased the canal, and the USACE built the canal we know today. The USACE has overseen the canal ever since. The canal provides a north–south shortcut for some 30,000 vessels each year, hundreds daily in summer. Water currents in the 32-foot-deep canal change direction every 6 hours.

Buzzards Bay Vertical Railroad Bridge is at the western end of the canal at the **Buzzards Bay Recreation Area.** At 270 feet high and 540 feet long, it's the third longest vertical railway bridge in the world. (Chicago, Illinois, and Long Island, New York, boast the other two.) The railroad bridge was completed the same year as the Sagamore and Bourne Bridges. When trains approach, it takes 2–3 minutes for the bridge to lower and connect with tracks on either side of it. The most reliable times to witness this event are at 5 PM and 6 PM (more or less), when trains haul trash off-Cape. Free parking. This is a good place to start the bicycle trail on this side of the canal.

Massachusetts Maritime Academy (508-830-5000), Taylors Point, off Main Street, Buzzards Bay. The academy's presence explains why you'll see so many young men with close-cropped hair jogging along the canal bicycle trail. Although tours of the 55-acre campus are no longer conducted for the general public, you can arrange to tag along on a tour for prospective merchant-marine cadets. Not only will you see the oldest maritime academy in the country (established in 1891) from an insider's perspective, but you'll also tour the 547-foot *Patriot State*, the cadets' training ship. At the end of August, freshmen learn basic skills in huge dories up on stilts on the expansive front lawn; it's quite a sight.

Aptucxet Trading Post and Museum (508-759-9487), 24 Aptucxet Road, Bourne. From the Cape-side Bourne Bridge rotary, follow signs for Mashnee Village, then Shore Road and Aptucxet Road; follow the signs. Open May to mid-October 10–5 weekdays, 2–5 Sunday (daily in July and August). Because two rivers converged here before the canal was built, English settlers thought the location perfect for a post to promote trade with their neighbors, the Wampanoag Indians and the Dutch from New Amsterdam. Furs, sugar and other staples, tools, glass, tobacco, and cloth were bought and sold; wampum (carved quahog shells made into beads) served as currency. Organized commerce was born.

The trading post you see today was built in 1930 by the Bourne Historical Society on the foundations of the original; a few bricks from the fireplace date to the Pilgrims. The hand-hewn beams and wide floor planks came from a 1600s house in Rochester, Massachusetts. On the grounds is the small Victorian railroad station used solely by President Grover Cleveland when he summered at his Gray Gables mansion in Monument Beach. You'll also find a Dutch-style windmill (which was intended merely "to add interest and beauty to the estate"), an 18th-century saltworks, an herb garden, a gift shop, and a shaded picnic area. Curator Eleanor Hammond is a treasure. Admission.

Bournedale Herring Run (508-759-4431), Route 6, about a mile south of the Sagamore rotary. Late April to early June. After the canal destroyed the natural herring run into Herring Pond, local engineers created an elaborate artificial watercourse so that the fish could migrate to the pond at spawning time. These three-year-old mature herring are returning to their birthplace. Each twice-daily tide brings thousands of the bony fish slithering upstream, navigating the pools created by wooden planks. With the aid of automated fish counters, it's estimated that upwards of 400,000 herring pass through the Bournedale run annually. Kids get a kick out of this spring ritual. During the season, this is the busiest fishing area in the state, with anglers catching their quota of herring and using them as bait for blues in the canal. Free.

&♫ **Marine Life Center** (508-759-8722; www.nmic.org), 120 Main Street, Buzzards Bay. Open 10–6 daily except Sunday; noon–6, late May to early September. Free. Plans are afoot to build a marine-animal rehabilitation hospital here for whales, dolphins, sea turtles, and seals that wash ashore on Cape Cod and need medical attention before they can be set free again. The center probably won't be ready until 2003, but it promises salt water pools, interactive exhibits, and a small science museum where we'll learn about the impact of humankind on the ocean. In the meantime, you can learn about the sea creatures that will eventually be brought here through displays, videos, artifacts, and a kids' activities table.

Briggs McDermott House & Blacksmith Shop (508-759-6120), 22 Sandwich Road, Bourne. Open 1–4 on Tuesday and Sunday mid-June to early September. This early-19th-century Greek Revival home with period gardens and a granite-walled barn is maintained by the Bourne Society for Historic Preservation. Docents discuss local architecture and former neighbor Grover Cleveland. When the house is open, blacksmiths operate the restored forge—complete with artifacts, tools, and a wagon—where President Cleveland's horses were shod.

Mashnee Island. From the Cape-side rotary of the Bourne Bridge, take Shore Road and follow signs for Mashnee Island. From the 2-mile-long causeway, there are lovely views of summer homes dotting the shoreline, sailboats on the still waters, and the distant railroad bridge and Bourne Bridge. Parking is nonexistent in summer, and as the island is private, you'll have to turn around at the end of the causeway.

Mashnee Island's celebrated, homespun Fourth of July parade consists of the current crop of island kids (and their parents) marching or riding their bikes through town.

Massachusetts Military Reservation (Otis Air Force Base) (508-968-4003), off the rotary at Routes 28 and 28A. The 21,000 acres east of Route 28 are a closed installation that contains Camp Edwards Army National Guard Training Site, Otis Air National Guard Base, the U.S. Coast Guard Air Station, the State Army Aviation complex, and the PAVE PAWS radar station, which detects nuclear missiles and tracks military satellites (it was established during the Cold War). Every other year in mid-August, Otis holds a 2-day air show and open house.

Although you won't read about it in most guidebooks, the MMR has long been designated by the Pentagon as a federal environmental "Superfund" site. Most experts agree that it will take decades to clean up the toxic Cold War–era pollutants that are contaminating an estimated 8 million gallons of groundwater a day. Other experts suggest it may be impossible to clean up the underground chemical plumes that resulted from various training exercises, landfill leaks, and oil spills.

OUTDOOR ACTIVITIES

BICYCLING/RENTALS

Cape Cod Canal. The canal is edged by level, well-maintained service roads perfect for biking. The mainland side has 7.7 miles of trail; the Cape side has about 6.5 miles. Clearly marked access points along the mainland side of the canal include the Scusset State Park off Scusset Beach Road; the Sagamore Recreation Area off Canal Road at the Sagamore rotary; near the Herring Brook Fishway in Bournedale; and beneath the Bourne Bridge. On the Cape side of the canal, there are access points from the U.S. Engineering Observation Station on Freezer Road in Sandwich; from Pleasant Street in Sagamore; and from the Bourne Bridge. If you want to cross the canal with your bike, use the Sagamore Bridge—its sidewalk is safer.

P&M Cycles (508-759-2830), 29 Main Street, Buzzards Bay. Open daily except Monday, March through December. Across from the railroad station and the canal path, this full-service bike shop rents bicycles ($10 for 2 hours or $25 per day) and offers free parking while you ride.

BOAT EXCURSIONS/RENTALS

Cape Cod Canal Cruises (508-295-3883), off Routes 6 and 28 at the Onset Bay Town Pier (a few miles west of the mainland-side Bourne Bridge rotary), Onset. Operated by Hy-Line Cruises, these 2- and 3-hour tours—with running commentary—are conducted from May to mid-October. It makes sense to experience the canal by boat. $10–12 adults, $5–6 children 5–12. There are also sunset cocktail cruises, Sunday-afternoon jazz trips, dance cruises, and a discounted family trip (children ride for free) every day at 4 PM.

Maco's Bait and Tackle (508-759-9836), at Routes 6 and 28, Buzzards Bay. Open daily April through October, Maco's rents 16-foot skiffs with motors.

FISHING

Freshwater licenses are available from the Bourne Town Hall (508-759-0613) on Perry Avenue. The banks of the Cape Cod Canal provide plenty of opportunities for catching striped bass, bluefish, cod, and pollack. Just bait your hook and cast away; no permits are required if you're fishing with a rod and line from the shore. There is no fishing, lobstering, or trolling by boat permitted on the canal.

Flax Pond and **Red Brook Pond** in Pocasset offer freshwater fishing.

See also Bournedale Herring Run under *To See*.

FOR FAMILIES

Water Wizz Water Park (508-295-3255), Routes 6 and 28, 2 miles west of the Bourne Bridge, Wareham. Open 10–6:30 daily, mid-June to early September. Southern New England's largest water park has it all: a 50-foot-high water slide with tunnels, a six-story tube ride, two more tube rides (one enclosed), a wave pool, two kiddie water parks, a river ride, and more mundane (and dry!) amusements like an arcade and mini-golf. Tickets: If you're taller than 4 feet, it's $25, otherwise it's $11; reduced admission after 4 PM.

Thunder Mine Adventure (508-563-7450), Route 28A and County Road, Cataumet. Open daily until 10 PM, late May through September. A revolving mill and flower gardens make this mini-golf park more attractive than most. It's not very challenging, but after battling with motorists at the rotaries and bridges, it might be just your speed.

Adventure Isle (508-759-2636), Route 28, 2 miles south of the Bourne Bridge. Open late May through October (daily 9 AM–11 PM in summer, Friday through Sunday 9 AM–6 PM in September and October). Diversions include go-carts, a bumper boat lagoon, laser tag, a game room, mini-golf, batting cages, a pirate ship in the kiddie area, a superslide, basketball, a little Ferris wheel, and a café after you've worked up an appetite. All-day passes cost $10.

Cartland of Cape Cod (508-295-8360), 3044 Route 6, East Wareham. Bumper boats, go-carts, an air cannon, slip track, game room, and railroad. Open daily in summer and weekends in spring and fall.

See also Cataumet Arts Center under *Selective Shopping*.

HORSEBACK RIDING

❄ **Grazing Fields Farm** (508-759-3763), 201 Bournedale Road, off Head of the Bay Road, Buzzards Bay. Private and semiprivate lessons are offered at the farm that held up the construction of I-495 in the early 1900s.

ICE SKATING

Gallo Ice Arena (508-759-8904), 231 Sandwich Road, Bourne. Call for variable public skating schedule.

SCUBA DIVING

Aquarius Diving Center (508-759-3483), 3239 Route 28, Buzzards Bay. This full-service dive shop offers rental equipment, instruction, general information, and charters that head off to explore the rocky bottom of Sandwich Town Beach (where you'll see lobsters scurrying about), the "backside" of Chatham, a wreck off Provincetown, and the Plymouth coast ($60–100 per person). Trips are usually scheduled on weekends, but in summer there are Wednesday-night dives.

SPECIAL PROGRAM

✐ **U.S. Army Corps of Engineers** (508-759-4431), Academy Drive off Main Street, Buzzards Bay. Junior ranger programs are offered for children 6–12, usually on Wednesday afternoon, from late June to early September. For 90 minutes, a different program each week explores canal history, water resources, environmental protection, water safety, and marine traffic control.

See also Cataumet Arts Center under *Selective Shopping*.

SWIMMING POOL

✐ **Bourne Scenic Park** (508-759-7873), Route 6 on the mainland side of the canal, Buzzards Bay. Open late March to late October. For a $2 day-use fee (free for children up to 18), you can swim in a saltwater swimming hole, fed by canal tides controlled by a system of floodgates. Reeds grow along the edges of the swimming hole, which has a sandy bottom and is surrounded by a chain-link fence. There are also picnic tables, a playground, and camping practically underneath the pylons of the Sagamore Bridge.

TENNIS
Public courts are located at **Bourne Memorial Community Building and Town Hall,** Shore Road in Buzzards Bay; the old **schoolhouse** on County Road in Cataumet; **Chester Park,** across from the old railroad station, Monument Beach; and **behind the fire station** on Barlow's Landing Road in Pocasset Village.

GREEN SPACE

BEACHES
Due to swift currents and heavy boat traffic, swimming is prohibited in the Cape Cod Canal.

Scusset and **Sagamore Beaches,** Cape Cod Bay, Sagamore. Both beaches are located off the Sagamore Bridge rotary via Scusset Beach Road. Facilities include changing areas and rest rooms.

Monument Beach, Buzzards Bay, on Emmons Road off Shore Road, Monument Beach. Facilities at this small beach include rest rooms and a snack bar. The warm waters of Buzzards Bay usually hover around 75 degrees in summer. Free parking.

Town Beach, Buttermilk Bay off Route 28 and Head of the Bay Road, Buzzards Bay. Free parking; no facilities.

WALKS
Cape Cod Canal. The U.S. Army Corps of Engineers (USACE; 508-759-4431), Academy Drive off Main Street, Buzzards Bay, offers numerous 1- to 2-hour guided programs from early July to mid-October. Look for walks and talks on Sagamore Hill history, managing canal maritime traffic, Bournedale history, astronomy, and dune-beach exploration. They also have biking and hiking along the canal. Call the Cape Cod Canal Recreation Hotline (508-759-5991) for up-to-the-minute recreational offerings and exact days. All free.

Red Brook Pond, Thaxter Road off Shore Road, Cataumet. Forty acres of wooded conservation land.

See also *Outdoor Activities—Bicycling/Rentals.*

LODGING

There really aren't many places to stay in this quiet corner of Cape Cod.
BED & BREAKFAST
Wood Duck Inn (508-564-6404), 1050 County Road, Cataumet 02534. This rustic 1848 farmhouse, with a sweeping lawn overlooking a cranberry bog

and on a rural road, offers one room and two suites, none of which will suit guests looking for pristine environs. Nonetheless, both suites have a separate sitting room and bedroom and a separate entrance from the rest of the bed & breakfast. The Garden Suite has stenciled walls and a king feather bed. Tree Tops, really an efficiency apartment geared to a family, has a little balcony overlooking the cranberry bog. All rooms have television, telephone, and refrigerator. In the morning innkeepers Dawn Champagne and Phil Duddy deliver a substantial breakfast-in-a-basket. There are miles of conservation paths near the inn, around the cranberry bog. May through October $99–120, $75–89 off-season. No credit cards.

CAMPGROUNDS

Bayview Campgrounds (508-759-7610), 260 Route 28 (1 mile south of Bourne) 02532. Open May to mid-October. About 50 of 430 sites are reserved for tenters, but RVers make up the majority of guests. $31 daily in-season, regardless of your sleeping quarters.

There is also camping at Bourne Scenic Park (see *Outdoor Activities—Swimming Pool*) and Scusset Beach State Reservation (see *Green Space* in "Sandwich"). Although there is no camping at the Midway Recreation Area (Route 6A on the Cape side of the canal in Bourne), **campfire programs** led by the Cape Cod Canal Rangers (508-759-4431) are held; call for days and times.

WHERE TO EAT

Despite the canal region's drive-through quality, there are a number of reasonable places to sit down and replenish your resources.

Chart Room (508-563-5350), Shipyard Lane off Shore Road at the Cataumet Marina. Open for lunch and dinner daily June through September; Thursday through Sunday in May and October. This low-slung building is well positioned on picturesque Red Brook Harbor. If you have to wait for a table—and you might, as the Chart Room does a high volume of business—there are a few Adirondack chairs and tables scattered across a short lawn. For the best sunset views, get a table on the edge of the outer dining room. The Chart Room, bustling and boisterous as it is, serves reliable sandwiches and seafood standards, including lobster salad, bisque, and grilled swordfish. Vinny McGuiness and Tom Gordon have been co-chefs since the early 1980s. Reservations recommended for dinner only. Entrées $9–18.

Sagamore Inn (508-888-9707), 1131 Route 6A, Sagamore. Open 11–9 daily except Tuesday, April to mid-November. Shirley and Joseph Pagliarani have served "Yankee Italian" food since 1963, and now their son Joseph Jr., who has been running around the restaurant since birth, is cooking. Inside the shuttered green-and-white building are signs of "old Cape Cod": shiny wooden floors, captain's chairs at round tables, a white tin ceiling, and wooden booths. The Yankee pot roast has been on the menu from the beginning, but homemade pies were added in 1994. There's a lot of very, very fresh seafood on the menu, including broiled, baked, and fried choices. Finish up with traditional Grape-Nut custard or bread pudding. Children's menu; takeout. Dishes $7–12.

❋ **The Courtyard** (508-563-1818), Route 28A and County Road, Cataumet. Open for lunch and dinner. In summer the outdoor **bar,** raw bar, and courtyard are hopping. And the food is pretty darn good, too: hot and cold sandwiches and fish-and-chips at lunch, whopping prime rib specials (Thursday through Sunday) for dinner; lighter salads, too. $11–17.

✎ **Lobster Trap** (508-759-3992), 290 Shore Road, Bourne. Open for lunch and dinner (weekends only in spring and fall). When familiar overtones are comforting, every town has one restaurant that overlooks water, has the requisite nautical paraphernalia, and features a menu of fried seafood, seafood rolls, and seafood plates. This is the one in Bourne. Children's menu; takeout. Dishes $5–14.

❋✎ **Parrot Bar & Grill** (508-563-6464), 1356 Route 28A, Cataumet. Open daily for lunch and dinner (closed Monday). In addition to a few burgers and pizzas, you can also get seafood dishes and prime rib. Nice local **bar.** Children's menu. Lunch $5–8, dinner $7–16.

❋✎ **The Bridge** (508-888-8144), 21 Route 6A, Sagamore. Open for lunch and dinner daily. On the Cape side of the Sagamore Bridge, this pleasant and friendly place has been in the Prete family since 1953. You can find something to suit everyone. For lunch the Bridge offers its renowned Yankee pot roast, as well as tuna melts, spaghetti with meat sauce, and burgers. At dinnertime the menu is Italian-influenced, with seafood entrées and a few well-executed Thai dishes to spice things up. Children's menu. Lunch $5–9, dinner $9–18.

❋ **Anthony's** (508-888-6040), Route 6A, Sagamore, next to the Christmas Tree Shop on the Cape side of the Sagamore Bridge. Tired of inching along in traffic? Stop here and get some ice cream or a sandwich or a pizza before tackling the last leg of your journey.

ICE CREAM
Emack & Bolio's (508-564-5542), Route 28A and County Road, Cataumet. Open seasonally. Try the local favorite—Cosmic Cataumet Crunch (vanilla ice cream with butterscotch, chocolate chips, and pralines).

FISH MARKET
❋ **Cataumet Fish** (508-564-5956), 1640 Route 28A, Cataumet.

ENTERTAINMENT

Band concerts, Buzzards Bay Park, off Main Street, Buzzards Bay. Concerts are held in July and August on Thursday at 7 PM.

❋♪ **Hoyt's Cinema** (508-759-3212), 105 Main Street, Buzzards Bay.

SELECTIVE SHOPPING

❋ Unless otherwise noted, all shops are open year-round.

ART AND ARTISANS

Pairpoint Crystal (508-888-2344; 1-800-899-0953), 851 Route 6A, Sagamore. Retail shop open daily; glassmaking weekdays 9–4:30, April through December. This place has existed under one name or another since 1837. Thomas Pairpoint, a glass designer in the 1880s, used techniques created by Deming Jarves. Master craftspeople still employ these techniques here today. Clear or richly colored glass is handblown, -sculpted, or -pressed on a 19th-century press. The crystal contains 34 percent lead. Through large picture windows you can watch the master glassblowers working on faithful period reproductions and cup holders or more modern lamps, paperweights, vases, and candlesticks. (See the introduction and *To See* in "Sandwich" for more about the glass industry.)

✎ **Cataumet Arts Center** (508-563-5434), 76 Scraggy Neck Road, off County Road and Route 28A, Cataumet. This community arts center has ever-changing exhibits; an airy gallery that shows crafts, paintings, wearable art, and whimsical wooden sculptures (among other art); artists' studios to rent; and a host of classes for children, printmakers, and others.

FACTORY OUTLETS AND MALLS

🏵 **Christmas Tree Shops** (508-888-7010), on the Cape side of the Sagamore Bridge, exit 1 off Route 6. This may be the first Christmas Tree Shop you see, but it won't be the last—there are six more on the Cape. This is the main outlet "where everyone loves a bargain," and they've gone all out to get your attention: You can't miss the revolving windmill and thatched roof. (Interestingly, the thatch, marsh grass from Canada, must be groomed every other year.) Merchandise has absolutely nothing to do with the end-of-the-year holiday. It revolves around inexpensive housewares, random gourmet food items, or miscellaneous clothing accessories—whatever the owners, Doreen and Charles Bilezikian, happen to get in close-out sales that week. Those who turn up their noses at the shops might be interested to know that the Bilezikians employ 1,700 to 2,200 year-round residents.

Cape Cod Factory Outlet Mall (508-888-8417), exit 1 off Route 6, Sagamore. Open daily. Surrounding a food court, 20 or more stores like London Fog, Bass, Corning-Revere, Carter's Children's Wear, Van Heusen, Reebok, Samsonite, Oshkosh B'Gosh, and Bannister Shoes tempt even the most harried.

Tanger Outlet Center (1-800-482-6437), at the Bourne Bridge rotary. Open daily. Liz Claiborne, Nine West, Izod, and Levi's.

SPECIAL SHOP

Bournedale Country Store (508-888-8853), 26 Herring Pond Road, off Route 6, Bournedale. Open March through December. This classic red building with wooden floors has been here about 200 years. On my last

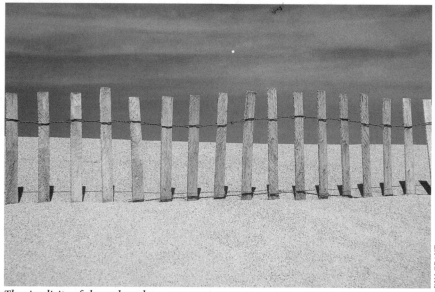

The simplicity of sky and sand

visit the aroma of baking brownies filled the store. What more could you ask for?

SPECIAL EVENTS

Mid- to late May: **Cape Cod Maritime Days** (508-862-0700). Coast Guard–operated lighthouses are open during this festival, including Nobska Light. In addition to focusing on the area's lighthouses, the Cape-wide event celebrates the region's fishing heritage, maritime villages, and seafaring way of life.

Fourth of July: **Mashnee Island's** celebrated, homespun Fourth of July parade consists of the current crop of island kids (and their parents) marching or riding their bikes through town.

Early August: Otis Air Force Base's **Cape Cod Air Show** (see Massachusetts Military Reservation under *To See*).

Early to mid-September: **Bourne Scallop Festival.** This weekend celebration is held in Buzzards Bay and along the shores of the canal. There are games, concerts, and lots of vendors and restaurants that create dishes that celebrate—what else?—the scallop. Rain or shine, as the eating takes place under a big tent; since 1969.

Early December: **Christmas in Old Bourne.** A traditional holiday celebration with tree lighting.

Sandwich

Sandwich is calm, even in the height of summer. Many visitors whiz right by it, eager to get farther away from the "mainland." Even people who know about the delightful treasures within historic Sandwich Village often return to Route 6 without exploring the back roads and historic houses off the beaten path. Those who take the time to explore will find that Sandwich is a real gem.

The oldest town on the Cape, Sandwich was founded in 1637 by the Cape's first permanent group of English settlers. The governor of Plymouth Colony had given permission to "tenn men from Saugust" (now Lynn, Massachusetts) to settle the area with 60 families. Sandwich was probably chosen for its close proximity to the Manomet (now Aptucxet) Trading Post (see *To See* in "Bourne") and for its abundant salt-marsh hay, which provided ready fodder for the settlers' cows. Agriculture supported the community until the 1820s, when Deming Jarves, a Boston glass merchant, decided to open a glassmaking factory. The location couldn't have been better: There was a good source of sand (although more was shipped in from New Jersey), sea salt was plentiful, salt-marsh hay provided packaging for the fragile goods, and forests were thick with scrub pines to fuel the furnaces. But by the 1880s, midwestern coal-fueled glassmaking factories and a labor strike shut down Sandwich's factories. The story is told in great detail at the excellent Sandwich Glass Museum. Glassblowers work in a few studios in town.

You could spend a day wandering the half-mile radius around the village center, a virtual time capsule spanning the centuries. Antiques shops, attractive homes, and quiet, shady lanes are perfect for strolling. Shawme Duck Pond, as idyllic as they come, is surrounded by historic houses (including one of the Cape's oldest), an old cemetery on the opposite shore, a working gristmill, swans and ducks, and plenty of vantage points from which to take it all in. Also pondside is a museum dedicated to the naturalist Thornton W. Burgess, a town resident and the creator of Peter Cottontail. Both children and adults delight in the museum and in the Green Briar Nature Center & Jam Kitchen down the road. Sandwich's greatest attraction lies just beyond the town center: Heritage Plantation of Sandwich, a 76-acre horticulturist's delight with superb collections of Americana and antique automobiles.

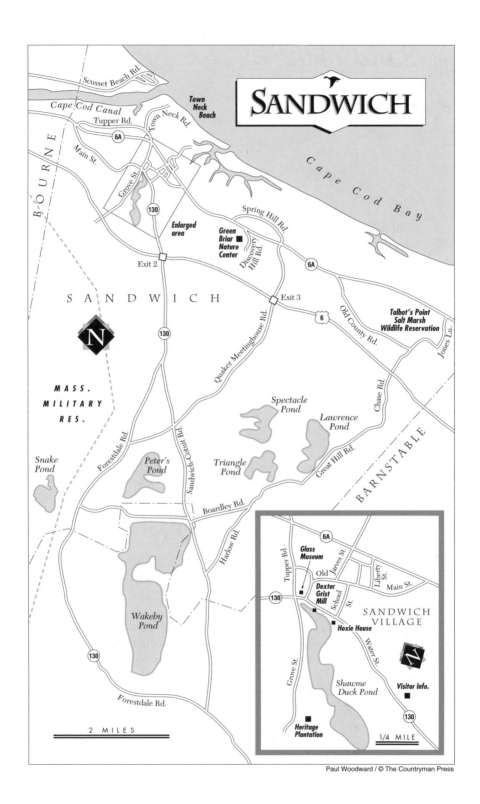

SANDWICH

Scusset Beach Rd.

Cape Cod Canal

Town Neck Beach

Tupper Rd.

6A

Main St.

Town Neck Rd.

Grove St.

130

Cape Cod Bay

Enlarged area

Spring Hill Rd.

Green Briar Nature Center

Discovery Hill Rd.

Exit 2

6A

Exit 3

6

Old County Rd.

Talbot's Point Salt Marsh Wildlife Reservation

Jones Ln.

S A N D W I C H

N

130

Quaker Meetinghouse Rd.

Chase Rd.

Spectacle Pond

Lawrence Pond

MASS. MILITARY RES.

Forestdale Rd.

Peter's Pond

Sandwich-Cotuit Rd.

Triangle Pond

Great Hill Rd.

BARNSTABLE

Snake Pond

Boardley Rd.

Harlow Rd.

Wakeby Pond

130

Forestdale Rd.

2 MILES

6A

Tupper Rd.

Glass Museum

Jarves St.

Old

Liberty St.

Main St.

130

Dexter Grist Mill

School St.

SANDWICH VILLAGE

N

Hoxie House

Grove St.

Water St.

Shawme Duck Pond

Visitor Info.

Heritage Plantation

1/4 MILE

130

Paul Woodward / © The Countryman Press

Beyond the town center, the Benjamin Nye Homestead is worth a visit; have a look-see, even if it's closed, because it sits in a picturesque spot. East of town on Route 6A, past densely carpeted cranberry bogs (harvested in autumn), you'll find a few farm stands, antiques shops, and artisans' studios. At the town line with Barnstable, you'll find one of the Cape's best beaches and protected areas: Sandy Neck Beach (see *Green Space—Beaches* in "Barnstable") and Sandy Neck Great Salt Marsh Conservation Area (see *Green Space—Walks* in "Barnstable"). The marina, off Tupper Road, borders the Cape Cod Canal with a recreation area. The often overlooked town beach is nothing to sneeze at, and there are numerous conservation areas and ponds for walking and swimming.

Although a surprising number of Sandwich's 18,000 year-round residents commutes to Boston every morning, their community dedication isn't diminished. Pick up a copy of the daily *Sandwich Broadsider* to glimpse the spirit that drives this town. A perfect example took place after fierce storms in August and October 1991 destroyed the town boardwalk, which had served the community since 1875. To replace it, townspeople purchased more than 1,700 individual boards, each personally inscribed, and a new boardwalk was built within eight months.

Sandwich was named, by the way, after the English town, not after the sandwich-creator earl, as many think. (The earl of that Sandwich was born 81 years after this town was founded.)

GUIDANCE

❄ **Cape Cod Canal Region Chamber of Commerce** (508-759-6000; www.capecodcanalchamber.org), 70 Main Street, Buzzards Bay 02532. The chamber is housed in an old railroad station in the center of Buzzards Bay. At press time the chamber was unable to provide details about hours. Sadly, I have found this chamber to be the least helpful and knowledgeable on the Cape. I hope you have better luck. While this office does have information on Sandwich, you can find a walking guide of Sandwich Village at many shops in town. A seasonal information booth is located on Route 130 as you head into Sandwich from Route 6.

PUBLIC REST ROOMS

Located in the chamber of commerce office in Buzzards Bay, they are open during business hours.

GETTING THERE

By car: Take the Sagamore Bridge to Route 6 east to exit 2 (Route 130 north) and travel 2 miles to Main Street. From exit 1 and Route 6A, you can take Tupper Road or Main Street into the village center.

By bus: There is no bus service to Sandwich proper, but Plymouth & Brockton (508-778-9767; www.p-b.com) buses bound for Boston stop at the Sagamore rotary, behind McDonald's in the commuter parking lot. For points south and west, Bonanza (1-888-751-8800; www.bonanzabus.com) buses stop nearby in Bourne.

GETTING AROUND
Sandwich Village is perfect for strolling, but you'll have to get back in your
   car to reach the marina and Heritage Plantation (see To See).

PUBLIC LIBRARY
🖎❄⚓**Sandwich Public Library** (508-888-0625), 142 Main Street, is open
   Tuesday through Thursday 9:30–8:30, and Friday and Saturday 9:30–4.
   From early September to late May, the library is also open Sunday 1–5.
   You can borrow toys and videos here.

MEDICAL EMERGENCY
   Call **911.**

TO SEE

In Sandwich Village

🖂⚓ **Sandwich Glass Museum** (508-888-0251; www.sandwichglassmuseum.
   org), 129 Main Street. Open 9:30–5 daily, April through December;
   9:30–4 Wednesday through Sunday, February through March. Closed
   January. During the 19th century, Sandwich glassmaking flourished at
   Deming Jarves's Boston & Sandwich Glass Company (1825–1888) and
   the Cape Cod Glass Works (1859–1869). Today, this internationally
   known museum, operated by the Sandwich Historical Society, chrono-
   logically displays thousands of decorative and functional glass objects,
   which became increasingly more elaborate and richly colored as the years
   progressed. The displays are dramatically backlit by natural light stream-
   ing through banks of windows. A video describes the rise and crash of the
   local glass industry, and a diorama displays how the glass was made. If
   you're in the habit of skipping town historical museums, break the habit
   this time; you won't be disappointed. Adults $3.50; children 6–16, $1.
   Personal guided tours $1 extra.

🖎 **Dexter Grist Mill** (508-888-1173), on Shawme Duck Pond, Water Street.
   Open 10–4:45 Monday through Saturday and 1–4:45 Sunday, mid-June
   to mid-September; 10–4:45 Saturday and 1–4:45 Sunday, mid-May to
   mid-June and mid-September to mid-October. The circa-1640 mill has
   had a multiuse past, and the site wasn't always as quaint as it is now. The
   mill was turbine powered during Sandwich's glassmaking heyday; it then
   sat idle until 1920, when it was converted into a tearoom. After the mills
   around it were torn down in the late 1950s, it was opened to tourists in
   1961, with the cypress waterwheel you see today. On-site miller and local
   schoolteacher Leo Manning describes the intricacies of the milling
   process. You can purchase stone-ground cornmeal—great for muffins,
   Indian pudding, and polenta. Nominal admission.

Artesian fountain, between the gristmill and Town Hall. Join residents by
   filling water jugs with what some consider the Cape's best water.

First Church of Christ, 136 Main Street. This Christopher Wren–inspired
   church with a tall white spire was built in 1847, but its brass bell, cast in

KIM GRANT

Tranquil Shawme Pond and the Dexter Grist Mill in Sandwich Village

1675, is thought to be the oldest in the country.

Town Hall (508-888-5144), Main Street. Sandwich has certainly gotten its money's worth out of this Greek Revival building, constructed at a cost of little more than $4,000 in 1834. It still serves as the center for town government.

Old Town Cemetery, Grove Street, on the shore opposite the Hoxie House and Thornton W. Burgess Museum. You'll recognize the names on many gravestones (including those of Burgess, Bodfish, and Bourne) from historic houses and street signs around town. Although the oldest marker dates to 1683, most are from the 1700s; many are marked with a winged skull, a common Puritan design.

✐ **Thornton W. Burgess Museum** (508-888-4668; 508-888-6870; www. thorntonburgess.org), 4 Water Street. Open 10–4 Monday through Saturday and 1–4 Sunday, April through October and the first two weekends in December. This Sandwich native and renowned children's author and naturalist wrote more than 15,000 stories and 170 books, featuring the escapades of Jimmy Skunk, Grandfather Frog, and the beloved Peter Cottontail (not to be confused with Beatrix Potter's Peter Rabbit). The house is crammed with Burgess's books, original Harrison Cady illustrations, a "see-and-touch room," and exhibits honoring Burgess's life and work. Don't miss story time, which takes place on Monday, Wednesday, and Saturday morning at 10:30 on the lawn in July and August; $1 per person. The Thornton Burgess Society was begun by local bookseller Nancy Titcomb (see *Selective Shopping—Bookstore*) in 1974 to celebrate the centennial of Burgess's birth. Donation suggested. (See also Green Briar Nature Center & Jam Kitchen under *Green Space*.)

🎗 **Hoxie House** (508-888-1173), 18 Water Street. Open 10–5 Monday through Saturday and 1–5 Sunday, mid-June to mid-October. For a long time this circa-1675 structure was thought to be the oldest on Cape Cod. Although it's impossible to know definitively—the Barnstable County Courthouse deeds were lost in a fire—that claim is now generally thought to be inaccurate. Nonetheless, the house has a rare saltbox roofline, small diamond-shaped leaded windows, and a fine vantage above Shawme Duck Pond. Thanks to loaner furniture from Boston's Museum of Fine Arts, the restored interior looks much as it did during colonial times. One of the most remarkable facts about this house is that it was occupied without electricity or indoor plumbing until the 1950s. The house was named for Abraham Hoxie, who purchased it in 1860 for $400. The Reverend John Smith lived here in 1675 when he came to be minister of the First Parish Church. Adults $1.50; children 12–16, 75¢. Combination ticket with Dexter Grist Mill: adults $2.50; children 12–16, $1.

Elsewhere around town

🎗 **Heritage Plantation of Sandwich** (508-888-3300; www.heritageplantation. org), Pine and Grove Streets. Open 10–5 daily, early May to late October (last tickets sold at 4:15). Established in 1969 by Josiah Lilly III, a descendant of the founder of the Eli Lilly Pharmaceutical Company, Heritage Plantation is an oasis for garden lovers, antiques and vintage-car buffs, and Americana enthusiasts. These 76 acres are planted with outstanding collections of rhododendrons, including the famous Dexter variety, which bloom from mid-May to mid-June. (Charles O. Dexter was the estate's original owner, and he experimented with hybridizing here.) There are also impressive collections of holly bushes, heathers, hostas, and almost 1,000 daylilies, which bloom from mid-July to early August. The estate is equally pleasant for an autumnal walk.

The **Military Museum** features a collection of 2,000 hand-painted miniatures, while the replica **Shaker Round Barn** houses the museum's outstanding vintage-car collection. A 1981 DeLorean, a 1930 Duesenberg built for Gary Cooper, and President Taft's White Steamer (the first official auto of the White House) are a few mint-condition classics.

The **Art Museum** features folk art, scrimshaw, cigar-store figures, weather vanes, carvings by Elmer Crowell, and Currier & Ives lithographs. Also on the grounds: an 1800 windmill, an operational Coney Island–style 1912 carousel, and the **Carousel Café.** The alfresco café has a limited but more-than-adequate menu of overstuffed sandwiches, salads, and desserts. A trolley transports people around the grounds, but it is not intended for sight-seeing. Keep your eyes peeled for museum special events, including plant sales and concerts (see also *Entertainment*). Adults $9; youths 6–18, $4.50; children 5 and under free.

Benjamin Nye Homestead (508-888-2368), 85 Old County Road, East Sandwich. Open noon–4:30 weekdays, mid-June to mid-October. Off

Route 6A, this 1685 homestead belonged to one of Sandwich's first settlers and has undergone many structural changes over the years. It began as a small peaked room with a central chimney; an addition turned it into a saltbox, and then a second floor created the full Colonial you see today. Although the interior is hardly a purist restoration, you'll see some of the original construction, early paneling, 18th-century wallpaper, a spinning wheel, and handwoven sheets. Small admission fee.

1641 Wing Fort House, 69 Spring Hill Road (off Route 6A), East Sandwich. Open 10–4 Tuesday through Saturday, mid-June to mid-September. The Wing house is the country's oldest home continuously inhabited by the same family. This circa-1646 house began as a one-room cottage when Stephen Wing, descendant of the Reverend John Wing, arrived with his new bride. In the mid-1800s, a second house was added to it to create the current three-quarter Colonial. Adults $2, children $1.

Friends Meeting House (508-888-4181), Quaker Road, off Spring Hill Road (from Route 6A), East Sandwich. Services Sunday at 10 AM. The building standing today was built in 1810, the third Quaker meetinghouse on this site. The congregation has been meeting since 1657, which makes it the oldest continuous meeting in North America. The interior is simple, with pews and a wood-burning stove stoked in winter for 25 or so congregants. The meetinghouse is flanked by handsome carriage barns.

✎❄ **Sandwich Fish Hatchery** (508-888-0008), Route 6A at Old Main Street. Open 9–3 daily. More than 200,000 trout at various stages of development are raised to stock the state's ponds. Throw in pellets of food (bring quarters for the vending machines) and watch 'em swarm.

✎ **Boardwalk,** Harbor Street off Factory Street. The boardwalk crosses marshland, Mill Creek, and low dunes to connect to Town Neck Beach (see *Green Space—Beaches*). Depending on the season, you might see kids jumping into the creek or blue heron poking around the tidal pools and tall grasses. There are expansive views at the end of the 1,350-foot walkway.

Yesteryears Doll Museum (508-888-1711), at Main and River Streets. At press time, I was unable to confirm any information about this "attraction."

OUTDOOR ACTIVITIES

BICYCLING/RENTALS
Cape Cod Bike Rentals/Sandwich Cycles (508-833-2453), 40 Route 6A. Open seasonally. Bicycles, mopeds, joggers, tandem bikes, in-line skates, and emergency repairs to your own bicycle, on-road if needed. On multiday rentals, Sandwich Cycles offers delivery to and pickup from your lodging. The shop is located between Sandwich's shady back

The beloved Sandwich boardwalk, rebuilt by townspeople after fierce storms destroyed it, leads over a picturesque marsh to the town beach.

roads and the Cape Cod Canal bike path (see *Outdoor Activities* in "Bourne").

BLUEBERRY PICKING

The Blueberry Bog, Spring Hill off Route 6A. In the 1940s, this former cranberry bog was turned into a blueberry farm. Today there are about 400 bushes on more than 4 acres. The fruit matures from early to mid-July through August; pick your own by the quart or pound.

CANOEING

Shawme Duck Pond, Water Street (Route 130), is actually linked to two other ponds, so you can do a lot of canoeing here.

Scorton Creek. Head east on Route 6A, turn right after the Sears auto store (on your left), and go down beyond the culvert to park. This is a good place for picnics, too.

Wakeby Pond, off Cotuit Road, South Sandwich.

FISHING

Freshwater fishing licenses and regulations can be procured from the Town Hall Annex (508-888-5144), Main Street. **Sandcastle Recreation Area** (at the Sandwich Marina) and **Scusset Beach State Reservation Pier** (off Scusset Beach Road from the rotary on the mainland side of the canal) are good places to cast a line into the Cape Cod Canal.

❊ GOLF

Holly Ridge (508-428-5577), off Route 130, South Sandwich. 18 holes, 3,000 yards, par 54.

Round Hill Country Club (508-888-3384), exit 3 (off Round Hill Road) off Route 6, East Sandwich. 18 holes, par 72.

MINI-GOLF

❧ **Sandwich Minigolf** (508-833-1905), 159 Route 6A. Open weekends mid-May to mid-October and daily in summer. Set on a cranberry bog, this course that boasts a floating raft for a green! An honest-to-goodness stream winds around many of the 27 holes.

TENNIS

Public courts are at **Wing Elementary School** on Route 130, **Oak Ridge School** off Quaker Meetinghouse Road, and **Forestdale School** off Route 130.

EVEN MORE THINGS TO SEE AND DO

FITNESS CLUB

❄ **Sportsite Health & Racquet Club** (508-888-7900), 315 Cotuit Road. Open daily. Two weight rooms, a cardiovascular area, aerobics classes, sauna, steam room, racquetball courts, spinning, and baby-sitting services while you work out. $50 for eight visits, $12 per day, or $25 per week.

SCENIC RAILROAD

❧ **Cape Cod Central Railroad** (508-771-3800; 1-888-797-7245; www.cape train.com), Main and Center Streets. Weekends in May, June, September, and October; daily except Monday in July and August. The 42-mile trip takes 2 hours and passes cranberry bogs and the Sandy Neck Great Salt Marsh. Since there are three trains daily, you take the first one, hop off in Hyannis, walk into town (the station is right in the center of town and close to the harbor), and then catch the last train back to Sandwich. Adults $11.75, children 11 and under $7.75.

GREEN SPACE

❧ **Green Briar Nature Center & Jam Kitchen** (508-888-6870; www.thorntonburgess.com), 6 Discovery Hill Road off Route 6A, East Sandwich. Trails open year-round; the Jam Kitchen is open the same hours as the Thornton W. Burgess Museum (see *To See*). Even in an area with so many tranquil spots, Green Briar rises to the top. Perhaps that's because it's run by the Thornton W. Burgess Society "to re-establish and maintain nature's fine balance among all living things and to hold as a sacred trust the obligation to make only the best use of natural resources." Located on Smiling Pond and adjacent to the famous Briar Patch of Burgess's stories, these 57 acres of conservation land have many short, interpretive nature trails (less than a mile long) and a lovely wildflower garden. The society hosts natural history classes, lectures, and nature walks, as well as other wonderful programs for children, adults, and families, throughout the year. Young children enjoy creeping along marsh creeks in search of hermit crabs, while older children take canoeing expeditions and learn Native American crafts and lore. Fees vary. Write or call for a schedule.

The Jam Kitchen was established in 1903 by Ida Putnam, who used her friend Fanny Farmer's recipes to make jams, jellies, and fruit preserves. Step inside the old-fashioned, aromatic, and homey place to see mason jars filled with apricots and strawberries and watch fruit simmering on vintage-1920 Glenwood gas stoves. Pick up a jar of beach plum jelly or try some of the original recipes in your own kitchen. Two-hour workshops on preserving fruit and making jams and jellies are also held. About this sweet and aromatic place, Burgess said to Putnam in 1939, "It is a wonderful thing to sweeten the world which is in a jam and needs preserving."

✎ **Shawme Duck Pond,** Water Street (Route 130), in the village center. Flocks of ducks, geese, and swans know a good thing when they find it. And even though this idyllic spot is one of the most easily accessible on the Cape, it remains a tranquil place for humans and waterfowl alike. Formerly a marshy brook, the willow-lined pond was dammed prior to the gristmill operating in the 1640s. It's a nice spot for canoeing.

🍴❄✎**Shawme-Crowell State Forest** (508-888-0351; reservations: 1-877-422-6762), Route 130. You can walk, bicycle, and camp ($10–12 nightly) at 285 sites on 742 acres. Often when the popular Nickerson State Park (see *Lodging—Campgrounds* in "Brewster") is full of campers, there are dozens of good sites still available here.

🍴❄✎**Scusset Beach State Reservation** (508-888-0859; reservations: 1-877-422-6762), on Cape Cod Bay, off Scusset Beach Road from the rotary on the mainland side of the canal. The reservation has 450 acres, some of which are set aside for camping (103 sites, primarily used by RVers, $17–20 nightly in-season), bicycling, picnicking, and walking. Campfire programs are held Thursday evening by Cape Cod Canal Rangers (see U.S. Army Corps of Engineers under *Guidance* in "Bourne"). Facilities include in-season lifeguard, rest rooms, changing rooms, and a snack bar. Parking $2.

See also Giving Tree Gallery and Sculpture Gardens under *Special Shops*.

BEACHES

Town Neck Beach, on Cape Cod Bay, off Town Neck Road and Route 6A. This pebble beach extends 1½ miles from the Cape Cod Canal to Dock Creek. Visit at high tide if you want to swim; at low tide, it's great for walking. Facilities include changing rooms and rest rooms. Parking $4.

Sandy Neck Beach, off Route 6A on the Sandwich/Barnstable line (see *Green Space—Beaches* in "Barnstable").

See also Scusset Beach State Reservation, above.

PONDS

Wakeby Pond (off Cotuit Road), South Sandwich, offers freshwater swimming.

WALKS

Talbot's Point Salt Marsh Wildlife Reservation, off Old County Road from Route 6A. This little-used, 1½-mile (round trip) hiking trail winds past red pines, beeches, and a large salt marsh.

See also Green Briar Nature Center & Jam Kitchen and Shawme-Crowell State Forest.

LODGING

✿❄ Sandwich's historic hostelries provide great diversity, something for everyone—from an unusually mod B&B to an incredibly impressive church conversion, a traditional B&B, and a large motor inn. Unless otherwise noted, all lodging is open year-round and in Sandwich 02563.

RESORT MOTOR INN

✍ **Dan'l Webster Inn** (508-888-3622; 1-800-444-3566; www.danlwebsterinn. com), 149 Main Street. The present building was modeled after the original 18th-century hostelry, which, before it was destroyed by fire, was a meeting place for Revolutionary patriots. The Catania family purchased the property in 1980 and vigilantly maintains its colonial charm. A full-time staff horticulturist oversees pleasant courtyards and an attractive pool area behind the inn. Most of the 54 rooms and suites are of the top-notch motel/hotel variety. Modern amenities include telephone, cable TV, turndown service, room service, and a daily newspaper at your door. Rooms in the Fessenden Wing overlook gardens. A few rooms are more innlike, more distinctive; these are in two separate older houses. There are four well-regarded dining rooms (see *Dining Out*). Guests have privileges at the nearby Sportsite Health & Racquet Club (see *Even More Things to See and Do—Fitness Club*). Late May to late October $169–199 for rooms and $229–379 for suites; off-season $109–279. Children under 12 free. Good off-season packages.

INN

Belfry Inne (508-888-8550; 1-800-844-4542; www.belfryinn.com), 8 Jarves Street. In the center of town, the Belfry Inne consists of the circa-1879 **Drew House** and its adjacent circa-1900 **Abbey.** Common space at the Drew House includes a front parlor, porch, and two-person treetop cupola; the Abbey has a second-floor sitting room. In total, there are 12 guest rooms with private bath, fine antiques, and tasteful and comfortable furnishings. While the Drew House rooms are certainly first-rate (I particularly like Kristina Drew on the third floor), the Abbey rooms are downright spectacular: stained glass, flying buttresses, fancy linens, bold colors, beds made from pews, gas fireplaces, Jacuzzis, and balconies. There isn't one I wouldn't highly recommend. Innkeeper Chris Wilson and his architect deserve awards for this conversion. The Abbey features a restaurant open to the public (see *Dining Out*). May through October Drew House $95–165, Abbey $165–195; off-season $85–135 and $135, respectively; full breakfast included except Sunday, when it's continental.

BED & BREAKFASTS

Captain Ezra Nye House (508-888-6142; 1-800-388-2278; www.captain ezranyehouse.com), 152 Main Street. Elaine and Harry Dickson have run this 1829 Federal-style bed & breakfast since 1986. The five rooms and one suite (all with private bath; one with a working fireplace; one with electric stove; all carpeted and with air-conditioning) are decorated with an eclectic assortment of antiques and objects the Dicksons have collected from around the world. The common front parlor is a bit formal, but there's a small TV room off the dining room that's more casual. Full breakfast included. Mid-May through October $85–110; $75–100 off-season.

The Village Inn at Sandwich (508-833-0363; 1-800-922-9989; www.capecodinn.com), 4 Jarves Street. Surrounded by perennial gardens and a white picket fence in the middle of town, this 1830s Federal house has a wraparound porch (decked with rocking chairs) and two living rooms for guests to enjoy. Six of eight guest rooms have private bath; third-floor rooms share a bath. All rooms have hardwood floors (some bleached) and down comforters. Full breakfast at individual tables included. May through October $95–120; $85–105 off-season.

Summer House (508-888-4991; 1-800-241-3609; www.capecod.net/summerhouse), 158 Main Street. This 1835 Greek Revival Cape has five rooms (all with private bath), furnished simply with antiques and quilts; many feature fireplaces, original hardware, and painted hardwood floors. A bountiful breakfast is served in the fanciful living/dining room with Chinese-red walls and a black-and-white checkerboard floor. Take your afternoon tea in the sunroom, in the English-style garden, or (very carefully) in the hammock. Late May through October $85–110; off-season $65-90.

Bay Beach (508-888-8813; 1-800-475-6398; www.baybeach.com), 1-3 Bay Beach Lane. Open mid-May through mid-October. Located right smack on a private beach with views of the Cape Cod Canal's east entrance, Emily and Reale Lemieux's contemporary house has seven luxurious rooms with air-conditioning, refrigerator, telephone, cable TV, and outdoor deck, and private bath (some with whirlpool and private deck). While I was unable to see guest rooms for this edition, the location is too special to ignore. Rooms $195–345, including full breakfast.

✎ **Windfall House** (508-888-3650; 1-877-594-6325), 108 Route 130 (Main Street). Within walking distance of the village, innkeeper Ted Diggle presides over a snug 1818 hostelry. The cozy gathering room boasts beamed ceilings, wide-pine floors, a working fireplace, cable TV, and beehive oven. Four colonial-style rooms and one suite, each with private bath, are furnished with homey and impressive antiques like carved cherry four-poster beds and wrought-iron beds. The Burbank Suite features a kitchenette and private entrance (with deck) and can accommodate a family or friends traveling together. A full breakfast, perhaps omelets and home fries, is included. Late May through October $75–125; off-season $55–110.

Dillingham House (508-833-0065), 71 Main Street. Open May through

October; by advance reservation in winter. Innkeeper Ryan Griffin's business card reads "a surprisingly different haunt." She's not kidding. But you'd never know it from the exterior of this circa-1650 three-quarter Cape, built by one of Sandwich's founders. Inside, your first hint of the dichotomy comes in the two living rooms, one with a large working hearth, one a former tack room. Both have wide-pine floorboards, but one is done in gold, and the other has a black ceiling and walls. The three rooms and one suite, all with private bath, are decorated in a similar vein. Despite what you might think about the color choice, Ryan has paid great attention to cleanliness and comfort. The adjacent **cottage** is great for longer stays. Oh, the inn is about a mile from the village center on Route 130. Rooms $110, suite and cottage $130, including a full breakfast in an upbeat dining room.

🐾 **Wingscorton Farm Inn** (508-888-0534), 11 Wing Boulevard, East Sandwich 02537. This circa-1758 working farm, on 13 acres of orchards and woods, once a stop on the Underground Railroad, has lots going for it, but I wasn't able to see rooms for this edition (the innkeeper, Sheila Weyers, was a bot overburdened when I stopped by) so I can't unequivocally recommend it. The house has low ceilings, wainscoting, wide-plank floors, rich paneling, and wood-burning fireplaces in the guest rooms. Two living rooms—one with the largest hearth in New England—provide plenty of common space for guests. Accommodations include three suites (each with private bath, refrigerator, period antiques, and canopy bed) and a two-story **carriage house** with a private deck and patio, full kitchen, and woodstove. A multicourse breakfast is served at a long harvest table in front of a working fireplace. Dogs and cats roam around the property, which is also home to pygmy goats, horses, and sheep. You can bring your own well-behaved pets. Free-range chickens and fresh eggs are sold from the barn. You can also walk to the inn's private bay beach. Suites from $135, carriage house from $175; $25–45 additional per child per night.

COTTAGES

✏ **Pine Grove Cottages** (508-888-8179), 358 Route 6A, East Sandwich 02537. Open May through October. These 10 tidy cottages with kitchens come in various sizes: There are tiny one-room, small one-bedroom, larger one-bedroom, and "deluxe" two-bedroom cottages. (Sandwich bylaws require two-bedroom units to measure 20 feet by 24 feet.) The cottages are freshly painted white. Although guests spend most of their time at the beach, there is also a new pool and play area in the pine grove. Mid-June to early September $394–713 (including tax) weekly for two to four people.

See also Dillingham House under *Bed & Breakfasts*.

MOTELS

Spring Garden Inn (508-888-0710; 1-800-303-1751; www.springgarden.com), 578 Route 6A, East Sandwich 02537. Open April to mid-Novem-

A cruise ship passes through the canal at the Sandwich Marina.

ber. Reserve early if you can; this is one of the best motels on Route 6A. Although modest from the street, from the back the bilevel motel overlooks a salt marsh and the Scorton River, particularly beautiful at sunset. The backyard is dotted with lawn chairs, grills, and picnic tables. Owners Stephen and Elizabeth Kauffman pay careful attention to the gardens. Eight carpeted rooms have knotty-pine paneling, two double beds, TV, air-conditioning, refrigerator, and telephone. In addition, there are two efficiencies and a two-room suite with a private deck. An outdoor pool is nicely shielded from Route 6A. Sandy Neck Beach is a 10-minute walk from here. Continental breakfast included. July and August $95–135; $72–99 off-season.

Shadynook Inn & Motel (508-888-0409, 1-800-338-5208; www.shadynook inn.com), 14 Route 6A. Sharon and Jim Rinaldi take well-deserved pride in their spiffy, shaded motel with lush landscaping and heated outdoor pool. The large rooms are typically appointed as far as motel rooms go, only a bit nicer. You'll also have a choice of two- and three-room suites, some of which are efficiencies. There are 37 rooms in total. Children under 12 free. Mid-June to early September $95–200 for two to four people; $65–175 otherwise.

CAMPGROUND

Peter's Pond Park (508-477-1775; www.campcapecod.com), 185 Cotuit Road. Open mid-April to mid-October. The park consists of 480 well-groomed campsites, walking trails, and a popular spring-fed lake for trout and bass fishing, boating, and swimming. There are organized children's activities at the playground in summer. On-site tepee rentals $250 weekly, $45 daily off-season; $27–39 campsites; two-bedroom cottages $650 weekly, $95 daily off-season. Rowboats and paddleboats rented by the day.

See also Shawme-Crowell State Forest and Scusset Beach State Reservation under *Green Space*.

RENTAL HOUSES AND COTTAGES

Real Estate Associates (508-888-0900), 2 Willow Street, has listings for seasonal rentals.

WHERE TO EAT

❋ Sandwich eateries run the gamut from fine dining in a former church and traditional dining in a conservatory to a tiny tea shop and fish houses. Unless otherwise noted, all entries are open year-round and in Sandwich.

DINING OUT

Belfry Inne Bistro (508-888-8550; 1-800-844-4542), 8 Jarves Street. Open for dinner. It took Chris Wilson nine months to renovate this former church, and it was worth every day of his time. The setting is dramatic: soaring beadboard ceilings, stained glass, flying buttresses, a confessional that's been converted into a tasteful **bar,** and a former altar set with tables. It's also elegant: candlelight, damask-linen-covered tables, a wood-burning fireplace. While I didn't get a chance to dine here for this edition, Chef Pelo's cooking comes recommended. The menu ranges from sautéed duck breast to grilled salmon to a seafood medley in a champagne cream sauce. Entrées $19–25.

✎ **Dan'l Webster Inn** (508-888-3622), 149 Main Street. Open for lunch and dinner daily year-round; Sunday brunch; breakfast daily mid-April to mid-November and on weekends mid-November to mid-April. In recent years, under the direction of chef-owner Robert Catania, the inn's dining room has gotten better and better, serving reliable, classic American dishes in four intimate dining rooms. The sunlit conservatory is an indoor oasis, especially for lunch and brunch, while the main dining room is more traditional. And in a nod to changing habits, the new **Tavern at the Inn** is more casual. Throughout the inn, the dress code is neat but informal. By the way, the inn has an excellent water-filtration system, and its water is perhaps the best tasting on the Cape. Children's menu; early specials. Brunch and lunch $7–14, dinner $17–26 (half entrées available, too).

EATING OUT

♿ **Bee-Hive Tavern** (508-833-1184), 406 Route 6A, East Sandwich. Open for lunch and dinner daily and for Sunday breakfast (Saturday, too, in summer). There are benches in front for a reason—there is often a wait due to the tavern's popularity. Low ceilings, barnboard, and booths make this dark, Colonial-style tavern a comfortable choice year-round. If you're tired of eating at picnic tables or in "quaint" clam shacks, try this place. Standard fare includes homemade soups, pasta, sandwiches (including the "roll-up" variety), and burgers. Full-fledged dinner entrées are more substantial: steaks, prime rib, lobster ravioli, and seafood. Part of the reason this place is so consistent is due to chef Mark Fitzpatrick, who's been here since opening day in 1992. Lunch $4.75–9, dinner $8–16.

Dunbar Tea Room & Shop (508-833-2485), 1 Water Street. Open daily 11 AM–4:30 PM. This tiny tearoom has been bustling since it opened. Try the authentic ploughman's lunch, or daily specials like seafood quiche (which sells out fast), or sweets like pies, cakes, scones, and Scottish shortbread. Afternoon English tea ($10 plus the cost of tea), with scones, finger sandwiches, and finger desserts, is offered 11–4:30 in the American-style country setting. Full afternoon dinners are offered on Sunday in the off-season. In summer, garden tables are an oasis; in winter, the fireplace makes it cozy indoors. Lunches average about $9.

&♪ **Aqua Grille** (508-888-8889), 14 Gallo Road, at the marina. Open for lunch and dinner mid-April to late October. The Aqua Grille's eclectic regional American menu features the ubiquitous fried seafood and lobster, but also pasta dishes, wood-grilled meats, and your choice of fish with your choice of sauces. Chef Gert Rausch spent many years in Austin and Aspen, so you'll find some modern interpretations of quesadillas (with cilantro, Vermont goat cheese, and bay shrimp, perhaps) on the menu. Specialty drinks from the **bar** are popular. It's a spacious, pleasant, and modern place with aqua walls, aqua-colored water glasses, and some Naugahyde, banquette-style booths. The marina and canal are visible from most tables. Children's menu. Lunch $7–15, dinner entrées $9–20.

♣♪ **Seafood Sam's** (508-888-4629), Coast Guard Road. Open for lunch and dinner daily, mid-March to mid-November. This casual spot near the marina serves fried and broiled seafood, seafood sandwiches, and seafood salad plates. Children's menu includes chicken and hot dogs. Dishes $6–12.

♣♪ **Marshland Restaurant** (508-888-9824), 109 Route 6A. Open for breakfast and lunch on Monday, all three meals Tuesday through Saturday 6 AM–9 PM, and breakfast Sunday 7 AM–1 PM. Primarily locals frequent this small, informal roadside place for coffee and breakfast muffins or lunch specials like homemade meat loaf, quiche with great salads, and chicken club sandwiches. They serve real mashed potatoes for dinner, too, along with prime rib. Eat at one of the Formica booths or on a swiveling seat at the U-shaped counter. Children's menu. Breakfast $5, lunch specials $6.25, dinner entrées $9.

♪ **Captain Scott's** (508-888-1675), 71 Tupper Road. Open 11:30–8:30-ish daily. This casual, inexpensive place is hopping with locals who come for the no-frills pasta dishes, fried seafood dinners, and baked or broiled fish. Early specials; children's menu. Entrées $5–15.

Horizons on Cape Cod Bay (508-888-6166), Town Neck Beach. Open April to late October. Horizons is the only beachfront eatery. It's a nice place for an afternoon drink on the deck; views are spectacular.

See also the Bridge and the Sagamore Inn under *Where to Eat* in "Bourne."

ICE CREAM

♪ **Twin Acres Ice Cream** (508-888-0566), 21 Route 6A near Bourne. Open

April to mid-October. The best in the area. The shop also boasts a lush lawn, little oak grove, and plenty of tables and chairs. (It sure beats standing in a parking lot.) It's lit at night, too. My only complaint: There's so much colorful signage describing the offerings that it's overwhelming. Come back often until you memorize the menu. Generous servings; banana boats, hot fudge sundaes, and an ample grill menu.

ENTERTAINMENT

As you enter Sandwich, there are a couple of well-placed marquees that will tell you what's happening that day or week.

Heritage Plantation of Sandwich (508-888-3300), Pine and Grove Streets, sponsors outdoor concerts—from big band to jazz, from chamber singers to ethnic ensembles. Mid-June to early September. (See also *To See.*)

✍ **Band concerts,** at the Wing School off Route 130, are given by the Sandwich Town Band on Thursday evening at 7 in July and August.

✍ **Opera New England of Cape Cod** (508-771-3600), a touring company from New York City, performs opera for adults in May and October and for children in November at the Cape Cod Community College in West Barnstable.

SELECTIVE SHOPPING

❋ Unless otherwise noted, all shops are open year-round. Still, don't expect many to be open during the week).

ANTIQUES

Brown Jug Antiques (508-833-1088), 155 Main Street. Open daily late March to late October. Antique glass (including Sandwich glass, of course, as well as Tiffany and Steuben), Staffordshire china, and English cameos are specialties.

Madden & Company (508-888-3663), 16 Jarves Street. Open by chance, as the owner is frequently on buying trips. Set up to resemble a country store (albeit an upscale one), Paul Madden's shop primarily offers antiques and Americana, but he also has decorative country-style household gifts and nautical items.

Sandwich Antiques Center (508-833-3600), 131 Route 6A. Open daily. A multidealer shop worth your time if you find something.

Maypop Lane (508-888-1230), Route 6A at Main Street. Open daily. With many dealers under one roof, you'll find a broad selection: decoys, quilts, clothing, jewelry, sterling, copper, brass, glass, furniture, and other collectibles and antiques.

ARTISAN

Glass Studio (508-888-6681), 470 Route 6A, East Sandwich. Open daily except Tuesday, April through December; Friday and Saturday, January through March. Artist Michael Magyar offers a wide selection of glass made with modern and century-old techniques. He's been plying his trade since 1980, and you can watch him work on Friday and Saturday, and possibly other days, too. Choose from graceful Venetian goblets, square vases, bud vases, handblown ornaments (some of which are sold during the Christmas in Sandwich celebration; see *Special Events*), and "sea bubbles" glassware, influenced by the water around him.

See also *Selective Shopping—Art and Artisans* in "Bourne."

AUCTIONS

Sandwich Auction House (508-888-1926), 15 Tupper Road. Consignment estate sales are held Wednesday in summer and Saturday off-season. Once a month (call for dates) they hold a superduper Oriental rug auction.

BOOKSTORE

Titcomb's Book Shop (508-888-2331), 432 Route 6A, East Sandwich. Open daily. It's hard to miss the wood carving of a colonist holding a book and walking stick. Titcomb's beacon draws you in. Book enthusiasts won't be disappointed; rare-book lovers will be even happier. This two-story barn is filled with more than 25,000 new, used, and rare books for adults and children, as well as a good selection of Cape and maritime books. The Titcombs have owned the shop since 1969 and, with the help of their eight children, have made hundreds of yards of shelves. It's a charming place, promoting browsing. By the way, owner Nancy Titcomb helped resurrect interest in Thornton W. Burgess, and, as you might imagine, she offers a great selection of his work.

SPECIAL SHOPS

Giving Tree Gallery and Sculpture Gardens (508-888-5446; www.giving treegallery.com), 550 Route 6A, East Sandwich. Open April through December. The gallery's logo might as well be "Where Art and Nature Meet." It's a wonderful and aesthetic place. Outdoor sculpture is exhibited on acres of marshland with nature paths, perennial gardens, and a bamboo grove, but don't overlook the indoor gallery, featuring the work of hundreds of artists.

The Weather Store (508-888-1200), 146 Main Street. Open Monday through Saturday, Sunday by chance or appointment, April through December. If it relates to weather and measuring or predicting weather, it's here: weather vanes, sundials, nautical gauges for yachts, "weather sticks" to indicate when a storm is headed your way, even whirligigs ("weather instruments" is broadly defined here).

Home for the Holidays (508-888-4388), 154 Main Street. Open daily from late May through December; Friday through Sunday the rest of the year. Each room of this 1850 house is filled with decorations and gifts geared to specific holidays or special occasions. Items in one room are changed every month, so there's always a room devoted to the current holiday.

Horsefeathers (508-888-5298), 454 Route 6A, East Sandwich. Open year-round; call ahead off-season. This small, aromatic shop sells linens, lace, Victoriana, teacups, and vintage christening gowns.

Collections Unlimited (508-833-0039), 365 Route 6A, East Sandwich. Open daily. Handcrafted items—wood objects, pottery, baskets, stained glass, and the like—from members of the Cape's longest-running cooperative (since 1990).

Crow Farm, Route 6A, East Sandwich. Open seasonally. Killer beach plum jam.

See also Green Briar Nature Center & Jam Kitchen under *Green Space.*

SPECIAL EVENTS

Mid-September: **Boardwalk celebration** (508-833-1625) includes a road race/walk, a kite festival, and a beachgoers' parade.

Early December: **Christmas in Sandwich** is a 3-week festival that includes caroling, hot cider at the Dan'l Webster Inn (see *Lodging—Resort Motor Inn*), open houses, trolley tours, and crafts sales.

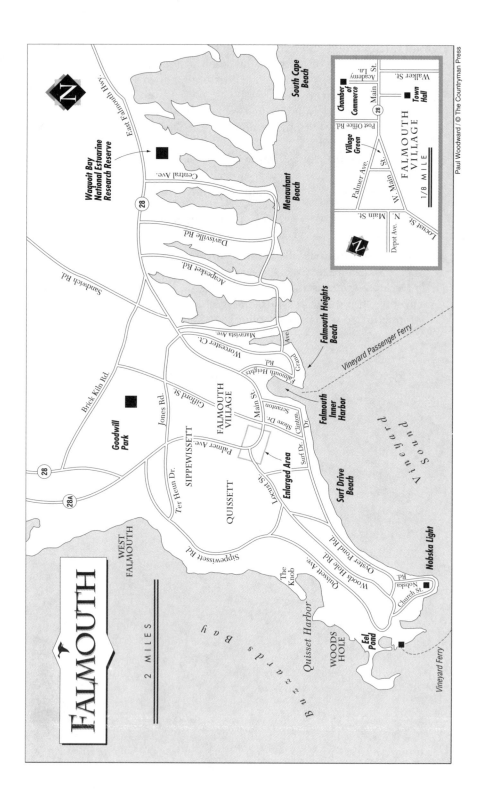

FALMOUTH

2 MILES

FALMOUTH VILLAGE
1/8 MILE

Chamber of Commerce
Post Office Rd.
Academy Ln.
Walker St.
Town Hall
Main St.
28
Village Green
Palmer Ave.
W. Main St.
N. Main St.
Depot Ave.
Locust St.

South Cape Beach
Waquoit Bay National Estuarine Research Reserve
East Falmouth Hwy.
Central Ave.
28
Menauhant Beach
Davisville Rd.
Acapesket Rd.
Sandwich Rd.
Falmouth Heights Beach
Maravista Ave.
Worcester Ct.
Grand Ave.
Falmouth Heights Rd.
Vineyard Passenger Ferry
Brick Kiln Rd.
Jones Rd.
Gifford St.
Main St.
Scranton
Clinton
Shore Dr.
Falmouth Inner Harbor
Goodwill Park
SIPPEWISSETT
Palmer Ave.
FALMOUTH VILLAGE
Enlarged Area
Surf Dr.
Vineyard Sound
28
28A
Ter Heun Dr.
QUISSETT
Locust St.
Surf Drive Beach
WEST FALMOUTH
Sippewissett Rd.
Quisset Harbor
The Knob
Quisset Ave.
Woods Hole Rd.
Oyster Pond Rd.
Nobska Rd.
Church St.
Nobska Light
Buzzards Bay
WOODS HOLE
Eel Pond
Vineyard Ferry

Paul Woodward / © The Countryman Press

Falmouth and Woods Hole

The Cape's second largest town, Falmouth has more shore and coastline than any other town on the Cape. In fact, it has 14 harbors, 12 miles of public beaches, and more than 30 ponds. Saltwater inlets reach deep into the southern coastline, like fjords—only without the mountains. Buzzards Bay waters lap the western shores of quiet North and West Falmouth and bustling Woods Hole. Falmouth's eight distinctive villages accommodate about 80,000 summer people, more than double the town's year-round population.

The villages differ widely in character. Quiet, restful lanes and residents who keep to themselves characterize Sippewissett and both North and West Falmouth. The West Falmouth Harbor (off wooded, scenic Route 28A) is tranquil and placid, particularly at sunset. Although Falmouth Heights is known for its opulent, turn-of-the-20th-century shingled houses on Vineyard Sound, its beach is a popular gathering spot for a younger crowd. You'll see them everywhere—playing volleyball, sunbathing, flying kites, and enjoying the warm water and comfortable, relatively inexpensive seaside apartments that line Grand Avenue and Menauhant Road. Falmouth Heights has early ties to the Kennedys: Rose Fitzgerald was vacationing here with her family when Joe Kennedy came calling.

East Falmouth is a largely residential area. There are several motels and grand year-round and summer homes lining the inlets of Green Pond, Bourne's Pond, and Waquoit Bay. Historic Danville was once home to whaling-ship captains and has a strong Portuguese and Cape Verdean fishing community and farming heritage.

The center of Falmouth, with plentiful shops and eateries, is busy year-round. And the village common, picture-perfect with historic houses (converted to beautiful bed & breakfasts) encircling the tidy green space, is well worth a stroll. Falmouth's Inner Harbor is awash with restaurants, boatyards, a colorful marina, and moderate nightlife. Two passenger ferries to Martha's Vineyard operate from here.

Four miles south of Falmouth, Woods Hole is more than just a terminus for the Steamship Authority auto and passenger ferries to the Vineyard. It is also home to three major scientific institutions: the National Marine Fisheries Service ("the Fisheries"), Woods Hole Oceanographic Institution (or WHOI, pronounced hooey), and the Marine Biological Laboratory (MBL).

Woods Hole, named for the "hole" or passage between Penzance Point and Nonamessett Island, was the site of the first documented European landing in the New World. Bartholomew Gosnold arrived here from Falmouth, England, in 1602.

GUIDANCE

✳ **Falmouth Chamber of Commerce** (508-548-8500; 508-548-8521 for 24-hour "fax-back" information; 1-800-526-8532; www.falmouth-capecod.com), Box 582, 20 Academy Lane, Falmouth 02541. Open 9–5 weekdays year-round; 9–5 weekends mid-May to mid-October. There is also a seasonal **satellite office,** open mid-May to mid-October, on Palmer Avenue. Both offices also have Woods Hole information, good foldout street maps and a fishing map, and the historical society's walking tour brochure. Check www.woodshole.com for more information on the tiny village.

PUBLIC REST ROOMS

In Falmouth, public rest rooms are located at the chamber of commerce office, Academy Lane; Peg Noonan Park and Town Hall on Main Street; and the Harbormaster's Office at Marina Park, Scranton Avenue. In Woods Hole, head to the Steamship Authority.

✎✳⛄PUBLIC LIBRARIES

The area has five libraries; call each for its hours:

Falmouth Public Library (508-457-2555), 123 Catherine Lee Bates Road, is excellent (it has coupons to local attractions);

East Falmouth Public Library (508-548-6340), 310 Route 28;

North Falmouth Public Library (508-563-2922), Chester Street;

West Falmouth Library (508-548-4709), 575 Route 28A;

Woods Hole Library (508-548-8961), 581 Woods Hole Road, Woods Hole. As you might imagine, there are lots of scientists and NPR "Science Friday" types at this branch.

GETTING THERE

By car: Via Route 28 south, Falmouth is 15 miles from the Bourne Bridge and 20 miles from the Sagamore Bridge. Route 28 turns into Main Street. In northern Falmouth, Route 28A parallels Route 28 and is much more scenic. Route 28 leads directly to Locust Street and Woods Hole Road for Woods Hole.

The directional signposts for Route 28 are a tad confusing from this point on. Although Hyannis and Chatham are east of Falmouth, the signpost from Falmouth to Chatham says ROUTE 28 SOUTH. This is because Route 28 originates in Bourne and does indeed head south to Falmouth before jogging east.

By bus: **Bonanza** (1-888-751-8800; www.bonanzabus.com) has service to Falmouth (stopping at the Depot Avenue terminal) and Woods Hole (stopping at the Steamship Authority) from New York, Providence, Connecticut, western Massachusetts, and Boston. There is direct ser-

The Falmouth village green

vice to Boston's Logan Airport. Some buses are intended to connect with ferries to Martha's Vineyard, although the ferry won't wait for a late bus. The round-trip fare from Boston's South Station to Woods Hole is $27.

GETTING AROUND

Whoosh (508-385-8326; 1-800-352-7155; www.capecodtransit.org) travels between major points of interest in and between Falmouth and Woods Hole. Tourists can hop on and off downtown and at shops and beaches. Whoosh operates about 9–7 daily, late May to late September; tickets cost $1 adults (50¢ kids 6–17). One-day passes are available from the chamber of commerce (see *Guidance*) or on board for $3 adults (half price kids). Pick up a schedule and route map at the chamber, Steamship Authority, shops, or any stop along the route. Trolleys are equipped with a bike rack. Parking is extremely limited in Woods Hole, and roads are congested, so take Whoosh if you're just visiting for the afternoon.

Trolley Tours (508-548-4857). Departing from the Julia Wood House on the town green on many Saturdays from mid-June to late August. Sponsored by the Falmouth Historical Society, this narrated 2-hour trip covers 10 miles and illuminates Falmouth's almost 350 years of maritime ties and rich history. Tickets $12 adults, $8 children under age 12. Purchase tickets at the chamber of commerce or Museums on the Green.

GETTING TO MARTHA'S VINEYARD

There is year-round automobile and passenger ferry service to Martha's Vineyard from Woods Hole; there are two seasonal passenger ferry services to the Vineyard from Falmouth Harbor. For complete information, see Getting There in "Martha's Vineyard."

Museums on the Green of the Falmouth Historical Society

MEDICAL EMERGENCY

Falmouth Hospital (508-548-5300), 100 Ter Heun Drive (off Route 28), Falmouth. Open 24 hours a day.

Falmouth Walk-In Medical Center (508-540-6790), 309 Route 28, Teaticket Highway. Walk-ins weekdays 8–5 year-round.

TO SEE

In Falmouth

Village green. The green is bordered by Colonial, Federal, Italianate, and Greek Revival homes, many built for wealthy ship captains and then converted to bed & breakfasts. Designated as public land in 1749 and now on the National Register of Historic Places, this large triangle of grass is enclosed by a white fence, surely as pastoral a sight today as it was more than 250 years ago. With these historic buildings surrounding you, it's not difficult to imagine local militiamen practicing marches and drills and townspeople grazing horses. In fact, a local militia reenacts maneuvers on July 4.

First Congregational Church, 68 Main Street, on the green. This quintessential New England church—with its high steeple and crisp white lines—is graced by a bell (which still rings) commissioned by Paul Revere. The receipt for the bell—from 1796—is on display; the inscription on the bell reads: THE LIVING TO THE CHURCH I CALL, AND TO THE GRAVE I SUMMON ALL. Today's church was built on the foundations of the 1796 church.

☙ **Museums on the Green of the Falmouth Historical Society** (508-548-4857; www.falmouthhistoricalsociety.org), 55–65 Palmer Avenue, just off the village green. Open 10–4 Tuesday through Saturday, July through September; additional weekend hours in June and October; archives by appointment year-round. The **Conant House,** a 1724 half house, contains sailors' valentines, scrimshaw, rare glass and china, and old tools. One room honors Katherine Lee Bates, a Wellesley College professor and composer of "America the Beautiful," who was born nearby in 1859 at 16 Main Street (not open to the public). Most Falmouth residents would lend support to the grassroots movement in the United States to change the national anthem from "The Star-Spangled Banner" to Bates's easier-to-sing, less militaristic song.

Next door, the early-19th-century **Julia Wood House** was home to Dr. Francis Wicks, known for his work with smallpox inoculations. When the restored **Dudley Hallett Barn** reopens in 2002, the educational center will center on a series of hands-on exhibits. There is also a lovely herb garden and a Nimrod cannon to explore. Tours by trained guides are included in the price: adults $5, children under 12 free.

See also Bourne Farm under *Green Space—Walks.*

In Woods Hole

☙※✓**Woods Hole Science Aquarium** (508-495-2001), Albatross Street. Open 10–4 daily, mid-June to mid-September, and 10–4 weekdays the rest of the year. When it opened in 1871, it was the first aquarium in the country. Today it's a fun place to learn about slippery fish, living shellfish (rather than the empty shells we're all accustomed to seeing), and other lesser-known creatures of the deep. Kids are encouraged to use microscopes and interact with lobsters, hermit crabs, and other crawling sea critters in a dozen tanks and shallow pools of icy-cold bubbling seawater. Even when the aquarium is closed, you can see seals in a tank out front. Free.

☙ **Woods Hole Oceanographic Institution (WHOI) Exhibit Center** (508-289-2663; 508-289-2252 for tour reservations; www.whoi.edu), 15 School Street. Open 10–4:30 Tuesday through Saturday and Sunday noon–4:30, May through October; also open Monday 10–4:30 in July and August. Closed January through March; weekend hours off-season. A Rockefeller grant of $2.5 million got WHOI off the ground in 1930, and since then the annual budget has grown to about $92 million. It is the largest independent oceanography lab in the country. About 1,000 students and researchers from all over the world are employed year-round. During World War II, WHOI worked on underwater explosives and submarine detection. Today, scientists study climate issues, undersea volcanoes, ocean and coastal pollution, deep-sea robotics and acoustics, and large and small marine life. Relatively unpolluted waters and a deep harbor make Woods Hole an ideal location for this work.

WHOI buildings cover 200 acres. One-hour guided walking tours are offered weekdays at 10 AM and 1:30 PM from mid-June to early September. The tour covers a lot of ground and is geared to adults and teenagers. A small exhibit center shows excellent videos; you'll also find an interactive display with marine-mammal sounds and a fascinating display of *Alvin*, the tiny submarine that allowed WHOI researchers to explore and photograph the *Titanic* in 1986. Suggested exhibit donation $2; walking tour free, but reservations required.

❋ **Marine Biological Laboratory (MBL)** (508-548-3705; 508-289-7623 for tour reservations; www.mbl.edu),100 Water Street. Visitors center open weekdays 10–4, June through August (additional hours vary because the center is staffed by volunteers). Tours, at 1, 2, and 3 PM only, are very popular and restricted in size, so reservations are required at least a week in advance. Founded in 1888 as "a non-profit institution devoted to research and education in basic biology," the MBL studies more than fish. It studies life at its most basic level, with an eye toward answering the question "What is life?" And marine creatures tend to be some of the most useful animals in that quest. Scientists (including 37 Nobel laureates over the years) study the problems of infertility, hypertension, Alzheimer's, AIDS, and other diseases. It's not hyperbole to say there's no other institution or academy like it in the world. Former researchers lead excellent tours that include a video about what goes on at the MBL. History buffs will be interested to note that one of the MBL's granite buildings was a former factory that made candles with spermaceti (whale oil). Free. Not appropriate for children under 10.

St. Joseph's Bell Tower, Millfield Street (north shore of Eel Pond). To encourage his colleagues not to become too caught up in the earthly details of their work and lose their faith in the divine, an MBL student designed this pink-granite Romanesque bell tower in 1929. He arranged for its two bells to ring twice a day to remind the scientists and townspeople of a higher power. (One bell is named for Gregor Mendel, the 19th-century botanist, the other for Louis Pasteur.) Nowadays, the bells ring three times, at 7 AM, noon, and 6 PM. The meticulously maintained **St. Mary's Garden** surrounds the tower with flowers, herbs, a bench, and a few chairs. Right on the harbor, this is one of the most relaxing places in the entire area.

Church of the Messiah, Church Street. Nine Nobel Prize winners are buried in the churchyard. This 1888 stone Episcopal church is admired by visiting scientists, tourists, and townsfolk alike. The herb meditation garden is a treasure.

🐚 **Woods Hole Historical Museum and Collection** (508-548-7270; www. woodsholemuseum.org), 579 Woods Hole Road. Open 10–4 Tuesday through Saturday, mid-June through September. Archives open year-round. A treasure. Near the top of the Steamship Authority parking lot, the **Bradley House** historical museum maintains a good library on maritime subjects, more than 200 local oral histories, a scale model of Woods Hole in the late 1800s, and a replication of Dr. Yale's 1890s workshop. Some exhibits change annually. Small historic boats that plied local waters are exhibited in the adjacent **Swift Barn.** There is a lovely view of Little Harbor from here, and staff give a free 90-minute walking tour around Eel Pond on Tuesday at 4 during July and August. Donations.

Nobska Light, Church Street, off Woods Hole Road. Open for free tours 1–3 some Saturdays and Thursdays, late May to mid-August. Built in 1828, rebuilt in 1876, and automated in 1985, the beacon commands a high vantage point on a bluff; the light is visible from 17 miles out at sea. It's a particularly good place to see the "hole" (after which Woods Hole was named), the Elizabeth Islands, the north shore of Martha's Vineyard, and to watch the sunset. More than 30,000 vessels—ferries, fully rigged sailing ships, and pleasure boats—pass by annually. The internationally regarded Falmouth Road Race also passes the picturesque lighthouse. During Cape Cod Maritime Days in mid-May, the Coast Guard opens many Cape lighthouses, including Nobska (see *Special Events*).

SCENIC DRIVE

Take Route 28A to Old Dock Road to reach placid **West Falmouth Harbor.** Double back and take Route 28A to Palmer Avenue, to Sippewissett Road, to hilly and winding Quissett Avenue, to equally tranquil **Quissett Harbor.** At the far edge of the harbor you'll see a path that goes up over the hill of **the Knob,** an outcrop that's half wooded bird sanctuary and half rocky beach. Walk out to the Knob along the water and back through the woods. It's a great place for a picnic or to take in the sunset. Sippewissett Road takes you to Eel Pond and Woods Hole the back way. Surf Drive from Falmouth to Nobska Light is also picturesque.

OUTDOOR ACTIVITIES

BICYCLING/RENTALS

Shining Sea Bike Path. The easygoing and level $3\frac{1}{3}$-mile (one way) trail is one of Falmouth's most popular attractions. Following the old Penn Central Railroad line between Falmouth and Woods Hole, the path parallels unspoiled beaches, marshes, and bird sanctuaries. It was named in honor of Katherine Lee Bates (see Conant House under *To See*), composer of "America the Beautiful." The last line of her song— "from sea to shining sea"—is a fitting description of the trail, which offers lovely views of Vineyard Sound, Martha's Vineyard, and Naushon Island.

The trail connects with several other routes: from Falmouth to Menauhant Beach in East Falmouth; from Woods Hole to Old Silver Beach in North Falmouth; and from Woods Hole to Quissett and Sippewissett. There is a trailhead and parking lot on Locust Street (at

Mill Road) in Falmouth, as well as access points at Elm Road and Oyster Pond Road. Park here; it's very difficult to park in Woods Hole.

Holiday Cycles (508-540-3549), 465 Grand Avenue, Falmouth Heights. Along with a wide variety of bikes (including tandems and surreys) and equipment (from child seats to locks), Holiday Cycles offers free parking. Ask for details about the **23-mile Sippewissett route.**

❆ **Corner Cycle** (508-540-4195), 115 Palmer Avenue, Falmouth, also rents bicycles.

BOAT EXCURSIONS/RENTALS

Cuttyhunk Cruise (508-548-2626) excursions aboard Patriot Party Boats in summer. These idyllic 5-hour trips depart twice weekly (probably noon–5 on Tuesday and Thursday, but you'll want to call ahead for reservations anyway) for the quaint little island of Cuttyhunk, one dot in the chain of Elizabeth Islands. It takes about 75 minutes to get there, cruising along the Vineyard Sound side, listening to on-board commentary about the private Forbes Islands, and back along the Buzzards Bay side. This means you have 2 hours on Cuttyhunk for a picnic lunch or lunch in a little café, or to walk around. You can see the whole island in that amount of time. Adults $30, kids 12 and under $20.

✐ **Ocean Quest** (508-457-0508), Water Street, Woods Hole. Mid-May to mid-October (but there are groups trips in spring and fall on which individuals may be able to tag along). Founder and director Kathy Mullin offers hands-on marine education for the entire family. A science teacher and naturalist, Kathy gives a brief overview of oceanography. The 90-minute trip costs $19 adults, $14 children 3–12. The boat departs four times each weekday in July and August.

❧ **Patriot Party Boats** (508-548-2626), 227 Clinton Avenue at Scranton Avenue, Falmouth. July to early September. This excellent outfit operates 2-hour sails on the *Liberté,* a 1750s schooner replica; adults $20, children 12 and under $14; sunset cruise $20 per person. The sunset trip cruises by six lighthouses and four harbors. Bring a picnic and BYOB. Soft drinks on board. The Tietje (pronounced teegee) family have been chartering boats since the mid-1950s, and they know the local waters like the backs of their hands. Captain Jim and his wife Maura are gems. Patriot also has **ferry shuttle service** to Oak Bluffs on Martha's Vineyard. Although they primarily service commuters, you can catch a ride for $6 one way.

CANOEING/KAYAKING

Waquoit Kayak at Edward's Boatyard (508-548-9722; 508-548-2216), 1209 Route 28, on Waquoit Bay, East Falmouth. From May to mid-October, you can rent canoes ($35 daily) and kayaks ($30 daily) to paddle around Waquoit Bay and over to Washburn Island. Half-day rentals also available. Ask about tours, too.

❧ **Cape Cod Kayak** (508-540-9377). Open late May through October. Exploring salt marshes, tidal inlets, freshwater ponds, and the ocean shoreline from the vantage point and speed of a kayak is a great way to experience the Cape. Cape Cod Kayak offers half-day, full-day, and weekend rentals, with delivery included. One- and two-seaters available. If you want to go kayaking and don't know where to go, owner Kim Fernandes will recommend spots or locations suited to your interests and level of ability. She also has organized tours with about five people per guide.

See also Cape Cod Kayak under *Kayaking* and Waquoit Bay National Estuarine Research Reserve under *Green Space.*

FISHING/SHELLFISHING

Contact Town Hall (508-548-7611) on Main Street for fishing and shellfishing licenses and regulations. It's open weekdays 8–4:30. The chamber of commerce (see *Guidance*) publishes a very good (free) fishing map and guide.

Fish for trout, smallmouth bass, chain pickerel, and white perch at **Ashumet Pond, Quashnet River,** and at the town landing on **Santuit Pond.** See Massachusetts Military Reservation under *To See* in "Bourne" for information about water quality at Ashumet. Surf-casting is great on **Surf Drive.**

✐ **Patriot Party Boats** (508-548-2626), 227 Clinton Avenue, Falmouth. The Goliath of boat tours in Falmouth also offers sport- and bottom fishing from late May to mid-October. Rate includes bait and tackle. Bottom fishing aboard the *Patriot II* costs $25 adults, $17 children 6–12, free age 5 and under. Sportfishing is offered a couple of times per week aboard the custom-outfitted *Minuteman.* Call for exact days of departure.

✿ ***Black Hawk*** (508-992-2038) offers sportfishing for one to four people ($450) in search of bass and blues. With friendly and hardworking Capt. Joe Cordeiro at the helm, you're sure to enjoy the 8-hour day. Oh yeah: He really knows where the fish are running, too. Trips depart from the Inner Harbor at the corner of Clinton and Scranton Avenues from May through October. The ***Dough Boy*** (508-299-8260), captained by Tom Danforth, also runs a good charter.

Susan Jean (508-548-6901), Eel Pond, off Water Street, Woods Hole. From late May to mid-October, Capt. John Christian's 22-foot Aquasport searches for trophy-size striped bass. This trip is for the serious angler— John usually departs in the middle of the night (well, more like 4 AM) because of the tides. $400 for an 8-hour trip for one to three people. Reservations necessary.

❋ **Eastman's Sport & Tackle** (508-548-6900), 150 Main Street, Falmouth. A good source for local fishing information; rod and reel rental, too.

❋ **GOLF**

Ballymeade Country Club (508-540-4005), 125 Falmouth Woods Road, North Falmouth. 18 holes, par 72. You'll have to play this tough semi-private course at least once before getting the hang of it.

Cape Cod Country Club (508-563-9842), off Route 151, North Falmouth. 18 holes, par 71. A scenic course with great variety.

Paul Harney Golf Club (508-563-3454), off Route 151, East Falmouth. 18

holes, 3,700 yards, par 59. Somewhat narrow fairways but generally within the ability of weekend golfers.

Woodbriar Golf Club (508-495-5500), 339 Gifford Street, Falmouth. A nine-hole, 1,285-yard, par-27 course that's quite forgiving.

Falmouth Country Club (508-548-3211), 630 Carriage Shop Road off Route 151, East Falmouth. Open March through November. A good mix of moderate and difficult pars. 18 holes, par 72.

HORSEBACK RIDING

✳ **Haland Stables** (508-540-2552), 878 Route 28A, West Falmouth. Open 9–5 Monday through Saturday; reservations absolutely necessary. Haland offers excellent English instruction, lessons, and guided trail rides through pine woods, fields, a bird sanctuary, cranberry bogs, and salt-marsh land.

ICE SKATING

Falmouth Ice Arena (508-548-9083; 508-548-0275 for recorded information), off Palmer Avenue, Falmouth. Call for variable public skating times. Skating $3; no rentals.

See also Edward's Boatyard under *Outdoor Activities—Canoeing.*

STRAWBERRY PICKING

✎ **Andrew's Farm Stand** (508-548-4717), 394 Old Meeting House Road, East Falmouth. Open daily, mid-June through December, since 1927. Strawberries, strawberries everywhere, and other produce, too, all reasonably priced (especially if you pick your own). From the looks of it, East Falmouth was once the strawberry center of the world! Strawberry season runs from early June to early July, more or less. You can also pick your own peas in June and tomatoes in August. Children welcome.

TENNIS

The following courts are public: at the **elementary school,** Davisville Road, East Falmouth; **Lawrence School**, Lakeview Avenue, Falmouth; the **high school,** Gifford Street Extension, Falmouth; **Nye Park,** North Falmouth; **Blacksmith Shop Road,** behind the fire station, West Falmouth; **Taft's Playground,** Bell Tower Lane, Woods Hole.

Ballymeade Country Club (508-540-4005), 125 Falmouth Woods Road, North Falmouth. Six outdoor Har-Tru and four hard courts; lessons and clinics.

Falmouth Sports Center (508-548-7433), Highfield Drive, Falmouth. Six indoor and three outdoor courts; $8–16 per person per hour, depending on the time you play.

Falmouth Tennis Club (508-548-4370), Dillingham Avenue, off Route 28 heading toward Hyannis. Open late May to early September. Three clay and three Har-Tru outdoor courts.

WINDSURFING

Cape Cod Windsurfing (508-540-9400), 134 Menauhant Road, East Falmouth. Open seasonally. Old Silver Beach gets a good, predominantly southwestern wind, so there is good windsuring here. You can take lessons or rent "nonmotorized" vessels like kayaks, canoes, and windsurfers in front of the Sea Crest Hotel (off Route 28A, North Falmouth) on Old Silver Beach.

EVEN MORE THINGS TO SEE AND DO

FITNESS CLUB
❄ **Falmouth Sports Center** (508-548-7433), Highfield Drive, Falmouth. For $6 daily, you have access to racquetball and a full array of bodybuilding equipment. Massages cost extra.

FOR FAMILIES
✎ Contact the Falmouth Chamber of Commerce (see *Guidance*) for its free publication *Children's Guide to Falmouth.*

SPECIAL PROGRAM
Sjöholm Bed and Breakfast (508-540-5706; 1-800-498-5706; www. sjoholminn.com), 17 Chase Road (off Route 28A), West Falmouth. Off-season, Barbara White organizes special-interest programs, including natural history field excursions, bird carving, personal retreats, rug hooking, and quilting. Programs are divided between hands-on activities and informal lecture-style weekends. Give Barbara a call to see if you like what she's offering. The price includes B&B (see *Lodging—Bed & Breakfasts*).

WINERY
Cape Cod Winery (508-457-5592), 681 Sandwich Road, East Falmouth. Open weekends early May to early December, noon–5 Wednesday through Sunday in July and August. Summer weekend tours at 2 PM. Tastings, too, of fruity wines, a Blanc de Blancs blend, Cabernet, Pinot Grigio, and Merlot. During harvesttime in late September and early October, visitors are invited to pick grapes in exchange for a gift certificate redeemable for that particular vintage, once it's bottled.

GREEN SPACE

Ashumet Holly and Wildlife Sanctuary (508-362-1426; www.audubon. org), 286 Ashumet Road (off Route 151), East Falmouth. Open daily sunrise to sunset. Local philanthropist Josiah K. Lilly III (of Heritage Plantation of Sandwich fame; see *To See* in "Sandwich") purchased and donated the land in 1961 after the death of Wilfrid Wheeler, who cultivated most of these plants. Wheeler had been very concerned about holiday overharvesting of holly. Crisscrossed with self-guided nature trails, this 45-acre Massachusetts Audubon Society sanctuary overflows with holly: There are more than eight species, 65 varieties, and 1,000 trees (from America, Europe, and Asia). More than 130 bird species have been sighted here: Since 1935, nesting barn swallows have made their home in the rafters of the barn from mid-April to late August. Other flora and fauna thrive as well. Rhododendrons and dogwoods bloom in spring. Large white franklinia flowers (named for Benjamin Franklin) make a show in autumn, and in summer Grassy Pond is filled with the blossoms of lotus plants. The sanctuary offers nature trips to Cuttyhunk Island and guided bird walks. Pick up the informative trail map before setting out. Adults $3, children $2; members free. See Massachusetts Military Reservation under *To See* in "Bourne" for information regarding water quality near Ashumet Pond.

Waquoit Bay National Estuarine Research Reserve (508-457-0495), off Route 28, East Falmouth. Headquarters open 10–4 Monday through Saturday in summer; 10–4 weekdays off-season. Part of a national system dedicated to research estuaries, there are four components to the reserve: South Cape Beach (see also *Green Space—Beach* in "Mashpee"), Washburn Island, Quashnet River Property, and the headquarters (which houses watershed exhibits). More than 2,500 acres of delicate barrier beaches surround lovely Waquoit Bay. Stop in at the headquarters for a trail map and schedule of July and August guided walks. In summer look for "Evenings on the Bluff" talks. Within the South Cape Beach State Park is the little-used, mile-long Great Flat Pond Trail (accessible year-round). It winds past salt marshes, bogs, and wetlands and along coastal pine forests. Guided walks are offered in July and August. The 330-acre, pine-filled Washburn Island is accessible year-round if you have a boat. The 11 primitive island campsites require a permit.

See also the Knob under *Scenic Drive.*

BEACHES

Along Buzzards Bay and Vineyard Sound, 12 miles of Falmouth's 68-mile shoreline are accessible to the public via four beaches. (There are eight additional town beaches.) Generally, waters are a bit warmer off Falmouth than off northside beaches because of the Gulf Stream. Weeklong cottage renters qualify for a beach sticker, obtainable at the Surf Drive Beach Bathhouse 9–4 daily in summer. The permit costs $40 for one week, $50 for 2 weeks. Some innkeepers provide beach stickers. Otherwise, you may pay a daily fee to park at the following beaches. (The Town Beach Committee, 508-548-8623, has further details.)

Menauhant Beach, on Vineyard Sound, off Route 28 and Central Avenue, East Falmouth. The best sound beach, by far. Waters are less choppy on Vineyard Sound than they are on the Atlantic. Parking is $10 weekends and holidays.

Old Silver Beach, on Buzzards Bay, off Route 28A and Quaker Road, North Falmouth. One of the longest and sandiest beaches in town, this is a good one for children, as an offshore sandbar creates shallow tidal pools. Facilities include a bathhouse, a lifeguard, and a snack bar. Parking is $10.

Surf Drive Beach, on Vineyard Sound, on Surf Drive, off Main and Shore Streets, Falmouth. This beach attracts sea kayakers, walkers, and swimmers who want to escape "downtown" beach crowds. It's accessible via the Shining Sea Bike Path (see *Outdoor Activities—Bicycling/Rentals*);

by foot it's 30 minutes from the center of Falmouth. Facilities include a bathhouse. Parking is $10.

Falmouth Heights Beach, on Vineyard Sound, Grand Avenue, Falmouth Heights. Although there is no public parking, the beach is public and popular. Facilities include lots of snack bars.

PONDS

Grews Pond, off Gifford Street at **Goodwill Park,** West Falmouth. Lifeguard in-season, as well as picnic and barbecue facilities and a playground. There are also hiking trails all around the pond.

WALKS

Beebe Woods, access from Ter Heun Drive off Route 28 or Highfield Drive off Depot Avenue, behind the College Light Opera Company (see *Entertainment*), Falmouth. The Beebes, a wealthy family originally from Boston, lived in Falmouth from the late 1870s to the early 1930s. Generous town benefactors, they were among the first to purchase land in Falmouth. Highfield Hall, built in 1878, was the centerpiece of the property, but it now stands in disrepair. (Friends of Highfield are working to save and restore the building.) The 387 acres around it contain miles of public trails for walking, mountain biking, and bird-watching. Locals often refer to these trails as the Dog Walks because so many of them walk their pets here. In autumn especially, it seems like the whole town takes the trail to the **Punch Bowl** (a kettle pond). It's particularly pretty in May when the lady's slippers bloom.

Spohr Gardens (508-548-0623), Fells Road off Oyster Pond Road from Woods Hole Road or Surf Drive. Thanks to Charles and Margaret Spohr (Charles won the citizen-of-the-year award in 1993), this spectacular 3-acre private garden is yours for the touring. Park on Fells Road, or tie up at the dock on Oyster Pond. More than 700,000 daffodils bloom in spring, followed by lilies, azaleas, magnolias, and hydrangeas. (You'll share the wide paths with geese and ducks.)

Waterfront Park, Water Street near the MBL, with shaded benches and a sundial from which you can tell time to within 30 seconds.

Eel Pond, off Water Street. The harborlike pond has a drawbridge that grants access to Great Harbor for fishing boats, yachts, and research vessels moored here. (The walk around the shore is lovely.) The little bridge goes up and down on the hour and half hour; in summer boats line up to pass through.

Bourne Farm (508-548-8484), Route 28A, North Falmouth. Grounds open year-round; house open by appointment. Owned by the nonprofit Salt Pond Areas Bird Sanctuaries, Inc., this 1775 historic landmark includes a restored and furnished farmhouse, a bunkhouse (now a private residence), a barn, and 49 acres of orchards, fields, and wooded trails. It's a perfectly tranquil spot overlooking **Crocker Pond,** complete with a picnic area under a grape arbor. Donations for trail fees. The property and barn are available for wedding rentals.

See also Ashumet Holly and Wildlife Sanctuary, Grews Pond, and Waquoit Bay National Estuarine Research Reserve.

LODGING

❄ Falmouth boasts arguably the Cape's most sophisticated place to stay, as well as lots of B&Bs around the town green, beachfront choices in Falmouth Heights, more secluded B&Bs in West and North Falmouth, and quite a few motels. Unfortunately, though, Falmouth has recently seen many of its family motels converted to time-share units. As for Woods Hole, most people staying there are heading to the Vineyard. Generally, your lodging dollars will go a long way in this part of the Cape. Unless otherwise noted, all lodgings in Falmouth are open year-round.

BED & BREAKFASTS

In Falmouth Heights 02540

🐾 **Inn on the Sound** (508-457-9666; 1-800-564-9668; www.innonthesound. com), 313 Grand Avenue. Open April through October. Renee Ross, a former interior designer with considerable talent, has transformed this shingle-style, turn-of-the-20th-century inn into an elegantly upscale yet casual oceanfront B&B. She's got a perfectly attuned sense of what people want. Nine of the 10 bedrooms, each with private bath and tasteful contemporary aesthetic, have a great view of the long Falmouth Heights Beach, Vineyard Sound, and Martha's Vineyard in the distance. Four rooms now have a private deck with water views. Fabrics are stylish but not overdone; in-room sitting areas are comfortable and substantial but seaside-breezy. The living room features a large stone fireplace, with couches perfectly situated to take advantage of the ocean view. On my last too-short visit, a breakfast basket, artfully presented in the form of a gift deposited on my doorstep, included coffee, various breads, and other epicurean delights. It was a joy to enjoy them on my private balcony. But you could take it to the beach, downstairs lounge, or your private breakfast table. May through October $95–225; otherwise $60–140; $30 additional for a third person.

🐾🏊 **Scallop Shell Inn** (508-495-4900; www.scallopshellinn.com), 16 Massachusetts Avenue. Fifty-two steps or one block from the ocean, with good water views nonetheless, the Scallop Shell, which opened in August 1999, boasts the most unusual policies and facilities of any place to stay on the Cape. There is no check-in or check-out time; there is a full, top-shelf bar with free drinks; there are no deposit or cancellation policies; there are no places off-limits in the inn; there is one staff person for each of the seven rooms; there is a 100 percent guarantee policy. I could go on and on. Innkeeper Betsy Cogliani (an interior designer) poured $1.5 million into the renovation, installing $1,000 hand-painted sinks, Brazilian mahogany floors, marble bathrooms (some with three-person whirlpool and gas fireplace), a cedar laundry (open to guests, of course) that replicates one at Hammersmith Farm in Newport, and a guest kitchenette where you can cook lobsters. Additional in-room amenities include European turndown service, plush robes, French milled toiletries, and hand-cut Belgian chocolates. As for the four-course breakfast, served 7 AM–2 PM, you might enjoy a lobster and asparagus omelet or steak and eggs along with homemade baked beans, fresh squeezed juice in chilled glasses, Kona coffee, and crème brûlée. Ah, I shouldn't forget to mention the billiards table and outdoor shower. Open late May through October, $225–300, off-season $180–225.

Bailey's on the Sea (508-548-5748; 1-866-548-5748; www.baileysonthesea.com), 321 Grand Avenue. This newly and completely renovated waterfront B&B boasts a wrap-around porch with a dozen picture windows, plenty of rocking chairs, and very comfortable but spare guest rooms. The accommodating innkeepers, Liz and Jerry Bailey, offer six rooms that can be rented with shared baths or as two-room suites. Decor ranges from Victorian to Japanese (the Baileys lived in Japan for almost eight years) to traditional. All rooms have bathrobes; TVs are available on request. If you're looking to spread out, third-floor rooms are quite spacious. A full breakfast, served on the porch, might include apple cranberry compote, eggs, hams, and scones; cinnamon buns are already a specialty. In case you're wondering, Bailey's Irish Cream is available in the evening. Mid-June to early September $120–185 with shared bath or $225–290 as a two-bedroom suite for four people. Off-season rates drop to $75–140 and $135–220, respectively.

Grafton Inn (508-540-8688; 1-800-642-4069; www.graftoninn.com), 261 Grand Avenue South. Open mid-March to mid-November. The Grafton Inn is a frilly but comfortable Victorian seaside B&B with five rooms overlooking the ocean. (Another five have decent oblique views.) In-room amenities include TV, bathrobes, and hair dryers. Innkeeper Liz Cvitan (who has owned the B&B with her husband, Rudy, since 1983) has "white noise machines" in each room for light sleepers. Falmouth Heights Beach (see *Green Space*) is across the street; the inn provides beach towels and chairs. A full, self-serve breakfast of eggs Benedict, French apple-stuffed pancakes, or crêpes with raspberry sauce is taken on the glassed-in front porch. Afternoon wine and cheese are included. $169–210 mid-June to mid-October; $105–170 off-season.

Beach House (508-457-0310; 1-800-351-3426; www.capecodbeachhouse.com), 10 Worcester Court. Open May through October. This unusually fanciful B&B has seven guest rooms. Each is hand painted with a different beach-inspired motif: Perhaps you'll get a room covered with fish and sea horses, or stars and moons, or a wave, or a lighthouse mural. The cottage furniture has been painted, too, but in solid colors. Down comforters and new bathrooms are the norm. There is also an adjacent bright and airy cottage suite. You can eat the continental breakfast buffet in the open kitchen or by the pool. May through September $139–169 rooms, $159–189 suite. Rates drop to $99 in October except over the Columbus Day weekend.

On or near the village green 02540

Palmer House (508-548-1230; 1-800-472-2632; www.palmerhouseinn. com), 81 Palmer Avenue. Adjacent to the village green, longtime innkeepers Joanne and Ken Baker run a tight ship, complete with an intercom buzzer and a formal portrait of themselves next to the reception desk. (I confess to being a tad mystified by the two large birdcages in one living room.) The Bakers preside over 17 "bedchambers," all with private bath, robes, lots of lace, TV, flowers, air-conditioning, triple sheeting, turndown service, and telephones. I particularly like the four rooms in the adjacent Guest House, perhaps because they afford greater privacy. Many have a gas fireplace. The main house is a Queen Anne beauty with stained-glass windows, shiny hardwood floors, and front-porch rockers. The upscale Victorian decor is fanciful but tasteful. Breakfast is elaborate and full, perhaps with blended juices, muffins, and an herb omelet with tomato and cheese. Loaner bikes are available for the asking. Mid-June to mid-October $105–260; off-season $75–199.

Captain Tom Lawrence House (508-540-1445; 1-800-266-8139; www. sunsol.com/captaintom), 75 Locust Street. Open March through December. This former 1861 sea captain's home with an impressive spiral staircase is now a pleasant and friendly B&B operated by Anne Grebert and Jim Cotter. Set back from the road, the inn offers six comfortable rooms with private bath, air-conditioning, mini-fridge, and cable TV. A few of the bathrooms are small, so if you are large, inquire. Most rooms are have wall-to-wall carpeting to keep down the noise. Families might appreciate the efficiency **apartment** with private entrance. A full breakfast (perhaps a frittata or strata) is served at one table in the spacious living/dining room. Mid-May through October $140–185 rooms, $200 for the efficiency apartment ($30 each additional person over age 12); off-season $100–155.

Village Green Inn (508-548-5621; 1-800-237-1119; www.villagegreeninn. com), 40 Main Street. Overlooking the village green, this pleasant B&B has five Victorian-style guest rooms and one suite, each with a unique feature (perhaps a pressed-tin ceiling). I particularly like Tripp, with a gas fireplace and sleigh bed, and Crocker, which has a parquet floor and stained-glass window. Traditionally furnished, the large and bright suite is well suited to long stays. Each room has air-conditioning, cable TV, and a phone. The friendly innkeepers, Diane and Don Crosby, provide loaner bikes. Common space includes two open porches and a small formal parlor filled with a collection of Lladros and dolls. Well-behaved children over 12 are welcome. A full breakfast, with blueberry puff pancakes perhaps, is served at 8:30. June through October $150–225; off-season $85–150.

✒ **Elm Arch Inn** (508-548-0133), 26 Elm Arch Way. Open April through October. This classic, old-fashioned hostelry is less than a block from Main Street, but it might as well be worlds away. Built in 1810 and bombed by the British in 1814 (there are still cannonball "scars" in the former dining room), the friendly inn has several common rooms downstairs and is chock-full of colonial touches, braided rugs, and easy chairs. A large, screened-in flagstone porch overlooks a small pool surrounded by lawn chairs. Half of the 20 guest rooms have private bath; others have an in-room sink; many can accommodate three people. In the main house, some of the colonial-style guest rooms have four-poster canopy beds, but beyond that they're quite modestly furnished. Across the street, rooms in the Richardson House are more modern. The inn has been in the Richardson family since 1926. $80–100 mid-June through September, coffee included. Inquire about the annex **cottage,** which sleeps five. No credit cards.

In West Falmouth 02574

✒ **Chapoquoit Inn** (508-540-7232; 1-800-842-8994; www.chapoquoit.com), 495 Route 28A. This rambling farmhouse is set on 3½ acres a couple of miles from the village center. It features a deep backyard complete with a gazebo and maturing gardens, which will seem like an oasis in the height of summer, and enthusiastic and helpful innkeepers. Within the circa-1841 house, innkeepers Kim and Tim McIntyre (and their young son) offer six rooms and a two-bedroom suite (a good value for families or couples traveling together) with private bath. Rooms are spacious and comfortably decorated with quilts and local art work. On my last visit a full breakfast—spiced lemon pancakes stuffed with cream cheese and Kim's grandmother's granola—was served on the deck and in the cheery dining room. Children younger than age 12 are welcome off-season. The inn is half a mile from Chapoquoit Beach, and loaner bikes are available. May through October $150–185 for rooms, $265 for four in a suite; off-season $95–125 and $225, respectively.

Inn at West Falmouth (508-540-6503; 1-800-397-7696; www.innatwest falmouth.com), 66 Frazar Road (off Route 28A). Well hidden on a side road, this turn-of-the-20th-century, shingle-style house features eight guest rooms furnished with English and Continental antiques. Many rooms have a private deck and fireplace; all have Italian marble bath. There are quiet nooks and common spaces aplenty, including a lushly landscaped deck overlooking the pool and a tennis court. The beach is a 10-minute walk away. Owner Stephen Calvacca divides his time between here and his law practice in Florida, while the inn is overseen by a succession of managers. May through October $195–345; off-season $130–225, with continental buffet breakfast.

✒ **Sjöholm Bed and Breakfast** (508-540-5706; 1-800-498-5706; www.sjoholm inn.com), 17 Chase Road (off Route 28A). On a quiet back road, enthusiastic hosts Barbara and Bob White preside over a laid-back 19th-century farmhouse where old-fashioned hospitality and shared experience predominate. Eight rooms in the "farmhouse gone sprawling" are simply furnished. (The adjacent 1930s Sail Loft, though, is very summer-camp rustic. Four rooms off a central hall share a bath, perhaps fine for a group of kids.) I didn't have a chance to see the two-bedroom cottage for this edition, so I can't recommend it. The innkeepers offer special-interest programs on off-season weekends (see *Even More Things to See and Do—Special Programs*). Mid-May through October $105–110 private bath in the farmhouse ($85–90 shared bath in the Sail Loft), including full breakfast.

In Woods Hole 02543

Woods Hole Passage (508-548-9575, 1-800-790-8976; www.woodshole passage.com), 186 Woods Hole Road. On the road connecting Woods Hole and Falmouth, this quiet B&B (with 2 acres of gardens enjoyed from a hammock and plenty of lounge chairs) has a welcoming feel, thanks to innkeeper Deb Pruitt. The attached barn has five completely renovated guest rooms; second-floor rooms are more spacious, with vaulted ceilings and exposed beams. Decor is crisp country modern, and each room has a bold splash of color. Full breakfast is included, as are loaner bikes, beach chairs, beach towels, and use of the outdoor shower. Children may be accommodated by advance arrangement. Mid-May to mid-September $125–165; otherwise $80–120.

MOTOR INN

Coonamessett Inn (508-548-2300), Jones Road and Gifford Street, Falmouth 02540. The Coonamessett has undergone some refreshing changes since 1996, when new owners came on board. Although it's billed as an inn, complete with a living room that's more like a foyer, the 28 units have something of a motel feel, with outside entrances. Choose between suites overlooking picturesque Jones Pond or two-bedroom apartment-style accommodations. There is one self-contained **cottage.** For family reunions, two rooms can be connected by an adjoining entryway. With 7 acres of meticulously landscaped lawns, the Coonamessett hosts its share of weddings and conferences. The inn is filled with the late Cotuit artist Ralph Cahoon's whimsical, neoprimitive paintings of outdoor scenes. Along with attentive service, you have a choice of four dining rooms (see *Dining Out*). Late June to early September $180 rooms, $260 two-bedroom suite, $260 cottage. Expanded continental breakfast included.

MOTELS

Seaside Inn (508-540-4120; 1-800-827-1976; www.seasideinnfalmouth. com), 263 Grand Avenue, Falmouth Heights 02540. Across the street from Falmouth Heights Beach (see Green Space—Beaches), this family-oriented 23-room motel was completely renovated and rebuilt in 1999 and 2000. It's right next to a park, another plus for families. Rates vary widely and are based on the degree of water view; whether the room has access to a deck, full kitchen, or kitchenette; and if the deck is shared or private. Rooms in the back building are the nicest, but the reservation folks won't guarantee a particular room. Too bad, since the third-floor rooms are outstanding. Late May through August $99–219, off-season $49–119. By the way, the **British Beer Company** (508-540-9600) is on the premises. I found it rather smoky but atmospheric, a fine place for an authentic stout or ale on tap. Too bad the service was so slow. If you're not in a hurry, wait for some fish-and-chips, a burger, or a hot sandwich for lunch or dinner.

        ♿ **Sands of Time** (508-548-6300; 1-800-841-0114; www.sandsoftime.com), 549 Woods Hole Road, Woods Hole 02543. Open April to mid-November. Some of the guests here missed the last ferry; others know that this is a convenient place to stay if you want to walk or bike around Woods Hole. There are 20 air-conditioned motel rooms (most with a delightful view of Little Harbor), an apartment with a kitchen, and 12 lovely and large innlike rooms in the adjacent 1870s Victorian Harbor House (many with a harbor view and working fireplace). Fresh flowers, lovely gardens, and a morning newspaper set this place apart. Small heated pool. $130–180 June through September; $80–150 otherwise.

EFFICIENCIES

Ideal Spot Motel (508-548-2257; www.idealspotmotel.net), Route 28A at Old Dock Road, West Falmouth 02540. Open April through October. In a quiet part of town, this nicely landscaped motel has two simple rooms (which can accommodate four people) and 12 efficiencies. There is a barbecue and picnic area. Mid-June to mid-September $98–110; $65–75 in spring and fall; weekly rates.

  ✎ **Mariner's Point Resort** (508-457-0300), 425 Grand Avenue, Falmouth 02540. Open mid-March to late November. This bilevel time-share offers 37 efficiency studios and apartments within a short stroll of Falmouth Heights Beach (see *Green Space—Beaches*). Most units overlook the pool area; a few have an unobstructed view of Vineyard Sound and a town-owned park popular with kite enthusiasts. Some units sleep up to six people, provided they're all very good friends. Mid-May through September $85 studio, $95–160 for up to six people; off-season $65–85.

See also Captain Tom Lawrence House under *Bed & Breakfasts*.

RENTAL HOUSES AND COTTAGES

Real Estate Associates, with four offices, has the local market covered. Depending on where you want to be, call the office in North Falmouth (508-563-7173), West Falmouth (508-540-3005), Falmouth (508-540-1500), or Pocasset (508-563-5266). Although first priority is given to monthly and seasonal rentals, they fill the holes in their schedule in April or early May. There are 100 or so listings.

See also Coonamessett Inn under *Motor Inn* and Elm Arch Inn under *Bed & Breakfasts*.

CAMPGROUNDS

✎**Sippewissett Campground and Cabins** (508-548-2542; 508-548-1971; 1-800-957-2267), 836 Palmer Avenue, Falmouth 02540. Open mid-May to mid-October. This is a well-run, private campground with 11 cabins and 100 large campsites for tents, trailers, and RVs; clean, large bathrooms and showers; and free shuttles to Chapoquoit Beach, the ferry to Martha's Vineyard, and other Falmouth-area locations. In-season camping $27 daily, cabins $300–540 weekly ($45–125 daily); off-season camping $20 daily, cabins $200–350 weekly ($35–75 daily). Pets permitted prior to Memorial Day and after Labor Day, but not in cabins.

See Waquoit Bay National Estuarine Research Reserve under *Green Space.*

WHERE TO EAT

❋ Falmouth and Woods Hole restaurants can satisfy all appetites, from fine dining and waterfront fish houses to taverns and upscale sandwich places. With an amazing array of choices for palates and budgets, everyone should do well here. Unless otherwise noted, all establishments are open year-round.

DINING OUT

In Falmouth

❦ **Chapoquoit Grill** (508-540-7794), 410 Route 28A, West Falmouth. Open for dinner daily at 5 PM. From the moment this eclectic New American bistro opened in mid-1993, it was a success. No longer did locals have to drive 45 minutes to get innovative cooking in a low-key atmosphere that didn't cost an arm and a leg. The popular wood-fired, thin-crust, garlicky pizzas are excellent. You can spot the regulars: They order from the nightly specials menu only. Swordfish and seafood dishes are always superb. No reservations are taken, so get there when it opens or be prepared for a long wait in the convivial **bar.** Entrées $7–18.

Coonamessett Inn (508-548-2300), Jones Road and Gifford Street. Open for lunch and dinner. This restaurant features traditional regional American fare with an emphasis on seafood—baked stuffed lobster, seafood Newburg, and lobster bisque. Each of the three dining rooms has something to recommend it: hot-air-balloon paintings by the late Ralph Cahoon, a view of secluded Jones Pond from an outdoor mahogany deck, and vines and tiny grapelike lights in the Vineyard Room. Reservations recommended. Entrées $11–30. **Eli's,** a tavern-style room with deep green trim, light wood, and brass pieces, is known for good service and conventional and conservative New England fare. Look for the day's specials (on Monday it's chicken Parmesan); otherwise, scallop dishes are usually quite good. Entrées $7–14.

EATING OUT

In Falmouth

❦ **The Quarterdeck** (508-548-9900), 164 Main Street. Open for lunch and dinner daily. This place enjoys a loyal local following, with good reason. With hand-hewn beams, barnboard walls, and a fire in the woodstove in winter, it has a warm, pubby feel. The service is also quite friendly. You could be happy with any number of dishes at lunch: fish-and-chips, quiche, and omelets, for example. For dinner I highly recommend the Seafarer's Catch (a daily New American seafood special with Asian or southwestern influences), the Old Salt's Notion (a nonseafood daily special of duck or ostrich, perhaps), and Commodore's Command (a scrod special). The baked seafood platter is always a popular standby. Children's menu. Lunch $8–12, dinner entrées $12–22.

✳ **TraBiCa** (508-548-2076), 327 Gifford Street, Falmouth. Open nightly (except Monday off-season). Trabica, derived from combining the first letters of trattoria, bistro, and café, takes its cues from the subtle differences between those types of eateries. You can get conventional family-style Italian dishes like shrimp scampi over linguini from the trattoria menu; unpretentious burgers from the café menu, and down-to-earth seasonal offerings from the bistro menu. (Rich seafood crepes, anyone?) It's not high cuisine, but the combination of moderate prices, comfortable surroundings, consistent preparation, and friendly service are unbeatable. No reservations, but try calling before leaving your lodging. Entrees $8–15.

Food for Thought (508-548-4498), 37 North Main Street. Open for breakfast daily (except closed Monday and Tuesday off-season). Locals are quite partial to this small and casual eatery—with good reason. If you're not staying at an inn that serves breakfast, this is an excellent choice. Most dishes are made from scratch. I particularly like their French-style omelets and anything with a southwestern flair. Daily specials keep patrons coming back. You'll often see owner/chief-cook-and-bottle-washer Charlie at the helm in the exposed kitchen. Takeout. Dishes $4–9.

Laureen's (508-540-9104), 170 Main Street. Open 8:30–5 daily except Sunday. Even without considering its prime downtown location, Laureen's would be a fine choice for casual lunches, homemade desserts, and good coffee. Busy sister-and-brother caterers Diane Harvey and John Marderosian offer eclectic dishes like a Middle East sampler plate, a vegetarian burrito plate, a few fancy feta pizzas, and sandwiches. There's table service as well as takeout.

The Chickadee (508-548-4006), 881 Old Palmer Avenue, West Falmouth. Open daily. On a quiet country road, the Chickadee at Peach Tree Circle Farm is surrounded by 6 acres of apple and peach orchards, and flower and vegetable gardens. You can dine alfresco or at a few tables inside. Light lunches—all homemade—of quiche, sandwiches, soups (the chowder is delicious), and seafood salads are recommended. Vegetables are particularly fresh. (Remember, this is a farm.) Or come for tea and a delectable sweet from the bakery. Lunch $3–10.

✑ **Clam Shack** (508-540-7758), 227 Clinton Avenue. Open mid-May to early September. Since 1962, chef-owner Jim Limberakis has operated this tiny and busy clam shack: There is rarely enough room inside. But it's just as well—head to the back deck to munch on fried clams, scallops, and fish while watching pleasure boats and fishermen come and go. Lunch and early dinner $5–10.

✍ **Seafood Sam's** (508-540-7887), Route 28. You can always count on Seafood Sam's for high quality fried seafood sandwiches and mixed plates. Dishes range from $5 for a fried shrimp roll to $11 for a lobster salad plate.

♿ **Peking Palace** (508-540-8204), 452 Main Street. Open from lunchtime until late daily. If you're tired of fried seafood platters or grilled fish and wishing for takeout from your favorite Chinese restaurant at home, the Peking Palace won't disappoint. If anything, it will make you think twice about your Chinese back home! It's definitely the best on the Upper or Mid-Cape. There must be 200 Mandarin, Szechuan, and Cantonese dishes on the menu. All furnishings and decor, by the way, have been imported from Taiwan. Lunch $3.50–6, dinner entrées $8–15.

✍ **Betsy's Diner** (508-540-0060), 457 Main Street, East Falmouth. Open for all three meals daily. This old-fashioned 1957 Mountain View Diner was transported by truck in 1992 from Pennsylvania to Main Street, on the former site of another diner. The boxy addition is not historic, just functional. The place is packed with locals and families who come for the inexpensive fare: club sandwiches, breakfast specials, or perhaps the famous roast turkey dinner. Specials are generally excellent and portions large. Breakfast is served all day to tunes from the '60s. Children's menu. Dishes $2–11.

✍ **Moonakis Cafe** (508-457-9630), 460 Route 28, Waquoit. Open for breakfast and lunch daily. Paul Rifkin and Ellen Mycock run a great breakfast joint. Specialties include homemade sausage, corned beef hash, and chowder, as well as fresh fruit waffles, crabcakes, and Reubens. Ellen is family-friendly: She'll make simple, small dishes for kids, depending on what they'll eat. $3–8.

Flying Bridge (508-548-2700), 220 Scranton Avenue (west side of Inner Harbor). Open 11:30 AM to 9 PM daily, mid-April through November; until 11 in summer. This enormous, 600-seat restaurant overlooks the busiest area of Falmouth's Inner Harbor, including the *Island Queen* dock. The view is the main attraction, so ask for a table on the deck. I nosh on appetizers or get a salad and sandwich. The same menu is served all day; dishes $5–25.

See also Nimrod, Liam Maguire's, and Boathouse under *Entertainment—Nightlife* and the British Beer Company at the Seaside Inn under *Lodging—Motels.*

In Woods Hole

🦞✍ **Fishmonger Cafe** (508-548-9148), 56 Water Street. Open for all three meals daily, mid-February to mid-December (except closed Tuesday off-season and no breakfast on Tuesday in summer). The Monger has been the most consistent place in town since Frances Buehler opened it in 1974; chef Harold Broadstock has been dishing up the eclectic, international fare since 1990. The menu features Thai spring rolls, tuna sate, and fried calamari, as well as fisherman's stew, tofu and veggies, and rice and refried beans. Specials change throughout the day and sometimes during a meal as well; keep an eye on the blackboard. Some savvy patrons order only off the specials menu. The location and atmosphere couldn't be better, overlooking the Eel Pond Bridge. And even though the Monger is always bustling, the friendly staff keep it comfortable. Evenings sparkle, thanks to candlelight, shiny wooden tables, and lots of little windowpanes. Children's menu and a friendly **bar.** Lunch $6–12, dinner $9–22.

Shuckers World Famous Raw Bar & Cafe (508-540-3850), 91A Water Street. Open for lunch and dinner May through October. Sit on the deck overlooking Eel Pond and enjoy twin lobsters on Tuesday night for $16. Also lobster bisque, lobster rolls, stuffed tomatoes with lobster, and lobster ravioli. Do you get the idea that lobster is a specialty? Of course, there is also raw and steamed seafood, and even mesquite- grilled fish and chicken. It's a fun place, kept consistent by the vision of a longtime chef owner. Children's menu. The dockside patio is heated on cool spring and fall evenings. Dishes $10–17.

Captain Kidd (508-548-8563), 77 Water Street. The tavern is open for lunch and dinner daily. The fancier waterfront section overlooking Eel Pond is open for dinner daily, mid-June to early September. The Kidd, as it's affectionately called, offers specialty pizzas, burgers, sandwiches, fish-and-chips, scrod, steaks, and blackboard fish specials. It's all very good. The glassed-in patio with a woodstove is a cozy place to be in winter. This local watering hole is named for the pirate who supposedly spent a short time in the environs of Woods Hole on the way to his execution in England. A playful pirate mural hangs above barrel-style tables across from the long, hand-carved mahogany bar. The primary drawback here: The staff are often more attentive to the TV at the bar than they are to patrons. Tavern lunch and dinner $7–15, waterfront dining entrées $15–25.

Landfall (508-548-1758), Luscombe Avenue. Open 11–10 daily, mid-April through October. The Landfall, in the Estes family since 1946, is one of the Upper Cape's best places to soak up local atmosphere: Preppies and weather-beaten fishermen are both regulars here. Bedecked with seafaring paraphernalia and built with salvaged materials, the large dining room is also cozy with hurricane lamps. The waterfront location is excellent: Try for a table overlooking the ferry dock. Fare is Cape Cod traditional: lobster and seafood like swordfish, cod, and scallops. Children's menu. Lunch $8–11, dinner $20–23.

Pie in the Sky (508-540-5475), 10 Water Street. Open 7 AM–5 PM weekdays and 7–3 Saturday; also open Sunday morning in summer. Strong coffee, good pastries, and deli sandwiches, too. There are a few tables inside and outside.

COFFEE & TEA

Coffee Obsession (508-540-2233), 110 Palmer Avenue, Falmouth. Open at least 7 AM–8 PM daily. Caffeine addicts flock to this bohemian place for bracing espressos, a slice of coffee cake, and a smidgen of counterculture à la Falmouth. Eggnog, apple cider, and other seasonal beverages, too. There's also a retail shop for all your chai- and coffee-related needs.

ICE CREAM

Dutchland Farms (508-548-9032), 809 Route 28, Falmouth. Open March to mid-December. On your way toward Hyannis, stop for excellent no-fat yogurt (Honolulu Crunch—coconut mango with macadamia nuts, is particularly good). All flavors are homemade and change daily.

See also Ben & Bill's Chocolate Emporium under *Special Shops*.

MARKETS

Windfall Market (508-548-0099), 77 Scranton Avenue. Open daily. Prepared foods, a deli section, trout, lobsters, homemade breads, and a fine wine selection with a knowledgeable staff.

West Falmouth Market (508-548-1139), 623 Route 28, West Falmouth. Open daily. This old-fashioned neighborhood market carries deli meats for sandwiches and hearty *pain d'Avignon*. You haven't tasted bread until you've tasted *pain d'Avignon*.

ENTERTAINMENT

✐ **Baseball,** Fuller Field, just off Main Street, Falmouth. The Commodores, one of 10 teams in the Cape Cod Baseball League, play in July and August. The chamber of commerce has a schedule (see *Guidance*).

✐ **Band concerts,** July and August. The Falmouth Town Band performs at Marina Park, on the west side of the Inner Harbor, on Thursday evening at 7:30 or 8. Bring a chair or a blanket and watch the kids dance to simple marches and big-band numbers. Or wander around and look at the moored boats. There are also free Friday concerts at 6:30 PM at Peg Noonan Park on Main Street in July and August.

College Light Opera Company (508-548-0668), Depot Avenue next to Highfield Hall, Falmouth. Open late June to late August. Performances Tuesday through Saturday at 8:30 PM and Thursday at 2:30. Founded in 1969, the talented and energetic collegiate company, which includes 32 singers, a 17-piece orchestra, and 12 technicians, has risen to the challenge of providing the only live musical and theatrical entertainment for area visitors. Music majors and theater arts students from across the country perform nine shows in nine weeks. Tickets $22 for those age 5 and older.

Woods Hole Folk Music Society (508-540-0320), Community Hall, Water Street, Woods Hole. Well-known touring folkies generally play on the first and third Sunday of each month, October to early May.

✳ ↑ **MOVIES**

    Nickelodeon Cinema (508-563-6510), Route 151, North Falmouth.

    Falmouth Mall Cinema (508-540-2169), Route 28 (Teaticket Highway).

NIGHTLIFE

✳ **Liam Maguire's Irish Pub & Restaurant** (508-548-0285), 273 Main Street, Falmouth. Open for lunch and dinner. It doesn't get any more "real" or more fun than this unless you go to South Boston or Ireland. Irish students serve shepherd's pie, Irish beef stew, corned beef and cabbage, or fish-and-chips in Irish beer batter for $8–10. Food is average, the sandwiches a bit better. Come for beer (Guinness on draft) and music. Liam himself plays some nights; sing-alongs after 9 PM.

✳ **The Nimrod** (508-540-4132), 100 Dillingham Avenue, Falmouth. Open for lunch and dinner. Listen to good jazz—piano, trios, and piano bar sing-alongs—nightly except Monday. Grab a seat at the bar or order traditional fare like shrimp scampi or a grilled chicken club sandwich. Luncheon specials at this "townie" place are a good deal at $6–10. Dinner entrées $15–30.

    The Boathouse (508-548-7800), 88 Scranton Avenue, Falmouth. Open late May through December. An attractive and pretty darn good restaurant by day, the Boathouse jumps with lively crowds and live music nightly in summer and on weekends in spring and fall.

SELECTIVE SHOPPING

✳ In recent years, the quality of Main Street stores in Falmouth has risen, sidewalks have been repaved, benches added, and flower beds and boxes are overflowing. Unless otherwise noted, all shops are open year-round and in Falmouth proper.

ARTISANS

Woods Hole Handworks (508-540-5291), 68 Water Street, Woods Hole. Open late June to mid-October and daily late November to late December. This tiny artisans' cooperative, hanging over the water near the drawbridge to Eel Pond, has a selection of fine handmade jewelry, scarves, weaving, beadwork, and tiles.

Under the Sun (508-540-3603), 22 Water Street, Woods Hole. An eclectic selection of handcrafted jewelry, pottery, glass, wood, and furniture. Although the quality is somewhat uneven, the "very good" far outweighs the "all right."

ART GALLERIES

Gallery 333 (508-564-4467; www.gallery333.com), 333 Old Main Road (near the intersection of Routes 151 and 28A), North Falmouth. Open afternoons Wednesday through Sunday, late May to mid-September. Arlene Hecht's gallery is housed in a wonderful 19th-century home that's been added on to many times over the last 200 years. Once the site of an asparagus farm, the house now showcases a medley of work by 40 local, regional, and national artists (both abstract and representational). Paintings, drawings, photography, ceramics, and limited edition prints. Don't miss the sculpture garden. On many Saturdays in summer, the gallery holds meet-the-artists receptions.

Woods Hole Gallery (508-548-4329), 14 School Street, Woods Hole. Open late June through September. Owner, curator, and all-around arbiter of fine art Edie Bruce has operated this gallery since 1963. It's hardly a pristine environment; the old house has low ceilings, walls are in need of a paint job, and the shag rug is worn. But amid the general feeling of clutter, with paintings stacked everywhere, you will find some real gems. Some are inexpensive, some are pricey. But any way you look at it, you can trust Edith's expertise about area artists.

The Open Door Gallery (508-540-8484), 544 Route 28A, North Falmouth. Open June to mid-October and for Christmas; Friday-evening hours in summer, too. One of the better contemporary fine art galleries in town offers exceptional furniture, fine art photography, and paintings in a whitewashed old house. "Art" for the garden, too. Make it a point to stop.

Falmouth Artists' Guild (508-540-3304; www.arts-cape.com/falag), 744 Main Street. Open 10–3 Tuesday through Friday, this nonprofit guild (active since the 1950s) holds 10 to 12 exhibitions a year, half of which are juried. They have a fund-raising auction in July and a big Arts Alive Festival in early August (see *Special Events*).

BOOKSTORES

Eight Cousins Children's Books (508-548-5548), 189 Main Street. This is an excellent shop, with very broad and deep roots in the community. And they're always changing and improving, eager for feedback from customers. Named for one of *Little Women* author Louisa May Alcott's lesser-known works, Eight Cousins stocks more than 14,000 titles and is a great resource, whether you're a teacher, a gift buyer, or entertaining a child on a rainy afternoon. It continues to excel with kids' programs, an extensive selection of titles, regular storytime, great service, and free gift wrapping.

Booksmith (508-540-6064), Falmouth Plaza, Route 28.

CLOTHING

Maxwell & Co. (508-540-8752), 200 Main Street. Absolutely fine men's and women's clothing.

Liberty House (508-548-7568), 89 Water Street, Woods Hole. Open mid-April through December. Good taste and reasonable prices for linen shorts and slacks, sundresses, and stacks of cotton T-shirts.

MALL

Falmouth Mall (508-540-8329), Route 28. A smaller version of the nearby Cape Cod Mall in Hyannis.

SPECIAL SHOPS

Twigs (508-540-0767), 178 Main Street. Practical, decorative, and functional accessories for the home and garden. (Do gardens need accessorizing? Think wind chimes.)

Bojangles (508-548-9888), 239 Main Street. This is a wonderfully tactile shop; in fact, it appeals to all the senses. It has a nostalgic feel but the goods are modern, funky, and contemporary. Stop in for high-end gifts: scarves, perfume bottles, hats, throws, candles, glassware, loose-hanging women's clothing, specialty place settings, unusual utensils.

Ben & Bill's Chocolate Emporium (508-548-7878), 209 Main Street. In this old-fashioned sweets shop, you'll be surrounded by walls of confections, some made on the premises. The excellent store-made ice cream is tasty, cheap, and served in abundant quantities.

SPECIAL EVENTS

Mid- to late May: **Cape Cod Maritime Days** (508-862-0700). Coast Guard–operated lighthouses are open during this festival, including Nobska. In addition to focusing on the area's lighthouses, the Cape-wide event celebrates the region's fishing heritage, maritime villages, and seafaring way of life.

Early June: **Illumination Weekend,** Woods Hole. Illuminated boats moored in Eel Pond, free crafts demonstrations, free open houses, a free concert, free cruises, a bagpipe jamboree, casino night, and more.

July 4: **Blessing of the Fleet** off Falmouth Heights Beach (see *Green Space—Beaches*); noon. Spectacular evening **fireworks** are displayed over Vineyard Sound. **Militia reenactment,** Falmouth (see Village green under *To See*).

Early to Mid-July: **Arts and Crafts Street Fair,** Main Street, Falmouth. Beginning at 10 AM, Main Street fills with crafts, artisans, and food stalls. **Fund-raising auction,** Falmouth Artists' Guild.

Late July: **Barnstable County Fair** (508-563-3200), Route 151, East Falmouth. Local and national music acts, a midway, livestock shows (including horse, ox, and pony pulls), and horticulture, cooking, and crafts exhibits and contests. A popular weeklong tradition, especially for teens and families with young children. $8 over age 12; otherwise free.

Late October: **The Cape Cod Marathon** (508-540-6959; www.capecodmarathon.com) is a high-spirited event which attracts several thousand long-distance runners, including relay teams. The 26.2-mile course loops around Falmouth and Woods Hole, beginning and ending on Falmouth's village green.

Early August: **Arts Alive Festival** (508-540-3304; www.arts-cape.com/falag), at the marina, including artists' demonstrations and a "wet auction" of paintings that were painted around town by local artists that morning.

Mid-August: **Annual Antiques Show,** held on the grounds of and sponsored by the historical society since 1970; $3.50.

Mid-August: **Falmouth Road Race** (508-540-7000; www.falmouthroad

race.com). This internationally renowned 7-mile race, limited to 9,500 participants, is the event of the year in Falmouth. Get your registration in before April 15 or you won't have a chance of running (Falmouth Road Race, Box 732, Falmouth 02541). Reserve your lodging before May; places usually fill up by then.

Early December: **Christmas by the Sea.** The weekend festivities, including tree lighting and caroling at the lighthouse and on the town green, culminate with a significant Christmas parade. **Annual House Tours,** quite popular, operated by the West Falmouth Library (508-548-4709).

Mashpee

Just east of Falmouth, fast-growing Mashpee is home to about 500 Wampanoag tribe members. For 1,000 years prior to the colonists' arrival, native Wampanoag Indians had established summer camps in the area, but with the settlement of Plymouth Colony, they saw larger and larger pieces of their homeland taken away from them and their numbers decimated by a plague. In 1617, three years after Capt. John Smith explored the area, six Native Americans were kidnapped and forced into slavery. In 1665, the missionary Reverend Richard Bourne appealed to the Massachusetts legislature to reserve about 25 square miles for the Native Americans. The area was called Mashpee Plantation (or Massapee or Massipee, depending on who's doing the translating), in essence the first Native American reservation in the United States. In 1870, the plantation was incorporated as the town of Mashpee. When the *Mayflower* arrived at Plymouth, the Wampanoag population was an estimated 30,000; there are a scant 500 Wampanoag in Mashpee today. Mashpee (which means "land near the great cove") is one of two Massachusetts towns administered by Native Americans (the other is Aquinnah, or Gay Head, on Martha's Vineyard).

Mashpee wasn't popular with wealthy 19th-century settlers, so there are few stately old homes there. The Wampanoag maintain a museum and church, both staffed by knowledgeable tribespeople. In the 1930s classic *Cape Cod Ahoy!*, Wilson Tarbel observed something about Mashpee that could still be said today: It's "retiring, elusive, scattered, a thing hidden among the trees."

The largest developed area of Mashpee is New Seabury, a 2,300-acre resort of homes, cottages, condos, several restaurants, golf courses, shops, and beaches. When developers won their lengthy legal battle with the Wampanoag, the tribe—and the town—lost much of its prettiest oceanfront property. The only noteworthy beach is South Cape Beach, a relatively pristine barrier beach with several miles of marked nature trails and steady winds that attract windsurfers. Compared with its neighbors, Mashpee is a quiet place.

GUIDANCE
❋ **Mashpee Chamber of Commerce** (508-477-0792; 1-800-423-6274; www.mashpeechamber.com), in the Cape Cod Five Cents Savings Bank

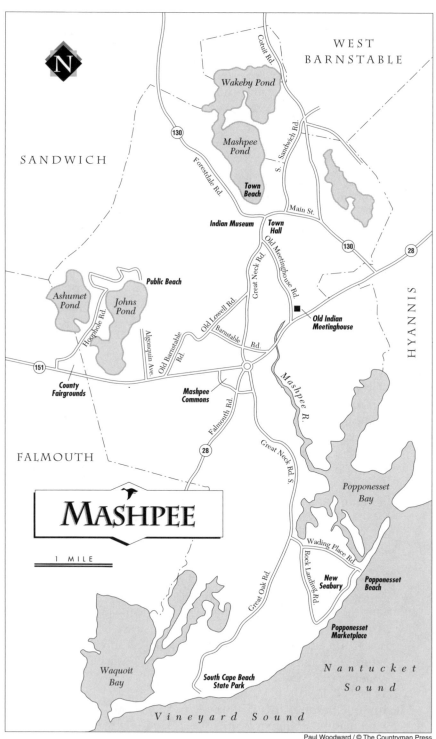

off the Mashpee rotary (Routes 28 and 151). Mailing address: P.O. Box 1245, Mashpee 02649. Open 9:30–4:30 weekdays.

PUBLIC REST ROOMS

Year-round rest rooms are available at the Mashpee Commons shopping area. Seasonal ones are located at South Cape Beach (at the end of Great Oak Road), and Johns Pond, a town park off Hoophole Road.

PUBLIC LIBRARY

✐❄↑**Mashpee Public Library** (508-539-1435), Route 151 across from Mashpee Commons, is open 9–5 Monday and Wednesday, 1–8 Tuesday and Thursday, 1–5 Friday, and 9–1 Saturday.

GETTING THERE

By car: From the Sagamore Bridge, take Route 6 east to Route 130 south to North Great Neck Road to the Routes 151 and 28 Mashpee rotary. The Mashpee Commons shopping area at the rotary acts as Mashpee's hub.

MEDICAL EMERGENCY

Mashpee Family Medicine (508-477-4282), Mashpee Health Center, 5 Industrial Drive at Route 28, accepts walk-ins weekdays 8–5 and Saturday 9–1.

TO SEE AND DO

HISTORIC HOUSES

Old Indian Meetinghouse (508-477-0208, Wampanoag Tribal Council), Meetinghouse Way off Route 28. Open 10–2 Wednesday and Friday in July and August. Located on the edge of what was once a Wampanoag-only cemetery ("They even took our burial ground away from us and made it theirs," laments a volunteer guide), this is the Cape's oldest surviving meetinghouse. It was built in 1684 and moved to its present spot in 1717. Inside, quilts commemorate the "glorious dead" tribe members; in the choir loft there are accomplished carvings of multi-masted ships whittled during lengthy 19th-century Baptist sermons.

✐❄ **Mashpee Wampanoag Indian Museum** (508-477-1536), on Route 130 across from Lake Avenue. Open 10–2 weekdays and by appointment. This small, early-19th-century house was built by Richard Bourne, minister and missionary to the Mashpee Wampanoag. Exhibits include tools, baskets, traditional clothing, arrowheads, a reconstructed wigwam, and a model of a pre-European-invasion tribal village. Although the displays aren't particularly enlightening, explanatory literature is available and the Wampanoag staff are happy to answer questions. (There is a herring run at the end of the parking lot.) Donations.

FISHING/SHELLFISHING

Obtain freshwater fishing and shellfishing licenses from the town clerk. The office (508-539-1416), at Town Hall, 16 Great Neck Road North, is open 8:30–4:30 weekdays year-round, 9–noon on Saturday in summer. Fish for trout, smallmouth bass, chain pickerel, and white perch at

Mashpee-Wakeby Pond, Johns Pond, and the **Mashpee River** (access from Quinnaquissett Avenue). See Massachusetts Military Reservation under *To See* in "Bourne" for information about water quality at Johns Pond. Surf casting is great at **South Cape Beach State Park** (see *Green Space—Beach*).

FOR FAMILIES

✿❈♈ **Cape Cod Children's Museum** (508-539-8788; www.capecodchildrens museum.pair.com), 577 Great Neck Road South. Open 10–5 Monday through Saturday, noon–5 Sunday. The most popular regularly scheduled activities include an enormous range of arts and crafts. Toddlers love the castle, puppet theater, and 30-foot pirate ship. Check out the Starlab Planetarium, too. Admission: $3.50 age 5 and over, $2.50 age 1–4. Membership, providing unlimited visits, cost $40 for the first person in a family, $5 each additional person.

GOLF

❈ **Quashnet Valley Country Club** (508-477-4412), Lowell Road, off Great Neck Road from Route 130. This semiprivate course winds around woods and cranberry bogs; ponds and marshes surround 12 of 18 holes; par 72.

New Seabury Country Club (508-477-9400), Shore Drive, New Seabury. Open to the public weekdays September to May. This semiprivate club has two excellent 18-hole courses.

TENNIS

Mashpee High School, 500 Old Barnstable Road (off Route 151), has public courts.

GREEN SPACE

BEACH

South Cape Beach State Park (508-457-0495), on Vineyard Sound, Great Oak Road. The 432-acre state park boasts a lovely 2-mile-long, dune-backed barrier beach and nature trails. Facilities include a concession stand, rest rooms, handicap ramp onto the beach, and lifeguards. Parking is $2 daily 9–3 late May to early September.

PONDS

Mashpee and **Wakeby Ponds,** off Route 130. Combined, these ponds create the Cape's largest freshwater body, wonderful for swimming, fishing, and boating. This area was a favorite fishing spot of both patriot Daniel Webster and President Grover Cleveland.

Johns Pond, off Hoophole Road from Route 151. Facilities include rest rooms, a snack bar, picnic tables, and grills. See Massachusetts Military Reservation under *To See* in "Bourne" for information regarding water conditions.

WALKS

Lowell Holly Reservation (781-821-2977), off Sandwich Road from Route 130. Open year-round but there is a ranger on duty 9 AM–5 PM

Old Indian Meetinghouse

daily, late May to early September, when parking costs $6 on weekends. Donated by Harvard University President Abbott Lawrence Lowell to the Trustees of Reservations in 1943, this tranquil 130-acre preserve contains an untouched forest of native American beeches and more than 500 hollies, as well as white pines, rhododendrons, and wildflowers. The Wheeler Trail circles the peninsula that separates Wakeby and Mashpee Ponds. There is a small bathing beach (no lifeguard).

Mashpee River Woodlands/South Mashpee Pine Barrens. Parking on Quinnaquissett Avenue (off Route 28 just east of the rotary) and at the end of River Road off Great Neck Road South. The 8-mile hiking trail winds along the Mashpee River, through a quiet forest, and along marshes and cranberry bogs. Put in your canoe at the public landing on Mashpee Neck Road. Free.

LODGING

Family-style accommodations are the rule in Mashpee.

RESORTS

New Seabury Resort (508-477-9400; 1-800-999-9033; www.newseabury. com), Rock Landing Road, New Seabury 02649. Open early March to early January. This self-contained resort, purchased by corporate raider Carl Icahn in 1998, is scattered across 2,300 acres fronting Nantucket Sound. The 13 "villages" of small, gray-shingled buildings offer a variety of rental accommodations (numbering about 130). Sea Quarters consists of one- and two-bedroom town houses, condominium-style, or stand-alone buildings. Maushop Village resembles Nantucket, with its lanes of crushed shells and weathered buildings; Tidewatch is a 1960s-style hotel near the golf course; Mews consists of contemporary California-influenced units. All one- and two-bedroom villas have fully equipped kitchens. Some overlook golf courses; some are oceanfront; others have more distant water views. Facilities include five restaurants (see Popponessett Inn under *Dining Out*), 16 tennis courts, two golf courses, a well-equipped health club, two outdoor pools, 3 miles of private beach on Nantucket Sound, bike rentals and trails, a small shopping mall, mini-golf, and a full schedule of activities for children. If it sounds like you don't have to leave this enclave to have a full vacation, you're right. That's the idea. Late June to early September $210–270 nightly for one bedroom, $305–400 two bedrooms; off-season $100–235 and $135–310, respectively. Weekly rates available in-season; inquire about golf and tennis packages.

❊ **Cape Cod Holiday Estates** (508-477-3377; 1-800-228-2968; www.vri vacations.com), 97 Four Seasons Drive. These 33 upscale time-share houses are operated by Vacation Resorts International. The airy two-bedroom and two-bath units have a full modern kitchen, Jacuzzi, central air-conditioning, separate living and family room, and private patio. On-premise activities and facilities include an indoor pool, shuffleboard, playground, tennis, basketball, and a nine-hole putting green. Late June to early September $245 nightly, $1,550 weekly; off-season $90–125 nightly, $600–750 weekly.

❊ **Sea Mist Resort** (508-477-0549; 1-800-228-2968; www.vriresorts.com), Great Neck Road South. Yes, they are time-share condos, but these one- and two-bedroom suites and town houses are a good value for families. There are 90 units. Facilities include tennis, an outdoor pool, mini-golf, and volleyball. Golf packages available. Late June to early September $125–165 nightly and $825–1,050 weekly for one bedroom, $210 nightly and $1,350 weekly for two bedrooms; off-season $60–90 nightly, $425–625 weekly.

RENTAL HOUSES AND COTTAGES

Century 21 Regan Realtors (508-539-2121), and **Real Estate Associates** (508-477-7771), both in Mashpee Commons, Routes 151 and 28, rent seasonal cottages and houses.

WHERE TO EAT

There aren't many choices in Mashpee, but the ones listed here are good. If you're not satisfied with these, stop at Mashpee Commons shopping area to see if there are any new restaurants.

DINING OUT

❊✿& **Popponessett Inn** (508-477-8258; 508-477-1100), Shore Drive, New Seabury. Open for dinner nightly in summer; call for off-season schedule. Within 50 feet of the ocean and with sweeping views of Nantucket Sound, this is the area's only choice for elegant dining. The Cape's largest resort village offers traditional New England seafood served in romantic dining rooms. Live entertainment throughout the summer under a big function tent. (This is a popular wedding location.) Reservations required; jackets preferred; children's menu. Entrées $17–25.

❋ **Contrast** (508-477-1299), Mashpee Commons. Open for lunch, dinner, and Sunday brunch. After opening the wildly successful Contrast Bistro and Espresso Bar in Dennis (and then selling it; they are no longer related at all!), Christian Soderstom thankfully came to Mashpee. At midday, the salads, creative sandwiches, and chicken potpie are deservedly popular. Dinner gets more creative with signature codcakes, lavash pizzas, and daily specials. There is also a convival **bar.** Lunch $7–12, dinner entrées $10–22.

♿ **The Flume** (508-477-1456), Lake Avenue, off Route 130 near the Mashpee Wampanoag Indian Museum. Open for dinner Tuesday through Sunday, April through November. Wampanoag and Mashpee native chef-owner Earl Mills trained at the Popponessett and Coonamessett Inns before opening his own restaurant in the early 1970s. His creative rendering of traditional recipes attracts food lovers from across New England to this small, casual restaurant built over a herring run. Fish figures prominently on the menu. Dishes include salt codfish cakes; marinated herring garnished with sour cream, red onion, and apple; and chowder. In spring, when the herring are running (along with Brewster, this is one of the oldest herring runs in the state), try the herring roe and bacon. Oysters are always a great choice. For dessert, try genuine Indian pudding, made with cornmeal, molasses, and ginger. Dishes $9–22 (baked stuffed lobster is more). Earl accepts only a few reservations so he can be sure of honoring them.

EATING OUT

Bobby Week's Raw Bar (508-539-4858, 508-477-9400), Popponessett Marketplace, New Seabury. Open May to late October (weekends only in spring and fall). You know this tiny place has something going for it when locals outnumber tourists. Part Cape Cod, part Caribbean, the raw bar boasts a loyal staff, incredibly fresh seafood, and an owner known for charity work.

ENTERTAINMENT

Boch Center for the Performing Arts (508-477-2580; www.capecod travel.com/boch), Mashpee Commons, Routes 151 and 28. The center is still in the capital fund-raising stages, but until it breaks ground, it sponsors performances at area venues.

Mashpee Commons (508-477-5400), Routes 151 and 28, Mashpee. Dozens of performances, including some free musical concerts, take place here. Keep your eyes peeled for current listings.

❋☂ **Hoyt's Cinema** (508-477-7333), Mashpee Commons, Routes 151 and 28.

SELECTIVE SHOPPING

MALL

❋ **Mashpee Commons** (508-477-5400), Routes 151 and 28. Open daily. If you're familiar with Seaside, the planned community of architectural note in Florida, you may recognize elements of this 30-acre outdoor shopping mall–cum–new town center. The buildings are pleasant and the layout is better than at most malls, but it still looks a bit contrived. (Developers went so far as to measure the sidewalk widths in an old, quintessential Vermont town and duplicate the dimensions here.) Having said that, it's won numerous awards for renovating a strip mall into a downtown commercial district. It's one of the most concentrated shopping venues on the Cape, boasting several good clothing stores, specialty boutiques, a movie theater, restaurants, cafés, and free outdoor entertainment in summer.

FLEA MARKET

Dick & Ellie's Flea Market (508-477-3550), Route 28 across from Deer Crossing Shopping Center. Open Wednesday through Sunday in summer; weekends only mid-April through June and September through October. More than 100 antiques and collectibles dealers peddle their wares here; other diversions include mini-golf and Four Seas ice cream (see *Where to Eat—Ice Cream* in "Barnstable").

SPECIAL SHOP

❋🐾 **Signature Gallery** (508-539-0029; www.signaturecraftgallery.com), 10 Steeple Street, Mashpee Commons, Routes 151 and 28. This exceptional gallery carries an eclectic selection by more than 600 distinguished American craftspeople. The acclaimed inventory includes jewelry, art glass, furniture, ceramics, wood, and wearable art.

SPECIAL EVENTS

✐ *Early July:* Mashpee Powwow (508-477-0208, Wampanoag Tribal Council) at the Barnstable County Fairgrounds on Route 151 in East Falmouth. The People of the First Light's Mashpee Wampanoag Powwow has been open to the public since 1924; the Mashpee Wampanoag Tribal Council has sponsored it since 1974. The powwow attracts Native Americans in full regalia from nearly every state as well as from Canada, Mexico, and some Central and South American countries. These traditional gatherings provide an opportunity for tribes to exchange stories and to discuss common problems and goals. Dancing, crafts demonstrations, and vendor booths. Kids are encouraged to join in the dancing and nearly constant percussive music. Adults $8; children under 12, $4.

II. MID-CAPE

Barnstable
Hyannis
Yarmouth
Dennis

Dune grass anchors shifting sands

KIM GRANT

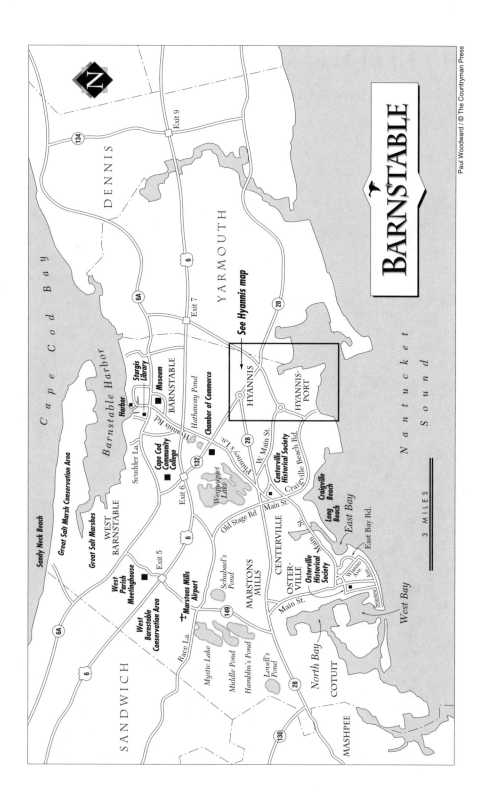

BARNSTABLE

See Hyannis map

Barnstable

The Cape's largest town covers 60 square miles and is home to 43,000 year-round souls. It's also the Cape's second oldest town, incorporated two years after Sandwich, in 1639. Barnstable actually comprises seven distinct villages—Cotuit, Marstons Mills, Osterville, Centerville, and Hyannis along Route 28, and West Barnstable and Barnstable along Route 6A. (Barnstable is sometimes referred to as Barnstable Village to distinguish it from Barnstable County, which embraces the whole of the Cape.)

On the Cape Cod Bay side, Route 6A (also called Old King's Highway and Main Street) winds through West Barnstable and Barnstable Village. Development—or lack of it—is rigidly controlled by the Old King's Highway Historical Commission, which regulates signage and does not allow gas stations, chain stores, or unconventional restorations within sight of the road. Sandy Neck, a haven for naturalists and beachgoers, is located off Route 6A, as are stately homes now converted into B&Bs.

On the southside, off Route 28, you'll find Centerville, Osterville, and Cotuit—parts of which front Nantucket Sound. Centerville's Main Street is full of handsome old homes built during the 19th century by affluent sea captains and businessmen. Osterville boasts some of the Cape's largest summer mansions, all with Nantucket Sound as their front yard. Osterville's Main Street is lined with upscale shops. At the turn of the 20th century, Cotuit was dubbed Little Harvard, as it was home to many academicians. Cotuit's Main Street is lined with impressive Federal, Greek Revival, and Queen Anne houses, with American flags and Adirondack chairs dotting the lawns. The popular Craigville Beach dominates this side of Barnstable.

Landlocked and wedged between Routes 28 and 6, Marstons Mills is tiny, quiet, and residentially developed. It was founded by the Marston family, who built and ran the mills driven by the Goodspeed River.

Barnstable was founded by English Congregationalist minister John Lothrop and a small band of religious renegades who felt that Plymouth Colony was a bit too settled for them. The neighborhood of Oysterville, as it was called, was purchased from the Native Americans in 1648 for "two copper kettles and some fencing." The area then was called Mattakeese, which translates as "plowed fields"—indeed, the land had already been cleared—but the settlers eventually named it after a similar harbor in Barnstaple, England.

GUIDANCE

❋ **Hyannis Area Chamber of Commerce** (508-362-5230; 1-800-449-6647 for 24-hour information; www.hyannischamber.com), 1481 Route 132, Hyannis 02601. Open 9–4:30 or 5 Monday through Saturday year-round; open 10–2 Sunday, late May to early September. A mile south of Route 6, the chamber has information about all Barnstable villages.

GETTING THERE

By car: Barnstable is 15 miles from the Sagamore Bridge. Take Route 6 to exit 5 for West Barnstable (Route 149 north) and Marstons Mills, Cotuit, and Osterville (Route 149 south). Take exit 6 for Barnstable Village (Route 132 west) and Centerville (Route 132 east).

By bus: The **Plymouth & Brockton** bus line (508-778-9767; www.p-b.com) connects Barnstable with other Cape towns, as well as with Boston's Logan Airport. The bus stops at the big commuter parking lot at Burger King, exit 6 off Route 6 at Route 132.

GETTING AROUND

The Villager (508-385-8326; 1-800-352-7155;www.capecodtransit.org) connects Barnstable's Route 6A (at the courthouse) with the malls in Hyannis on Route 132, the P&B bus terminal in the center of Hyannis, the West End Rotary, and Star Market. Schedules are available from the chamber of commerce (see *Guidance*). Purchase tickets on board. Fares: $1 over age 5.

PUBLIC LIBRARY

See Sturgis Library under *To See and Do.*

MEDICAL EMERGENCY

Cape Cod Hospital (508-771-1800), 27 Park Street, Hyannis. Open 24 hours.

TO SEE AND DO

Along or near Route 6A

West Parish Meetinghouse (508-362-8624), Route 149 at Meeting House Way, West Barnstable. Open daily 10–4 late May to mid-October and for Sunday services at 10. This majestic example of early Colonial architecture is the second oldest surviving meetinghouse on Cape Cod. (Its senior, the 1684 Old Indian Meetinghouse, is in Mashpee.) Its members belong to the oldest Congregationalist church fellowship in America, established in 1639 and descended from London's First Congregationalist Church. Founding pastor John Lothrop and his small band of followers erected their first meetinghouse in 1646. But by 1715 the Congregational church had become so popular that Barnstable split into two parishes; the building you see today was constructed in 1717. Its bell tower, topped by a gilded rooster, holds a bell cast by Paul Revere in 1806; it still rings. Until 1834 the meetinghouse doubled as a town hall—so much for separation of church and state! In the 1950s, the meetinghouse was fully restored to its original modest, neoclassical beauty. Donations.

⛪❄ **William Brewster Nickerson Memorial Room at Cape Cod Community College** (508-362-2131), Route 132, West Barnstable. Open 9–3 Tuesday and 8:30–4 Monday, Wednesday, and Friday. Rainy day or not, visitors with more than a passing interest in the social history, literature, institutions, and people of the Cape and islands owe it to themselves to stop here. Students voted in 1966 to set up this collection to honor the college's second president, a Vietnam War hero and *Mayflower* descendant. The significant collection contains more than 5,000 documents: religious treatises, biographies, autobiographies, oral histories, letters by dune poet Harry Kemp, scrimshaw, ship registers and logs, early diaries, U.S. Lifesaving Service reports, telephone directories from 1886 on, and aerial photographs. Several excellent books have been written using solely these materials.

✿⛪❄**Sturgis Library** (508-362-6636; www.capecod.net/sturgis), 3090 Route 6A, Barnstable Village. Open 10–5 Monday, Wednesday, and Friday; 1–8 Tuesday and Thursday; 10–4 Saturday; 1–5 Sunday (except closed Sunday in July and August). William Sturgis went off to sea at age 15 when his father died, and returned four years later as a captain. Although he received no formal education, this self-made man obtained reading lists from a Harvard-educated friend. Sturgis was born in the original part of the building, which he deeded to the town as a library. Researchers from all over the country (including entrepreneurs looking for shipwrecks) visit the country's oldest public library building. It boasts one of the finest collections of genealogical records, dating to the area's first European settlers; an original 1605 Lothrop Bible; more than 1,500 maps and charts; and archives filled with other maritime material. $5 fee for the genealogy and research collection; otherwise, free. The library has a very good children's corner.

Barnstable County Courthouse (508-362-2511), 3195 Route 6A, Barnstable Village. Built in 1831–1832, this imposing, granite, Greek Revival building is one of few reminders that tranquil Barnstable is the county seat for the Cape. (It's been the county seat since 1685.) Look for original murals and a pewter codfish in the main courtroom. On the side lawn, a bronze sculpture commemorates James Otis Jr., a West Barnstable "patriot" who wrote the famous 1761 Writs of Assistance speech. President John Adams said that Otis was the "spark by which the child of Independence was born."

Lothrop Hill Cemetery, Route 6A, just east of Barnstable Village. Slate headstones are scattered across this little hillock, where John Lothrop and other Barnstable founders rest. Near the stone wall along Route

6A, look for a large granite memorial bearing the following inscription: "In this cemetery lie the mortal remains of Capt. John Percival known as 'Mad Jack.' Born April 3, 1779. Died September 17, 1862 in command of Old Ironsides around the world 1844–1846."

Barnstable Harbor, Mill Way Road off Route 6A. Fishing charters and whale-watching trips depart from this small harbor.

Donald G. Trayser Memorial Museum Complex (Old Customs House) (508-362-2092), 3353 Route 6A, Barnstable Village. Open 1:30–4:30 Tuesday through Sunday, mid-June to mid-October. Before Barnstable Harbor filled with silt around 1900, it was the Cape's busiest port. As such, the Old Customs House was built in 1856 to oversee the enormous stream of goods passing through the harbor. When harbor activity diminished, the brick Italian Renaissance Revival building served as a post office, until the Barnstable Historical Commission made it their headquarters in 1959. The commission restored the beautiful building, painted it deep red, and opened this museum complex. It contains a second-floor custom keeper's office (with a harbor view), Native American arrowheads, Sandwich glass, ivory, and children's toys. Adjacent is a shed with a horse-drawn hearse, an 1869 velocipede, and a 1900 wooden-frame bicycle. Also on the grounds is a circa-1690 jail cell, complete with colonial "graffiti." Donations.

Off Route 28

Cahoon Museum of American Art (508-428-7581; www.cahoonmusuem. org), 4676 Route 28, Cotuit. Open February through December, 10–4 Tuesday through Saturday. This magnificent 1775 Georgian Colonial farmhouse was once a stagecoach stop on the Hyannis-to-Sandwich route. Today it houses a permanent collection of American art, featuring the whimsical and often humorous paintings of neoprimitive artists, including the late Martha and Ralph Cahoon. The building's low ceilings, wide floorboards, fireplaces, and wall stenciling provide an intimate backdrop for the artwork. Don't miss it. The museum also offers summer classes in watercolor, bird carving, and other fine and applied arts. Gallery talks on many Friday mornings at 11. Donations.

Centerville Historical Society Museum (508-775-0331), 513 Main Street, Centerville. Open 12:30–4:30 Wednesday through Saturday, June to mid-October. The 1840s Mary Lincoln House (no relation to Abraham) was built by Mary's father, Clark, a local tinsmith. Charles Ayling, a wealthy Cape businessman and philanthropist, endowed much of the museum, although many of the mid-19th-century furnishings were donated by Centerville folks. Ayling also assembled an entire Cape Cod colonial kitchen, complete with large open fireplace and dozens of iron utensils. The 14 rooms are filled with rare Sandwich glass, Civil War artifacts, maritime artifacts, historic quilts, costumes from 1750 to 1950, children's toys and games, perfume bottles, and A. E. Crowell's miniature duck carvings. Adults $3; children under 12 free.

KIM GRANT

The Osterville Historical Society Museum

❄ **The 1856 Country Store** (508-775-1856), 555 Main Street, Centerville. Beyond a selection of cutesy country and perfumed things, you'll find large pickles in a barrel of brine and wheels of cheddar cheese. The store is more picturesque outside than inside, although the original wood floors have been preserved.

Osterville Historical Society Museum (508-428-5861), 155 West Bay Road, Osterville. Open 1:30–4:30 Thursday through Sunday, mid-June through October. The society maintains a complex of three properties. The **Captain Jonathan Parker House,** built circa 1790, contains period art, antiques, furniture, and dolls, as well as paintings and porcelain from the China trade. The one-room-deep **Cammett House,** a simple Cape Cod farmhouse built circa 1790, is furnished with period pieces. And the **Crosby Boat Shop Museum** showcases the famous Crosby-designed Catboat *Cayuga,* built in 1928, and the *Wianno Senior* and *Junior.* Half models, tools, and historic Osterville waterfront photographs are also displayed. Don't miss the period colonial gardens maintained by the Osterville Garden Club. Admission $2 adults (kids free).

Samuel B. Dottridge House (508-428-0461), 1148 Main Street, Cotuit. Open 2:30–5 Thursday through Sunday, mid-June to early September; Saturday until mid-October. Owned by the Sansuit and Cotuit Historical Association, this 1790 house contains historical but otherwise fairly unremarkable objects pertaining to daily 19th-century life.

SPECIAL PROGRAMS

✸ **Tales of Cape Cod** (508-362-8927; www.capehistory.com), 3018 Route 6A at Rendezvous Lane, Barnstable Village. This simple, white-clapboard building served as the Barnstable County Courthouse from 1772 to 1832, when the "new" granite structure down the road was built. The secular Old King's Colonial Courthouse then became a Baptist church until it was purchased in 1949 by Tales of Cape Cod, a nonprofit organization that preserves Cape folklore and oral histories. The organization sponsors an excellent lecture series Tuesday evening at 7:30 in July and August. Subject titles range from "Inventors, Entrepreneurs, and Opportunists of Cape Cod" to "Cape Cod Attics: Antique Appraisal Evening," "Whale Rescues," "Shipwrecks," and "Growing Up on Cape Cod in the 1930s." Talks are delivered by knowledgeable townspeople. $5 per person. (The refreshments alone are worth the price of admission.)

See also Barnstable Comedy Club under *Entertainment.*

OUTDOOR ACTIVITIES

AIRPLANE RIDES

❋ **Cape Cod Soaring Adventures** (508-420-4201; 1-800-660-4563), Marstons Mills Airport, Route 149, Marstons Mills. Open year-round, weather permitting; reservations highly recommended. (On a sunny winter day, you can see for 80 miles, far better than on an average hazy summer day, when visibility peaks at about 5 miles. The key is low humidity and seasonably cool days.) Fall is perhaps the best time to fly, with spring a close second. Flying with Randy Charlton's glider at 5,000 feet and 40 mph, you'll see butterflies, seagulls, and hawks. The unrestricted views and the quietness are like nothing you've ever experienced. One person at a time: $65–85 for 20–35 minutes; $105 for 30–40 minutes.

Cape Cod Flying Service (508-428-8732; 1-888-247-5263), Marstons Mills Airport, Route 149, Marstons Mills. April through November, weather permitting. Biplane rides—in an open cockpit while Chris flies in back—cost $80 for two people; $60 for one. Thirty-minute sightseeing trips, which can go virtually anywhere on the Cape, cost $70 for one to three people. For twice the price and time you can head up to Wellfleet. This is the Cape's only grass-strip airport.

BICYCLING

If you don't have a friend with a summer place in the exclusive Wianno section of town, the best way to enjoy the village of Osterville is to cycle or drive along Wianno Avenue to Seaview Avenue, then turn right onto Eel River Road to West Bay Road and back into town.

FISHING/SHELLFISHING

Freshwater fishing licenses are obtained from the town clerk's office (508-790-6240) in Town Hall, 367 Main Street, Hyannis. Shellfishing permits are required and may be obtained from the Department of Natural Resources (508-790-6272), 1189 Phinney's Lane (which runs between Routes 28 and 132), Centerville. You can also get freshwater fishing permits here.

Wequaquet Lake in Centerville has plenty of largemouth bass, sunfish, and tiger muskies to go around. Park along Shoot Flying Hill Road. Marstons Mills has three pretty ponds stocked with smallmouth bass, trout, and perch: **Middle Pond,** Race Lane; **Hamblin's Pond,** Route 149; and **Schubael's Pond,** Schubael Pond Road off Race Lane.

Barnstable Harbor Charter Fleet (508-362-3908), 186 Millway, off Route 6A. Late May to mid-October. A fleet of seven boats takes up to six passengers each for 4- to 8-hour fishing expeditions in Cape Cod Bay.

Sea Witch (508-776-1336; 413-283-8375 off-season), Barnstable Harbor. May through September. Capt. Bob Singleton, who's been fishing these waters since 1960, uses a custom-built, 32-foot sportfishing boat. Captain Bob supplies the tackle and a money-back guarantee: If you don't return with fish, you get your money back. Up to six people for 4-, 6- and 8-hour trips.

FOR FAMILIES

Cape Cod YMCA (508-362-6500), Route 132, West Barnstable. In addition to a fitness center and cardiovascular center, the YMCA offers a number of programs where short-term visitors are welcome: open swims, Saturday-evening "Teen Nights," and Friday "Kids' Night Out." Drop off the kids and go out to dinner while they do arts and crafts. The Y also has a summer camp with weekly sessions. Fees vary.

Main Street Playground, adjacent to the recreation building, Centerville. Built by local volunteers in 1994, there are swings for big kids and toddlers, slides, a fancy jungle gym, sand for digging and building, climbing rings, and picnic tables.

GOLF

Cotuit Highground Country Club (508-428-9863), Crocker Neck Road, Cotuit. A popular nine-hole, 1,500-yard, par-28 course.

Olde Barnstable Fairgrounds Golf Course (508-420-1142), 1460 Route 149, Marstons Mills. An 18-hole course (par 70) so close to the airport that you can see the underbellies of approaching planes from the driving range.

TENNIS

Public courts are located at the **Centerville Elementary School** on Bay Lane; at the **Cotuit Elementary School** on Highland Avenue; at the **Osterville Bay School** off West Bay Road between Eel River Road and Main Street; and at the **Marstons Mills East Elementary School** on the Osterville–West Barnstable Road.

WHALE-WATCHING

Hyannis Whale Watcher Cruises (508-362-6088; 1-888-942-5392), Mill Way off Route 6A, Barnstable Harbor. Daily departures, April through October. A convenient Mid-Cape location and a new, fast boat make this a good choice for whale-watching. An on-board naturalist provides commentary. There are also sunset cruises in summer. Adults $26; children 4–12, $16.

GREEN SPACE

BEACHES

Sandy Neck Beach, on Cape Cod Bay, off Route 6A, West Barnstable. One of the Cape's most stunning beaches. The entrance to this 6-mile-long barrier beach is in Sandwich. Encompassing almost 9,000 acres, the area is rich with marshes, shellfish, and bird life. Sandy Neck dunes protect Barnstable Harbor from the winds and currents of Cape Cod Bay. Sandy Neck was the site of a Native American summer encampment before the colonists purchased it in 1644 for three axes and four coats. Then they proceeded to harvest salt-marsh hay and boil whale oil in tryworks on the beach. Today, a private summertime cottage community occupies the far eastern end of the beach. Known locally as the Neck, the former hunting and fishing camps, built in the late 19th century and early 20th, still rely on water pumps and propane lights. Beach facilities include rest rooms, changing rooms, and a snack bar. Parking $10. Permits for four-wheel drives are purchased at the gatehouse (508-362-8300). If you live outside Barnstable, the cost is $40 from early September to mid-April or $80 per calendar year. Six items must be in your car when the permit is issued: a spare tire, jack, jack pad, shovel, low-pressure tire gauge, and something to tow the car.

Millway Beach, just beyond Barnstable Harbor. Although a resident parking sticker is needed in summer, in the off-season you can park and look across to Sandy Neck Beach.

Craigville Beach, on Nantucket Sound, Centerville. This crescent-shaped beach—long and wide—is popular with college crowds and families. Facilities include rest rooms, changing rooms, and outdoor showers. Parking $15–20 per day, $40 per week.

Long Beach, on Nantucket Sound, Centerville. Centerville residents favor Long Beach, at the western end of Craigville Beach; walk along the water until you reach a finger of land between the sound and the Centerville River. Long Beach is uncrowded, edged by large summer shore homes and a bird sanctuary on the western end. Although a resident sticker is required, I list it anyway because it's the nicest beach.

PONDS

Hathaway Pond (508-790-6345), Phinney's Lane, Barnstable Village, is a popular freshwater spot. Facilities include a bathhouse and lifeguard; parking $5. The following freshwater locations require a resident sticker: **Lovell's Pond,** off Newtown Road from Route 28, Marstons Mills; **Burgess Park,** off Route 149 in Marstons Mills; **Hamblin's Pond,** off Route 149 from Route 28, Marstons Mills; and **Wequaquet Lake,** off Shoot Flying Hill Road from Route 132 (Iyanough Road), Centerville.

WALKS

Sandy Neck Great Salt Marsh Conservation Area (508-362-8300), West Barnstable. First things first: Hike in the off-season when it's not so hot.

The trailhead is located off Sandy Neck Road. The 9-mile (round trip) trail to Beach Point winds past pine groves, wide marshes, low blueberry bushes, and 50- to 100-foot dunes. It takes about 4 hours to do the whole circuit. This 4,000-acre marsh is the East Coast's largest. Be on the lookout for endangered piping plovers nesting in the sand. Eggs are very difficult to see and, therefore, very easily crushed. Parking $10.

St. Mary's Church Gardens, 3005 Route 6A (across from the library), Barnstable Village. Locals come to these peaceful, old-fashioned gardens to escape the swell of summer traffic on Route 6A. In spring, they're full of crocuses, tulips, and daffodils. A small stream, crisscrossed with tiny wooden bridges, flows through the property; it's rather like an anglicized Japanese garden.

Tidal flats, Scudder Lane, off Route 6A, West Barnstable. At low tide you can walk onto the flats and almost across to the neck of Sandy Neck.

West Barnstable Conservation Area, Popple Bottom Road, off Route 149 (near Route 6), West Barnstable. Park at the corner for wooded trails.

Cape Cod Horticultural Society Park, Route 28 near East Bay Road, Osterville. This park has shaded picnic tables, wooded walking trails with identified specimens, and a wetland walkway—it's a lovely place.

LODGING

✲ A number of historic B&Bs line Route 6A, but I have only included a selective selection. To get off the beaten path (with more modest accommodations) head "inland" to Marstons Mills or Centerville. The only beachfront option is a motel. Unless otherwise noted, all lodgings are open year-round.

BED & BREAKFASTS

✤ **Honeysuckle Hill** (508-362-8418; 1-966-444-5522; www.honeysucklehill. com), 591 Route 6A, West Barnstable 02668. Seasoned and welcoming innkeepers Mary and Bill Kilburn hail from a wonderful Vermont inn and have applied their talents to making this 1810 cottage a new favorite. They have four rooms and a two-bedroom Honeysuckle Suite (an extremely good value), all with private bath, feather bedding, air-conditioning, robes, fine toiletries, and marble baths. They're comfortably elegant and modestly furnished with a mix of white wicker and antiques. I particularly like Magnolia with a pineapple poster bed, but Wisteria is the largest and boasts its own entrance. They're a breath of fresh air and you can't go wrong with any of them. Common space includes a living room with fireplace and a screened-in porch where you'll find lots of extra amenities. Rates include a full breakfast of "Dutch Babies" (small puffy pancakes) and citrus salad or perhaps eggs with feta and herbs, served at one table. May through October $125–155 rooms, $200 suite (for two to four—kids 12 and over are accommodated); off-season $100–130 and $180, respectively.

Beechwood (508-362-6618; 1-800-609-6618; www.beechwoodinn.com), 2839 Route 6A, Barnstable Village 02630. This 1853 Queen Anne–style house is named for the copper beeches that flank the house. Beechwood offers six romantic guest rooms furnished with high Victorian charm and modern air-conditioning. Rooms are all very different from one another, decide whether you're interested in a canopy bed, private entrance, marble fireplace, or steeply angled walls. (The Garret Room is tucked under third-floor eaves.) A wide veranda overlooks the beeches, and a privacy hedge separates the inn from Route 6A. The dining room—a full breakfast is included—features tongue-and-groove paneling and a pressed-tin ceiling. Innkeepers Debbie and Ken Traugot love talking with guests. May through October $150–185; off-season $95–140.

🐾🔊 **Lamb and Lion Inn** (508-362-6823; 1-800-909-6923; www.lambandlion.com), 2504 Route 6A, Barnstable 02630. Proprietors Alice Pitcher and Tom Dott have worked hard to upgrade this property, which consists of 10 rooms (including a **cottage** and **"barn-stable"** that can accommodate families) surrounding a heated swimming pool. Although the physical setup is rather like a U-shaped motel, the diverse rooms are quite pleasant with wicker and antiques, and the long hallways have been delightfully brightened with sky murals. Because the rooms are so different, ask for a complete description. I particularly like room 9, which gets great afternoon sun. All rooms have TV and phone; most have a fireplace, more than half have a kitchenette, and most have spiffy motel-style bathrooms. An expanded continental breakfast is included and available on a sunporch, by the pool, or on the back deck. Before leaving, ask to see the triple-sided fireplace in the original 1740 house. I've never seen anything like it. You'll enjoy the relaxing and congenial atmosphere here. In-season $125–160 rooms, $180–250 cottage, suite, and barn; off-season $85–130 and $115–170, respectively.

The Inn at the Mills (508-428-2967), 71 Route 149 (at Route 28), Marstons Mills 02648. If you didn't know this circa-1780 red farmhouse and barn was a B&B, you'd remark on how picturesque it was but you'd drive right by. There's no sign because innkeeper Bill Henry has plenty of business with weddings and word of mouth. On a knoll overlooking a pond, gazebo, and pool, the inn has six lovely rooms. Common rooms include a formal front living room and a wicker-filled sunroom. Continental breakfast included. In-season $95–145; $10 less off-season.

🔊 **Adam's Terrace Gardens Inn** (508-775-4707; www.bedandbreakfast.com), 539 Main Street, Centerville 02632. If you're looking for an unpretentious place off the beaten path, this circa-1830s sea captain's house is it. All eight rooms have television and homey furnishings; five have private bath. Host Louise Pritchard serves a full breakfast. Late May to mid-September $90–115 private bath, $75–80 shared bath. Off-season $80–100 private, $65–70 shared. Children $20 extra. No credit cards.

Heaven on High (508-362-4441; 1-800-362-4044), 70 High Street, West

Barnstable 02668. Open April through October. In a contemporary home on a quiet road just off Route 6 and half a mile west of Route 149, hosts Deanna and Gib Katten offer three very large rooms with private bath. The living room is filled with their collectibles, which also make their way up the stairs and into guest rooms. Common space includes a great room and separate living room. A full breakfast is served alfresco or with linen and sterling in the dining room. The real draw is the expansive panorama of Great Salt Marsh and dunes, enjoyed from the guest rooms and large back deck. Putting green. Late May to late October $155–165, off-season $130–145.

MOTEL

& **Trade Winds Inn** (508-775-0365; 1-877-444-7966; www.twicapecod.com), Craigville Beach, Centerville 02632. Open May through October. The raison d'être for this four-building, 6-acre, 46-room complex: Craigville Beach is across the street. (The motel maintains its own private stretch of this beach.) Ocean-view rooms and efficiencies have sliding glass doors that open onto balconies. Less expensive non–ocean view rooms (some with kitchen) are also available, as are suites. All rooms have TV and air-conditioning. Adults will like the putting green; kids will flock to the small lake with swans, geese, and ducks. Of all your area lodging choices, this motel is the best, about two miles from downtown Hyannis. Mid-June to early September $119–189, continental breakfast included; off-season $70–110. Discounts for longer stays.

RENTAL HOUSES AND COTTAGES

Craigville Realty (508-775-3174), 648 Craigville Beach Road, West Hyannisport 02672. This agency specializes in two- to four-bedroom rental houses in quiet neighborhoods within a mile of Craigville Beach. At any given time there are about 125 houses in the rental pool; $725–5,000 weekly in-season.

See also Lamb and Lion Inn under *Bed & Breakfasts*.

CAMPGROUND

& **Sandy Terraces Nudist Family Campground** (508-428-9209), Box 98C, Marstons Mills 02648. Open mid-May to mid-October. Geared toward couples and families, this 10-acre campground has 12 wooded sites, a sandy beach on a mile-long lake, a redwood sauna, and lots of activities and cookouts. Call or write in advance of your visit.

WHERE TO EAT

Barnstable doesn't have a plethora of restaurants, but it does boast perhaps the finest dining on the Cape, a waterfront restaurant, an excellent local tavern, and the best homemade ice cream on the Cape. What else do you want?

DINING OUT

& **The Regatta of Cotuit** (508-428-5715), 4613 Route 28, Cotuit. Open for

dinner. Early three-course dinners (5–6 PM) are an exceptional value at $24–28. Dollar for dollar, this is one of the Cape's top two or three restaurants—at once elegant and relaxed. Brantz and Wendy Bryan's superb restaurant, housed in a 200-year-old Federal mansion—a former stagecoach stop—is more romantic, with eight intimate dining rooms. The menu features Asian and European pairings of traditional New England meats and seafood. Plan on ending your gastronomic romp with Chocolate Seduction with *sauce framboise*. Or get the sampler plate of four desserts for $12.50. While you might fear haughty service with such sublime dishes, this is not the case whatsoever. A jazz pianist performs in the tavern most evenings. Reservations suggested. Entrées $24–36.

❄ **Dolphin** (508-362-6610), 3250 Route 6A, Barnstable. Open for lunch and dinner. A local favorite watering hole, complete with a long **bar** separated from the main dining room, the taverny Dolphin has an extensive menu specializing in seafood. At midday you'll find everything from crabcakes and oysters to salads, specialty sandwiches, and baked and fried seafood. At dinner it's a bit more elaborate, with grilled swordfish and braised salmon. Lunch $6–11, dinner entrées $17–22.

EATING OUT

Mattakeese Wharf (508-362-4511), 271 Mill Way, Barnstable Harbor. Open 11:30–9 daily, May through October. Nobody beats the quintessential harborside location and million-dollar water views. Get a table about an hour before sunset so you can watch the fishermen and pleasure craft come and go in this quiet harbor. Entrées include almond-coated swordfish steak, large burgers, mussels with your choice of sauce—Dijon or marinara—and boiled lobster. Mattakeese has been under Ken LaCasse's guidance since 1968. Lunch $6–9; dinner entrées $13–19.

⬢ **Mill Way Fish and Lobster Market** (508-362-2760), 276 Mill Way, Barnstable Village. Open April through September and during the year-end holiday season. Culinary Institute of America–trained chef Ralph Binder puts his heart into this unordinary market. He does a booming business in prepared foods for seafood lovers and vegetarians, as well as take-out fried seafood and grilled fish. His specialty is "shellfish sausage," designed for the grill and made with shrimp, lobster, and scallops. He mails them all over the country.

❄ **Osterville Cheese Shop** (508-428-9085), 29 Wianno Avenue, Osterville. Open daily. Osterville residents and summer folks order imported and domestic cheeses and other gourmet goodies for their cocktail parties here. Enjoy a thick sandwich, soup, breakfast pastries and breads, a slice of chicken pie, or a pint of pasta salad, all wrapped up to take away.

❄ **Breaking Grounds** (508-420-1311), 791 Main Street, Osterville. Open for breakfast and lunch daily. This pleasant place serves omelets, pancakes, and a limited menu of soups, salads, and hot sandwiches. Large selection of flavored coffee and espresso drinks. Patio dining in warm weather. $3–6.

❋ **Barnstable Tavern** (508-362-2355), 3176 Route 6A, Barnstable Village. Open for lunch and dinner, but I only recommend you stop for a drink on the front patio at this old tavern in Barnstable's historic district.

See also Dolphin under *Dining Out* and Cotuit Pizza Factory under *Special Shops*.

ICE CREAM
🚗🍴♿**Four Seas** (508-775-1394), 360 South Main Street, at Centerville Four Corners. Open 9 AM–10:30 PM daily, mid-May to mid-September; sandwiches served 10–2:30. Founded in 1934, Four Seas has been owned by Dick Warren since 1960, when he bought the place from the folks who gave him a summer job as a college student. It's named for the four "seas" that surround the Cape: Buzzards Bay, Cape Cod Bay, the Atlantic Ocean, and Nantucket Sound. The Cape's absolute best ice cream is made every day, using the freshest ingredients. For instance, Dick makes beach plum ice cream only once a year—when the beach plums are ripe. The walls of this funky place, a former garage, are lined with photos of preppy summer crews, newspaper articles about Four Seas (it wins national ice cream awards every year), and poems written for Four Seas' 60th anniversary. Lobster salad sandwiches are great, too.

ENTERTAINMENT

✍ **Baseball.** The Cotuit Kettlers play at Lowell Park in Cotuit from mid-June to mid-August.

Barnstable Comedy Club (508-362-6333), 3171 Route 6A across from the Barnstable Tavern, Barnstable Village. November through June. Call for exact production schedule. First things first: This is not a comedy club! Founded in 1922, the country's oldest amateur theater group performs more than comedies—look for musicals and straight though not heavy or provocative theater. Since 1922 its motto has been "To Produce Good Plays and Remain Amateurs." (Kurt Vonnegut got his feet wet here.) A 200-seat theater; tickets $12–14.

SELECTIVE SHOPPING

❋ All shops are open year-round unless otherwise noted.

ANTIQUES
Harden Studios (508-362-7711), 3264 Route 6A, Barnstable Village. This late-17th-century house was beautifully restored by Charles M. Harden in 1993 and now functions as a two-story antiques shop–cum–gallery. It's a true family affair: Harden's son Charles operates an etching press and art gallery in the adjacent shed, and son Justin researches the fine antiques collection. American antiques from the early 1700s to the 1840s; Empire and Federal pieces; Oriental rugs, lamps, and chandeliers.

Sow's Ear Antiques (508-428-4931), Route 28 at Route 130, Cotuit. Open daily except Monday. Americana and primitive folk art and furniture sold from an 18th-century house; some garden antiques, too.

Cotuit Antiques (508-420-1234), 70 Industry Road, behind Cotuit Landing off Route 28, Cotuit. Henry Frongillo enjoys people and keeping his shops folksy. Since he buys estates, you never know what you'll find. Primarily, though, he offers fine furniture, hot collectibles, some art pottery, and lots of great old signage and advertising memorabilia.

ART GALLERIES

Cape Cod Art Association (508-362-2909), 3480 Route 6A, Barnstable Village. This nonprofit was founded in 1948 and displays a fine range of juried art and artists in a beautiful and airy gallery. Shows change monthly. Classes and workshops offered, both indoors and outdoors.

Tao Water Art Gallery (508-375-0428), 1989 Route 6A, West Barnstable. This contemporary Asian gallery, representing over 20 artists from post–Cultural Revolution China and the States, runs the gamut from exceptional abstract painting to landscapes and sculpture. One of the largest galleries on the Cape, with over 5,600 square feet, Tao Water holds regularly changing exhibits. They also offer Chinese tea ceremony and calligraphy classes in the off-season, as well as antique furniture and handmade crafts and gifts from all over Asia.

Cummaquid Fine Arts (508-362-2593), 4275 Route 6A, Cummaquid. Open Thursday through Sunday, plus additional weekdays as the weather warms. Gallery owners Jim Hinkle and Roy Hammer promote work by living, resident Cape Cod artists. You'll find landscapes, still lifes, coastal scenes, and figure studies within this 18th-century house.

See also Harden Studios under *Antiques.*

ARTISANS

The Blacks Handweaving Shop (508-362-3955), 597 Route 6A (about half a mile west of Route 149), West Barnstable. The Blacks create beautiful woven pieces with a variety of textures, colors, and materials: chenille, mohair, wool, and cotton. They are quite well known for custom, one-of-a-kind jacquard coverlets and throws, signed and dated. Bob Black—who's been weaving since he was 14 and studied at the Rhode Island School of Design—and his wife, Gabrielle, have been working at their looms in this post-and-beam shop since 1954.

Oak and Ivory (508-428-9425), 1112 Main Street, Osterville. If you've always wanted a Nantucket lightship basket but haven't made it to Nantucket, this is the off-island place for you. The baskets are expensive (from about $700 to several thousand dollars), reflecting the fine craftsmanship and 35–45 hours of work that go into each delicate piece. But basket makers Bob and Karen Marks (he a Nantucketer, she a wash-ashore) primarily offer traditional 18th century coastal New England artwork and gifts like scrimshaw, Wedgwood china with lightship basket patterns, sailors' valentines, and hand-carved shorebirds. Reproduction furniture, too.

BOOKSTORES

Baker Books (508-428-4635), 13 Wianno Avenue, Osterville. Proprietor Debbie Baker has extensive local connections to the community.

Isaiah Thomas Books & Prints (508-428-2752), 4632 Falmouth Road, at Routes 28 and 130, Cotuit. Open year-round (weekends January through March). Jim Visbeck offers more than 60,000 antiquarian, first-edition, and slightly used books, as well as books for children. They're divided by age group and interest. He also offers appraisals, search services, archival materials, and lectures on book collecting. This place is marvelous; you could easily spend an afternoon here.

SPECIAL SHOPS

West Barnstable Tables (508-362-2676), Route 149, West Barnstable. Open daily. Dick Kiusalas is a master craftsman and artist. As it's difficult (not to mention prohibitively expensive) to find antique tables anymore, he makes tables using 18th- and 19th-century wood scavenged from houses about to be demolished. His creations are exquisite and worth admiring even if you don't have a couple of thousand dollars to spare. Less expensive pieces include windowpane mirrors and primitive cupboards made with old painted wood and found objects. Dick also offers Windsor and thumback chairs for sitting at his beautiful tables. Furniture maker Stephen Whittlesey shares the big barn; his fanciful, whimsical, primitive folk art pieces are equally worthy.

Tern Studio (508-362-6077), Route 149, West Barnstable. Wood turner Albert Barbour creates artful bowls and vases using local woods, including driftwood that washes ashore during hurricanes. His work is very organic.

Maps of Antiquity (508-362-7169), 1022 Route 6A, West Barnstable. Open May to mid-October; limited hours mid-October to mid-December. Rare antique and reproduction maps of the 19th century and earlier, from around the world. Because the worldwide supply of originals is limited, they get snapped up quickly when discovered. If you want to know what the Cape or a specific town looked like 100 years ago, these folks will have a reproduction map that will tell you. This place is a treasure trove.

Margo's Practically Unusual (508-428-5664), 27 Wianno Avenue, Osterville. The name dictates the buying: "unusual" picture frames, serving pieces, hand-painted furniture and home accessories, handmade lamps with "unusual" finials, bed linens, jewelry, scarves, and sweaters.

Cotuit Grocery/Cotuit Pizza Factory (508-428-6936; 508-420-1994), Main Street, Cotuit. This old multiuse building would go unnoticed in Vermont, but on the Cape it's an anomaly. On the one hand it's simply a convenience store–cum–wine shop. But owners Steve and Jan Gould also sell Jan's jewelry, a few antiques, and pizza. It's a prime example of year-rounders doing whatever they have to do to enjoy the Cape in all seasons.

SPECIAL EVENTS

Late April: **Osterville Village Daff-O'Ville Day** (talk to Gail at 508-428-6327). Hayrides, musical entertainment, some crafts, a dog show, and daffodil flower arrangements made by the garden club gracing all the shop windows.

Mid-July: **Osterville Village Day** (talk to Gail at 508-428-6327). Always on the third Saturday in July, and held since 1976, this event includes a crafts and antiques fair, road race, children's events, and a parade.

Late July: **Barnstable County Fair** (508-563-3200), Route 151, East Falmouth. Local and national music acts, a midway, livestock shows (including horse, ox, and pony pulls), and horticulture, cooking, and crafts exhibits and contests. A popular weeklong tradition, especially for teens and families with young children. $8 over age 12; otherwise free.

Mid-August: **Centerville Old Home Week.** Until 1994 this event hadn't been held for 90 years. Main Street open houses.

Late September: **Osterville Village Fall Festival Day** (talk to Gail at 508-428-6327). Wine tasting, an arts and crafts show, entertainment, antiques show, dog show, and food. Always held on the Saturday before Columbus Day weekend.

Mid-December: **Osterville Christmas Open House and Stroll** (talk to Gail at 508-428-6327). Since 1972, the village has gussied itself up with traditional decorations. Despite what you might think about Nantucket's stroll, this is the Cape's oldest and New England's second oldest stroll. Upwards of 2,000 to 3,000 participate in Friday-evening festivities, which include hayrides, trolley rides, wine tastings, and more. Bell ringers, too.

Hyannis

Hyannis is the Cape's commercial and transportation hub: An astonishing 1 million people take the ferry from Hyannis to Nantucket every year. Most Cape visitors end up in Hyannis at some point, whether by choice or from necessity.

Among Cape visitors, Hyannis seems to be everyone's favorite whipping boy: A sigh of sympathy is heard when someone mentions he "has" to go into Hyannis in July or August. Yes, traffic is gnarly and Route 28 is overbuilt, but those same Cape residents and off-Cape visitors who moan about congestion in Hyannis couldn't live as easily without its services, including many fine restaurants. They come to buy new cars, embark to the islands, visit doctors, shop at malls. Thus, because it is so distinct from the rest of Barnstable, I have given it its own chapter even though Hyannis is technically one of Barnstable's seven villages.

Hyannis's harborfront and Main Street were revitalized in the 1990s, thanks in part to the encouragement of Ben Thompson, architect of Boston's Quincy Market shopping complex and other successful urban waterfront development projects. Watching the boating activity on Lewis Bay is an easy way to while away dusk and a sunset. It's pleasant to mill around Main Street, lined with benches and hanging flower baskets. Main Street also has its share of T-shirt shops and a growing crop of congregating youth. (Hyannis is, after all, the closest thing to a "city" that the Cape has.) Yes, Hyannis has a bit of everything: discount outlets, more than 60 eating establishments in the waterfront district alone (a number of them quite good), some quiet cottages and guest houses, plenty of motels geared to overnight visitors waiting for the morning ferry, harbor tours, and lots of lively bars and nightlife.

Then there's the Kennedy mystique. Hyannisport—a neighborhood within Hyannis but quite distinct from Hyannis—will forever be remembered as the place where, in the early 1960s, President John F. Kennedy and Jacqueline sailed offshore and played with children Caroline and John. Visitors who come in search of the "Kennedy compound" or in hopes of somehow experiencing the Kennedy aura will find only a residential, Yankee-style community of posh estates.

Hyannis's harbor area was inhabited about 1,000 years ago by ancestors of the Eastern Algonquian Indians, who set up summer camp-

117

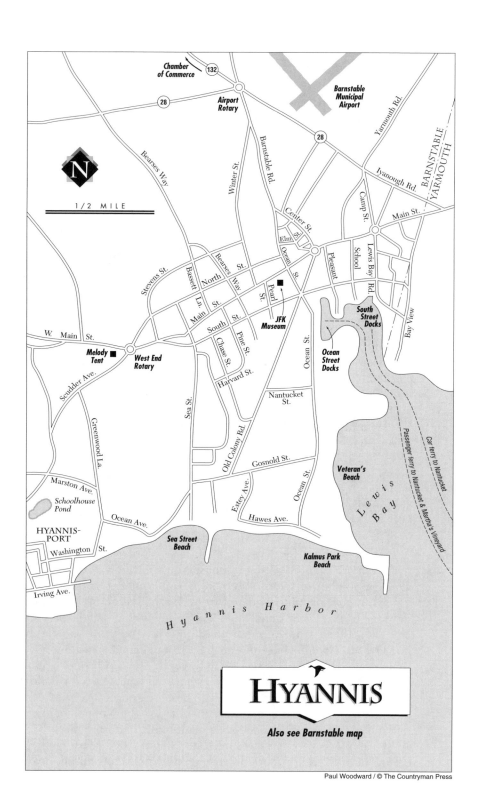

Chamber of Commerce
132
28
Airport Rotary
Barnstable Municipal Airport
BARNSTABLE
YARMOUTH
Yarmouth Rd.
28
Iyanough Rd.
N
1/2 MILE
Bearses Way
Winter St.
Barnstable Rd.
Camp St.
Main St.
Center St.
Elm St.
Ocean St.
School
Lewis Bay Rd.
Stevens St.
Bassett Ln.
North St.
Bearses Way
Pleasant
Bay View
Pearl St.
South Street Docks
W. Main St.
Main St.
JFK Museum
Ocean Street Docks
Melody Tent
West End Rotary
South St.
Pine St.
Chase St.
Scudder Ave.
Sea St.
Harvard St.
Nantucket St.
Ocean St.
Greenwood La.
Old Colony Rd.
Gosnold St.
Veteran's Beach
Marston Ave.
Schoolhouse Pond
Estey Ave.
Ocean St.
Lewis Bay
HYANNIS-PORT
Ocean Ave.
Hawes Ave.
Washington St.
Sea Street Beach
Kalmus Park Beach
Irving Ave.
Passenger ferry to Nantucket & Martha's Vineyard
Car ferry to Nantucket

Hyannis Harbor

HYANNIS

Also see Barnstable map

sites south of what is now Ocean Street. The first European to reach Cape Cod, Bartholomew Gosnold, anchored in the harbor in 1602. Shortly thereafter, settlers persuaded Native American sachem Yanno to sell them what is now known as Hyannis and Centerville for £20 and two pairs of pants.

Main Street was laid out in 1750, and by the early 1800s Hyannis was already known as the Cape's transportation hub. The harbor bustled with two- and three-masted schooners. When the steam-train line was extended from Barnstable in 1854, land-based trade and commerce supplanted the marine-based economy. Tourists began arriving in much greater numbers by the end of the century. Pleasure-seeking yachts filled the harbor by the 1930s, until John Kennedy (who tied up at the Hyannisport Yacht Club) renewed interest in traditional local sailboats, known as Catboats, in the 1950s. More and more big boats return as the economy improves.

GUIDANCE
❋ **Hyannis Area Chamber of Commerce** (508-362-5230; 1-800-449-6647 for 24-hour information; www.hyannischamber.com), 1481 Route 132, Hyannis 02601. Open 9–4:30 or 5 Monday through Saturday year-round; open 10–2 Sunday, late May to early September. A mile south of Route 6, the chamber has information about all Barnstable villages. There is also a small visitors booth at the JFK Hyannis Museum (see *To See*) on Main Street, staffed in summer only.

PUBLIC REST ROOMS
Public rest rooms are located at the beaches (see *Green Space—Beaches*), behind the JFK Hyannis Museum on Main Street, and at the Ocean Street Docks (Bismore Park).

PUBLIC LIBRARY
❋✎ꕯ**Hyannis Public Library** (508-775-2280), 401 Main Street. This charming little house has a much larger facility tacked onto the rear. It's open weekdays 11–5 (until 8 PM on Tuesday and Wednesday) from early June to mid-September. Off-season hours are Tuesday and Wednesday 11–8, Thursday through Saturday 11–5. Buy your paperbacks here to benefit the library.

GETTING THERE
By car: To reach Hyannis, about 30 minutes from either bridge, take exit 6 off Route 6; follow Route 132 south to the airport rotary (at the junction of Routes 28 and 132). Take the second right off the rotary onto Barnstable Road, which intersects with Main, Ocean, and South Streets (for the harbor).

By bus: The **Plymouth & Brockton** bus line (508-778-9767; www.p-b.com), Center and Elm Streets, connects Hyannis with other Cape towns, as well as with Boston's Logan Airport. **Bonanza Bus** (508-775-6502; 1-800-751-8800; www.bonanzabus.com), Center and Elm Streets, connects Hyannis to Providence, T. F. Green Airport, and New York

KIM GRANT

The Steamship Authority ferry from Nantucket docks in Hyannis.

City. In-season there are six daily trips from New York City. The trip takes about 6 hours, and coaches are equipped with movies.

By air: **Barnstable Municipal Airport** (508-775-2020), at the airport rotary, at the junction of Route 28 and Route 132, Hyannis. Small carriers flying in and out of Hyannis include **Colgan Air** (partnered with Continental; 1-888-265-4267), offering year-round service between Hyannis and La Guardia Airport in New York. **Cape Air** and **Nantucket Air** (508-790-1980; 1-800-352-0714; www.flycapeair.com) have year-round service from Boston to Hyannis; Cape Air provides year-round service from Providence, too. Cape Air and Nantucket Air have grown considerably in the recent past; they currently fly more than a quarter of a million people to the Cape and islands each year. Service is excellent.

GETTING AROUND

By car: Hyannis suffers from serious summer traffic problems. Parking on Main Street is free if you can get a space. If not, try North Street, one block north of Main Street and parallel to it. Main Street (one way) is meant for strolling, but it's a long walk from end to end.

    Rental cars. Hyannis is one place where it's convenient to get a rental car. Call the big agencies based at the airport: **Hertz** (1-800-654-3131), **National** (1-800-227-7368), **Avis** (1-800-331-1212), **Budget** (1-800-527-0700), and **Thrifty** (508-771-0450; 1-800-367-2277). Or try **Trek** (508-771-2459), near the bus terminal, but they'll pick you up from the airport.

By shuttle: **Hyannis Area Trolley** (508-385-8326; 1-800-352-7155;

www.capecodtransit.org). The state- and town-funded summertime HAT shuttle is very popular and makes a loop down Main Street to Sea Street, the beaches, and South Street. Buses operate daily, every half hour, from late June to early September. Fare $1.

The **H₂O** (508-385-8326; 1-800-352-7155; www.capecodtransit. org) bus line, used by more locals than visitors, travels along Route 28 between Hyannis and Orleans daily except Sunday year-round. In Hyannis it stops at the Cape Cod Hospital and the P&B bus terminal.

YES (Yarmouth Easy Shuttle) (508-385-8326; 1-800-352-7155; www.capecodtransit.org) operates late June to early September. Funded by a state grant, the shuttle begins at the Plymouth & Brockton bus terminal in Hyannis and runs along Route 28 to various family-oriented points (including beaches) in Yarmouth. Flag down the driver, who will pull over to pick you up. (It sure beats traffic.) Adults $1 one way; kids age 6–17, 50¢ One-day passes ($3) and tickets are purchased aboard the trolley or at the chamber of commerce (see *Guidance*).

Sea Line (508-385-8326; 1-800-352-7155; www.capecodtransit. org). Operating daily year-round, Sea Line connects Hyannis to Barnstable, Mashpee, Falmouth, and Woods Hole. The fare depends on the distance traveled; children 5 and under ride free. Look for a schedule for complete details.

The Villager (508-385-8326; 1-800-352-7155; www.capecodtransit. org) connects Barnstable's Route 6A (at the courthouse) with the malls in Hyannis on Route 132, the P&B bus terminal in the center of Hyannis, the West End Rotary, and Star Market. Schedules are available from the chamber of commerce (see *Guidance*). Purchase tickets on-board. Fares: $1 over age 5.

GETTING TO THE ISLANDS

From Hyannis, there is year-round auto and passenger service to Nantucket from Hyannis and seasonal passenger service to Martha's Vineyard. For complete information, see *Getting There* in "Martha's Vineyard" and "Nantucket." *Note:* You can also fly to the islands.

MEDICAL EMERGENCY

Cape Cod Hospital (508-771-1800), 27 Park Street. Open 24 hours.

TO SEE

T **John F. Kennedy Hyannis Museum** (508-790-3077), 397 Main Street in the Old Town Hall. Open 10–4 Monday through Saturday, 1–4 Sunday, mid-April through October; 10–4 Wednesday through Saturday the rest of the year except closed completely in January. This museum opened in 1992 to meet the demands of visitors making a pilgrimage to Hyannis in search of JFK. People wanted to see "something," so the chamber gave them a museum that focuses on JFK's time in Hyannisport and on Cape Cod. The museum features more than 100 photographs of Kennedy from

1934 to 1963, arranged in themes: JFK's friends, his family, JFK the man. JFK said, "I always go to Hyannisport to be revived, to know the power of the sea and the master who rules over it and all of us." (If you really want to learn something about the president and his administration, head to the JFK Museum in Boston.) Adults $3, free for children under 16.

JFK Memorial, Ocean Street. The fountain, behind a large presidential seal mounted on a high stone wall, is inscribed: I BELIEVE IT IS IMPORTANT THAT THIS COUNTRY SAIL AND NOT SIT STILL IN THE HARBOR. There is a nice view of Lewis Bay from here.

Kennedy compound. Joe and Rose Kennedy rented the Malcolm Cottage in Hyannisport from 1926 to 1929 before purchasing and remodeling it to include 14 rooms, nine baths, and a private movie theater in the basement. (It was the first private theater in New England.) By 1932 there were nine children scampering around the house and grounds, which included a private beach, dock, tennis court, and pool. In 1956, then Senator John Kennedy purchased an adjacent house (at the corner of Scudder and Irving Avenues), which came to be known as the Summer White House. Bobby bought the house next door, which now belongs to his widow, Ethel. Sen. Edward Kennedy's former house (it now belongs to his ex-wife, Joan) is on private Squaw Island. Eunice (Kennedy) and Sargent Shriver purchased a nearby home on Atlantic Avenue. If you drive or walk around this stately area, you'll see nothing but high hedges and fences. Those who can't resist a look-see will be far better off taking a boat tour (see *Outdoor Activities—Boat Excursions/ Rentals*); some boats come quite close to the shoreline and the white frame houses. It was at Malcolm Cottage that JFK learned he'd been elected president, at Malcolm Cottage that Jacqueline and the president mourned the loss of their infant son, at Malcolm Cottage that the family mourned the deaths of the president and Bobby Kennedy, at Malcolm Cottage that Sen. Edward Kennedy would annually present his mother with a rose for each of her years, and at Malcolm Cottage that matriarch Rose Kennedy died in 1995 at the age of 104. Regardless of the fact that Kennedy sightings are rare, the Kennedys are still Hyannis's number one "attraction."

St. Francis Xavier Church, 347 South Street. When Rose Kennedy's clan was in town, they worshiped here. The pew used by JFK is marked with a plaque, while the altar is a memorial to JFK's brother, Lt. Joe Kennedy Jr., killed during World War II. More recently, Maria Shriver and Arnold Schwarzenegger were wed here.

Town green, adjacent to the JFK Hyannis Museum. Note the life-size bronze of the sachem Ivanough, chief of the Mattakeese tribe of Cummaquid and friend to the Pilgrims, created in 1995 by Osterville sculptor David Lewis.

Weeping Beech Tree, in the courtyard behind Plush & Plunder (605 Main Street). To the town's knowledge, this is one of seven remaining weeping beeches in the entire country. (Another is in Yarmouth.) It's an awesome, magnificent 200-year-old specimen.

SCENIC DRIVE

Hyannisport is by far the loveliest section of Hyannis, but don't come expecting to see the Kennedys. The "compound" is wedged between Scudder and Irving Avenues. From Main Street, turn left onto Sea Street, right onto Ocean Avenue, left onto Hyannis Avenue, left onto Iyanough Avenue, right onto Wachusett Avenue, and left onto Scudder Avenue.

OUTDOOR ACTIVITIES

AIRPLANE RIDES

✳ **Cape Flight** (508-775-8171), Barnstable Municipal Airport, East Ramp, Routes 132 and 28. Flights by reservation. Get away from the traffic in a Cessna 172. On the 30-minute trip, you can head east to Chatham Light or west to the Cape Cod Canal (one to three people $69). An hour-long trip goes to the outer beaches and Pilgrim Monument in Provincetown (up to three people $129). The Grand Tour lasts 2 hours and takes you all over the Cape and out to the islands (up to three people $200). You can basically go wherever you want; talk to the pilot.

BICYCLING/RENTALS

✳ **Cascade Motor Lodge** (508-775-9717), 201 Main Street. One block from the harbor and bus and train stations, Cascade rents mountain, 10-, and 3-speed bikes daily April to mid-November (year-round, weather permitting).

BOAT EXCURSIONS/RENTALS

✐ **Hyannisport Harbor Cruises** (508-778-2600; www.hy-linecruises.com), Ocean Street Docks. Mid-April to late October. Lewis Bay and Hyannis Harbor are beautiful, and the best way to appreciate them is by water. Also, if you're like 85,000 other visitors each season and you want the best possible view of the Kennedy compound, take this hour-long Hy-Line excursion. The boat comes within 500 feet of the shoreline. Hy-Line also offers a special deal for families: From late June to early September, children ride free on early-morning and late-afternoon boats. During the height of summer, there are also two sunset trips; a Sunday-afternoon family cruise with Ben & Jerry's ice cream sundaes; Wednesday lobster luncheons; Thursday-evening jazz cruises; Friday blues cruises; and Saturday-evening cocktail cruises. Adults $10–16; children 5–12; $5–8.

✐ *Cat Boat* (508-775-0222), Ocean Street Docks. Mid-April to late November. Look for the big cat on the sail. *Eventide* has a full complement of trips; head down to the dock to see what they offer.

✐ **Cape Cod Duck Mobile Tours** (508-362-1117), 448 Main Street. Early April to mid-October. These amphibious tours last 45 minutes and go splashing around Hyannis Harbor, then roll along the street, rather like a duck out of water. Adults $12; children over 5, $8.

FISHING/SHELLFISHING

Freshwater fishing licenses are obtained from the town clerk's office (508-790-6240) in Town Hall, 367 Main Street, Hyannis. Shellfishing permits are required and may be obtained from the Department of Natural Resources (508-790-6272), 1189 Phinney's Lane (which runs between Routes 28 and 132), Centerville. You can also get freshwater fishing permits here.

❋ **Sports Port** (508-775-3096), 149 West Main Street. Surely you've seen the statue of a yellow guy in a red rowboat? That means the store is open—which it has been since Karen Hill unlocked the doors in 1958. References for charters and tours; supplies for freshwater, saltwater, and fly-fishing; ice fishing, too.

Hy-Line Fishing Trips (508-790-0696), Ocean Street Docks. "Bottom-fishing" and deep-sea fishing for fluke and blues from late April to late October. Half day, $22 adults, $14 children. Inquire about full-day trips and night trips.

❋ The supercruiser ***Helen-H*** (508-790-0660), Pleasant Street Docks, goes in search of big fish, too. You'll find cod all year long, bottom fish in the spring, and blues in summer.

FITNESS CLUB

❋ **Barnstable Athletic Club** (508-771-7734), 55 Attucks Way, Independence Park, off Route 132. Racquetball, basketball, squash, aerobics classes, fitness machines, tanning booths, and day care for $10 daily, $25 weekly. Fees permit access to pools at the Ramada Inn and Comfort Inn, too. Both are on Route 132.

❋ ## GOLF

Hyannis Golf Club (508-362-2606), Route 132. An 18-hole, par-71 course.

Twin Brook Golf Course (508-775-7775), West End Circle. Sheraton's course is 18 holes, 2,621 yards, and a par 54.

ICE SKATING

Kennedy Memorial Skating Rink (508-790-6346), Bearses Way. Public skating mid-October through March. Skate rentals $2.

✍ ## MINI-GOLF

Storyland Miniature Golf (508-778-4339), 70 Center Street. April to mid-October. Bumper boats and a 2-acre mini-golf course. Adults might take this opportunity to teach their kids a little about regional architecture and history, as some holes are modeled after local landmarks. Adults $6, children $5.

Carousel & Funhouse Arcade (508-790-0167), 541 Main Street, offer a break from walking around.

SPECIAL PROGRAMS

Eastern Mountain Sports (EMS) (508-362-8690), 1513 Iyanough Road (Route 132). In addition to renting kayaks (great for navigating herring rivers, creeks, and inlets), the Cape's largest purveyor of outdoor gear offers free instructional clinics every couple of weeks throughout the year. Topics range from outdoor cooking to mastering compass skills. Check the bulletin board for a schedule.

TENNIS
Public courts are located at **Barnstable High School** on Route 28 and at **Barnstable Middle School** on West Bay Road.

EVEN MORE THINGS TO SEE AND DO

FOR FAMILIES
✐✝ **Cape Cod Potato Chip Factory** (508-775-7253), Breed's Hill Road, Independence Park, off Route 132. Open 9–5 weekdays year-round and 10–4 Saturday in July and August. Chatham resident Steve Bernard began the company in 1980, parlayed it into a multimillion-dollar business, sold it to corporate giant Anheuser-Busch in 1986, and moved on to the business of purveying Chatham Village Croutons. But in late 1995, when Anheuser-Busch wanted to sell or close it, Bernard bought the company back, saving 100 year-round jobs. Take the 15-minute self-guided tour of the potato-chip-making process, then sample the rich flavor and high crunchability resulting from all-natural ingredients cooked in small kettles. You, too, will be glad Bernard saved the company.

See also Cape Cod YMCA under *Outdoor Activities—For Families* in "Barnstable."

SCENIC RAILROAD
✐ **Cape Cod Central Railroad** (508-771-3800; 1-888-797-7245; www.capetrain.com), Main and Center Streets. Weekends in May, June, September, and October; daily except Monday in July and August. The 42-mile trip takes 2 hours and passes cranberry bogs and the Sandy Neck Great Salt Marsh. Since there are three trains daily, you take the first one, hop off in Sandwich, walk into the picturesque village (it's about a 10-minute walk), and then catch the last train back to Hyannis. Adults $11.75, children 11 and under $7.75.

GREEN SPACE

BEACHES
Weekly cottage renters can purchase beach stickers 9–4 Monday through Saturday and 9–12 Sunday, mid-May to early September, at the Recreation and Human Services Department (508-790-6345), 141 Bassett Lane, behind the skating rink.

Kalmus Park Beach, on Nantucket Sound, at the end of Ocean Street. This beach is good for windsurfing. The land, by the way, was donated by Technicolor inventor Herbert Kalmus, who also owned the Fernbrook estate in Centerville. Facilities include a rest room, snack bar, and bathhouse. Parking $10.

✐ **Veterans Beach,** on Hyannis Harbor (Lewis Bay), off Ocean Street. A good beach for children because the waters are fairly shallow and calm, and a good place to watch harbor sailboats (the Hyannis Yacht Club is next door). Facilities include a rest room, bathhouse, snack bar, swings, grills, and a big wooded area with picnic tables. Parking $10.

Sea Street Beach, on Nantucket Sound, off Sea Street. Facilities include a rest room and bathhouse. Parking $10.

LODGING

Hyannis has hordes of nondescript motels, a small but good selection of B&Bs, and many good family-oriented cottages. All properties are located in Hyannis unless otherwise noted. The zip code for Hyannis is 02601.

RESORT MOTOR INNS

Sheraton Hyannis Resort (508-775-7775; 1-800-325-3535; www.sheraton hyannis.com), West End Circle. These 224 standard-issue rooms, equipped with a king bed or two doubles and cable TV, are pleasant enough. The bilevel motel has plenty of facilities, including a large indoor pool overlooking an 18-hole golf course, heated outdoor pool, tennis courts, health club, massage and treatments at the spa, a bar, and a dining room. Ask for a garden- or golf-course-view room. About $169–209 late June through August, $79–99 in winter, $119–159 in spring and fall. Kids under age 17 free. Rates seem to fluctuate hour to hour, based on tourist traffic.

Sheraton Four Points (508-771-3000; 1-800-325-3535; www.fourpoints hyannis.com), Route 132 at Bearses Way. Open April to mid-November. About 3 miles from the center of town, this two-story motel has 251 rooms, an indoor and heated outdoor pool, kiddie pool, restaurant and bar, fitness center, game room, tennis courts, and access to its sister property's golf course. Late June through August $129–169; $89–119 in spring and fall. Kids under age 17 free. Again, rates seem to fluctuate according to demand.

BED & BREAKFASTS

Inn on Sea Street (508-775-8030; www.capecod.net/innonsea), 358 Sea Street. Open May through October. Innkeepers Sylvia and Fred LaSelva rent nine pristine and lovely rooms, most with private bath, air-conditioning, and TV. Some are furnished with Victorian antiques, including the Garden Room, which has a private entrance. The most popular rooms, completely refurbished and decorated with English country antiques and canopy beds, are across the street. One has a particularly large bathroom; another has a private porch. The inn also boasts one of the sweetest places to stay on the Cape—a small but airy, all-white **cottage** with peaked ceiling, kitchen, separate bedroom, and sitting room. Other pluses: There's plenty of common space; it's located a 2-minute walk from the beach; and the inn never has a minimum-night stay. Breakfasts are rich—

crab scramble, cream cheese coffee cake, and buttery oatmeal bread on lacy-clothed tables set with china. $150 cottage, $85–125 rooms.

Mansfield House (508-771-9455; www.mansfieldhouse.com), 70 Gosnold Street. Open mid-May to mid-October. Innkeeper Don Patrell, a very helpful "people person," continues to upgrade his B&B, providing more and more value each year. For a simple but nice, relatively inexpensive place to stay within walking distance of a beach (three beaches, actually!), it doesn't get any better. There are four fresh and comfortable guest rooms, all with private bath, TV, and VCR. Two rooms have raised ceilings, which lends an airiness to them, while the smallest room compensates with a private deck. Outdoor space includes a porch and garden patio. Children are accommodated in the same room as their parents for an additional $10. $85–95 mid-June to mid-September; $10 less off-season; rates include breakfast.

Sea Breeze Inn (508-771-7213; www.seabreezeinn.com), 270 Ocean Avenue. These 14 rooms (all with private bath, some with two beds) are within a stone's throw of the beach. Although the rooms aren't fancy or filled with antiques, they are certainly comfortable, clean, and pleasant. Expanded continental breakfast included. Mid-June to mid-September $80–140; off-season $55–110.

Memories by the Sea (508-775-9300; 1-877-737-9300; www.memoriesby thesea.com), 162 Sea Street. For families weary of motels and cottages, hosts Debbie and Eric Hubler offer three fine guest rooms with private bath in their 1880s house. Each room has a cable TV, sitting area, air-conditioning, and a fireplace; VCRs are available. The inn is half a mile from the beach, with a convenience store in between them for picnic lunches and drinks. Since the Hublers can set you up with beach chairs and towels, you'll be all set. Afterward, relax on the front porch with a drink or in the spacious living room. Expanded continental breakfast included. May through September $120, off-season $90; each additional person $15. Inquire about various packages.

Simmons Homestead Inn (508-778-4999; 1-800-637-1649; www.capecodtravel.com/simmonsinn), 288 Scudder Avenue. This is one of the Cape's more unusual places to stay. Innkeeper Bill Putman relishes his quirkiness and has furnished the restored 1820s sea captain's home to reflect his offbeat tastes. The basics: There are two suites and 12 antiques-appointed guest rooms with private bath; some have a fireplace and canopy bed; outdoor space includes porch rockers, well-placed hammocks, and a hot tub. As for the idiosyncrasies: The place has been taken over by carved, stuffed, and painted animals (each room has a different animal theme); the living room is chock-full of bric-a-brac—ceramic and papier-mâché—and plants; Datsun hoods from Bill's old racing cars stand in the hallway; guests use "all-purpose drinking mugs." The adjacent annex, with family-appropriate accommodations, has its own living room and billiards room. A full breakfast and wine at "6-ish" are included. May through October $175–225 rooms, $350 suites; off-season $120–175 rooms, $250 suites; $0–20 per additional child, depending on age. Smokers take note: Bill smokes and allows you to, too. Wintertime single-malt Scotch tastings from Bill's collection of almost 300 kinds. For all you fanatics out there, Bill also indulges in sports cars.

COTTAGES AND EFFICIENCIES

Harbor Village (508-775-7581; www.harborvillage.com), 160 Marstons Avenue, Hyannisport 02647. Open April through November. Delightfully off the beaten path but still centrally located, Tim Fuller's one- to four-bedroom cottages can sleep 3–12 people. Each of the 14 cottages has a living room, dining area, fully equipped kitchen, individual heat, a fireplace, deck or patio with grill, cable TV, and VCR. Midweek housekeeping is provided, but you need to bring your own beach towels and chairs. On a private, wooded, 17-acre compound, Harbor Village is within a 2-minute walk of Quahog Beach. Late June to early September $1,250–1,300 for a two-bedroom, $1,400–1,500 for a three-bedroom weekly. Cottages are rented nightly (with a 3-night minimum) off-season: $110–125 for a two-bedroom, $125–145 for a three-bedroom. Service charge of $30 per week added; no credit cards; pets with prior approval (fee).

The Breakwaters (508-775-6831; www.capecodtravel.com/breakwaters), Sea Street Beach. Open May to mid-October. Within a sandal shuffle of Sea Street Beach, these 16 well-maintained cottages accommodate two to six people. Kitchens are small but complete and updated. All cottages have a private deck or patio; some have ocean views. While it's on the beach, Breakwaters also has a heated pool with a lifeguard; swimming lessons are sometimes offered. Late June to late August $925–1,000 weekly for one bedroom, $1,450 for two bedrooms, $2,000 for three bedrooms; off-season $560–725, $900, and $1,200, respectively; spring and fall $68–160 daily, depending on unit size. No credit cards.

Rose Garden Cottage (508-771-7213; www.capecodcottagerentals.com), 256 Ocean Avenue. Open April through November. Owned by the Sea Breeze Inn (see *Bed & Breakfasts*), this three-bedroom, two-bathroom house (complete with a lovely rose garden) is fully equipped for longer stays. There are also two studio efficiencies, one with a whirlpool and canopy bed. House $2,000 weekly, mid-June to mid-September; $1,200 off-season. Efficiencies $690–1,000 weekly in-season; $600 off-season. Inquire about the five-bedroom **Ripple Cove Cottage,** which is just a minute or so from a private beach.

Capt. Gosnold Village (508-775-9111; www.captaingosnold.com), 230 Gosnold Street. Open mid-April to mid-November. Although some motel rooms are a tad dull, most of the knotty-pine-paneled cottages are spacious and have a private deck. Request a newer cottage with three bedrooms, and you'll also get three bathrooms and three televisions. Daily maid service; fully equipped kitchens. Bring your own beach towels. Children enjoy the wooded and grassy grounds with a fenced-in

Fencing and deep roots keep sands from retreating

pool and lifeguard, lawn games, and a play area. In a residential area near the harbor, Gosnold's is a short walk to the beach. Thirty-one units. Mid-June to early September $90 rooms, $105 studios, $170 one-bedroom cottages, $240–280 two- and three-bedroom cottages. Off-season $55 rooms, $65 studios, $100 one-bedroom cottages, $140–160 two- and three-bedroom cottages. Three-night cottage minimum, 2 nights for other lodging. A service charge is added.

See also Inn on Sea Street under *Bed & Breakfasts*.

TOWN HOUSES

✻✔ **The Yachtsman** (508-771-5454; 1-800-695-5454), rental office at 500 Ocean Street, Apt. 14. These privately owned townhouse condominiums, with their own private stretch of beach between Kalmus and Veterans Beaches (see *Green Space*), are right on Lewis Bay. During the summer, about 50 of the 125 units are available for rent. Although the decor varies from one unit to another, all must meet certain standards. Multilevel units have a full kitchen, 2½ baths, private sundeck, sunken living room, and two to four bedrooms. About half have water views; half overlook the heated pool. Late June to early September $1,450–2,595 weekly; about 30 percent less in spring and fall, 40 percent lower in winter.

MOTOR INN

See Tidewater under *Lodging—Motor Inns* in "Yarmouth."

WHERE TO EAT

✎ With more than 60 eateries, most open nearly year-round, you can find everything from fine Continental to Tex-Mex. Reservations are recommended at all the establishments under *Dining Out.* Unless otherwise noted, all restaurants are open year-round.

DINING OUT

Penguins Seagrille (508-775-2023), 331 Main Street. Open for dinner year-round except January. Despite a constant parade of upstart competitors, Penguins still serves the best seafood in town. In fact, the whole menu (and its winning execution) is the most innovative and creative around. Dishes sail the globe, from French to Italian to Asian, from wood-grilled meats (a specialty) to Szechuan salmon (excellent), from a vegetable quesadilla to a feast of seafood stewed in marinara sauce. Your taste buds will be tickled; trust your instincts when ordering. There are usually half a dozen daily fish specials, while pastas and risottos make regular menu appearances. Chef-owners Bobby and Portia Gold have been at the helm since 1980; kudos. Save room for Chocolate Seduction at dessert. Oh, the wine list is lengthy and well chosen. Early specials. Entrées $16–20.

RooBar City Bistro (508-778-6515), 586 Main Street. Open for dinner. This is one happening place, especially when the **bar** crowd reappears. Part of the name is apropos: With an exposed kitchen, high ceilings, and steel-based art (does a car grille hanging on the wall constitute art?), the bistro could well have been transported from Boston's South End. As for the "Roo," the cuisine is about as far from kangaroos as you can get. Fortunately, the food keeps up with a hip and fast-paced city rather than the outback. Some tables are linen covered, some polished wood. The innovative menu is best described as internationally influenced New American fusion. During my last visit it highlighted Wellfleet oysters, grilled swordfish with roasted corn and cilantro salsa, and a fire-roasted chicken rubbed with toasted fennel and cumin seed marinade. Check it out. Fancy and fabulous brick-oven pizzas ($10), too. Entrées range from $14 for vegetarian rigatoni to $20 for steak *au poivre* with herbed mashed potatoes and a nice brandy sauce.

✍❀♿**Alberto's Ristorante** (508-778-1770), 360 Main Street. Open for dinner. Catering to a loyal following from the minute it opened in 1984, chef-owners Felis and Donna Barreiro's popular restaurant is elegant and romantic, all done up in pink and off-white. While it may look formal, the service is professional but not stuffy at all. The extensive menu features homemade pasta and northern Italian specialties such as eggplant parmigiana, lobster diavolo, seafood ravioli, and veal Sienese, a mushroom lover's delight. They do an excellent job and are deserving of their fine reputation. Portions are large. Top off your meal with a rich cappuccino. Children's menu. Early-dinner specials 4–5:45 PM are $11–16; dinner entrées $13–26.

✍❀♿**Sweetwaters Grille & Bar** (508-775-3323), 644 Main Street. Open for dinner nightly year-round and lunch Friday through Sunday in-season (daily off-season). Sure as coyotes howl and adobe is made of mud and straw, Southwestern cuisine has come to Hyannis. After Steve and

Colleen Jais opened it in 1991, the place was so popular with locals that seating mushroomed from 40 to 140. While the extensive and consistent menu has its share of sizzling fajitas and burritos, the kitchen is really much more creative than that. Nightly specials are always a good bet (I relished a pan-bronzed striped bass with mango beurre blanc and roasted corn and black bean salsa), as are the Thai-, Caribbean-, and Cuban-influenced dishes. I would order every dish from my last visit again: grilled portobello mushroom caps, vegetarian ravioli, Baja-grilled shrimp, and "seafood salina." Although the brownie and Toll House cookie dessert is the most popular, the warm orange Grand Marnier flan is out of this world. A screened-in porch opens for summer dining. There are always lots of families here in the early evening; children's menu. Sunday brunch $9–11, lunch $7–10, dinner entrées $10–20.

❄️♿ **Fazio's Trattoria** (508-775-9400), 294 Main Street. Open for dinner. Chef-owners Tom and Eileen Fazio hail from San Francisco's Italian North Beach neighborhood. Hyannis is not North Beach, but you'd never know it inside this trattoria. The storefront bistro space has a good feel, with high ceilings, pale yellow walls, and exposed air ducts. But it's topped by excellent homemade pasta dishes (like *fettuccine rosmarino con pollo*) and a few chicken and veal specialties. Thin-crust, brick-oven pizzas have no equal. Dinner $11–17.

❄️♿ **Roadhouse Cafe** (508-775-2386), 488 South Street. Open for dinner nightly. This pleasant place—with polished floors, Oriental carpets, hanging plants, tongue-and-groove ceilings with paddle fans, candlelight, and two fireplaces—is also very dependable, thanks to the long tenure of owners Dave and Melissa Colombo and chef Tim Souza. Come for a romantic interlude or with a group for fun. The extensive Italian and seafood menu features large portions. You might consider splitting an entrée and pairing it with a couple of appetizers. You really can't go wrong here. Try seared codcakes or tender calamari marinara to start, and move on to almost any chicken, veal, or beef dish imaginable. Creative, thin-crust pizzas are offered in the **Back Door Bistro** (see *Entertainment—Nightlife*), which has a clubby feel with dark paneling and a mahogany bar. It has a large selection of wine by the glass and 40 brands of beer. Early specials from 4 to 6 PM. Dinner entrées $14–24.

Naked Oyster (508-778-6500), 20 Independence Drive, off Route 132 and across from Sam Diego's. Open for lunch and dinner. I didn't get a chance to eat at this eclectic new place, but reliable innkeeper friends have given me good reports. From the longtime owners of the Roadhouse Cafe, this is a very cosmopolitan place off the beaten path. In addition to a raw bar starring clams and oysters, you can get a Caesar salad with salmon or appetizers like tuna sashimi or a softshell crab sandwich. Dinner tends toward lobster, roasted statler chicken breast, and ribeye steaks. Lunch $8–15, dinner entrées $16–24.

✐ **The Paddock** (508-775-7677), West End rotary. Open for lunch and dinner

April to mid-November. If you're in the mood for traditional seafood and Continental cuisine, the main dining room's Victorian airs provide the requisite backdrop. It sports dark beams, upholstered armchairs, and frosted glass. Luncheon, frequented by an older crowd and business-people in summer, is served in a garden-style setting heavy on rattan and pastel. The Zartarian family has operated this institution since 1970, and John Anderson has been the chef since 1973. Stick to salads, chowder, and sandwiches at lunch. At dinner the Paddock offers standards like 2-pound lobsters, rack of lamb, and Black Angus steaks. When there's an event at the Melody Tent, stay away until after 9 PM. The wine list is excellent; children's menu $8; early specials 30 percent off. Lunch $5.25–9.50, dinner entrées $14–25.

EATING OUT

Baxter's Boat House Club and Fish 'n Chips (508-775-4490), 177 Pleasant Street. Open for lunch and dinner, mid-April to mid-October. It's mostly about location rather than food here, and it's better for lunch than dinner. Built on an old fish-packing dock near the Steamship Authority terminal, Baxter's has attracted a crowd since 1956, from beautiful people tying up at the dock to singles meeting at the bar, from families to folks who just purchase a soda and go through the side door to a harborfront picnic table. It's really the best waterfront table in town. The fried and broiled seafood is usually consistent, too, if not exemplary. Dishes $10–17.

Tugboats (508-775-6433), 21 Arlington Street, behind the hospital off Willow Street. Open for lunch and dinner mid-April to mid-October. This casual place overlooking the harbor—with an outdoor deck—has lots of food, especially fried seafood, but beyond that, the salmon is very good and the lobster specials are priced out of this world. Dishes $6–20.

Ying's (508-790-2432), 59 Center Street. Open for lunch and dinner. While Ying's boasts arguably the best Thai on Cape Cod, the noodle, Japanese, and Korean dishes are nothing to sneeze at either. Lunch specials are all $7–9, and dinner dishes are only slightly more. **Ying's Noodles** (508-771-9464), 453 Main Street, only serves more than 100 noodle dishes. The atmosphere is tasteful, rather like an indoor garden. All available for takeout.

Pastiche & The Blue Room (508-778-7200), 415 Main Street. Open for lunch and dinner, Sunday brunch. The outdoor patio overlooking Main Street at this so-called eclectic New American bistro is key. I found the service here less than stellar, but I' still come back for an alfresco martini and appetizer. Inside, there are a few upscale **bars** with entertainment.

La Petite France (508-771-4445), 349 Main Street. Open daily (except Sunday off-season) April through December. This informal café serves fresh salads, sandwiches, and soups. Owner Lucien (Lu) Degionanni hails from the south of France, so many homemade offerings are distinctly French—like the onion soup; cold tomato, feta, and basil salad;

and baguettes and pastries. In a nod to his current home, he also makes great clam chowder and roasts his own beef, turkey, and ham for sandwiches. As might be expected, the café also serves a good cup of coffee. There are half a dozen tables; otherwise, take a picnic to the park. Dishes $4–5.50.

❦ **Common Ground Cafe** (508-778-8390), 420 Main Street. Open Monday through Thursday 10–9 and Friday 10–3. When you step inside, let your eyes adjust to the darkness for a minute: You'll find hand-hewn booths resembling hobbit houses and an anachronistic community (a religious collective actually) of folks serving honest food. With the exception of baked salmon offered most Monday and Wednesday nights, the menu is limited to a few wholesome sandwiches, "south-of-the-border" dishes like burritos, and salads. Everything is made from scratch. Note that the restaurant is closed on weekends, when members prefer to spend time with their families rather than pursue the almighty buck. There's also a **juice bar** upstairs. Dishes $4–12.

Black Cat (508-778-1233), 165 Ocean Street. Open for lunch and dinner year-round except January. Although it's a bit noisy and pubby, the Black Cat serves the best fried scallops and fried clams in town. (It's not a fry joint, though.) Dine alfresco surrounded by a white picket fence and flowering baskets (across the street from the harbor) or indoors. Lunch $7–15; dinner entrées average about $19.

✐ **Sam Diego's** (508-771-8816), 950 Iyanough Road. Open 11:30 AM–1 AM; dinner until midnight; takeout until 4 PM on weekdays. Decorated with little white lights, colorful serapes, toucans, and sombreros, this fun place is often full of families. They come for reliable southwestern- and Mexican-inspired fare like chicken fajitas, barbecued ribs, burritos, and enchiladas. In warm weather, there is a large outdoor patio for dining. For weekday lunches (year-round), try the all-you-can eat chili, soup, and taco bar for $6, $2.95 for kids 8 and under. Children's menu. Dishes $5–13.

✐ **Starbuck's** (508-778-6767), Route 132. Open 11:30 AM–midnight daily. Part bar, part family restaurant, part roomy barn with bric-a-brac (and no relation to the coffee chain), Starbuck's opened in 1985 with a diverse menu: pastas, Tex-Mex, Thai hot-peppered shrimp, burgers, and chicken sandwiches. Many people come just for the frozen drinks and 20-ounce cocktails, though. Children's menu; live entertainment in the **bar** (nightly except Monday). Dishes $5–15.

Harry's (508-778-4188), 700 Main Street. Open for lunch and dinner daily. This small, local **bar**/hangout features Cajun dishes, BBQ, seafood (including popular stuffed quahogs), and homemade soups. Lunch leans heavily toward New Orleans with "hoppin' John" (rice with black-eyed peas), jambalaya, and blackened chicken. The joint jumps with live blues and jazz nightly except Monday. Lunch $5–8, dinner $9–17.

❦✐ **Mayflower Cape Cod Diner** (508-771-3554), 50 Sea Street. Open daily for breakfast and daily except Sunday for lunch year-round; also open for dinner late June to early September. A refreshingly inexpensive and simple alternative, this calculatingly retro diner is bright and fun, with aquamarine upholstered booths, swivel bar stools, and a shiny tin ceiling. Short-order specialties prevail: hash, omelets, and scrambled eggs with biscuits and gravy (that is, breakfast) are served all day. Burgers and hot and cold sandwiches are offered at lunch; meat loaf, seafood platters, and sirloin are on at dinnertime. Try the weighty and delectable morning glory muffins! Or for a change, check out Greek specialties like spinach pie and pastitso. Children's menu. Dishes $2–9.

The Egg & I (508-771-1596), 521 Main Street. Open for breakfast 6–1, March through November. This charming half-timber house is not your run-of-the-mill breakfast joint. It's a Hyannis institution, dishing up seafood omelets, crabcakes, fancy pancakes, waffles, and French toast creations with pralines, along with corned beef hash, since 1971. Children's menu. Dishes $4–11.

Box Lunch (508-790-5855), 357 Main Street. Open for lunch daily (except Sunday in winter). More than 50 kinds of sandwiches, all wrapped up in pita bread. Convenient for the beach and taking anywhere, really.

See also Sweetwaters Grille & Bar under *Dining Out.*

COFFEE

Spiritus (508-775-2955), 500 Main Street. Open daily. If you can make your way past the loitering teens and Gen-Xers, you'll be rewarded with strong coffee; hot slices of pizza decked with broccoli, eggplant, and sun-dried tomatoes; tasty focaccia sandwiches; and buttery ice cream. After 10 PM the congregation of kids out front swells to a "wild" level for Cape Cod.

Caffe e Dolci (508-790-6900), 430 Main Street. Open for pastries and sandwiches until 11 in summer, about 5 the rest of the year. All you 40-somethings who aren't interested in Spiritus or The Prodigal Son have an alternative. Strong espresso and flavored coffee drinks share the stage here with foccaccia sandwiches and pastries. There's some indoor seating.

The Prodigal Son (508-771-1337), 10 Ocean Street. Open from about 9:30 AM to 1 AM. This 20-something coffeehouse with offbeat art features microbrews, wine by the glass, strong coffee drinks, and specialty sandwiches. There's a full calendar of live entertainment scheduled: acoustic folk, blues, jazz, open-mike nights on Wednesday. Dishes $4.25–7.

See also La Petite France under *Eating Out.*

ICE CREAM

The contest is basically local versus regional: **Maggie's Ice Cream** (508-778-8118), 570 Main Street; **Ben & Jerry's** (508-790-0910), 352 Main Street; and **Emack & Bolio's** (508-775-2955), within Spiritus (see *Coffee*), 500 Main Street (open year-round).

DINNER TRAIN

Cape Cod Dinner Train (508-771-3800; 1-888-797-7245; www.capetrain.com), Main and Center Streets. I didn't have a chance to personally try this newly resurrected Victorian-style dinner train. But I can give you the details; ask your innkeeper about its current reputation. The train runs on weekends (Saturday evening and Sunday afternoon, with some Friday evenings) from October through June (except January) and from Wednesday through Sunday evening July through September. The vintage 1920s cars run at "soup speed" for a 3-hour trip to the canal and back. During that time you'll enjoy a five-course meal, which you will have chosen 48 hours in advance. (*Hint:* Reservations are required.) Tickets cost $50 per person; alcohol and tipping are additional. Inquire about the summertime family supper train.

ENTERTAINMENT

MUSIC

Cape Cod Melody Tent (508-775-9100 tickets; 508-775-5630 information), West Main Street. Shows June through September. When this big white tent was erected in 1950, entertainment was limited to Broadway musicals. Today it's the Cape's biggest and best venue for top-name comics and musicians like Joan Rivers, Tony Bennett, Julio Iglesias, Lyle Lovett, Wynonna, Kenny Rogers, and Little Feat. There are **children's shows** ($6) Wednesday morning in July and August. Profits are poured into arts programs and education on the Cape and Boston's South Shore.

Cape Symphony Orchestra (508-362-1111). About 15 concerts for children and adults, September through May. The orchestra plays at a new 1,400-seat auditorium, the Barnstable Performing Arts Center, at Barnstable High School, West Main Street in Hyannis.

SPECTATOR SPORTS

Baseball. The Hyannis Mets play mid-June to early August.

The Cape Cod Crusaders (508-790-4782), a professional soccer team, play 12 home games from early May to mid-August at the Dennis-Yarmouth High School (exit 8 off Route 6). Formed in 1991 as one of 60 teams within the USISL (United Systems Independent Soccer League), the Crusaders are a Division 3 farm team for the New England Revolution. They're the Cape's only pro team of any sort. Tickets $8 adults, $5 children 14 and under. Call for game times and dates.

MOVIES

Hoyt's Cinema Center (508-771-7460), Routes 132 and 28, at the Cape Cod Mall. The Cape's only stadium-seating megacomplex, with 12 screens.

NIGHTLIFE

Back Door Bistro at the Roadhouse Cafe (508-775-2386), 488 South Street. Live jazz on Monday night year-round, piano by Lou Colombo nightly in summer, and piano Friday and Saturday off-season.

Hyannisport Brewing Company (508-775-8289), 720 Main Street. If you consider a sampler rack of beer "entertainment," this is the place for you. Unfortunately, the food doesn't live up to the beverages.

See also RooBar City Bistro under *Dining Out;* Pastiche, Starbuck's, and

Harry's under *Eating Out;* and the Prodigal Son under *Coffee.*

SELECTIVE SHOPPING

❆ Unless otherwise noted, all shops are open year-round.

ART GALLERY AND CRAFTS

The Spectrum (508-771-4554), 342 Main Street. Textiles, jewelry, lamps, glass objects, wooden boxes and business-card holders, musical instruments, and ceramics—all creatively handcrafted by contemporary American artists.

Red Fish Blue Fish (508-775-8700), 374 Main Street. The most fun and whimsical "gallery" in town (in the area, for that matter), with unusual gifts and crafts. When it's not too busy, you can watch owner Jane Walsh making handblown jewelry in the store. When the shop is closed, a video runs in the front window. Do stop by.

Just Africa (508-775-0448), 364 Main Street. Open May through December. Displaying powerful work from the entire continent, this gallery specializes in contemporary Zimbabwe stone sculpture, but there are also extensive inventories of textiles, brass and copper jewelry, ceramics, stoneware, wood carvings, batik, and paintings. Decorative folk art, ceremonial masks.

Guyer Barn Gallery (508-790-6370), 250 South Street. Weekly shows hung from mid-June through October. The Barnstable Arts and Humanities Council established this art gallery in 1986. Openings on Sunday.

BOOKSTORES

Barnes & Noble (508-771-1400), Route 132, just north of the airport rotary. Although there are a few smaller new- and used-book stores on Main Street, if you want a particular book, it's probably here.

Borders Books, Music, Cafe (508-862-6363), Route 132, north of the airport rotary. A superstore with a café.

Rodney's Bookstore (508-790-3448), 580 Main Street, is just one of a few bookstores on Main Street. Rodney's deals in used hardcovers and nonfiction; I've always found the staff very helpful.

CLOTHING

Plush & Plunder (508-775-4467), 605 Main Street. Vintage and eccentric used clothing adorns those marching to an offbeat drummer, including fabled customers like Cyndi Lauper, Joan Baez, and Demi Moore. You don't have to be an entertainer to stop here, although you'll end up entertained and entertaining (if you purchase something). Thousands of hats hang from the rafters like bats in the Carlsbad Caverns. Need gold lamé, a boa, or other retro accessories? Don't miss this great place.

Europa (508-790-0877), 37 Barnstable Road at North Street. Fine and fun clothing, in a full range of sizes, made of natural fibers from around the world. Plus a really great selection of accessories, including sterling jewelry and scarves.

FACTORY OUTLETS

Christmas Tree Shops (508-778-5521), between Route 28 and Route 132, next to the Cape Cod Mall. Of the seven Christmas Tree Shops on the Cape, this Victorian-style one is the largest.

Dansk Factory Outlet (508-775-3118), Route 132, across from the Cape Cod Mall. Contemporary designs for the kitchen and table.

MALL

✐ **Cape Cod Mall** (508-771-0200; www.shopsimon.com), Routes 132 and 28. Open daily. The Cape's only "real" mall—as distinguished from a plethora of strip malls—is anchored by big retailers and supplemented by more than 100 other stores, a large food court, and four cinemas. To keep kids occupied, there is an arcade and Venetian carousel, too.

SPECIAL SHOPS

Cellar Leather (508-771-5458), 592 Main Street. Quality coats, vests, shoes, clogs, sandals, briefcases, hats, and wallets—if you have any money left over.

Hyannis Antique Center (508-778-0512), 500 Main Street. More flea market than antiques outlet, the co-op is worth a look-see. You never know what you'll find: jewelry, prints, collectibles.

Play It Again Sports (508-771-6979), 25 Route 28. Whether it's new or used equipment you're after, this shop has it all.

All Cape Cook's Supply (508-790-8908), 237 Main Street. Useful gadgets for pros and amateurs.

Kandy Korner Gifts (508-771-5313), 474 Main Street. Closed January. Watch the saltwater taffy and fudge being made in the front windows before heading in to indulge your sweet tooth with old-fashioned candy.

SPECIAL EVENTS

May: **Annual Figawi Sailboat Race Weekend.** The largest sailboat race in New England goes from Hyannis to Nantucket.

Early July: **Blessing of the Fleet,** downtown and on the waterfront. Street parade, fireworks, and boat parade.

Late July: **Regatta.** Since the early 1940s at the Hyannis Yacht Club.

Early August: **Pops by the Sea.** Boston Pops Esplanade Orchestra on the town green. In the past, guest conductors have included Mike Wallace, Julia Child, Olympia Dukakis, and Walter Cronkite. Reserved-seating and general-admission tickets.

Early December: **Harbor Lighting.** Parade of boats includes the arrival of Santa; entertainment with a holiday theme.

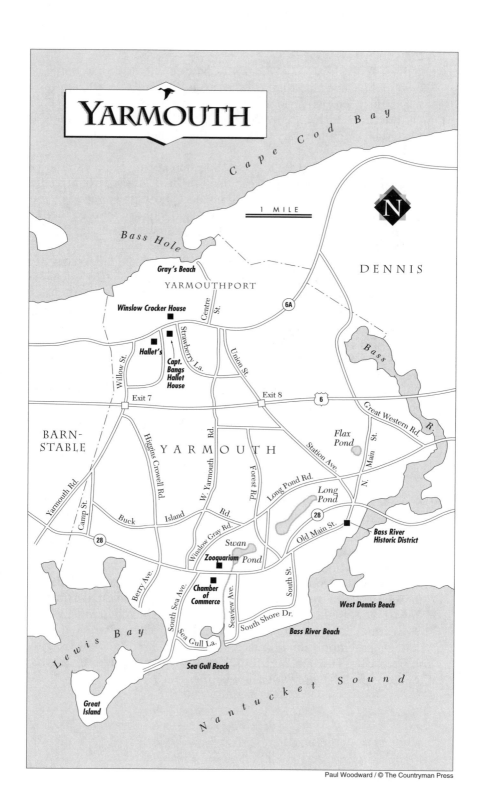

YARMOUTH

Cape Cod Bay

1 MILE

N

Bass Hole

Gray's Beach

YARMOUTHPORT

DENNIS

Winslow Crocker House

Centre St.

6A

Hallet's

Strawberry La.

Bass

Capt.
Bangs
Hallet
House

Union St.

Willow St.

Exit 7

Exit 8

6

Great Western Rd.

R.

BARN-
STABLE

YARMOUTH

Rd.

Flax
Pond

N. Main St.

Higgins Crowell Rd.

W. Yarmouth

Station Ave.

Yarmouth Rd.

Camp St.

Buck

Island

Rd.

Forest Rd.

Long Pond Rd.

Long
Pond

28

Old Main St.

Bass River
Historic District

28

Winslow Gray Rd.

Swan

Berry Ave.

Zooquarium

Pond

South Sea Ave.

Chamber
of
Commerce

Seaview Ave.

South St.

South Shore Dr.

West Dennis Beach

Sea Gull La.

Bass River Beach

Lewis Bay

Sea Gull Beach

Nantucket Sound

Great
Island

Paul Woodward / © The Countryman Press

Yarmouth

Stephen Hopkins, a *Mayflower* passenger, built the first house in Yarmouth in 1638 (off Mill Lane); the town was incorporated just one year later. Yarmouth's active ports bustled in the 19th century: Packets sailed to Boston from Yarmouthport and boats sailed to New York and Newark from South Yarmouth at Bass River. Both villages (the former on Route 6A, the latter on Route 28) have lovely historic districts lined with houses built for and by rope makers, sea captains, bankers, and shipbuilders. At one time, a mile-long section of Yarmouthport was referred to as Captain's Row, as it was home to almost 50 sea captains. Today, Yarmouth is the third most populous town on the Cape, with 22,000 year-round residents.

Yarmouth, like neighboring Dennis, stretches from Cape Cod Bay to Nantucket Sound; it unfolds along quiet Route 6A and congested Route 28. It's a family-oriented town, with many golf courses, tennis courts, and town-sponsored sailing lessons, as well as quite a few southside oceanfront resorts. There are almost 4,000 beds to rent in Yarmouth.

Although Yarmouth's 5.3-mile section of Route 28 was planted with more than 350 trees in 1989 (on its 350th birthday), the road is still a wall-to-wall sea of mini-golf courses, shops, fast-food places, and family-style attractions like a combination zoo-aquarium, a billiards emporium, and boating on the Bass River. A larger-than-life plastic polar bear, lunging shark, and elephant bear witness to the Cape's kitschier side. They're alternately viewed as icons and eyesores by locals. It's difficult to imagine that Route 28 was once open land dotted with small farms. The scenic Bass River and South Yarmouth Historic District provide a delightful detour south of Route 28.

On the north side, Route 6A was settled in the 1600s, was traveled by stagecoaches in the 1700s, and reached its height of prosperity in the 1800s. Many former sea captains' houses are now attractive bed & breakfasts. Meander along tranquil Route 6A and you'll find crafts and antiques shops, a former apothecary with a working soda fountain, a quiet village green, a couple of fine historic houses open to the public, walking trails, and an antiquarian bookstore. Take any lane off Route 6A to the north, and you'll find picturesque residential areas.

GUIDANCE

❋ **Yarmouth Area Chamber of Commerce** (508-778-1008; 1-800-732-1008; www.yarmouthcapecod.com), 657 Route 28, West Yarmouth 02673. Open 9–5 Monday through Saturday and 10–3 Sunday, early May to mid-October; 9–5 weekdays mid-October to early May. The chamber booklet is filled with money-saving coupons, and the chamber staff are very helpful. Pick up two self-guided historical tours of Yarmouth and Old South Yarmouth here.

PUBLIC REST ROOMS

Public rest rooms are located on Route 6 between exits 6 and 7, and at Gray's Beach (open seasonally, off Centre Street from Route 6A).

❋✍🏠PUBLIC LIBRARIES

With such variable hours, it's best to call ahead:
South Yarmouth Library (508-760-4820), 312 Main Street;
West Yarmouth Library (508-775-5206), 391 Route 28;
Yarmouthport (508-362-3717), 297 Route 6A.

GETTING THERE

By car: Yarmouth is 26 miles from the Bourne Bridge; take Route 6 to exit 7 for the north side (Yarmouthport and points along Route 6A). For points along Route 28 on the south side, take exit 7 south to Higgins Crowell Road for West Yarmouth, or exit 8 south for South Yarmouth and the Bass River.

GETTING AROUND

YES (Yarmouth Easy Shuttle) (508-385-8326; 1-800-352-7155; www.capecodtransit.org) operates late June to early September. Funded by a state grant, the shuttle begins at the Plymouth & Brockton bus terminal in Hyannis and runs along Route 28 to various family-oriented points (including beaches) in Yarmouth. Flag down the driver, who will pull over to pick you up. (It sure beats traffic.) Adults $1 one way; kids age 6–17, 50¢. One-day passes ($3) and tickets are purchased aboard the trolley or at the chamber of commerce (see *Guidance*).

❋ The **H₂O** (508-385-8326; 1-800-352-7155; www.capecodtransit.org) bus, primarily used by residents, travels along Route 28 between Hyannis and Orleans daily except Sunday year-round. It stops in South Yarmouth on Main Street, Star Market, and Stop & Shop; in West Yarmouth it stops at Higgins Crowell Road.

MEDICAL EMERGENCY

Call **911**.

Bass River Chiropractic (508-394-1353), 833 Route 28, South Yarmouth. Open daily except Sunday. When I'm researching a guidebook, I spend a lot of time driving around and at my computer. Without Dr. Reida or Dr. Allen, I'd continue with pain. They're both health savers, full of quiet wisdom.

TO SEE

🍄 **Hallet's** (508-362-3362; www.hallets.com), 139 Route 6A, Yarmouthport. Open April through December. Hallet's has been a community fixture since it was built as an apothecary in 1889 by Thacher Taylor Hallet. T. T. Hallet's great-grandson Charles owns and operates the store, which boasts an old-fashioned oak counter and a marble-topped soda fountain. As time stands still, sit on a swivel stool or in one of the wrought-iron, heart-shaped chairs beneath the tin ceiling, and relax over a light breakfast, ice cream soda, or lunchtime sandwich. The second floor has been turned into something of a museum, documenting Yarmouth's history as seen through one family's annals and attic treasures. In addition to being a pharmacist (old medicine bottles are on display), T. T. Hallet was a postmaster (during his tenure, only 15 families had mail slots), selectman (the second floor was used as a meeting room from 1889 to the early 1900s), and justice of the peace. The charming displays include store posters from the last 100 years and historical photographs. Donation for the museum.

    Village pump, Route 6A near Summer Street, Yarmouthport. This wrought-iron pump has served the community since 1886. It's located just west of the Old Yarmouth Inn, the oldest inn (and stagecoach stop) on the Cape, dating from 1696. The pump's iron frame, decorated with birds, animals, and a lantern, is supported by a stone trough from which horses drank. Horse-drawn carriages traveling from Boston to Provincetown stopped here.

🍄 **Captain Bangs Hallet House** (508-362-3021), 2 Strawberry Lane (park behind the post office on Route 6A), Yarmouthport. Open Thursday through Sunday, June to mid-October, for tours at 1, 2, and 3. The original section of this Greek Revival house was built in 1740 by town founder Thomas Thacher, but it was substantially enlarged by Capt. Henry Thacher in 1840. Captain Hallet and his wife, Anna, lived here from 1863 until 1893. The house, maintained by the Historical Society of Old Yarmouth, is decorated in a manner befitting a prosperous sea captain who traded with China and India. Note the original 1740 kitchen and don't miss the gracious weeping beech behind the house. Adults $3, children 12 and under 50¢.

🍄 **Winslow Crocker House** (508-362-4385; www.spnea.org), 250 Route 6A, Yarmouthport. Tours hourly between 11 AM and 4 PM on weekends, June to mid-October. Set back from Route 6A, this two-story Georgian home was built in 1780 with 12-over-12 small-paned windows and rich interior paneling. The house was constructed for a wealthy 18th-century trader and land speculator and moved to its present location in 1936 by Mary Thacher. Thacher, a descendant of Yarmouth's original land grantee, was an avid collector of 17th-, 18th-, and 19th-century furniture, and she used the house as a backdrop for her magnificent collection. The house was donated to the Society for the Preservation of New England Antiquities (SPNEA) and is the only SPNEA property on Cape Cod. Sara Porter and Jim McGuinness administer the house and will regale you with stories. Adults $4; children 5–12, $2; members and Cape Cod residents free.

Baxter Grist Mill, Route 28, West Yarmouth. Usually open 10–2 weekends, early June through August, and on holiday weekends (Memorial Day, Labor Day, and Columbus Day). The original mill was built in 1710 with an exterior waterwheel. In 1860, when water levels in Mill Pond became so low that the wheel froze, an inside water turbine was built. (This is the Cape's only mill with an inside water turbine.) Kids can help grind corn with "the Mill Man." Free.

Windmill Park, off River Street from Old Main Street, South Yarmouth. Now on the Bass River, this eight-sided windmill was built in 1791 and moved here in 1866. There are plans to restore the windmill and open it to the public. This scenic spot also has a small swimming beach.

SCENIC DRIVES

South Yarmouth and the Bass River Historic District, on and around Old Main Street (off Route 28), South Yarmouth. The Pawkannawkut Indians (a branch of the Wampanoag tribe) lived, fished, and hunted on a tract of land Yarmouth set aside for them along Long Pond and the Bass River in 1713. By the 1770s, a smallpox epidemic wiped out most of the Native population. In 1790 David Kelley (a Quaker) acquired the last remaining Pawkannawkut land from the last surviving Pawkannawkut, Thomas Greenough. Quakers then settled the side streets off Old Main Street near Route 28 and built handsome homes. The simple traffic rotary at River and Pleasant Streets is thought to be the oldest in the country. The Historical Society of Old Yarmouth publishes a walking tour to Old South Yarmouth, which you can purchase at the chamber of commerce (see *Guidance*).

Yarmouthport: From Route 6A, turn onto Church Street across from the village green. Follow it around to Thacher Shore Drive and Water Street. When Water Street turns left, head right down a dirt road for a wide-open view of marshland. Continue on Water Street across Keveney Bridge, which crosses Mill Creek; Keveney Lane takes you back to Route 6A. Turn left to head east, back into Yarmouthport. This scenic loop is nice for a quiet walk, a bicycle ride, or an early-morning jog.

OUTDOOR ACTIVITIES

BICYCLING/RENTALS

All Right Bike (508-790-3191), 627 Route 28, West Yarmouth, near Parker's River. Open March through December. Here you can rent 3-speeds, 10-speeds, BMX, mountain bikes, tandems, and mopeds.

☀⚡ BILLIARDS, BOWLING, AND ARCHERY

Classical Billiards (508-771-5872), 657B Route 28, West Yarmouth. Open daily. This family-oriented billiards room has 14 tables, darts, fooseball, video games, Ping Pong, and snooker.

Ryan Family Amusement Center (508-394-5644), 1067 Route 28, South Yarmouth. Open 9 AM–10 PM daily. When rain strikes, head indoors to bowl away the blues. Ten-pin and candlepin.

Riverview Bait & Tackle (508-394-1036), 1273 Route 28, South Yarmouth, has an indoor archery range.

☀ FISHING/SHELLFISHING

Shellfishing permits and freshwater fishing licenses are required. Obtain them from Town Hall (508-398-2231), Route 28, South Yarmouth.

Truman's Bait & Tackle (508-771-3470), 608 Route 28, West Yarmouth. One-stop shopping for rod rentals, repairs, freshwater licenses, and local maps and charts. A great resource.

Riverview Bait & Tackle (508-394-1036), 1273 Route 28, South Yarmouth. Among other services, the staff will direct you to local fishing spots, including the Bass River and High Bank Bridges, Sea Gull Beach at Parker's River, and Smugglers Beach off South Shore Drive. Riverview also has an indoor archery range.

FITNESS CLUB

Mid-Cape Racquet Club (508-394-3511), 193 White's Path (off South Yarmouth Road), South Yarmouth. For a day-use fee of $10, you have access to racquetball and squash courts, basketball, Nautilus, free weights, and kick boxing. Additional fee for the nine indoor courts, Pilates, spinning, and child care. It's obviously a full-service kind of place.

FOR FAMILIES

Zooquarium of Cape Cod (508-775-8883), Route 28, West Yarmouth. Open 9:30–5 daily, February to late November, until 6 PM in summer. Part zoo (with a petting area), part aquarium (with performing sea lions), this place is packed on cloudy days, but if you come at the beginning or end of a sunny beach day, you can avoid the crowds. Although the place may conjure up thoughts of the movie *Free Willy*, keep in mind that many of these animals would have died if they hadn't been brought here. Some arrive injured or blind. With the exception of the farm animals, all land and sea creatures are native. Small endangered animals educate small children at the **Zoorific Theater.** Children 10 and older $8; children 2–9, $5.

Jump On Us (508-775-3304), Route 28, West Yarmouth. This trampoline center is open late May to mid-October.

Playgrounds. Flax Playground is on Old Main Street off Route 28 in South Yarmouth; another is on Route 6A at old Church Street in Yarmouthport.

See also Bass River Sports World under *Mini-Golf.*

GOLF

King's Way (508-362-8870), off Route 6A, Yarmouthport. Open March

Some mini-golf courses tower above the competition

through November. A challenging 18-hole, 4,100-yard, par-59 course designed by Cornish and Silva and opened in 1988.

Bayberry Hills (508-394-5597), off West Yarmouth Road, West Yarmouth. Open early April to late November. A town-owned, 18-hole, par-72 course with driving range.

❄ **Bass River Golf Course** (508-398-9079), off Highbank Road, South Yarmouth. Open year-round, weather permitting. Founded in 1900, this town-owned, 18-hole, par-72 course offers great views of the Bass River.

❄ **Blue Rock Golf Course** (508-398-9295), off Highbank Road, South Yarmouth. Open year-round, weather permitting. A short 18-hole, par-54 course.

KAYAKING

✎ **Ripple Creek Kayaking** (508-362-2891), at Red Jacket Beach Resort, South Shore Drive, South Yarmouth. Open mid-May to mid-October for rentals, guided tours (up the river and on the ocean), and fishing trips. They also have paddleboats for kids. Their popular 3½ -hour organized river paddle costs $55 per double kayak, $45 single.

✎ MINI-GOLF

Pirate's Cove Adventure Golf (508-394-6200), 728 Route 28, South Yarmouth. Open daily mid-April to late October. At the granddaddy of all Cape mini-golf courses, kids have their choice of two 18-hole courses complete with lavish landscaping, extravagant waterfalls, dark caves, and pirate-themed holes. Kids receive eye patches, flags, and tattoos.

Bass River Sports World (508-398-6070), 928 Route 28 at Long Pond Road, South Yarmouth. Open weekends March to mid-May and daily mid-May to late September. In addition to a "Swiss Family Treehouse" adventure mini-golf, Bass River lures families with baseball and softball batting cages, soccer cages, a game room, and a driving range.

PAINTBALL

✳✦ **SLAM Paintball** (508-398-6919), Bass River Sports World, 934 Route 28, South Yarmouth. If you haven't heard of paintball (a high-action "pursuit" game), it goes like this: Small gelatinlike balls of water-based paint are shot with an air-powered pump at the "enemy" in games like Capture the Flag, the Fox and the Hound, and Elimination. Games are played rain or shine on eight fields of differing terrain. It's for frustrated commando types, and Green Beret preparation for the kids, I imagine. Games are played 10–4-ish daily from late May to early September and during school holidays; weekends year-round.

TENNIS

The public can play at **Flax Pond,** which has 4 courts (off North Main Street from Route 28 in South Yarmouth); at **Sandy Pond,** which has 4 courts (from Route 28 in West Yarmouth, take Higgins Crowell Road to Buck Island Road); and at **Dennis-Yarmouth High School,** which has 10 courts (from Route 28, take Station Avenue to Regional Avenue in South Yarmouth). All free.

See also Mid-Cape Racquet Club under *Fitness Club*.

GREEN SPACE

BEACHES

Some lodging places offer discounted daily beach stickers; don't forget to ask. Weekly stickers for cottage renters are available for $40 at Town Hall (508-398-2231), 1146 Route 28, South Yarmouth. If you take the Easy Shuttle (see *Getting Around*), there is no fee to walk onto the beach.

Sea Gull Beach, off South Sea Avenue from Route 28, West Yarmouth. This is the longest, widest, and nicest of Yarmouth's southside beaches, which generally tend to be small, narrow, and plagued by seaweed. The approach to the beach is truly lovely, with views of the tidal river. (The blue boxes you see, by the way, are fly traps—filled with musk oil, they attract the dreaded biting greenhead flies that terrorize beaches in July.) Parking $10; facilities include a bathhouse, rest rooms, and food service.

Bass Hole (or **Gray's**) **Beach,** off Centre Street from Route 6A. The small protected beach is good for children, but the real appeal lies in the **Bass Hole Boardwalk,** which extends across a marsh and a creek. From the benches at the end of the boardwalk, you can see across to Chapin Memorial Beach in Dennis. It's a great place to be at sunset, although you won't be alone. The 2½-mile **Callery-Darling Trail** starts from the parking lot and crosses conservation lands to the salt marsh. As you walk out into the bay, a mile or so at low tide, recall that this former harbor used to be deep enough to accommodate a schooner shipyard in the 18th century. Free parking; handicap ramp.

KIM GRANT

Bass Hole Boardwalk at Gray's Beach in Yarmouthport

WALKS

Botanical Trails of the Historical Society of Old Yarmouth, behind
the post office and Captain Bangs Hallet House (see *To See*), off Route
6A, Yarmouthport. This 1½-mile trail, dotted with benches and skirting
60 acres of pines, oaks, and a pond, leads past rhododendrons, holly,
lady's slippers, and other delights. The trail begins at the gatehouse,
which has a lovely herb garden. A spur trail leads to the profoundly
simple **Kelley Chapel,** built in 1873 as a seaman's bethel by a father
for his daughter, who was mourning the untimely death of her son. The
interior contains a few pews, an old woodstove, and a small organ. It
may be rented (508-362-3021) for small weddings and special events.

Bray Farm, Bray Farm Road South, off Route 6A near the Dennis town
line. The Bray brothers purchased this land in the late 1700s and created a successful shipyard and farm. Now town owned, this working
farm offers a short walking trail and tidal-marsh views. It's a nice place
for a picnic. Whoever said "old Cape Cod" doesn't exist? You can't help
but take a deep breath of fresh air here.

See also Bass Hole (or Gray's) Beach under *Beaches*. Also, don't forget about
the walking tour brochure published by the Historical Society of Old
Yarmouth (see *Guidance*).

LODGING

Route 6A is lined with lovely B&Bs, while the southside generally appeals
to families (with a couple of notable exceptions).

RESORTS

∂ **Red Jacket Beach Resort** (508-398-6941; 1-800-672-0500; www.redjacket inns.com/redjacket), South Shore Drive, South Yarmouth 02664. Open early April through October. Occupying 7 acres at the end of South Shore Drive, wedged between Nantucket Sound and Parker's River, this extensive complex attracts families—with good reason. Two-room family suites cost just $30 more than a single room. Amenities include a large private beach bordered on one side by a jetty; indoor and outdoor pools; a supervised children's program; tennis; parasailing; jet-boat, kayak, and paddleboat rentals; and a putting green. A pleasant, family-style restaurant serves all three meals. All accommodations (150 rooms and 13 cottages) have their own deck or patio and in-room fridge. Room and cottage rates vary considerably, according to view: near the hotel entrance, riverside or poolside, ocean view, and oceanfront (from least to most expensive). July to late August $195–265; off-season $90–145; two children under age 8 free in parent's room. Inquire about myriad packages as well as weekly rates in the two- and three-bedroom **town houses** and **cottages.**

BED & BREAKFASTS

✳✳❀ **Wedgewood Inn** (508-362-5157; www.wedgewoodinn.com), 83 Route 6A, Yarmouthport 02675. An elegant and sophisticated 1812 B&B with helpful hosts neither fussy nor overbearing, the Wedgewood Inn is one of the top two or three inns on Route 6A. It offers nine spacious rooms in two buildings, all with private bath and air-conditioning. Within the main inn, the antiques-filled rooms are furnished with pencil-post beds, quilts, and wing chairs. Most have a fireplace and hardwood floors covered with Oriental carpets or hooked rugs. Two rooms have their own screened-in porch. The expertly renovated two-story **carriage house/barn** is more private, great for romantic getaways and off-season jaunts. It's the most authentic and tasteful renovation of its kind on the Cape. The dramatic and lofty entry boasts original wainscoting, barnboard, and a sliding barn door. Rooms are lovely, with custom-made tiger maple bureaus, sculpted mantels, wood-burning fireplaces, four-poster beds, quilts, TV, and luxurious bathrooms. Two of the three rooms have private decks overlooking the shaded back lawn. Back in the main inn, Gerrie cooks and Milt serves a full breakfast on fine china at individual tables. June through October $135–195; off-season $115–155.

✳ **Liberty Hill Inn** (508-362-3976; 1-800-821-3977; www.capecod.net/ libertyhillinn), 77 Route 6A, Yarmouthport 02675. New innkeepers Ann and John Cartwright are breathing renewed life into this former 1825 whaling tycoon's home. On a knoll set back from Route 6A, there are nine comfortable rooms with private bath in the main house and adjacent modern carriage house. Rooms in the main inn profit from lofty ceilings and a dramatic spiral staircase, while next door, rooms might have a whirpool, fireplace, or canopy bed. A full breakfast at individual tables is included. Mid-June to mid-September $115–185, off-season $90–160.

❄ **Captain Farris House** (508-760-2818; 1-800-350-9477; www.captainfarris. com), 308 Old Main Street, South Yarmouth 02664. Located within a small pocket of historic homes off Route 28, the 1845 Captain Farris House offers understated elegance and luxurious modern amenities. Lovely window treatments and fine antiques fill the guest rooms. Other nice touches include fine linens, damask duvets, down comforters, thick white towels, and Jacuzzi tubs. Of the 10 rooms (all with private bath), 4 are suites, a few have private decks, and most have a private entrance. A fancy three-course breakfast is served at individual tables in the courtyard or at one long formal dining room table. Afternoon tea is set out year-round, while five rooms with fireplace are well suited to off-season cocooning. May through September $105–160 rooms, $160–225 suites; off-season $95–150 rooms, $130–210 suites.

🐾🐕❄**Lane's End Cottage** (508-362-5298), 268 Route 6A, Yarmouthport 02675. Down a quiet lane off Route 6A, this circa-1710 cottage is surrounded by flowers and woods, and its back patio is encircled by potted geraniums. Host Valerie Butler presides (along with Chloe, an adorable Rescue League cocker spaniel), attending to your needs and whipping up a full breakfast and afternoon refreshments. The three guest rooms, each with private bath, are simply furnished. One has a fireplace and French doors leading to its own cobblestone terrace. The living room is "lived-in comfortable," with American, English, and country antiques and a fireplace. $120–135. No credit cards.

🐾 **August House** (508-760-0412), 175 Old Main Street, Bass River 02664. Open May through October. Delightfully off the beaten path in a neighborhood of historic homes, the August House is a mile from Nantucket Sound beaches. (It's a 5-minute walk to the small Windmill Beach.) The late-18th-century house has three modestly furnished guest rooms (one with private bath, two with shared bath, all with TV, and two with fireplace) that are well suited to a family or couples traveling together. (Roll-aways cost $15 nightly.) Host June Augustine encourages guests to use the house as if it were their own. (That could mean, perhaps, eating takeout in front of the TV or fireplace in the large living room.) $70–80, including continental breakfast served on the patio in good weather. No credit cards.

🏅 **Inn at Lewis Bay** (508-771-3433; 1-800-962-6679; www.innatlewisbay.com), 57 Maine Avenue, West Yarmouth 02673. Open April through October. In a residential neighborhood near a small, protected beach, this Dutch Colonial has six guest rooms (all with private bath, two with an ocean view). Innkeepers Liz and Rick Latshaw include a full breakfast, afternoon tea, beach towels, and beach chairs. $128 in summer, $98–108 off-season.

🐾 **Village Inn** (508-362-3182), 92 Route 6A, Yarmouthport 02675. Open May through December. In keeping with the delightfully old-fashioned idea of providing a place for travelers to relax and interact, there are two comfortable living rooms that fit like an old shoe—they are immediately comforting. There's also a wicker-filled, screened-in porch overlooking the backyard. The 10 guest rooms (some smaller than others) are modestly furnished with prices to match: $89–119 for a private bath, $50–75 for a shared bath. A full breakfast, served on Cape Cod place mats, is included. They don't make 'em like this anymore. This historic colonial landmark has been operated by the Hickey family since 1952.

COTTAGES

Seaside (508-398-2533), 135 South Shore Drive, South Yarmouth 02664. Open May to late October. These 43 one- and two-room cottages, built in the 1930s but nicely upgraded and well maintained, are very popular for their oceanfront location. Reserve by mid-March if possible; otherwise, they'll probably be full. Sheltered among pine trees, the shingled and weathered units are clustered around a sandy barbecue area and sit above a 500-foot stretch of private beach. (A playground is next door.) Kitchens are fully equipped, and linens are provided. Many of the tidy units have a working fireplace. The least expensive units (without views) are decorated 1950s style. One-room studio units sleep two to four; one-bedroom efficiencies sleep four to six. Don't bother with the motel efficiencies. Late June to early September $795–1,125 weekly for one-room units, $1,125–1,495 weekly for two-room units; off-season $75–120 and $110–160 daily, respectively.

See also Red Jacket Beach Resort under *Resorts* and Ocean Mist under *Motor Inns.*

MOTOR INNS

Beach House at Bass River (508-394-6501; 1-800-345-6065), 73 South Shore Drive, Bass River (South Yarmouth) 02664. Open late March through October. This tasteful bilevel motor inn sits on a 110-foot stretch of private Nantucket Sound beach. Each of the 26 rooms is decorated differently (some with antiques), but generally the oceanfront rooms are a bit spiffier, with country-pine furnishings. Most rooms have private balconys; all have a refrigerator. Cliff Hagberg built the tidy complex in the 1970s and still operates it. July to early September $140–185 (ask about discounts for early bookings); off-season $90–120; children under 10 free in parent's room; free cribs and use of microwave for heating baby bottles and such. Expansive buffet breakfast included.

Ocean Mist (508-398-2633; 1-800-248-6478; www.capecodtravel.com/oceanmist), 97 South Shore Drive, South Yarmouth 02664. Open early February through November. This shingled three-story complex fronting a 300-foot private Nantucket Sound beach offers 32 rooms and 32 loft suites. Each of the contemporary rooms has a wet bar or full efficiency kitchen, two double beds, and air-conditioning. Loft suites feature an open, second-floor sitting area—many of the rooms have ocean views, all have a sofa bed; many of these have skylights and two private balconies.

There's a small indoor pool on the premises. July to early September $179–289; June and mid-September to mid-November $79–239; off-season $59–209; three children up to age 15 stay free in parent's room.

Tidewater Motor Lodge (508-775-6322; 1-800-338-6322; www.tidewaterml.com), 135 Route 28, West Yarmouth 02673. For inexpensive accommodations close to the Nantucket ferry, this is the best of the lot. 100 rooms, with indoor and outdoor pools. July and August $99–125, off-season $39–75; two children under 12 free with adults.

TOWN HOUSES

Clipper Ship Cove (508-394-6044; www.clippershipcove.com), 183 South Shore Drive, South Yarmouth 02664. Open April through October. The grounds surrounding this cluster of 14 freestanding, two-story town houses are nicely landscaped with brick walkways, green lawns, rosebushes, and privacy fences. Newly built, most town houses accommodate four people comfortably in two bedrooms. Each is complete with hardwood floors, a fireplace, 1½ bathrooms, cable TV, outdoor patio furniture, washer and dryer, central air-conditioning, and a modern kitchen. You provide the linens. July to early September $1,675–2,050 weekly; June and September $1,050–1,600 weekly; off-season $850–1,050 weekly. No credit cards.

RENTAL HOUSES AND COTTAGES

Great Island Ocean Club (508-775-9085), South Sea Avenue, West Yarmouth 02673. Open April through November. This gated residential community has about 30 rental homes, located on or within a quarter mile of a private Nantucket Sound beach. Off by itself, it's a real find, perfect for families. Fully equipped houses have one to six bedrooms. Send for the detailed list of where each house is located and its particulars. Shared facilities include a clubhouse, tennis courts, and pool. Reservations by mail only, until mid-March. Mid-June to early September $950–1,800 weekly for two bedrooms, $1,700–3,000 for three bedrooms; about 40 percent lower off-season.

Crocker & Flinksterom (508-362-3953), Cranberry Court, 947 Route 6A, Yarmouthport 02675. Nancy and Charlie Flinksterom rent 30–40 houses each season (by the week, month, or longer). For the best pick, call in January.

Century 21–Sam Ingram Real Estate (508-362-8844; 1-800-697-3340), 938 Route 6A, Yarmouthport 02675. This agency rents 100 or so private homes that go for as little as $550 weekly for a one-bedroom to as much as $9,000 weekly for a spectacular six-bedroom waterfront unit. Call in January or February. Rentals are shown throughout winter by appointment.

WHERE TO EAT

Route 6A has a couple of excellent restaurants, and while Route 28 is lined with dozens, most are not discernible from one another. I have only reviewed a few that are. If you're staying on the southside, and want more choice, check the entries under "Dennis." Unless otherwise noted, all restaurants are open year-round.

DINING OUT

❧ **Inaho** (508-362-5522), 157 Route 6A, Yarmouthport. Open for dinner nightly except Monday (and Sunday off-season). Alda and Yuji Watanabe have done it again, giving patrons plenty of reasons to remain loyal. They offer some of the most sophisticated and authentic Japanese cuisine east of Tokyo. Yaki-Nasu, a broiled eggplant appetizer topped with a delicate blend of miso and sesame, is particularly savory. While fearless diners are handsomely rewarded, less adventurous diners revel in traditional tofu, teriyaki, bento box combinations, and miso soup. Then there is tempura, an exemplary metaphor for life: Wait too long to eat it, and the fleeting, perfect moment passes by. Meanwhile, over at the sushi bar, intense concentration is focused on the Zen of sushi wrapping. Don't miss bananas tempura on an oversize plate for dessert or the beautiful garden in the rear. If you feel like switching palates, Alda's flourless chocolate cake is great, too. Takeout. Dishes $12–23.

❧ **Abbicci** (508-362-3501), 43 Route 6A, Yarmouthport. Open for lunch and dinner. If you're filled to the gills with seafood served in nautically challenged surroundings, this mod bistro will delight you. Housed in a mustard yellow 1775 cottage, its style is more apropos of New York's SoHo than of conservative Route 6A. Check out the stunning trompe l'oeil floors, track lighting, a sleek **bar,** and a hip but friendly waitstaff. Sophisticated and contemporary Italian cuisine, infused with olive oil and garlic, includes such creations as a seafood stew with lobster, clams, mussels, fish, and shrimp in a saffron broth; and roasted duck with sweet-and-sour sauce and apricots. Marietta Hickey's menu changes seasonally. Early, three-course dinner specials for $14–18 are a great value. Dinner entrées $17–28. Reservations recommended.

✍ **Old Yarmouth Inn** (508-362-9962), 223 Route 6A, Yarmouthport. Open for lunch, dinner, and very popular and extensive Sunday buffet brunch. You have a choice to make at this 1696 inn, the oldest on the Cape: casual dining in the pub or fine dining in one of three dining rooms. I prefer the low-key **tavern,** a former stagecoach stop, which is just the perfect atmosphere for a grilled chicken Caesar, cup of clam chowder, or great burger. In addition to lighter fare, you can get serious with lobster ravioli with a fresh tomato and cream sauce or a broiled seafood platter. All entrées are served with wonderfully dense bread. Children's menu. Lunch $9–17, brunch $14 per person, dinner entrées $9–24.

EATING OUT

❧✍ **Keltic Kitchen** (508-771-4835), 415 Route 28, West Yarmouth. Open for breakfast all day, 6 or 7 AM–2 PM. Owner and Irishman Dave Dempsey and his staff still carry thick brogues from the old country when they take your orders for Irish farmhouse breakfasts with rashers and black and white pudding or Keltic Bennys with poached eggs on an English muffin and corned beef hash. Despite having no ties to Ireland, the cranberry French toast, made with Portuguese bread, is particularly light. This family operation, where Dave's father did tromp l'oeil artwork on walls, is friendly and cozy. Come once and you'll come back again and again. Try the beef and barley soup for lunch. Dishes $2.50–6.50. No credit cards.

Stefani's Restaurant (508-760-2929), at the Bayberry Hills Golf Course, 635 West Yarmouth Road. Open 6–6 daily April through November. Longtime caterer and restaurateur Stefani Wright offers baked goodies that are gobbled up as soon as she puts them out in jars, great clam chowder, and hot and cold sandwiches like turkey Reubens, chicken BLT roll-ups, burgers, and grilled roast beef with horseradish mayo. While the pleasant café overlooks the course, this place isn't just for golfers. Sandwiches $5-ish.

&✎ **Oliver's** (508-362-6062), Route 6A, Yarmouthport. Open for lunch and dinner daily. Serving generous portions in cozy, tavernlike surroundings, the wide-ranging menu also features reduced portions. Chef-owner Dale Ormon attracts an older crowd at lunchtime, longtime Cape residents who like to keep things simple, and families who need to satisfy everyone. Specialties include broiled seafood, but hearty sandwiches, burgers, and veal parmigiana are also quite popular. Thankfully, specials come in two portion sizes and two prices. Children's menu; early specials. At press time, there were plans afoot to build an outdoor dining deck. Live entertainment on weekends. Dishes $9–18.

🍴✎ **Jack's Outback** (508-362-6690), 161 Route 6A, Yarmouthport. Open for breakfast and lunch daily. Classic American down-home cooking is served from an exposed, dinerlike kitchen that revels in its no-nonsense attitude. Their shtick goes like this: "Go away, the food is good, but the service stinks." While the tone is far from charming, this place has been a local institution for years. (It's already changing, though, as Jack becomes less and less involved each season.) Patrons help themselves to coffee, write their own orders after looking at the wall menu, and take their plates back to the pine-paneled dining room. Meals $2–6.

✎ **Clancy's** (508-775-3332), 175 Route 28, West Yarmouth. Open for lunch and dinner. This is the kind of no-surprises place that appeals to a variety of palates and budgets: chicken fingers and shrimp cocktail appetizers; Reubens and smoked turkey sandwiches; burgers; eggplant Parmesan and chicken cordon bleu for dinner. The pleasant decor is classic Victorian, with wainscoting. Generous portions. Children's menu. Lunch $5–11, dinner entrées $14–23.

Black Rock Grille (508-771-1001), 633 Route 28, West Yarmouth. Open 4 PM to "late." This handsome grill specializes in wild game. For the red-meat lovers in your party who like red wine and béarnaise sauces, this place is a winner. Early specials. Try their specialty seasonal ales. Entrées $10–40.

See also Hallet's under *To See*.

PICNICS
Lambert's (508-790-5954), 325 Route 28, West Yarmouth. Open daily. A large, veritable "rainbow basket" of bread, deli items, fruit, and drinks to take to the beach.

ENTERTAINMENT

✍ **Band concerts** (508-778-1008), Mattachesse Middle School band shell, Higgins Crowell Road, West Yarmouth. Since 1970, concerts have been held on Monday nights at 7 in July and August.
✍ **Baseball.** The Cape League sponsors the Yarmouth-Dennis Red Sox. Games are held from mid-June to early August at 5 PM at the Dennis-Yarmouth High School, Station Avenue, South Yarmouth. Free.
✍ **Soccer.** The Cape Cod Crusaders (508-790-4782), the Cape's only pro team of any sort, play from late April to early August on many Saturdays at 7:30 at Dennis-Yarmouth High School. Tickets cost $8 adults, $5 children 14 and under.

MOVIES
↑❊ **Hoyt's Entertainment Cinemas** (508-394-1100), Patriot Square Mall, Route 134, South Dennis.

SELECTIVE SHOPPING

❊ Unless otherwise noted, all shops are open year-round.
Bass River Boatworks (508-398-4883), 1361 Route 28, South Yarmouth. Barely west of the Bass River, these two crammed shops will satisfy the nautical fanatic in your party. Copper weather vanes, lightship baskets, marine antiques, custom-made glass display cases, lighthouse models, and the largest number of ship-model kits on the Cape. They also do lots of ship-model restoration.

ANTIQUES
Town Crier Antiques (508-362-3138), 153 Route 6A, Yarmouthport. Open May to mid-October. Five dealers share this space, where you can find plates, glassware, collectibles, silver, brass, and small furniture.
Yarmouthport Antiques (508-362-3599), 431 Route 6A, Yarmouthport. Open April through October. Three dealers, who collect formal and country furniture, glass, decorative accessories, decoys, pewter, paintings, and folk art, share this barnlike space that's fun to browse.

ARTISANS
Pewter Crafters of Cape Cod (508-362-3407; www.pewtercraftercape cod.com), 933 Route 6A, Yarmouthport. Open daily except Sunday and Monday. Ron Kusins has been toiling at this ancient craft, creating and selling traditional and contemporary designs, since the late 1970s. Finishes are either satin or bright; forms are functional. This is one of only half a dozen pewter studios in the country (and the only one on the

Cape), so now may be the time to get an up-close view of pewter making.

BOOKSTORE

Parnassus Book Service (508-362-6420), 220 Route 6A, Yarmouthport. Deliberately avoiding signs and categories, proprietor Ben Muse wants people to browse and dig around, perhaps finding a first edition of James or Melville among the stacks! Specializing in maritime, Cape Cod, and ornithology, Muse has been selling new, used, and rare books since 1960. Bookshelves line the wall outside (under a little roof), where the books are available for browsing or purchase on a 24-hour honor system. In its former incarnations, this 1840 building served as a general store and as a church; it was once home to the Yarmouth Society of the New Jerusalem. This really is one unique shop with one unique guy running it.

SPECIAL SHOPS

Design Works (508-362-9698), 159 Route 6A, Yarmouthport. Open daily. Festive and fanciful Mackenzie-Childs pottery, Scandinavian country antiques, home furnishings, and accessories like throws, pillows, and linens.

Peach Tree Designs (508-362-8317), 173 Route 6A, Yarmouthport. Open daily. Homebodies will delight in this two-floor shop filled to the brim with an assortment of decorative accessories for gracious living.

Cape Home Emporium (508-362-1514), 169 Route 6A, Yarmouthport. This small historic house offers gifts, home accessories, and antiques. It's set up appropriately: The kitchen and pantry are stocked with glassware and old china; the bathroom has coarse oatmeal soap for sale; there is a playroom with toys; and the former dining and living rooms . . . well, you get the idea.

SPECIAL EVENTS

Late May to late September: The **Yarmouth Art Guild** sponsors outdoor art shows on many Sundays (10–5); Route 6A in Yarmouthport at the Cape Cod Cooperative Bank.

Late July: **Circus Smirkus.** By overwhelming demand, these kids age 9–19 entertain locals and visitors alike with their high-spirited antics. $13 adults, $5 kids, free under age 12.

Mid-October: **Seaside Festival.** Begun in 1979, this festival has featured jugglers, clowns, fireworks, field games, a parade, sand-castle competitions, arts and crafts, and bicycle, kayak, and road races.

Early December: **Yarmouthport Christmas Stroll** includes a tree lighting on the village common, caroling, and special children's activities. Wreaths for sale.

Dennis

Located at the Cape's geographic center, Dennis is a convenient base for day trips. Some visitors are drawn to Dennis for fine summer theater, others come for family-style attractions along Route 28. Indeed, to outsiders (including the 40,000 or so summer visitors), Dennis suffers from a split personality. Luckily, the 13,000 year-round residents have long since reconciled the village's conflicting natures.

On the north side of town, Route 6A continues along its scenic way, governed by a historical commission. Skirting Dennis and East Dennis, Route 6A is lined with a smattering of antiques shops, crafters, and sea captains' gracious homes. (During the 19th century, more than 400 sea captains called Dennis home.) Colonial side roads off Route 6A lead to beach communities, Quivett Neck (settled in 1639), and Sesuit Marsh and Sesuit Harbor, where the fishing industry once flourished and fishing charters now depart. Note the streets in this area, named after methods of preserving fish: Cold Storage Road and Salt Works Road. The center of Dennis has a quintessential white steeple church, town green, and bandstand. The oldest cranberry bog is also off Route 6A; Dennis resident Henry Hall cultivated the first cranberries in 1807. He discovered that the berries grow much better when covered with a light layer of sand. It wasn't until the 1840s, when sugar became more readily available, that anyone could do much with these tart berries, though.

On the southern side of town, the 6-mile-long Bass River is the largest tidal river on the eastern seaboard. It serves as a natural boundary between Yarmouth and Dennis, offering numerous possibilities for exploration, fishing, and birding. Although it's never been proved, it's widely believed that Viking explorer Leif Eriksson sailed up the Bass River about 1,000 years ago, built a camp, and stayed awhile. Follow Cove Road off Route 28 and Main Street for nice views of the Bass River and sheltered Grand Cove. (The villages of South Dennis and West Dennis were once connected by a bridge here.) In Dennisport, kids will enjoy the smaller Swan River in a paddleboat.

Each side of Dennis has its own nice, long beach: Chapin Memorial Beach on Cape Cod Bay and West Dennis Beach on Nantucket Sound. Head to Scargo Tower for an expansive view.

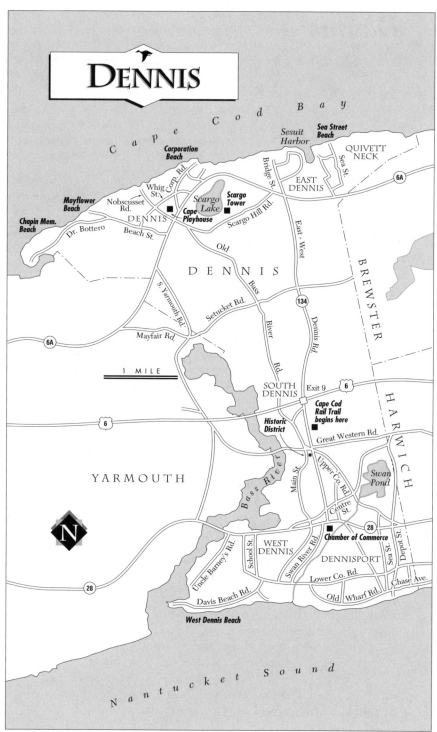

DENNIS

Cape Cod Bay

Corporation Beach

Sesuit Harbor

Sea Street Beach

QUIVETT NECK

Bridge St.

EAST DENNIS

Sea St.

6A

Whig St.

Corp. Rd.

Scargo Lake

Scargo Tower

Mayflower Beach

Nobscusset Rd.

Cape Playhouse

Scargo Hill Rd.

DENNIS

East - West

BREWSTER

Chapin Mem. Beach

Dr. Bottero

Beach St.

Old

DENNIS

Bass

134

Dennis Rd.

S. Yarmouth Rd.

Setucket Rd.

River

6A

Mayfair Rd.

Rd.

1 MILE

SOUTH DENNIS

Exit 9

6

HARWICH

6

Cape Cod Rail Trail begins here

Historic District

Great Western Rd.

YARMOUTH

Bass River

Upper Co. Rd.

Swan Pond

Main St.

Centre St.

N

28

Chamber of Commerce

Uncle Barney's Rd.

School St.

WEST DENNIS

Swan River Rd.

DENNISPORT

Sea St.

Depot St.

28

Lower Co. Rd.

Chase Ave.

Davis Beach Rd.

Old Wharf Rd.

West Dennis Beach

Nantucket Sound

GUIDANCE

✳ **Dennis Chamber of Commerce** (508-398-3568; 1-800-243-9920; www.dennischamber.com), Routes 134 and 28, West Dennis. Open 10–4 daily from late May through September and 10–2 weekdays from October to late May, plus Saturday in spring and fall 10–2. Chamber members are knowledgeable and proud of the long hours they staff their booth. As this booth doesn't face Route 28, you might miss it if you're not looking for it. There are lots of discount coupons in the member-sponsored information booklet. There is also an unstaffed satellite **outlet** at 821 "Rear" Route 6A, Dennis, just east of the Scargo Cafe, that's open 9–5 daily year-round.

PUBLIC REST ROOMS

Public rest rooms are located at Sesuit Harbor in East Dennis and at Town Hall, Main Street, South Dennis.

✳ ⌀ ⚓ PUBLIC LIBRARIES

There are five village libraries; it's best to call each for their hours.

Dennis Memorial Library (508-385-2255), 1020 Old Bass River Road, Dennis;

Dennis Public Library (508-760-6219), 673 Route 28;

Jacob Sears Memorial Library (508-385-8151), Center Street, East Dennis;

South Dennis Free Public Library (508-394-8954), 389 Main Street (see *To See—Scenic Drive*);

West Dennis Village Library (508-398-2050), 272 Route 28.

GETTING THERE

By car: Take exit 9 off the Mid-Cape Highway (Route 6). Head north on Route 134 to Route 6A for Dennis and East Dennis. Head south on Route 134 to Route 28 for West Dennis and Dennisport. The tiny historic district of South Dennis is just west of Route 134 as you head south. Depending on traffic, it takes 20–30 minutes to get to various points in Dennis from the canal.

GETTING AROUND

As the crow flies, Dennis is only about 7 miles long from Cape Cod Bay to Nantucket Sound; it's 2–5 miles wide. When navigating, keep a couple of things in mind: South Dennis is in the geographic center of Dennis (not the south), and Dennisport (the southeastern portion of town) doesn't have a harbor on the ocean as you might expect it to. In general, there isn't much to interest travelers between Routes 6A and 28. Year-rounders make their homes here, visit doctors' and lawyers' offices, and buy food and gardening supplies. Concentrate your meandering north off Route 6A and around the tiny historic district on Main Street in South Dennis.

Coach of Dennis Trolley (508-385-8326; 1-800-352-7155; www.capecodtransit.org) operates late June to early September. It travels along Route 134 and 28 to Patriot Square and Windmill Plaza as well as a few beaches. There are connections to Harwich and Yarmouth and on to Hyannis, as well. Flag down the driver when you see her. Purchase tokens and get a map route at the chamber of commerce (see *Guidance*). Adults $1, kids half price, children 5 and under free.

The **H₂O** (508-385-8326; 1-800-352-7155; www.capecodtransit.org) bus, generally used by locals, travels along Route 28 between Hyannis and Orleans daily except Sunday year-round. It stops at the central shopping area in Dennisport, Patriot Square in South Dennis, and School Street in West Dennis.

MEDICAL EMERGENCY
Call **911**.

TO SEE

🐾❄️🍴**Cape Museum of Fine Arts** (508-385-4477; www.cmfa.org), Route 6A, Dennis. Open 10–5 Tuesday through Saturday, 1–5 Sunday year-round, and 10–5 Monday June to mid-October. On the grounds of the Cape Playhouse (see *Entertainment*), Cape Cod's important artists—both living and dead—are represented by more than 800 works on paper and canvas as well as sculpture. The museum, which opened in 1985, also sponsors trips to artists' studios, classes for adults and children, and lectures. The Reel Art cinema features first-run independent and foreign films in the museum's 92-seat auditorium. One of the most popular events is a Secret Garden Tour in late June, which features local artists painting scenes inspired by Dennis's most lovely gardens; tickets $45 (see *Special Events*). Adults $5, children under 16 free; films $5.

🐾 **Scargo Tower,** off Scargo Hill Road from Route 6A, Dennis. The 28-foot stone tower sits 160 feet above sea level atop the area's tallest hill. On a clear day the panoramic view extends all the way to Provincetown. Even on a hazy day you can see the width of the Cape: from Nantucket Sound to Cape Cod Bay. Scargo Lake (see *Green Space—Ponds/Lakes*), a glacial kettle pond, is directly below the tower.

🐾 **Josiah Dennis Manse Museum** and **Old West Schoolhouse** (508-385-2232), 77 Nobscusset Road at Whig Street, Dennis. Open 10 AM–noon Tuesday and 2–4 Thursday, late June through September, and 2–4 Saturday in September. This 1736 saltbox was home to the Reverend Mr. Dennis, for whom the town is named. The house is set up much as it would have been during his time, with a keeping room, child's room, maritime wing, and spinning exhibit in the attic. The 1770 one-room schoolhouse, filled with wooden and wrought-iron desks, was moved to its present location in the mid-1970s. There is also a small exhibit on Nobscusset Indians. Donations.

South Congregational Church (508-394-5992), 234 Main Street, South Dennis. The church itself is not open, but the church office is (weekdays 9–noon), and staff are happy to let folks inside. The chapel in this 1835 church features a chandelier made with Sandwich glass and a 1762

Snetzler pipe organ, the country's oldest still in use. The church is also called the Sea Captain's Church because more than 100 of its founding members were sea captains.

✎ **Jericho House and Barn Museum** (508-398-6736), Trotting Park Road and Old Main Street, West Dennis. Open 10–noon Wednesday and Friday in July and August and by appointment. The 1801 full-Cape-style house contains period furnishings, and the 1810 barn is filled with antique tools, carriages, and a fanciful collection of folk art animals (a veritable "driftwood zoo") crafted in the 1950s by Sherman Woodward. Donations.

SCENIC DRIVE

The **South Dennis Historic District,** on and around Main Street from Route 134, gets very little traffic and wonderful afternoon light. Escape the crowds that bypass this little gem; it's worth a short drive or quiet walk. Note the South Dennis Free Public Library (circa 1858) on Main Street, a cottage-style building covered with wooden gingerbread trim. **Liberty Hall,** which was used for concerts, fairs, lectures, and balls when the second story was added in 1865, is also noteworthy. Edmond Nickerson, founder of the Old South Dennis Village Association, deserves much of the credit for initiating fund-raising drives and overseeing restoration projects.

OUTDOOR ACTIVITIES

BICYCLING/RENTALS

Cape Cod Rail Trail is a well-maintained asphalt bikeway that follows the Old Colony Railroad tracks for 26 miles from Dennis to Wellfleet. The trail begins off Route 134 in South Dennis across from Hall Oil. Parking and bike rentals are available at the trailhead from **Barbara's Bike and Sports Equipment** (508-760-4723), 430 Route 134. Bikes are about $10 for 2 hours, $20–25 per day. The shop also rents in-line skates and stays open from late March to late October. On the southside, rent from the even more seasonal **Pizazz** (508-760-3888), 633 Route 28, Dennisport, about 1½ miles from the Rail Trail. The free chamber of commerce booklet available here details seven undeveloped bicycle routes through Dennis.

BOAT EXCURSIONS/RENTALS

The Schooner *Freya* (508-385-4399), Town Marina, Dennis. Take a 2-hour Cape Cod Bay sail aboard a 63-foot ship captained by Frank and Elaine Meigs. Adults $16; children 2–12, $10. The morning sail is $4 less. Sunset trips are $18 per person. No credit cards.

✎ **Water Safari's *Starfish*** (508-362-5555), Bass River Bridge, Route 28, West Dennis. These 90-minute narrated trips of the Bass River, the largest tidal river on the East Coast, operate late May to mid-October. Along the shoreline you'll see windmills, luxurious riverfront estates, sea captains' homes, and lots of birds. The flat-bottomed aluminum boat (which has an awning) accommodates almost 50 people. Adults $12; children age 1–11, $7.

🖋 **Cape Cod Waterways** (508-398-0080), Route 28 near Route 134, Dennisport. Open May to mid-October. The small and winding Swan River heads about ¾ mile north to the 200-acre Swan Pond and 2 miles south to Nantucket Sound. Cape Cod Waterways rents electric and manual paddleboats, canoes, and kayaks that can accommodate a family with two small children.

FISHING/SHELLFISHING

Freshwater fishing is good at **Scargo Lake,** stocked with smallmouth bass and trout. Obtain a state fishing license at **Town Hall** (508-394-8300), Main Street, South Dennis, or at **Bass River Bait & Tackle** (508-394-8666), Bass River Bridge, Route 28, West Dennis.

Shellfishing permits are required and can also be obtained at Town Hall.

Bass River Bridge, Route 28, West Dennis. Park on one side and try your luck; or just stop and watch.

A number of competitively priced, seasonal fishing charters depart from Sesuit Harbor, off Route 6A in East Dennis. Among them: *Prime Rate* (508-385-4626), *Albatross* (508-385-3244), and *Blue Fish* (508-385-7265). Expect to pay about $25 adults, $18 kids under 12.

FITNESS

Lifecourse, South Dennis, is a 1½-mile trail through the woods with 20 exercise stations along the way. Take Route 28 to Route 134 north; turn left onto Bob Crowell Road to the pavilion.

FOR FAMILIES

🖋 **Cartwheels** (508-394-6755), 11 South Gages Way, across from Tony Kent Arena, South Dennis. Open 10–10 daily in the summer. "Indy-style" go-carts; batting cages.

❊ ### GOLF

Dennis Highlands (508-385-8347), Old Bass River Road, Dennis. This 18-hole, par-71 course is wider and more forgiving than Pines; it also has a geat driving range and practice putting greens.

Dennis Pines (508-385-8347), off Route 134, East Dennis. This is a tight and flat 18-hole, par-72 course; it's also more competitive than Highlands.

The Longest Drive (508-398-5555), 131 Great Western Road, South Dennis. This driving range with covered enclosures also offers lessons and clinics.

ICE SKATING

❊ **Tony Kent Arena** (508-760-2400; 508-760-2415 for a human being), 8 South Gages Way, South Dennis. Off Route 134, this rink served as Olympic silver medalist Nancy Kerrigan's training ground. Public skating hours vary, so it's best to call. Rental skates, too.

IN-LINE SKATING

See Barbara's Bike and Sports Equipment under *Bicycling/Rentals.*

KAYAKING

❊ **Sesuit Creek Outfitters** (508-385-1912), 22 Bridge Street. Kayak rentals, demos, and guided tours.

MINI-GOLF

✎ **Holiday Hill** (508-398-8857), Route 28, Dennisport. Open late April to mid-October. Route 28 is lined with mini-golf courses similar in quality, but can others claim that they plant more than 12,000 flowers annually, as Holiday Hill can?

SAILING

✎ **West Dennis Yacht Club** (508-398-9757), 259 Loring Way. Sailing school for kids 5–14. The 3-hour morning and afternoon classes cost $40 and are geared to "pre-sailors," beginners, and advanced students.

TENNIS

🎖 **Mashantum Tennis Club** (508-385-7043 in-season; 413-567-1803 prior to opening), off Nobscusset Road, off the beaten path, Dennis. Open mid-June to late October. Four well-maintained clay courts and value pricing are the draw. This family-oriented nonprofit club offers morning classes for children and adult afternoon play. Courts aren't reserved or rented by the hour; members play on an "informal share-and-share-alike basis." Fees are $50 weekly for individuals, $80 weekly for families, but Lucy Shepard says it's also possible to pay on a daily basis. Well worth seeking out.

❄ **Sesuit Tennis Centre** (508-385-2200), 1389 Route 6A, East Dennis. Open year-round, depending on weather. The center offers three Har-Tru clay courts (rented hourly), a ball machine, open tournaments, and instruction.

GREEN SPACE

BEACHES

Cottage renters may purchase a weekly parking pass for $34 at Town Hall (508-394-8300), Main Street, South Dennis. Day-trippers can pay a daily fee of $10 to park at the following beaches.

✎ **West Dennis Beach** (off Davis Beach Road) on Nantucket Sound is the town's finest and longest beach (it's more than a mile long). Like many Nantucket Sound beaches, though, it's also rather narrow. There's parking for more than 1,000 cars, and the lot rarely fills. If you drive to the western end, you can usually find a few yards of beach for yourself. The eastern end is for residents only. Facilities include 10 lifeguard stations and a snack bar at the eastern end. It's difficult to imagine that fishing shanties, fish weirs, and dories once lined the shores of West Dennis Beach. But they did.

Chapin Memorial Beach, off Chapin Beach Road on Cape Cod Bay, is open to four-wheel-drive vehicles; it's a nice, long, dune-backed beach. As you drive up to Chapin, you'll probably notice an incongruous-looking building plunked down in the marshes and dunes. In fact, it's the headquarters for the Aquaculture Research Corporation (known as the Cultured Clam Corp.), the only state-certified seller of shellfish seed. Begun in 1960, the company is a pioneer in the field of aquaculture. There's no better place to study shellfish.

Tidal flats at Chapin Memorial Beach stretch into Cape Cod Bay for more than a mile.

Corporation Beach, off Corporation Road on Cape Cod Bay, is also backed by low dunes and was once used as a packet-ship landing by a group of town residents who formed the Nobscusset Pier Corporation (hence its name). The crescent-shaped beach has concession stands.

Mayflower Beach, off Beach Street on Cape Cod Bay, has a boardwalk, rest rooms, and a concession stand; **Sea Street Beach,** off Sea Street, and **Howes Street Beach,** off Howes Street and backed by low dunes, both have boardwalks. The Sea Street parking lot fills up by noon. These three beaches are relatively small and good for families with young children because the water is shallow. As at Corporation and Chapin Memorial Beaches, at low tide you can walk a mile out into the bay.

There are about eight other public beaches on Nantucket Sound, but all are small.

PONDS/LAKES

Scargo Lake, a deep, freshwater kettle hole left behind by retreating glaciers, has two beaches: **Scargo Beach** (off Route 6A) and **Princess Beach** (off Scargo Hill Road). Princess Beach has a picnic area; bathers at Scargo Beach tend to put their beach chairs in the shallow water or on the narrow, tree-lined shore. There are two legends concerning the lake's creation; you decide. Did an Indian princess have the lake dug for fish that she received as a present or did a giant named Maushop dig the hole as a remembrance of himself to the local Native Americans?

Swan Pond Overlook, off Centre Street from Searsville Road and Route 134. Beach, picnic area, and bird-watching area.

WALKS

Indian Lands Conservation Area, South Dennis. This easy, 2-mile round-trip walk skirts the banks of the upper Bass River. In winter you'll see blue herons and kingfishers; lady's slippers bloom in May. From the northern end of the Town Hall parking lot on Main Street, follow the power-line right-of-way path for half a mile to the trailhead.

LODGING

Only one place off Route 6A really stands out on the northside, while the southside is loaded with family places (with one exception). Most lodgings on the southside are on or quite close to the beach.

RESORT

🦉🖉&**Lighthouse Inn** (508-398-2244; www.lighthouseinn.com), off Lower County Road, West Dennis 02670. Open mid-May to mid-October. On Nantucket Sound, this old-fashioned, family-friendly resort has 68 rooms and tidy cottages set on 9 grassy acres of waterfront property. The working Bass River Lighthouse tops the main inn. The resort, expertly operated by the Stone family since 1938, has all sorts of amenities: a full program of supervised children's activities, a special children's dinner, a heated pool, tennis, shuffleboard, mini-golf, volleyball, and the **Sand Bar Club and Lounge.** On rainy days guests gather in the common rooms of the lodge-style main building, stocked with games, books, and a television. Lunch is served on the deck or poolside; dinner is served in the large oceanside dining room (see *Dining Out*). A full breakfast is included. You can't miss the giant pirate-ship playhouse in front. July and August $196–270; $136–210 off-season. Children sharing a room with their parents cost an additional $35–55 daily, depending on age. Rates including dinner are an additional $22 per night per adult, $10 per child.

BED & BREAKFASTS

🦉 **Isaiah Hall Bed and Breakfast Inn** (508-385-9928; 1-800-736-0160; www.isaiahhallinn.com), 152 Whig Street, Dennis 02638. Open mid-April to mid-October. On a quiet street behind the Cape Playhouse off Route 6A (see *Entertainment*), this rambling 1857 farmhouse is one of the most comfortable places Mid-Cape. Innkeeper Marie Brophy's enthusiasm is infectious and her garden a delight. Rooms in the main house are comfortably furnished with country-style antiques. Rooms in the attached carriage house are newer, each decorated with stenciling, white wicker, and knotty-pine paneling. All rooms are air-conditioned and equipped with TV, VCR, and phone. There is plenty of indoor and outdoor common space, including a cathedral-ceiling great room and a deep lawn that leads to the Cape's oldest cranberry bog. (Isaiah Hall's brother, Henry, cultivated the first cranberries, and cooper Isaiah patented the barrels used to transport the harvest.) An expanded continental breakfast is served at one long table. Mid-June to early September $100–140, $170 for the king-bedded suite with balcony; off-season rates slightly lower.

🦉 **English Garden B&B** (508-398-2915; 1-888-788-1908; www.theenglish

gardenbandb.com), 32 Inman Road, Dennisport 02639. Open mid-May to early December. Within a 2-minute walk of the beach, this completely "gutted" guest house has eight tasteful rooms outfitted with quilts and hardwood floors. Each has a private bath and deck, perhaps more aptly called a small Juliet balcony. Some have a whirlpool and ocean view. Both airy common rooms are the kind of places where you could spend a rainy afternoon, reading in front of the fireplace. A full breakfast is included and served at individual tables in a spacious, bright, and contemporary breakfast room. You'll always have a choice of eggs any style. At press time, there were two apartment suites under construction that should be complete in mid-2001; do inquire. Late May to early September $115–129, off-season $65–95.

✎ **By The Sea Guests B&B** (508-398-8685; 1-800-447-9202; www.bythesea guests.com), Chase Avenue at Inman Road, Dennisport 02639. Open May through November. This Inman Beach guest house has 12 renovated rooms, each with a very nicely and newly tiled bathroom, refrigerator, and cable TV with HBO. The large rooms are basically but pleasantly outfitted with well-maintained 1950s-style cottage furniture, white cotton bedspreads, and white curtains. It's all very summery, charming, and breezy. Some rooms have two double beds. On rainy days, head to the enclosed porch overlooking the private beach (just steps away) or to the large living room with stereo, books, games, and a ready supply of fruit and cookies. July to early September $80–135, $15 each additional person. Off-season $50–105, $10 each additional person. Inquire about the five new one- and two-bedroom suites that were under construction at press time; I have high expectations for them.

✎ **Beach House Inn Bed & Breakfast** (508-398-4575), 61 Uncle Stephen's Road, West Dennis 02670. Off a sandy lane in a residential area (well off Route 28), the Beach House is well suited to families who want to be right on the beach. Parents can watch their kids from the glassed-in breakfast porch or from the deck overlooking the private beach. Although the living room has a beach-worn appearance, the seven guest rooms with wood floors (each with a private bath, TV, and private deck) are nicely decorated. Each room can accommodate two adults and two children, who sleep in sleeping bags on futons. Guests have access to the fully equipped kitchen. An expanded continental breakfast buffet is included in-season; picnic, barbecue, and play areas on the premises. Mid-June to mid-September $500–700 weekly; there are a few nightly slots available; mid-October to mid-May $79 for 3 nights or $500 for the whole house for a whole weekend.

✎ **Captain Nickerson Inn** (508-398-5966; 1-800-282-1619; www.bbonline. com/ma/captnick/), 333 Main Street, South Dennis 02660. Open April through October. Just off Route 28 in a lovely and tranquil part of town, innkeepers Pat and Dave York offer four comfortably modest and air-conditioned rooms (all with private bath and TV/VCR). Within the

Queen Anne Victorian sea captain's home, there is one room that can accommodate parents and a young child (for no extra charge). The backyard has a play set and sandbox. Bicycles are complimentary; the Cape Cod Rail Trail is only half a mile away. A full breakfast of crêpes or pancakes is included. Stuffed-shirt types won't be happy here. July to early September $97–115 double; $150 for a family suite; off-season $80–90; extended-stay packages.

COTTAGES

Dennis Seashores (508-398-8512; 508-432-5465 for advance inquiries), 20 Chase Avenue, Dennisport 02639. Open May through October. These 33 housekeeping cottages, rented weekly in-season, are some of the best on Nantucket Sound; make reservations a year in advance. The two-, three-, and four-bedroom shingled cottages, with knotty-pine paneling and fireplaces, are decorated and furnished in a "Cape Cod Colonial" style. Cottages, with fully equipped kitchens, towels, and linens, are either beachfront or nestled among pine trees; each has a grill and picnic table. The resort's private stretch of beach is well tended. Early July to early September $975–1,195 weekly for a two-bedroom, $1,475–3,095 for a three- and four-bedroom; off-season $425–525 weekly for a two-bedroom. Three-night rentals in May, June, September, and October. No credit cards.

RENTAL HOUSES AND COTTAGES

For summer rentals, try the friendly and helpful **Peter McDowell Associates** (508-385-9114; www.capecodrentals.com), 585 Route 6A in Dennis. They have over 150 houses ranging from $2,800 weekly for a two-bedroom on the water to $2,200 off the water. You can spend as little as $600, though, or as much as $7,000 for a weekly rental.

See also Century 21–Sam Ingram Real Estate in "Yarmouth."

WHERE TO EAT

Dennis has plenty of restaurants to satisfy every budget and taste bud.

DINING OUT

Ocean House (508-394-0700), 3 Chase Avenue, at the end of Depot Street, Dennisport. Open for dinner April through November. Don't let appearances deceive you: The boxy brick building belies the ocean views within. All the action is on the other side, where chef Roy Breiman prepares distinctive seasonal contemporary American dishes. His dishes are fresh and light. Depending on what's available, you might find bouillabaisse, salmon with lobster mashed potatoes, swordfish Provençal, or short ribs with potato puree. If you don't want to wait for a table (patrons come from as far away as Sandwich and Chatham), you can get full meals at the **bar,** which also serves gourmet pizzas and appetizers. Definitely save room for dessert. Look for special wine dinners once a month in the off-season. Entrées $14–29.

❄ **Red Pheasant Inn** (508-385-2133), Route 6A, Dennis. Open for dinner. Low ceilings, wood floors, and exposed beams set a rustic and romantic tone in the dining rooms, located in a 200-year-old renovated barn (a former ship chandlery on Corporation Beach). Local arts grace the white-linen-covered tables: glassware from Sydenstricker, pieces from Scargo Pottery (see *Selective Shopping—Artisans*), and Bill Block's Victorian lighting. The Red Pheasant usually enjoys a fine reputation for attentive service, fine cuisine, and excellent wine. Roast duckling, lamb and game dishes, and lobster are among the regional American specialties offered. Chef-owner Bill Atwood and his wife, Denise, have been here since 1980. Entrées $16–28. Reservations highly recommended.

♿ **Gina's By The Sea** (508-385-3213), 134 Taunton Avenue, Dennis. Open for dinner Thursday through Sunday, April through November; nightly June through September. Gina's is a friendly place, with a low-key **bar,** knotty-pine walls, a fireplace, and exposed beams. The northern Italian menu features signature dishes like garlicky shrimp scampi, mussels marinara, and chicken "gizmondo." Gina's has been a fixture in this beachside enclave since 1938 and chef Chris Lemmer has been cooking since 1990. It really is as consistently good as everyone says. Because the restaurant is small, very popular, and doesn't take reservations, arrive early or wait until after 9 PM. Otherwise, put your name on the waiting list and take a walk on nearby Chapin Memorial Beach (see *Green Space—Beaches*) or have a drink and watch the sunset. Dinner $9–22.

🍷❄⌀♿**Scargo Cafe** (508-385-8200), Route 6A, Dennis. Open for lunch and dinner. This bustling, renovated former sea captain's house is awash in wood: paneling, wainscoting, and floors. The friendly staff are adept at getting patrons to Cape Playhouse shows (see *Entertainment*) on time without hurrying them. Light bites and finger foods such as potato skins, Arizona shrimp, and pesto bruschetta are served in the pleasant **bar.** Always-dependable specials include "wildcat chicken" with Italian sausage and mushrooms; a vegetable and Brie sandwich; seafood strudel; grilled lamb; and Grape-Nut custard, a regional dessert favorite. Brothers Peter and David Troutman have presided over the extensive and well-executed menu since 1987. Early specials in summer for those seated by 5:30; children's menu. Lunch $6–14, dinner $7–22.

⌀♿ **Lighthouse Inn** (508-398-2244), off Lower County Road, on the road to West Dennis Beach. Open for breakfast and dinner, mid-May to mid-October, and for lunch in July and August. The extensive dinner menu features reasonably priced seafood as well as pork chops and New York sirloin. On my last visit I had a house specialty: chicken hazelnut, a boneless breast lightly encrusted with nuts and sautéed in a Dijon sauce. Steamed lobster is always a popular choice. All the desserts, and the dinner rolls, are baked on the premises. The cuisine, as well as the decor, is at once decidedly old-fashioned and surprisingly modern. Tables are draped with white linen and the service is professional. The large and open dining room has peaked ceilings, flags hanging from the rafters, knotty-pine paneling, and a full wall of windows overlooking the ocean. Casual luncheons are nice, served on the oceanfront deck, they include sandwiches, burgers, and light salads. Cocktails are served on the deck after 4 PM. Breakfast is a hot or cold buffet ($11 and $7, respectively). Children's menu; early specials. Lunch $7–12; dinner entrées $15–20. Reservations suggested in summer.

✒ **Ebb Tide** (508-398-8733), 94 Chase Avenue, Dennisport. Open for dinner early May to mid-October. The McCormick family have been serving well-prepared old-fashioned New England cuisine since 1959. They take great pride in what they do and also teach at the Cape Cod Community College's culinary arts and management program. The Ebb Tide is fine dining without the customary formality, the kind of place that serves sorbet between courses but that also has a children's menu. Baked stuffed scrod with lobster stuffing, broiled swordfish with béarnaise sauce, prime rib, lobster, and seafood Newburg are among the specialties. Extensive early menu 4:30–5:30. Entrées $13–26.

❄ **Max's** (508-385-8888), 800 Route 6A, Dennis. Open for lunch and dinner. Next to the post office in the center of town, this new Italian place is intimate and a welcome addition to the village. Although I didn't get a chance to eat there for this edition, reliable innkeeper friends assure me that their customers have found it consistent and very good. The signature dish includes artichoke ravioli with a lemon, cream, and Parmesan sauce. At midday, try a roast turkey sandwich with Havarti or grilled salmon. Lunch $6–12, dinner entrées $15–23.

EATING OUT

🍴❄✒**Marshside** (508-385-4010), 25 Bridge Street, East Dennis. Open for all three meals and Sunday brunch. A local favorite, Marshside is noted for its casual atmosphere (with country-floral tablecloths, for instance), good food (shrimp scampi, lobster, salads, sandwiches, and veggie melts), and reasonable prices (you can get a teriyaki chicken salad for $6.50). It's a family-oriented restaurant that provides coloring books, toys, and contests for children, along with a children's menu. Some tables overlook the namesake marsh, with a view of Sesuit Harbor. Lunch $5–10, dinner $9-16.

🍴✒ **Bob Briggs' "Wee Packet"** (508-398-2181), Depot Street, Dennisport. Open 11:30–8:30 daily, May through September; open for breakfast late June to early September. This spick-and-span little restaurant, regarded with great affection by hordes of repeat customers, was opened in 1949 by Bob Briggs. (In case you're wondering, a "wee packet" is a small ship.) Today, Bob's son Rob and daughter Sheila carry on the tradition. An exposed kitchen, counter-style seating, and a dining room with shiny yellow tables and bright yellow walls lend the place a homespun feel. As for the food, specialties include Cape Cod bay scallops, onion rings, fried lobster, and Sheila's homemade desserts, including blueberry shortcake. Children's menu. Look for the new, old-fashioned doughnut shop/bakery next door. Dishes $3–13.

✔✳ **The Breakfast Room** (508-398-0581), 675 Route 28, West Dennis. Open for breakfast 7 AM–2 PM daily, April through November; weekends year-round. This place is classic, a local fixture. In addition to griddle cakes, you can order no-nonsense egg dishes or go whole hog and chow down on steak, eggs, and potato pancakes. Belgian waffles, French toast, and a children's menu, too. Even in the off-season, you can wait an hour for a table. Dishes $4–10.

🍴✔ **Captain Frosty's** (508-385-8548), 219 Route 6A, Dennis. Open 11 AM–8 or 9 PM early April through September; closed Monday off-season. One of the Cape's best roadside clam shacks, Frosty's takes pride in its hooked (not gillnetted) Chatham cod, Gulf shrimp, native fried clams, small sea scallops, clam fritters, lobster rolls, and grilled chicken. Seafood and onion rings are deep-fried in 100 percent canola oil. There are always daily specials. Casual dining room, outdoor seating at a brick patio surrounded by rhododendrons, and takeout. Dishes $3–14. Run, don't walk. No credit cards.

🍴✳✔**Bob's Best Sandwiches** (508-394-8450), 613 Route 28, Dennisport. Open for breakfast and lunch year-round and dinner in summer. There really is a Bob, and his sandwiches are made with thick slices of homemade bread (like oatmeal) and thick slices of home-smoked turkey or roast beef. If you're a Texas chili fan, Bob's rules. For breakfast, you have a choice of veggie omelets, homemade French toast, and the like. Children's menu; early specials. $3–6.

✔   **Swan River Seafood** (508-394-4466), 5 Lower County Road, Dennisport. Open for lunch and dinner, late May to late September; takeout, too. This casual restaurant's appeal is fresh, fresh, hook-caught fish, thanks to the attached fish market. Cynthia Ahern, chef-owner since the mid-1970s, keeps it simple with lobster, clams, oysters, and the catch of the day. Despite doing a large volume of business, tables next to the big picture windows are available for those who arrive early. It overlooks a river, marsh, and windmill. Children's menu. Lunch $5–10, dinner $12–17.

✳   **The Mercantile** (508-385-3877), 766 Route 6A, Dennis. Open daily for breakfast and lunch. Located behind the post office, this "gourmet" deli and bakery makes fancy cold salads, sandwiches, and homemade soups and breads. Breakfast offerings include egg sandwiches, bagels, muffins, granola, quiche of the day, and pastries. There are tables upstairs and down and on the back patio; otherwise, have a picnic. Dishes $4–6.

   Clancy's Fish 'n Chips and Beach Bar (508-394-6900), 228 Lower County Road, Dennisport. Open for lunch and dinner mid-May to early September. New in 1998. You'll get reliable seafood in pleasant and casual surroundings here. Food arrives in plastic baskets at outdoor tables under canvas umbrellas, within the screened-in porch, or at shiny wooden tables with director's chairs. Try the boneless Buffalo wings. A convivial **bar,** too. Dishes $6–19.

✔   **Kream 'n' Kone** (508-394-0808), Route 28, Dennisport. Open February through October. Honest-to-goodness kitsch, not imported from any consultant who says kitsch is cool among a certain crowd. Self-serve fried seafood, ice cream, and clams eaten in booths. Although it's campy, a family can spend $50 here easily.

🏵 **The Dog House** (508-398-7774), 189 Lower County Road, Dennisport. Open seasonally. This old-fashioned hot dog stand dispenses dogs with sauerkraut or bacon and cheese or lots of other combinations for $2–6. After you've ordered from the take-out window, have a seat at one of a few covered picnic tables. Green Mountain coffee, too.

See also Woolfies Home Bakery, under *Sweets;* Devon Tea Room and Contrast Bistro and Espresso Bar, under *Coffee and Tea.*

COFFEE AND TEA

❄ **Contrast Bistro and Espresso Bar** (508-385-9100), 605 Route 6A, Dennis. On my most recent visit, I found dinner disappointing (and overpriced relative to the setting and quality), but the cappuccino sure is strong. For a quick lunch there are plenty of salads, lavish pizzas, and hot and cold sandwiches. The decor screams hip and artsy: bright blue ceilings, red walls, and oversize modern paintings.

Devon Tea Room (508-394-6068), 294 Route 28, West Dennis. Open April through December. Open for lunch, afternoon tea, and desserts. With no whiff of sexism, hear me out: This is a nice spot for lunching ladies. Tables are rather close to one another, with a gift shop spilling into the dining area. Devonshire cream teas ($6 per person)—with scones, strawberry preserves, and Devon cream—are popular. You can also enjoy a ploughman's lunch with Stilton cheese, a savory tea with assorted tea sandwiches, or simply a pot of tea. The shop has an extensive array of teas, accessories for tea, aprons, cozies, and imported food items from England and Ireland.

SWEETS

❄ **Stage Coach Candy** (508-394-1791), 411 Main Street, Dennisport. Ray and Donna Hebert originated the ultimate chocolate-covered cranberry! They'll make chocolates in any shape, including computer boards and TV remote controls.

Sundae School Ice Cream Parlor (508-394-9122), 387 Lower County Road, Dennisport. Open mid-April to mid-October. This old-fashioned parlor has a marble soda fountain, round marble tables, old-fashioned tin signage, and a nickelodeon. Some confections are delightfully modern: Frozen yogurt and ice cream are made with two-thirds less fat. Fruit sundaes are very good, too. Open until 11 PM in-season, for that late-night fix. No credit cards.

Woolfies Home Bakery (508-394-3717), 279 Lower County Road, Dennisport. Open daily May to mid-October. From a small red Cape on Dennis's south side, Terri Moretti whips up honey wheat bread for the morning and raspberry nut squares and éclairs for the afternoon. It's frankly not so much what she whips up as it is having an inviting and low-key place to relax in. Typical breakfast selections and lunch items like focaccia and pizza are also offered. Wednesday through Saturday

KIM GRANT

Go fly a kite!

Woolfies stays open until 10 PM, when indoor tables and the outside patio furniture are candlelit. Otherwise, the shaded front lawn has rocking chairs and benches.

Ice Cream Smuggler (508-385-5307), 716 Route 6A, Dennis. Open late March to late October. Homemade ice cream—including a great mocha chip—and frozen yogurt.

See also Bob Briggs' "Wee Packet" under *Eating Out*.

ENTERTAINMENT

Cape Playhouse (508-385-3838; 508-385-3911 box office; www.cape playhouse.com), Route 6A, Dennis. Shows daily but with a limited Sunday schedule, mid-June to early September. The Cape Playhouse was established in 1927 by Californian Raymond Moore, who initially went to Provincetown to start a theater company but found it too remote. Moore's attitude when he purchased this former 1830s Unitarian meetinghouse for $200 was, "If we fix it up, they will come." The playhouse proudly claims the title of the country's oldest continuously operating professional summer theater and the Cape's only full Equity theater. Basil Rathbone starred in the company's first production, *The Guardsman.* Over the years, the playhouse has featured the likes of Helen Hayes, Julie Harris, Olivia de Havilland, and Jessica Tandy, when they were already "stars." Henry Fonda, Bette Davis, Humphrey Bogart, and Gregory Peck acted here before they were "discovered." On Friday morning in July and August there is **children's theater.** If you make it to only one summer production, let it be here. Tickets $15–35; children's theater $6.

Band concerts, whether the music be country or American classics, are held on both town greens in July and August. Head to Dennis on Route 6A on Monday and Dennisport off Route 28 on Tuesday. Check with the chamber (see *Guidance*) for an exact schedule of places and times.

Christine's (508-394-7333), 581 Route 28, West Dennis. This restaurant and show club features a full lineup of jazz, cabaret, comedy, dance, and party bands—groups you've heard of—nightly in summer.

MOVIES

Cape Cinema (508-385-2503; www.capecinema.com), Route 6A, Dennis. Screenings daily, mid-April through October. Built in 1930 as a movie theater, Cape Cinema continues to bring fine art films, foreign films, and independent productions to Cape audiences. The exterior was designed after the Congregational church in Centerville, while the interior ceiling was designed by Rockwell Kent to represent his view of heaven, filled with comets and constellations. Jo Mielziner supervised the painting of the 6,400-square-foot art deco mural, which was done by the Art Students League in a New York theater and shipped by train to the Cape. Kent refused to set foot in Massachusetts because he was protesting the 1921 verdict in the Sacco and Vanzetti trial. There are about 300 seats in this theater, which was chosen to premiere *The Wizard of Oz* in 1940. Don't miss catching a flick here; screening times are usually 4:30, 7, and 9. Tickets $7 adults, $4 children.

Hoyt's Cinemas (508-394-1100), Patriot Square Mall, South Dennis. Take exit 9 off Route 6.

See also Cape Museum of Fine Arts under *To See.*

SELECTIVE SHOPPING

❈ Unless otherwise noted, all shops are open year-round.

ANTIQUES

Dennisport center is fast becoming a quiet mecca for year-round antiques browsers. There are more than half a dozen shops within a block, chief among them **Main Street Antique Center** (508-760-5700), 691 Route 28. With more than 100 dealers, it's just one of many retailers revitalizing the little district. Also, stop into **Antiques at 671 Main** (508-398-0100) and **South Side Antique Center** (508-394-8601).

Webfoot Farm Antiques (508-385-2334), 1475 Route 6A, East Dennis. Open daily except Wednesday off-season. Each of the four tasteful rooms in this 1845 captain's house is crammed with impressive Continental, American, and English decorative arts and fine antiques. (The house shows off pieces quite nicely indeed.) The collection of sterling is strong, as are the Oriental porcelains and pottery.

Gloria Swanson Antiques (508-385-4166), 608 Route 6A, Dennis. This shop is crammed with Flow Blue, Mulberry, and Staffordshire china, early glass and bottles, teapots, and tins. It's a treasure.

Antiques Center of Cape Cod (508-385-6400), 243 Route 6A, Dennis. Open daily except Wednesday in January through March. With more than 150 dealers, this two-story former building supply store is the Cape's largest cooperative, offering items large and small. Don't miss it or the giant warehouse next door. Most objects sell for under $200 and are classified as "old," "vintage," or "collectible" rather than "antique."

Antiques 608 (508-385-2755), 608 Route 6A, Dennis. This multidealer shop deals more in what owner Marcia Cardaropoli calls "junque," but if you hunt through the stuff you'll find antiquarian books, daguerreotypes, and ephemera.

Finders Keepers (508-760-3440), 257 Lower County Road, Dennisport. Antiques, nautical items, glass, toys, even fishing poles. This shop has a little of everything and is great fun.

ART GALLERIES

Grose Gallery (508-385-3434), 524 Route 6A, Dennis. This barn-gallery features the work of illustrator and printmaker David Grose, who created the wood engravings and pen drawings for three of John Hay's books: *The Great Beach, Nature's Year,* and *The Run.* He also has produced serigraphs of Dennis landmarks.

The Artists Gallery (508-385-4600), 593 Route 6A, Dennis. While the art may be a bit uneven, you do have the opportunity to buy direct from the artists at this cooperative. That means that prices are often lower than at other galleries, which take a 50 percent commission.

Wilson Gallery (508-385-0856), 800 Route 6A, Dennis. The directors here, a father-and-son team, thankfully see no reason to traffic in Cape Cod landscapes and scenics. Their Newbury Street gallery was quite sophisticated and the art here speaks for itself, too. It's refreshing.

Kate Nelson at **Ross Coppleman** (508-385-7900), 1439 Route 6A, East Dennis. Open April through December. Kate's work is some of the most sophisticated abstraction I've seen on the Cape. Her nonrepresentational paintings and prints are extraordinary and, as she says, "everchanging, like the path to the outgoing tide on the Brewster flats." She continues to fuse the experience of exterior landscape with the "inscape," the inner landscape of psyche and spirit.

ARTISANS

Fritz Glass (508-394-0441; www.fritzglass.com), 36 Upper County Road, Dennisport. Open 11–4 Monday, Wednesday, and Friday in summer, and by appointment. Although this is primarily a wholesale glass blowing operation, the colorful and striking showroom is filled with extraordinarily beautiful, artful creations, decorative functional creations. You can watch Fritz Lauenstein work and check out the inventory of fun and intricate marbles (sold in museums around the country) and sand dollars, honey pots and bud vases. Chances are that Fritz's wife, June, and daughter Coco will be in the shop, too.

Scargo Pottery (508-385-3894), 30 Dr. Lord Road South, off Route 6A, Dennis. Down a path through the woods, potter Harry Holl, his four daughters (Tina, Kim, Mary, and Sarah), and son-in-law (Kevin) make whimsical and decidedly untraditional birdhouses, fountains, and architectural sculptures, among other things. Harry has been working here since 1952. It's a magical world that you won't want to miss: Pieces hang from tree branches and sit on tree stumps. The work isn't cheap, but it isn't runof-the-mill, either. There's no question that this is pottery as art.

A Touch of Glass (508-398-3850), 711 Route 28, West Dennis. These stained-glass lamps and lampshades have been fused and blown, assembled using the same techniques employed by Tiffany.

AUCTIONS

Eldred's Auctions (508-385-3116), 1483 Route 6A, East Dennis. This high-end auction house—the largest on the Cape, with more than $5 million in sales—moves magnificent collections. In July the weekly auctions center on books, collectibles, marine items, and paintings. In August there is an Americana auction the first week of the month, and a fine and decorative arts auction the second week. A weeklong Oriental auction takes place late in the month. In spring and fall there are generally specialty auctions once a month; call for a schedule.

BOOKSTORES

Arm Chair Bookstore (508-385-0900; www.chapterstogo.com), 619 Route 6A, Dennis. Open 8:30 AM–9 PM in summer; shorter hours off-season. This fantastic, family-owned and -operated shop has a devoted following, with obvious reason. There simply isn't a more inviting bookstore on the Cape. Patty Barnes began the shop, and now her two daughters Elly and Sarah (and Sarah's husband, Greg) are involved. They've even spun off adjacent businesses. (See *Special Shops* below for the adjacent Arm Chair Cottage and Wee Cottage Baby.)

Paperback Cottage (508-760-2101), 927 Route 28 at Route 134, next to the chamber of commerce booth, South Dennis. Open daily in summer; Thursday through Monday in spring and fall; Saturday through Monday in winter. In addition to selling books the old-fashioned way, Joan Sullivan rents books by the week. Good children's section, too.

The Book Seller (508-760-4516), 84 School Street, just off Route 28, West Dennis. One of the best used-book stores I've found. Paul Gauthier, the proprietor, is a gem.

JEWELERS

Baska Studio (508-385-5733), 766 Route 6A, Dennis, and **Ross Coppelman** (508-385-7900), 1439 Route 6A, East Dennis, have both fashioned stunning designs as goldsmiths for more than 20 years. Both men work on the premises; Michael Baska is open year-round (but closed on Sunday) and Coppelman is open April through November. Ross's shop is a special-occasion kind of place; his creations have lots of zeros on the price tags. If you're serious about having a stone set or buying something in gold or silver, don't overlook **Jewelry by Etta** (508-394-8964), 530 Route 28, West Dennis. Open daily year-round except Monday off-season. Many people who don't venture to the southside are unaware of Etta and unwittingly bypass a fine, singular shop.

SPECIAL SHOPS

Arm Chair Cottage (508-385-4808; www.armchaircottage.com), 611 Route 6A, Dennis. Look no farther for that distinctive summery cottage look. Stuffed with a combination of Maine cottage furniture and Nantucket/Cape Cod cottage home accessories, this fun store has diverse price points, appealing to all budgets. Offerings are built around colors, which makes shopping all that much easier and more tempting. Also, affordable, nautically inspired gold jewelry.

Wee Cottage Baby (508-385-2929), 623 Route 6A, Dennis. This small shop is devoted to baby gifts and items.

Grandma Daisy's (508-394-3373), 444 Lower County Road. Open early May to mid-December. This former blacksmith's barn is crammed with tasteful gifts for any occasion, books, and distinctive home accessories. Great browsing and buying.

Tobey Farm, Route 6A, Dennis. This colorful farm has been in the same family since 1678, when it was given to Thomas Tobey for his service during King Philip's War.

Pizazz (508-760-3888), 633 Route 28, Dennisport. Giant blow-up beach toys and summer novelties. There are dozens of other similar shops, but they just don't have pizzazz, so to speak.

See also Devon Tea Room, under *Coffee and Tea.*

SPECIAL EVENTS

Mid- to late June: **Secret Garden Tour,** sponsored by the Cape Museum of Fine Arts. Tour gardens and watch artists paint their inspiration. Tickets $50.

Mid- to late August: **Dennis Festival Days.** Billed as the Cape's oldest festival (since 1958), this 5-day celebration includes a crafts fair, an antique auto parade, kite-flying and sand-castle-building contests, puppet shows, fireworks, and band concerts.

III. THE LOWER CAPE

Brewster
Harwich
Chatham
Orleans

KIM GRANT

Puffy hydrangea blossoms burst from cottage window boxes

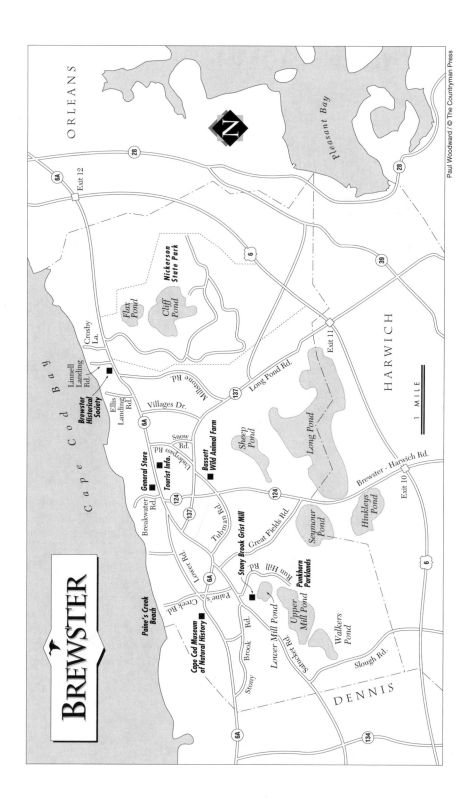

BREWSTER

ORLEANS

Pleasant Bay

28

6A
Exit 12

28

39

Cape Cod Bay

Nickerson State Park

Flax Pond

Cliff Pond

6

Crosby La.

HARWICH

Exit 11

Linnell Landing Rd.

Brewster Historical Society

Ellis Landing Rd.

Villages Dr.

6A

137

Long Pond Rd.

Millstone Rd.

1 MILE

Snow Rd.

Bassett Wild Animal Farm

Sheep Pond

Long Pond

General Store

Underpass Rd.

Tourist Info.

124

124

Breakwater Rd.

137

Tubman Rd.

Great Fields Rd.

Brewster - Harwich Rd.

Exit 10

Hinkleys Pond

Seymour Pond

6

Paine's Creek Beach

Lower Rd.

6A

Stony Brook Grist Mill

Run Hill Rd.

Punkhorn Parklands

Cape Cod Museum of Natural History

Creek Rd.

Paine's

Lower Mill Pond

Upper Mill Pond

Walkers Pond

Stony Brook Rd.

Satucket Rd.

Slough Rd.

DENNIS

6A

134

Paul Woodward / © The Countryman Press

Brewster

Brewster, settled in 1659 and named for *Mayflower* passenger Elder William Brewster, wasn't incorporated until 1803, when it split from Harwich. By then the prosperous sea captains who'd built their homes on the bay side wanted to distance themselves from their less-well-off neighbors to the south. Between 1780 and 1870, 99 sea captains called Brewster home (although they sailed their clipper ships out of Boston and New York), a fact that even Henry David Thoreau commented on during his 1849 trip. Many of these beautiful houses on Route 6A have been converted to bed & breakfasts and inns.

In the early 1800s, Breakwater Beach was a popular landing for packet ships, which transported salt and vegetables to Boston and New York markets and brought tourists to the area. Salt making was big business in 1837, when more than 60 saltworks dotted Brewster beaches. Windmills pumped seawater into 36-by-18-foot vats, where it was left to evaporate (this process was developed in Dennis). During the late 18th and early 19th centuries, Brewster's Factory Village sold cloth, boots, and food to people all over the Cape.

You could spend a charmed week in Brewster and still find plenty to occupy you. While the 2,000-acre Nickerson State Park boasts facilities for a dozen outdoor activities, there is also Punkhorn Parklands, an undeveloped, 800-acre parcel of conservation land in town. Although Brewster has only 8,700 year-round residents, it has more than its share of attractions, including two good golf courses, horseback-riding trails, an outstanding museum of natural history, a few smaller museums, and exceptional dining choices.

Brewster's section of Route 6A is a vital link in the 80-square-mile Old King's Highway Historic District. Known for its selection of fine antiques shops, Brewster also attracts contemporary artists, who are drawn to a landscape more evocative of the countryside than the seaside—the land south of Route 6A is dotted with ponds, hills, and dales.

GUIDANCE

Brewster Visitor Information Center (508-896-3500; www.cape codtravel.com/brewster or www.brewstercapecod.org), 2198 Route 6A (P.O. Box 1241), about half a mile east of Route 124, in the rear of the

Town Offices. Open 9–3 daily late June to early September; 9–2 or 3 Tuesday through Saturday from late April to late June and early September to mid-October. Jan Moore and the staff here are very friendly and quite knowledgeable.

PUBLIC LIBRARY
See Brewster Ladies' Library under *To See*.

PUBLIC REST ROOMS
Public rest rooms are located at Nickerson State Park and the Visitor Information Center, both on Route 6A.

GETTING THERE
By car: Brewster is 30 minutes from the Cape Cod Canal (take Route 6 east to exit 9, to Route 134, to Route 6A); it is 45 minutes from Provincetown, at the tip of the peninsula.

GETTING AROUND
Brewster is very easy to get around. There's no real "center" to the town; places of interest are strung along Route 6A.

MEDICAL EMERGENCY
Call **911**.

TO SEE

𝕋✳︎✎**Cape Cod Museum of Natural History** (508-896-3867; www.ccmnh.org), 869 Route 6A. Open 9:30–4:30 Monday through Saturday, 11–4:30 Sunday. Cofounded by naturalist John Hay in 1954, this is one of the best resources for learning about the Cape's natural world. The museum takes its mission seriously: to "inspire and foster an understanding and appreciation of our environment through education, and a means to sustain it." There are marine tanks (containing crabs, lobsters, mollusks, turtles, eels, and frogs), whale displays, and a natural history library. There are also many interactive, hands-on exhibits for kids. The gift shop is packed with fun and educational toys, books, and games. The John Wing Trail—just one trail traversing the museum's 80 acres of marshes, beaches, and woodland—begins from here (see *Green Space—Walks*). Adults $5; children 5–12, $2; fee for some programs. (Also see *Even More Things to See and Do—For Families* for special children's day camps.)

Stony Brook Grist Mill and Museum and Herring Run (508-896-6745), 830 Stony Brook Road. Open April through June, 2–5 Thursday through Saturday, and 2–5 Friday in July and August. This millside pond is one of the Cape's most picturesque places, especially during the spring migration, when the herring are "running" and the natural "ladders" are packed with the silver-backed fish. In 1663 America's first water-powered mill stood on this location. The present gristmill, constructed on 1873 woolen mill foundations (part of the 19th-century Factory Village), contains old milling equipment and a 100-year-old loom on which age-old techniques are sometimes demonstrated. Donations.

KIM GRANT

Locals and visitors enjoy coffee and the morning paper at the 1866 Brewster Store.

The Brewster Store (508-896-3744), 1935 Route 6A at Route 124. Open daily. Purveying groceries and general merchandise since 1866, this two-story, quintessentially Cape store was built in 1852 as a Universalist church. Beneath red, white, and blue bunting and at small-paned windows covered by gingham curtains, locals and visitors sit on old church pews, sip coffee, read the morning newspaper, eat penny candy and ice cream, and watch the world go by. Four generations of families have relied on the store. Upstairs has been re-created with memorabilia from the mid-1800s to the mid-1900s; downstairs has a working antique nickelodeon and oft-used peanut roaster.

✳✍️**Brewster Ladies' Library** (508-896-3913), 1822 Route 6A. Open 10–8 Tuesday and Wednesday, 10–6 Thursday, and 10–4 Friday and Saturday. In 1852 two teenage Brewster girls established this "library," which began as a shelf of books lent from the girls' houses. After local sea captains donated funds in 1868, the ever-expanding library moved to a handsome red Victorian building. The two original front-parlor rooms—each with a fireplace, stained-glass windows, and armchairs—are filled with portraits of sea captains and ships. The library has a large children's area, videos, audios, periodicals, and newspapers. They also sponsor musicals, lectures, and art exhibits.

Higgins Farm Windmill and **Harris-Black House** (508-896-9521), 785 Route 6A, Drummer Boy Park. Open 1–4 Tuesday through Friday in July and August. These two structures are operated by the Brewster Historical Society. Members are on hand to tell you that a family raised

10 children in the one-room house (possibly the "last remaining primitive one-room house on the Cape"), and that the 1795 windmill is known for its octagonal design, while its top resembles a boat's hull. Donations.

New England Fire & History Museum (508-896-5711), 1439 Route 6A. Open 10–4 weekdays and noon–4 weekends, late May through August; open 12–4 weekends, September to mid-October. Surrounding a 19th-century New England–style town common, the complex includes an apothecary's shop, a blacksmith shop, antique fire-fighting equipment, a diorama of the 1871 Chicago Fire, a "Boston Burns 1872" exhibit, 10 life-size figures of firefighters through the centuries, and 35 working fire engines. Some exhibits are on loan from the Smithsonian. Picnic area. Adults $5; children 5–12, $2.50.

Brewster Historical Society Museum (508-896-9521), 3341 Route 6A. Open 1–4 weekends in mid- to late June and early to mid-September; 1–4 Tuesday through Friday in July and August. Free. Highlighting Brewster's rich heritage, the small museum has an 1884 barbershop, an 1830s sea captain's room, dolls and toys, the old East Brewster Post Office, and antique gowns. A walking trail originates from the house (see Spruce Hill Conservation Area under *Green Space—Walks*).

Crosby Mansion (508-896-1744), Crosby Lane off Route 6A. This yellow and white Colonial Revival, once the elegant home of Albert and Matilda Crosby, sits on 19 acres of bayside property. Massachusetts acquired the land (and the house by default) by eminent domain in 1985 so the public could access Cape Cod Bay from Nickerson State Park. Because the state cannot afford to maintain it (the 28-room mansion needs about $1.5 million in repairs), a volunteer group, the Friends of Crosby Mansion, stepped in. They've done an impressive job repairing the worst structural damage and much of the interior. Albert Crosby owned the Chicago Opera House and fell in love with one of the showgirls, Matilda. When she came to live in Albert's modest turn-of-the-20th-century house, she was so unhappy that Albert had a mansion built for her—around his original four-room house! (Kids compare stepping into the smaller house to what Alice must have felt like in Wonderland.) Matilda is said to have entertained in the larger mansion while Albert stayed in his interior boyhood home. The mansion is open 6 days per season—the first and third Sunday in July and August and during the weekend of Brewster in Bloom (see *Special Events*)—but you can always peek in the oversize windows.

Tidal flats. At low tide, you can walk 2 miles out onto the tidal flats of Cape Cod Bay. During Prohibition, townspeople walking on the flats would often stumble onto cases of liquor thrown overboard by rumrunners. Encounters are tamer these days: Kids discover tidal pools, play in channels left by receding tides, and marvel at streaked "garnet" sand. On a clear day you can see from the Provincetown Monument to Sandwich. You can reach the flats from any of the beaches.

First Parish Church (508-896-5577), 1969 Route 6A, on the town green, also nicknamed the Egg because of its shape and natural depression. The 1834 clapboard exterior is marked by Gothic windows and a bell tower, while interior pews are marked with names of prominent Brewster sea captains. Wander around the graveyard behind the church, too.

OUTDOOR ACTIVITIES

BICYCLING/RENTALS
Because the **Cape Cod Rail Trail** runs through Brewster, and **Nickerson State Park** (see *Green Space*) has its own network of bicycle trails linked to the trail, there are many places to rent bicycles in town. Look for **Rail Trail Bike & Blades** (508-896-8200), 302 Underpass Road. It rents and sells bikes year-round and will deliver bikes. **Brewster Bike** (508-896-8149), 442 Underpass Road, is open seasonally. All shops offer plenty of parking. In-season rates are about $10 for 2 hours, $22 for 24 hours, $48 for 3 days, $70 weekly. Pick up the excellent, free Nickerson trail map.

If you're not renting bikes, there is **Rail Trail** parking on Route 137, on Underpass Road off Route 137, and at Nickerson State Park on Route 6A.

Trailers and alleycats (rented above) for hauling kids are great for this stretch because it's shady and fairly flat. Nickerson trails are a bit more hilly.

BOATING/RENTALS
Jack's Boat Rentals (508-896-8556), within Nickerson State Park, Route 6A. Open seasonally. Jack's rents canoes, kayaks, Sunfish, and other modes of water transportation on Flax Pond.

CANOEING/KAYAKING
Cape Cod Coastal Canoe & Kayak/Paddle Cape Cod (508-564-4051; www.paddlecapecod.com). Trips April to mid-October, and later by appointment and weather permitting. Under the auspices of the Cape Cod Museum of Natural History (see *To See*), naturalists Fred and Shirley Bull, who wrote the guidebook *Paddling Cape Cod*, lead trips all over the Cape. Half-day trips for explorers age 6 and older cost $50 per person and are well worth it. Children are free when in the same canoe as parents. Call for specific schedule, since locations and departures are dependent on the tide.

FISHING/SHELLFISHING
Brewster has almost 50 freshwater ponds; required state fishing licenses are obtained from the Town Offices (508-896-3701), 2198 Route 6A. The following ponds are stocked: **Sheep Pond,** off Route 124, and **Flax, Little Cliff,** and **Higgins Ponds** within Nickerson State Park.

Shellfishing permits are also obtained weekdays year-round from the Town Offices. In July and August shellfishing is permitted only on

Thursday and Sunday. (In June, it's AOK daily.) Shellfish beds at **Saint's Landing Beach** (off Lower Road from Route 6A) are seeded in summer. Quahogs and sea clams are harvested June to mid-September; steamers are harvested October to mid-April. Nonresident permits cost $15 weekly.

Brewster Flats Fishing & Outfitters (508-896-2460), 2655 Route 6A (Foster's Square). Sporadic hours. Half- and full-day charters for up to six people explore bayside tidal flats, 7 miles of which are in Brewster. The flats are full of sandbars, channels, grassy patches, clam beds, and fish. It takes a local to navigate them successfully enough to outwit the fish.

FOR FAMILIES

✍ **Playground by the Bay,** Drummer Boy Park, Route 6A. Shaped like a packet ship to honor Brewster's seafaring history, this play structure has separate areas for toddlers and older kids. Picnic tables.

❄ GOLF

Captain's Golf Course (508-896-5100; 508-896-1716 pro shop), 1000 Freeman's Way off Route 6A. There are 36 holes at the Port and Starboard Courses. Rated by *Golf Digest* as one of the top 25 public courses in the country. Holes are named after Brewster sea captains. The adjacent practice center is quite extensive.

Ocean Edge Golf Club (508-896-5911), Villages Drive off Route 6A. This 18-hole, tournament-caliber course designed by Cornish and Silva has Scottish-style bunkers and one hole that crosses a cranberry bog. Ocean Edge Resort (see *Lodging—Resort*) offers a "resident" and "commuter" golf school (1-800-343-6074) from late April through July.

❄ ✍ HORSEBACK RIDING

Moby Dick Farm (508-896-3544), Great Fields Road, between Stony Brook Road and Route 124. Open for instruction (inquire about fees) and trail rides ($40 per person per hour). Because the farm has access to 1,000 acres of conservation land, its regularly scheduled trail rides at 10 AM and 2 PM are quite popular; reservations are highly suggested.

Woodsong Farm Equestrian Center (508-896-5555), 121 Lund Farm Way. Open daily by appointment. Established in 1967, Woodsong offers riding instruction, boarding, training, coaching for competitive riders, children's day programs (Horsemasters for experienced riders age 8–18 and Pony Kids, an introductory program, for kids 5–13), horse shows, two-phase events, and an on-premises tack shop.

IN-LINE SKATING

❄ **Rail Trail Bike & Blades** (508-896-8200), 302 Underpass Road. Skate rentals daily.

SAILING

Cape Sail (508-896-2730), out of Brewster and Harwich Harbors; call to arrange trips from late May to mid-October. Since 1983, Capt. Bob Rice has offered customized sailing lessons and an overnight sailing school. The price for two people for instruction and an overnight to

Nantucket (accommodations on-board) is $750; $125 each additional person up to six. Otherwise, the 6-hour basic course takes place over 3 days and costs $360 for one person, $540 for two. Bob also does custom charters ($625 to Nantucket without lessons, for example) and sunset and moonlight cruises. He doesn't have any set schedule, so call him to discuss your interests.

TENNIS

Four public courts are located **behind the Fire and Police Department** near the Town Offices, Route 6A. Free.

Ocean Edge Resort (508-896-9000) offers a 4-day tennis school for resort "residents" and "commuters" from May through August. The extensive program includes both instruction and supervised play. Folks staying at Ocean Edge ("residents") have one additional option: daily tennis clinics from mid-June to early August.

EVEN MORE THINGS TO SEE AND DO

COOKING SCHOOL

❄ **Cooking School at the Captain Freeman Inn** (508-896-7481; 1-800-843-4664; www.captainfreemaninn.com), 15 Breakwater Road (see *Lodging—Bed & Breakfasts*). Many weekends from late November to late April. Chef/instructor/innkeeper Carol Edmondson, an enthusiastic and talented woman, leads the Saturday class in healthy—without hitting you over the head with it—gourmet cooking. You'll start by making bread for a tangible sense of accomplishment. Throughout the day, you'll pick up lots of useful techniques. Carol specializes in cuisines of the Mediterranean region, including southern Europe, northern Africa, and the Middle East. Each year the emphasis switches among countries. The price ($450–580) includes 2 nights at the inn, plus a Saturday-evening wine tasting and dinner for two. By the end of the weekend, the group comes together like one big party. Carol manages to satisfy serious foodies as well as people who can't boil water—in the same class.

FOR FAMILIES

Bassett Wild Animal Farm (508-896-3224), 620 Tubman Road, off Route 124. At press time this 20-acre wooded area with a petting zoo was closed and there were no firm details about whether it will reopen. Just so you know, it used to be home to free-ranging goats and peacocks, domestic and exotic birds, porcupines, llamas, and even a lion and a cougar. There were picnic areas, pony rides, and hayrides.

Day camps (508-896-3867), 869 Route 6A, at the Cape Cod Museum of Natural History (see *To See*). Day camps lasting 2 hours, 2 days, or 2 weeks are offered for children age 3–15. Classes explore "incredible insects," "marine mania," tidal flats, archaeology, and Monomoy's barrier beach. The emphasis is on fun, outdoor adventure, and education. Adults are catered to with canoe trips, and excursions to Monomoy (see *Outdoor*

Activities—Boat Excursions/Rentals in "Chatham") and Nauset Marsh (see *Outdoor Activities—Boat Excursions* in "Orleans"). Call for a schedule of programs.

Baseball clinics. The Brewster Whitecaps sponsor weeklong clinics (508-896-3913) from mid-June through July for boys and girls. Meet at the Cape Cod Tech High School on Route 124 in Harwich.

See also Cape Repertory Theatre under *Entertainment.*

GREEN SPACE

Nickerson State Park (508-896-3491; www.state.ma.us/dem), 3488 Route 6A. Open dawn to dusk, daily. This former estate of Chatham native Roland Nickerson, a multimillionaire who founded the First National Bank of Chicago, contains more than 2,000 acres of pine, hemlock, and spruce and includes eight kettle ponds. Nickerson and his wife, Addie, who entertained such notables as President Grover Cleveland, had a fairly self-sufficient estate, with their own electric generator, ponds teeming with fish, vegetable gardens, and game that roamed the land. When the mansion that Roland's father, Samuel, built for him burned down in 1906, a disconsolate Roland died 2 weeks later. (The "replacement" is now the Ocean Edge Conference Center.) Addie ultimately donated the land in 1934 to honor their son, who died in the 1918 influenza epidemic.

Nickerson State Park has been developed with walking trails, bicycling trails, jogging paths, picnic sites, boat launches, and sandy beaches (further details for various activities can be found under *Outdoor Activities* and *Lodging—Campgrounds*). Winter conditions often provide for ice skating and ice fishing and sometimes for cross-country skiing. (Snow rarely stays on the ground for more than a few days, though.) If you're at all interested in the out-of-doors, don't bypass Nickerson, one of the Cape's real treasures. Almost 300,000 people visit each year. Day use is free.

BEACHES

Brewster has 8 miles of waterfront on Cape Cod Bay and eight public beaches, none of which is particularly spacious and all of which are located off Route 6A. Daily ($8), weekly ($25), and seasonal parking permits are purchased at the Visitor Information Center (508-896-4511), 2198 Route 6A, 9–3 daily from mid-June to early September. No permit is required at any town beach after 3 PM.

Paine's Creek Beach, Paine's Creek Road off Route 6A. This is one of Brewster's most picturesque beaches because of the creek that feeds into it. Parking fee.

PONDS

Long Pond and **Sheep Pond,** both off Route 124, have freshwater swimming and sandy beaches. Long Pond has a lifeguard. Long and Sheep

Ponds are among the best of Brewster's more than 50 ponds. Parking permits required for both residents and visitors.

Flax Pond and **Cliff Pond,** within Nickerson State Park, Route 6A. Flax Pond has the best public beach in the park; it has picnic tables and a bathhouse, but no lifeguard. Cliff Pond is ringed with little beaches, but bathers share the pond with motorized boats. (It's not really a problem, though.)

WALKS

John Wing Trail, South Trail, and **North Trail,** at the Cape Cod Museum of Natural History (see *To See*), 869 Route 6A. Named for Brewster's first settler, a Quaker forced to leave Sandwich due to religious persecution, the John Wing Trail (about 1½ miles round trip) meanders past a sassafras grove and salt marshes, which provide habitat for diverse plants and animals. Traversing a tidal island, it ends on the dunes with a panoramic bay view. South Trail is on the opposite side of Route 6A and extends for about a mile past Stony Brook, a beech grove, and the remnants of a cranberry bog. The short North Trail wends around the museum's immediate grounds, crossing a salt marsh. Naturalist-led walks depart from the museum daily in summer and on weekends off-season. Call 508-896-3867 for times.

Punkhorn Parklands, Run Hill Road, off Stony Brook Road. Miles of scenic trails on more than 800 acres—some overlooking kettle ponds—traverse oak and pine forests, meadows, and marshes. Trails are used by birders and mountain bikers, even coyotes and foxes. Pick up a detailed trail and off-road map from the Visitor Information Center ($1; see *Guidance*).

Spruce Hill Conservation Area, behind the Brewster Historical Society Museum, 3341 Route 6A. This trail, and the uncrowded little beach at the end of it, is a secret treasure. The 30-minute, round-trip trail follows a wide old carriage road—probably used for off-loading fish and lumber and rumored to have been used by bootleggers during Prohibition—that runs from the museum to the bay and a private stretch of sandy beach. The Conservation Commission manages the 25-acre area.

See also Nickerson State Park under *Green Space*.

LODGING

Brewster has it all, from first-class inns and homey B&Bs to resort condos and family cottages. The zip code for Brewster is 02631.

RESORT

✳🐾 **Ocean Edge Resort** (Great Vacations booking agent: 508-896-2090, 1-800-626-9984; Resort and Conference Center: 508-896-9000, 1-800-343-6074; www.oceanedge.com), 2660 Route 6A. Open year-round if booking directly through the hotel; town houses available through Great Vacations late May to mid-October. Once part of the vast Roland

Nickerson estate (see *Green Space*), this 380-acre complex includes a Gothic and Renaissance Revival stucco mansion (now a hotel and conference center) and 17 private, contemporary condominium "villages." I recommend renting condos through Great Vacations. Units are configured as **apartments,** two-story **town houses** (with one, two, and three bedrooms), and Cape **cottages.** Some units are bayside; others overlook the golf course. All have "real" backyards, and most are within walking distance of resort facilities. Great Vacations is good at matching your needs with the right unit. If you want to stay at the hotel/mansion, book directly through the resort. Resort facilities include indoor and outdoor pools, a private 1,000-foot bayside beach (for bayside rentals only), four restaurants, a fitness center, a playground, and organized programs for kids age 4–10 (for a fee). Golf and tennis packages, with and without instruction, are available through the resort on a "pay-as-you-play" basis. Condos booked with Great Vacations: July to early September, $975–2,400 weekly for two bedrooms, $1,825–2,500 weekly for three bedrooms (Saturday-to-Saturday rentals), more for bayside rentals. Stay in June or after Labor Day in September and shave about $300–500 off these rates. Inquire about off-season 3-night minimums and hotel-room rates.

INNS

Bramble Inn (508-896-7644), 2019 Route 6A. Open mid-May to late October. Innkeepers Cliff and Ruth Manchester opened the historic Bramble Inn in 1985 and offer eight comfortable rooms in two mid-19th-century buildings. The cozy guest rooms are really Cliff's domain and he has meticulously high standards. I particularly like the rooms in the adjacent building with a shared living room. Room 5 is typical of the country traditional rooms, featuring wide sanded floors, antiques, Oriental carpets, and a lacy four-poster canopy bed. All have air-conditioning. Ruth Manchester, a very talented chef (see *Dining Out*), includes a full breakfast of, perhaps, strata, bacon, and breads. $115–165.

Chillingsworth (508-896-3640; 1-800-430-3640; www.chillingsworth. com), 2449 Route 6A. Open late May to late November. This 1689 house, believed to be Brewster's second oldest house, rents three European-style guest rooms above the restaurant (see *Dining Out*). The antiques-filled Stevenson Room boasts a private entrance and four-poster bed—it's the largest and nicest of the rooms. The Foster Room has views of the back gardens and gazebo, and although the Ten Eyck Room is small and without a view, it's nonetheless charming. All have private bath, TV, and air-conditioning. If you are traveling with a child, there is a small single that shares a bath with the Foster Room and rents for $20. Room rates include afternoon wine and cheese, a full breakfast, access to a private beach at the end of the street, and privileges at a private club with an indoor/outdoor pool, tennis courts, and golf. $110–150.

Brewster's Stony Brook Grist Mill

KIM GRANT

&.✿Old Sea Pines Inn (508-896-6114; www.oldseapinesinn.com), 2553 Route
6A. Open late April to late December. In 1907 the Old Sea Pines Inn was
the Sea Pines School of Charm and Personality for Young Women.
Today, longtime, hospitable hosts Michele and Steve Rowan combine
1920s and '30s nostalgia with modern comforts. All 21 rooms and two
suites are pleasant, furnished with old brass or iron beds and antiques.
The less expensive "classrooms" are small and share baths—it will be easy
to imagine yourself as a young girl at boarding school. Rooms in the rear

annex are handicap accessible and more modern, with TVs. Four economical family suites each sleep four people. The house is set on 3½ acres, and there's plenty of space to relax inside, too, including a large, comfy living room with fireplace that leads onto the wraparound porch set with rockers. On Sunday evening in summer, the Cape Repertory Theatre holds a Broadway musical dinner revue here (see *Entertainment*), and cocktails and hors d'oevres are served under the canopied deck. Full breakfast included. July and August $85–135 double, $125–135 for three or four people in a family suite; $5–20 less off-season.

✿ **High Brewster** (508-896-3636; 1-800-203-2634), 964 Satucket Road. Open April through November. On a 3½ -acre countryside parcel overlooking a pond, High Brewster offers three lovely **cottages** and two antiques-appointed inn rooms (best suited to independent travelers). The 1738 homestead, in one family for more than 200 years, retains its Colonial charm, right down to the low-ceiling dining rooms (see *Dining Out*) and steep, narrow stairs that lead to the guest rooms. As for the cottages, Brook House has a full kitchen, two bedrooms, a fireplace, and a large deck; Barn Cottage also sleeps four with a loft, full kitchen, fireplace, patio, and private yard. My favorite is the romantic Pond Cottage—bright white with a large screened-in porch and an efficiency kitchen. Rooms $95–115 nightly; cottages $1,000–1,400 weekly in July and August, $165–220 nightly. Pets permitted in cottages for slight additional charge.

BED & BREAKFASTS

❄ **Captain Freeman Inn** (508-896-7481; 1-800-843-4664; www.captain freemaninn.com), 15 Breakwater Road. Next to the Brewster Store (see *To See*) on the town green, the 1866 Captain Freeman Inn has been gussied up with four-poster canopy beds, sanded hardwood floors, designer window treatments, and air-conditioning. It's one of the best inns on Route 6A, innkeeper presence being one of the prime reasons. Two other big factors are a private pool and the most decadently healthy breakfasts on the Cape. Of the 12 rooms, 6 are upscale suites with television, VCR, mini-fridge, fireplace, and whirlpool bath on a private enclosed porch. One particularly secluded room (off the dining area) overlooks the garden. Some traditional quarters, many of which are large corner rooms, boast inlaid floors and oversize windows. All rooms have sitting areas, but there are also two living rooms, the cozier one with a working wood fireplace. Innkeepers Carol and Tom Edmondson offer a full breakfast. Perhaps you'll feast on a pint of blueberries with fat-free crème fraîche on the side and strawberry rhubarb cobbler served in individual ramekins. Carol is an expert cook who specializes in tasty low-fat creations; she holds cooking classes on many winter weekends (see *Even More Things to See and Do—Cooking School*). Mid-May through October $140–250; off-season $115–190.

❀ **The Blue Cedar Bed & Breakfast** (508-896-4353; www.thebluecedar.

com), 699 Route 6A. Open mid-May to mid-October. New in 2000, this 1840 farmhouse has been completely renovated but still retains wide pine flooring, latch doors, and some exposed post-and-beam construction. Innkeepers Diane and Clyde Mosher have only three rooms, all with private bath, and all with tranquil colors. Room 1 was the original Brewster farmhouse and boasts a large bathroom and pencil-post bed. Room 2 is quite large, with a spiffy bathroom combining contemporary black and white tilework with traditional wainscoting. Room 3 is even larger. Thankfully, the rooms are not overdecorated; devoid of knick-knacks. An expanded continental breakfast is served on the screened-in, wicker-filled patio. $100–125.

Ruddy Turnstone (508-385-9871; 1-800-654-1995), 463 Route 6A. Open March through October. This is one of only two B&Bs on Route 6A with a view of Cape Cod Bay and the salt marsh. And what a view it is! If the weather is good, you'll enjoy it from the garden, under the fruit trees, or from a hammock. If it's cold or rainy, a second-floor common room has a large picture window with an unobstructed view. This early-19th-century Cape-style house has four guest rooms and one large suite (which boasts a fireplace and view) appointed with antiques, Oriental carpets, and luxurious feather beds. The adjacent barn, recently restored and furnished with pencil-post canopy beds and quilts, offers a bit more privacy. It's also rustic—in a good way. Hosts Swanee and Sally Swanson offer a full breakfast. June through October $110–175; off-season $80–135.

🏅 **Old Manse Inn** (508-896-3149; www.oldmanseinn.com), 1861 Route 6A. Open April through December. This recently renovated, historic 1801 inn has eight guest rooms with air-conditioning, private bath, and newly redone bathrooms. Most have cable TV. I particularly like room 4, the largest, with hardwood floors and a spacious bathroom, and room 3, completely redecorated with a four-poster pencil-post bed. Third floor rooms benefit from high, mansard-ceiling rooflines. One room can accommodate an extra person. A full buffet breakfast, with particularly noteworthy pastries and baked goods, is included. On my last visit it included baked Swedish pancakes filled with fruit, with a side of broiled tomatoes. There are always sweets and teas left out on the sideboard. The inn has a fine dining room (see *Dining Out*). $115–135.

❄ **Brewster Farmhouse Inn** (508-896-3910; 1-800-892-3910; www.brewster farmhouseinn.com), 716 Route 6A. This Greek Revival farmhouse has a light-infused reception area with one large dining table and a small sitting area with a fireplace. The inn boasts three luxurious suites within the newly constructed, adjacent carriage house. Each has a gas fireplace and whirlpool tub. I prefer the upstairs suites, because they feel more spacious. Within the main house, there are four more very stylish guest rooms and a two-bedroom suite (rented as separate rooms with shared bath off-season). These also feature luxurious amenities like thick towels, fine bedding, and nightly turndown with chocolates. One room has a private deck; another has a fireplace. The back deck, where afternoon tea is served, leads to a heated pool and hot-tub area nicely landscaped with big blue hydrangeas. Full breakfast included. Late May to mid-October $165–225; off-season $145–175.

* **Greylin House** (508-896-0004; 1-800-233-6662; www.capecodtravel.com/greylin), 2311 Route 6A. Open April through November. Built in 1837, this snug house is light and airy, featuring a comfortably gracious, antiques-filled living room with fireplace. With the exception of the yellow room, most second-floor guest quarters are on the small side but with nice sanded floors; all are air-conditioned. Included in the rates: morning newspaper, afternoon tea, and a continental breakfast enjoyed fireside or on the quiet, back-side patio. Mid-May to mid-October $85–125; off-season $70–85. Well-behaved dogs ($15 fee) with prior approval.

COTTAGES AND APARTMENTS

Linger Longer By The Sea (508-240-2211; www.capecodtravel.com/lingerlonger), 261 Linnell Landing Beach. Open April through November. Off a sandy lane and within a sandal shuffle of a private stretch of Linnell Landing Beach, this place is perfect for families who appreciate not having to pile into a car or cross a busy street to get to the beach. A few of the 10 cottages have been completely remodeled, and all of the six apartments overlook Cape Cod Bay. All have decks, barbecue grills, linens, and picnic tables. Some have a fireplace. Late June through August $800–1,175 weekly for a studio or one-bedroom unit, $950–1,725 weekly for a two-, three-, or four-bedroom. Off-season, cottages and apartments are rented with a 2-night minimum.

Ellis Landing Cottages (508-896-5072), Ellis Landing. Open late May to mid-October. Only dune grasses and sandy lanes separate these 15 cozy waterfront and water-view cottages from the bay. In Gil Ellis's family since the 1930s, most of the refurbished and simply furnished house-keeping cottages were built by his father in the 1940s and 1950s. At the end of a quiet side road off Route 6A, the pine-paneled cottages have complete kitchens; many have fireplaces. Some are more rustic than others. My favorite is the cozy Rest Haven Cottage, once the East Brewster railroad station. It was moved here in the 1930s by Gil's grandfather and converted into a cottage. It features a private garden, screened-in porch, and three bedrooms. Late June to early September $1,800 weekly for a three-bedroom waterfront cottage, $1,600 weekly for a two-bedroom waterfront cottage, $1,000 weekly for a two-bedroom off-the-water cottage. Off-season, cottages go for $700–1,000 weekly or can be rented for a 3-night minimum. No credit cards.

* **Michael's Cottages** (508-896-4025; 1-800-399-2967), 618 Route 6A. Open late March to late October. Set back from the road in a pine grove, these five tidy cottages (one is really a small house) are a good bargain; proprietor Michael DiVito maintains them nicely. Most have a screened-

in porch, all have air-conditioning, four have a fireplace. The small house sleeps six and features a full living room. It's a 15-minute walk to a bayside beach. Linen service is included in the price. July and August $625–700 weekly for two, $15 each additional person over age 5; $1,025 weekly for four in the small house; $75–105 nightly off-season. Credit cards not accepted in-season.

See also High Brewster under *Inns*.

RENTAL HOUSES AND COTTAGES

Stonecroft-Abbott Real Estate (508-896-2290), Foster Square, 2655 Route 6A. A friendly agency with good listings.

Vacation Cape Cod/Kinlin-Grover GMAC (508-896-7004; www. vacationcapecod.com), 1900 Route 6A. This agency has about 200 listings, from studios to two-bedroom knotty-pine cottages and year-round-like homes with four bedrooms. The bulk of rentals are booked November through March (for the following summer), but if you wait until July, they can still probably find something for you.

See also Ocean Edge Resort under *Resort*.

CAMPGROUNDS

Nickerson State Park (1-877-422-6762 for high-season reservations; 508-896-3491 for general information), 3488 Route 6A. Open year-round. Since Nickerson is the second busiest campground in the state, summer reservations are absolutely essential and are accepted six months in advance for 80 percent of the 418 available sites. In summer, other sites are first come, first served—you often can't even get one for 5 days or so, even after waiting in line at 6 AM. (You'd think you were waiting in line for Rolling Stones tickets.) There is a 14-day limit in summer. $12–15; pets permitted. (See also Green Space.)

Alternatives to Nickerson State Park include **Shady Knoll Campground** (508-896-3002), Route 6A at Route 137, and **Sweetwater Forest** (508-896-3773), off Route 124, set on 60 acres abutting a freshwater lake. Both accept reservations. Sweetwater is open year-round.

WHERE TO EAT

Brewster has a wide variety of really great restaurants. In fact, with the exception of Provincetown, no other town has a better selection. Even if you're staying in an adjacent town, I bet you'll cross the town line to dine in Brewster at least once. When you exhaust these possibilities, head to Cape Sea Grille in Harwich.

DINING OUT

Bramble Inn (508-896-7644), 2019 Route 6A. Open for dinner weekends mid-May to late October and nightly except Monday in summer. The exceptional New American and internationally inspired cuisine, gracious service, and five intimate dining rooms are the result of chef-owner Ruth Manchester's creative talents. Place settings are mix-and-

194   THE LOWER CAPE

match antique china, elegantly casual and romantic. Dine by candle-light from a broad, prix fixe menu that changes every few weeks. House specialties include veal with Shiitake mushrooms, parchment-roasted chicken with grilled lobster, and assorted seafood curries. This place is underrated; I've never talked with a diner who was less than wholly satisfied. There's no entertainment in the dining room, unless you con-sider Ruth's husband Cliff; they've presided here since 1984. Four-course dinners $43–68; by reservation only.

Old Manse Inn (508-896-3149), 1861 Route 6A. Open for dinner April through December (nightly except Monday in-season). This old inn got a new lease on life in 1997 when Culinary Institute of America gradu-ates David and Suzanne Plum took over. (Suzanne has cooking in her genes; Ruth Manchester—see Bramble Inn, above—is her mother.) The far-reaching intercontinental bistro menu changes every 4 to 6 weeks and might include an olive-crusted or Szechuan shellacked seared salmon; curried coconut shrimp soup or Indian chicken mulligatawny soup; *chiles rellenos de bacalao,* homemade lamb sau-sage, or Long Island duck breast. I recently enjoyed plump seared scal-lops with soba noodles in a ginger carrot broth. My spinach salad with figs was delicately dressed. Vegetarians are not overlooked here either. Suzanne bakes breads and desserts in the morning and hostesses in the evening. Save room for double-crust cinnamony peach pie with homemade ice cream or a chocolate and red raspberry flourless torte. The dining rooms, with muted yellow and aquamarine walls further enlivened by local art, are elegantly casual and the waitstaff professional and knowledgeable about wine pairing. While it's a romantic place, the affair is really with the center-stage cuisine. Entrées $18–35.

Brewster Fish House (508-896-7867), 2208 Route 6A. Open daily for lunch and dinner, early April to early December. Run, don't walk. This small roadside bistro doesn't look like much from the outside, but inside it is quite pleasant, with white table linens, Windsor chairs, fresh flowers, high ceilings, and a small bar. There is always a steady stream of customers who appreciate a friendly staff and consistently well-prepared, very fresh seafood at somewhat reasonable prices. With the exception of luncheon specials (which are quite creative), the midday choices are simple: grilled and broiled seafood and fish served on mod plates. Try the chowder or lobster bisque, which has a nice spicy kick to it. For dinner, try any of David and Vernon Smith's (chef-owners) innovative specials. Sea scal-lops with sun-dried tomatoes, garlic, and tarragon is a good bet. Save room for crème brûlée at dinner. Arrive before 7 PM or expect to wait at least an hour—as much as an hour and 45 minutes in summer—no reservations accepted. Put your name on the list and walk across the street to the beach; they'll honor your position on the list when you return. Lunch $8–12, dinner entrées $15–25.

Chillingsworth (508-896-3640; 1-800-430-3640), 2449 Route 6A. Open for lunch and dinner, late May to late November (fine dining closed Monday in July and August); off-season schedule varies. There is nothing I can say about Chillingsworth that hasn't been said before, by *Bon Appétit*, *Gourmet*, and other arbiters of haute cuisine. Seven-course, prix fixe French/California-style dinners are served at two seatings (one off-season); choose the early seating, unless you want to be eating until 11:30 or midnight. The small, candlelit dining rooms, filled with antiques (some dating to Louis XV), feel rather like salons; service is well paced and discreet. There are always a dozen or so appetizers and entrées on the menu, which changes daily. Do pace yourself. An exclusive gazebo degustation menu is offered with advance notice. Gourmands might want to inquire. For those with less of an appetite (and wallet), a bistro menu is served in the airy greenhouse or alfresco. À la carte luncheons in the greenhouse (or alfresco) are a relaxing, decadent endeavor. Chef "Nitzi" Rabin and his wife, Pat, proudly preside. Bistro lunch $10–14, dinner $15-25; fine dining $55–65. Reservations required for fine dining, suggested for the bistro; jacket suggested for dinner.

High Brewster (508-896-3636), 964 Satucket Road. Open for dinner April through November (Wednesday through Sunday in the shoulder seasons). High Brewster remains a top choice for dining, thanks to the tenure of chef Robert Hickey. On my last visit, we enjoyed two specialties: rack of lamb with pink peppercorn demiglaze and polenta, as well as broiled swordfish topped with tomatoes, bread crumbs, and Asiago and served with scallion fritters. Three charming dining rooms in this 1738 farmhouse are romantic: candlelight, low ceilings, exposed beams, wood floors, antique paneling, fresh flowers, and ladder-back chairs. Four-course dinners range from $38 for the vegetarian meal to $65 for the rack of lamb. Reservations required.

EATING OUT

✳✿ **Cafe Alfresco** (508-896-1741), Lemon Tree Village, 1097 Route 6A. Open for breakfast and lunch year-round. This modest café offers breakfast (eggs any style, omelets, and croissants), lunch sandwiches (lobster rolls, grilled chicken, and smoked salmon), great soups and homemade bread, and nightly specials like fish-and-chips, scallop rolls, and chicken salad. The grilled portobello mushroom sandwich is particularly good. There are a few outdoor tables where you hear trickling water fountains, but most people sit inside. Children will find plenty to their liking here. Coffee drinks and dessert, too. Dishes $4–10.

Breakwater Fish (508-896-7080), 235 Underpass Road. Open mid-March through December. Cyclists on the Rail Trail can get serious eats at this fish market: oysters, clamcakes, smoked salmon rolls. If you're renting a cottage, these folks have excellent fish and lobsters, too. They'll even steam lobsters for you.

✿ **JT's** (508-896-3355), 2689 Route 6A, across from Ocean Edge. Open for lunch and dinner mid-April to mid-October. Picnic-style fried seafood platters, seafood rolls, and crabcakes at reasonable prices. I always choose from the specials board, which has never disappointed. Expect to spend about $10–12 per adult; children's menu.

🖋 **Cobie's** (508-896-7021), 3260 Route 6A. Open for lunch and dinner, mid-May to mid-September. Serving northside patrons since 1948. I like Cobie's seafood shack for its charbroiled burgers and covered picnic tables near the pine trees. It's convenient for Rail Trail cyclists (see *Outdoor Activities—Bicycling/Rentals*). Children's menu. Lunch $3–6, dinner $8–12.

PICNICS, SEAFOOD, SNACKS, AND ICE CREAM

Le Bistrot (508-896-3640), 2449 Route 6A. Open late May to late November. Assorted gourmet picnic fixings—from pâté and focaccia to cheeses and pastries, from lemon tea cakes to chocolate roulade.

Satucket Farm Stand (508-896-5540), Route 124 just off Route 6A. Open seasonally. An old-fashioned open-air stand with farm-fresh produce including great corn, pies, soups, salads, baked goods, jams, honey, and cheeses; a popular spot for local chefs.

Brewster Scoop (508-896-7824), Route 6A. Open mid-June to early September. Behind the Brewster Store, this small shop is a purveyor of Bliss Dairy's sugar-free ice cream and nonfat frozen yogurt.

❄ **Brewster Express** (508-896-6682) and **Box Lunch** (508-896-1234), both on the bike trail on Underpass Road, offer ice cream and sandwiches to hungry cyclists. Box Lunch has exceptional Four Seas ice cream from Centerville, but Brewster Express has picnic tables under scrub oaks. It boils down to this: Do you like your sandwich meats and cheese rolled up in pita bread or more traditional?

See also Breakwater Fish, under *Eating Out*.

ENTERTAINMENT

🖋 **Band concerts** (508-896-7770), Drummer Boy Park, Route 6A, 1½ miles west of Route 137. July and August concerts Sunday at 6 PM at the gazebo.

🖋❄ **Cape Repertory Theatre** (508-896-1888 for schedule information; www.caperep.org), 3397 Route 6A. Under the directorship of Bob Troie, who has New York credits to his name, the company presents engaging open-air theater in the woods (on the former Crosby estate), performances at its new 140-seat indoor theater, and a musical dinner revue at the Old Sea Pines Inn (see *Lodging—Inns*) on Sunday night in summer. Indoor shows daily except Sunday and Monday, May through November. Tickets $14–18 adults, $7–8 children. Children's productions $6 on Tuesday and Friday morning.

🖋 **Baseball.** The Brewster Whitecaps, which joined the Cape Cod Baseball League in 1988 as an expansion team, play at the Cape Cod Technical High School, Route 124, Harwich. From June to early August, games begin at 5 PM.

SELECTIVE SHOPPING

❄ Unless otherwise noted, all shops are open year-round.

ANTIQUARIAN BOOKS

Punkhorn Bookshop (508-896-2114), 672 Route 6A. Open daily except Monday. David Luebke deals in rare, quality used books from the ground floor of his house. Specialties include Cape Cod, New England, natural history, fine arts, and biographies. Selections are well organized and categorized by the Dewey decimal system. Free search service.

Kings Way Books and Antiques (508-896-3639), 774 Route 6A. Proprietor Dick Socky specializes in out-of-print and rare books. The collection includes medieval and modern history, biography, architecture, archaeology, and nature books. The antique cherrywood shelves were salvaged from the New Haven, Connecticut, public library. As for their select small antiques, most are book-related items. Free search service.

ANTIQUES

Dozens of antiques shops line Route 6A; only a sampling follows.

Breton House Antiques (508-896-3974), 1222 Stony Brook Road. After 20 years in business, it's no surprise that the three floors of antiques leave very little room to maneuver.

Wysteria Antiques, Etc. (508-896-8650), 1199 Route 6A. Open May through October. Between the purple exterior, an overwhelming scent of wisteria once you cross the threshold, and three rooms filled top to bottom with purple glassware and porcelain, it's safe to say this is one unusual establishment. The owners have a good eye, even if the presentation is over the top.

Spyglass Antiques (508-896-4423), 2257 Route 6A. Eighteenth- and 19th-century American furniture and accessories.

ARTISANS

Brewster Pottery (508-896-3587), 437 Harwich Road. Open April through December. Potter Marion Eckhardt moved to this house in 1947 and opened her shop in 1960. Since then she's had young apprentices from all over the country learning hand-built and wheel-thrown pottery. One young man came to learn the craft when he was 15 and is still here (now in his 40s). Marion's functional and whimsical porcelain and stoneware (birdbaths, birdhouses, fountains) are lovely, made all the more so by watching her work.

Heart Pottery (508-896-6189), 1145 Route 6A. Open daily except Sunday. Specializing in functional and decorative porcelain, raku, and stoneware, Diane Heart spends most days at her wheel here in the shop. Her raku, using an ancient Japanese firing technique, is particularly fine.

Clayworks (508-255-4937), 3820 Route 6A. A bit more unconventional than other Cape potters, Clayton Calderwood works in porcelain, stoneware, and terra-cotta and creates interesting abstract sculptures, large fish platters, and mammoth urns.

Kemp Pottery (508-385-5782), 258 Route 6A. Open daily except Sunday, May through September. Stoneware and porcelain: fountains, garden sculpture, abstract pieces, stained glass, and decorative and functional forms made with sand from Nauset Beach. Kemp also has a bigger shop in Orleans.

The Woodwright (508-896-3393), 2091 Route 6A. Open weekdays, and Saturday by appointment. Before you leave home, measure your needy window casings or door frames and have Leonard Courchesne replace them for you. He's an expert in restoration, reproduction, custom design, and millwork.

ART GALLERIES

Underground Art Gallery (508-896-6850; 508-896-3757), 673 Satucket Road. This working studio sits beneath 100 tons of soil and is supported by 10 tree trunks. The gallery features the work of watercolorist Karen North Wells, who also uses oil and acrylic for her seascapes and landscape florals. Her husband, Malcolm Wells, who is also a painter, designs earth-covered solar buildings like this one. Passing bicyclists are encouraged to make use of Malcolm's composting toilet.

Maddocks Gallery (508-896-6223), 1283 Route 6A. Open March through December and by appointment off-season. James Maddocks paints nostalgic traditionalist and representational Cape Cod scenes. His gallery, where you'll often find him painting and where he's also happy to talk with visitors, is an 1840s carriage house attached to his home. Less expensive limited-edition prints, too.

Ruddeforth Gallery (508-255-1056), 3753 Route 6A. Watercolors, oils, and lithographs of Cape Cod scenes, florals, and still lifes by Debra Ruddeforth (a signature member of the Copley Society in Boston). Husband Tom Ruddeforth's color and black-and-white photographs are also displayed.

Franny Golden (508-896-6353; www.frannygolden.com), 502 Harwich Road. The road sign proclaims FINE ART; the work within Franny's home/ studio defies easy interpretation. There are some portraits, some landscapes (sort of), some expressionist abstracts, many visual journals that have to do with experience. She works a lot with process. Franny teaches part time at Cape Cod Community College (the "4Cs") and does a local public TV cable show. This is not your standard Cape fare. Bigger pieces go for $2,000–8,000.

Millstone Sculpture Gallery (508-896-2452), 3090 Route 6A. Open late April through October. In a converted four-bay garage, Benton Jones displays his personal explorations of the dark unconscious and shadow sides. Employing various metals and materials, his pieces might be titled BALANCE (with four heads on a balance beam) or CONTAINED (a person pushing within the confines of a box). This is not your typical Route 6A art.

Struna Galleries (508-255-6618), 3873 Route 6A. Working from copper plates to make dry point engravings, artist Tim Struna creates sweet little renderings of Cape Cod scenes. They're a nice (and affordable) reminder of why life on the Cape is so special. Since his studio is here, you'll often find Tim hard at work. He also sells larger watercolors.

BOOKSTORE

Brewster Book Store (508-896-6543), 2648 Route 6A. A large and excellent offering of children's books within a small space. Also Cape Cod titles, games, toys, story time, and book signings.

SPECIAL SHOPS

Eve's Place (508-896-4914), 564 Route 6A. Eve Roulier lived for eight years in Hawaii, where she learned all about pearls. Now, from this modest little Cape house, she buys directly from growers, strings her own pearls, sells antique pearls, and talks extensively about rare black Tahitian pearls, pearls from Kobe, Japan, and freshwater pearls from China. She'll tell you that cultured pearls are created by injecting an irritant into an oyster's shell and that about 40 percent of the oysters die as a result of the injection. Those that don't die secrete a substance (nacre, the basis of the pearl) in reaction to the irritant. It then takes about three or four years for the pearl to mature. Whether you're ready to buy, just want to learn about pearls, or need some pearls restrung, Eve is the one to talk to.

Spectrum (508-385-3322), 369 Route 6A. This shop, which opened in 1966, displays a most wonderful collection of high-quality contemporary crafts and fine art. It represents more than 500 craftspeople from all over the country. I hesitate to itemize even a few of their pieces, because I don't want to limit your imagination. Two floors of beautifully designed objects (blown glass, woodworking products, handmade jewelry, textiles), plus sculpture that spills out-of-doors.

Sydenstricker Galleries (508-385-3272), 490 Route 6A. Open daily. Glass-fusing demonstrations, using a technique developed by Brewster native Bill Sydenstricker (who died in 1994), are given 10–2:30 daily except Sunday. Sydenstricker glass is used in two American embassies and displayed in museum collections around the country.

Spyglass (508-896-4423), 2257 Route 6A. Although this exceptional shop is best known for its telescope collection, there are all sorts of nautical antiques like barometers, sextants, maps, charts, and even a few paintings and sea captain portraits. It's great to poke around when you begin to lose sight of the Cape's maritime connection.

The Cook Shop (508-896-7698), Lemon Tree Village, Route 6A. Open daily. Although you probably didn't come to the Cape with thoughts of cookware, this shop has just about everything a serious or would-be cook needs to outfit an impressive kitchen. Apparently many other people think so, too; the shop has been here since 1978.

Great Cape Cod Herb, Spice & Tea Co. (508-896-5900; or 1-800-427-7144; www.greatcape.com), 2628 Route 6A. Open daily. With more than

170 varieties of Western and Chinese herbs in stock, this herbal apothecary may well be the largest retailer of its kind in New England. Proprietor Stephan Brown (who opened the rustic shop in 1991) also stocks a selection of New Age literature on health and well-being. The herb farm is certified organic for medicinal herbs; ginkgo trees are a specialty. Weekly herb-identification "weed walks" May through September.

SPECIAL EVENTS

April to early May: **Herring run.** Hundreds of thousands of alewives (herring) return from the salt water to lay their eggs in the same freshwater ponds where they were born (see Stony Brook Grist Mill and Museum and Herring Run under *To See*).

Last weekend in April: **Brewster in Bloom.** Faith Dibble proposed the idea to plant 100,000 daffodils in 1983. Today, there's an annual festival celebrating the bright yellow flowers that line the already picturesque streets. Events include an arts and crafts festival, food festival, and parade.

Mid-September: **Bird Carvers Exhibit,** at the Cape Cod Museum of Natural History (Route 6A; see *To See*). One of the premier exhibits of its kind in the country boasts carving and painting demonstrations. A fundraising event for the museum since 1976.

Harwich

Harwich isn't nearly as developed as its westerly neighbors, although its stretch of Route 28 does have its share of bumper boats, mini-golf courses, and go-carts. In fact, the town exudes a somewhat nonchalant air. It's as if the 11,000 year-rounders are collectively saying, "This is what we have and you're welcome to come and enjoy it with us if you wish"—which is not to say that Harwich doesn't attract visitors. It boasts a wide range of places to stay and eat, from the fanciest Victorian inn to the most humble B&B, from fine French cuisine to roasted chicken-on-a-spit. At the same time, although Harwich has more saltwater and freshwater beaches than any other town on the Cape, only a few have parking for day-use visitors.

Harwich, mostly blue collar and middle class, comprises seven distinct villages and is blessed with one of the most picturesque harbors on the Cape, Wychmere Harbor. Nearby, lovely Saquatucket Harbor is reserved for fishing charters and ferry service to Nantucket. It's worth poking around the quiet center of Harwich, with its historic homes standing in marked contrast to the heavily developed areas just a mile or so away. Harwich, which bills its annual Cranberry Harvest Festival as "the biggest small-town celebration in the country," lays claims to cultivating the first commercial cranberry bog.

GUIDANCE

Harwich Chamber of Commerce (508-432-1600; 1-800-441-3199; www.harwichcc.com), Route 28, P.O. Box 34, Harwichport 02646. Open 9–5 daily late May to mid-September; 9–5 on weekends, mid-September to mid-October. An informed chamber staff and a well-organized, townwide publication make Harwich an easy place to navigate. Pick up their good biking and walking trail maps. For information in the off-season, head four doors down to the Cape Cod Five Cents Savings Bank. You can park for free in the booth's large parking lot and walk to Bank Street Beach.

❄☙↑ PUBLIC LIBRARIES

Call for hours:

Brooks Free Library (508-430-7562), 739 Main Street, Harwich; newly renovated and expanded;

Chase Library (508-432-2610), Route 28, West Harwich;

Harwichport Library (508-432-3320), 47 Banks Street.

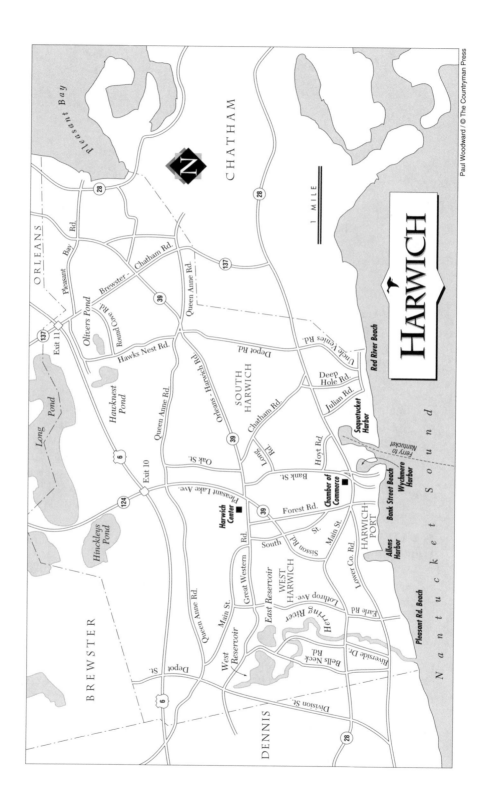

PLEASANT BAY

ORLEANS

CHATHAM

28

N

28

1 MILE

Pleasant Bay Rd.

Brewster - Chatham Rd.

Queen Anne Rd.

137

39

Olivers Pond

Round Cove Rd.

Exit 11

137

Hawks Nest Rd.

Depot Rd.

SOUTH HARWICH

Uncle Venies Rd.

Red River Beach

HARWICH

Hawknest Pond

Long Pond

6

Queen Anne Rd.

Orleans - Harwich Rd.

Chatham Rd.

Deep Hole Rd.

Julian Rd.

Saquatucket Harbor

Nantucket Sound

39

Long Rd.

Hoyt Rd.

Ferry to Nantucket

Exit 10

Oak St.

Bank St.

Chamber of Commerce

Bank Street Beach

Wychmere Harbor

124

Hinckleys Pond

Pleasant Lake Ave.

Harwich Center

39

Forest Rd.

St.

Main St.

HARWICH PORT

Allens Harbor

Rd.

South

Sisson Rd.

Lower Co. Rd.

BREWSTER

Queen Anne Rd.

Main St.

Great Western

East Reservoir

WEST HARWICH

Lothrop Ave.

Earle Rd.

Herring River

Pleasant Rd. Beach

Nantucket Sound

Depot St.

West Reservoir

Bells Neck Rd.

Riverside Dr.

6

Division St.

DENNIS

28

INTERNET ACCESS

✻✿ **CyberDocks** (508-430-1555), 565A Route 28, Harwichport. Computer games, networked so kids can play together, and Internet access on a dozen computers. $5 for 30 minutes, but other increments available. Check your e-mail while you're away without carrying your laptop.

PUBLIC REST ROOMS

Public rest rooms are located at the chamber parking lot (see *Guidance*) and at Brooks Park on Route 39 and Oak Street.

GETTING THERE

By car: Take Route 6 from either bridge across the canal to exit 10 (Route 124 south and Route 39 south) to Route 28, or take exit 11 to Route 137 for East Harwich. It takes 35–40 minutes to reach Harwich from the canal.

By bus: The **Plymouth & Brockton** bus line (508-778-9767; www.p-b.com) connects Harwich with Hyannis and other Cape towns, as well as with Boston's Logan Airport. The bus stops at the commuter lot near the intersection of Routes 6 and 124.

GETTING TO NANTUCKET

By ferry: There is seasonal passenger ferry service to Nantucket from Harwichport. For many people, this service is more convenient than going into Hyannis to catch a boat. For complete information, see Getting There in "Nantucket."

GETTING AROUND

By car: Route 28 is also called Main Street. (This is not to be confused with the Main Street—aka Route 39—in the center of Harwich, which is inland.) Although most points of interest are located along or off the developed Route 28, head inland to explore Harwich's ponds and conservation areas.

By bus: The **H₂O** (508-385-8326; 1-800-352-7155; www.capecodtransit.org) bus line, used by more locals than visitors, travels along Route 28 between Hyannis and Orleans daily except Sunday year-round. It stops at Star Market in Harwichport.

MEDICAL EMERGENCY

Long Pond Medical Center (508-432-4100), off Route 137, Harwich. Walk-ins 9–4:45 weekdays and 9–noon Saturday.

OUTDOOR ACTIVITIES

All listings are in Harwich Center unless otherwise noted.

BICYCLING/RENTALS

About 5 miles of the **Cape Cod Rail Trail** run through Harwich; you can pick up the trail near the Pleasant Lake General Store on Route 124 and off Great Western Road near Herring Run Road. The chamber of commerce publishes a good biking map. **Harwichport Bike Company Inc.** (508-430-0200), 431 Route 28, rents bicycles.

Harwich cultivated the country's first commercial cranberry bog; it celebrates with a Cranberry Harvest Festival in mid-September.

BOATING AND CANOEING

Red River Beach, off Depot Road. Canoes may be launched from the east end of this beach (see *Green Space—Beaches*).

✳ **Cape Water Sports** (508-432-5996), at the junction of Routes 28 and 124. The Herring River, which runs north to a reservoir and south to Nantucket Sound, is great for canoeing. This shop rents canoes by the day ($65) or week ($350); you can also rent Sunfish.

Saquatucket Harbor, Route 28. With 200 berths, this is the largest municipal marina on the Cape; about 10 slips are reserved for transient visitors.

Wychmere Harbor, Harbor Road off Route 28. A large fleet of sloops is often moored here, making it one of the most scenic (albeit man-made) harbors on the Cape. In the late 1800s, Wychmere Harbor was simply a salt pond, around which a racetrack was laid. But locals, disapproving of horse racing, convinced the town to cut an opening from the pond into Nantucket Sound. Thus the harbor was born.

Allens Harbor, on Lower County Road, is the town's other picturesque, well-protected, and man-made harbor; it has a docking ramp.

See also Herring River/Sand Pond Conservation Area under *Green Space— Walks.*

FISHING/SHELLFISHING

Shellfishing permits ($15 per nonresident family per day, $30 per season) are obtained from the Town Hall (508-430-7513) on Route 39 weekdays 8:30–4, and from the harbormaster (508-430-7532) at Saquatucket Harbor 8–4 on weekends, June through September.

A number of charter fishing boats depart from Saquatucket Harbor, Route 28, including the **Yankee** (508-432-2520). From Wychmere Harbor off Route 28, the **Golden Eagle** (508-432-5611) offers deep-sea-fishing trips, $21–30 per person, for 2- or 6-hour trips, mid-May to mid-October. Rod, reel, bait, and fish bag included.

Try your luck casting from a jetty at Red River Beach (see *Green Space— Beaches*) or the Herring River Bridge in West Harwich.

❄ **Fishing the Cape** (508-432-1200), Routes 137 and 39, Harwich commons. From May through August, the king of fly-fishing—Orvis—offers a 2 ½-day saltwater fly-fishing course for $430. (The price includes lunch for you and food for the fish.) Guided fishing trips, too. A full line of Orvis supplies, flies, and tackle is sold at the shop, open year-round.

FOR FAMILIES
Grand Slam Entertainment (508-430-1155), 322 Route 28. Open late May to mid-September (9 AM–11 PM daily in summer). Batting cages with varying degrees of difficulty and bumper boats for toddlers to teens. Also, a radar pitching cage and one of the world's only Wiffle ball cages for kids.

Trampoline Center (508-432-8717), 296 Route 28. Open weekends only, late May to late June and early September to mid-October; 9 AM–11 PM daily, late June to early September. There are no age or height restrictions; the only limit at this outdoor center is that kids can't do flips.

Bud's Go-Karts (508-432-4964), 9 Sisson Road, at Route 28. Open 9 AM–11 PM daily, mid-June to early September, and weekends only from mid-April to mid-June and early September to mid-October. Kids have to be more than 54 inches tall and at least 8 years old to ride without parents at this busy track. Six minutes for $5.

Castle in the Clouds, behind the Harwich Elementary School, South Street. A fun playground. There are also picnic tables and a playground at **Brooks Park,** Route 39, Harwich.

GOLF
Cranberry Valley Golf Course (508-430-7560; 508-430-5234), Oak Street, off Main Street which turns into Route 39. Open March through December. This 18-hole, par-72 course also has a driving range and practice putting green. One junior clinic is offered in summer.

❄ **Harwichport Golf Club** (508-432-0250), South and Forest Streets. A nine-hole, par-34 course.

IN-LINE SKATING
Harwich Skate Park (508-430-7554), Brooks Park at Route 39, Harwich. Full protective gear required. Open 2–4 during the school year; longer hours and night skating in summer. Call before going, as it's supervised by volunteers.

MINI-GOLF
Harbor Glen Miniature Golf (508-432-8240), Route 28, West Harwich. Open April to mid-October. With fountains and imitation rocky water-

falls, this place packs 'em in, especially at night. Perhaps it's due to the adjacent restaurant, which offers kids' meals and ice cream.

Club House Mini Golf (508-432-4820), Route 39 near Route 137. Open daily, mid-June to early September, and weekends only during the month preceding and following.

SAILING

See Cape Sail under *Sailing* in "Brewster."

TENNIS

Four public courts are located at **Brooks Park** (508-430-7553), Route 39 and Oak Street. Free.

Wychmere Harbor Tennis Club (508-430-7012; 508-394-3511), 792 Route 28. Open late May to mid-September. Primarily for members, this full-service facility offers nine clay and two hard courts, instruction, a pro shop, and clinics to nonmembers only when members haven't booked up all the time slots. It's still worth calling.

EVEN MORE THINGS TO SEE AND DO

HISTORIC BUILDINGS

☂ **Brooks Academy Museum** (508-432-8089; www.capecodhistory.org/harwich), Routes 124 and 39 at Main Street. Open 1–4 Tuesday through Friday, mid-June to early September, and by appointment year-round. This imposing 1844 Greek Revival schoolhouse was home to the country's first vocational school of navigation, established by Sidney Brooks. Now operated by the Harwich Historical Society, it exhibits a history of cranberry farming, historical photographs, and Native American and maritime artifacts. There are also collections of glass, furniture, decorative art objects, textiles, and art by C. D. Cahoon. Genealogical resources and a significant manuscript collection round out the research facility. Also on the premises: a gunpowder house used from 1770 to 1864 and a restored 1872 outhouse. Donations.

First Congregational Church, Routes 124 and 39, Harwich Center. Built in the mid-1700s, this church is surrounded by a white picket fence and anchors the tiny town center.

BIRD CARVINGS

Cape Cod Five Cents Savings Bank (508-430-0400), Route 28 in the center of Harwichport, displays a fine collection of carved miniature shore- and songbirds by hometown artist Elmer Crowell.

✍ FOR FAMILIES

❄ **Harwich Junior Theatre** (508-432-2002), Division and Willow Streets, West Harwich. This semiprofessional theater—the country's oldest children's theater, established in 1952—produces eight shows in July and August and another four or so the rest of the year. In summer children age 7–15 star in kids' roles, manage the sound and lighting, and sell refreshments. Classes or workshops are offered year-round. Whether your child is considering acting or you want to introduce him or her to theater, this is an imaginative alternative to another round of mini-golf. Summer performances late June to late August; $10-14.

Baseball clinics (508-432-2000; 508-432-4298), Whitehouse Field, off Oak Street from Route 39, behind the high school in Harwich Center. Weekly clinics (9–noon) are held for kids age 6–12 from late June to mid-August; $50. Sign up on Monday morning at the field.

GREEN SPACE

BEACHES

Weekly beach stickers ($25) are required for all but one of Harwich's 16 public saltwater beaches . If you can show that you're renting a cottage, call 508-430-7555 or 508-430-7553 to find out where to pick up a parking sticker.

Red River Beach, off Depot Road or Uncle Venies Road from Route 28, is the only beach with parking for day visitors. Parking $5 weekdays, $10 weekends. Facilities include rest rooms, concessions, and a lifeguard.

Pleasant Bay, off Route 28, is salt water, but calm, like a pond. It's open to nonresidents.

PONDS

Hinckleys Pond and **Seymour Pond,** both off Route 124, are open to nonresidents. You can also swim at **Bucks Pond,** off Route 39, where there is a lifeguard.

Long Pond has two beaches, although both require parking stickers. One is located off Long Pond Drive from Route 124, the other off Cahoons Road from Long Pond Drive from Route 137.

Sand Pond is off Great Western Road.

WALKS

The chamber of commerce (see *Guidance*) publishes a good walking trail map.

Herring River/Sand Pond Conservation Area (park off Bell's Neck Road from Great Western Road) in West Harwich. These 23 acres (which also go by the name of **Bells Neck Conservation Area**) of marshland, tidal creeks, reservoir, and riverway are great for birding and canoeing. You may see cormorants, ospreys, and swans.

🐾 **Thompson's Field,** Chatham Road, south of Route 39. This 87-acre preserve, with dirt-road trails for you and your canine friends, is full of wildflowers in springtime. This gives you an idea of what the Cape must have looked like 100 years ago.

LODGING

❄ Unless otherwise noted, all lodgings are open year-round.

BED & BREAKFASTS

Augustus Snow House (508-430-0528; 1-800-320-0528; www.augustus snow.com), 528 Route 28, Harwichport 02646. This 1901 Queen Anne

Victorian mansion—complete with turrets, gabled dormers, a gazebo, and a wraparound porch—has five large guest rooms furnished in authentic Victorian style to complement the luxuriously outfitted bathrooms. All rooms have gas fireplace and TV; some have a Jacuzzi. Innkeepers Joyce and Steve Roth serve a full breakfast at individual tables in the elegant breakfast room. Mid-May to mid-October $160–200; off-season $105–150. Ask about off-season packages.

House on the Hill (508-432-4321), 968 Route 28, South Harwich 02661. Although located on Route 28, this 1832 Federal-style farmhouse is set back from the road with lots of open space around it. It's been in host Allen Swanson's family since 1948, when he was 18 years old; Swanson and his wife, Carolyn, began taking guests in 1986. The house has three charmingly simple guest rooms, all with private bath. The homey living room and breakfast room feature original pine wainscoting, handwrought door latches, a beehive oven, and fireplaces. Continental breakfast included. It's conveniently located only ½ mile from a ferry to Nantucket. $65–75; $10 additional for a child in the same room. No credit cards.

Blue Heron Bed & Breakfast (508-430-0219; www.theblueheronbb.com), 464 Pleasant Lake Avenue, Harwich 02645. The main draw for this pleasant and homey 19th-century B&B is its proximity to the Cape's largest freshwater lake and to the Rail Trail: Both are across the street. (The beach is private.) Off the beaten path, these three simple rooms (one with private bath, all with air-conditioning) rent for $65–85, including an expanded continental breakfast.

Lion's Head Inn (508-432-7766; 1-800-321-3155; www.capecodinns.com), 186 Belmont Road, West Harwich 02671. On a quiet residential street within walking distance of a beach, this modest B&B has some nice attributes. Four of the six guest rooms can accommodate three people; one room has a private deck and original pine floors. The Huntington Suite is large, with a sitting area, TV, and private entrance to the pool. Nineteenth-century common rooms include two comfortable parlors, one with fireplace. The sunny breakfast room/terrace overlooks the nicely landscaped pool. Inquire about the two moderately priced cottages; they're darkish and more rustic than the B&B, but fully equipped for a family of five. June through September $90–145; off-season $65–110. Expanded continental breakfast included. Cottages $650–800 weekly in-season.

Barnaby Inn (508-432-6789; 1-800-439-4764; www.barnabyinn.com), 36 Route 28, West Harwich 02671. Although this rambling farmhouse is on busy Route 28, it's set back from the road. Innkeepers Bill and Eileen Ormond purchased this formerly ramshackle place in 1995 and set about gutting and refurbishing it. (Bill grew up 300 yards from the inn.) Most of the four rooms and two suites (really deluxe rooms) are modest, each with new carpeting and private bathroom. Two have a fireplace and Jacuzzi. A brand-new two-bedroom **cottage,** with complete kitchen, is a bargain at

Wychmere Harbor in Harwichport

$800 weekly in summer, $600 weekly off-season. Breakfast is delivered to all inn rooms. Well-behaved pets are accepted. Late May through September $100–150; off-season $60–100.

GUEST HOUSES

Cape Winds By-The-Sea (508-432-1418; www.capewinds.com), 28 Shore Road, West Harwich 02671. There are four quiet and airy rooms with across-the-street views of Nantucket Sound; a studio that can accommodate three people; and a two-room efficiency **apartment.** A continental breakfast is included and coffee is best enjoyed from a front-porch rocker. The beach is just a 5-minute walk away. Mid-June to early September $95–105 rooms, $120 studio, $150 efficiency; $16 each additional person. No credit cards.

Seadar Inn By-The-Sea (508-432-0264; 1-800-888-5250; 508-842-4525 off-season; www.seadarinn.com), Braddock Lane at Bank Street Beach, Harwichport 02646. Open May through October. Just a short shuffle from the beach in a quiet neighborhood, the rambling and shingled Seadar Inn has 23 air-conditioned rooms decorated in early American style. Bill Collins's family has proudly hosted guests at this old-fashioned hostelry since 1970; his is only the fourth family to own the Seadar since it opened in 1946. A buffet breakfast, served in the colonial-style dining room, is included. Mid-June to mid-September $95–205; $20 each additional person in a room.

Winstead Inn & Beach Resort (508-432-4444; 1-800-870-4405; www.winsteadinn.com), 4 Braddock Lane, Harwichport 02646. Owners Gregg Winston and David Plunkett have transformed this formerly modest beachfront house into a very upscale establishment with 14 deluxe rooms off a central hallway. All but two offer a beach view; some have a private deck. All rooms have air-conditioning, private bath (some with Jacuzzi), TV, and refrigerator. The back porch, sheltered by *Rosa rugosa*, leads to multilevel decks set with lounge chairs. There's nothing between the decks and the ocean except a private beach. Extensive continental breakfast buffet included. Mid-June to mid-September $195–325; off-season $135–205.

COTTAGES

Tern Inn (508-432-3714; 1-800-432-3718; www.coastalinnkeepers.com), 91 Chase Street, West Harwich 02671. Open May through October. A 10-minute walk from the beach, these six nicely maintained and recently renovated cottages and efficiencies (one of which is shaped like a gazebo) are set on a 2-acre wooded lot. The Tern Inn also rents eight rooms in a half-Cape house. A pool and basketball court are on the premises. Mid-June through August $99–130 for rooms, $500–900 weekly for cottages; off-season $75 nightly for rooms.

See also Cape Winds By-The-Sea under *Guest Houses* and Barnaby Inn and Lion's Head Inn under *Bed & Breakfasts.*

MOTELS

Harbor Breeze (508-432-0337; 1-800-455-0247; www.harborbreezeinn. com), 326 Lower County Road, Harwichport 02646. Across from Allens Harbor, Harbor Breeze offers 10 pleasant rooms (all with private entrance, a few with private deck) delightfully off the beaten path. Rooms are clustered around a garden courtyard, next to a hidden pool. Decorated with wicker and country florals, many rooms can accommodate a family of four; others can be connected as family suites; cribs and cots are available. All rooms have private bath, TV, and refrigerator; one suite has a fireplace. Expanded continental breakfast included; grills available for the picnic area; microwave in the breakfast room. Rooms $105–225 May through October; $12.50 per additional person.

Wychmere Village Lodging (508-432-1434; 1-800-432-1434; www. wychmere.com), 767 Route 28, Harwichport 02646. Open April through November. This motor inn complex, set on 3 piney acres and surrounded by a white picket fence, operated by an enthusiastic couple, is so tidy and sweet that I can't help but recommend it even though it's on Route 28. It's location is great—just half a mile from the beach or the Nantucket ferry. The 24 traditional motel-style rooms are configured with either one or two double beds or a king; cribs and cots are available for families. Some rooms have a kitchenette; all have cable TV, air conditioning, and refrigerator. Request a room facing the pool rather than Route 28. One **cottage** sleeps a family of five. After the beach, kids will enjoy shuffleboard, table tennis, volleyball, and a playground with swings and games. Mid-June to mid-September $99–115 rooms, $145 two-bedroom unit, $899 weekly for cottage. Off-season $65–70, $95, $750, respectively.

Sandpiper Beach Inn (508-432-0485; 1-800-433-2234; www.coastal innkeepers.com), 16 Bank Street, Harwichport 02646. Open April through October. Fronting its own private beach, this U-shaped building is constructed around a well-tended grassy courtyard. All 20 renovated and redecorated rooms have TV, refrigerator, telephone, and air-conditioning. Some can sleep three to five people; most have a private patio. The duplex **cottage** that opens directly onto the beach is stunning, but it's often booked a year in advance for July and August. Continental breakfast included. Mid-June to mid-September $125–195 rooms, $320 beachfront cottage rooms; off-season $85–145 rooms, $170–210 beachfront; $30 per additional person.

Commodore Inn (508-432-1180; 1-800-368-1180; www.commodoreinn. com), 30 Earle Road, West Harwich 02671. Open mid-April through October. At first glance, this complex looks like just another cluster of motel rooms set around a pool. But on closer inspection, it's quite a large (heated) pool, and the 27 rooms are nicely outfitted with wicker furniture and white cotton bedspreads. Some even have Jacuzzi, gas fireplace, wet bar, and microwave. Many can sleep a family of four in two double beds. Ask for a room with a vaulted ceiling; they feel much more spacious. It's a 1-minute walk to the beach, and there's a good play area. Mid-June to mid-September $165–215; off-season $95–175; $35 per additional person. Full buffet breakfast included in summer; otherwise it's continental.

RENTAL HOUSES AND COTTAGES

The Real Estate Place (508-430-4606; 1-877-760-6606), 72 Route 28, West Harwich. Talk to Pam Reida-Allen; she's friendly and knowledgeable about the local market, whether you're buying or renting, seasonally or year-round. She has 30–40 listings all around the area—South Yarmouth, Dennis, Harwich, and Chatham—from small cottages up to seven-bedroom houses.

WHERE TO EAT

Harwich has two of the best restaurants on the Cape, a great hole-in-the-wall, and a bunch of places in between: You won't go hungry here.

DINING OUT

& **Cape Sea Grille** (508-432-4745; www.seagrille.com), 31 Sea Street, Harwichport. Open for dinner April through November; closed Tuesday off-season. This contemporary bistro easily makes my short list of favorite places to eat on the Cape. Easily. Chef-owners Jim and Beth Poitrast offer exceptionally well-prepared New American cuisine served by candlelight in a lovely old sea captain's home. You simply can't go wrong here. In fact, I've never found anyone who didn't rave about their little secret. (It's a mightily undersung restaurant.) Outstanding specialties include a bountiful seafood paella and a mixed grill of roasted lobster, herb-crusted salmon fillet, and swordfish wrapped in bacon. (You might want to share that one after a couple of appetizers.) One particularly perfect meal began with a delicate pumpkin ravioli and ended with a warm chocolate cake, still soft in the center. My dining companions swore by the apple tart and banana in phyllo dough. You'd better save room or, better yet, come back again and again. There is a three-course sunset menu 5–5:45. Reservations suggested. Entrées $15–25.

❋ **L'Alouette** (508-430-0405), 787 Route 28, Harwichport. Open for dinner Tuesday through Sunday, year-round except February. Danielle Bastres and her chef husband, Louis, have developed a loyal clientele since they opened L'Alouette in 1986. Bastres's consistently well-prepared and -presented French cuisine appeals to a sophisticated older crowd that doesn't necessarily think that more is better. Specialties include country-style pâté and sautéed escargots to start, and braised fillet of sole and bouillabaisse for entrées. If you've had a hankering for châteaubriand, this is the place to have it. Reservations suggested. Dinner $16–21.

Brax Landing (508-432-5515), 705 Route 28, Harwich. Open for lunch, dinner, and Sunday brunch April through December. Overlooking Saquatucket Harbor, this popular and casual tavernlike restaurant has a varied menu. Look for fish and chicken sandwiches, fried seafood, seafood stew, and sautéed lobster. Their steamers are particularly good. A few indoors seats have choice views, but the real draw is outdoor seating on the tranquil harbor. Well, on Sundays, the real draw is a bountiful buffet. Entrées $13–17, brunch $12.

EATING OUT

❋ All entries under *Eating Out* are open year-round unless otherwise noted.

❦ **Ay! Caramba Cafe** (508-432-9800), 703 Main Street, Harwich Center. Open 11–9:30-ish daily. Overlooking the town green and church, this tiny and cheery hole-in-the-wall has excellent, authentic, and fresh Mexican dishes: *carne asada*, combo plates with *chiles rellenos* or *flautas*, burritos and tacos, tortas and tostadas. You know the menu; you probably didn't know it was this good, though . . . unless you're lucky enough to have a grandmother who cooks like this. In summer, the patio is pleasant. In cooler weather, the tables are quite limited. Dishes $4–9.

❦ **New Moon** (508-432-9911), 551 Route 28, Harwichport. Open for lunch and dinner. In the center of town, this value-packed **bar** and grill offers a healthy selection of salads, soups, grilled sandwiches (Cajun chicken with roasted red peppers and Boursin), thin crispy pizzas (with spinach, broccoli, feta, and plum tomatoes), a few pasta dishes (chicken with sun-dried tomatoes, pine nuts, Swiss chard, and four-cheese ravioli), and some traditional and creative entrées like filet mignon or salmon brushed with truffle honey. You're bound to find something to suit your taste buds and wallet. Dishes $6–18.

❦❧ **Bonatt's Restaurant & Bakery** (508-432-7199), 537 Route 28 at Sea Street, Harwichport. Open for breakfast and lunch year-round (closed Tuesday from December through April). Bonatt's successfully fulfills four important missions: to dish up good breakfasts from the short-order kitchen; to offer luncheon specials like fish-and-chips, fisherman's platters, and open steak sandwiches in the pleasant dining rooms; to provide box lunches for the beach (call an hour in advance in summer or be prepared to wait, as this place is always hopping); and to boast its famous "meltaway" sweet bread from the bakery. Children's menu. Dishes $4–10.

The Mason Jar (508-430-7600), 544 Route 28, Harwichport. Open daily in-season and closed Sunday off-season. Because the owners are also caterers, you can rightfully expect this tiny shop to have great "specialty" sandwiches, grilled chicken breast box lunches ("totes"), and pastries. Cheeses and pâtés. There are a few tables outdoors.

Stewed Tomato (508-432-2214), 707 Main Street, Harwich Center. Open for breakfast and lunch daily. This bright and cheery neighborhood place, established in 1983, is delightfully off the beaten path. Fare is simple but well done: homemade soups, baked goods, a few sandwiches (crab roll), burgers (get the one with tomatoes and fried onions), and omelets (the "kitchen sink" has everything thrown into it!). Breakfast and lunch $3–7.

400 East (508-430-1800), Route 39 and 137, East Harwich. Open for lunch and dinner. 400 East is a friendly place, good for families. The menu features standards like "gourmet" pizza, charbroiled steaks and burgers, and pasta dishes like fettuccine Alfredo. Children's menu and crayons. Many think 400 East is better than its more visible cousin, **The 400** on Route 28 in Harwichport. Dishes $4.50–16.

Seafood Sam's (508-432-1422), 302 Route 28, Harwichport. Open for lunch and dinner, February through October. You can always count on Sam's for reliable, informally presented, reasonably priced fried or broiled seafood. Outdoor seating, chicken, burgers, and ice cream, too. Children's menu. Lunch $5–7, dinner $8–12.

SNACKS

Thompson's Farm Market (508-432-5415), 710 Route 28, Harwichport. Open daily in-season; closed Sunday and Monday mid-October to mid-May. This upscale market and deli is an appealing place to gather picnic fixings. Café seating, where you can enjoy baked goods and coffee in an air-conditioned setting, is also an option.

Sundae School Ice Cream Parlor (508-430-2444), 606 Route 28, Harwichport. Open mid-May to late October. The place to go for homemade ice cream and sundaes.

Pleasant Lake General Store (508-432-5305), Route 124. A good old-fashioned store, perfectly situated for cyclists on the Rail Trail (see *To Do—Bicycling/Rentals*).

ENTERTAINMENT

The **Harwich Mariners** (508-432-2000) play baseball at Whitehouse Field behind the high school in Harwich Center, off Oak Street from Route 39. Games begin at 7 PM and are played from early June to early August. Free.

Band concerts are held Tuesday evening at 7:30 in Brooks Park, at Route 39 and Oak Street.

✐ See also Harwich Junior Theatre under *Even More Things to See and Do—For Families.*

SELECTIVE SHOPPING

❄ All establishments are open year-round unless otherwise noted.

ANTIQUES

The Barn at Windsong (508-432-8281), 245 Bank Street, Harwichport. Open April through October. A variety of dealers offer a variety of goods: quilts, silver, toys, linen, glassware, and furniture.

The Mews Antiques at Harwichport (508-432-6397), 517 Route 28, Harwichport. Open mid-May through October. A few dealers have joined forces to offer decoys, folk art, early American glass, primitives, "country smalls," kitchen collectibles, and mirrors.

ARTISANS AND CRAFTS

♿ **Always & Forever** (508-430-2237), 791 Route 28, Harwichport. Open daily. This truly outstanding contemporary American crafts gallery represents national as well as homegrown craftspeople and artists. Curator Joel Roberts has a great eye and travels to ACC Crafts Fairs in search of exceptional work. He is also a fine potter himself, creating sculptural as opposed to functional clay pieces. By all means, stop in.

Pamela Black/Paradise Pottery (508-432-1713), 928 Route 28, South Harwich. Black creates and displays her whimsical and functional stoneware and raku (as well as hand-cut paper designs) in an old barn next to her house. This is a self-serve kind of place; don't be shy.

BOOKSTORES

Wychmere Book & Coffee (508-432-7868), 587 Route 28, Harwichport. This fine bookshop, with enough seats to make browsing enjoyable, stocks a good selection displayed in aesthetic environs. Story time Tuesday 10–noon in summer.

Sea Street Books (508-430-1816), 537 Route 28, Harwichport. Newly expanded.

SPECIAL SHOPS

Monahan & Co. (508-432-3302; 1-800-237-4602), 540 Route 28, Harwichport. Prices for Monahan's high-end jewelry (which is purchased from estate auctions and taken on consignment) range from the double digits to six figures. The shop has been in Michael Monahan's family for generations; they claim it's America's oldest family-owned jewelry store.

Cape Cod Tileworks (508-432-7346), 705 Main Street, Harwich Center. Open daily except Sunday. This colorful shop sells nothing but tile: ceramic, marble, limestone, and hand-painted. Custom designs and installation, too.

Cape Cod Bonsai Studio (508-432-8400), 1012 Route 28, Harwich. Closed January. In addition to selling more bonsai trees than you've ever seen, they also sell all the bonsai paraphernalia you'll need. Classes and workshops are offered on creating miniature bonsai and on rock planting. Check out their large private bonsai collection and koi pond.

Cape Cod Braided Rug Co. (508-432-3133), 537 Route 28, Harwichport. In 1910 Romeo Paulus, great-grandfather of the current generation of employees, was the first American to make these old-fashioned braided rugs on a machine. All sizes and shapes and color combinations are available—the in-store inventory is large but you can also have them custom-make a rug in 6 weeks for about the same price.

SPECIAL EVENTS

July and August: **Guild of Harwich Artists** sponsors Monday **"Art in the Park"** at Doane Park, off Lower County Road. (Rain date is Wednesday.) Look for members' work at the Pilgrim Congregational Church (Route 28, Harwichport), too.

Mid-September: **Cranberry Harvest & Arts and Crafts Festival.** This popular 10-day celebration has an attendance of almost 40,000 people. Activities include fireworks, "A Taste of Harwich" (a gala event with almost 20 participating restaurants), and a parade. Also, 300 top-notch crafters set up their wares in five massive tents. A nice community spirit prevails.

Early December: **Christmas Weekend in the Harwiches.** Hayrides, strolling minstrels, a choral group, and B&B tours.

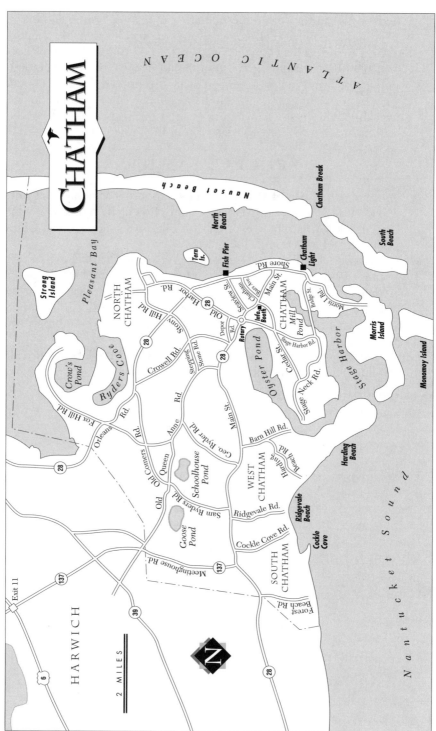

CHATHAM

ATLANTIC OCEAN

Nauset Beach

Chatham Break

North Beach

South Beach

Pleasant Bay

Strong Island

Tern Is.

Fish Pier

Chatham Light

NORTH CHATHAM

Shore Rd.

Stony Hill Rd.

Harbor Rd.

Old

28

Seaview St.

Chatham St.

Main St.

Park Ave.

Depot Rd.

Info. Booth

Cross St.

Morris Ltd.

Bridge St.

CHATHAM

Crow's Pond

Ryder's Cove

Crowell Rd.

Cedar St.

Stepping Stone Rd.

Rotary

Oyster Pond

Mill Pond

Stage Harbor Rd.

Stage Harbor

Morris Island

Fox Hill Rd.

Orleans Rd.

Anne Rd.

Main St.

Stage Neck Rd.

Monomoy Island

Queen

Old Comers Rd.

Geo. Ryder Rd.

Schoolhouse Pond

Barn Hill Rd.

WEST CHATHAM

Harding Beach Rd.

Harding Beach

Old

Sam Ryders Rd.

Goose Pond

Ridgevale Rd.

Ridgevale Beach

Meetinghouse Rd.

Cockle Cove Rd.

137

SOUTH CHATHAM

Cockle Cove

Forest Beach Rd.

Nantucket Sound

Exit 11

137

HARWICH

39

6

2 MILES

28

N

Harding Beach

Paul Woodward / © The Countryman Press

Chatham

Although Chatham is less accessible from Route 6 than are its neighbors, even the most hurried Cape visitors stop here. Occupying the tip of Cape Cod's elbow, the town offers a good mix of archetypal Cape Cod architecture, a classic Main Street, a refined sensibility, plenty of beaches and shops, and a rich seafaring history.

When Samuel de Champlain and his party tried to land at Stage Harbor in 1606, they were met with stalwart resistance from the Native inhabitants. Fifty years later, though, Yarmouth's William Nickerson purchased a great deal of land from Chief Mattaquason. By 1712, the permanent "settlers" had incorporated the town.

Among Cape towns, Chatham is known for its calm, genteel, independent spirit. The town's vigilant zoning commission has kept tourist-trap activity to a minimum. Bordered on three sides by water, the town is populated by descendants of its oceangoing founders, many of whom continue in their ancestors' footsteps. Despite the difficulty in navigating the surrounding waters, Chatham sustains an active fleet of fishermen and leisure-time sailors. Sailors, fishermen, shop owners, and an increasing number of retirees live quietly in this delightfully traditional village.

Chatham, along with the spectacularly desolate Monomoy National Wildlife Refuge, boasts 65 miles of shoreline. Chatham's beaches are varied: Some are hit by pounding surf, others are sheltered by inlets; some are good for shell collecting, others are wide and sandy. A walk along the shore reveals long sandbars and beautiful seafront homes. An inland drive or bicycle ride takes you past elegant shingled cottages and stately white houses surrounded by picket fences and boasting primroses and tidy lawns.

In the center of Chatham, Main Street is chock-full of upscale shops, offering everything from tony antiques and nautically inspired gifts to jewelry, clothing, and culinary supplies. This central part of town has excellent restaurants and inns, and some of the Cape's finest bow-shaped roof houses (so named because they're shaped like the bow of a ship turned upside down). North Chatham, primarily residential, is dotted with several picturesque inlets. West and South Chatham border the beaches; you'll find lots of rental houses, summer cottages, and piney woods here.

GUIDANCE

Information booth (508-945-5199; 1-800-715-5567 for recorded information year-round; www.chathamcapecod.org), 533 Main Street, Chatham 02633. Open 10–5 daily mid-May to mid-October (until 6 late June to early September). The map-lined walls come in handy when you're planning an itinerary or looking for a specific place—as does the walking guide.

There is also a seasonal welcome center with the same hours at the historic Bassett House, Routes 137 and 28, South Chatham. Even if you don't need information, this is a great old house.

PUBLIC LIBRARY

❄☞♪**Eldredge Public Library** (508-945-5170), 564 Main Street. Open Monday, Wednesday, Friday, and Saturday 10–5; Tuesday and Thursday 1–9. This three-story municipal building is one of the Cape's best libraries. Modern literature, genealogical records, books on tape, free Internet access on six computers, and newspapers and magazines. The genealogical department is only staffed Tuesday and Thursday 1–5.

PUBLIC REST ROOMS

Year-round public rest rooms are located behind the town offices on Main Street and at the Fish Pier on Shore Road. Additional summertime facilities are located at Kate Gould Park (off Main Street) and the welcome center (see *Guidance*) at Routes 137 and 28.

GETTING THERE

By car: Take Route 6 east to exit 11 (Route 137 south) to Route 28 south. The center of Chatham is 3 miles from this intersection, about 45 minutes from either bridge.

By bus: There is no bus service to Chatham; you'll have to catch the **Plymouth & Brockton** bus line (508-778-9767; www.p-b.com) in Orleans or Barnstable to reach other Cape towns or Boston's Logan Airport.

By air: **Chatham Municipal Airport** (508-945-9000), George Ryder Road, is a full-service airport for charters, private planes, and sight-seeing (see *Outdoor Activities—Airplane Rides*).

GETTING AROUND

Chatham is crowded in July and August, and you'll be happiest exploring Main Street on foot. It's about a 15-minute walk from mid–Main Street to the lighthouse and another 15 minutes from the light to the pier (one way). There is free parking at Town Hall (off Main Street), the Colonial Building (off Stage Harbor Road), one block west of the rotary at the elementary school, and on Chatham Bars Avenue behind the Impudent Oyster restaurant off Main Street.

The **H₂O** (508-385-8326; 1-800-352-7155; www.capecodtransit.org) bus line, used by more locals than visitors, travels along Route 28 between Hyannis and Orleans daily except Sunday year-round. It stops on Shore Road in North Chatham, at the rotary in the center of Chatham, and on Morton's Road in South Chatham.

MEDICAL EMERGENCY
Call **911.**

TO SEE

Chatham Light, Main Street and Bridge Street. Built in 1828 and rebuilt in 1876, the lighthouse has a beacon visible 23 miles out to sea. The U.S. Coast Guard–operated lighthouse is open to visitors only during Cape Maritime Days in mid-May (see *Special Events*). Parking limit of 30 minutes during the summer.

Chatham Break. Coin-operated telescopes across from the lighthouse allow visitors to take a closer look at the famous Chatham Break, the result of a ferocious nor'easter on January 2, 1987. Low dunes were flattened, tidal waters rose, and eventually waves and high winds forced a channel through the barrier beach (the lower portion of Nauset Beach) that had previously protected Chatham Harbor from the open ocean. Boating around the harbor's strong currents is now more difficult than ever. In a matter of hours rather than over the natural course of 50 years, the break also created circumstances that destroyed prime pieces of waterfront realty. Ocean currents have a mind of their own; in 1846 a previous break in South Beach repaired itself. Chatham Light Beach is directly below the lookout area; South and North Beaches are visible across the harbor (see *Green Space—Beaches*).

Fish Pier, Shore Road at Bar Cliff Avenue. Chatham's fleet of fishing boats returns—from as far away as 100 miles—to the pier daily about 2–4. From the pier's second-floor observation deck you can watch fishermen unloading their catch of haddock, lobster, cod, halibut, flounder, and pollack. While you're at the pier, take a gander at the **Fisherman's Monument.** A 1992 call for designs attracted nearly 100 applicants from around the world, but the committee chose Sig Purwin, a Woods Hole sculptor, to memorialize the town's fishermen.

In recent years, as stocks have begun to dwindle, fishermen have increasingly turned to shellfish harvesting. (Bay scallops harvested in late fall are like nothing you've ever tasted.) In fact, more commercial licenses are purchased yearly in Chatham (about 500) than anywhere else on the Cape. And while Chatham has particularly rich, natural beds, many fishermen are turning to organized aquaculture farming. The harvest goes on amid a contentious debate over the regulation of this new industry.

Railroad Museum (508-945-0342), 153 Depot Road. Open 10–4 Tuesday through Saturday, mid-June to mid-September. This carefully restored 1887 depot—on the National Register of Historic Places—is chock-full of Victorian details, from a turret to its gingerbread trim. Inside you'll find treasures such as a 1910 New York Central train caboose and photos, models, and equipment pertaining to the Cape's railroad history. Donations.

Digging for clams at low tide in Pleasant Bay

⚓☞ **Old Atwood House** (508-945-2493; www.atwoodhouse.org), 347 Stage
Harbor Road. Open 1–4 Tuesday through Friday, mid-June through
September. The gambrel-roofed Atwood House, built by a sea captain in
1752, has been maintained by the Chatham Historical Society since 1926.
(Note the low doorways and how much we've grown over the last two
centuries by eating our vegetables!) The museum houses antique dolls,
tools, toys, portraits of sea captains, seashells from around the world,
Sandwich glass, and other Chatham seafaring artifacts. The adjoining
train barn features a three-panel mural by Alice Wright that depicts more
than 130 townspeople with a "modern Christ." Adults and children over
12, $3; children under 12 free.

Mayo House (508-945-4084), 540 Main Street. Open 11–4 Tuesday
through Thursday, late June through September. Built in 1818 by Josiah
Mayo (who served for 40 years as Chatham's first postmaster) and filled
with period antiques, the Mayo House is the headquarters of the
Chatham Conservation Foundation. The tiny, yellow three-quarter
Cape isn't the "best this" or the "oldest that"; it's just a nice little old
house. Donations.

SCENIC DRIVES

Chatham is one of the most scenic Cape towns. Route 28 toward Orleans is
quite scenic, with views of Pleasant Bay to the east. Shore Road passes
handsome cedar-shingled houses. The causeway to Morris Island affords harbor views as well as views of the open ocean beyond tall grasses
and sandy shores. And the road to Cockle Cove Beach from Route 28 in
South Chatham runs along a picturesque salt marsh and tidal river.

OUTDOOR ACTIVITIES

AIRPLANE RIDES
Cape Cod Flying Circus (508-945-9000; 508-945-2363), Chatham Municipal Airport, George Ryder Road. Reserve a day in advance in summer. To really appreciate Chatham's shoreline and the fragility of the Outer Cape landscape, head 900 feet above it in a three-seater Cessna. These wonderful sight-seeing rides are a bargain (25 minutes, $70; 55 minutes, $135). Prices are per ride, whether it's one person or three (max).

BICYCLING/RENTALS
With gentle inclines and quiet lanes accessible from any street in town, Chatham is a nice place for bicycling. It's also easy: There is a well-marked 2³/₄-mile route around town. **Bert & Carol's Lawnmower and Bicycle Shop** (508-945-0137), 347 Route 28, North Chatham, offers rentals and makes personalized routes and recommendations based on your level and needs. They also carry a full line of accessories like roof racks, baby seats, and trail-a-bikes. Open from April through December, with parking on the premises. For extensive cycling, look for the $2.99 Chatham bike trail map.

See also Bikes & Blades under *In-Line Skating*.

BOAT EXCURSIONS/RENTALS
Monomoy Wildlife Refuge Cruises (508-896-3867), sponsored by the Cape Cod Museum of Natural History, are offered mid-June to mid-October. The 4-hour North Monomoy trip costs $40 per person; it's not appropriate for kids under age 12. The South Monomoy voyage is a whopping 7-hour adventure and costs $65 per person. Trips only depart once weekly, so call for a current schedule. At that time, you should also ask what the on-board naturalists will be discussing during the trip. Plans were subject to change at press time.

Outermost Harbor Marine (508-945-2030; www.outermostharbor.com), Seagull Road, off Morris Island Road. Late June to mid-September. This outfit offers seal cruises and on-demand shuttles to South Beach and Monomoy Island between 8 AM and 4:30 PM. To South Beach, adults $10; children under 12, $5; Monomoy is a bit more expensive. As for seal trips, hour-long excursions are by appointment only; minimum cost $70. Otherwise, $16 adults, $8 children under 12.

Monomoy Island Ferry *(Rip Ryder)* (508-945-5450; www.monomoy islandferry.com), Wikis Way, off Morris Island Road. Boats April through October; make reservations the night before. Regular launches to North Monomoy and South Beach. When the captain drops you off, tell him what time you want to be picked up. Inquire about fly-fishing, birding, surf-casting, and seal trips.

Beachcomber (508-945-5265; www.sealwatch.com), from the Fish Pier, Ryders Cove, and Stage Harbor. These folks shuttle you across the inlet to North Beach. Like most other outfits, they also do 90-minute seal trips, but they use a faster boat so you spend more time watching seals and less time traveling. In this case it's the destination, not the journey. Beachcomber also takes fishermen to North Beach.

Cape Water Sports (Nauti Jane's Boat Rentals), Pleasant Bay at the Wequassett Inn (508-432-5400; 508-430-6893), Route 28, You can rent daysailers, kayaks, catamarans, surf bikes, powerboats, and Sunfish from the beachfront Wequassett Inn location (see *Lodging—Resorts*) from May through October. Make reservations for lessons. Cape Water Sports also operates at Ridgevale Beach (508-432-4339) with a more limited season, mid-June to early September.

Boats can be rented at **Oyster River Boatyard** (508-945-0736), Barn Hill Lane extension, off Route 28, West Chatham.

FISHING/SHELLFISHING

See the town clerk (508-945-5101) at 549 Main Street for a freshwater fishing license. Shellfishing licenses are required, too; contact the Permit Department (508-945-5180) on George Ryder Road in West Chatham.

✎ **The Fishin' Bridge.** Follow Stage Harbor Road to Bridge Street, where Mill Pond empties into Stage Harbor. You'll probably haul in several crabs, small flounders, eels, and perhaps even a bluefish. Locals will certainly be there with long rakes, harvesting shellfish. Stop even if you don't fish; it's picturesque.

North Beach is a good choice for surf-casting for striped bass.

Schoolhouse Pond off Schoolhouse Road via Sam Ryders Road and **Goose Pond** off Fisherman's Landing offer freshwater fishing for rainbow trout. (In-season there is resident-only parking at Schoolhouse.)

For sportfishing charters (May through November, weather permitting), you have a few choices: try Bob Miller's ***Booby Hatch*** (508-430-2312) and Ron McVickar's ***Banshee*** (508-945-0403), both out of Stage Harbor Marine in Chatham.

Capt. Jack Wesley Randall (508-432-4630) leads guided charter fly-fishing trips. Stop in for custom tackle, supplies, rod rentals, and more charter information at **Top Rod Fly & Surf Fish Shop** (508-945-2256), 1082 Route 28, next to Ryders Cove, North Chatham.

See also Beachcomber under *Boat Excursions/Rentals,* and Monomoy Outdoors under *Selective Shopping.*

FOR FAMILIES

✎& **Play-a-Round Playground,** on Depot Road behind Chatham Elementary School. This wonderful, multilevel wooden structure includes an area for disabled children and a fenced-off area for toddlers.

GOLF

❅ **Chatham Seaside Links** (508-945-4774), 209 Seaview Street, next to the Chatham Bars Inn (see *Lodging—Resorts*). Open year-round, weather permitting; off-season, pay on the honor system. A nine-hole, par-34 course.

From Chatham's Fish Pier

IN-LINE SKATING

❄✍ **Bikes & Blades** (508-945-7600), 195 Crowell Road. Rentals of just what the name implies: bicycles and in-line skates. Bikes are $15 daily for kids and adults; skates $20. Half-day, 3-day, and weekly rates, too. You can park here.

KAYAKING

For rentals see Monomoy Outdoors under *Selective Shopping* and Cape Water Sports under *Boat Excursions/Rentals*.

SEAL CRUISES

About 300 gray and harbor seals summer off the shores of Chatham, and unlike human beings, who migrate in the opposite direction in the same multiples, about 3,000 seals rally here in winter. While the shores of Chatham have been a hangout for the personable seals since the early 1980s, Monomoy has been a haven only since the 1991 hurricane created a break in the barrier beach. For information on cruises, see Monomoy Island Ferry, Outermost Harbor Marine, and Beachcomber under *Boat Excursions/Rentals*.
See also Wellfleet Bay Wildlife Sanctuary under *Green Space* in "Wellfleet."

TENNIS

Public courts are located on **Depot Road** by the Railroad Museum (see *To See*) and at **Chatham High School** on Crowell Road. Free.

Chatham Bars Inn (508-945-0096), Shore Road. Mid-May to mid-October. CBI has three waterfront courts made out of synthetic "classic-clay" (which play like clay but are much easier to maintain) that rent to nonguests for $30 an hour ($20 off-season). Lessons are $55–65 per hour plus the court fee.

WINDSURFING
Monomoy Sail & Cycle (508-945-0811), 275 Route 28, North Chatham, rents sailboards and Sunfish. Pleasant Bay enjoys easterly and northeasterly winds, while Forest Beach receives southwesterly winds.

EVEN MORE THINGS TO SEE AND DO

ART CLASSES
❋ **Creative Arts Center** (508-945-3583), 154 Crowell Road. The center offers classes in pottery, drawing, photography, painting, jewelry making, and other fine arts. Work is shown at the center's on-site **Edward A. Bigelow Gallery.** Since 1971, the center has held an annual art festival in August (see *Special Events*), where you may meet the artists and purchase their works.

FOR FAMILIES
✎ **Baseball clinics** (508-945-5511) are sponsored by the Chatham A's from late June to mid-August. There are weekly sessions ($50) for youngsters; register at Veterans Park (Route 28 just west of the rotary) on Monday morning at 8:15.

GENEALOGY
Nickerson Family Association (508-945-6086), 1107 Orleans Road. Think you have ties to over 350,000 other descendants of William Nickerson, who founded Chatham? This genealogical research center will help you find out. In addition to Nickersons, the volunteer association has cast a wide net, inadvertently compiling information on folks associated the Nickersons and original settlers of Cape Cod and Nova Scotia.

HEALTH CLUB
❋ **Chatham Health & Swim Club** (508-945-3555), 251 Crowell Road. A full-service place with a five-lane lap pool and weekly fee of $75.

GREEN SPACE

Monomoy National Wildlife Refuge. North and South Monomoy Islands, acquired by the federal government as part of a wildlife refuge in 1944, comprise a 2,700-acre habitat for more than 285 species of birds. Birds and seaside animals rule the roost; there are no human residents, no paved roads, no vehicles, and no electricity. (Long ago the island did support a fishing community.) It's a quiet, solitary place. Monomoy, one of four remaining "wilderness" areas between Maine and New Jersey, is an important stop for shorebirds on the Atlantic Flyway—between breeding grounds in the Arctic and wintering grounds in South America. Conditions here may well determine whether the birds will survive the journey. Some beaches are closed from April to mid-August to protect threatened nesting areas for piping plovers and terns. The lovely old lighthouse, built in 1823 and not used since 1923, was restored in 1988.

In 1996, the U.S. Fish and Wildlife Service embarked on a long-term management project to restore avian nesting diversity to Monomoy NWR by creating habitat for terns, which historically numbered in the thousands. (By 1995, only hundreds of common terns remained, and between 1988 and 1995 only one pair of roseate terns nested.) Restoring the nesting space was controversial because the government considered it necessary to "remove" (with bread chunks laced with poison) 1,700 of the 12,500 seagulls that also nested here. From 1996 to 1999, the number of nesting terns, including 18 pairs of roseate terns, increased dramatically. There are protesters who still argue that the Fish and Wildlife Service took this action under pressure from off-road-vehicle drivers, who are often banned from driving on mainland beaches because of nesting endangered birds.

Monomoy was attached to the mainland until a 1958 storm severed the connection; a storm in 1978 divided the island in two. The islands are accessible only by boat (see *Outdoor Activities—Boat Excursions/Rentals*), and only under favorable weather conditions. Guided tours are available from the Cape Cod Museum of Natural History (508-896-3867 for reservations; see *To See* in "Brewster") and the Wellfleet Bay Wildlife Sanctuary (508-349-2615 for reservations; see *Green Space* in "Wellfleet"). Groups of six or more must obtain a permit from the refuge headquarters on Morris Island (508-945-0594). The 40-acre Morris Island is accessible by car and foot: Head south from Chatham Light and turn left onto Morris Island Road, then take your first right and continue on Morris Island Road to the end.

Chase Park, on Cross Street, is a tranquil vest pocket of parkland just a couple of blocks from the summertime madness on Main Street. It's perfect for a picnic lunch and overlooks a tranquil windmill.

Hydrangea Walkway. As you head north on Shore Road from Main Street, the road is lined with stately private homes overlooking the ocean. One house on the left, in particular, is really eye-catching from July through September, when its front walkway is awash with more than 25 blooming hydrangea plants.

BEACHES

Weekly beach stickers for cottage renters are purchased at Hardings, Ridgevale, and Cockle Cove Beaches (see below). From late June to early September, parking (508-945-5158) is $8 daily, weekly $35.

Hardings Beach, on Nantucket Sound. From Route 28, take Barn Hill Road to Hardings Beach Road. Small dunes. Rest rooms, lifeguard, and concession stand.

Ridgevale Beach, on Nantucket Sound. Take Ridgevale Road off Route 28. Rest rooms, lifeguard, and snack bar.

✍ **Cockle Cove Beach,** protected from Nantucket Sound by Ridgevale Beach. Take Cockle Cove Road off Route 28. Gentle waves and soft sand make Cockle Cove a good choice for families with small children. Picturesque waterways and inlets line the way to the beach. Lifeguard.

✐ **Pleasant Bay Beach,** Route 28, North Chatham. The 7,000-acre inlet and bay has been called breathtakingly beautiful, and it is. It's also on the state's list of 25 areas of "critical environmental concern." This beach is narrow but great for children because the water is so shallow.

North Beach, on the Atlantic Ocean. North Beach, which is actually the southern end of Nauset Beach, is accessible only by boat (see *Outdoor Activities—Boat Excursions/Rentals* for water-taxi services). It's well worth the effort and expense to get here.

Chatham Light Beach or **South Beach,** below the lighthouse, on the Atlantic Ocean. There's only 30-minute parking, but you can bicycle or walk to the lane off Morris Island Road just beyond the lighthouse; a sign points the way to South Beach. If you're day-tripping to Chatham, pay to park at the Eldredge Taxi parking lot, 365 Main Street, and take its shuttle to the beach. The most desolate part of the beach requires quite a long walk, but the early sections are very nice, too. Many ferries (see *Outdoor Activities—Boat Excursions/Rentals*) take passengers to the farthest, most remote reaches of the beach. One of the best aspects of this beach is that you've got surf on the east side and calm bay waters on the west.

POND

Oyster Pond Beach, off Stage Harbor Road, near the rotary. This inland saltwater pond is connected to Nantucket Sound by way of Oyster Creek and Stage Harbor. Good for families, its shores are calm and its waters are the warmest in town. Free parking; lifeguard.

WALKS

Conservation Foundation. More than 500 acres in Chatham have been donated by private citizens to the Conservation Foundation. Walking trails traversing marshes, wetlands, and meadows in four distinct areas have been developed; contact the town information booth on Main Street (see *Guidance*) for directions.

🐾 **The Dog Runs,** as it's known locally. Walk 10 minutes along Bridge Street from the lighthouse to find the entrance to this forested coastal trail that runs along Stage Harbor. Take a picnic, and enjoy it in the cattail marshes.

See also Monomoy National Wildlife Refuge, above.

LODGING

Generally, Chatham is one of the most expensive places to stay on Cape Cod. Two-night minimum stays in July and August are normal, and many of Chatham's most notable places are booked for July and August well before July 4. Unless otherwise noted, all lodging is in Chatham 02633.

RESORTS

❋✐&**Chatham Bars Inn** (508-945-0096; 1-800-527-4884; www.chathambars inn.com), Shore Road. This quintessential, grand, historic seaside resort was built in 1914 as a hunting lodge. The grande dame's gracious elegance is rivaled by only a handful of places in New England. Scattered over 20 acres, the main inn and adjacent cottages have undergone extensive, multimillion-dollar renovations and now total 205 rooms and suites. Unfortunately, on a recent stay, the resort seemed to be expanding faster than they could keep up with; service requests also went unanswered. Nonetheless, grounds are lushly landscaped and the seaside setting nearly perfect. Rooms and cottages, many with fireplaces, are comfortably decorated with wicker, hand-painted furniture, and understated florals. Some rooms have private balconies or decks with lovely ocean views. One- and two-bedroom suites within lodge-style cottages share a living room and fireplace. The inn boasts a lot of extras: private beach, heated outdoor pool, four tennis courts, croquet, fitness room, nine-hole golf course, launch service across Pleasant Bay to the southern tip of Nauset Beach, and a full schedule of daytime activities and complimentary children's programs. There are many dining rooms (see *Dining Out, Eating Out,* and *Drinks*). In addition, a lavish buffet is laid out every morning. The hotel also has an expansive veranda and very comfortable, grand living rooms. It's a 10-minute walk from town. Mid-June to mid-September $210–420 for rooms; $100–265 off-season. Inquire about rates for one- and two-bedroom suites, off-season packages, and special-event weekends.

Wequassett Inn (508-432-5400; 1-800-225-7125; www.wequassett.com), 2673 Route 28. Open mid-April through November. A 10-minute drive north of Chatham on picturesque Pleasant Bay, the Wequassett is a first-class resort. The complex consists of 18 buildings set on 23 beautifully landscaped acres, a fine restaurant (see *Dining Out*), four tennis courts, sailing, and a 68-foot outdoor pool bordered by a strip of private beach on Pleasant Cove. (There isn't a more perfectly situated pool on the Cape.) The inn is renowned for its attentive staff, knowledgeable concierge, and exceptional level of service. As for the rooms, most cottages have cathedral ceilings and their own decks, though not all have views of boat-studded Round Cove. Triple sheeting, morning delivery of the newspaper, and turndown service are standard. The early American–style and country-pine furnishings are lovely. Other resort amenities include a tennis shop, fitness center, complimentary transport to nearby golf courses, boat rentals, and baby-sitting. The inn also ferries guests across the bay to an uncrowded section of the Cape Cod National Seashore. The resort offers guests the exclusive rights to play on the otherwise private Cape Cod National Golf Course, a challenging course designed by Cornish and Silva. Green fees are $100 per person. Back at the resort, light lunches, snacks, and cocktails are served poolside. Late June to early September $315–395 non-water-view rooms, $500–635 water views, $895 suite; shoulder seasons $125–250 rooms, $450 suite.

HOTEL

✻ **Chatham Wayside Inn** (508-945-5550; 1-800-391-5734; www.waysideinn. com), 512 Main Street. Welcoming visitors since 1860, this historic hostelry (which looks brand new these days) was renovated from top to bottom in 1994. Disgruntled locals think it lacks soul these days; there's certainly no subtlety to its domination of Main Street. Nonetheless, the 53 guest rooms and three suites are furnished with flair and a decorator's sure touch. Triple sheeting, thick towels, and top-notch bathroom amenities are standard. Each room has a canopy or four-poster bed, private bath, air-conditioning, TV, and reproduction period furniture. Some rooms have a fireplace, whirlpool tub, or a private patio or balcony. Views are of the town green, golf course, or parking lot. Summer and winter, cocktails are served fireside in the pub and dining room (see *Dining Out*). Outdoor swimming pool and tennis courts. Late June to late August $165–365; otherwise, $95–285 (off-season packages).

BED & BREAKFASTS

✿✔ **The Moorings** (508-945-0848; 1-800-320-0848; www.capecodtravel.com/ moorings), 326 Main Street. Open February through December. It's hard to say what I like best about this B&B: the large private, landscaped backyard; the comfortably elegant guest rooms; or the relaxed atmosphere. The gardens certainly are a riot of color, and there are plenty of tables and chairs from which to enjoy them. I also appreciate how, when Roberta and Frank Schultz renovated this fine old house, they thankfully retained its "old-house feel." The centrally located spacious B&B has 15 rooms, only 5 of which are in the main house. Of these, the yellow room is the best and brightest, although all are quite lovely. The large and comfortable living room is equally soothing, with high wainscoting and Oriental carpets. Rooms in the adjacent building are quite large and feature private decks, gas fireplaces, and fresh bathrooms. Some rooms have a whirlpool. The hideaway **cottage** is charming and completely renovated, too. A full breakfast— perhaps strata with ham and zucchini and homemade applesauce—is served in the cheery, bright dining room. The beach is a 10-minute walk, and the B&B has loaner beach chairs. Mid-June to mid-September $138–225; $255 nightly or $1,765 weekly for the cottage; off-season $98–165, $210 nightly or $1,100 weekly for the cottage; even less from November through April.

✻ **Port Fortune Inn** (508-945-0792; 1-800-750-0792; www.capecod.net/ portfortune), 201 Main Street. This B&B has a most enviable location, a couple of hundred yards from the excellent Chatham Light Beach (see *Green Space—Beaches*). Innkeepers Renee and Mike Kahl completely renovated the property's 13 rooms in 1997 and they continue to improve it. Each room has a tasteful, modern feel, with private bath, air-conditioning, telephone, and reproduction furnishings. Most rooms have four-posters, refrigerator, and TV; room 9 gets a warming southern exposure. The front building boasts two ocean-view rooms. On rainy days, there are two comfortable common rooms, one with a gas fireplace. Beach towels and chairs are provided. Shops and restaurants on Main Street are a 10-minute walk away. Mid-June to mid-September $135–180, spring and fall $115–155, November through April $95–125, including expanded continental breakfast buffet.

❋ **Captain's House Inn of Chatham** (508-945-0127; 1-800-315-0728; www.captainshouseinn.com), 369–377 Old Harbor Road. This traditional and elegant Greek Revival inn enjoys a privileged position. Jan and Dave McMaster, innkeepers since 1993, preside over an enthusiastic British hotel management staff, 2 acres of well-tended lawns and gardens, and 16 handsome rooms and sumptuous suites in an adjacent cottage, carriage house, and converted "stables." The Captain's Cottage contains one particularly historic room with wood-burning fireplace, walnut-paneled walls, and pumpkin-pine flooring; a hideaway attic suite; and a honeymoon-style room with a double whirlpool. The new Stables rooms are luxurious with gas fireplace, private patio or balcony, whirlpool tub, TV/VCR, and robes. Antiques-filled inn rooms are more traditional, and all very different, but I personally like the Garden Room with direct access to the grounds. All rooms have triple sheeting, air-conditioning, and a telephone; most have a fireplace and TV/VCR. The full breakfasts—perhaps French toast served with slivers of almonds, powdered sugar, and blueberries—are served on tables set with linen and silver in a wonderfully airy room. Smoked salmon graces the sideboard every morning, and an authentic English tea including savories and sweets is offered every afternoon. Loaner bikes. $165–375 mid-May through October, $145–295 November to mid-May.

🌸❋✔**Bow Roof House** (508-945-1346), 59 Queen Anne Road. A 5-minute walk from town—and a 2-minute walk from the town beach—Vera Mazulis's late-18th-century B&B is a real find. After seeing so many fancied-up inns, decorated with designer this and that, the Bow Roof House is a breath of fresh air. It feels authentic. Of the six guest rooms (all with private bath), I prefer the ones on the first floor. Room 1 features an old beehive oven, antiques, and two double beds. The comfy living room, with woodstove, leads to a deck. A continental breakfast is served at one table in the plant-filled dining room. Vera has owned this B&B since 1975 and allows children. $75–80 double.

🌸✔ **Blowin' A Gale Guest House** (508-945-9716), 210 Old Harbor Road. Open mid-June to mid-October. Enclosed by a white picket fence and blossoming garden, this snug and weathered 1888 house is operated by Nancy Petrus (who grew up across the street) and husband Bob. They rent only one room (or two rooms to a family), but it's very comfy and well looked after. As for common space, the first-floor sitting room is separate from the owners' quarters and the back porch overlooks conservation land. An expanded continental breakfast is served on the porch in warm weather. $125 double, $200 as a two-room suite.

❋ **Carriage House Inn** (508-945-4688; 1-800-355-8868; www.capecodtravel.

com/carriagehouse), 407 Old Harbor Road. Patty and Dennis O'Neill run
a friendly B&B on the edge of town. Of the six air-conditioned guest
rooms, my favorites are the more private ones in the adjacent Carriage
House. Each has a peaked ceiling, private ground-floor deck, and
fireplace. The guest living room has a large-screen TV and Steinway
grand piano for those so inclined. $170–195 late June to early September,
$140–165 spring and fall, $105–130 November through April. Full
breakfast and afternoon refreshments included.

❋ **Cranberry Inn** (508-945-9232; 1-800-332-4667; www.cranberryinn.com),
359 Main Street. Located toward the end of Main Street, a 10-minute
walk from the Chatham Light and the beach, this completely renovated
two-story inn has 18 traditional rooms off a long hallway. It's more like a
small hotel than a B&B in attitude and decor. Common space includes a
traditional living room that also serves as a reception area and a small,
handsome bar. Upscale guest room furnishings are a mix of period
antiques and reproductions. Many have a fireplace, private balcony, and
wet bar; all have private bath and air-conditioning. Guests enjoy rocking
in the chairs on the long veranda. Your innkeepers are Kay and Bill
DeFord, who include an expanded continental breakfast buffet. Behind
the inn is a little nature trail and an unharvested cranberry bog. Early May
to late October $150–260; off-season $100–180.

COTTAGES

Metter's Cottages (508-432-3535), Chat Harbor Lane, West Chatham
02669. Open May through October. These three water-view cottages
are more like homes than cottages. Talk with George and Donna Metter
about your needs when reserving; there's probably a cottage with your
name on it. July to early September $1,000–1,300 weekly for a water-
view three-bedroom; off-season $700–900. Reservations are taken af-
ter January 1 for the upcoming summer.

See also The Moorings under *Bed & Breakfasts*.

EFFICIENCIES AND MOTELS

Chatham Highlander I and II (508-945-9038; www.realmass.com/high-
lander), 946 Route 28. Open April through November. An excellent
choice for budget-minded travelers, this is one of my favorite motels
because of the friendly and hands-on proprietors, Mike and Pauline
Holly. They take deserved pride in maintaining and upgrading their
place. Just a stone's throw from the center of town, the two adjacent
motels sit on a little knoll above a well-traveled road. Each of the 28 rooms
has a TV, small refrigerator, tiled bathroom, and air-conditioning; most
have two double beds. Decor is quite cheery, albeit old-fashioned; aspects
are charmingly retro. Rooms are sparkling white, freshened with new
mattresses and spreads. I'm more partial to units at the Highlander II.
There are two heated pools. Mid-June to early September $109, off-
season $60–85; $10 per additional child, $20 per additional adult.

Chatham Tides Waterfront Motel (508-432-0379; www.allcapecod.com/

chathamtides), 394 Pleasant Street, South Chatham 02659. Open mid-May to mid-October. Delightfully off the well-trodden path, this quiet beachfront complex of 24 rooms and suites is a real find: It's been in Ellen and Ed Handel's family since 1966 and is still maintained with impressive care. Fronted by dunes and ocean, the view alone is worth the price. After staying here once, you'll probably return again and again. In fact, you might try booking in February after the repeat guests get their pick of the litter in January. Rooms with kitchenette, air-conditioning, decks: $155–180 daily, $1,000–1,200 weekly from late June through August; $115–145 daily and $700–925 weekly off-season. Town houses $1,300–1,900 weekly in-season.

Hawthorne Motel (508-945-0372; www.thehawthorne.com), 196 Shore Road. Open mid-May to mid-October. About a 10-minute walk from Chatham's main shopping district, this motel is popular because nothing stands between it and Pleasant Bay except green grass and a path down to the motel's private beach. The 16 rooms are 1960s style, and the 10 efficiencies are "summer campish," but who cares—you're coming for the easy access to sunning, swimming, and lazing on the beach. There are four much larger corner rooms; some rooms have a kitchenette. Mid-June to mid-September, $165 rooms with a view ($145 without); $300 two-bedroom cottages; $155 efficiencies.

✎ **Pleasant Bay Village Resort Motel** (508-945-1133; 1-800-547-1011), Route 28. Open May through October. About a mile from town, this place will forever change your opinion of a motel complex. The 6 acres of lush, Japanese-style landscaping and tasteful pool are reason enough to recommend it, and the assortment of room types is extensive. Accommodations are well maintained, too. Some rooms have a sundeck, while others overlook exotic gardens and a cascading waterfall; some are spacious, others are snug; some have their own grills, while others have fully equipped kitchens. Walk across the street and down Route 28 to Pleasant Bay Beach (see *Green Space—Beaches*). Late June to early September $135–255 rooms, $185–255 efficiencies, $285–355 one-bedroom suites for four people, $345–455 two-bedroom suites for four. The lower end of these ranges is for late June to late July. Inquire about weekly rates. Children $15–20 additional per day.

LIGHTHOUSE

South Monomoy Lighthouse (508-896-3867; www.ccmnh.org). Overnights permitted late May to early October. Administered by the Cape Cod Museum of Natural History, this 30-hour Monomoy Island overnight includes transportation to and from the island and time with a naturalist, who will end up cooking your dinner by kerosene lamp. Breakfast and a substantial lunchtime snack are also included, since your departure is tide dependent. The rustic keeper's house has three bedrooms with air mattresses and cots. This overnight is very popular; you'd be well advised to make reservations after late January, if you can. $200 per person.

RENTAL HOUSES AND COTTAGES

Sylvan Rentals (508-432-2344), 1715 Route 28, South Chatham 02659, has listings ranging from basic beach cottages to luxury homes.

WHERE TO EAT

Dining in Chatham runs the gamut from elegant to child-friendly places. Reserve ahead on summer weekends or be prepared for a lengthy wait.

DINING OUT

At the risk of alienating some Chatham friends, your fine-dining dollars are more reliably spent (with perhaps one exception) in the neighboring towns of Brewster and Harwich.

❄ **Sosumi Asian Bistro & Sushi Bar** (508-945-0300), 14 Chatham Bars Avenue. Open daily for lunch and dinner. I was thrilled to learn of this mod bistro's opening in 2000. The exciting tastes and exotic flavors have really ignited the traditional dining options in Chatham. I treat the menu like a tapas menu, ordering assorted appetizers, soups, and salads as I go along. I have never met a dish I didn't like. Try the grilled eggplant with plum paste, shrimp toast with sweet-and-spicy cucumber noodles, lobster bisque, spicy seaweed salad, house-made parsnip chips, or pungent purple pickles. While the menu is quite far-reaching, you can always stick to sushi, grilled tuna teriyaki, or scallops tempura. The tuna burger with wasabi mayo and slaw is also a treat. Live big and order a sake sampler with five varied rice wines (warm and cold). Appetizers $5–12, entrées $15–23.

Vining's Bistro (508-945-5033), 595 Main Street (on the second floor). Open for dinner April through November (often closed Sunday and Monday off-season). The bistro, with high ceilings and exposed beams, specializes in wood grilling, but the menu really roams the world, although it is strongly influenced by the West Coast. Seasonal possibilities include: North African vegetable curry, warm lobster taco, and Thai crabcakes. This is one of the more adventurous restaurants in town, thanks to the vision of owners Lynda and Steve Vining. Entrées $16–24.

Le Petit Cafe (508-945-0028), 155 Crowell Road. Open for dinner April to mid-January. While I didn't get a chance to dine at this casual little café, my innkeeper friends all rave about it. Rest assured, the modest surroundings belie the quality of cuisine. Creative and well-priced dishes like bouillabaisse and lobster medallions on tagliatelle pasta in a lobster reduction sauce keep pace with steak *frites* in a red wine shallot sauce and roasted magret duck breast. (The menu is predominantly seafood, though.) Entrées $15–24.

❄♿✎**Campari's** and **Benedetto's** (508-945-9123), 323 Route 28 (Northport Shopping Plaza). Campari's is open for dinner daily, June to mid-October (less frequently the rest of the year); Benedetto's is open for dinner daily. Perhaps it's the location—just outside of town with plenty of parking—or perhaps it's Bob and Lisa Chiappetta's fine reputation that inspired loyalists to follow when they moved here in 1998. Whatever the case, there is more than ample reason to dine here on Italian-inspired seafood and vegetable dishes like shrimp and mussel scampi on capellini pasta, veal Piccata, and eggplant stuffed with ricotta and spinach. The choices are extensive, servings large, and bistro pricing right. Benedetto's is a much more casual, family-style alternative, with pizza, pastas, burgers, and grinders on the menu. Both places are always hopping, as is the **bar.** Children's menu. Campari's entrées $17–28, Benedetto's dishes $4–17.

Wequassett Inn (508-432-5400), Route 28, North Chatham (just over the Harwich town line, actually). Open for lunch and dinner, mid-April to mid-November. Although the Wequassett Inn is technically within the sliver of Harwich fronting Pleasant Bay, I include it in "Chatham" because its sensibility matches Chatham far more than it does Harwich. Having said that, executive chef Frank McMullen oversees regional American cuisine at the genteel **Eben Ryder House,** and a charming maître d' oversees the understated, elegant dining room. McMullen's strong suit is local seafood prepared traditionally; the menu changes seasonally. The lounge is livened by a pianist in July and August. Down by the pool, the more casual **Outer Bar & Grill,** with a large and open deck, serves lobster salad and seafood at lunch and dinner. The setting, right on the water, is lovely. Reservations recommended. Lunch $9–15, dinner entrées $25–38.

Queen Anne Inn (508-945-0394), 70 Queen Anne Road. Open for dinner early May to late October. This independently operated fine dining room serves sophisticated palates. During the 2000 season, the Austrian chef offered pheasant breast glazed with an apple–black currant preserve and grilled tenderloin with a sherry–rosemary glaze. The service is as gracious as the dining room is romantic. Reservations recommended. Entrées $20–26.

✍ **Chatham Bars Inn** (508-945-0096; 1-800-527-4884), Shore Road. Open for breakfast year-round, dinner late May to mid-November. Panoramic ocean views and romantic candlelit ambience are this conservative dining room's main claims to fame. Executive chef Yamamoto's international cuisine and seafood preparations are classic and conventional: clam chowder, Maine salmon, sweet local lobster, scallops chanterelles, and pecan-crusted rack of lamb. Save room for a sweet treat at the end—this is the place to indulge in desserts you might normally forgo. The grand **Sunday-night buffet,** accompanied by an a cappella group, is legendary. On Saturday evening a swing band entertains, while on Tuesday a pianist performs. Children's menu. Breakfast buffet $15 adults, $8 children; dinner entrées $18–34. Jacket and tie requested at dinner; reservations highly recommended.

❄✍ **Impudent Oyster** (508-945-3545), 15 Chatham Bars Avenue. Open for lunch and dinner nightly. The atmosphere is pleasant enough: peaked ceiling with exposed beams, skylights, and hanging plants. And the extensive menu highlights internationally inspired fish and shellfish dishes. Follow the lead of the regulars, though, and order from the daily specials. The beer-battered fish fry is popular at lunch, and the butternut bisque is rich all the time. Children's menu at dinner. Reservations recommended. Lunch $7–13; dinner entrées $17–24.

✳✿⚑**Christian's** (508-945-3362), 443 Main Street. "Upstairs" open for dinner nightly year-round; "downstairs" open for dinner nightly in-season. Owned by the Chatham Wayside Inn, Christian's has a split personality. Downstairs is quiet and comfortable, while upstairs, a traditional pub-style room with mahogany paneling, is more boisterous and casual, more appropriate for families. Fairly unadventurous Continental and American seafood dishes like grilled filet mignon and roast duck are popular, as are the seafood platter and lobster. In addition to the "downstairs" menu, burgers and pizza are available upstairs. Don't be surprised by spontaneous piano sing-alongs. Children's menu upstairs. Entrées $9–23.

✳✿ **Chatham Wayside Inn** (508-945-5550), 512 Main Street. Open daily for all three meals except closed Monday off-season. Simply because of its prominent in-town location and a constant parade of strollers-by, this pleasant room, featuring a 360-degree mural of Chatham, really packs visitors in at lunch. The midday menu is dominated by sandwiches and salads, perhaps a grilled chicken Caesar salad. As for atmosphere, the newly renovated room is filled with shiny wooden tables, Windsor chairs, and lots of windows. For breakfast, try the eggs Benedict made with Portuguese sweet muffins. Dinner is more ambitious (but sadly, the kitchen fell short on a recent visit): duck with pineapple, or cod with pesto, bread crumbs, and lemon beurre blanc. But the Wellfleet oysters and Chatham littlenecks are always very fresh. Children's menu. Breakfast $5–8, lunch $5–12; dinner entrées $13–22.

EATING OUT

✿ **Beach House Grill** (508-945-0096; 1-800-527-4884), Shore Road. Open for breakfast, lunch, and theme dinners mid-June to early September. Across from its parent Chatham Bars Inn (see *Dining Out*), this is the area's only alfresco oceanside dining. As it epitomizes easy summer living, you'd think there would be more places like it on the Cape. But there aren't. The deck is anchored in the sand, overlooking a wide, golden beach. When the kids finish eating before you do, they can run and play on the hotel's private beach. On foul-weather days, move indoors, enclosed by wall-to-wall sliding glass doors. The menu features upscale seaside standards: burgers, summer salads, smoked salmon plate, peel-and-eat shrimp, and fried seafood platters. The breakfast buffet ($15 adults, $8 children) features an omelet station. Check out the various theme dinners, all with apropos live music—Monday family beach barbecues, Wednesday clambakes, and Thursday Caribbean cuisine. Lunch $7–16.

✿✳✿⚑**Chatham Squire** (508-945-0945 restaurant; 508-945-0942 tavern), 487

Main Street. Open for lunch and dinner daily. Chatham's best family restaurant offers something for everyone—from burgers and moderately priced daily seafood specials to a raw bar, multi-ethnic dishes, and excellent chowder. Paisley carpeting, low booths, captain's chairs at wooden tables, exposed beams, and pool tables (off-season only) add to the family-den feel of the place. Drop in for a drink in the busy and colorful **tavern** (a haven for 20-somethings in summer until locals take it back for the off-season). Children's menu. Lunch $5–14; double that for dinner entrées.

Carmine's (508-945-5300), 595 Main Street. Open for lunch and dinner April through December (weekends only in fall and spring). For quick and inexpensive eats, try Carmine's, which offers slices of pizza (and whole pies, for that matter).

Chatham Village Cafe (508-945-2525), 400 Main Street. Open for breakfast and lunch. Tired of walking in and out of all the Main Street shops? When the boutiques and galleries start to peter out, this upscale deli will beckon you with dozens of creative sandwiches for $5.75. There are a couple of picnic tables in front.

Luscious Louie's (508-945-5223), 1603 Route 28, West Chatham. When a place uses seven-grain bread for its sandwiches, you know you're in luck. Owned by a pastry chef and the former executive chef at the Chatham Bars Inn, this is not your average picnic purveyor. After feasting on baked cod with focaccia crumbs or grilled salmon with an herbed compound butter from the deli case, try a tart Key lime tart or giant éclair or blueberry and white chocolate cheesecake. Portions are enormous. There are a few indoor tables. The shop is a couple of miles west of the rotary, far from the madding crowds.

Chatham Provisions (508-432-7126), 1403 Old Queen Ann Road. At the corner of Route 137, and a mile north of Route 28, this picnic provision place is run by very friendly folks intent on making their customers happy. Put together a morning pick-me-up of pastries and croissants or a lunchtime meal with sesame snap peas, pesto tortellini, and tuna salad with practically no filler.

Marion's Pie Shop (508-432-9439), 2022 Route 28. Open mid-March to late December. Marion's savory pies are a delicious alternative to prepared sandwiches or salads. Perfect for busy families that can reheat them at home, Marion's pies come in large and small sizes. You can't go wrong with the chicken potpies, clam pies, beefsteak pies, fruit pies, or the breakfast baked goods (especially the cinnamon rolls). Takeout only from this humble but humming little house. I highly recommend calling in your order! Careful with the kids; misbehaving ones "will be made into pies."

The Tavern (508-945-0096), Shore Road, at the Chatham Bars Inn. Open for lunch and dinner daily. The atmosphere is sumptuously casual, clubby, with dark and handsome paneling, a long **bar,** and a big central fireplace.

There's plenty of time for reflection at the beach.

The menu is easygoing, too, and features seafood, a mixed grill, club sandwiches, and the like. Children's menu. Lunch $7–16, dinner entrées $14–25.

Break Away Cafe (508-945-3637), Chatham Municipal Airport, George Ryder Road. Open for lunch in July and August and breakfast late April to early November (only on weekends in the off-season). You don't have to charter an airplane to eat here. But you'll enjoy sitting outside watching the planes take off at this tiny airstrip. Before Sue and Tim Roth set up shop out here, they had a popular breakfast place near the beach. Omelets, eggs, and waffles in the morning; salads, sandwiches, burgers, and dogs for lunch. Starbucks coffee. Dishes $2–10.

See also Concerts (lobster suppers) under *Entertainment* and Benedetto's, Impudent Oyster, and Chatham Wayside Inn under *Dining Out*.

DRINKS

Chatham Bars Inn (508-945-0096), Shore Road. The grand hotel's terrace, overlooking the ocean, makes a picture-perfect setting for a late-afternoon drink.

SPECIALTY OUTLETS

Farmer's Market, Veterans Park (Route 28, just west of the rotary), is held late May to early September, 8–noon on Tuesday.

❄ **Clambake Celebrations** (508-945-7771; 1-877-792-7771), 1223 Route 28. Lobsters and steamers (clams) are air-shipped (or you can order them and pick them up at the shop) in a cooking pot layered with seaweed. Just add water and steam for 30 minutes. Packages also include mussels, corn on the cob, new potatoes, onions, and sweet Italian sausage, as well as claw crackers, bibs, forks, and moist towelettes. Clambake for four people is $228 (including FedEx delivery); for two, $146; combinations priced accordingly. Local pickup prices are lower.

❅ **Chatham Fish & Lobster Company** (508-945-1178), Route 28, Cornfield Market Place. For those of you with cooking facilities: They hook 'em, you cook 'em.

ENTERTAINMENT

Monomoy Theatre (508-945-1589), 776 Main Street. Performances late June to late August. Operated by Ohio University, the Monomoy is among the Cape's better-known and oldest (1930) playhouses. A new production—anything from a Rodgers and Hammerstein musical to Shakespeare—is staged every week. There isn't a bad choice among the 263 seats. Evening curtain at 8 or 8:30, matinees at 2.

✐ **Band concerts** at Kate Gould Park, off Main Street. Every Friday night at 8, early July to early September, this brass-band concert is the place to be. As many as 6,000 lighthearted visitors enjoy music and people-watching as they have for the past 60 years. Dance and swing to Sousa marches, big-band selections, and other standards. The bandstand, balloons tied to strollers, bags of popcorn, blankets on the grass, and the Star-Spangled Banner that closes the program—it hasn't changed a "whit" since it began. (Except that beloved Whit Tileston, who led the band for almost 50 years, passed away in 1995.)

✐ **Concerts (lobster suppers),** First United Methodist Church (508-945-0474), 16 Cross Street. The church sponsors free choral, jazz, big-band, light classical, and a cappella concerts Sunday summer evenings at 8. Since the mid-1960s, the church has also held popular Friday lobster roll suppers at 4:30 PM prior to the concerts in Kate Gould Park. Adults $10, children $4.

✐ **Baseball,** Veterans Park, Route 28, just west of the rotary. The Chatham A's (the Athletics), one of 10 teams in the Cape Cod Baseball League, usually play ball at 7 PM from mid-June to mid-August; the information booth (see *Guidance*) has schedules.

Bands. In the off-season, locals flock to the Chatham Squire (see *Eating Out*) for live bands.

SELECTIVE SHOPPING

❅ Depending on your age and interests, Chatham's Main Street just could be the Cape's best shopping street. (Merchants and visitors loyal to Provincetown's Commercial Street may have something to say about that.) Instead of organizing shops by category like I usually do, I list them here in the order you'll encounter them while strolling. Unless otherwise noted, all shops are open year-round. Note, though, that many places listed as open year-round are only open on weekends in winter.

West of the rotary

Chatham Glass Company (508-945-5547), 758 Main Street. Open daily
except Sunday. James Holmes designs and creates unique, colorful glass
items—candlesticks, goblets, platters, bud vases, and marbles—sold in
Barneys, Neiman-Marcus, and Gump's. The working studio is just behind the brilliantly lit displays, so you can watch the creative process of
glassblowing.

East Wind Silver Co. (508-945-8935), 878 Main Street. This gallery features more than sterling jewelry. Look for foil floor cloths, watercolors
with a local angle, hand-thrown pots with metallic raku glazes, Tiffany-
style art glass, and water fountains.

Munson Gallery (508-945-2888), 880 Main Street. Open June through
November. Munson's has been in business since 1955 as one of *the* Cape
galleries for paintings, photographs, and sculpture by area artists. It
would be a shame not to stop in. The collection is fine, with something
for everyone, it seems—in both price and taste. The gallery is housed in
a wonderfully restored barn, right down to horse stalls hung with art.

Ivy Cottage Shop (508-945-1809), 894 Main Street, Munson Meeting
Complex. Buyer Peggy DeHan has a good eye for both vintage and new
stuff—linens, place settings, decorative home accessories, framed
prints, painted furniture—that would look perfect in a country cottage
or summerhouse. Pieces are affordable and well priced (unlike at many
shops in Chatham), in the $40–100 range. She haunts flea markets and
scours the countryside so you don't have to. And she keeps you coming
back with new acquisitions daily.

Kingsley Brown Galleries (508-945-6408), 902 Main Street. You
probably didn't come to the Cape looking for African art, but this gallery
has a great selection of masks, sculptures, textiles, and other art. There
is another location on the other side of the rotary at 499 Main Street.

Rose Cottage Shop (508-945-3114), 1281 Route 28. Richard Morris, an
expert at restoring and renovating old houses, also has a talent for decorating their interiors. He's been in Chatham quite a while and has developed a loyal following. This expansive showroom offers mostly larger
pieces, tasteful country-pine antiques, fine reproductions, and unique
home accessories. Richard travels to England several times a year,
where he finds most of his pieces.

The Cooperage at the 1736 House (508-945-5690), 1731 Route 28, West
Chatham. It's worth stopping here simply to walk through the oldest
house in Chatham. But watch out: It's tantalizingly easy to spend money
on period antiques shown in a period house! Anthony and Barbara
Bridgewater, a lovely English couple, have also filled a series of barns
behind the house with antiques and items from their Cape Cod Cooperage (see below). Check out the sturdy lobster-pot chairs, a truly
unique marriage of form and function invented by a Chatham commercial fisherperson.

Chatham Pottery (508-430-2191), 2058 Route 28, South Chatham. Open daily. Gill Willson and Margaret Willson-Grey's large studio offers a wide array of functional, decorative stoneware for everyday use— hand-thrown pots, pitchers, sinks, plates, bowls, tiles, and tables. They also carry a few other items to "accessorize" their pottery, including wrought iron, rugs, and handcrafted glass.

Chatham Jam and Jelly Shop (508-945-3052), Route 28, West Chatham. Almost 2 miles east of the intersection of Routes 28 and 137, this colorful shop sells dozens and dozens of varieties of homemade jams and jellies. Feel free to taste them before committing. Try the wild beach plum, elderberry, or damson plum. They're hard to resist and make nice gifts.

Cape Cod Cooperage (508-432-0788), 1150 Queen Anne Road at Route 137. Within a rambling barn, floors covered in sawdust, this cooperage has made containers to hold fish and cranberries for shipment to Boston and New York since the late 1800s. At the state's only remaining cooperage, coopers here still use the 100-year-old methods. Three-hour and daylong painting and stenciling classes are offered throughout the year. The cooperage also has well-priced furniture to paint yourself, primitive folk-style painted furniture, and slate WELCOME signs.

See also Creative Arts Center under *Even More Things to See and Do—Art Classes.*

East of the rotary

Main Street Pottery (508-945-0128), 645C Main Street. Barbara Parent works here, so you can watch her making pots similar to the one you're purchasing.

Cabbages and Kings (508-945-1603), 628 Main Street. New hardcovers, paperbacks, and many children's books and toys in a light-filled shop. Long live the independents!

Spyglass (508-945-9686), 618 Main Street. Although this exceptional shop is best known for its telescope collection, there are all sorts of nautical antiques like barometers, sextants, maps, charts, and even a few paintings and sea captain portraits. It's great to poke around when you begin to lose sight of the Cape's maritime connection.

Monomoy Outdoors (508-945-9499), 593 Main Street. Open for all your retail fishing needs, as well as guided fishing trips and kayak rentals.

The Epicure (508-945-0047), 534 Main Street. Fine wines and specialty beers.

Yankee Ingenuity (508-945-1288), 525 Main Street. This eclectic assortment of "cool things" extends from art glass and jewelry to clocks and lamps. Prices run $2–1,500. If you don't get something here the day you see it, it may be gone tomorrow.

Yellow Umbrella Books (508-945-0144), 501 Main Street. Owner Eric Linder has gathered a fine selection of Cape Cod titles and some used books, too, for all ages and interests. Ditto on the earlier "long-live-the-independents" remark.

Falconer's (508-945-2867), 492 Main Street. Get your limited-edition Friday-night band concert lithographs here. Actually, there are many different Cape scenes available in lithograph, and original oil paintings, too.

Mark August Designs (508-945-2600), 490 Main Street. Functional and fun, creative and artsy decorative items for your house. Jewelry, too. If you don't like the background music, you're probably too old to be shopping here.

Regatta Shop (508-945-4999), 483 Main Street. Open March through December. Seaside motifs and sailing-oriented gifts for your favorite sailor or sailor wannabe. Prints of ships, lighthouses, and beach scenes; hand-painted furniture; sterling pendants and charms; foul-weather gear; and colorful blankets to ward off chills aboard your yacht or sofa.

Chatham Candy Manor (508-945-0825; 1-800-221-6497), 484 Main Street. Open daily. They've made hand-dipped chocolate, fudge, and liqueur-flavored truffles since 1955.

The Mayflower (508-945-0065), 475 Main Street. Established in 1885, this venerable, old-time general store is beginning to look out of place on swanky Main Street. Let's hope it survives.

The Patten Gallery (508-945-5313), 459A Main Street. The subject matter of Nick Patten's hand-colored lithographs and mezzotints is brooding, spare interiors, still lifes that create a sense of quiet. He works in the front of the gallery and enjoys discussing the work.

Demos Antiques (508-945-1939), 447 Main Street. Open daily May through October and weekends off-season. You'll find funky treasures here—from a dressmaker's dummy to an antique nutmeg grater—as well as estate jewelry and miniature gold Nantucket lightship baskets. Also, Tiffany lamps, Sandwich whale oil lamps, fine glass, china, sterling, coins. You can't miss the place, with items spilling out onto the front lawn. Cynthia Demos went to school in Chatham, and her family have had this shop, in one form or another, since 1956. If they don't have it, you don't need it.

Odell's Studio and Gallery (508-945-3239), 423 Main Street. Open daily except Sunday year-round, and evenings by chance in summer. Tom and Carol Odell, metalsmith and painter, respectively, have lived and worked in their lovely old home since 1975. They've turned it into a bright and airy gallery space. Carol does colorful nonobjective, multimedia paintings, monotypes, gouaches, and screens. Her work complements Tom's jewelry and sculpture, which he fashions from precious metals and alloys. Tom's recent work shows evidence of a Japanese aesthetic. I must admit that this is my favorite shop in town; artistry oozes from the walls.

Mermaids on Main (508-945-3179), 410 Main Street. Open late May through December. Kids will love this colorful place, bursting at the seams with purple- and aquamarine-colored playthings. Hold on to your wallets. (Actually, items are well priced.) Books, bubble bath, candles, rubber stamps, mobiles, and small stuffed and rubber creatures, among hundreds of other things.

Forest Beach Design (508-945-7334), 402 Main Street. Chatham's Main Street has been sprouting upscale jewelry shops recently, and this small shop is the best among them.

SPECIAL EVENTS

Early May: **Spring Fling** opens the summer season. Bake sales, a crazy-hat contest, jugglers and clowns, and a treasure hunt for children.

Mid- to late May: **Cape Cod Maritime Days** (508-862-0700). Coast Guard–operated lighthouses are open during this festival, including Chatham Light, Monomoy Light, and Stage Harbor. In addition to focusing on the area's lighthouses, the Cape-wide event celebrates the region's fishing heritage, maritime villages, and seafaring way of life.

July 4: **Independence Day arade** from Main Street to Veterans Park; strawberry festival with shortcake at the First United Methodist Church (16 Cross Street) postparade.

Mid-August: **Chatham Festival of the Arts,** Chase Park. On the third weekend in August, the Creative Arts Center sponsors more than 100 exhibitors, from painters to quilters to sculptors (see *Even More Things to See and Do—Art Classes*).

Mid-October: **Seafest,** an annual tribute to Chatham's maritime industry. There are exhibits and demonstrations on net mending, casting techniques, quahog raking, the proper way to eat a lobster, fishing skills, boating, filleting fish, and rigging.

Late November to mid-December: **Christmas by the Sea and Christmas Stroll.** This annual 2-week event includes a tree-lighting ceremony, candy-cane-making demonstrations, caroling, mulled cider served at the Mayo House (see *To See*), hayrides, open houses, and much more.

New Year's Eve: **First Night Celebration.** Fireworks over Oyster Pond (see *Green Space—Pond*). Chatham limits the number of buttons sold to residents and visitors so the town won't be overrun.

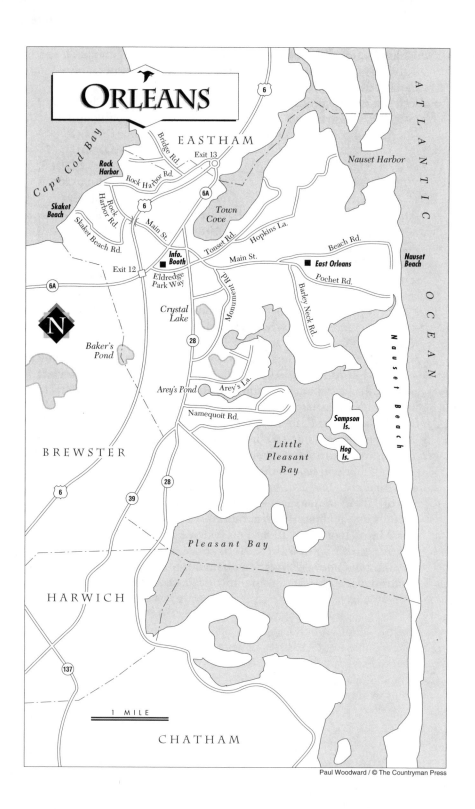

ORLEANS

EASTHAM

Cape Cod Bay

ATLANTIC OCEAN

Bridge Rd.

Exit 13

Rock Harbor

Rock Harbor Rd.

6

6A

Nauset Harbor

Skaket Beach

Rock Harbor Rd.

Town Cove

6

Main St.

Skaket Beach Rd.

Tonset Rd.

Hopkins La.

Beach Rd.

Nauset Beach

Info. Booth

Exit 12

Main St.

■ **East Orleans**

6A

Eldredge Park Way

Monument Rd.

Pochet Rd.

Barley Neck Rd.

Nauset Beach

Crystal Lake

N

28

Baker's Pond

Arey's Pond

Arey's La.

Namequoit Rd.

Sampson Is.

Little Pleasant Bay

Hog Is.

BREWSTER

28

6

39

Pleasant Bay

HARWICH

137

1 MILE

CHATHAM

Paul Woodward / © The Countryman Press

Orleans

Many could argue, with some success, that Orleans's biggest draw is Nauset Beach, an Atlantic Ocean barrier beach more than 9 miles long. It can accommodate hundreds of sun seekers and sandcastle builders in summer. But in the off-season, you'll be practically alone, walking in quiet reflection, observing shorebirds and natural rhythms. It's a beautifully haunting place during a storm—so long as it's not a huge storm. Nauset Beach also has historical significance. It was explored by Gosnold in 1602 and Champlain in 1605. It was the location of the first recorded shipwreck on the eastern seaboard, in 1626, when the *Sparrow Hawk* ran aground near Pochet. It is the only place in the continental United States to be fired upon in the War of 1812 (by the British) and in World War I (in 1918 it was shelled by a German submarine). Most recently, two Englishmen set off from nearby Nauset Harbor to row successfully across the Atlantic Ocean.

The real charm of Orleans, which has few historical sights, lies not in the sand but in the waters that surround the town. A large number of fingerlike inlets creep into the eastern shoreline from aptly named Pleasant Bay, dotted with tiny islands. And most of these quiet inlets are accessible via back roads and town landings. Excursion boats explore the rich habitat of Nauset Marsh to the north, while bayside, Rock Harbor is home to the Cape's most active charter fishing fleet.

Because Routes 6, 6A, and 28 converge in Orleans, traffic is heavy in summer; getting anywhere takes time. But Orleans straddles the two distinct worlds of the Outer and Lower Cape. On the one hand, Orleans serves as a year-round commercial and retail center for the area. It offers plenty of activities and a variety of dining and lodging options. On the other hand, Orleans has its share of exclusive residential areas and plenty of quiet, waterside spots.

Orleans is the only Cape town without a Native American or English name. Incorporated in 1797 after separating from Eastham, Orleans was named for Louis Philippe de Bourbon, duke of Orléans (and later king of France), who visited this Orleans in 1797 during his exile.

GUIDANCE

Orleans Chamber of Commerce Information Booth (508-240-2484 booth; 508-255-1386 administration office; www.capecod-orleans.com),

P.O. Box 153, Orleans 02653. Booth open 10–6 daily, late May to early September, 10–4 daily until mid-October; weekends 10–4 through October. The booth is on Eldredge Parkway (just off Route 6A), south of the Orleans rotary. The administrative office, located at 44 Main Street, is open year-round. Like all Cape towns, Orleans publishes a helpful booklet (which you can pick up here), but the booth is also full of menus.

PUBLIC LIBRARY

✳♨⊤**Snow Library** (508-240-3760), Main Street at Route 28. Open 10–5 Monday, 10–8 Tuesday and Wednesday, 10–5 Thursday and Friday, 10–4 Saturday. It's only open Sunday 2–4 from November through March.

PUBLIC REST ROOMS

Public rest rooms are located at the information booth on Eldredge Parkway; and at the Community Building, 44 Main Street.

GETTING THERE

By car: Take Route 6 east from either the Sagamore Bridge or the Bourne Bridge for about 48 miles to exit 12. Route 6A east takes you directly into town.

By bus: The **Plymouth & Brockton** bus line (508-778-9767; www.p-b.com) connects Orleans with Hyannis and other Cape towns, as well as with Boston's Logan Airport. It stops at the CVS on Main Street.

GETTING AROUND

East Orleans Village and Nauset Beach are 3 miles east of the center of Orleans (which is located along Route 6A); Rock Harbor and Skaket Beach are 1.5 miles west of the center.

The **H$_2$O** (508-385-8326; 1-800-352-7155; www.capecodtransit.org) bus, used more by locals than visitors, travels along Route 28 between Hyannis and Orleans daily except Sunday year-round. It makes about five stops in Orleans, so it's best to call them for locations. With all the stops it makes along the way, it takes about 90 minutes to get from Orleans to Hyannis.

MEDICAL EMERGENCY

Orleans Medical Center (508-255-9577), Route 6A or exit 12 off Route 6. Walk-ins accepted weekdays year-round.

TO SEE

⊤ **Meeting House Museum** (508-255-1386), at Main Street and River Road. Open 10–1 Thursday through Saturday in July and August. Built in 1833 as a Universalist meetinghouse, and now operated by the Orleans Historical Society, the museum contains artifacts documenting Orleans's early history. Among the items are an assessor's map of Orleans homes in 1858, photographs, Native American artifacts, and a bicentennial quilt. The building is a fine example of Greek Revival Doric architecture. Free.

⊤ **French Cable Station Museum** (508-240-1735), Route 28 at Cove Road. Open 1–4 Monday through Saturday in July and August; 1–4 Friday through Sunday in June and September; otherwise, by special appointment. Before the advent of the "information superhighway" and wireless communications, there was the French Cable Station. Direct transmissions from Brest, France (via a 3,000-mile underwater cable), were made from this station between 1890 and 1941, at which time transmissions were automated. Among the relayed news items: Charles Lindbergh's successful crossing of the Atlantic and his 1927 Paris landing, and Germany's invasion of France. Much of the original equipment and instruments are still set up and in working order. (Alas, the cable is no longer operational.) The displays, put together with the help of the Smithsonian Institution, are a bit intimidating and confusing, but someone is on hand to unravel the mysteries. Free.

Jonathan Young Windmill (508-240-1329), on Route 6A at Town Cove Park; you can park at the Orleans Inn. Open 11–4 daily in July and August; 11–4 weekends mid-May through June and September to mid-October. This circa-1720 gristmill was built in East Orleans, transported to the center of town in 1839, moved to Hyannisport in 1897, and returned to Orleans in 1983. Although it's no longer operational, the windmill is significant because of its intact milling machinery. Within the mill are interpretive exhibits, a display of a 19th-century miller's handiwork, and a resident miller—who explained the origins of "keep your nose to the grindstone": Because grain is highly combustible when it's ground, a miller who wasn't paying close attention to his grain might not live to see the end of the day. The setting, overlooking Town Cove, provides a nice backdrop for a picnic. Free.

Rock Harbor, on Cape Cod Bay, at the end of Rock Harbor Road from Main Street. This protected harbor, the town's first commercial and maritime center, served as a packet landing for ships transporting goods to Plymouth, Boston, and Maine. When the harbor filled with silt, several old houses in the area were built from the lumber of dismantled saltworks. During the War of 1812, Orleans militiamen turned back Britain's HMS *Newcastle* from Rock Harbor. In case you're wondering about the dead trees in the harbor entrance, they mark the channel that is dredged for the charter fishing fleet.

SCENIC DRIVES

Pleasant Bay, Little Pleasant Bay, Nauset Harbor, and Town Cove creep deep into the Orleans coastline at about a dozen named inlets, ponds, and coves. With the detailed centerfold map from the Orleans Chamber of Commerce guide in hand (see *Guidance*), head down the side roads off Tonset Road, Hopkins Lane, Nauset Heights Road, and Barley Neck Road to the town landings. After passing beautifully landscaped residences, you'll be rewarded with serene, pastoral scenes of beach grass and sailboats. Directly off Route 28 heading toward Chatham there are two particularly lovely ponds with saltwater outlets: **Arey's Pond** (off Arey's Lane from Route 28) and **Kescayogansett**

Pond (off Monument Road from Route 28). There's a little picnic area with limited parking at **Kent's Point** near here, off Frost Fish Lane from Monument Road.

OUTDOOR ACTIVITIES

BICYCLING/RENTALS

The Cape Cod Rail Trail runs near the center of town, right past Orleans Cycle (508-255-9115), 26 Main Street, which is open April through December. Expect to spend about $12 for 3 hours, $17–20 daily, $40 for 3 days; less for kids' bikes.

BOAT EXCURSIONS

Nauset Marsh Cruise (508-255-4250), Town Cove, behind the Goose Hummock Outdoor Center, off Route 6A. Mid-June to early October. Since this 2-hour catamaran voyage only departs two or three times a week, it's best to call for departure times and days. Along with informative on-board narration, kids and adults enjoy hauling traps from the marsh and getting acquainted with the on-board touch tank. Adults $30; children 12 and under $25.

CANOEING/KAYAKING

The protected, calm waters of northern **Pleasant Bay** offer delightful canoeing opportunities. (Southern Pleasant Bay can be treacherous; talk with the folks at the Goose Hummock Outdoor Center before setting off.) There is limited parking at each of the numerous town landings, but it's free.

Goose Hummock Outdoor Center (508-255-2620), off Route 6A on Town Cove. Shop open year-round; rentals mid-May to mid-October. Pick up the Nauset Harbor tide chart and rent a canoe or recreational kayak ($25 for four hours, $45 daily, $100 for 3 days; more for big touring sea kayaks). For 24-hour rentals, the center throws in a loaner roof rack. If you're new to kayaking, take their 3½ -hour course ($65) to learn basic paddle strokes and skills. Otherwise, consider one of the center's organized half-day trips ($65), which require 24 hours' notice to put together.

See also Nauset Sports under *In-Line Skating.*

FISHING/SHELLFISHING

Freshwater fishing requires a state permit, obtainable at the town clerk's office (508-240-3700), 19 School Road, off Main Street. Check **Pilgrim Lake,** off Kescayogansett Road and Monument Road, and **Crystal Lake,** off Monument Road (see *Green Space—Ponds*). There are at least a dozen fresh- and saltwater town landings in Orleans. Anglers looking for trout and perch will most likely find them in Crystal Lake. Contact the harbormaster (508-240-3755), Route 28, Orleans, about a shellfishing permit and regulations before you head out with your shovel, rake, and bucket.

Casey Jones (508-896-4048) offers an unusual service. If you've always

KIM GRANT

Early morning and low tide on Nauset Marsh

wondered how people find clams and how they dig with those shovels and rakes, Casey will teach you how and where. Casey, who has a commercial permit, has been clamming all her life. This tide-dependent activity is not as easy as it looks, but after searching out littlenecks, cherrystones, and mussels with Casey, you'll be a pro. $35 per person for a 2½ - to 4-hour adventure, plus an inexpensive seasonal shellfish permit (per family). Inquire about children's rates. All equipment provided. At press time, Casey was in the middle of writing a cookbook devoted to clams.

Bruce Scott (508-896-4048) knows the ins and outs of Nauset Inlet. Yes, he'll help you catch striped bass, but he'll also teach you about finding your own bait and observing where the birds feed. This will increase your chances of landing stripers no matter where you go on the Cape. If you want to get away from the crowds, a quiet paddle through this fragile inlet will do it. $85 per person for a 4- to 6-hour trip. Special motorboat trips available, too; inquire about prices.

✳ **Goose Hummock Outdoor Center** (508-255-2620), Town Cove, Route 6A at the rotary, Orleans. This outfitter will fulfill all your fishing-related needs, including rod rentals, fishing trips, instruction, and wintertime fly-tying seminars. Shellfishing equipment, too. The staff offers lots of free advice and information.

✐ **Rock Harbor Charter Fleet** (508-255-9757; 1-800-287-1771 within Massachusetts), Rock Harbor. Trips daily mid-May to mid-October; harbor booth staffed from June through September. These 18 boats comprise the largest charter fleet in New England. U.S. Coast Guard–licensed captains offer 4- and 8-hour trips for groups in search of bluefish, striped bass, and mackerel. Children welcome. $100 per person for a 4-hour trip,

$120 per person for an 8-hour trip. If you round up six people, it costs $400 for a half day, $600 for a full day.

IN-LINE SKATING

Nauset Sports (508-255-4742), Jeremiah Square, Route 6A at the Orleans rotary. Open year-round, but rentals are only provided in-season: in-line skates, tennis rackets, surfboards, kayaks, boogie boards, and wet suits.

MINI-GOLF

Cape Escape (508-240-1791), Canal Road, off Route 6A near the Orleans rotary. Open seasonally.

See also Kadee's Lobster & Clam Bar under *Eating Out*.

SAILING

Arey's Pond Boat Yard (508-255-0994), Arey's Lane off Route 28, South Orleans. Late May to early September. They offer 10 hours of beginning and intermediate sailing instruction over the course of 5 weekdays for $170. A popular weekly kids' camp ($275) is offered 8–12:30 weekdays. Group and private lessons by appointment. Private lessons cost $60 per hour, with a 2-hour minimum.

TENNIS

Public courts are located at **Eldredge Park** (off Route 28 at Eldredge Parkway) and the **elementary school** (off Eldredge Parkway). Free.

See also the Recreational Department under *Even More Things to See and Do—For Families* and Nauset Sports under *In-Line Skating*.

EVEN MORE THINGS TO SEE AND DO

BOWLING

Orleans Bowling Center (508-255-0636), 191 Route 6A. Okay, so you didn't come to the Cape to go bowling, but if it's raining and you've got kids in the car, it's an idea.

FITNESS CENTER

Willy's Gym and Fitness Center (508-255-6826), 21 Old Colony Way, off West Road from Route 6A, Orleans Marketplace. Open daily. One of the Cape's best fitness centers, Willy's has an extensive array of cardiovascular machines, free weights, sauna and steam rooms, classes, supervised child care, and a café. $12 per day, $30 for a 3-day weekend, $39 weekly.

FOR FAMILIES

Baseball clinics (508-255-0793). The Orleans Cardinals hold a 7-week baseball clinic for boys and girls 6–13 that begins in early June. As many as 60–70 kids might show up, but there is always a good ratio of player-instructors to kids. The cost is $55 for the first week, $50 each additional week.

Recreational Department (508-240-3785), 44 Main Street, offers instructional tennis for adults and kids over age 7, a playground program for kids 7–14, and swimming lessons. Call for schedule details and registration.

Nauset Beach, the 9-mile-long barrier beach in Orleans

SKATING

❊⍣ **Charles Moore Arena** (508-255-2971), O'Connor Way, near the town
landfill; look for signs at the information booth (see *Guidance*). The 85-
by-200-foot arena is reserved most of the year, but there are times in
spring and fall set aside for public skating; it's best to call. Every Friday 8–
10 PM year-round is Rock Night, when the strobe-lit rink is reserved for
9-to 14-year-olds.

SPECIAL PROGRAMS

❊⍣ **Academy of Performing Arts** (508-255-5510 for the school), 5 Giddiah Hill
Road. The academy offers Cape-wide instruction to more than 500
students of all ages, including jazz, tap, and ballet dance classes; musical
instrument instruction; and drama and creative writing courses. Two-
week sessions (concentrating on musical theater, ballet, and drama
production) in July and August end with a public performance. Children's
summer matinees at 10 every Friday.

GREEN SPACE

BEACHES

⍣ **Nauset Beach** (508-240-3780), on the Atlantic Ocean, off Beach Road,
beyond the center of East Orleans. It doesn't get much better than this:
good bodysurfing waves and 9 miles of sandy Atlantic shoreline, backed
by a low dune. (Only about a half-mile stretch is covered by lifeguards;
much of the rest is deserted.) A gently sloping grade makes this a good
beach for children. Facilities include an in-season lifeguard, rest rooms,
a snack bar, chairs and umbrellas for rent, and plenty of parking (parking

is rarely a problem). Parking costs $10 daily ($35–40 weekly), mid-June to early September; $5 on late-May, early-June, and off-season holiday weekends. Free after 4:30.

Four-wheel-drive vehicles with permit are allowed onto Nauset Beach except during certain bird-breeding and nesting periods. From May to mid-October, obtain permits at the beach or from the harbormaster behind the Orleans Police Station if it's a weekend in July and August). Off-season, by appointment only, head to the Parks and Beaches Department (508-240-3775), 18 Bay Ridge Lane.

Skaket Beach (508-255-0572), on Cape Cod Bay, off Skaket Beach Road. Popular with families, as you can walk a mile out into the bay at low tide; at high tide the beach grass is covered. The parking lot often fills up early, creating a 30-minute wait for a space. Parking $10 daily from mid-June to early September. (The parking fee is transferable to Nauset Beach on the same day.) Amenities include an in-season lifeguard, rest rooms, and a snack bar.

Pleasant Bay Beach, Route 28, South Orleans. A saltwater bayside inlet beach with limited roadside parking.

PONDS

Crystal Lake, off Monument Road and Route 28, and **Pilgrim Lake,** off Monument Road from Route 28, are good for swimming. Pilgrim Lake has an in-season lifeguard, rest rooms, changing rooms, picnic tables, a dock, and a small beach; parking is $8 daily. At Crystal Lake, parking is free but limited.

WALKS

Paw Wah Point Conservation Area, off Namequoit Road from Eldredge Parkway, has one trail leading to a nice little beach with picnic tables.

Rhododendron Display Garden, Route 28 and Main Street. A nice place for a picnic.

Sea Call Farm, Tonset Road, just north of the intersection with Main Street. Overlooking Town Cove, this is a nice place for a picnic.

LODGING

All in all, lodging in Orleans is a very good value. You'll find everything from contemporary studios to friendly B&Bs, from almost-beachfront motels to family motor inns.

RESORT MOTOR INN

The Cove (508-255-1203; 1-800-343-2233; www.thecoveorleans.com), 13 Route 28, Orleans 02653. As the name implies, this well-kept complex of 47 rooms and suites is situated on 300 feet of shorefront along Town Cove. A gazebo, a dock for sunning and fishing, picnic tables, and grills are well situated to exploit the view. There is also an outdoor heated pool. In summer the Cove offers a free boat tour of Town Cove and Nauset Beach. There are deluxe rooms with a sitting area and sofa bed; waterfront rooms with a shared deck overlooking the water; two-room suites with a kitchen (and some with a fireplace and private deck); and inn rooms with a bit more decor (some of these also have a fireplace and private deck). From late June to early September $109–189; mid-October through May $65–95. Service charge of $25 per visit added in high season. Children under 18 free in parent's room.

BED & BREAKFASTS

Nauset House Inn (508-255-2195; www.nausethouseinn.com), Beach Road, East Orleans 02643. Open April through October. These 14 rooms (8 with private bath) are the best in the area for many reasons. The inn has genuinely hospitable hosts; it's half a mile from Nauset Beach; guest rooms are thoughtfully and tastefully appointed; a greenhouse conservatory is just one of the many quiet places to relax. You'll have Diane and Al Johnson, their daughter Cindy, and her husband, John, to thank; they've owned and constantly upgraded the 1810 farmhouse since 1982. Rooms in the carriage house are generally larger than those in the inn, while the rustic **cottage,** with peaked ceiling, is quite private and cozy. $75–140; full breakfast included. One single room rents for $65.

❋ **Morgan's Way** (508-255-0831; www.capecodaccess.com/morgansway/), Morgan's Way, Orleans 02653. Page McMahan and Will Joy opened their contemporary home, about a mile south of town, to guests in 1990. Lush landscaping extends across 5 acres, and a multilevel deck wraps around a 20-by-40-foot heated pool. The interior is spacious; guests may use the open, second-floor living room, complete with TV, VCR, and wood-burning stove, and enjoy panoramic views beyond the pool. One of the two guest rooms has a small attached greenhouse. The delightful **poolside guest house** is bright and modern, with a full kitchen and private deck. This is a real find. Rooms: $125 May through October, $95 November through April, including a full breakfast. Pool house: $900 weekly May through October; $700 otherwise. No credit cards.

❋ **Parsonage Inn** (508-255-8217; 1-888-422-8217; www.parsonageinn.com), 202 Main Street, East Orleans 02643. This very pleasant, rambling, late-18th-century house has eight guest rooms (all with private bath) comfortably furnished with country antiques. (Only two rooms have adjoining walls, so there is plenty of privacy.) Wide pine floors, canopy beds, and newly redone bathrooms are common. The studio apartment Willow has a kitchenette and private entrance, while the roomy Barn, recently renovated with exposed beams and eaves, has a sitting area and sofa bed. Longtime innkeepers Elizabeth and Ian Browne, who hail from England, serve a full breakfast of apple crêpes or lemon ricotta pancakes at individual tables or on the brick patio. June through September $110–140; October through May $80–120.

MOTELS

& **Nauset Knoll Motor Lodge** (508-255-2364), Nauset Beach, East Orleans 02643. Open mid-April to mid-October. Nauset Knoll, located a few steps from Nauset Beach, is often booked long before other places because of the expansive views of dune and ocean. You can watch the sun as it rises over the ocean from lawn chairs atop the lodge's namesake knoll. The 12 simply furnished rooms (à la 1950s) with large picture windows are in three separate units, distinctively modeled after a barn, shed, and Cape-style cottage. Mid-June to early September $140; off-season $80–100.

Barley Neck Inn (508-255-0212; 1-800-281-7505; www.barleyneck.com), Beach Road, East Orleans 02643. Open May through November. After purchasing this neglected 18-room, bilevel motel in mid-1994, Joe and Kathi Lewis completely rehabbed it, much to the appreciation of area residents. It offers a good value for families: There is no charge for two children under age 12. Rooms are tastefully appointed, albeit with hotel/motel-style furnishings. There is a fenced-in swimming pool, but, alas, without any landscaping per se. The Barley Neck is well positioned between Orleans and Nauset Beach, about a mile from the beach. Late June to mid-September $129–159; off-season $79–109.

COTTAGES AND ROOMS

Rive Gauche (508-255-2676; fhogan@capecod.net), 9 Herringbrook Way, Orleans 02653. Open mid-May to mid-October. Artist Ruth Hogan's light and airy studio is located in a carriage house in a residential neighborhood about a mile south of town. It's situated above a saltwater pond (just 100 feet from a freshwater lake), and guests are welcome to use the Hogans' dock and canoe. With a complete kitchen and a deck overlooking the pond, it's easy to settle into this treehouse hideaway for a week. $875 weekly.

Hillbourne House (508-255-0780; www.capecodtravel.com/hillbourne house), 654 Route 28, South Orleans 02662. Open year-round except February. Since 1984, hosts Barbara and Jack Hayes have offered a variety of accommodations atop a hill commanding views of Pleasant Bay. The main house was built in 1798 and served as a stop on the Underground Railroad. The carriage house, which sleeps five people in three bedrooms, has a full kitchen and a large living room. The cottage has a great view of Pleasant Bay. Each of the three motel-style rooms in the former paddock has two double beds. Request the room in front; it has the best view. An expanded continental breakfast is included for inn and "paddock" guests; all guests have use of the private beach and private dock. No charge for children under 6. Mid-June to mid-September $70–125 for rooms, $650–725 weekly for cottage and carriage house for four people; otherwise, $65–95 rooms, $500–575 weekly for cottage and carriage house. No credit cards.

Ridgewood Motel & Cottages (508-255-0473; www.ridgewoodmotel.com), junction of Routes 28 and 39, South Orleans 02662. Cottages open May to late October. These six tidy housekeeping cottages, constantly upgraded since 1980 by the Knowles family, are a couple of miles south of Orleans center and 1 mile from the saltwater Pleasant Bay Beach. I particularly like units 12, 17, and 18—all very comfortable in an "olde" Cape Cod way. A large pool, grill and picnic area, lawn games, and playground are set within the wooded compound. Weekly cottage rates, mid-June to early September, are $360–510 for two or three people, $440–620 for five or six people. Rates go as low as $300 and $350, respectively.

EFFICIENCIES

Kadee's Gray Elephant (508-255-7608), 216 Main Street, East Orleans 02643. Open February through November. In 1992 Kris Kavanagh opened these fanciful accommodations next to her wildly popular Kadee's Lobster & Clam Bar (see *Eating Out*). (The 200-year-old former sea captain's house had belonged to her grandmother.) Every surface of woodwork and furniture has been whimsically painted lavender, sea green, and bright pink. Each of the six efficiencies (some carpeted) has cable TV, phone, and air-conditioning. Kitchens are equipped with a coffeemaker, electric burners, a microwave, refrigerator (stocked the first morning), and portable cooler. Don't come here if you're looking for a touchy-feely B&B experience; these studios are for independent travelers who want to come and go without anyone noticing. In summer $140 nightly; off-season $95.

See also Morgan's Way under *Bed & Breakfasts*.

RENTAL HOUSES AND COTTAGES

Compass Vacation Cape Cod (508-240-7600), Route 6, Main Street Mercantile, Unit 23, Eastham 02642. Listings $600–3,500, from Harwich to Truro, from cottages that sleep 2 to houses that sleep 10.

WHERE TO EAT

❊ Orleans has an excellent variety of restaurants, the great majority of which are open year-round (unless otherwise noted).

DINING OUT

Christian's Ocean Grill (508-240-1585), 2 Academy Place at Route 28. When Christian Schultz left his longtime namesake restaurant in Chatham, legions of loyal patrons went into mourning. After a couple of years of catering (due to a noncompete clause), he's back! His menu changes constantly, but look for the likes of sole Française (dipped in egg, a-la-minute, and topped with lobster and orange beurre blanc); "clams Christian" (as opposed to clams casino, untraditional with macadamia nuts and apricots); swordfish with a basil glaze; a daily roasted duck preparation; and a goat-cheese-and-pistachio-crusted napoleon. All entrées include two or three vegetables. (Christian probably presses 10–15 different vegetables into action daily.) Order a salad just to try Christian's ruby red vinaigrette salad dressing. Entrées $19–24.

⚘ **Captain Linnell House** (508-255-3400), 137 Skaket Beach Road. Open for dinner; closed March. Chef-owner Bill Conway's fine fare matches the graceful ease of this former sea captain's mansion. Dining is romantic, with candles, fine china, and linens. One dining room overlooks a small water garden; the salon overlooks the side garden. Start with oysters sautéed with julienned vegetables and champagne-ginger sauce and move to rack of lamb or scallops and shrimp sautéed in a tarragon lobster sauce. Prime rib specials are always popular. Chef Conway will also dish out small portions for children with refined palates. If you're seated by 5:45, you'll receive a complimentary lobster bisque or chowder and dessert. Bill and his wife, Shelly, have owned and been restoring this gem since 1988. Reservations strongly suggested. Entrées $19–30.

    Barley Neck Inn (508-255-0212), Beach Road, East Orleans. Open weekends, late April through December, for dinner; nightly, early May to mid-October. The Barley Neck offers a well-balanced New American menu prepared with flair and French accents by chef Franck Champely (on board since 1996). It's served in four lovely, intimate, romantic dining rooms. My last meal was truly outstanding, although there was a bit of a wait (even with reservations). While the menu changes frequently, I found the sea scallop ravioli with wild mushrooms and beurre blanc and "tuna Tokyo" (wrapped in seaweed with saffron-steamed potatoes and ginger-soy beurre blanc) particularly noteworthy. Other popular dishes include duck aiguillette and various salmon preparations. Leave room for dessert, and for coffee that stands up to milk. Reservations highly recommended. Entrées $16–24.

Nauset Beach Club (508-255-8547), 222 Main Street, East Orleans. Open nightly for dinner except Monday and Tuesday from mid-October to mid-May. Within this former duck-hunting cottage, peach walls and lovely tableware set the stage for sophisticated northern Italian dining. One recent meal featured unusual crabcakes and a lobster tart to start, followed by an untraditional Saltimbuca. Desserts might include pineapple upside-down polenta or a chocolate torte with pignoli nuts and a gooey ganache center. Many of the recipes that Bob Furst's chefs use have been handed down to Bob from family members. The select, reasonably priced wine list includes an impressive 20 wines by the glass. Reservations recommended. Entrées $19–28.

EATING OUT

Cap't Cass Rock Harbor Seafood, Rock Harbor. Open 11–2 and 5–9 daily except Monday in July and August; 11–2 and 5–8 on Friday and Saturday, 11–2 on Sunday, from April through June and September and early October. This classic roadside lobster shack on the harbor, adorned with colorful buoys on the outside and checkered tables on the inside, is as good as they come. The food is a cut above: The lobster roll ($12) hasn't a shred of lettuce in it, and the homemade chowder and clam dinners are great, too. The menu is written on poster board, as it's been done since 1958. There really is a Captain Cass, by the way; George Cass, his wife, Betty, and their daughter Sue run the place. Lunch $6–11, dinner $10–30. BYOB. No credit cards.

🏵 **The Beacon** (508-255-2211), 23 West Road. Open for lunch and dinner. On the way to Skaket Beach, this intimate bistro offers sizable portions of well-presented dishes at reasonable prices. Dishes range from stuffed portobello caps as a starter to pasta (quite popular), halibut, sole Piccata, and chicken Saltimbuca for dinner. Sandwiches and burgers are offered at lunch ($7–8) on the deck. Dinner entrées $14–22.

👤🏵 **Joe's Beach Road Bar & Grille** (508-255-0212), Beach Road, East Orleans. Within the Barley Neck Inn (see *Lodging—Motels*), Joe's is a hopping joint, a lively and loud **bar**-happy place that also happens to serve very good food—and lots of it. Relative to the quality of food, the menu is a very good value, too. It's the kind of place where everybody knows your name. As Joe himself works the room with great ease, locals continue to flock here even as the summer crowds swell. Housed in a rustic, barnlike space with barnboard walls and a large fieldstone fireplace, Joe's offers hearty and simple dishes like lobster prepared five different ways each night. Other specialties include a revolving selection of Asian dishes and locally caught sushi. For lighter appetites and thinner wallets, you can also get pizza, pasta, soup, and main-course salads. Off-season, the most popular dishes from the main dining room (see *Dining Out*) are also offered at Joe's. While the crème brûlée is popular, the dessert quesadilla is special. Entrées $10–20.

🏵 **Rosina's Cafe** (508-240-5513), 15 Cove Road off Route 6A near Main Street. Open for dinner. Since the chef was a fisherman in Sicily, you can trust him to know something about handling seafood and fish. Devoted patrons flock here for Italian food that's not outrageously priced. What more could you want? Something specific to hang your hat on? The sole is terrific. The dining room is understated with etched glass and lots of wood. If you have to wait, there's a nice **bar.** Early specials and takeout. Dinner entrées $11–26.

🏵 **Binnacle Tavern** (508-255-7901), 20 Route 28. Open nightly for dinner, May to mid-October; Wednesday through Sunday the rest of the year. Barnboard walls, low lighting, "oldies" top-40 music, and a ubiquitous nautical motif pervade the interior of this cozy, popular tavern. An enclosed outdoor patio is heated in the shoulder seasons. The Binnacle is deservedly well known for its appetizers and designer pizzas, but it also serves seafood and homemade pasta. This place is always lively, even in the dead of winter. Entrées $10–17.

🏵✍ **Land Ho!** (508-255-5165), Route 6A. Open daily. John Murphy, owner since 1969, is responsible for this favorite local hangout. Don't miss it. It's very colorful (literally), from red-and-white-checked tablecloths, to old business signs hanging from the ceiling, to a large blackboard menu. Newspapers hang on a wire to separate the long bar from the dining area. Land Ho! serves club sandwiches, fried seafood dishes, and burgers and hot dogs. Specialties include fish-and-chips, barbecued ribs, stuffed clams, clam pie, chowder, and kale soup. You'll find lots of families, college students, and old-time locals here. Dishes $8–16.

&✍ **The Lobster Claw** (508-255-1800), Route 6A, near the Orleans rotary. Open 11:30–9 daily, April through October. Since 1970 the entire extended Berig family have been involved in dishing up fresh seafood to visitors at their large, convenient, family-style restaurant. It's a very pleasant place, proudly maintained, and decorated with the requisite nautical motif. The Berigs offer straightforward and consistent preparations that people can understand. I recommend the delicately broiled fisherman's platters, Marylou's homemade crabcakes, and fried clams. Lobster sandwiches and salads are popular at lunch. Children's menu, early specials from 4 to 5:30, and a "waiting lounge" upstairs. Grape-Nut custard flies out of the place after dinner. Lunch $4–15, dinner entrées $10–19.

&✍ **Kadee's Lobster & Clam Bar** (508-255-6184), 212 Main Street, East Orleans. Open for lunch and dinner daily, late May to early September. A summer tradition since 1975 because of its location (on the way to Nauset Beach), Kadee's serves fresh local seafood. The setting is casual, at shellacked picnic tables under an open-air structure (enclosed in cool or inclement weather) or on the deck at umbrella-covered tables next to the parking lot. Choose from oysters on the half shell; broiled, steamed, or fried seafood; their special kale soup; or a rich "seafood simmer" with lobster, shrimp, and scallops in a sherry wine sauce. Lighter salad plates are a good lunch idea. Portions are large, but there is a hefty plate charge if you share. Frozen drinks are quite popular, as is the single dessert choice: chocolate-marbled cheesecake. Children's menu and a rudimentary mini-golf course if the kids finish eating before you. Be careful or expect the prices to add up. Lunch $6–14; dinner entrées $10–18.

✍ **Old Jailhouse Tavern** (508-255-5245), 28 West Road. Open for lunch, dinner, and late-night light fare daily. This casual tavern with is always crowded and boisterous. The food is okay. It's a good choice when everyone in your party wants something different: nachos, soup and salad, fish-and-chips, or a broiled seafood sampler. Eat in one of the booths, on the atriumlike terrace overlooking the garden, at the long oak bar, or within the rock walls of the old jail. In the early 1800s the town constable offered the use of his front bedroom, complete with bars on the windows, as an overnight lockup facility. This room now serves as a cozy dining room. Dishes $10–21.

🍴✍ **Sir Cricket's Fish 'n Chips** (508-255-4453), Route 6A. Open daily. This tidy hole-in-the-wall, next to the Bird Watcher's General Store (see *Special Shops*), dishes out pints of fried seafood, fish sandwiches, and mixed platters. You'll also find chicken tenders and hot dogs for the kids. Plan on takeout, as there are only a couple of tables. Dishes $5–9.

🍴✍ **Hearth 'n Kettle** (508-240-0111), on West Road at Route 6A. Open daily. This early American–themed, family-style restaurant (one in a chain operated by the Catania family) offers reliable service, good food, and moderate prices. Breakfast is served until 2 on weekends, and there are early specials (like chicken teriyaki and broiled scrod) until 6. Meals $5–15.

A clam shack on the Cape Cod Rail Trail

The Hole (508-255-3740), Route 6A within Main Street Square. Open 5 AM–4 PM (until 3 on Sunday). The Hole is pleasant and airy place, a real local hangout. It's packed at breakfast time and friendly all day. $2–6.

SNACKS

The Hot Chocolate Sparrow (508-240-2230), Lowell Square, off Route 6A. Open 7 AM–10 PM daily, this place makes the best cappuccino, lattes, and hot chocolates between Beantown and Provincetown. Proprietor Marje Sparrow sends her staff to "espresso lab" to make sure they know the hows and whys of making a consistent cup. In addition to a blackboard menu of drinks like frozen "hot" chocolate, caffe mocha Sparrow (espresso with "real" hot chocolate), and chai tea, they also make luscious hand-dipped chocolates and sweet treats. At press time, the Sparrow was moving: Look for it behind the CVS store on Old Colony Way, across from the Rail Trail (see *Outdoor Activities—Bicycling/Rentals*).

Cottage St. Bakery (508-255-2821), Cottage Street near Routes 6A and 28. Open 6 AM–6 or 9 PM late June to early September, until 6 the rest of the year. JoAnna Keeley, buttering up the community since 1984, has a number of oddly named specialties, including "dirt bombs," an old-fashioned French doughnut recipe that requires baking, not frying, and "fly cemeteries," puff-pastry squares, knotted on top and filled with currants and nuts. Her breads—cinnamon butter bread, multigrain breads, and a garlic and herb oregano "Milan" bread—are also great. Knead I say more? Okay, I will: You can get homemade soups and sandwiches here, too. There are a few indoor and outdoor tables.

Fancy's Farm (508-255-1949), 199 Main Street, East Orleans. Open daily late March through December. Fancy's is more than your average farm stand. You can assemble a gourmand's feast with cold pastas, Thai salads, roasted chicken, and sesame noodles. There's a salad bar, too.

Kim's Cafe (508-255-7469), 210 Main Street, adjacent to the East Orleans post office. On the way to Nauset Beach, stop for a bagel sandwich, soup, sweet treats, or a cup of Seattle's Best coffee. It's open 7–3 daily.

New York Bagels (508-255-0255), 125 Route 6A. Open daily. Bagels are par-baked by H&H in Manhattan and finished off here. Add salmon, smoked whitefish, or kosher pastrami, or opt for potato pancakes, knishes, bialys, or challah.

Phoenix Fruit & Vegetable (508-255-5306), Orleans Marketplace, Route 6A. Open daily. This tiny shop, tucked into the corner of a strip mall, is a delight for foodies. If you have cooking facilities, you'll appreciate organic greens, locally grown Shiitake mushrooms, locally made clam pies, and hearty *pain d'Avignon*.

Choose your ice cream parlor based on location, as both shops offer sublime flavors. **Emack & Bolio's** (508-255-5844) is on Route 6A, and the **Sundae School** (508-255-5473) is at 210 Main Street in East Orleans. (Tasters rave about the black raspberry and Grape-Nut ice cream.)

COFFEE

See the Hot Chocolate Sparrow under *Snacks*.

FISH MARKETS

Young's Fish Market (508-255-3366), Rock Harbor. Open mid-June to mid-September. Call ahead and they'll cook lobster to order for you; otherwise, the lobster rolls are always good. The market, by the way, has been in the Harrison family since 1962, when they bought it from the Youngs.

ENTERTAINMENT

✐ **Baseball.** The Orleans Cardinals (508-255-0793) play ball at Eldredge Park Field, off Route 28 at Eldredge Parkway, from mid-June to early August.

✳ **Academy Playhouse** (508-255-1963 box office), 120 Main Street. The performance space for the Academy of Performing Arts, this 162-seat playhouse occupies the Old Town Hall, built in 1873. It holds a prominent position high above Main Street. Over the years the building has been host to local government, record hops, movies, and theater. The theater company (established in 1975) stages 10–12 dramas, comedies, and musicals throughout the year. Since 1986, the season has kicked off with a literary cabaret, *A Night of New Works*. The eagerly awaited March event brings established and unknown Cape writers (who have been holed up working all winter) together with audiences. Tickets $14–16.

SELECTIVE SHOPPING

❋ Unless otherwise noted, all shops are open year-round.

ANTIQUES

Pleasant Bay Antiques (508-255-0930), 540 Route 28, South Orleans. Most of these high-quality, 18th- and 19th-century American antiques come from area residents rather than auctions. They're displayed in a lovely old barn.

Continuum (508-255-8513; www.oldlamp.com), 7 Route 28. Open daily except Sunday in the off-season. Dan Johnson sells expertly restored antique lamps and textures from the Victorian to the art deco period. He also sells old advertising signs, folk art, and wooden fish decoys.

Countryside Antiques (508-240-0525), 6 Lewis Road, behind the Box Lunch on Main Street, East Orleans. Open March through December. Deborah Rita has been traveling the world since 1984 in order to fill these eight rooms with English, Irish, Scandinavian, European, and Chinese antiques and fine reproductions.

ART GALLERIES

Addison Holmes Gallery (508-255-6200; www.addisonart.com), 34 Route 28. Helen Addison and Herb Holmes represent both new and established artists working in realistic and traditional realms, lithographs, photography, and modern classic sculpture. It's a comfortable gallery for both the serious collector and the uninitiated art buyer.

Tree's Place (508-255-1330; 1-888-255-1330; www.treesplace.com), Route 6A at Route 28. Open daily year-round, except closed Sunday early January to mid-April. When Elaine and Julian Baird bought this place in 1981, they really put the Lower Cape on the art map. Tree's offers a vast collection of unusual gifts (like Russian lacquerware) displayed throughout nine small rooms; an excellent collection of representational New England painters; and a tile shop. Meet-the-artist champagne receptions 5–7 Saturdays in summer.

Hogan Art Gallery (508-240-3655), 39 Main Street. Open 10–5 Monday through Saturday in summer; hours vary off-season. Ruth Hogan has amassed a fine body of work: primitive white-line woodblock prints, impressionistic landscape paintings, and lovely pastels. Husband Frank offers a collection of 20th-century regional paintings. The Hogans also feature Ginny Boyland's fanciful furniture and Susanne Strenz-Thibault's trompe l'oeil furniture.

ARTISANS

Orleans Carpenters (508-255-2646), Commerce Drive. Orleans Carpenters makes magnificent reproduction Shaker nesting oval boxes, oval trays, oval carriers, and music boxes from cherry and bird's-eye maple. These traditional oval boxes are so expertly made and durable that you could put your full weight on one and it would feel more sturdy than a stepladder. Work by the Orleans Carpenters has been presented to the king and queen of Norway, to Gorbachev, and has been purchased by Ronald and Nancy Reagan. Although Paul and Beth Dixon's business is primarily a wholesale shop with museum customers, the front of the unprepossessing shop has a small display of goods. The "seconds," which look perfect to all but the most expert eyes, go very quickly in summer. Orleans Carpenters is hard to find, off Finlay Road (from Route 28), behind Brewster Welding.

Nauset Lantern Shop (508-255-1009; 1-800-899-2660), 52 Route 6A. Just north of the Bird Watcher's General Store, Ken Alman expertly hand-crafts copper and brass colonial- and early American–style lanterns. Most of the nautical and onion lanterns are for exterior use, but he also makes sconces and indoor accessories. Watch him work.

Kemp Pottery (508-255-5853), Route 6A near the Orleans rotary. Open daily except Sunday. Steven Kemp creates unusual designs from this unassuming location. Utilizing Nauset Beach sand, Kemp makes functional porcelain and stoneware pieces like bird feeders and bathroom sinks, as well as less common decorative objects for the garden, like pagodas, torsos, and moated castles. He also works with stained glass.

BOOKSTORES
Compass Rose Book Shop (508-255-1545), 43–45 Main Street. Extensive selections about Cape Cod, nature and the environment, science, history, biographies, and books by local authors.

Booksmith/Musicsmith of Orleans (508-255-4590), Skaket Corners, Route 6A. Paperbacks and best-sellers.

CLOTHING
Karol Richardson (508-255-3944), 47 Main Street, and **Hannah** (508-255-8234), 47 Main Street, both sell stylish women's clothing and are open year-round. Across the street, **XO Clothing Store** (508-255-4407) offers loose-fitting styles made of natural fabrics and sold at refreshing prices.

FARMER'S MARKET
Orleans Farmer's Market, 19 West Road, off Route 6A near exit 12. Pick up local produce and shellfish 8–noon every Saturday in June, July, and August.

SPECIAL SHOPS
Bird Watcher's General Store (508-255-6974; 1-800-562-1512; www.birdwatchersgeneralstore.com), Route 6A near the Orleans rotary. Open daily. If it pertains to birds or watchers-of-birds, this store has it: bird feeders in every size and shape, birdseed in barrels (a ton of seed is sold daily), fountains, bird note cards, bird kitchen magnets, bird playing cards. As important as commerce is, though, this place is an invaluable resource for news of where and when birds have been sighted or will be sighted. (This place isn't just for the birds!)

Oceana (508-240-1414), 1 Main Street Square. Carol Wright stocks lovely household items and jewelry inspired by the sea and nature. A percentage of total sales from her Ocean Information Center is donated to the Center for Coastal Studies (see *Even More Things to See and Do—Special Programs* in "Provincetown.")

Orleans Whole Food Store (508-255-6540), 46 Main Street, Orleans. Open daily. Healthy foods, pizza on Tuesday and Thursday, vitamins, books, and items that promote holistic living.

Baseball Shop (508-240-1063), 26 Main Street. The shop carries more than 1,000 caps, as well as trading cards, clothing, and other baseball paraphernalia.

Cape Cod Photo & Art Supply (508-255-0476), 38 Main Street. Open daily except Sunday. One-hour film processing, and painting supplies if you become inspired by the wonderful Cape Cod light.

SPECIAL EVENTS

Late June through August: **Antiques and Craft Shows,** Nauset Regional Middle School, Route 28. Many weekends in June, July, and August.

Late August: **Pops in the Park.** The Cape Cod Symphony performs a concert in Eldredge Park, off Route 28 at Eldredge Parkway.

Late September/early October: **Fall for Orleans Festival.** Activities include a car show, pet parade, and pancake breakfast.

Mid-August to late September: **Nauset Painters,** sponsors of the Cape's oldest juried outdoor art shows, at various town locations and on various days; look for the current flyer. Painting demonstrations are often held on Sunday.

IV. THE OUTER CAPE

Eastham
Wellfleet
Truro

The play of light and shadow

KIM GRANT

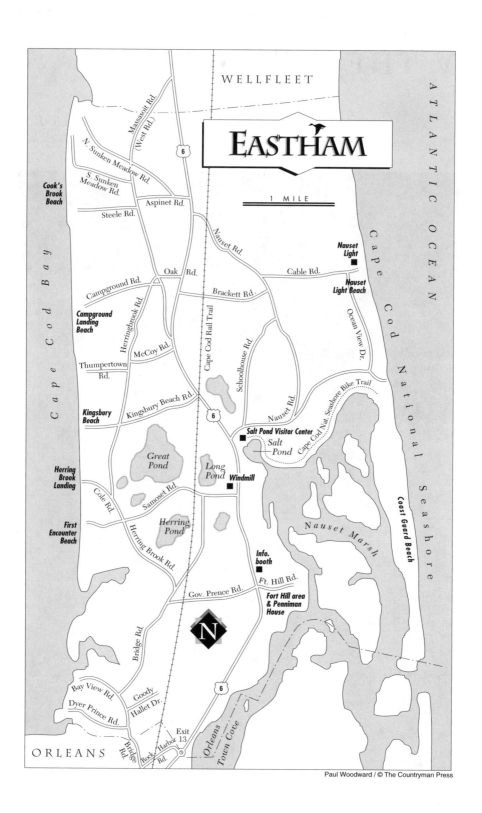

WELLFLEET

EASTHAM

1 MILE

Massasoit Rd. (West Rd.)

N. Sunken Meadow Rd.

S. Sunken Meadow Rd.

Cook's Brook Beach

Aspinet Rd.

Steele Rd.

Nauset Rd.

Nauset Light

Cape Cod Bay

Oak Rd.

Cable Rd.

Campground Rd.

Brackett Rd.

Nauset Light Beach

Campground Landing Beach

Herringbrook Rd

McCoy Rd.

Cape Cod Rail Trail

Schoolhouse Rd.

Ocean View Dr.

Thumpertown Rd.

Kingsbury Beach Rd.

Nauset Rd.

Kingsbury Beach

Cape Cod Nat. Seashore Bike Trail

Salt Pond Visitor Center

Salt Pond

Herring Brook Landing

Great Pond

Long Pond

Windmill

Cole Rd.

Samoset Rd.

First Encounter Beach

Herring Pond

Herring Brook Rd.

Info. booth

Nauset Marsh

Coast Guard Beach

Ft. Hill Rd.

Gov. Prence Rd.

Fort Hill area & Penniman House

Bridge Rd.

N

Bay View Rd.

Goody Hallet Dr.

Dyer Prince Rd.

Bridge Rd.

Rock Harbor Rd.

Exit 13

Orleans Town Cove

ORLEANS

ATLANTIC OCEAN

Cape Cod National Seashore

Paul Woodward / © The Countryman Press

Eastham

Settled by the Pilgrims in 1644, Eastham is content to remain relatively undiscovered by 21st-century tourists. In fact, year-round residents (fewer than 5,000) seem downright pleased that any semblance of major tourism development has passed them by. There isn't even a Main Street or town center per se.

What Eastham does boast, as gateway to the Cape Cod National Seashore (CCNS), is plenty of natural diversions. The Salt Pond Visitor Center, one of two CCNS headquarters, dispenses a wealth of information and offers ranger-guided activities and outstanding nature programs. Take an informative boat trip onto Nauset Marsh, a fragile ecosystem that typifies much of the Cape. In addition, a marvelous network of bicycle and walking trails traverses this part of the seashore, including the Fort Hill area. The Cape's renowned, uninterrupted stretches of sandy beach, backed by high dunes, begin in earnest in Eastham and extend all the way up to Provincetown. One of them, Coast Guard Beach, is also where exalted naturalist Henry Beston spent 1928 observing nature's minute changes from a little cottage and recording his experiences in *The Outermost House.*

Eastham is best known as the site where the *Mayflower's* Myles Standish and a Pilgrim scouting party met the Nauset Indians in 1620 at First Encounter Beach. The "encounter," in which a few arrows were slung (without injury), served as sufficient warning to the Pilgrims: They left and didn't return for 24 years. When the Pilgrim settlers, then firmly entrenched at Plymouth, went looking for room to expand, they returned to Eastham. Led by Thomas Prence, they purchased most of the land from Native Americans for an unknown quantity of hatchets.

Although the history books cite these encounters as the beginning of Eastham's recorded history, the 1990 discovery of a 4,000-year-old settlement (see Coast Guard Beach under *Green Space—Beaches*) is keeping archaeologists and anthropologists on their toes.

GUIDANCE

Eastham Information Booth (508-255-3444; 508-240-7211 year-round; www.easthamchamber.com), near Fort Hill on Route 6 (P.O. Box 1329, Eastham 02642). Open 9–7 daily, July to mid-September, 10-5 daily, mid-June to late June; and 10–5 Friday through Sunday, late May to mid-June and mid-September to late September.

❦T❄**Salt Pond Visitor Center** (508-255-3421; www.nps.gov/caco), off Route 6. Open daily 9–5 in summer and daily 9–4:30 the rest of the year. In 1961, newly elected President John F. Kennedy, Sen. Leverett Saltonstall, and Rep. Hastings Keith introduced a bill that would turn more than 43,000 acres into the **Cape Cod National Seashore** (CCNS), protected forever from further development. (About 500 private homes remain within the park.) Today, the CCNS is visited by over 5 million people annually. The information center is an excellent resource for first-time and repeat visitors alike. Short films on Thoreau's Cape Cod, Marconi, and the ever-changing natural landscape are shown in the auditorium throughout the day. Ranger-guided activities include sunset campfires on the beach, talks on Cape geology and tidal flats, and bird walks. There is a presentation of some sort nightly in summer. The fine museum includes displays on the salt and whaling industries and the diaries of Captain Penniman's wife, who accompanied him on several voyages. I learn something every time I stop here. Free.

PUBLIC LIBRARY

❄T❧**Eastham Library** (508-240-5950), west of the windmill, 190 Samoset Road. Open Monday, Friday, and Saturday 10–4, Tuesday and Thursday 10–8 in summer. Call for off-season hours. Story time and summer events for children, plus PCs and Macs with Internet access.

PUBLIC REST ROOMS
Public rest rooms are located in the Salt Pond Visitor Center.

GETTING THERE
By car: Eastham is 40 miles from the Sagamore Bridge via Route 6.

By bus: The **Plymouth & Brockton** bus line (508-778-9767; www.p-b.com) connects Eastham with Hyannis and other Cape towns, as well as with Boston's Logan Airport. The bus stops at the Town Hall on Route 6.

GETTING AROUND
Eastham is only a few miles wide and 6 miles long. Beaches and places to stay and eat are all well marked along or off Route 6. The CCNS is to the east of Route 6.

MEDICAL EMERGENCY
Call **911.**

TO SEE

Edward Penniman House (508-255-3421), off Route 6 in the Fort Hill area, CCNS. Open intermittently; call for current schedule. At age 11, Penniman left Eastham for the open sea. When he returned as a captain 26 years later, he had this 1868 house built for him. Rumor has it that he used ship's carpenters because he didn't trust landlubber architects. Boasting indoor plumbing and a kerosene chandelier, this French Second Empire–style house has Corinthian columns, a mansard roof, and a cupola that once afforded views of the bay and ocean. Although

KIM GRANT

The National Park Service's Edward Penniman House is graced by the jawbone of a whale.

the house is only partially restored and contains a few period furnishings, the ever-helpful National Park Service guides are on hand to dispense lots of historical information. Even if it's closed, peek in the windows. Free.

Swift-Daley House and **Tool Museum** (508-240-1247), next to the post office on Route 6. Open 1–4 weekdays in July and August and 1–4 on Saturday in September. In 1998 one of the seashore dune shacks (see Dune shacks under *To See* in "Provincetown") was moved to this site. Although it's difficult to imagine what dune-shack life might have been like, this helps. As for the Swift-Daley House, it's a completely furnished full-Cape Colonial built by ship's carpenters in 1741. It has wide floorboards, pumpkin-pine woodwork, narrow stairways, and a fireplace in every room on the first floor. The Tool Museum behind the house displays hundreds of old tools for use in the home and in the field. Free.

Old Schoolhouse Museum (508-255-0788), off Route 6 across from the Salt Pond Visitor Center. Open 1–4 weekdays in July and August and 1–4 on Saturday in September. This former one-room schoolhouse served the town from 1869 until 1936. During that time there were separate entrances for boys and girls. Inside you'll learn about Henry Beston's year of solitude spent observing natural rhythms on nearby Coast Guard Beach. Thanks to the Eastham Historical Society, you can also learn about the town's farming history, daily domestic life, Native Americans, offshore shipwrecks, and the impressive Lifesaving Service. Free.

Oldest windmill, on Route 6 at Samoset Road. Across from Town Hall, the Cape's oldest working windmill was built in Plymouth in the 1680s and moved to Eastham in the early 1800s. Corn is sometimes ground here in summer, when longtime Eastham resident Jim Owens is usually on hand to explain the gristmill's operation.

First Encounter Beach, off Samoset Road and Route 6. A bronze marker commemorates where the Pilgrims, led by Capt. Myles Standish, first met the Native Americans. The exchange was not friendly. Although arrows flew, no one was injured. The site goes down in history as the place where the Native Americans first began their decline at the hands of European settlers. On a more modern note of warfare history, for 25 years the U.S. Navy used an offshore ship for target practice. Until recently, it was still visible on a sandbar about a mile offshore. The beach, with its westward vista, is a great place to catch a sunset.

Doane Homestead Site, between the Salt Pond Visitor Center and Coast Guard Beach, CCNS. Only a marker remains to identify the spot where Doane, one of Eastham's first English settlers, made his home.

Old Cove Cemetery, Route 6. Many graves date back to the 1700s, but, in particular, look for the memorial to the three *Mayflower* Pilgrims who were buried here in the 1600s.

Three Sisters Lighthouses and Nauset Light, at the corner of Cable Road and Ocean View Drive, CCNS. In 1838 this coastal cliff was home to three brick lighthouses that provided beacons for sailors. They collapsed from erosion in 1892 and were replaced with three wooden ones. When erosion threatened those in 1918, two were moved away; the third was moved in 1923. Eventually the National Park Service acquired all three and moved them to their present location, nestled in the woods far back from today's coastline. (It's a rather incongruous sight, lighthouses surrounded by trees, unable to reach the water.)

In 1996, when Nauset Light was just 37 feet from cliff's edge, the large red-and-white steel lighthouse, too, was moved—via flatbed truck—from the eroding shoreline. This trip took a mere 3 days. Originally the light was moved from Chatham, where it was built in the 1870s, one of twins. For now, the cast-iron behemoth sits a respectable 250 feet from the shoreline, its beacon still stretching 17 miles to sea. To reach Three Sisters from Nauset Light, take the paved walkway from the parking lot.

Nauset Light (508-240-2612) is open Sunday 4:30–7:30 PM July to early September, and Sunday 1–4 from early September to late October. Like all Cape Cod lighthouses, it is open the weekends during Maritime Days (see *Special Events*) in mid-May and Heritage Week in mid-June. Free.

OUTDOOR ACTIVITIES

BICYCLING/RENTALS

Cape Cod Rail Trail. This scenic, well-maintained, 26-mile (one way) paved path winds from Dennis to Wellfleet. Park at the Salt Pond Visitor Center (see *Guidance*).

Nauset Bike Trail, CCNS. This 1²/₃-mile (one way) trail connects with the Cape Cod Rail Trail and runs from the Salt Pond Visitor Center, across Nauset Marsh via a boardwalk, to Coast Guard Beach. The trail passes large stands of thin, tall black locust trees not native to the area—they were introduced to return nitrogen to the soil after overfarming.

Rental prices are about the same at the "conglomerate" **Idle Times Bike Shop** (508-255-8281), on Route 6 about 1 mile north of the Salt Pond Visitor Center, open year-round, and the family-owned **Little Capistrano Bike Shop** (508-255-6515), across from the Salt Pond Visitor Center behind the Lobster Shanty, open April to mid-November. Rentals cost about $18 a day for a mountain bike or hybrid, $45 for 3 days, $10 for 2 hours; less for children's bikes. Both shops do repairs, but Little Cap also sells bikes.

FOR FAMILIES

Poit's Place (508-255-6321), Route 6. Open mid-May to mid-September. Families have stopped here since 1954 for mini-golf, ice cream, pizza slices, hot dogs, and fish-and-chips. Will yours?

T-Time Family Sports Center (508-255-5697), Route 6, North Eastham. Open daily in summer, weekends in spring and fall, mid-May to mid-October. If you're desperately in need of a bucket of balls to belt out, this will suffice. The mini-golf is a bit run-down, but the Outer Cape has slim pickings.

FISHING/SHELLFISHING

Purchase your required freshwater fishing license at any bait and tackle shop or the Town Hall (508-240-5900) on Route 6 and then head to the stocked, spring-fed **Herring Pond** (see *Green Space—Ponds*). Contact the Department of Public Works (Department of Natural Resources; 508-240-5972), 555 Old Orchard Road (off Route 6 or Brackett Road), for shellfishing permits and regulations. Open 9–4 weekdays, plus Saturday 9–4 in summer. Shellfishing is permitted at Salt Pond (Route 6) and Salt Pond River only on Sunday.

Connie Codner (508-255-1308), the women's world line record holder for striped bass, teaches novices how to cast from shore from June through October. The informative and fun 3-hour sessions cost $50 per person. Demonstrations and discussions include knot tying, when to use which bait, and where you'll have the best luck. Shorts and sneakers are the order of the day, unless it's chilly, when waders and boots are de riguer. (You'll have to bring your own; otherwise, Connie provides all the equipment.) Meet at Blackbeard's Bait & Tackle on Brackett Road in North Eastham.

TENNIS

Nauset Regional High School, Cable Road, North Eastham. The public can use the courts after school gets out for a small fee; call the recreation director at 508-240-5974.

See also *Even More Things to Do—Fitness Club.*

EVEN MORE THINGS TO DO

FITNESS CLUB

❄ **Norseman Athletic Club** (508-255-6370), Route 6. Open daily. Facilities include racquetball and squash courts, Nautilus and free weights, a lap pool, saunas and steam rooms, a whirlpool, six indoor tennis courts, and aerobics, yoga, and spinning classes. Daily $12; weekly, 3-day weekend, and family rates.

SPECIAL PROGRAMS

Cape Cod Photo Workshops (508-255-6808), North Eastham. These diverse, creative, and fun hands-on workshops offer a chance to learn from professional photographers (including me) from around the country. Location work, view camera use, portraiture, darkroom classes, critiques; weekend and weeklong; beginner and advanced. Owner Linda McCausland puts together an excellent program.

✎ **Recreational programs** (508-240-5900) are held 9–noon, late June to mid-August. Visitors and summer residents are encouraged to bring their children (age 6–16) to the playground at Nauset Regional High School (on Cable Road, North Eastham) to participate in various programs including archery, arts and crafts, and soccer. Supervised swimming and instruction are offered at Wiley Park (on Great Pond; see *Green Space— Ponds*) for children age 3–16 on weekday mornings. Register ($10) any weekday at 9. Fees for some specific programs vary.

GREEN SPACE

BEACHES

Coast Guard Beach, CCNS, on the Atlantic Ocean. This long beach, backed by grasses and heathland, is perfect for walking and sunning. Facilities include excellent changing rooms, rest rooms, and in-season lifeguards. In summer a shuttle bus ferries visitors from a well-marked parking lot. Parking $7 per day (good all day on any CCNS beach); seasonal pass $20; walkers and bicyclists free.

At times during the winter, you might be lucky enough to spot gray seals and small brown harbor seals congregating at the southern tip of Coast Guard Beach. They feed on the ever-present sand eels. Take the walk at low tide and allow an hour to cover the 2 miles.

Henry Beston wrote his 1928 classic, *The Outermost House*, during the year he lived in a two-room bungalow on Coast Guard Beach. The book chronicles Beston's interaction with the natural environment and records seasonal changes. The cottage was designated a national literary landmark in 1964, but the blizzard of 1978 washed it into the ocean. Bundled up (tightly!) against the off-season winds, you'll get a glimpse of the haunting isolation Beston experienced.

After a brutal 1990 storm washed away a large chunk of beach, an amateur archaeologist discovered evidence of a prehistoric dwelling on Coast Guard Beach. (Watch the video at the Salt Pond Visitor Center.) It is one of the oldest undisturbed archaeological sites in New England, dating back 4,000 years to the Early Archaic and Woodland cultures. Because Coast Guard Beach was then 5 miles inland, the site provided a safe encampment for hunters and gatherers.

The Coast Guard Station at the top of the cliff was decommissioned in 1958 and now serves as the Environmental Educational Center for the CCNS. The U.S. Coast Guard evolved from the Lifesaving Service established in 1872 in response to the thousands of ships that were wrecked off the treacherous coast. When the Cape Cod Canal was built in 1914, and ships could pass through instead of going around the Cape, fatalities decreased dramatically.

Nauset Light Beach, CCNS, on the Atlantic Ocean. An idyllic, long, broad, dune-backed beach. Facilities include changing rooms, rest rooms, and a lifeguard in-season. Parking $7 daily in-season (transferable to any CCNS beach).

First Encounter Beach, Campground Landing Beach, and **Cook's Brook Beach.** These bayside town beaches are well suited to kite flying and shelling. Because of the shallow water and gradual slope, they are safe for children. Parking is $8 daily in-season. Weekly stickers ($30) are available from the Department of Natural Resources (508-240-5972), 555 Old Orchard Road (off Route 6 or Brackett Road). The office is open 9–4 Monday through Saturday (except it closes at noon on Wednesday).

PONDS

Herring Pond and **Great Pond,** west of Eastham Center off Samoset, Great Pond, and Herring Brook Roads. Parking $8 daily in-season. Great Pond has more parking and a bigger beach. Furthermore, it also has two swimming areas, including **Wiley Park,** with a beach, playground, and new bathhouse.

WALKS

Fort Hill area, CCNS; trailhead and parking off Route 6. The trail—one of my all-Cape favorites—is about 1$\frac{1}{2}$ miles round trip with a partial boardwalk, some log steps, and some hills. It offers lovely views of Nauset Marsh, especially from Skiff Hill, but also winds through the dense Red Maple Swamp and past the Edward Penniman House (see *To See*). Birders enjoy this walk year-round, but it is particularly beautiful in autumn when the maples turn color. Pastoral Fort Hill was farmed until the 1940s, and rock walls still mark boundaries.

Nauset Marsh Trail, CCNS; trailhead behind the Salt Pond Visitor Center (see *Guidance*). About 1 mile round trip; some log steps. This trail runs along Salt Pond and yields expansive vistas of Nauset Marsh, which was actually Nauset Bay when it was charted by French explorer Samuel

The Nauset Light Trail boardwalk crosses below the Coast Guard station.

de Champlain in 1605. As the barrier beach developed, so did the marsh. Along those same lines, Salt Pond was a freshwater pond until the ocean broke through from Nauset Marsh. This complex ecosystem sustains all manner of ocean creatures and shorebirds.

Buttonbush Trail, CCNS, trailhead at the Salt Pond Visitor Center. The trail is half a mile, with some boardwalk, some log steps. It was specially designed with Braille markers for the blind and visually impaired.

Eastham Hiking Club (508-255-3021). From September through June, the club, led by Hortense Kelly since 1984, meets at 9 AM on Wednesday for a vigorous 2-hour walk somewhere between Yarmouth and Provincetown. Generally about 45 or 50 people gather for the 5- to 6-mile hike. Call for the week's location.

LODGING

Route 6 is lined with cottage colonies, but there are a few notable B&B alternatives.

HOTEL

✳♪⚓♿ **Four Points Hotel at the National Seashore** (508-255-5000; 1-800-533-3986), Route 6, Eastham 02642. This bilevel Sheraton hotel has all the amenities you'd expect: an indoor and an outdoor pool, a whirlpool, a fitness center, and two tennis courts. The odd thing is that you just don't expect to see a Sheraton on the Outer Cape. About half of the 107 nicely appointed rooms and two suites overlook the tasteful indoor pool area, which resembles an inverted ship's hull. The other rooms overlook woods; these are slightly larger and brighter and have small refrigerators. Restaurant on the premises. July and August $219 (always ask for the "best available rate"), off-season $119, but if you head to the Outer Cape without a reservation, you'll often find rooms advertised for less. Children under 17 free in parent's room.

BED & BREAKFASTS

   ᐊ **Whalewalk Inn** (508-255-0617; www.whalewalkinn.com), 220 Bridge Road, Eastham 02642. Open April through November and select winter weekends. One of the top five or six places on the whole Cape and delightfully off the beaten path, this 19th-century whaling captain's home has been operated with flair and grace by Carolyn and Dick Smith since 1990. The Smiths offer a range of accommodations, including a luxurious new **carriage house** (smartly designed to look 19th century) outfitted with four-poster king-size beds and gas fireplaces. Most of these six rooms have a small private deck or balcony, while some have a large whirlpool. There are three large suites in other buildings that afford great privacy; all have a kitchen and fireplace. There is also a lovely, airy, romantic **cottage.** The four inn rooms are decorated with country sophistication, a smattering of fine antiques, and breezy floral fabrics. I particularly like the quiet brick patio where a creative full breakfast (perhaps crab-and-spinach quiche) is served and afternoon drinks and hors d'oeuvres can be had. The inn also has loaner bikes. Late May through mid-October $160–300; off-season $140–225.

   ❃ **Fort Hill Bed and Breakfast at Sylvanus Knowles House** (508-240-2870; www.forthillbb.com), 75 Fort Hill Road, Eastham 02642. Across from the Edward Penniman House (see *To See*), Jean and Gordon Avery's two-room B&B has one of the best locations on all of Cape Cod. The 19th-century Greek Revival farmhouse is idyllically perched on a little knoll overlooking Nauset Marsh. As if that weren't enough, the hosts are friendly, there is a separate guest entrance, and the living room is elegantly appointed and boasts a fireplace to take off the winter chill. The two-room Emma Suite has its own library and piano, as well as an oversize tub. On the second floor, Lucille is charming with slanted eaves, wide pine floors, a separate dressing room, and a contemporary wrought-iron bedstead. Both suites have TV and air-conditioning. A full breakfast—perhaps zucchini quiche, eggs Benedict, or pear and almond pancakes—is included. This casually refined place is a charmer; book well in advance. By our publication date, the Averys expected to have another suite with its own secluded garden, ocean views, and a fireplace. $145–180 May through October, $125–145 off-season; 3-night minimum in summer, 2 nights the rest of the year. No credit cards.

   🐶 **700 Samoset** (508-255-8748), 700 Samoset Road, Eastham 02642. Open May through October. Sarah Blackwell moved this abandoned 1870 Greek Revival farmhouse to its present location on the bay side of Route 6, on a quiet road near the bike trail. She did a wonderful job restoring it, sanding floors and woodwork, and blending period pieces with contemporary accents like a painted checkerboard floor and tin lamps. There are only two guest rooms, each with private bath and king or twin beds. From the open country kitchen, guests enjoy an expanded continental breakfast of muffins, bagels, cereal, yogurt, and fruit. Plan your day from the front porch rocking chairs. July and August $95–110, off-season $70–85.

❊❦❧**Over Look Inn** (508-255-1886; www.overlookinn.com), 3085 Route 6, Eastham 02642. On the Rail Trail, this big yellow Victorian house is difficult to see even though it's on Route 6, across from the Salt Pond Visitor Center. The common rooms are unusual: There's a billiards room with Nigerian art, a library dedicated to Winston Churchill, and a parlor with velveteen curtains. Afternoon tea is served amid a collection of Andrew Wyeth prints, while the hallways are lined with the hosts' son's large canvases. The 14, generally airy guest rooms all have private bath, lace curtains, and antique furnishings; some have cathedral ceiling and skylight. The Garden Room, my favorite, has a private porch and fireplace. There is also a **cottage** behind the inn that can accommodate a family (and the family pet). An adjacent carriage house has three rooms, which share a butler's pantry, that are geared toward families. Nan Aitchison and her family have been welcoming guests with their Scottish hospitality since 1983. Full breakfasts include such hearty dishes as kedgeree (smoked cod and rice, sautéed with onions). Late May to mid-October $175; off-season $125.

❊ **Penny House Bed & Breakfast** (508-255-6632; 1-800-554-1751; www.pennyhouseinn.com), 4885 Route 6, North Eastham 02651. From the street, this bow-roofed Cape doesn't look nearly as old as it is; sections date back to the mid-1700s, though. The dining room (where a full breakfast is served) has wide floorboards, original beams, and barnboard walls. The rest of the house has a newer feel: Each of the 12 guest rooms (of varying sizes and styles) has a new bathroom and comfortable furnishings; most have air-conditioning; some have a TV. (Ask for a room with a phone if that's important.) The mother-daughter team of Margaret and Becky Keith have been particularly helpful innkeepers ever since they opened in 1988. Common space includes the great room with a working fireplace, and a brick patio in the back of the house. $120–205 June through September; $110–190 off-season.

COTTAGES

❦❧ **Cottage Grove** (508-255-0500; 1-877-521-5522; www.grovecape.com), 1875 Route 6, Eastham 02642. Open May through October. You can tell this is not your average cottage colony just by the unusual fence that fronts Route 6. (It has the double function of cutting road noise.) Hosts Greg Wolfe and Chris Nagle have renovated a total of eight cozy cottages (studios and one- and two-bedroom units) and a "meeting house," all on 3 acres and set back from the road. The cottages are rustic, with knotty-pine walls, but they have upgraded bathrooms and kitchens, firm new mattresses with cotton sheets, phones, and a smattering of antiques. In the off-season, this is a nice place for a group get-together. Continental breakfast included. Mid-June to mid-September $90–160 for studio or one-bedroom, $225 for two-bedroom; off-season $60–100 and $165, respectively; weekly rates.

✆ **Midway Motel & Cottages** (508-255-3117; 1-800-755-3117; www.midway motel.com), Route 6, North Eastham 02651. Open April through October. Pine and oak trees shield this reasonably priced complex of **motel units** and cottages from the road. The tidy grounds, over which Ron and Sally Knisely have presided since 1983, feature a nice children's play area, shuffleboard, badminton, horseshoes, picnic tables, grills, and direct access to the Cape Cod Rail Trail (see *Outdoor Activities—Bicycling/ Rentals*). One of the two cottages has three bedrooms. In-season $86–92 for rooms (each additional person $8), $710–850 per week for cottages; off-season $54–90 rooms, $425–590 per week cottages. Children under 16 free, as is the morning coffee and tea.

Cranberry Cottages (508-255-0602; 1-800-292-6631; www.sunsol.com/ cranberrycottages), 785 Route 6, Eastham 02642. This cottage colony has been in Lisa Grant's family since 1964, when her grandparents began operating it. She and her husband, Guy, have been refurbishing the 14 cottages, set back from the highway, since the mid-1990s. Two-bedroom housekeeping cottages have fully equipped kitchens. You'll want one of the significantly bigger units. Cottages without kitchens, which can accommodate two adults and a child, are rented on a nightly basis ($86– 92) April through November. In-season $675–775 weekly; off-season $48–65 nightly.

Saltaway Cottages (508-255-2182; www.saltawaycottages.com), Aspinet Road, North Eastham 02651. Open May through early November. The seven cottages are sited in a pine grove half a mile off the much-traveled Mid-Cape Highway. The shellacked knotty-pine walls lend the one- and two-bedroom cottages an immaculate feel. Kitchens are fully equipped and furnishings tasteful. Brewster Cottage has a fireplace. Playground and games for the kids. Late June to early September $550–705 weekly for two to four people; off-season $370–525 weekly.

Marsh View Cottage (508-247-9408), 2170 Route 6, Eastham 02642. Open June through October. This two-story barn commands a beautiful, distant view of Nauset Marsh. Two bedrooms upstairs have twin beds, while the first floor consists of a good-size kitchen and separate living room. A screened-in porch with cement floor faces the marsh. June and October $775 weekly; July through September $875 weekly.

Gibson Cottages (508-255-0882), off Samoset Road from Route 6. Open April through November. Down a little dirt road marked only with GIBSON, you'll find some of the best lakeside cottages on the Cape. Jerry and Mary Jane Gibson have owned the seven cottages since 1966 and take great pride in maintaining them. Each of the well-spaced one-, two-, and three-bedroom cottages has a screened porch or deck and fully equipped kitchen. They're very neat and tidy, freshly painted white. A swimming dock, sailboat, rowboats, and barbecue area are shared by all. There are also two bike trails on the other side of the pristine lake, which boasts a private, sandy beach. One "quiet" pet per cottage is permitted. This is a gem. Call as soon as you can to get a cottage. $800–1,000 weekly late June to early September; $500–700 weekly off-season. The Gibson's also rent their former five-bedroom house for $2,400 in-season.

See also Over Look Inn under *Bed & Breakfasts.*

RENTAL HOUSES AND COTTAGES

Anchor Real Estate (508-255-4949), 4761 Route 6, North Eastham 02651.

HOSTEL

Hostelling International Mid-Cape (508-255-2785; www.hi-travel.org; 1-800-909-4776 for in-season reservations; 617-531-0459 or enecreservations @juno.com for reservations prior to the start of the season), 75 Goody Hallet Drive, off Bridge Road, Eastham 02642. Open mid-May to mid-September. Located in a quiet residential neighborhood off the Orleans rotary, this hostel is open to people of all ages and promotes cross-cultural understanding through educational travel. The hostel sponsors programs on environmental topics, budget travel, bike repair (note the bike weather vane), stargazing, and such. It's a warm, cooperative environment with 50 beds in eight cabins. Well-maintained facilities include a common kitchen, bike shelter, a volleyball and basketball court, a game room, table tennis, and a barbecue area. It's about a mile to the nearest bay beach. Reservations are essential in July and August. $15–17 for AYH members, $18–21 for nonmembers; children under 14 are half price. Lockout 10–5.

WHERE TO EAT

There aren't many restaurants—good or bad—in Eastham.

Eastham Lobster Pool (508-255-9706; 508-255-3314 for takeout), 4360 Route 6, North Eastham. Open 11:30–9 daily, April through October. Although this place has the requisite fried fish and seafood platters, you can also order fish poached, broiled, or grilled ($14–18). Or just snack on peel-and-eat shrimp (10 for $11) and a side of clam chowder ($3.50). The choices and combinations are practically endless. Weekly and daily specials (like a lobster shore dinner for $21) are usually a good bet. The indoor dining room is pleasant, with wooden tables and chairs. There's outdoor dining and less expensive takeout, too. Although the Pool offers burgers and steaks, stick to the fish.

Arnold's Lobster & Clam Bar (508-255-2575), 3580 Route 6. Open 11–8 daily (until 10 in summer), mid-May to mid-September. A raw bar complements the usual assortment of fish rolls and fried seafood baskets. Order a generous side portion of fried shrimp or clam strips or a weekday lunch special for $3. Onion rings are excellent; during the summer of 1998 they sold 4,000 pounds of them! Choose nondescript indoor dining, the open-air patio, or tables under pine trees. Dishes $7–16. No credit cards.

❄︎✍ **Box Lunch** (508-255-0799), Route 6, North Eastham. Open daily year-round, until 4 PM off-season. If you've got a hungry family or a hankering for a sandwich made with pita bread, stop at this inconspicuous strip mall. (In case you didn't know, they roll their sandwich meats in pita bread at this ubiquitous Cape franchise.) Sandwiches $4–9.

SNACKS

Ben & Jerry's (508-255-2817), Route 6 at Brackett Road. Open April through November. The trademark black-and-white cows of Vermont have migrated to the warmer pastures of Cape Cod. The Bluesberry frozen yogurt, with blueberries, strawberries, and raspberries, can't be beat; or choose from dozens of creamy, crunchy, and chunky ice cream offerings.

ENTERTAINMENT

First Encounter Coffee House (508-255-5438), Samoset Road. Open year-round except December and May. Performances on the second and fourth Saturday of each month; open mike every first Saturday. Acoustic, folk, blues, and bluegrass reign here, attracting musicians with national reputations—including Wellfleet's very own Patty Larkin and Vineyarder Livingston Taylor. The coffeehouse has been home to the 1899 Unitarian-Universalist church (aka Chapel in the Pines) since 1974. The intimate venue has only 100 seats, beneath stained-glass windows. Off-season, it's a very local affair, where everybody knows your name and knows to arrive early to get a good seat. On my last visit (when I arrived late), it was difficult to hear the performers while folks were cleaning up in the open kitchen. Tickets are usually $10–15; children free; open mike $3.

Band concerts. Fund-raising efforts were well under way at press time for a gazebo-style bandstand to be sited in the windmill park by May 2001.

SELECTIVE SHOPPING

ARTISAN

❄︎ **Sunken Meadow Basketworks & Pottery** (508-255-8962), North Sunken Meadow Road, North Eastham. Open year-round, but call first in winter. Look for Hugh and Paulette Penney's well-executed handwoven baskets, wall sculptures, stoneware, and jewelry in a newly constructed barn.

ART SHOWS

Eastham Painters' Guild, at the Old Schoolhouse Museum (see *To See*). Outdoor art shows are held here most Thursdays and Fridays in July and August, as well as over the Memorial Day, Labor Day, and Columbus Day weekends.

SPECIAL SHOPS

❊ Unless otherwise noted, all shops are open year-round.

Collector's World (508-255-3616), Route 6. Since 1974, Chris Alex has been selling an eclectic lineup of antiques, gifts, and collectibles like Russian lacquer boxes, scrimshaw, pewter, and wooden nutcracker soldiers. It's one of the wackiest collections on the Cape.

The Chocolate Sparrow (508-240-0606), 4205 Route 6. Marjorie Sparrow opened this shop in 1989 to sell her luscious hand-dipped chocolates and homemade fudge. It's for the chocoholics among us who aren't trying to overcome the affliction.

Gristmill Gallery (508-240-0033), 2320 Route 6. Open seasonally. These one-of-a-kind pieces, made from antique wood and vintage hardware, are a treasure, unpretentious and unconventional. Also, some antiques, prints, and nautical items.

Exposure (508-255-6808), 135 Oak Leaf Road, North Eastham. One of the few Cape places that process black-and-white film, Exposure does such a fantastic job that I even mail them my 4-by-5 sheet film from Boston and beyond when I'm traveling!

Eastham Pottery & Loomworks (508-255-1556; www.capecodpotters. com/easthampottery.htm), 105 Gigi Lane, North Eastham. Just south of the Wellfleet town line, opposite the drive-in, Brian Brader has opened a small studio and showroom barn. His pots, platters, sculpture, and stoneware reflect his interest in the natural world. Lisa, Brian's wife, is a weaver who takes commissions.

Four Winds Leather (508-240-7998), 5130 Route 6, North Eastham. You probably didn't come to the Cape in search of sheepskins and moccasins, but these are the real thing. The store is piled high with Native American art, leather coats, wallets, and the like. Tom and Doris Ficca also do leather repairs and custom work.

SPECIAL EVENTS

Yearlong: **350th anniversary.** The town is celebrating it in 2001 with special events every month throughout the year.

Mid- to late May: **Cape Cod Maritime Days** (508-862-0700). Coast Guard–operated lighthouses are open during this festival, including Nauset Light and Three Sisters. In addition to focusing on the area's lighthouses, the Cape-wide event celebrates the region's fishing heritage, maritime villages, and seafaring way of life.

Mid-September: **Windmill Weekend.** This community festival is staged for locals and features a road race, band concert, arts and crafts show, square dancing, and a parade.

Wellfleet

Although a whopping 70 percent of Wellfleet is conservation land, the town is perhaps best known as an art stronghold. Wellfleet's two principal thoroughfares, Main Street and Commercial Street, are dotted with 20 or so galleries, some of them in little weathered cottages reminiscent of fishing shacks. The galleries represent a wide gamut of art: from souvenir works to images that transcend their media. Many artists and artisans who exhibit here call Wellfleet home, at least for a short time each year, gaining inspiration from pristine landscapes and an unrelenting ocean.

Wellfleet appeals to a distinct crowd, many of whom have returned year after year for decades. When shopkeepers and restaurateurs begin dusting off the shelves in early to mid-June, it feels like a real homecoming—old friends catching up over a coffee in a café, neighbors renewing relationships as they tend their gardens, and acquaintances greeting a faintly familiar face from the previous summer. Nonnative families—wash-ashores—rent houses here for the entire summer. (The *Boston Globe* reports that two-thirds of Wellfleet's 3,700 houses are unoccupied in the off-season.) And although Wellfleet is very popular with vacationing psychiatrists, there's also a notable contingent of lawyers, professors, and writers. They've all come for the same purpose—to commune with their thoughts, recharge batteries, and lead a simpler life (albeit only temporarily). The visiting August vacationers purchase seven times as many *New York Times* and *Boston Globes* as are sold off-season. They also venture out of their cocoons to dine on wonderful food in laid-back settings, to square dance outdoors, and to engage in lively conversation. No enterprise in town is more fondly supported than the adventurous Wellfleet Harbor Actors Theater.

Even so, Wellfleeters are an independent bunch. Almost 30 percent of the 2,500 year-rounders are self-employed (proverbial Jacks and Jills of all trades), more than in any other Cape town. Most of the town rolls up its shutters from mid-October to mid-May, when unemployment climbs to 20 percent. Even on a weekday in mid-June, though, Wellfleet may feel eerie, like a ghost town. The off-season has its own allure, however. If you visit midwinter, you'll find a few warm beds and a hot meal or two, and the frozen bay is a romantic sight on an overcast day.

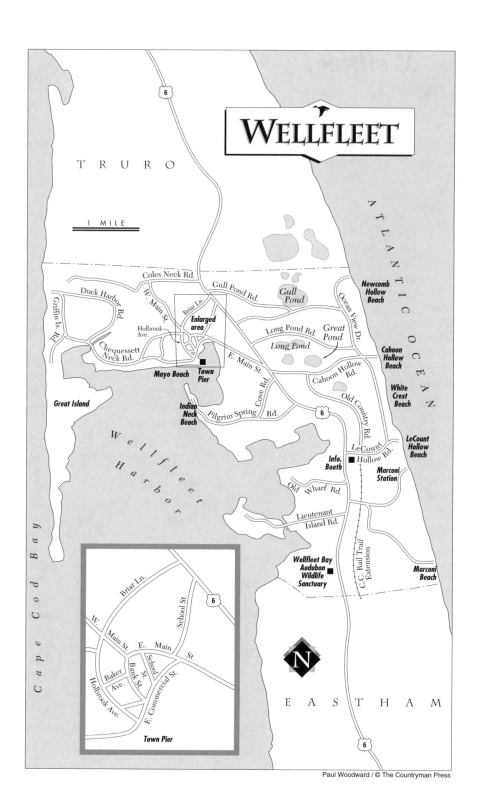

WELLFLEET

T R U R O

1 MILE

Coles Neck Rd.

Duck Harbor Rd.

Griffin Is. Rd.

W. Main St.

Gull Pond Rd.

Gull Pond

Briar Ln.

Enlarged area

Holbrook Ave.

Chequessett Neck Rd.

Long Pond Rd.

Long Pond

Great Pond

Ocean View Dr.

Newcomb Hollow Beach

Cahoon Hollow Beach

White Crest Beach

Mayo Beach

Town Pier

E. Main St.

Cahoon Hollow Rd.

Great Island

Indian Neck Beach

Pilgrim Spring Rd.

Cove Rd.

Old Country Rd.

6

LeCount Hollow Rd.

LeCount Hollow Beach

W e l l f l e e t   H a r b o r

Info. Booth

LeCount Hollow

Marconi Station

C a p e   C o d   B a y

Old Wharf Rd.

Lieutenant Island Rd.

C.C. Rail Trail Extension

Marconi Beach

Wellfleet Bay Audubon Wildlife Sanctuary

Briar Ln.

W. Main St.

E. Main

School St.

6

St.

School St.

Baker Ave.

Bank St.

E. Commercial St.

Holbrook Ave.

Town Pier

N

E A S T H A M

6

A T L A N T I C   O C E A N

Paul Woodward / © The Countryman Press

In addition to art, Wellfleet's draw is its natural environment. The Audubon Society's outstanding Wellfleet Bay Wildlife Sanctuary offers practically unparalleled opportunities for observing marine and bird life through a variety of guided activities and self-guided walks. A mostly sandy, 8-mile-long trail on Great Island, part of the Cape Cod National Seashore (CCNS), yields solitude and commanding views of Wellfleet Bay. On the other side, the broad, uninterrupted beaches east of Route 6 are backed by dunes and cliffs. Any of Wellfleet's meandering roads are perfect for cycling, leading you past ponds, salt marshes, heathlands, and scrub pines.

Wellfleet was most likely named after a town in England, which, like "our" Wellfleet, was also renowned for its oyster beds. As early as the 17th century, when Wellfleet was still a part of Eastham known as Billingsgate, the primary industries revolved around oyster and cranberry harvesting. Whaling, fishing, and other related industries also flourished until the mid-1800s. And by the 1870s, commercial markets had really opened up for littlenecks, cherrystones, and clams for chowder. Today, with the depletion of natural fish and shellfish stocks, year-round fishermen have turned to aquaculture. Currently about 50 or so aquaculturists lease 120 acres of Wellfleet Harbor; you'll see them off Mayo Beach at low tide. Shellfish like quahogs and oysters are raised from "seed," put out in "protected racks," and tended for two to three years while they mature. Since as many as 2 million seeds can be put on an acre of land, this is big business. For those looking for fishing charters, though, the harbor and pier are still centers of activity.

In the name of "progress," houses and businesses were assigned street numbers in 1995. Although they're helpful to the fire department, they're of relatively little use to visitors, as many shops don't post the numbers—and when they do, numbers are often not in consecutive order. Don't despair, Wellfleet's a small town; you won't have trouble finding what you're looking for.

GUIDANCE
Wellfleet Chamber of Commerce (508-349-2510; www.wellfleet chamber.com), Route 6, P.O. Box 571, Wellfleet 02667. Open 10–4 Friday through Sunday, mid-May to mid-October; 9–6 daily late May to early September. The **information booth** is well marked, right off Route 6 in South Wellfleet. The frequently overworked chamber publishes a rudimentary foldout map of Wellfleet bicycle routes.

PUBLIC LIBRARY
❄☞☂**The Wellfleet Public Library** (508-349-0310), West Main Street. Open Monday, Wednesday, and Thursday 2–8; Tuesday and Friday 10–5; and Saturday noon–5. Housed within the former Candle Factory, this outstanding library is available to all Wellfleet vacationers; call for children's story hour times.

PUBLIC REST ROOMS

Public rest rooms can be found in summer at Bakers Field across from Mayo Beach (see *Green Space—Beaches*), as well as at the Town Pier and the Marina (both at the end of Commercial Street). Throughout the year, during business hours, head to the basement of Town Hall on Main Street.

GETTING THERE

By car: Wellfleet is 50 miles beyond the Sagamore Bridge via Route 6.

By bus: The **Plymouth & Brockton** bus line (508-778-9767; www.p-b.com) connects Wellfleet and South Wellfleet with Hyannis and other Cape towns, as well as with Boston's Logan Airport. The bus stops in front of the Town Hall on Main Street in Wellfleet and at D&D Market on Route 6 in South Wellfleet.

GETTING AROUND

By car: From Route 6, take Main Street to the town center or veer from Main to Commercial Street to the colorful harbor. There is free parking at the Town Pier (at the end of Commercial Street) and behind Town Hall on Main Street. As the seagull flies, the town is anywhere from 2 to 5 miles wide.

MEDICAL EMERGENCY

Outer Cape Health Services (508-349-3131), Route 6, Wellfleet. Open for walk-ins 8–5 daily in summer (some evenings, too). Off-season, walk-ins are taken weekdays 8–8:45 AM only.

TO SEE

Marconi Wireless Station, CCNS, off Route 6 at the Marconi Area. Guglielmo Marconi began construction of the first wireless station on the U.S. mainland in 1901. Two years later the first U.S. wireless transatlantic message was transmitted between this station and England: President Roosevelt sent King Edward VII "most cordial greetings and good wishes." (Canada beat the United States in sending a wireless transatlantic message by one month.) The station was closed in 1917 for wartime security reasons and was dismantled and abandoned in 1920 because of erosion and the development of alternative technologies. There are few remains today, save the concrete foundation of the transmitter house (which required 25,000 volts to send a message) and sand anchors that held guy wires to the 210-foot towers. The Cape Cod peninsula is at its narrowest here, and from a well-positioned observation platform you can scan the width of it—from Cape Cod Bay, along Blackfish Creek, to the Atlantic Ocean.

Wellfleet Historical Society Museum (508-349-9157), 266 Main Street. Open 10–4 Tuesday and Friday and 1–4 Wednesday and Thursday, late June to early September. The society has collected photographs, toys, shipwreck detritus, marine artifacts, displays on Marconi and oystering,

Wellfleet's winter "skyline" from across Duck Creek at low tide.

and household items to illustrate and preserve Wellfleet's past. Adults $1, children under 12 free. Inquire about the good 75-minute walks around town on Tuesday and Friday during the summer ($3).

First Congregational Church of the United Church of Christ (508-349-6877), 200 Main Street. The church office is open 9–noon Wednesday through Friday year-round; they'll let you in. While the church was organized in 1721, this meetinghouse dates to 1850. The interior is graced with a brass chandelier, pale blue walls, curved pews, and a Tiffany-style stained-glass window depicting a 17th-century ship similar to the *Mayflower*. On Sunday evening at 8 in July and August, concerts are given on the restored Hook and Hastings pipe organ. The church's architecture is Greek Revival, except for the bell-shaped cupola, which was added in 1879 after a storm destroyed the traditional one. (It was thought that a bell-shaped tower would be more sturdy—perhaps it has been.)

Town clock, First Congregational Church, Main Street. According to the arbiter of strange superlatives, *Ripley's Believe It or Not*, this is the "only town clock in the world that strikes ship's time." Listen for the following chimes and try to figure out what time it is for yourself: Two bells distinguish 1, 5, and 9 o'clock; six bells signify 3, 7, and 11 o'clock; eight bells toll for 4, 8, and 12 o'clock. To make matters even more interesting, the half hours are signified by adding one chime to the corresponding even hours. (After all these years, I still double-check my "newfangled" wristwatch!)

Our Lady of Lourdes Church (508-349-2222), Main Street. On the occasion of the country's 1976 bicentennial, two troubadours expressed their thanks to the town after a long celebration by donating these handsome painted carvings attached to the doors, which are thankfully kept open for all to see.

Samuel Rider House, Gull Pond Road. Although the house is not open to the public, it's a fine early-1700s Outer Cape farmstead.

Atwood Higgins House (508-255-3421), Bound Brook Island Road, off Pamet Point Road. Under the auspices of the National Seashore, this homestead conducts an open house on Thursday 1–4 PM from late May to mid-October. The pastoral 5-acre property has a little store and post office, but the tour only discusses the architecture and versatility of the 18th-century full Cape that was restored by its early-20th-century owners. Free.

SCENIC DRIVES

Ocean View Drive. Take LeCount Hollow Road to Ocean View (despite its name, it has only limited views) and head back to Route 6 via Gull Pond Road. You'll pass heathlands, cliffs, and scrub pines.

Chequessett Neck Road. Cross the dike at Herring River and head to the end of the road for magnificent sunset views. Although there is room for only a few cars at the very end of the road, you can park near the Great Island Trailhead and walk down to the beach (about 15 minutes).

Pilgrim Spring Road. Not to be confused with the Pilgrim Spring Trail in Truro, where the Pilgrims got their first taste of fresh water, this quiet road offers lovely inlet and cove views; at the end of the road, look back to Wellfleet Harbor.

OUTDOOR ACTIVITIES

BICYCLING/RENTALS

Cape Cod Rail Trail. Extended in the mid-1990s, the trail now terminates in Wellfleet at LeCount Hollow Road (where there is parking), just east of Route 6.

Wellfleet Cycles (508-349-9322), 54 East Commercial Street, is open seasonally for rentals.

Idle Times Bike Shop (508-349-9161), Route 6. Open mid-May to early September. A full line of bicycles for the whole family.

BOAT EXCURSIONS/RENTALS

Jack's Boat Rentals (508-349-7553), Gull Pond. Open late May to early September. Jack's offers guided kayak and canoe tours (about twice daily) through estuary marshes and along the tidal Pamet and Herring Rivers. Jack's also rents canoes, boogie boards, kayaks, double kayaks, and Sunfish. If you want to paddle somewhere besides Gull Pond, pick up a boat at the shop (508-349-9808) on Route 6.

Wellfleet Marine Corp. (508-349-2233), Town Pier. From mid-June to mid-September, you can rent Stur-Dee Cat sailboats, sloops, and fishing skiffs by the hour or by the day.

See also *Fishing/Shellfishing.*

FISHING/SHELLFISHING

Obtain a freshwater fishing permit at Town Hall (508-349-0301) on Main
Street. Freshwater fishing holes include **Great Pond, Gull Pond,** and
Long Pond (see *Green Space—Ponds*).

Shellfishing permits are required for the taking of oysters, clams, and qua-
hogs. Permits cost $40 for a four-month seasonal nonresident permit.
Wellfleet's tidal flats are wondrous places at low tide. Contact the **Beach
Sticker Booth** (508-349-9818) on the pier in July and August or the
Town Hall (508-349-0300) the rest of the year. Try your luck surf-casting
early in the morning or at night at **Newcomb Hollow, White Crest
Beach, LeCount Hollow** (all on the Atlantic), or at **Duck Harbor** on
the bay side.

Black Duck Sports Shop (508-349-9801), off Route 6, South Wellfleet.
Open mid-April to mid-October. Get your tide chart, live eels, squid,
worms, and sand eels here, along with outdoor maps and camping
equipment.

For half- and full-day fishing charters, contact *Snoop* (508-349-6113) and
Jac's Mate (508-255-2978; 508-237-3289 mobile). Both are docked at
the Wellfleet Harbor Marina and offer charters mid-May through September, although *Jac's* has a slightly longer season.

Navigator (508-349-6003), also at the Wellfleet Harbor Marina. With more
than 30 years of experience plying Cape Cod waters, Capt. Rick Merrill
offers a little bit of everything: morning and afternoon fishing trips in
July and August and a marine-life cruise with seal-watching in conjunc-
tion with the Audubon Society in spring and fall. The boat holds 49 people.

GOLF

Chequessett Yacht & Country Club (508-349-3704), Chequessett Neck
Road. Open April through November, weather permitting. This nine-
hole, par-35 course offers beautiful views of Wellfleet Harbor.

MINI-GOLF

✐ **At the Wellfleet Drive-In** (508-349-2520), Route 6. Open May to mid-
October. This 18-hole course is nothing special, but it's the only game in
town and it's conveniently located next to the flea market and drive-in
(see *Entertainment*); there's also an adjacent, classic dairy bar.

SAILING

✐ **Chequessett Yacht & Country Club** (508-349-0198), Chequessett Neck
Road, offers sailing lessons. Junior and adult sailing programs run from
early July to late August. Group instruction by the week and individual
instruction (for one or two people) by the hour.

SEAL CRUISES

✳ **Wellfleet Bay Wildlife Sanctuary** (508-349-2615; www.wellfleetbay.org).
Trips most weekends and some weekdays; call for the tide-dependent
schedule. The Audubon Sanctuary offers a 2-hour Sea Bird and Seal
Cruise departing out of Wellfleet Harbor in late fall on an open commercial fishing vessel; a 90-minute trip off South Beach and Monomoy Island

KIM GRANT

A boardwalk crosses the dunes to the National Seashore

departing out of Chatham in summer (10 people maximum); and a longer winter trip out of Harwichport on a big ferry with indoor heated seating. On-board naturalists expound on the habits and habitats of the hundreds of harbor and gray seals sunning themselves or bobbing in the water. Tickets: $25–35 for nonmembers; $5 less for members.

SPECIAL PROGRAMS

Wellfleet Bay Wildlife Sanctuary Natural History Day Camp (508-349-2615), South Wellfleet 02663. July and August. Intended for children 4–14, these excellent weeklong, half-day, and daylong programs are designed to "expand curiosity about and respect for the environment through hands-on outdoor experiences . . . and to develop skill in discovering the natural world using the principles of scientific inquiry." $65 for nonmembers ($55 members) for a half day; $175–200 nonmembers for a full day.

Wellfleet Bay Wildlife Sanctuary Adult Field School (508-349-2615). Four weeklong, hands-on courses are given in July and August on Cape Cod natural history; ornithology; marine life; and nature photography. Six-day mini-courses are also given on field archaeology; the geology of the Cape; local endangered habitats; and sketching in the field. Expert instruction. Programs range $185–455. Shared accommodations are available on-site for an additional fee.

Summer recreation programs (508-349-0330), Bakers Field and Gull Pond. Weekdays 9–noon, early July to mid-August. Sports, arts and crafts, and swimming lessons. Nonresidents $40 per week per child.

TENNIS

Town courts are on **Mayo Beach,** Kendrick Street.

Oliver's Clay Tennis Courts (508-349-3330), Route 6. Open daily May through October, weather permitting. You'll notice Saabs parked in front before you see the seven well-hidden clay courts and one Truflex court. Matches can be arranged and racquets restrung.

Chequessett Yacht & Country Club (508-349-3704), Chequessett Neck Road. Open March through December, weather permitting. Five all-weather courts are available to the public for a fee.

GREEN SPACE

Wellfleet Bay Wildlife Sanctuary (508-349-2615; www.wellfleetbay.org), off Route 6, South Wellfleet. Trails open daily sunrise to sunset; center open daily 8:30–5, year-round, except closed Monday from November through April. The sanctuary encompasses almost 1,000 acres of pine, moors, freshwater ponds, tidal creeks, salt marsh, and beach. This is one of the most active sanctuaries in New England and an excellent resource for Cape Cod naturalists. Even nonnaturalists will appreciate the relative lack of human presence after a day of gallery hopping and sunbathing. In 1993 an environmentally friendly visitors center was built as a result of the efforts of director Bob Prescott; its composting toilets save 100,000 gallons of water per season.

The sanctuary offers a steady stream of activities throughout summer (plenty year-round, for that matter): canoe trips, sunset walks, night hikes, marine-life cruises in Pleasant Bay and Cape Cod Bay, birding expeditions for beginners and aficionados, cruises on Nauset Marsh, and trips to Monomoy Island (see *Green Space* in "Chatham"). Summertime evening bayside talks focus on the Cape's natural history. Wintertime seal cruises to Monomoy Island and South Beach are also popular (see *Outdoor Activities—Seal Cruises*). Drop in or write for a detailed schedule. Trails free to members, $3 for adult nonmembers, $2 for children nonmembers. Members may tent in the wooded, natural setting.

BEACHES

Marconi Beach, CCNS, on the Atlantic. A boardwalk and steep staircase lead to the long, narrow beach backed by dramatic dunes. In-season amenities include lifeguards, outdoor showers, and superb changing facilities. Parking $7 (permit valid all day at any CCNS beach); seasonal pass $20. The cost to enter on foot or bicycle is $1.

Cahoon Hollow Beach and **White Crest Beach,** town beaches on the Atlantic Ocean. Sandy shoals create shallow, warm pools of water here. Although each beach is wide and sandy, local townsfolk favor the sea grass and dunes of White Crest, and hang gliders and surfers appreciate the surf. (Hang gliders are allowed only before 9 AM and after 5 PM.) White Crest has more parking. Amenities include lifeguards and rest rooms. Parking $10 per day.

Mayo Beach, Kendrick Street. Parking is free, but the beach is nothing to write home about. From here you can see some of the offshore areas—marked by yellow buoys—where modern aquaculture thrives in the form of constructed shellfish farms.

The following beaches require a town sticker: **LeCount Hollow Beach** and **Newcomb Hollow Beach,** both off Ocean View Drive on the Atlantic Ocean; **Burton Baker Beach** (the only place in town where windsurfing is permitted) and **Indian Neck Beach,** both off Pilgrim Spring Road on the bay side; **Powers Landing** and **Duck Harbor,** both off Chequessett Neck Road on the bay side. Cottage renters may purchase a sticker at the well-marked **Beach Sticker Booth** (508-349-9818) on the Town Pier from early July to early September, the only time you'll need a sticker. $30 per week, $100 per season.

PONDS

Great Pond, Long Pond, and **Gull Pond** offer freshwater swimming. Resident parking stickers are required (and can be purchased at the **Beach Sticker Booth,** 508-349-9818, on the Town Pier). All ponds have lifeguards.

WALKS

Wellfleet Bay Wildlife Sanctuary (see full listing above). The sanctuary offers three trails totaling more than 5 miles: Silver Spring Trail, a lovely, wooded walking trail alongside a long pond; Goose Pond Trail, past ponds, woodlands, a marsh, and heathland (a boardwalk leads to the bay from here); and Bay View Trail.

Great Island Trail, CCNS, off Chequessett Neck Road. About 8 miles round trip, this trail is relatively flat, but soft sand makes for a challenging trek. Walk at low tide when the sand is more firm. (Jeremy Point, the tip of land farthest out to sea, is covered at high tide.) You'll be rewarded with scant human presence and stunning scenery during the 4-hour round-trip hike. Bring plenty of water and sunscreen. The trail is best on a sunny spring day or a crisp autumn one. It's great for birders.

This area was once an island, hence its name. But over time Cape Cod Bay currents deposited sandbars that eventually connected it to the mainland. Long ago, Great Island was home to various commercial enterprises—oystering, cranberry harvesting, and shore whaling—and the land was dotted with lookout towers used to spot whales. There was even a local watering hole and overnight hostelry, the Great Island Tavern, built in 1690 and used until about 1740. But as shore whaling died, so did the community on Great Island. By 1800 the island was deserted and deforested. (Pines have been planted in an effort to keep erosion under control.)

Atlantic White Cedar Swamp Trail, CCNS, Marconi Area. The early and latter parts of this 1½-mile round-trip trail traverse steep stairs and soft sand; the swamp is navigable via a boardwalk. The swamp has a primordial feel, and the dense overhead cover keeps the trail cool even on the most stifling of days. Because white cedar was prized by the settlers for its light weight and ease of handling, a century of overuse took its toll. Recently the swamp (in places, 24 feet deep with peat) has begun to recover. Nature has its own cycles, however, and the red maples will eventually choke the white cedars out of existence. For now, appreciate one of the few remaining stands of white cedar on the Cape. In August, wild trailside blueberries are ripe for the picking.

Uncle Tim's Bridge, East Commercial Street. The often photographed wooden footbridge connects Commercial Street to a small wooded island, crossing a tidal creek (Duck Creek) and marshland. Short, sandy trails circle the island.

LODGING

Most summer visitors to Wellfleet stay in cottages and houses, rented by the week or, most probably, longer, but there are places for short-term guests as well. Unless otherwise noted, all lodging is in Wellfleet 02667.

INN

Inn at Duck Creeke (508-349-9333; www.capecod.net/duckinn), 70 Main Street. Open early May to mid-October. Half a mile from the town center is a rambling, old-fashioned 1800s inn situated between an idyllic duck pond (rooms 26 and 27 overlook the water) and a salt marsh (rooms 21 and 30 overlook it). Of all the simple guest rooms, my favorites are in the Saltworks Cottage (they share a homey living room) and the carriage house (they have a spiffed-up, romantic cabin feel). Rustic, air-conditioned rooms on the third floor of the main inn, referred to as the soccer field, are well suited to groups and families. Otherwise, rooms are on the small side, but at least they're priced accordingly. In-season $85–95 with private bath, $70–85 with shared bath; off-season $50–85.

BED & BREAKFASTS

Aunt Sukie's Bayside Bed & Breakfast (508-349-2804; 1-800-420-9999; www.auntsukies.com), 525 Chequessett Neck Road. Hidden by a fence from a road less traveled, this beachfront B&B is full of picture windows facing the bayside setting sun. It takes just 30 seconds to walk from the shingled house, with a contemporary addition, across a boardwalk marsh to their private bay beach, with shallow waters warmed by the tide. Sue and Dan Hamar have lived here since 1984 but have been taking in guests only since 1994. The suite, with a separate sitting room in the original 1830 section of the house, features a fireplace, wide pine floors, Oriental carpets, and its own private patio. One of the three rooms can accommodate a child over 8 years old. Two of the contemporary rooms boast private decks and splendid bay views. They face the setting sun. The common room is dotted with antiques and overflowing with "Aunt Sukie's" history. Expanded continental breakfast on the bayside deck, weather permitting. On my last visit Dan served homemade bread with his son's beach plum jam made from bushes on the premises. May through October $140–200; shoulder seasons $120–170. Inquire about the nearby **three-bedroom house,** perfect for families ($1,100–1,400 weekly in July and August, $1,000 weekly in June and September).

❦ **Blue Gateways** (508-349-7530; www.bluegateways.com), 252 Main Street. Closed February and March. In 1996, Bonnie and Richard Robicheau opened what Wellfleet had previously lacked: a comfortable, cheery, completely refurbished B&B in the center of town. Since Richard is a builder, the house has been expertly renovated, right down to latch doors and sanded floors. The three crisp guest rooms share an upstairs reading room and a downstairs TV room, complete with one of the house's three working fireplaces. An expanded continental breakfast is served on the light sunporch, overlooking the little reflecting pool (a great place for a second cup of coffee). Bonnie obviously enjoys taking care of people. Late May to early September $100–120; $10 less off-season.

❦ **Sea Cliff** (508-349-3753; 212-645-5028 off-season), 740 Ocean View Drive. Open mid-June to mid-October. Although Marla Perkel has only one guest accommodation, what a room it is! The guest house, which is separate from the main house, is perched 110 feet above the Atlantic on a 2,200-square-foot deck. All you can see is the falling away of beach grass and the endless sky and ocean. That sense of scale has a way of easing life back into perspective. Room amenities include a microwave, refrigerator, TV, VCR, and outdoor shower (there's an indoor one, too). You can easily settle into a weeklong stay here. There is no direct beach access, but there are beaches a quarter mile in either direction. Marla, a charming well-traveled woman who winters in Manhattan, sets out an expanded continental breakfast on the deck each morning and enjoys talking with her guests. You may even be invited over for a sunset glass of wine. $175 nightly (3-night minimum, 7-night maximum). No credit cards.

❋✐ **Stone Lion Inn** (508-349-9565; www.stonelioncapecod.com), 130 Commercial Street. Innkeepers Janet Loewenstein and Adam Levinson have completely renovated and redecorated the B&B to reflect the era of a 1871 sea captain's house but also their contemporary sensibilities as former Brooklynites. The three guest rooms, all with private bath and queen-size bed, are located on the second floor. One has a small but private deck. The first floor is given over to common space, including a very comfortable living room with TV, VCR, and lots of art, and a dining room where a breakfast buffet—perhaps cranberry nut muffins and a bacon and onion quiche—is laid out. The color palette of muted lavenders, yellows, and greens is very tranquil. Neither the **apartment** nor the **three-bedroom cottage** has received the same attention as the B&B renovation, but they may work for you. The cottage was in need of some sprucing up, but families may wish to inquire about weekly rentals. The low-key **apartment** has a rudimentary kitchenette and a second-floor

KIM GRANT

Low tide abstractions

bedroom reached via a spiral staircase. Mid-June to early September $125–140 for rooms, off-season $90-120; if you're interested, inquire about rates at the apartment and cottage.

COTTAGES

✳🐾 **Surf Side Cottages** (508-349-3959; www.capecod.net/surfside), Ocean View Drive, South Wellfleet 02663. Open April through October; one cottage is open year-round. The 1950s-style housekeeping cottages aren't much to look at on the outside (unless you count the private outdoor showers). But what's really important is the location, in the CCNS and within a minute's walk of the dunes. Nothing separates them from the ocean except other Surf Side cottages and scrub pines. A few of the 18 units have ocean views. Most larger cottages have a roof deck; each has a screened-in porch and wood-burning fireplace. Modern kitchens, knotty-pine paneling, and tasteful rattan furnishings are the norm. Bring sheets and towels and leave the cottage clean and ready for the next tenants. Reserve early. Pets accepted off-season. Weekly, June to mid-October, $750 for one bedroom, $1,100–1,350 for two or three bedrooms; off-season, $70–125 per day, $450–700 per week.

The Colony (508-349-3761), 640 Chequessett Neck Road. Open late May to late September. This is not your average cottage colony. It was built as a private club in 1949 by Ned Saltonstall (a trustee of Boston's Institute for Contemporary Arts), who decided to open an art gallery and ended up hanging paintings in the cottages as well. These days guests flock to the Colony for its calming atmosphere and excellent service (including turndown service and flowers on arrival) provided by Eleanor Stefani, who purchased the place in 1963. Each of the 10 units has a different view of the adjacent golf course or Cape Cod Bay and its own charm. Each of the patios or decks has a view of the natural, preserved surroundings. In addition, they all have daily maid service, working fireplaces, original artwork, and picture windows. Galley kitchens and enclosed dining porches are standard features of the one- and two-bedroom units. The 1949 low-slung duplexes were built in the Bauhaus style, intent on doing the most with the least. There are no hard-and-fast rules about renting from Saturday to Saturday, just one of the refreshing changes about the low-key style of the Colony. $1,050–2,000 per week, $165–300 daily, with a 3-night minimum.

✐ **The Even'tide** (508-3410; 1-800-368-0007 within Massachusetts; www.eventidemotel.com), Route 6, South Wellfleet 02663. Open April through October. These nine cottages are a cut above. Wooded and set back from Route 6, the complex has a nice children's play area and a 30-by-60-foot heated indoor pool. The Cape Cod Rail Trail runs along the back of the property, and a ¾-mile walking trail leads to Marconi Beach. All cottages have cable TV, telephone, fully tiled bathrooms, and full kitchens (except Tern). Rates for two of these cottages include linens and maid service. Bedrooms in the peak of the A-frame cottages get warm in summer. Also available: 31 above-average **motel rooms** and suites that rent for $89–120 nightly in-season. Weekly, in July and August, $700 for four, $785–925 for six; $515–925 weekly for four to six people off-season (or $74–94 nightly for two people).

See also Stone Lion Inn under *Bed & Breakfasts* and Maurice's Campground under *Campgrounds*.

MOTELS

&❄ **Wellfleet Motel & Lodge** (508-349-3535; 1-800-852-2900; www.wellfleetmotel.com), Route 6, South Wellfleet 02663. The highly visible sign proclaiming SQUEAKY CLEAN ROOMS begs inspection and, fortunately, the 65 rooms and suites live up to the boasting. Located across from the Wellfleet Bay Wildlife Sanctuary, the bilevel, 1960s-style motel units are typically appointed and air-conditioned. Rooms in the nicely landscaped lodge, built in 1986, are generally more spacious than the motel rooms. A gas grill, whirlpool, restaurant, and indoor and outdoor pools are on the premises. There is direct access to the Cape Cod Rail Trail. July and August $125–225 double, $10 each additional person; off-season $60–100 double.

See also the Even'tide under *Cottages*.

CAMPGROUNDS

🐾✐ **Paine's Campground** (508-349-3007; 1-800-479-3017; www.campingcapecod.com), off Old County Road from Route 6, South Wellfleet 02663. Open mid-May to late September. At this tenters' haven there are designated areas for "quiet" campers, youth groups, and families, as well as sites to which you must lug your tent. Of the 150 sites, only 6 are reserved for RVs. You can walk from the campground to the National

Seashore. Freshwater swimming is found in nearby kettle ponds. Sites $9–12 per person. Children 6 and under stay free.

Maurice's Campground (508-349-2029; www.mauricescampground.com), Route 6. Open late May to mid-October. 180 wooded sites for tents and trailers. There are also a few **cottages** that can sleep four and **cabins** that can sleep three with a cot. Direct access to the Cape Cod Rail Trail. $24 for two; additional adults $5, additional children $2. Cottages $450 weekly for two, $470 for four. Cabins $70 nightly.

See also Wellfleet Bay Wildlife Sanctuary under *Green Space.*

RENTAL HOUSES AND COTTAGES
Starfish Properties (508-349-6396), Cove Corner, Route 6.

See also Aunt Sukie's Bayside Bed & Breakfast under *Bed & Breakfasts.*

WHERE TO EAT

Wellfleet oysters are renowned: Legend has it that England's Queen Victoria served Wellfleet oysters at her state dinners (no others would do). According to aficionados, Wellfleet oysters taste better when harvested from the cooler waters in the off-season, but you'll have little choice if you vacation in July or August; order them anyway. Wellfleet is also known for its hard-shell quahog and steamer clams. In fact, these waters yield more than $2 million worth of shellfish annually.

Although there are many restaurants listed here, look closely and you'll find that most are closed prior to mid-June and after early autumn. Most of the opening and closing dates are quite fluid, too, wholly dependent on weather and tourist traffic.

DINING OUT
Aesop's Tables (508-349-6450), 316 Main Street, next to Town Hall. Open for lunch in July and August and dinner mid-May to mid-October. Accolades over the years for Wellfleet's premier dining spot are deserved. Aesop's is best known for local seafood, coastal cuisine influenced by other places that are also influenced by the sea: Italy, France, Japan, Thailand, and New Zealand. Of the six dining rooms decorated with local art, avoid the rear one next to the kitchen. Although the small tables and table settings undersell the quality of the food, you must remember: This befits low-key, understated Wellfleet. A bar menu (see Upstairs Bar at Aesop's Tables under *Eating Out*) is served at lunch indoors and on the brick terrace overlooking Main Street. Children's menu. Reservations highly recommended. Lunch $7–15; dinner entrées $14–26.

Painter's (508-349-3003), 50 Main Street. Open for dinner mid-May to mid-November. Kate Painter—who apprenticed at Biba and Hammersley's in Boston and Stars in San Francisco before graduating from college—has been serving New American bistro cuisine to Wellfleet audiences since 1992. She moved from an offbeat waterfront joint to this more refined, 18th-century space in the mid-1990s. It's friendly, casually elegant, and hip. Local seafood and homemade pasta dishes are creative and ambitious. I'm partial to the corn and cod chowder, Gorgonzola baked in terra-cotta, myriad oysters, Portuguese seafood stew, and pan-seared (rare) tuna. **Bar** and **dinner theater** off-season (call 1-800-950-9471). Entrées $10–23.

❄ **Finely JP's** (508-349-7500), 554 Route 6, South Wellfleet. Open for dinner nightly in July and August and Wednesday or Thursday through Sunday the rest of the year. Don't let appearances fool you. You'd probably drive by this nondescript roadside place if someone didn't recommend it. But chef-owner John Pontius has been serving large portions of Italian cuisine (seafood and pasta, red clam sauce) here since 1991. The pine paneling and decor are simple, but candlelight and linens make it more special. Loyal vacationers have been known to return many nights during a 14-day vacation. No reservations taken, but you can try calling ahead and putting your name on the waiting list. If you arrive after 6 PM, you'll be waiting. Entrées $12–16.

EATING OUT

Moby Dick's (508-349-9795), Route 6. Open 11:30–9 or 10 daily, early May to mid-October. Pride of ownership has its rewards. Although the place is always packed, would you really want to patronize an establishment that wasn't? There's good reason business is so brisk: Since 1983 Todd Barry and his team have provided the best and largest portions of fresh seafood in town. Order from the big blackboard over the counter and take a seat surrounded by the weathered nautical paraphernalia or on the spacious, open upper level and listen to the breeze rustle through the reeds outside. The friendly waitstaff bring your order. You know the fare (it's just not normally this good): fried seafood, unusually presented onion rings (I'll say no more), local steamers (clams) caught off Chatham's Monomoy Island, lobsters, burgers, and seafood rolls (with only a bare hint of mayo). The clam chowder, loaded with big chunks of clams and tender potatoes, really tastes like clam chowder should. Tart Key lime pie is just the thing for a hot afternoon. BYOB. Children's menu. Entrées $8–20.

Flying Fish Cafe (508-349-3100), 29 Briar Lane, between Route 6 and Main Street. Open early April through October. Breakfast and dinner daily in July and August; breakfast Thursday through Sunday and dinner on Friday and Saturday off-season. The vegetarian and ethnic menu is more interesting than the simple decor suggests: modest tables, local art, a natural-wood counter, and a partially visible kitchen. For breakfast, try crêpes or omelets or scrambled tofu with veggies or green eggs and ham (even if you can't proclaim, "Sam I am"). Keep dinner simple with a vegetable stir-fry or spice it up with jerk chicken Caribe. Don't pass up appetizers such as baked Brie and Eastham mussels. Breakfast $4–8, dinner $11–20.

Captain Higgins Seafood Restaurant (508-349-6027), next to the Town Pier. Open noon–9 daily, mid-June to mid-September. The thing here is to sit outside on the large deck surrounded by tall grasses and enjoy the boats moored across the street at the town dock. Although I always order from the daily specials, the crab and lobster rolls (always on the menu) are also a good bet. Other reliable specialties include well-prepared native bluefish, Wellfleet sea scallops, lobsters, and oysters and littlenecks from the raw bar. Some pasta dishes, too, when you tire of seafood. Children have their own menu, coloring books, and crayons for the paper table-cloths. Dave Balch and Jeanne Coser have run this family business since 1968. Lunch $6–10, dinner $12–22.

Duck Creeke Tavern Room (508-349-7369), 70 Main Street. Open for dinner and late-night appetizers mid-May to mid-October. Wellfleet's oldest tavern is a cozy, lively, and fun place offering well-priced, less formal dishes like steak and ale, burgers, seafood stew, and—in a nod to "bistro fare"—roasted eggplant on basil focaccia. A fireplace, beamed ceilings, greenery, and a **bar** fashioned from old doors set the tone for live entertainment Thursday through Sunday. Melodies range from jazz to folk, piano, pop, and blues. Children's menu. Entrées $12–17.

Upstairs Bar at Aesop's Tables (508-349-6450), 316 Main Street. Open mid-May to mid-October. Low lighting, plush chairs, and velvety di-vans make this converted attic space a comfortable place to end an evening. Sip an apéritif or special coffee with your Death by Chocolate, a dense chocolate mousse with a brownie crust. There's no better way to go. (A substantial tavern menu including salads, barbecued ribs, and steak sandwiches is also available.) Entertainment on occasion.

Mac's Seafood and Harbor Grill (508-349-0404), Town Pier. Open late May to mid-October. Mac buys seafood direct from boats throughout the day and offers a raw bar, sushi, smoked pâté, chowder, and mussels or littlenecks with linguine in white wine. You'll also find fried seafood, burritos, clambakes-to-go, and vegetarian dishes. Regardless of whether you eat in or take out, the harborside location and casual outdoor patio at sunset aren't matched; BYOB. Entrées $10–15.

Bookstore Restaurant (508-349-3154), Kendrick Avenue. Open mid-February through December. Because owner Michael Parlante raises oysters from his harbor shellfish beds, I recommend you come simply for oyster appetizers, preferably raw as they're so fresh. You can't go wrong with lobsters either.

Box Lunch (508-349-2178), 50 Briar Lane. Proprietor Owen Macnutt's original branch of the ever-expanding chain is open daily, for breakfast too. "Rollwiches" are perfect for the beach or to take on a Great Island hike. Roast beef, ham, tuna salad, seafood salad, or a vegetarian alterna-tive like guacamole is rolled up tight in a piece of pita bread for $2–7. A lot of folks swear by "Porky's Nightmare"; I'll leave it to you to see what's in it.

The Lighthouse (508-349-3681), 317 Main Street. Open for breakfast, lunch, and dinner daily year-round (except closed in March). A locals' hangout and a fixture in the center of town since 1930, the Lighthouse offers no-nonsense omelets, waffles, and two eggs any style (until noon). Try to get a table in the quieter, glassed-in dining room to the side. Children's menu (in summer for dinner); Guinness on tap.

🖋 **On the Creek Cafe** (508-349-9841), 55 Commercial Street. Open for breakfast and lunch mid-May to mid-October. Because of the tranquil location and outdoor seating on the edge of Duck Creek, you might find yourself here despite the "laid-back" service. This depot-style place is simple and cheery, and the offerings are simple, too: eggs, bagels, and pancakes for breakfast; sandwiches, seafood stew, Greek salads, and PB&J or fluffernutter for the kids at lunch. Blackboard specials; home-garden–grown lettuce, tomatoes, and snow peas in-season. Dishes $4–9.

🖋 **Van Rensselaer's Restaurant** (508-349-2127), Route 6, opposite Marconi Station. Open for breakfast and dinner April through October. Van Rensselaer's is a deservedly popular roadside breakfast place offering Belgian waffles and eggs Benedict. If you're renting a house and don't want to do dishes first thing in the morning, you'll want to know about this place. Children's menu.

See also Beachcomber and Wellfleet Drive-In under *Entertainment*.

DESSERT

See Upstairs Bar at Aesop's Table under *Eating Out*.

COFFEE

Outer Cup Coffeehouse (508-349-0004), 50 Main Street. At Painters, or next door (the location was uncertain at press time), you'll probably find this place open 7 AM–noon most days year-round. Rich and flavorful espresso served with a selection of homemade scones, H&H bagels, coffee cakes, and the like.

ENTERTAINMENT

♿ **Wellfleet Harbor Actors Theater** (508-349-6835; www.what.org), 1 Kendrick Avenue, Wellfleet. Performances mid-May to mid-October (nightly in July and August, Thursday through Sunday off-season); 90 seats. Known locally as WHAT, it's clear why this highly regarded theater company doesn't receive funding from the current National Endowment for the Arts: You'd never see Jesse Helms at one of its experimental, new-wave, and sometimes misunderstood shows. WHAT produces plays by new writers and directors as well as established folks like David Mamet and David Wheeler of the American Repertory Theater in Cambridge, Massachusetts. Radical interpretations of Chekhov, too. A fixture in the community since 1985, WHAT can always be counted on to be provocative. Founder Gip Hoppe (a marvelous actor) writes some of the plays himself (he is perhaps best known for *Jackie: An American Life*) and shares the co–artistic director title with Jeff Zinn, son of historian Howard Zinn. Tickets $18; half-price "student rush" just prior to curtain time.

🎭 **Cape Cod Tales from Past and Present** (508-349-0103). In July and August (Wednesday through Friday at 7:30 PM) at the Wellfleet United Methodist Church on Main Street, master storyteller Jim Wolf does very dramatic (read: loud and highly interpretive) storytelling that's entertaining for both adults and children. Stories are related to the Cape, of course.

♞ **Square dancing,** Town Pier. On Wednesday evening in July and August, the pier takes on a different tone. Dancing begins at 7 or 7:30, and the steps get progressively more difficult until 10 or so.

✍ **Wellfleet Drive-In** (508-349-7176; 508-349-2450 for a human being; 1-800-696-3532), Route 6. Shows late May to mid-September. One of the last holdouts of a vanishing American pastime, this drive-in has lured patrons since 1957, when the number of U.S. drive-ins peaked at 4,000. Today there are fewer than 800 left, only a handful in New England, no others on the Cape. Hence, it remains a treasured local institution. Late owner John Jentz, a former engineering professor at MIT, designed the screen with his MIT pals; perhaps that's why it's withstood hurricanes with winds up to 135 mph. Double features are shown nightly at dusk (about 8 PM in summer). Movies change up to three times a week, and there's a play area behind the reasonably priced **Intermission Bar & Grill.** The box office opens at 7. Films are generally family-oriented. Tickets: $6.50 adults (less if you purchase a burger or sandwich or fried fish platter over $5.75), $4 kids 5–11.

❄☂ **Wellfleet Cinemas** (508-349-7176; 1-800-696-3532), Route 6. Adjacent to the drive-in, the only cinema on the Outer Cape that's open year-round. First-run movies on four screens.

Beachcomber (508-349-6055; www.thebeachcomber.com), off Ocean View Drive on Cahoon Hollow Beach. Open daily noon–1 AM from late May to early September. In its former incarnation, this 1850 structure was one of the Outer Cape's nine lifesaving stations. Today, this 350-person-capacity operation, perched on a bluff right above the beach, is better known as a bar and club, but it also serves food. When the sunken pirate ship, the *Whydah,* was being excavated a couple of miles down the beach, JFK Jr. would hang out here with project boss Barry Clifford and his crew. There's nothing else like it on the Cape and it's simply amazing that it's survived this long, as a college-age bar surrounded by National Park Service land. Be careful about wandering out onto the beach after a couple of drinks; the first step is a doozy! Hip Boston bands and national blues artists perform in the evenings, but the club is perhaps best known for its Sunday-afternoon concerts and reggae-filled happy hours (frozen mudslides are very popular). By day, shuffle from the beach to hang out with a 20-something crowd on the outdoor deck, complete with a 40-foot-long, cabana-style raw bar. Burgers, boneless Buffalo wings, and a full children's menu are also offered. Inside is dark, with wooden booths. Only appetizers and pizza are available after 9 PM. Dishes $5–15.

Band concerts. On Sundays at 8 PM during July and August, visitors and locals congregate at the First Congregational Church on Main Street.

See also Painter's, Duck Creeke Tavern Room, and the Upstairs Bar at Aesop's Tables under *Where to Eat.*

SELECTIVE SHOPPING

Arts and crafts shows are held on many Mondays and Tuesdays in July and August next to the Wellfleet Drive-In (see *Entertainment*) on Route 6. This is generally high-quality stuff, from oils and watercolors to pottery, jewelry, and objets de wood or glass.

Wellfleet Flea Market (508-349-2520; 1-800-696-3532), at the Wellfleet Drive-In, Route 6. Open Saturday, Sunday, and Monday holidays mid-April to mid-October, as well as Wednesday and Thursday in July and August. With more than 300 stalls, there's more junk than treasure, but you never know what you'll find: name-brand clothing, a hat to ward off the summer sun, used and antique furniture, and trinkets, tea sets, and colored glasses. Wander in with the intention of spending a few minutes and a few dollars and you'll probably find that hours have passed and you've bought more than you bargained for! It's the Cape's biggest and best. Admission $1–2 per car.

ART GALLERIES

Wellfleet is an art town; the **Art Gallery Association** (508-349-9546) publishes a complete list of galleries, some of which are excellent, others of which cater to souvenir art. In July and August, many galleries host wine-and-cheese openings on Saturday evening.

Cherry Stone Gallery (508-349-3026), 70 East Commercial Street. Open late May to late September. Sally Nerber has collected and sold works by Abbott and Atget, Motherwell and Rauschenberg (and emerging artists) since 1971. Unpretentious and friendly, this small place is for the serious collector. A top Cape gallery.

❋ **Left Bank Gallery** (508-349-9451), 25 Commercial Street. Open June to mid-October, weekends off-season. Audrey and Gerald Parent converted the former American Legion Hall in 1972; head past the paintings to the craft-filled potter's room, which has lovely works. All in all, a wonderfully diverse collection.

The Nicholas Harrison Gallery (508-349-7799), 275 Main Street. Open spring through fall. Laura and Mark Evangelista catapult contemporary crafts into the fine art category with this collection. Laura was schooled in ceramics at RISD, but the two of them have amassed an outstanding assortment of glass objects, metalwork, fountains, lighting, woodworking, collages, jewelry, and other wearable art. Don't miss it, really.

❋ **Left Bank Small Works & Jewelry** (508-349-7939), 3 West Main Street. Open daily late May to mid-October, weekends off-season. Works on paper and contemporary jewelry are highlighted.

Kendall Art Gallery (508-349-2482), Main Street. Open late May to mid-October. In town since the early 1960s, Walter and Myra Dorrell sell not only Walter's paintings but also work by some 40 other artists and craftspeople. There are a few buildings behind the 1840s Greek Revival house filled with even more paintings and ceramics. In addition, they probably carry more sculpture in more media—bronze, aluminum, and marble—than any other gallery on the Cape. The sculpture garden is tranquil.

Blue Heron Gallery (508-349-6724), 20 Bank Street. Open mid-May to mid-October. Royal and Jocelyn Thurston pack a lot of art and crafts (Cape scenes, jewelry, and pottery) into a seemingly endless series of small rooms. More than 30 representational contemporary artists and artisans are shown.

Cove Gallery (508-349-2530), 15 Commercial Street. Open mid-June to mid-October. Open since 1968, this gallery feature oils and pastels and also has a lively sculpture garden overlooking Duck Creek.

The Davis Gallery (508-349-0549), 2766 Route 6. Open mid-May to mid-October. It's worth stopping at this unusual assortment of contemporary sculpture, crafts, and painting.

ARTISANS

❄ **Salty Duck Pottery** (508-349-3342), 115 Main Street. Katherine Stillman was attracted to Wellfleet because of its reputation as a community of tolerant eccentrics. Now she's one of them, living and shaping her clay beside a salt marsh. Her lead-free vessels gracefully combine simple lines with utilitarian purposes. Fellow potter Maria Juster makes blue-green stoneware pottery, tiles, mirrors, and tables.

Wellfleet Pottery (508-349-6679), Commercial Street. Open June through September. Trevor and Kathleen Glucksman have been making pottery in Wellfleet since 1970. He designs and crafts the small-scale china, employing all methods of casting, throwing, and pressing to achieve the desired results. Kathleen glazes and hand paints them with simple depictions of wildflowers and grasses. The umber country china (a very strong china good for daily use) is displayed as sparingly as it's "decorated."

Narrow Land Pottery (508-349-6308), 3 West Main Street. Open April through December. Joe McCaffery, who studied at the School of the Museum of Fine Arts, throws pots, vases, mugs, lamp bases, and plates. His glazes, porcelain, and stoneware come in a variety of colors.

BOOKSTORES

Herridge Books (508-349-1323), 11 East Main Street. Open late May to late September. This is the place to go for used books covering a wide range of subject matter.

CLOTHING

Style-conscious women are in luck (in-season) in Wellfleet. Loose-fitting designs in cotton, linen, rayon, and earth tones reign. Try **Hannah** (508-

349-9884), 234 Main Street; **Eccentricity** (508-349-7554), 361 Main Street (beautiful kimonos and tactile and ethnic pieces); **Eccentricity's Off Center** (508-349-3634), across the street; and **Karol Richardson** (508-349-6378), nearby at 11 West Main Street.

FARM STAND

Hatch's Fish Market/Hatch's Produce (508-349-2810), behind Town Hall on Main Street. Open late May to late September. Although you might find better prices at the supermarket, the fish and produce here are fresh and beautifully displayed, and the location can't be beat. Hatch's smokes its own fish, pâté, and mussels.

SPECIAL SHOPS

❄ **Jules Besch Stationers** (508-349-1231), 15 Bank Street. Open May to mid-October; weekends mid-October to late December and February through April. The area's most tactile shop carries products that will make you want to take pen (perhaps an antique 1880s pen or a quill) to paper (perhaps some handmade paper or a bound journal). It also sells unique wrapping paper, collectible postcards, artsy boxed note cards, specialty albums, and blank books. Parts of the shop mimic a study, set up with writing tables, leather blotters, and stylish desk lamps. Jules is very well known for his calligraphy and verse. Buy a blank card and ask him to personalize it. He maintains a healthy backlog of wedding and other invitations to inscribe.

The Chocolate Sparrow (508-349-1333), Main Street. Open late June to early September. As long as anyone can remember, Wellfleet has had a penny-candy store. The Chocolate Sparrow opened in 1990 to continue the tradition, and added rich, hand-dipped chocolates.

I Used to Be a Tree (508-349-1234), 326 Main Street. Open weekends June through October and daily in summer. This "tree-mendous" little shop carries all sorts of products, gifts, and games made from wood pulp or relating somehow to forested gentle giants.

SPECIAL EVENTS

July 4: **Independence Day parade.**

Late July: **House tours.** An annual event sponsored by the Historical Society (508-349-9157).

Mid-October: **Scholarship auction.** The Inn at Ducke Creek hosts a benefit auction, and prior to bidding, the items—original art, wine, and spring bulbs, for instance—are displayed at Eccentricity, 361 Main Street.

Truro

Considered to be the last vestige of "old Cape Cod," Truro has no stop-lights, no fast-food outlets, no supermarket, no automatic teller machine. No one even sells motorboat gasoline at Pamet Harbor. It does have, though, the last working farm on the Outer Cape. Truro "center" consists of a tiny strip mall and a nearby gourmet food shop. That's it. And local folks and summer people (vacationing writers and urban professionals who have built large houses in the rolling hills and dunes) are determined to keep it that way.

North Truro is also tiny but has blue-collar ties to Provincetown. Compare Dutra's Market (an old institution) to Jams (a fancy food shop born in the '80s) and the differences are readily apparent. As you head toward Provincetown, the only real development—in a nod to the tourist industry—consists of hundreds of tiny cottages, motels, and houses lining a narrow strip of shore wedged between Cape Cod Bay and the dramatic Parabolic Dunes on Pilgrim Lake. It's an odd juxtaposition, but one I always look forward to.

There aren't many human-made sites to explore, except for Highland Light and the Truro Historical Museum, but there are plenty of natural ones. Almost 70 percent of Truro's 42 square miles (one of the largest towns on the Cape, in acreage) falls within the boundaries of the Cape Cod National Seashore (CCNS). There are hiking and biking trails as well as long expanses of beach. Rolling moors and hidden valleys characterize the tranquil back roads east and west of Route 6. Wind-swept dunes, lighthouses, beach grass, and austere shorelines will inspire you, as they did Edward Hopper. The painter built a summer-house in Truro in the 1930s and worked there until 1967.

Truro, established in 1697, has endured many name changes. Originally it was called Payomet or Pamet, after the Native American tribe that inhabited the area before the Pilgrims. In 1705 it was known as Dangerfield because of the large number of offshore sailing disasters. Eventually it was named Truro, after a Cornish coastal town in England.

Although today Truro is sleepy and rural, it has been, at times during the last few centuries, a hotbed of activity. The *Mayflower's* Myles Standish spent his second night ashore in Truro. His band of 16 fellow

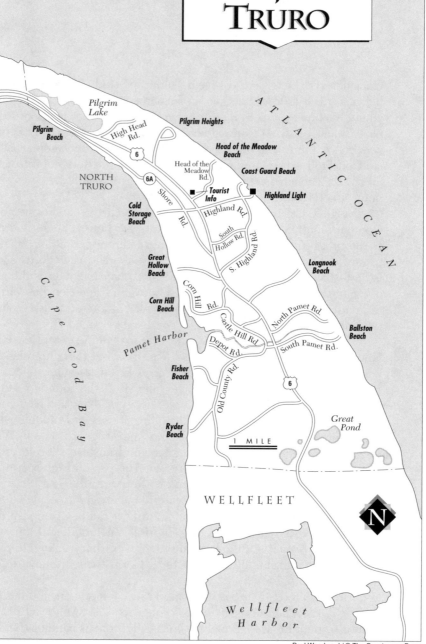

TRURO

ATLANTIC OCEAN

Pilgrim Lake

Pilgrim Heights

Pilgrim Beach

High Head Rd.

6

Head of the Meadow Beach

Head of the Meadow Rd.

NORTH TRURO

6A

Coast Guard Beach

Shore Rd.

■ *Tourist Info*

■ *Highland Light*

Cold Storage Beach

Highland Rd.

South Hollow Rd.

S. Highland Rd.

Great Hollow Beach

Longnook Beach

Corn Hill Rd.

Corn Hill Beach

North Pamet Rd.

Ballston Beach

Cape Cod Bay

Pamet Harbor

Castle Hill Rd.

Depot Rd.

South Pamet Rd.

Fisher Beach

Old County Rd.

6

Great Pond

Ryder Beach

1 MILE

WELLFLEET

N

Wellfleet Harbor

Paul Woodward / © The Countryman Press

Pilgrims found their first fresh water in Truro, as well as a stash of corn (which belonged to the Native Americans) from which they harvested their first crop. Although you wouldn't know it today, since Pamet Harbor choked up with sand in the mid-1850s, Truro's harbor once rivaled neighboring Provincetown as a whaling and cod-fishing center. By the late 1700s, shipbuilding was thriving and the harbor bustling. Vessels bound for the Grand Banks were built here, and a packet boat sailed from Truro to Boston. The whaling industry also owes a debt to early Truro residents, one of whom (Ichabod Paddock) taught Nantucketers how to catch whales from shore.

In 1851 the population soared to a rousing 2,000 souls. But in 1860 the Union Company of Truro went bankrupt due to declining harbor conditions, and townspeople's fortunes and livelihoods sank with it. Commercially, Truro never rebounded. Today, the year-round population is about 1,550; the summer influx raises that number tenfold. And at the height of the season, about seven times as many *Boston Globes* and *New York Times* are sold as in the off-season.

GETTING THERE

By car: The center of Truro is about 60 miles from the Sagamore Bridge via Route 6. Route 6A and Shore Road are synonymous.

By bus: The **Plymouth & Brockton** bus line (508-778-9767; www.p-b.com) connects Truro with Hyannis and other Cape towns, as well as with Boston's Logan Airport. The bus stops at the Post office (and the Jams store) in the center of town.

GETTING AROUND

Beaches, sites, and roads are well marked off Route 6. Generally, the CCNS is east of Route 6. The Shore Road exit in North Truro takes you into North Truro and eventually to Beach Point, choked with motels as it approaches Provincetown. At its narrowist, Truro is only a mile wide, while it stretches for 10 miles north to south.

The excellent **Summer Shuttle** (508-385-8326; 1-800-352-7155; www.capecodtransit.org) operates daily late May to mid-October. The bus runs from Dutra's Market in North Truro along Route 6A and up to Provincetown, with stops in Provincetown on Bradford Street, Mac-Millan Wharf, the A&P grocery store, Pilgrims Park, and Herring Cove Beach. Buses run every 20 to 30 minutes 7:15 AM–12:15 AM (until 8 PM in spring and fall). Fares are $1 one way (kids 50¢ up to age 17).

GUIDANCE

Truro Chamber of Commerce (508-487-1288), Route 6, P.O. Box 26, North Truro 02652. Open 10–5 daily, late June to early September; 10–5 Friday and Saturday, noon–4 Sunday, late May to late June and early September to mid-October.

PUBLIC LIBRARIES

❄️🍷✒️**Truro Public Library** (508-487-1125), off Standish Way, north of North Truro, new in 1999, is open 9:30–8 Tuesday and Wednesday, 9:30–6 Thursday, 9:30–4 Friday, and 9:30–2 Saturday.

PUBLIC REST ROOMS
Public rest rooms are found at the Pilgrim Heights area in summer.

MEDICAL EMERGENCY
Outer Cape Health Services (508-487-9395, Harry Kemp Way, Province-town, and 508-349-3131, Route 6, Wellfleet) is open year-round; call for summer walk-in hours.

TO SEE

Cape Cod Light or **Highland Light,** CCNS, Highland Light Road, off South Highland Road, North Truro. The original lighthouse that guarded these treacherous shores was erected in 1798, the first light-house on Cape Cod. It was rebuilt in 1853, the year that 1,200 ships passed by within a 10-day period. Henry David Thoreau stayed in the lighthouse during one of his famous walks along the Outer Cape. The spot where he once stood and proclaimed that here a man could "put all America behind him" is thought to be 150 feet offshore now, thanks to erosion. One of only four working lighthouses on the Outer Cape, it was the last to become automated, in 1986. The original light shone with whale oil from 24 lamps, while later lamps were fueled with lard and kerosene. The modern light has a 1,000-watt bulb. Visible 30 miles out to sea, it's the brightest lighthouse on the New England coast. At 120 feet above sea level, the lighthouse is aptly named Highland.

In July 1996 the National Park Service, Coast Guard, Truro His-torical Society, and the state joined forces to avert a looming disaster. If the lighthouse was not moved soon, engineers cautioned, it would crumble into the ocean. Erosion, at the rate of 3 to 4 feet per year, had chewed away the cliff upon which the lighthouse was built. (Thanks to ferocious storms in 1990, some 40 feet were lost in that one year alone!) And when cliffs erode to within 100 feet of a lighthouse, it is too dan-gerous to bring in the heavy equipment needed to move it. So at a cost of $1.6 million, the 410-ton historic lighthouse was jacked up onto steel beams and pushed along steel tracks by hydraulic rams. The project took 18 days (that's about 25 feet a day), including moving the light keeper's house. It was moved 450 feet west and 12 feet south (that is, inland), to a spot on the golf course. It should be safe for another 150 years, unless we get a lot of nor'easters.

Daily lighthouse tours (508-487-1121), which include a short video and exhibit in the Keeper's House, are offered daily early May to late October, 10–5 (until about sunset in the summer), for $3 per person. Combination tickets ($5) include a visit to the Highland House Mu-seum (see below). No children under 51 inches. An observation deck, where the lighthouse recently stood, overlooks the ocean.

Highland House Museum (508-487-3397; www.capecod.net/ths), High-land Light Road, North Truro. Open 10–4:30 daily June through Septem-

KIM GRANT

Truro's First Congregational Parish Church and cemetery

ber. Operated expertly by the Truro Historical Society and housed in the circa-1907 Highland House, this large building is wholly dedicated to preserving Truro's maritime and agricultural past. Items on display include a pirate's chest, fishing and whaling gear, 17th-century firearms, photos of Truro residents and places, toys, and scrimshaw. One room is dedicated to Courtney Allen, the Truro Historical Society founder, artist, model maker, and wood carver. The old Highland House is a fine example of the fashionable, once prominent, turn-of-the-20th-century summer hotels. Adults $3, children under 12 free; combination ticket with lighthouse $5.

Jenny Lind Tower, CCNS, off Highland Light Road, North Truro. Between the Highland Golf Links (see *Outdoor Activities—Golf*) and the former **North Truro Air Force Base** is a 55-foot tower of granite that seems out of place. In fact, it is. In 1850, P. T. Barnum brought Swedish singing legend Jenny Lind to America. He oversold tickets to a Boston concert, and when Lind heard the crowds were going to riot, she performed a free concert from the roof tower for the people in the street. When the building was to be destroyed in 1927, a Boston attorney purchased the tower and brought it here (he owned the land at that time). The CCNS owns the property now and the entrance is blocked, but the granite tower still stands 150 feet above sea level, visible to passing ships and those of us on the ground.

Congregational church and **cemetery,** Meetinghouse Road (off Castle Road), Truro. A marble shaft commemorates the terrible tragedy of the October Gale, when seven ships were destroyed and 57 crew members died. Renowned glassmakers of Sandwich made the church windows, and Paul Revere cast the steeple bell.

SCENIC DRIVES

It's difficult to find an unpicturesque Truro road. Both North and South Pamet Roads, connected prior to a breach at Ballston Beach, wind past bayberry, beach plums, and groves of locust trees. From Truro center, Castle Road to Corn Hill Beach is lovely. From North Truro, Priest Road to the bay and to Bay View Road offer great bay views.

OUTDOOR ACTIVITIES

BICYCLING/RENTALS

High Head Road, CCNS, off Route 6, North Truro. Just south of Pilgrim Lake, this 4-mile bikeway runs from High Head Road, past salt marshes and dunes, to Head of the Meadow Beach (see *Green Space—Beaches*). Four-wheel-drive vehicles with proper stickers can enter the dunes here, too.

Bayside Bikes (508-487-5735), 102 Shore Road (Route 6A), North Truro, rents and repairs cycles; free parking and easy access to Head of the Meadow bike trail, Provincetown, and three of Truro's bayside beaches.

BOATING

Pamet Harbor, off Depot Road, Truro. There are no boats to rent, but you can contact the harbormaster (508-349-2555) for launching information.

FISHING/SHELLFISHING

Permits for freshwater fishing and shellfishing are available from Town Hall (508-349-3635) on Town Hall Road, off Bridge Road from Route 6, Truro. Kids love fishing from the grassy shores off **Pond Road** (which leads to **Cold Storage Beach**); it's tranquil for picnicking and watching the sun set, too. Surf-fishing is good all along the Atlantic coastline. For freshwater fishing, try **Great Pond,** off Savage Road from Route 6 in southern Truro.

GOLF

❊ **Highland Golf Links** (508-487-9201), Highland Light Road, off South Highland Road, North Truro. Open year-round; clubhouse open 7-7 from mid-May to mid-October. Perched on a high windswept bluff, this is the Cape's oldest course (founded in 1892) and one of the country's oldest, too. At the turn of the 20th century, the course was part of the Highland House resort (now a museum, see *To See*), which drew Boston visitors by train. Today, the museum sits between the eighth and ninth holes. The course exemplifies the Scottish tradition, with deep natural roughs, Scotch broom, heath, unirrigated open fairways, occasional fog, and spectacular ocean views. That's why golfers come to this nine-hole, par-35 course. That, and dime-size greens, whale sightings from the sixth tee in summer, and the view of Highland Light adjacent to the seventh hole. Avoid the crowds by playing on Sunday. It's the only public course between Orleans and Provincetown. $20 for nine holes, regardless of age; annual pass $400.

TENNIS

Pamet Harbor Yacht & Tennis Club (508-349-3772), 7 Yacht Club Road, on the harbor. When not reserved to club members, these three courts are available for rental to nonmembers.

EVEN MORE THINGS TO SEE AND DO

SPECIAL PROGRAMS

🖉 **Truro Center for the Arts at Castle Hill** (508-349-7511; www.castlehill. org), Castle and Meetinghouse Roads, Truro. Classes July and August. A nonprofit educational institute, Castle Hill was founded in 1972 and has evolved into an important cultural voice on the Outer Cape art scene. Classes and workshops are offered in a converted 1880s barn to people of all ages in painting, drawing, writing, printmaking, book arts, photography, clay, and sculpture. Castle Hill also sponsors events like a mid-August open house, lectures, concerts, and artist receptions. Nationally renowned artists and writers lead classes that last for 1 or 2 days or 4 or 5 sessions; a few classes stretch for 10–14 days. Register by mail prior to June 1 or by phone after June 1.

WINERY

Truro Vineyards of Cape Cod (508-487-6200), South Hollow Vineyards, Route 6A, North Truro. Tastings 12–5 late May through October; Friday through Sunday in November and December. Call for schedule of tours. Feel free to bring lunch, buy a bottle of wine, and enjoy a picnic amid the huge antique wine casks. Look for notices of special events and festivals held on the grounds.

GREEN SPACE

BEACHES

Town parking stickers are required from July 1 to September 1. Weekly cottage renters may purchase parking stickers ($20 weekly) at the **Beach Commission** (508-349-3635) behind the Truro center post office.

Head of the Meadow Beach, on the Atlantic Ocean. Half the beach is maintained by the town, half by the CCNS. The only difference is that the latter half has changing rooms and rest rooms; otherwise it's the same wide, dune-backed beach. Parking $5 in-season. Both beaches have lifeguards.

Corn Hill Beach, off Corn Hill Road, on Cape Cod Bay. This is the only other town-managed beach where nonresidents can pay a daily parking fee ($5). Facilities include Porta-Potties and a large parking area. Backed by a long, low dune, the width of Corn Hill Beach decreases measurably as the tide comes in. There's good windsurfing, too.

Long Nook Beach, off Long Nook Road, on the Atlantic Ocean. Although this wonderful beach requires a town parking sticker, in the off-season anyone can park here.

Coast Guard Beach, off Highland Road, and **Ballston Beach,** off South Pamet Road; both on the Atlantic Ocean. Each is owned by the town and requires a resident sticker, but anyone can bicycle in for free. (This Coast Guard Beach is not to be confused with Henry Beston's Coast Guard Beach in Eastham, under the auspices of CCNS.) Lifeguard, no; Porta-Potties, yes. *Note:* Use caution because of the treacherous undertow.

WALKS

Pilgrim Heights Area (508-349-3785), CCNS, off Route 6, North Truro. Two short walks yield open vistas of distant dunes, ocean, and salt marsh. As the name implies, the easy ¾-mile round-trip **Pilgrim Spring Trail** leads to the spot where the Pilgrims reportedly tasted their first New England water. One subsequently penned: "We . . . sat us downe and drunke our first New England water with as much delight as ever we drunke in all our lives." A small plaque marks the spot.

Small Swamp Trail (about the same distance) was not named for the size of the swamp or trail but rather after the farmer (Mr. Small) who grew asparagus and corn on this former 200-acre farm. By August, blueberries are ripe for the picking. Wooded picnic area. In spring, look for migrating hawks.

Cranberry Bog Trail, North Pamet Road, Truro. You won't want to pick this tangy and sour fruit come late September, but take the lovely walk—partially over a boardwalk—around the bog. The trailhead is located at the parking lot below the youth hostel (see *Lodging—Hostel*).

LODGING

BED & BREAKFAST

Truro Vineyards of Cape Cod (508-487-6200), Route 6A, North Truro 02652. Open May through December. Judy Wimer and Kathy Gregrow opened this 19th-century, Federal-style farmhouse in 1994 after renovating it from top to bottom. Just before that, they planted the 5-acre property with vinifera grapes, and voilà, three years later they were bottling wine! (See *Even More Things to See and Do—Winery*.) The first floor of the large house is kind of dark and sparsely furnished, with a slate floor, large hearth, heavy beams, and burgundy and deep green color scheme. (It's very cool in summer.) The five guest rooms, all with private bath, have four-poster beds. A continental breakfast is served on the brick patio or deck overlooking the vineyard. Late May through October $99–129; off-season $89–119.

✳✍ **The Moorlands Inn** (508-487-0663), 11 Hughes Road, North Truro 02652. On a back road, this massive house is a great place for family reunions and children of any age. The main house has four rooms (two with private bath) and a suite. Each has a phone, most have a TV, and one has a deck. Although I didn't get to see the rooms, based on the decor, feeling, and attention given to the first-floor living space by innkeepers Skipper and Bill Evaul, I feel confident recommending them. B&B rooms include continental breakfast. Adjacent to the B&B is a two-story carriage house with a kitchen and private courtyard hot tub. Two **cottages** sleep three and have a full kitchen, TV, and phone. An **apartment,** which takes up the third floor of the inn, has a private entrance. July and August $79–149 rooms, $895–995 weekly for carriage house, $695–775 weekly for cottages, $129–149 for apartment. Inquire about shorter stays in the carriage house and cottages, as well as off-season rates.

COTTAGES AND EFFICIENCIES

✒ **Kalmar Village** (508-487-0585; 617-247-0211 in winter; www.kalmarvillage. com), Route 6A, North Truro 02652. Open mid-May to mid-October. On a strip chock-full of cottage colonies, Kalmar stands out. The Prelacks have owned the place since 1968, and you can spot their care and attention in the details: well-tended, trim lawns around the pool, black-and-white chimneys atop the shingled cottages, and six new waterfront cottages. All cottages are delightfully roomy inside, with modern kitchens. Other perks include daily housekeeping and private outdoor space. There are also small, large, and two-room efficiencies and three **motel rooms**. This is a great place for families, since Kalmar sits on 400 feet of private oceanfront beach. The 45 cottages are rented by the week in July and August, $985–1,240 for one- and two-bedroom cottages; $1,650–1,870 for the newer two-bedroom units. Off-season they rent for $500–1,075 weekly, $83.50–180 nightly. In July and August efficiencies rent for $655–840 weekly, $110–140 nightly.

✒ **East Harbour** (508-487-0505; www.eastharbour.com), 618 Route 6A (Shore Road), North Truro 02652. Open April through October. Although Truro has dozens of small cottage colonies, Sonja Soderberg's easily rises to the top. These tidy, paneled two-bedroom beachfront cottages (some are "mere" water-view units) enjoy daily maid service and manicured lawns and gardens. In total, there are seven cottages (fully equipped), nine motel rooms (with microwaves and refrigerators), and one suite. Grills, deck chairs, and umbrellas are available. Although some guests have been coming for five generations, Sonja's kept up with the times and is appealing to modern families, too. Late June to early September $825–925 weekly; $100 per additional child, $200 per additional adult; cottages rent by the night off-season, when they are available, or $525–625 weekly. Motel rooms $105–120 in-season, $55–80 off-season. Make reservations in January if you can.

Day's Cottages (508-487-1062), Route 6A (Shore Road), North Truro 02652. Open May to late October. These little green-and-white cottages, all 23 of them lined up like ducks in a row, are something of a local icon. When you see them, you know you're just about to the tip of

Rows of identical cottages face the setting sun and line the bayside of Route 6A in North Truro.

the Cape. Although each is only a few feet from the next, people love them. Perhaps because there's nothing between them and the ocean, except for a couple of lawn chairs (albeit on a cement slab). And perhaps because they face due west, toward the setting sun. Late June to early September $840 weekly; $520 weekly in autumn; $490 weekly, $70 nightly in May.

MOTEL

Top Mast (508-487-1189; www.capecodtravel.com/topmast), Route 6A, North Truro 02652. Open May to mid-October. Owned by the Silva family since 1971, this nicely maintained two-story motel flanks Route 6A well before the congestion begins. Beachfront units are built right on sandy Cape Cod Bay, and each opens onto an individual balcony with lawn chairs. Poolside garden rooms rent by the night, even in high season. There are 33 rooms and two 2-bedroom **apartments.** Swimming pool. Mid-June to early September: $775 weekly for beachfront efficiencies, $1,100 weekly for apartment for four people, $80 nightly for poolside room; in the shoulder seasons, all rooms are $65–70 nightly, $440–475 weekly.

RENTAL HOUSES AND COTTAGES

Duarte/Downey Real Estate (508-349-7588), 12 Truro Center Road, in the center of town next to Jams, is one of the big Truro names renting condos, houses, and cottages.

CAMPGROUNDS

North of Highland Camping Area (508-487-1191), Head of the Meadow Road, North Truro 02652. Open mid-May to mid-September. On 60 acres of scrub pine within the CCNS, these 237 sites are suitable for tents and tent trailers only (no hookups, though) and are a 10-minute walk from Head of the Meadow Beach (see *Green Space—Beaches*). There are strict quiet hours. From mid-July to mid-August, reservations must begin and end on a Saturday or Sunday. $20 for two people with one car.

🏵🐾 **North Truro Camping Area** (508-487-1847), Highland Road, North Truro 02652. Open April through December. Within the CCNS, these 22 acres of wooded sites can accommodate 350 tents and RVs. It's less than a mile to Coast Guard Beach (see *Green Space—Beaches*), and only 7 miles to Provincetown. $16 per day for two, more for hookups.

HOSTEL

🏵 **Hostelling International, Truro** (508-349-3889; www.hi-travel.org; 1-800-909-4776 for in-season reservations; 617-531-0459 or enecreservations @juno.com for reservations prior to the start of the season), North Pamet Road, Truro 02666. Open late June to early September. Originally a U.S. Coast Guard station, the hostel commands a dramatic location—amid dunes, marshes, and a cranberry bog. The hostel is within the CCNS and just a 7-minute walk from Ballston Beach (see *Green Space—Beaches*). National Park Service interpreters host special programs each week; they're free to all and not to be missed. Each of 42 dormitory beds rents for $15–17 per night to members, $18–21 to nonmembers.

WHERE TO EAT

EATING OUT

🕭🏵✒**Adrian's** (508-487-4360), Route 6, North Truro. Open for breakfast and dinner daily, mid-June to early September; breakfast on weekends and dinner Thursday through Monday from mid-May to mid-June and early September to mid-October. Chef Adrian Cyr and his wife, Annette, have wooed and won a decidedly loyal and ever-growing following since they opened their first area restaurant in 1985. Dine on regional Italian cuisine on the outdoor deck up on a bluff or in the dining room with candlelight, large picture windows, and well-spaced tables. There are so many well-priced, exceptional choices that you'll need to return again and again: make-your-own brick-oven pizzas, inspired pasta al pesto (the essence of summer), traditional pasta alla puttanesca, a generous and sublime cold insalate and mixed antipasto, and specials like cayenne-crusted salmon with grilled polenta. For breakfast, try huevos rancheros, specialty omelets, and cranberry pancakes. Children's menu. You can also come just for dessert or coffee, but I really recommend you come for more than that. The waitstaff are perfectly accommodating. Breakfast $3–8; dinner entrées $8–23.

🏵 **Terra Luna** (508-487-1019), Route 6A, North Truro. Open for dinner, mid-May to mid-October. High ceilings, large canvases, assorted objets d'art, shellacked wooden tables, and candlelight transform this otherwise unassuming roadside eatery with barnboard walls into a hip space. Deftly executed New American and Italian cuisine includes spinach tortellini with crab and tofu strudel. Dinner $14–20.

&♿ **Village Cafe** (508-487-5800), in the center of North Truro. Open daily 7 AM–10 PM in July and August, 7–5 May through June and September to mid-October. This pleasant sandwich place has a big brick courtyard where you can take your H&H bagel with smoked mozzarella and sun-dried tomato. Turkey sandwiches on baguettes, hearty soups, muffins, scones, pastries, espresso, desserts, and Four Seas ice cream too.

❄🍴 **Montano's** (508-487-2026), Route 6, North Truro. Open nightly. This slightly upscale family restaurant serves dependable Italian favorites like seafood fra diavolo and steak umbriago, with unlimited refills on the garden salads, a full children's menu, and early specials (4:30–6) for about $11. Montano's gets big points in my book for serving hungry explorers in the dead of winter. Entrées $9–21.

❄   **Blacksmith Shop** (508-349-6554), off Route 6A near Pamet Road, Truro. Open for dinner year-round. This simple roadside tavern offers poached sole, chicken dishes, haddock almondine, and the like. It always seems more appealing in winter. Most entrées $13–15.

SEAFOOD MARKETS
Pamet Seafood (508-349-7044), 14 Truro Center Road, behind the post office in Truro center; **Nana Molly's** (508-487-2164), on Route 6 next to the Hillside Farm Stand. Both open mid-May to mid-October. Fish, lobsters, and clambakes-to-go.

SNACKS AND COFFEE
🍴 **Jams** (508-349-1616), off Route 6 in Truro center. Open 7:30 AM–"closing" daily, late May to early September. Jams caters to sophisticated palates who need their *New York Times*, tonic water, truffles, and pesto pizzas. Coffee aficionados, take note: Jams serves rich espresso and lattes. Basic groceries share the stage with sun-dried tomatoes, rotisserie-roasted chicken, and Port Salut cheese. For those of you who don't live nearby, carry your picnic fixings to the small field across the street, perfect for bicyclists and the car-weary. Jams makes PB&J and bologna sandwiches for the kids. Sandwiches $4–7.50; salads by the pound.

SELECTIVE SHOPPING

Susan Baker Memorial Museum (508-487-2557), Route 6A, Truro. Open late May to early September and by appointment. One of the most irreverent painters on the Cape, Baker is a humorist at heart. She has a great body of work exploring the history of Provincetown and a more recent one from Italy.

❄   **Atlantic Spice Co.** (508-487-6100; 1-800-316-7965), Route 6 at 6A, North Truro. Open daily except Sunday. Culinary herbs and spices, botanicals, make-your-own potpourri, teas, spice blends, nuts, and seeds. They're here, they're fresh, and they're in a cavernous warehouse. Although this is primarily a wholesaler, you can purchase small quantities (less than the usual 1-pound increments) of most products. At the very least, utilize the mail-order form.

Secrest Studio (508-349-6688), 54 Old King's Highway, Truro. Take Longnook Road, turn right on Higgins' Hollow Road, and watch for signs. Open in summer and by appointment year-round. Philip and Rosamond Secrest make functional and decorative clay and steel pieces.

Truro Crafters (508-487-3239), South Highland Road, North Truro. Open June to mid-October. Jobi pottery, scrimshaw, "clamshaw," and wood carvings.

Whitman House Quilt Shop (508-487-3204), Route 6, North Truro. Open mid-May to mid-October, daily in summer and weekends off-season. This former schoolhouse is packed with Amish quilts.

Banyan Trading Company (508-349-6220), 2 Truro Center Road. Imported Indonesian indoor and outdoor furniture, as well as lava rock-garden ornaments.

Trifles and Treasures (508-349-9509), Truro center. Open weekends April through December and daily May to mid-October. A little bit of art, a few quilts, some pine furniture, and a few collectibles.

SPECIAL EVENTS

Mid- to late May: **Cape Cod Maritime Days** (508-862-0700). Coast Guard–operated lighthouses are open during this festival, including Highland Light. In addition to focusing on the area's lighthouses, the Cape-wide event celebrates the region's fishing heritage, maritime villages, and seafaring way of life.

Mid-September: **Truro's Treasures.** Since 1992, this folksy 3-day weekend features a craft fair, parade, beach bash, road race, pancake breakfast, and parade. The highlight, attended by more than 300 townsfolk, is the dump dance—held at the recycling center (aka the town dump).

V. PROVINCETOWN

Dune shacks, in better condition than Harry Kemp's old shack, are scattered along the National Seashore.

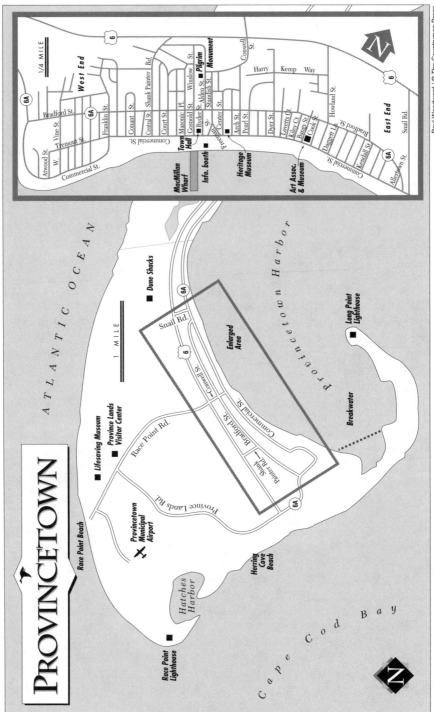

PROVINCETOWN

Race Point Beach

ATLANTIC OCEAN

■ Lifesaving Museum
■ Province Lands Visitor Center

■ Dune Shacks

Race Point Rd.

Province Lands Rd.

✈ Provincetown Municipal Airport

Hatches Harbor

■ Race Point Lighthouse

Herring Cove Beach

Snail Rd.

6A

6

Conwell St.

Bradford St.

Commercial St.

Shank Painter Rd.

Enlarged Area

6A

Provincetown Harbor

Breakwater

Long Point Lighthouse

Cape Cod Bay

1 MILE

Enlarged Area

1/4 MILE

West End

6

6A

Bradford St.

6A

Franklin St.

Commercial St.

Atwood St.
W. Vine St.
Tremont St.

Commercial St.

Conant St.

Central St.

Court St.

Masonic Pl.

Gosnold St.

Ryder St.

Alden St.

Winslow St.

Standish St.

Center St.

Freeman St.

Arch St.

Pearl St.

Dyer St.

Harry Kemp Way

Lovetts Ct.

Kiley Ct.

Bangs St.

Cook St.

Daggett Ln.

Kendall St.

Commercial St.

Allerton St.

Howland St.

Bradford St.

Snail Rd.

Conwell St.

Pilgrim Monument

East End

6

6A

Town Hall

MacMillan Wharf

■ Info. booth

Heritage Museum

Art Assoc. & Museum

N

Provincetown

As you cross into Provincetown, where high dunes drift onto Route 6, you begin to sense that this is a different place. This outpost on the tip of the Cape, where glaciers deposited their last grains of sand, attracts a varied population. Whether seeking solitude or freedom of expression in the company of like-minded souls, visitors relish Provincetown's fringe status. P-town, as it's often referred to by nonlocals but never by locals, is perhaps best known as a community of tolerant individuals—gay men and lesbians, artists, Portuguese fishermen, and families all call it home and welcome those who are equally tolerant.

Visitors parade up and down Commercial Street, the main drag, ducking in and out of hundreds of shops and galleries. The town has a carnival-like atmosphere, especially in July and August, testing the limits of acceptability. As you might imagine, people-watching is a prime activity. On any given Saturday, the cast of characters might include cross-dressers, leather-clad motorcyclists, barely clad in-line skaters, children eating saltwater taffy, and tourists from "Anytown, USA," who can't quite figure out what they've stumbled into.

Provincetown's history began long before the *Mayflower* arrived. It's said that Leif Eriksson's brother, Thorvald, stopped here in 1004 to repair the keel of his boat. Wampanoag Indians fished and summered here—the tiny strip of land was too vulnerable to sustain a year-round settlement. In 1620 the Pilgrims first set foot on American soil in Provincetown, anchoring in the harbor for five weeks, making forays down-Cape in search of an agreeable spot to settle. By the late 1600s and early 1700s, only 200 fishermen lived here.

But from the mid–18th to the mid–19th century, Provincetown was a bustling whaling community and seaport. After the industry peaked, Portuguese sailors from the Azores and Cape Verde Islands, who had signed on with whaling and fishing ships, settled here to fish the local waters. The Old Colony Railroad was extended to Provincetown in 1873, transporting iced fish to New York and Boston. Upwards of four trains a day departed from the two-room station, located where Duarte Motors parking lot is today, two blocks from MacMillan Wharf. But by the early 1900s, Provincetown's sea-driven economy had slowed. Trains stopped running in 1950. Today, although a small fishing industry still exists, tourism is the steam that drives the economy's train.

In 1899 painter Charles W. Hawthorne founded the Cape Cod School of Art. He encouraged his Greenwich Village peers to come north and take advantage of the Mediterranean-like light. By 1916 there were six art schools in town. By the 1920s, Provincetown had become as distinguished an art colony as Taos, East Hampton, and Carmel. Hawthorne encouraged his students to flee the studio and set up easels on the beach, incorporating the ever-changing light into their work. By the time Hawthorne died in 1930, the art scene had a life of its own, and it continues to thrive today.

Artistic expression in Provincetown wasn't limited to painting, though. In 1915 the Provincetown Players, a group of playwrights and actors, staged their works in a small waterfront fish house. In their second season they premiered Eugene O'Neill's *Bound East for Cardiff* before moving to New York, where they are still based.

Provincetown's natural beauty isn't overshadowed by its colorful population.

Province Lands, the name given to the Cape Cod National Seashore (CCNS) within Provincetown's borders, offers bike trails, horseback riding trails, and three remote beaches, where, if you walk far enough, you can find real isolation. Most summertime visitors venture onto the water—to whale-watch or sail and windsurf in the protected harbor. A different perspective comes with a dune or aerial tour.

Provincetown is a delight in late spring and again in fall, when the 40,000 summer visitors return home. Commercial Street is navigable once again, and most shops and restaurants remain open. Tiny gardens still bloom profusely, well into October. From January to March, though, the town is given back to the 3,500 hardy year-rounders—almost half of whom are unemployed during this time. Although it's said that 80 percent of the businesses close for January and February, there are still enough guest houses (and a handful of restaurants, especially on the weekends) open all winter, luring intrepid visitors with great prices and stark natural beauty. Steel yourself against the wind and take a walk on the beach, attend a reading at the Fine Arts Work Center, or curl up with a good book.

GUIDANCE

❄ **Chamber of Commerce** (508-487-3424; www.ptownchamber.com), 307 Commercial Street at MacMillan Wharf, P.O. Box 1017, Provincetown 02657. Open 9:30–4:30 daily May through October; open daily except Wednesday and Sunday in April, November, and December; open Monday, Tuesday, Thursday, and Saturday January through March. I've always found this particular chamber to be the most informative and helpful on the Cape.

Provincetown Business Guild (508-487-2313; 1-800-637-8696; www.ptown.org), 115 Bradford Street, Provincetown 02657. Open 9–2:30

weekdays. The guild, established in 1978 to support gay tourism, promotes about 275 gay-owned businesses.

Women Innkeepers of Provincetown (www.womeninnkeepers.com).

☙✍♿**Province Lands Visitor Center** (508-487-1256; www.nps.gov/caco), Race Point Road, Cape Cod National Seashore (CCNS). Open daily 9–5, early April to late November. First things first: Climb atop the observation deck for a 360-degree view of the outermost dunes and ocean. The center offers informative exhibits on Cape history, local flora and fauna, and dune ecology, along with frequent short films. Organized activities include sunset campfires and storytelling, birding trips, dune tours, and a junior ranger hour for children age 8–12.

WEB SITES AND INTERNET ACCESS

www.ptownchamber.com (chamber of commerce)

www.provincetown.com (an townwide site)

Log on at the library (see below) for a requested minimal donation or at Mailspot Express (508-487-6650), 170 Commercial Street.

PUBLIC LIBRARY

❉✍♪**Provincetown Public Library** (508-487-7094; www.ptownlib.com), 330 Commercial Street (at Freeman Street). Open Monday 10–5, Tuesday and Thursday noon–8, Wednesday 10–8, Friday 10–5, Saturday 10–2; Sunday (off-season only) 1–5.

PUBLIC REST ROOMS

Public rest rooms are located behind the chamber of commerce at the MacMillan Wharf parking lot (open daily in-season and Friday through Sunday, off-season) and in the Provincetown Town Hall at 260 Commercial Street (open weekdays year-round).

GETTING THERE

By car: Provincetown is the eastern terminus of Cape Cod, 63 miles via Route 6 from the Bourne Bridge and 128 miles from Boston and Providence. It takes almost 2½ hours to drive from Boston.

By boat from Boston: **Bay State Cruise Company, Inc.** (508-487-9284 seasonally on MacMillan Wharf; 617-748-1428 on Boston's Commonwealth Pier, Northern Avenue; www.baystatecruisecompany.com). There are two boats, a fast one and a slow one. The **Provincetown Express** takes 2 hours and operates twice daily from late May to mid-October. The boat departs Boston at 8 AM and 4 PM. Boats depart Provincetown at 10:30 AM and 6:30 PM. You could conceivably take the first boat to Provincetown in the morning, have 6 hours in town and at the beach, and be back in Boston by 8:30 PM. The fare is the same for adults and kids: $49 return ($28 one way) Friday through Monday and $39 return ($25 one way) Tuesday through Thursday. Bikes cost $10 return.

As for the regular ferry, ***Provincetown II,*** there are weekend departures late May to late June and early September to mid-October; daily departures late June to early September. Boats leave Boston at 9

AM and return at 3:30 for the 3-hour voyage. Return tickets cost $30 adults, $21 children, $10 bicycles. The schedule doesn't permit much a day trip to Boston from Provincetown, but you could spend the night in Boston and take the morning boat back to Provincetown.

Boston Harbor Cruises (617-227-4321; www.bostonharbor cruises.com) operates one or two daily fast boats from Boston's Long Wharf to Provincetown from early May to mid-October. The 90-minute trip aboard a catamaran costs $39 adults (return), $30 kids 12 and under (return), $10 bikes (return).

By boat from Plymouth: **Cape Cod Cruises** (Capt. John's Boats) (508-747-2400), State Pier (next to the *Mayflower*) in Plymouth and Fisherman's Wharf in Provincetown. The ferry schedule is designed so that you leave Plymouth at 10 AM, spend about 5 hours in Provincetown, and are back in Plymouth by 6 PM. You even get a narrated history of Plymouth Harbor as the boat pulls away from shore. Weekends late May to late September; daily mid-June to early September; Tuesday and Wednesday in September, too. Round-trip tickets: $26.50 adults; $17.50 children under 12; $2 bicycles. Free parking on the waterfront.

By bus: The **Plymouth & Brockton** bus line (508-778-9767; www.p-b.com) connects Provincetown with Hyannis and other Cape towns, as well as with Boston's Logan Airport. The bus stops behind the chamber of commerce. Purchase tickets on board. There are five buses a day in summer, two between early September and early May; travel time is 3½ hours and requires a bus change in Hyannis; $23 one way.

By air: **Cape Air** (508-487-0241, 508-771-6944; 1-800-352-0714; www.flycapeair.com) provides extensive daily, year-round service from Boston to Provincetown Municipal Airport. The flight takes 25 minutes, and the airport is 3 miles north of town. Summer fares $140–200 round trip; off-peak fares, too; $770 for a book of 10 one-way tickets, including tax.

GETTING AROUND

By car: The first exit off Route 6 (Snail Road) leads to the East End. (Street numbers in the East End are higher than in the West End.) Take the second exit for MacMillan Wharf and Town Hall, where street numbers are in the 300s. Shank Painter Road, the third exit, leads to the West End. Follow Route 6 to its end for Herring Cove Beach. A right off Route 6 takes you to the Province Lands section of the CCNS.

Provincetown's principal thoroughfare, Commercial Street, is narrow, one way, and 3 miles long. When you want to drive from one end of town to another quickly, use Bradford Street, parallel to Commercial. There are no sidewalks on Bradford, known as Back Street in the days when Provincetown had only a front and a back street. About 40 narrow cross-streets connect Commercial and Bradford.

Finding free on-street parking is a problem. There are municipal lots next to the Pilgrim Monument off Bradford Street; on MacMillan

Wharf; off Commercial Street; off Bradford Street; and one at the end of Commercial Street near the Breakwater.

- *By bus:* The excellent **Summer Shuttle** (508-385-8326; 1-800-352-7155; www.capecodtransit.org) operates daily late May to mid-October. The bus runs from Herring Cove Beach to Pilgrims Park and the A&P grocery store, down Bradford Street, with a detour at MacMillan Wharf, and down Route 6A to Dutra's Market in North Truro. Flag down the bus anywhere along the route. Buses run every 20 to 30 minutes 7:15 AM–12:15 AM (until 8 PM in spring and fall). Fares are $1 one way (kids 50¢ up to age 17).

- *By boat:* **Flyer's Shuttle** (508-487-0898), 131A Commercial Street. From mid-June to mid-September, an hourly shuttle takes bathers and picnickers to and from remote, unspoiled Long Point (see *Green Space—Beaches*). Fare is $7 one way, $10 round trip; children under 7 free. The boat runs from about 10 to 5:30-ish, when the last pickup is made at Long Point.

- *Sight-seeing tours:* **Art's Dune Tours** (508-487-1950), at Commercial and Standish Streets, offers daily trips mid-April to mid-November. The Costa family have led tourists on these narrated, hour-long trips through the CCNS dunes since 1946. The GMC Suburbans stop at least once (on the beach or atop a high dune or both) for photos, so you can take in the panoramic views. Rates $12–15 per person. Highly recommended. Reservations necessary for sunset trips. Ask about sunset clambakes and sunrise trips, too.

Provincetown Trolley, Inc. (508-487-9483), Commercial Street at Town Hall. These 40-minute, narrated sight-seeing trips depart approximately every half hour 10–4 and on the hour 5–8 daily, May through October. You can get on and off at the Provincetown Art Association & Museum (see *To See*); the Provincetown Inn next to the breakwater (see *Green Space—Walks*), at the western end of Commercial Street; and the Province Lands Visitor Center (see *Guidance*). Adults $8, children 12 and under $5.

MEDICAL EMERGENCY

Outer Cape Health Services (508-487-9395), Harry Kemp Way. Open year-round by appointment. Call for summer walk-in clinic hours.

Lyme disease. Ticks carry this disease, which has flu-like symptoms and may result in death if left untreated. Immediately and carefully remove any ticks that may have migrated from dune grasses to your body. Better yet, wear long pants, tuck pants into socks, and wear long-sleeved shirts whenever possible when hiking. Avoid hiking in grassy and overgrown areas of dense brush.

TO SEE

Listings are from east to west.

Commercial Street. Until Commercial Street was laid out in 1835, the shoreline served as the town's main thoroughfare. Because houses had been oriented toward the harbor, many had to be turned around or the "front" door had to be reconstructed to face the new street. Some houses, however, still remain oriented toward the shore.

❄⛵ **Provincetown Art Association & Museum** (508-487-1750; www.paam. org), 460 Commercial Street. Open noon–5 daily and 8 PM–10 PM on Friday and Saturday, late May to mid-October (plus 8 PM–10 PM daily in July and August); noon–4 or 5 on Saturday and Sunday the rest of the year. Organized in 1914 by a few artists to "promote education of the public in the arts, and social intercourse between artists and laymen," PAAM members have included Ambrose Webster, Milton Avery, and Marsden Hartley. One of the country's foremost small museums, its four galleries feature established and emerging artists. Selections from the permanent collection of 1,700-plus works change frequently. Special exhibitions, juried shows, and other events are sponsored throughout the year. The bookstore specializes in the local art colony. Suggested adult admission $3, kids $1.

⛵ **Provincetown Heritage Museum** (508-487-7098), Commercial and Center Streets. Open 10–5:30 daily, late May to mid-October. This former 1861 Methodist church is topped with a 162-foot-high steeple that serves as a landmark for fishermen sailing into the harbor. The museum contains the world's largest indoor model (66 feet long) of a fishing schooner. *Rose Dorothea* was built from scratch in Francis Santos's workshop at Flyer's boatyard (see *Outdoor Activities—Boat Excursions/Rentals*) and assembled upstairs in the museum. Impressive as it is, the museum has more to offer: local artwork, an offshore whaling boat, 19th-century fishing artifacts, and a trap-fishing boat. Before you leave, you might want to purchase three inexpensive **walking pamphlets**—for the East End, Center, and West End—which are full of historical anecdotes. Adults and children 12 and over, $3.

MacMillan Wharf. By 1800 Provincetown was already one of the country's busiest seaports; 50 years later it was second largest whaling port. By the 1880s, when cod fishing reached its peak and Provincetown boasted the Cape's largest population, MacMillan Wharf was just one of 56 wharves jutting into the harbor. (MacMillan Wharf, built in 1873, was originally called Old Colony Wharf after the railroad that met Boston packets, but was ultimately named for native son Adm. Donald MacMillan, who explored the North Pole with Peary.) The town bustled with herring canning, cod curing, whaling, and fishing. Although only a few wharves are still standing, MacMillan Wharf remains true to its original purpose: Even though the fishing industry has recently suffered because of overfishing, some boats still unload their afternoon catch here. And instead of whaling ships, the wharf now is lined with whale-watching boats. The view of town from the end of the pier is expansive.

⛵ **Expedition *Whydah*** (508-487-8899; www.whydah.com), 16 MacMillan

KIM GRANT

Only a handful of the dozens of wharves that once jutted out into the bay still survive.

Wharf. Open daily 10–5 April to mid-October, weekends through January. This museum, new in 1996, is devoted solely to chronicling the story of the *Whydah*, the only pirate ship ever salvaged. It sank 1,500 feet offshore from Wellfleet's Marconi Beach (see *Green Space—Beaches* in "Wellfleet") on April 26, 1717, and it was raised in 1984 by Cape Codder Barry Clifford. Adults $5; children 4–12, $3.50.

Provincetown Town Hall, 260 Commercial Street. Constructed in 1878, the building serves as the seat of local government and community agencies. The auditorium is also used for concerts. Look for the Works Progress Administration (WPA)–era murals of farmers and fishermen by Ross Moffett and the portrait by Charles Hawthorne.

Provincetown Tales (508-487-6786), Whaler's Wharf, 237 Commercial

Street. Open mid-April through December. This new exhibition space and 71-seat cinema in the newly rebuilt Whaler's Wharf engages visitors in the rich history of this truly unique seaside village. The film and exhibit will change yearly, but the story will loosely follow the theme of "History, Legends, Rumors, and Downright Lies." In 2001 the film explored the horrendous February 1998 fire that engulfed the building, making national headlines. Tickets $7 adults, $4 children under 12; 4-person family $20.

Pilgrim bas-relief, Bradford Street, behind Town Hall. Sculptor Cyrus Dalin's memorial commemorates the Mayflower Compact, which has been called the "first American act in our history." After traveling from England for almost two months, the *Mayflower* sat in the harbor until the compact was drawn up. No one was allowed to go ashore until he signed the document, attesting to his willingness to abide by laws. One relief memorializes the five Pilgrims who died before reaching Plymouth. (Three Pilgrims are buried near the center of town.) The other relief contains the text of the compact and the names of the 41 people who signed it.

✳❧**Pilgrim Monument** and **Provincetown Museum** (508-487-1310), High Pole Road, off Winslow Street from Bradford Street. Open 9–7 daily in July and August; 9–5 daily April through June and September through November. Last admission is 45 minutes before closing. The 252-foot monument (the tallest all-granite U.S. monument) commemorates the Pilgrims' landing in Provincetown on November 11, 1620, and their 5-week stay in the harbor while searching for a good place to settle. President Theodore Roosevelt laid the cornerstone in 1907, and President Taft dedicated it in 1910. Climb the 116 stairs of the monument—modeled after the Torre del Mangia in Siena, Italy—for a panoramic view of the Outer Cape. On a clear day you can see 30 miles to Boston.

One wing of the museum is devoted to early Pilgrim travails: the *Mayflower's* first landing, finding corn and fresh water, the unsuccessful search for a place to settle. The other wing contains dioramas and changing exhibits dedicated to a whaling captain's life ashore, shipwrecks, dolls and toys, the Lower and Outer Cape, and local art. Free parking for 2 hours; but beware—your car will be towed if you linger or park illegally. Adults $5; children 4–12, $3.

✳ **Universalist Meetinghouse** (508-487-9344), 236 Commercial Street. Generally open 9–1 Sunday through Thursday. This 1847 Greek Revival church contains trompe l'oeil murals (by Carl Wendt, who painted similar murals for Nantucket's Unitarian Universalist Church), a Sandwich glass chandelier, and pews made with Provincetown pine. The pews are decorated with medallions carved from whales' teeth.

Pilgrim plaque, at the western end of Commercial Street. Provincetown's version of Plymouth's Rock—a plaque in the middle of a landscaped traffic circle—commemorates the Pilgrims' landing.

On the outskirts of town

Old Harbor Lifesaving Station (508-487-1256), Race Point Beach. Open 1:30–2:30 daily late May through June and early September to mid-October; 3–5 daily except Thursday July to early September. This 1872 structure, one of nine original Lifesaving Service stations on the Outer Cape, was floated by barge from Chatham to its present location in 1977. The Lifesaving Service, precursor to the Coast Guard, rescued crews from ships wrecked by shallow sandbars and brutal nor'easters. The boat room contains the original equipment, but on Thursday at 6 PM (confirm the time before going), hour-long demonstrations are given using the old-fashioned techniques. "Surfmen" launch a rescue line to the wrecked ship and haul in the distressed sailors one at a time. Plaques lining the boardwalk to the museum explain how the service worked. Suggested donation $3 adults, $1 kids 16 and under. You have to pay an additional $7 to park at Race Point Beach.

Dune shacks, beyond the end of Snail Road. In the dunes between Race Point and High Head in North Truro, on 2 miles of ridges and valleys, stand about 17 weather-beaten dune shacks. Constructed between 1935 and 1950 of driftwood and scavenged materials, they are the subject of local legend. Over the years, notable writers and artists have called them home for weeks, months, even years: Among the tenants have been Jack Kerouac, e. e. cummings, Norman Mailer, Jackson Pollock, poet Harry Kemp, and Eugene O'Neill.

When the CCNS was created in 1961, the federal government set up 25-year or lifelong leases with squatters who were living in the shacks. (Only one of the inhabitants held a clear title to the land.) Some shacks are still occupied. In 1985, Joyce Johnson, a dune dweller since the early 1970s, founded the Peaked Hill Trust to oversee some of the shacks. Members of the trust win stays through the lottery system; write to P.O. Box 1705, Provincetown 02657, for membership information. Since Province Lands was added to the National Register of Historic Places in 1989, the maintenance and fate of most of the historic shacks have fallen to the National Park Service. In 1996 the park service set aside a few shacks for artists in residence.

In May 2000, two days before I won a weeklong stay in one of two shacks owned by Hazel Hawthorne Werner and "rented" through Peaked Hill, Hazel died. At press time, it was unclear if the National Park Service would allow Peaked Hill Trust to maintain them or whether the NPS would destroy them or use them for some other purposes. During my visit I didn't produce anything approaching Cynthia Huntington's *The Salt House*, which she wrote over many, many months of living there. It's well worth reading.

There are a few off-road parking spots at the end of Snail Road. Take the short woodland trail and hike up the first steep dune, then over the next two crests; the shacks will appear in the distance. You can

Early morning surf fishing at Race Point

also reach the shacks by walking east from Race Point Beach. Remember, however, that most shacks are still occupied, and people live out there for privacy, to pursue the creative process uninhibited, to contemplate in isolation.

OUTDOOR ACTIVITIES

AIRPLANE RIDES
Willie Air Tours (508-487-9989), Provincetown Municipal Airport, Race Point Road, offers rides late May to early October. Gwen Bloomingdale and Barbara Gard offer 15-minute trips in a 1930 Stinson Detroiter that help you grasp how narrow and vulnerable this strip of land is. A flight costs about $50 for one person, $80 for a group of four. Purchase tickets at the airport.

BICYCLING/RENTALS
Province Lands. Eight miles of hilly paved trails—around ponds, cranberry bogs, and sand dunes—wind through Province Lands' 4,000 acres. Spur trails lead to Herring Cove and Race Point Beaches (see *Green Space—Beaches*). Access is from Race Point Road near Route 6. Parking areas are at the Beech Forest Trailhead (see *Green Space—Walks*), Province Lands Visitor Center (see *Guidance*), and Race Point and Herring Cove Beaches.

Rentals. All shops are open seasonally, from April through October. Bike rentals cost about $3–4 hourly, $14–19 daily, $60–70 weekly, depending on what kind of bike you get. **Arnold's** (508-487-0844), 329 Commercial Street, since 1937, enjoys a prime location right in the middle of town. Beach umbrellas and chairs for rent, too. **Galeforce Beach Market** (508-487-4849), 144 Bradford Street Extension, is on the western edge of town with free parking. **Nelson's Bike Shop** (508-487-0034), 43 Race Point Road, is located about 100 yards from the bike trails, with free parking.

BOAT EXCURSIONS/RENTALS

Provincetown Harbor Cruises (508-487-4330; 508-487-0898), MacMillan Wharf. Captain Carla departs every hour from 11 to 7 daily, late June through September. The 45-minute trip, around one of the world's largest deep-water ports, costs $10 for adults (children are free).

Bay Lady II (508-487-9308) and *Schooner Hindu* (508-487-0659), both on MacMillan Wharf. Mid-May to mid-October. These 2-hour harbor sails into Cape Cod Bay are aboard traditionally gaff-rigged schooners. Four trips a day in-season (two off-season), including a sunset trip. Adults $10–15; children under 12, $6.

Flyer's Boat Rentals (508-487-0898), 131A Commercial Street. Daily 8–6, May through October. Flyer's, in business since 1965, has a rental boat to suit your needs: Sunfish, catamaran, sloop, kayak, "surf bike," powerboat, rowboat. Sailboats are $16–25 hourly, $50–100 daily; single kayaks cost $25 for 4 hours, $40 daily; or try your hand at cycling on the water with a surf bike for $15 per hour. Flyer's also offers an equivalent to early-bird dinners—early-bird fishing specials: For 4 hours (8 AM–noon), you get a boat, bait, and two rods for $40. Two-hour sailing instruction is also offered for $60 per person; the price for additional people is negotiable.

FISHING

Surf-casting is great on Race Point Beach in the early morning or after sunset. There is no shellfishing allowed by nonresidents.

Cee Jay (508-487-4330), MacMillan Wharf. From June to mid-October there are three daily departures on half-day bluefishing and fluke excursions. The third-generation crew will fillet your fish if you have a place to cook it. $25 per person.

Nelson's Bait & Tackle (508-487-0034), 43 Race Point Road. Open mid-April to mid-October. If you're not hiring a charter boat (which supplies the necessary equipment), Nelson's is the source for rod rentals, live and frozen bait, and fresh- and saltwater tackle.

See also Flyer's Boat Rentals under *Boat Excursions/Rentals.*

FOR FAMILIES

Playgrounds are located at both ends of town: at Bradford and Howland Streets (East End) and at Bradford and Nickerson Streets (West End).

HORSEBACK-RIDING INSTRUCTION

Bayberry Hollow Horse Farm (508-487-6584), West Vine Street Extension, offers horseback-riding instruction but no trail rides.

IN-LINE SKATING

Skating is off-limits on the National Seashore bike trails.

KAYAKING

Kayak Tours & Rentals (1-877-785-2925; www.offthecoastkayak.com), Whaler's Wharf or 3 Freeman Street, right behind Napi's. (The shop was moving at press time.) Open seasonally. Rent kayaks to paddle out to Long Point, Great Island in Wellfleet, or Pamet Harbor in Truro. Or let these folks lead the way on a tour, which includes snacks and refreshments or even a full-blown clambake. Four-hour rentals $25; all day $40. Tours $40–60 per person; tours vary daily.

SAILING LESSONS

See Flyer's Boat Rentals under *Boat Excursions/Rentals*.

TENNIS

Town courts are located at **Motta Field** off Winslow Street.

Provincetown Tennis Club (508-487-9574), 286 Bradford Street. Open 8 AM–7 PM daily, late May to mid-October. Five clay and two hard courts are available for non–club members. Tournaments in July and August.

Bissell's Tennis Courts (508-487-9512), Bradford Street Extension behind the Moors restaurant (see *Dining Out*). Five red clay courts and lessons are offered late May to late September.

WHALE-WATCHING

Located just 8 miles from Provincetown, the fertile feeding grounds of Stellwagen Bank attract migrating finback and humpback whales. Although the bank was designated the country's first National Marine Sanctuary in 1992, the government's attempts to control the ocean's intricate ecosystem don't always work out as planned. For instance, whales feed on sand lance, which thrive when herring populations are small. (Herring eat sand lance larvae.) But since the government began protecting dwindling stocks of herring, the number of sand lance larvae has decreased. Some naturalists theorize that humpbacks are heading elsewhere in search of more abundant food supplies. Fear not, though; a whale-watching trip without a whale sighting is rare.

Most whale-watch cruises last about 3½ hours and have an onboard naturalist. Bring a sweater (even in summer), and seasickness pills if you think you'll need them.

Check the chamber of commerce brochure rack (see *Guidance*) or with your lodging for money-saving coupons.

Dolphin Fleet Whale Watch (508-349-1900; 1-800-826-9300), MacMillan Wharf. Mid-April through October. Scientists aboard the Dolphin Fleet, the best outfit in town, hail from the Center for Coastal Studies. Adults $19–20; children 7–12, $16–17; children under 7 free.

Portuguese Princess **Whale Watch** (508-487-2651; 1-800-442-3188), MacMillan Wharf. May to mid-October. Early-morning trips are a bit less expensive. Park at their lot on Shank Painter for $5 in summer, free off-season. (It's then a 20-minute walk into town.)

EVEN MORE THINGS TO DO

❊ **FITNESS CLUBS**
Mussel Beach Health Club (508-487-0001), 35 Bradford Street. Open daily, the club has state-of-the-art equipment, free weights, and cardiovascular equipment. Day-use fee $12; "punch card" for multiple visits (5 for $49, 10 for $75).

Provincetown Gym (508-487-2776), 81 Shank Painter Road. Open daily. Cardiovascular machines and free weights; perhaps less intimidating for women. Day-use fee $12, or six visits (which can be transferred between people) for $54.

SPECIAL PROGRAMS

❊ **Fine Arts Work Center** (508-487-9960; www.capecodaccess.com/fineartsworkcenter), 24 Pearl Street. The center was founded in 1968 by a group of writers, artists, and patrons, including Robert Motherwell, Hudson Walker, Stanley Kunitz, and Myron Stout. The intent was to provide a place for emerging artists to pursue independent work within a sympathetic community of their peers. In 1972 the center purchased Days Lumber Yard, where artists have worked in small studios since 1914. (Frank Days Jr., who had been concerned about the plight of artists, built 10 studios over his lumberyard. Charles Hawthorne was one of the first tenants in 1914.) Writing and visual arts residencies, which include a monthly stipend and materials allowance, run October through April; the deadline for applications is February 1. Twenty candidates are chosen from a pool of about 1,000. Readings, seminars, workshops, and exhibits year-round are open to the public. There's also a summer program for creative writing and visual arts, as well as weeklong and weekend workshops in printmaking, sculpture, fiction writing, and the like.

✎ **Provincetown Museum School** (508-487-1750), 460 Commercial Street at Bangs Street. Open early July to late August. Printmaking, painting, etching, monotypes, and watercolor are some of the classes taught by notable artists at the Provincetown Art Association & Museum (PAAM). Children's painting and drawing classes are held Monday and Thursday, 9:30–noon.

Cape Cod School of Art (508-487-0101; www.capecod.net/artschool), 48 Pearl Street. Workshops June through September. This excellent program carries on Provincetown's impressionist tradition established by Charles Hawthorne in 1899, and is the first U.S. art school dedicated solely to outdoor painting, "plein air." (The CCSA was basically responsible for Provincetown developing into an art mecca.) Workshops in a variety of media, mostly held outdoors, are available for practically all ages and levels. Director Lois Griffel was a longtime student of Henry Hensche, Hawthorne's successor.

✳ **Campus Provincetown** (508-487-9666; www.campusprovincetown.org). For those who never stop learning, a consortium of cultural and scientific institutions has banded together to offer educational courses, workshops, field studies, and stage productions through Campus Provincetown. Additionally, a new collaborative, Provincetown International Art Institute, offers college-credit courses through the Cape Cod Community College.

Center for Coastal Studies (508-487-3622), 59 Commercial Street. Library open to members year-round. This independent, nonprofit, membership-supported institution is dedicated to research, public education, and conservation programs for the coastal and marine environments. Educational programs include trips and lectures for school groups and Elderhostel. The center supplies naturalists for the Dolphin Fleet whale-watch trips (see *Outdoor Activities—Whale-Watching*). Among other things, researchers study endangered right whales (there are only about 300 in the world) and have raised important environmental questions about Boston's Outfall Pipe, which will discharge treated sewage just 16 miles from Stellwagen Bank and 36 miles from Provincetown. Center scientists are always on the scene when pods of pilot whales strand themselves on area beaches. (With the possible exception of a spot or two in New Zealand and Australia, Cape Cod has more whale strandings than any other place in the world. It happens primarily on the bayside beaches between Brewster and Provincetown in November and December. Scientists are at a loss to explain these mysterious mass suicides.) The center is also the only East Coast organization authorized to disentangle whales trapped in fishing nets.

✳🖉 **Provincetown Community Center** (508-487-7097), 44 Bradford Street. In addition to a host of classes sponsored by the Provincetown Recreation Department and held here, the center has a weight room, karate classes for adults and children, dance, and yoga classes. Call for current schedule, offerings, and fees.

SWIMMING POOL

Provincetown Inn (508-487-9500), 1 Commercial Street. This outdoor, Olympic-size pool is free and open seasonally.

See also the Boatslip Beach Club under *Entertainment*.

GREEN SPACE

BEACHES

After you look at a map or take an airplane tour—to see the long spit of sand arching around the harbor—you won't doubt there are about 30 miles of beach within the CCNS in Provincetown.

Race Point Beach, CCNS, off Route 6. Race Point faces north, and, as such, it gets sun all day; it also has long breaking waves coming in off the Atlantic Ocean. Surrounded by dunes as far as the eye can see, Race

The tradition of open-air painting classes began in Provincetown and still flourishes here.

Point feels as remote as it is. In spring, with binoculars, you might see whales spouting and breaching offshore. Amenities include lifeguards, showers, and rest rooms. Parking from mid-June to early September is $7 daily (permit transferable to and valid all day at any CCNS beach); entering on foot or bicycle is $1; a yearly pass is $20.

Herring Cove Beach, CCNS, at the end of Route 6. The water here is calmer and "warmer" (it's all relative) than at Race Point. Because the beach faces due west, you'll often find large groups gathering for spectacular sunsets. Lifeguards, showers, rest rooms, and a snack bar. Parking is the same as at Race Point (see above). Both lots fill up by 11 AM in summer; usually there is no charge to park after 5:30 PM.

Harbor Beach is about 3½ miles long and parallels Commercial Street. Although there is little beach at high tide, and few public access points, it's great to walk the flats at low tide.

Long Point. Long Point is easily accessible by boat in summer (see Flyer's Shuttle under *Getting Around*), although few people make the effort. You'll be rewarded if you do, but don't forget to pack a picnic and plenty of water. You can walk atop the breakwater (see *Walks*), but it takes about 2 hours. **Long Point Lighthouse,** at the tip of the spit, was built in 1816, two years before a community of fishermen began to construct homes out there. By 1846 there were 61 families on Long Point, all of whom returned to town during the Civil War. (Two Civil War forts were built on Long Point.) As you walk around town, notice which old houses sport a blue enamel plaque in the shape of a barge. This plaque identifies Long Point houses that were floated across the harbor on barges. (Locals call them "floaters.")

WALKS

Beech Forest Trail, CCNS, off Race Point Road from Route 6. This sandy, 1-mile trail circles a freshwater pond before steep stairs cut through a forest of beech trees. Warblers migrating from South America pack the area from mid- to late May, but the trail is also beautiful in autumn.

Breakwater, at the western end of Commercial Street (at the Provincetown Inn) and Bradford Street Extension, is a mile-long jetty doubling as a footpath to the secluded Long Point beach. But even if you walk out only partway, it's a great place to watch the tide roll in. **Wood End Lighthouse** (1872) is to the north; **Long Point Lighthouse** is at the tip.

Hatches Harbor. From Herring Cove Beach, at the end of Route 6, walk about 10 minutes toward Race Point Light to the entrance of Hatches Harbor. There's a dike along the back of the salt marsh and tidal estuary that you can walk across.

See also Dune shacks under *To See* and Province Lands Trail under *Outdoor Activities—Bicycling/Rentals.*

LODGING

If you care about where you stay, don't go to Provincetown in summer without reservations. In fact, try to reserve a condo or apartment in January for July or August. Although there are more than 100 places to stay, good ones fill up fast. If you must wait until the last minute, there are often vacancies midweek in July. Most places have lengthy minimum-night stays during special events and holiday weekends—again, reserve early. Rates for holiday weekends are always higher than I've reported. Since the East End tends to be quieter than the West End, I've indicated where each lodging is located, unless it's in the middle of town. All guest houses included below welcome everyone: gay and straight. If you want to know the specific disposition of a guest house (Is their clientele more straight than gay in summer? Are there more men in summer than women? . . . and so on), *ask* the innkeepers. You won't be offending anyone. Finally, Provincetown has a limited water supply; try to conserve.

The zip code for Provincetown is 02657.

BED & BREAKFASTS/GUEST HOUSES

&   **The Brass Key** (508-487-9005; 1-800-842-9858; www.brasskey.com), 67 Bradford Street. Open mid-April through mid-November. More like a small hotel or a luxurious private enclave—fenced in and gated—the Brass Key has catapulted Provincetown accommodations to a different level. It's all very elegant and sophisticated and friendly, thanks to proprietor Michael MacIntyre's expertise and his staff. All 33 rooms, around an enclosed courtyard with pool, spa, and lounge chairs, are completely different from one another. A few generalizations can be made, though: Look for vaulted ceilings, working fireplaces, multiperson

KIM GRANT

Parabolic dunes on the National Seashore

showers, whirlpool baths, fancy amenities, nightly turndown service, antiques, and plenty of style and grace. Some rooms have a private balcony; all have access to a rooftop widow's walk and two living rooms. An expansive continental breakfast buffet with lots of fruit and delectable pastries is served in the country-inn-style Gatehouse. Iced tea and lemonade are always available. Wine and beer and cheese and crackers are offered each afternoon. Mid-June to mid-September $225–425; off-season $115–325.

❀❄ **Fairbanks Inn** (508-487-0386; www.fairbanksinn.com), 90 Bradford Street. This 1770s sea captain's house, the first in town to have indoor plumbing, is a Federal-style beauty. In the 1800s it was owned by the town's wealthiest individual, David Fairbanks, who began Seamen's Bank. The house is a restored jewel, one brought up to 21st-century standards without sacrificing historical integrity. Period antiques, wood-burning fireplaces, and wide-plank floorboards complement fine amenities and plush bedding. Although rooms in two adjacent buildings are less historic, they are still very desirable. In fact, there isn't a single room I'd hesitate to recommend. Stylish and thoughtful touches are everywhere. An expanded continental breakfast is served in a wicker-filled, glassed-in porch; in the Revolutionary-era dining room; or on the quiet brick patio. Innkeeper Lynette Molnar has an expert staff (including Kay Halle) to help with this 14-room inn. $109–225 mid-June to mid-September and holidays; $75–145 the rest of the year.

❄ **Copper Fox** (508-487-8583; www.provincetown.com/copperfox), 448 Commercial Street (East End). Innkeeper John Gagliardi worked his tail off to renovate this three-story Federal sea captain's B&B into the wonderfully relaxing hostelry that it is today. Set back from the road, the deep front lawn and covered porch offer plenty of places to relax. Inside, the sunporch and living room are a treat on inclement days. The three guest rooms and two suites have top-notch furnishings and are meticulously maintained. For longer stays, John has two **apartments** with kitchens and separate entrances. Mid-June to mid-September $140–169 for rooms, $185 apartments; off-season $85–95 and $100, respectively.

☕✴ **Inn at Cook Street** (508-487-3894; 1-888-266-5655; www.innatcookstreet. com), 7 Cook Street (East End). Owners Paul Church and Dana Mitton operate a mixed house (gay, straight, men, women), which is just the way they like it. It's a gracious 1836 Greek Revival sea captain's house, with four rooms and two suites. They are all very tasteful and highly recommended. Pick your room based on its sleigh bed (Gable), how much sun it gets (the Hobbit Suite is very bright), or its deck access (some have a private deck.) All have TV, telephone, private bath, and air-conditioning. A hammock in the private, shady backyard is enticing, a rare amenity for Provincetown B&Bs. Continental breakfast. June to mid-September $125–175; off-season $90–120.

✴ **Land's End Inn** (508-487-0706; 1-800-276-7088), 22 Commercial Street (West End). After the Masthead and Watermark, Land's End has the best views in town. As you walk up the hidden path, catching glimpses of turrets and decks, you'll quickly realize this is the most unusual place to stay in town. (No description can really prepare you.) At the end of the West End, perched atop Gull Hill, many rooms have wonderful ocean views. The dark interior is a visual feast, chock-full of Victoriana, wood carvings, stained glass, and Oriental rugs atop floral carpets. (I wouldn't want to be the housekeeper here—too many things to dust; but someone does an admirable job.) The inn offers 16 rooms (all with private bath) and three **apartments;** the tower rooms and loft suite are spectacularly situated. Some rooms sleep four. There are lots of common spaces in which to relax; it's all very tranquil. Continental breakfast; on-site parking. Late May through September $120–190 for rooms, $140–150 for apartments, $285 for suite; off-season $87–165 for rooms, $97–110 for apartments, $185 for suite; rates are for two people; each additional person $25 per day. (Inn profits are donated to local arts organizations via a trust dedicated to David Adam Schoolman, who owned the inn from 1972 to 1995.)

✴ **Beaconlight Guesthouse** (508-487-9603; 1-800-696-9603; www.capecod. net/beaconlight), 12 Winthrop Street (West End). Innkeepers Stephen Mascilo and Trevor Pinker—and their golden retrievers—have a knack for creating warm and homey surroundings. There's a palpable sense of it within the two living rooms (one with a grand piano begging to be played) and a country-style kitchen, scene of fine expanded continental breakfasts and lively conversation that extends well into the late morning. The 10 rooms (2 with shared bath) are elegantly furnished and named after lighthouses; Cape Ann is particularly spacious. All have television and VCR; some have a fireplace and separate sitting room. There are two decks (arguably the largest roof deck in town, with panoramic views); an outdoor hot tub is on the lower deck. Mid-June to late September $120–245 for rooms and suites; $65–165 the rest of the year.

❄ **Oxford Guesthouse** (508-487-9103; 1-800-456-9103; www.capecod.net/oxford), 8 Cottage Street (West End). Innkeepers Stephen and Trevor (of the Beaconlight, above) opened this refined, hospitable, and sophisticated English-style B&B in 1998. The lovely living room, furnished with plump sofas and a fireplace, is the kind of place you'd be happy in on a rainy day. The five (two with shared bath) guest rooms have central air-conditioning, television and VCR, robes, and telephone. For more privacy, there is a studio **apartment** with cooking facilities. An expanded continental breakfast is included, and served in an elegant but relaxed dining room. Outdoor space is limited to a front porch overlooking a side street and a few shaded tables behind the house. Ask about a newly renovated and self-contained two-story **cottage** that was being readied at press time. Mid-June through September $120–195 rooms, $210–245 suites; off-season $65–115 rooms, $145–165 suites.

❄🐾 **Six Webster Place** (508-487-2266; 1-800-693-2783; www.sixwebster.com), 6 Webster Place. This 18th-century guest house sits at the end of a quiet lane behind Provincetown Town Hall. It was handsomely and authentically restored in 1985 to reflect its colonial origins. Most of the seven rooms have a working fireplace and private bath; all have cable TV, air-conditioning, and telephone. Common areas include a small living room, a sunny reading nook, gardens, and decks or patios. One- and two-bedroom **apartments** are contemporary and sophisticated. Hosts Ray Boylan and Stanley Wilson offer an expanded continental breakfast. On-site parking; year-round Jacuzzi. July to mid-September $110 shared bath, $145–190 private bath, $1,500–2,000 weekly for apartments; off-season $60–140 for rooms, $125–185 nightly for apartments.

🏅 **Windamar House** (508-487-0599; www.provincetown.com/windamar/), 568 Commercial Street (East End). Open May through December. This circa-1840 sea captain's house has six modest rooms (two of which have private bath) and two **apartments.** Bette Adams, innkeeper since 1980, has filled them with antiques, local art, and coordinated fabrics and wallpapers. The small common room, where a continental breakfast is set out, has a refrigerator and TV. The most spectacular guest room overlooks the garden and grape arbor, while one large and airy **apartment** has cathedral ceilings and a view of the harbor. The well-manicured lawns and gardens in the backyard are an oasis. On-site parking. Late May to mid-September $65–125 for rooms; off-season $55–115. In-season $795–895 weekly for apartments; mid-September to mid-October $695–795 weekly; off-season $85–100 nightly. No credit cards.

See also White Horse Inn under *Apartments, Cottages, and Studios.*

APARTMENTS, COTTAGES, AND STUDIOS

❄ **Watermark Inn** (508-487-0165;www.watermark-inn.com), 603 Commercial Street (East End). These 10 contemporary suites are on the water's edge. They have triangular gable windows, skylights, modern bathrooms, spacious living areas, cable TV, and either a full kitchen or a kitchenette (two rooms have a fireplace). Sliding glass doors open onto decks, many of which are private; at high tide the water laps at the deck. A 20-minute walk from town; parking. Late June to early September weekly $1,025–2,150; nightly off-season $85–170 (excluding holiday weekends); discounts for some off-season stays.

🐾❄ **White Horse Inn** (508-487-1790), 500 Commercial Street (East End). Frank Schaefer has presided over this low-key, artsy hostelry since 1963, intent on providing clean, comfortable rooms at good prices. Six studio apartments are individually decorated with an eclectic, bohemian flair. Some are light and airy, some are dark and cozy. All defy description; even Frank has a hard time describing them to people over the phone. (On my last visit, though, he did describe one bathroom aptly as postmodern nautical.) Suffice it to say, each is a work of art in progress. Although the 12 **guest rooms** are basic (most with a shared bath), they are filled with local art from the last 30 years. They're a real find; in fact, as many Europeans find their way here as Americans. Mid-June to early September $75–80 ($50–80 single) rooms, $125–140 studio apartments with a 3-night minimum. Off-season $50–60 ($40–50 single) rooms, $75–90 studios. Weekly studio rates. No credit cards.

❄🐾 **The Masthead** (508-487-0523; 1-800-395-5095; www.capecodtravel.com/masthead), 31–41 Commercial Street (West End). At the far end of the West End, about a 15-minute walk from the center of town, the Masthead offers a superb variety of well-maintained apartments, cottages, and **rooms.** The neatly landscaped complex, operated by the Ciluzzi family since 1959, has a boardwalk with lounge chairs and access to the 450-foot private beach below. Each cottage has a large picture window facing the water. Units, in buildings more than 100 years old, have fully equipped kitchens, low ceilings, pine paneling, and Early American furnishings that are a bit dated but nonetheless charming and comfortable. Although most units can accommodate four people, one sleeps seven. The brochure contains a very accurate and detailed description of each room. Great for families; children under 12 stay free. Limited on-site free parking. July to early September $158–321 for two to four people ($81–197 for rooms); off-season $76–168 ($63–108 for rooms). In-season weekly rates $992–1,905.

❄🐾 **Bay Shore & Chandler Houses** (508-487-9133; www.provincetown.com/bayshore), 493 Commercial Street (East End). This complex consists of six buildings, four of which are waterside, clustered around landscaped grounds, lounge chairs, and a beach. (Units across the street have access to the lawn and beach.) Most of the 26 units have private decks or patios and large picture windows facing east; all have well-equipped kitchens; a few have fireplaces. The shingled, traditional exteriors belie individually and newly decorated interiors. I particularly like the completely renovated Chandler House units, more contemporary and bright. All of these have a fireplace and very good to spectacular views. Although this is a condominium complex, managers Ann Maguire and Harriet Gordon keep standards consistent and high. The rate sheet details each unit's special features. About a 15-minute walk from the center of town. Ann and Harriet also recently began renting, by the week, two new units adjacent to their own house in the West End. I highly recommend them. Mid-June to early September $1,195–1,695 weekly for one and two bedrooms (studio $950–995 weekly); off-season $85–175 nightly. Rates are for two to four people, depending on the unit. (Since pets are accepted, those who don't have dogs may not appreciate these barking guests.)

Capt. Jack's Wharf (508-487-1450), 73A Commercial Street (West End). Open late May to late September. On a rustic old wharf, these 13 colorfully painted bohemian apartments (condos actually) transport you back to Provincetown's early days as an emerging art colony. Many units have whitewashed interiors, with skylights and lots of windows looking onto the harbor. Some first-floor units have narrow cracks between the planked floorboards—you can see the water beneath you! I particularly like Australis, a two-story unit with a spiral staircase and more than 1,000 square feet of space. The wharf is strewn with bistro tables, pots of flowers, and Adirondack chairs. Late June to mid-September $850–1,350 weekly; off-season $650–1,350 weekly, $93–140 nightly (3-night minimum). No credit cards.

🍷 **Ship's Bell Inn and Motel** (508-487-1674), 586 Commercial Street (East End). Open mid-May to mid-November. This hospitable and old-fashioned place is fine for a family on a budget or two people wanting lots of space to spread out. Most of these 11 apartments and seven studios have decks with water views across Commercial Street. A few units sleep as many as five or six people; all have fully equipped kitchens. Ship's Bell also rents eight **motel rooms** off a cozy fireplaced living room, but they're less impressive. On-site parking; daily maid service; private access to the beach across the street. July and August $600–730 weekly for rooms, $1,260–1,530 weekly for apartments. Off-season, take about 30 percent off the above. Rates are for two people; each additional person is $15 per night.

See also B*ed & Breakfasts/Guest Houses*, and Surfside Inn under *Motels*.

MOTELS

🍷 **Bill White's Motel** (508-487-1042; www.oncapecod.net/billwhitesmotel/), 29 Bradford Street Extension (West End). Open early May to late October. Across the street from the dunes at the very end of town, this small, 12-unit, family-run motel provides arguably the best value in town.

KIM GRANT

Although the fishing fleet at Provincetown is dwindling, boats still unload their daily catch here.

Owners Maggie and John Tinkham welcome a mixed crowd of families and couples. Rooms are simple but well maintained, and the Portuguese hospitality is warm. Rooms have one queen or two full beds and cable TV. It's 15 minutes to the beach, 20 to MacMillan Wharf; the shuttle also goes right by here. July to early September $80 for two people, $15 each additional; off-season $60 double.

✂ **Best Western Tides** (508-487-1045; 1-800-528-1234; www.bwprovince town.com), 837 Commercial Street (East End). Open mid-May to mid-October. This 6-acre complex on the Provincetown/Truro line sits right on Cape Cod Bay. Most of these pleasantly upgraded motel rooms are waterfront, within a shuffle of the motel's 600-foot private beach. Ground-floor rooms open onto the beach. All rooms have a king-size bed or two doubles and a refrigerator and coffeemaker. On-site parking, but be sure to bring bikes so you can ride into town rather than drive. July and August $120–200; off-season $89–180. Children under 18 free in parent's room.

🐾 **Surfside Inn** (508-487-1726; 1-800-421-1726; www.surfsideinn.cc), 543 Commercial Street (East End). Open late April through November. At four stories, this is the tallest commercial building in Provincetown. One building sits on the private harborfront beach; the other overlooks the large heated pool. The 84 rooms are of the modern motel variety, with VCR, cable TV, telephone, small refrigerator, and balcony. And they're clean and well maintained. The best accommodations are the three new **apartments** which sleep four to six people and have fully equipped kitchens. Dogs are permitted in some ground-floor poolside units for $20 per pet, per day. On-site parking. Early July to early September $139–189; off-season $55–129; continental breakfast included.

LIGHTHOUSE

🐚✒ **Race Point Light** (508-487-9930; www.lighthousefoundation.org). Open late April to mid-October. After the Coast Guard decommissioned this light in 1972, it stood empty for more than 20 years before the nonprofit New England Lighthouse Foundation took over. Now that it's renovated, overnight stays are wonderful for families and groups. There is no electricity, but there is a propane-powered refrigerator and stove in the shared kitchen. Bring your own food. The keeper's house has three different-size bedrooms that share 1½ baths as well as a living room. It's glorious out here—with the Atlantic Great Beach on one side and Hatches Harbor, a tidal estuary with shallow warm water, on the other. First-time visitors tend only to come for 1 night, but those in the know come for 2 or 3. After making reservations (as soon as possible), you'll arrange a meeting point so that a volunteer can drive you out to the lighthouse. $135–155 double; each additional person $25.

CAMPGROUNDS

🐚✒🌑**Dune's Edge Campground** (508-487-9815), off Route 6. Open May through September. One hundred wooded lots, mostly for tents, on the edge of the dunes; $23–26 for two people tenting without electricity. Reservations recommended in summer and on holidays. No credit cards.

Coastal Acres Camping Court, Inc. (508-487-1700), West Vine Street Extension. Open April through October. Wooded sites on the western edge of town; $23 for two in a tent, $32 with hookups.

HOSTEL

The Outermost Hostel (508-487-4378), 28 Winslow Street. Register in cabin 4. Open mid-May to mid-October. Personally, I'd rather camp in the rain than stay here. Nonetheless, for the record, this independent hostel (not affiliated with the American Youth Hostel—AYH—system) has 30 well-worn bunks in five tiny cabins, each with a bath in need of upgrading. The hostel is in a quiet area near downtown, across from a soccer field and tennis courts. $15 per person nightly.

RENTAL HOUSES AND COTTAGES

❄ **The Point** (508-896-2797), 5–7 Point Street (West End). Tucked one block off Commercial Street at the virtual tip of town, this three-bedroom/three-bath second-floor condo features a quiet backyard and a little deck overlooking it. In the height of summer, you'd never know you were in hectic Provincetown. The completely renovated 19th-century house is a "floater," the nickname for former fishing cottages that once lined the bay beach and were floated via barge to town. On-Cape owners Cindy Rosenbaum and Rebecca Bruyn treat the house as a personal off-season retreat, so you can safely assume it's well outfitted. (Mattresses are firm and stemware fine; there is also a gas grill.) The U-shaped layout effectively segregates the eat-in kitchen and a living room from the bedrooms. Weekly mid-May through September $1,650–1,950; rates negotiable for 3-night weekends the rest of the year. In-season, sheets and towels are included; off-season, BYO. No pets; no credit cards.

In Town Reservations (508-487-1883; 1-800-677-8696), 4 Standish Street, represents hundreds of condos, houses, and apartments, rented on a Saturday-to-Saturday basis in-season. One-bedrooms start at $850 weekly, two-bedrooms at $2,000, and a few three-bedrooms at $3,500. In Town Reservations also acts as a free reservation service for guest houses, B&Bs, and motels in town.

Swan Associates Real Estate (508-487-2990), 374 Commercial Street, and **Pat Shultz Real Estate** (508-487-9550), 406 Commercial Street, have listings for weekly and longer stays in Provincetown. You might get lucky and find a two-bedroom waterfront for $1,100 weekly, but listings go up to $3,500 weekly. Also, if you wait until June to line up a rental, you'll probably still find something, but the pickings will be slim. Call on January 2 if you can.

CANINE ACCOMMODATIONS

✳🐾 **KC's Animal Resort** (508-487-7900), 79 Shank Painter Road. Since so few inns and guest houses accept pets, this kennel seemed an obvious idea to KC in late 1998. Bring your dog on vacation with you, take her to the beach and on bike rides, drop her off overnight, and then play together again after you've had breakfast the next day. Adjacent veterinary facilities.

WHERE TO EAT

The quality of Provincetown restaurants continues to impress me. In fact, it has the greatest concentration of fine restaurants of any town on the Cape. You'll have plenty of choices to suit your budget and taste buds. Instead of listing places in order of preference (as I usually do), listings are from east to west relative to Commercial Street. The opening and closing months listed here are only a guideline. Although many places are closed certain days of the week, I generally don't mention that because it's so changeable. Better for you to call ahead than rely on information that changes so quickly. If you have your heart set on a particular place, call ahead off-season, and make reservations when you can, especially in summer.

DINING OUT

✳🍽 **Ciro & Sal's** (508-487-6444), 4 Kiley Court at Commercial Street. Open for dinner. Opened as a coffeehouse and sandwich shop for artists in the early 1950s, today this is a popular northern Italian restaurant. Ciro and Sal are no longer involved, and the restaurant was sold to longtime cook Larry Luster, who is married to Cynthia Packard (of the painting family—see *Galleries*). The menu is extensive, with traditional signature dishes like veal Marsala and a nice infusion of specials like rack of veal with herbed risotto. You'll find lots of seafood, too. Upstairs, Ciro & Sal's has a nice **bar,** candlelight dining, and Italian opera music playing in the background. The ground-floor wine cellar is cozy, with brick and plaster walls and Chianti bottles hanging from the low rafters. Reservations recommended. Children's menu. Entrées $13–27; pasta dishes about $16.

🎗 **Lorraine's** (508-487-6074), 436 Commercial Street (at Banks Street). Open for dinner mid-April through October. This authentic Mexican hideaway serves upscale south-of-the-border alternatives like carnitas enchiladas, featuring the owner's third-generation recipe for pork tenderloin with mole sauce. Vegetarians will gravitate to Estelle's Enchiladas; and for seafood with a twist, try specials like blackened sea scallops ensalada and blackened tuna soft-shell tacos. The menu tops out with paella. There is a great margarita **bar** open until 12:30 AM. Entrées $15.50–25.

❋♿🎗**Mews Restaurant and Cafe** (508-487-1500), 429 Commercial Street (between Kiley and Lovetts Courts). Open for dinner nightly and Sunday brunch. When I asked our waiter what the restaurant was particularly known for, his response was immediate: "Fabulous food." After the meal it was easy to excuse his lack of humility: It's true. It is fabulous. Arguably Provincetown's most sophisticated and consistent restaurant, the beach-front Mews is always a pleasure and worth every penny. Downstairs is elegant and romantic, awash in peach tones and bleached woods. Longtime chef Laurence deFreitas offers a popular mixed seafood grill and dishes like peppercorn tuna with ginger horseradish mashed potatoes (sublime), a delicate but robust bouillabaisse, blackened Wellfleet scallops, and duck appetizers. Servers are very knowledgeable. Sauces are rich and delicious. The exceptionally smooth white chocolate crème brûlée—like butter—might be the best I've ever tasted. The more casual **upstairs café,** with the same great water views and "American Fusion" menu, also has fancy burgers, appetizers, salads, and pasta. It's a great place for a before-dinner drink or after-dinner dessert and coffee; the Mews stocks over 60 types of vodka, perhaps the largest selection in New England. There's also entertainment in summer. Reservations recommended. Dine before sunset to better appreciate the water view. Brunch $9–12; dinner entrées $18–26.

Chester (508-487-8200), 404 Commercial Street (between Dyer and Washington Streets). Open for dinner May through December. Housed in a Greek Revival sea captain's house with candlelit tables, banquettes, and local art warming the sophisticated rooms, Chester made an impressive debut in 1998. With a seasonal New American menu, Chester emphasizes fresh food prepared and presented simply and beautifully, and enhanced by complex sauces. Chef Michael McGrath's menu might include a light corn and tomato bisque or smoked mushroom tart (both excellent) and move to lobster with saffron, carrots, and couscous or black Angus sirloin. While some hearty diners might find the portions a tad small, they weren't for my appetite. Save room for tasty homemade ice cream or an assortment of farmhouse cheeses at dessert. The award-winning and intriguing wine list is very well chosen and moderately priced; there are wines by the glass as well as microbrews. Come early and have a Harrison margarita and "bar savories" at the small **bar.** Reservations suggested. Entrées $19–29.

The Bistro at the Commons (508-487-7800), 386 Commercial Street (between Law and Pearl Streets). Open for dinner April through December; for lunch daily late May through August. This eclectic place offers wood-fired pizzas, Mediterranean specialties, and entrées like root vegetable cake with smoked salmon, grilled halibut with black beans, and duck confit. (The menu changes frequently.) Chef Chach Briseno, who earned her stripes at Stars in San Francisco, also worked at Front Street before coming here in 1997. She fuses southwestern influences with Asian, Italian, and French bistro fare. I particularly like the sidewalk tables (warmed by heaters late into the season), but there is a covered second-floor deck and indoor dining, too. Lunch $7–15; dinner entrées $14–24.

Dancing Lobster Cafe (508-487-0900), 373 Commercial Street. Open for dinner May to mid-October. After chef-owner Nils "Pepe" Berg moved to this larger location in the late 1990s and started accepting reservations, things changed, perhaps chief among them the attitude of the service. As for the food, Pepe honed his considerable skills at his family's namesake restaurant, but he now uses olive oil to bring out delicate Tuscan and Mediterranean flavors. Simple, flavorful specialties include homemade pasta with lobster fra diavolo and scaloppine of veal. Entrées $16–32.

Edwige at Night (508-487-2008), 333 Commercial Street (at Freeman Street). Open for dinner mid-May to mid-October. With sophisticated cuisine that surpasses the lovely atmosphere, the Edwige is one of Provincetown's top places to dine. Although Edwige is a hopping breakfast place (see *Eating Out*), by night it's romantic, with subdued lighting and solicitous service. Chef Steven Frappolli's eclectic Thai and international menu—with an American flair—changes seasonally. If you're lucky you'll see a few of these dishes on the menu: fried rock shrimp cocktail served in a martini glass, Thai vegetable shrimp salad, risotto with littlenecks and fiddleheads, Maine crabcakes, and Chilean sea bass. The food and presentation are both fun, the staff colorful, and the creative salads loyal standbys. You can't go wrong here. Partner Rocco Carulli keeps the place humming. During the 2000 season, Edwige mixed a killer cosmopolitan, concocted from homemade vodkas. Entrées $18–24.

Napi's (508-487-1145), 7 Freeman Street at Bradford Street. Open for lunch September through May; dinner year-round. Chef-owners Helen and Napi Van Dereck built this unusual restaurant in 1973 and have filled it chockablock with local art, plants, stained glass, and lively objects to stir your imagination. The eclectic menu has an international flair: dishes made with Portuguese sausage (linguiça), organic salads, a large selection of vegetarian dishes, fresh fish, pasta dishes, and stir-fry. Health-conscious

Napi's also accommodates no-fat and low-salt diets. A favorite of local artists, townsfolk, and the "Old Guard," Napi's is even more lively off-season. For a quick bite, you can always get cold snacks and appetizers at the **bar.** Reservations recommended, essential in summer. Parking on the premises; children's menu; early specials. Dinner entrées $14–22.

🦪 **Front Street** (508-487-9715), 230 Commercial Street (between Gosnold and Masonic Streets). Open for dinner May through December. One of the Outer Cape's most consistent places, this bistro-style restaurant is located in the cozy brick cellar of a Victorian house. The convivial atmosphere is enhanced by candlelight, small tables placed close together, antique booths, and local artwork. Service is provided by unobtrusive, attentive, and longtime waitresses. Donna Aliperti, chef-owner since opening the restaurant in 1987, reigns over a kitchen serving much-lauded "Mediterranean-American fusion." The creative repertoire of Italian, French, and Continental dishes changes weekly, but might include selections as varied as rack of lamb, tea-smoked duck, and softshell crabs. Leave plenty of room for pastry chef Kathy Cotter's delicious finales. (Kathy is also the sous-chef.) Front Street wins *Wine Spectator* awards for excellence. A full Italian-only menu is also served off-season. The small, popular **bar** is open until 1 AM. Reservations highly recommended. Entrées $13–23.

🦪 **Grand Central** (508-487-7599), 5 Masonic Place. Open for dinner mid-May through October. Across from the Atlantic House, this intimate, ivy-covered bistro is easy to miss. But since 1995, executive chef Kevin Fletcher has put together some very good meals: Tuscan-style penne pasta with artichoke hearts, eggplant, and roasted red peppers; steak frites or pan-roasted free-range chicken with pistachio sauce and roasted potatoes. There's a stylish but casual upstairs **wine bar,** too. Reservations suggested. Entrées $13–24.

♿🦪 **11 Carver** (508-487-2119), 11 Carver Street (at Bradford Street). Open for dinner April through December; take-away sandwiches for lunch April through October. For the money, this newly renovated airy bistro within the Gifford House is a very good bet. Chef-owner Kelly Weiss executes an eclectic and somewhat northern Italian menu: pasta with shrimp and vodka cream sauce, duck breast with green peppercorn sauce and mashed sweet potatoes, spicy tuna with watermelon relish and a coconut risotto cake. Or come for a few appetizers like grilled portobello mushrooms, steamed mussels, and crab- and lobster cakes. The menu changes seasonally. Entrées $15–22.

❄ **Martin House** (508-487-1327), 157 Commercial Street (at Atlantic Street). Open for dinner. Siblings Glen and Gary Martin preside over one of my favorite Cape restaurants. The circa-1750 whaling captain's house is rustic colonial through and through: exposed beams, wall sconces, stenciling, sloping dormers, fireplaces, low ceilings, wainscoting, and a series of small dining rooms. The cuisine, decidedly modern for the surroundings, is complemented by well-paced service. Chef Alex Mazzocca's internationally influenced dishes include innovative variations on game, black Angus beef, roast duck, and local seafood. Halibut is extremely popular. My most recent inspired meal centered on a melt-in-your-mouth tuna tartare followed by intensively prepared marinated and braised octopus. Oysters Claudia are particularly renowned and usually transcend the seasonal menu changes. Vegetarians, don't despair: You will not be slighted here. Save room for dessert, which almost overshadows the meal: We almost died over our caramelized banana and lime tart and summer peach and raspberry crumble. In summer, meals are also served in a lovely garden with harbor views. Reservations required. There's a small, convivial **bar,** too. Entrées $16–30.

✳ **Gallerani's Cafe** (508-487-4433), 133 Commercial Street (between Pleasant and Franklin Streets). Open for dinner (closed December). Barry Barnes's candlelit café opened in 1986 to rave reviews and continues to be packed by loyal and sophisticated patrons. With three walls of small-paned windows, the bistro-style dining room has always had a warm, neighborhood feel to it. It's a fun place with a friendly staff; you never know what's going to happen. Perhaps it will be a spur-of-the-moment dress-up night—pajama night, for example. Chef Ginny Palmer's menu encourages you to mix and match half orders of grilled meats, seafood, and pasta dishes. Specialties include chicken stuffed with roasted red peppers, mozzarella, and pear chutney, and almost anything off the grill. Sauces tend to be simple but very tasty. Reservations for parties of five or more. Full entrées $13–21.

🐾🍷♿**Sal's Place** (508-487-1279), 99 Commercial Street (at Cottage Street). Open for dinner early May through October; long weekends in spring and fall. Reserve a waterside table on the deck covered in grapevines, and enjoy southern Italian dishes as you listen to the waves lapping at the deck pilings. There's no better to way to spend a summer evening. One of the two indoor dining rooms is classic trattoria: Chianti bottles hang from the ceilings and red-and-white-checked cloths cover the tables. Two or three nightly specials like scampi Adriatico (grilled shrimp with squid in pesto) supplement classics like *melanzane alla parmigiana* and a 28-ounce *bistecca pizzaiola.* Service is very friendly but "relaxed," portions large, and the *tiramisu* heavenly, thanks to longtime chef-owners Lora and Jack Papetsas (Jack has presided over the kitchen since 1964). Children's portions; reservations recommended. Entrées $10–25.

🍷 **The Moors** (508-487-0840), Bradford Street Extension. Open for dinner mid-April through October. The Moors has been serving classic Portuguese dishes since 1940 (chef Ryan Roderick has been at the helm since 1975), and locals love it, particularly those from Wellfleet and Truro, as parking is easy. This is the place to try Portuguese kale soup, *lagosta Viera a moda de Peniche* (lobster and scallop casserole with an herb tomato sauce and wine and brandy), or their version of an old favorite: Scampi

Moors (with a cheese, garlic, and mustard flavor). For the less adventurous, there are lobsters and standard seafood entrées. The Moors is lively and rustic, with low ceilings, nautical flotsam and jetsam, and barnboard and driftwood walls. The candlelit dining room is so dark that the friendly waitstaff regularly offer flashlights to patrons reading the menu. The wine list is reasonably priced. Reservations suggested. Children's menu; early specials. Seasonal entertainment downstairs in the **bar**. Dinner $13–21.

EATING OUT

❄ **Fat Jack's** (508-487-4822), 335 Commercial Street (at Freeman Street). Open for lunch and dinner year-round, except closed in December. This tavernlike, storefront eatery is casual and local, particularly well suited to the colder off-season months. Fat Jack's serves burgers, fish-and-chips, sandwiches, and grazing foods like guacamole and potato skins. Lunch $5–10, dinner entrées $10–20.

🏵 **Cafe Edwige** (508-487-2008), 333 Commercial Street (at Freeman Street). Open for breakfast from early May to late October; dinner also served (see *Dining Out*). If you don't get here in the morning by 9:30 or so, expect a short wait; loyal locals know a good thing when they find it. Proprietor Nancyann has worked at this institution since 1974, dishing up frittatas, excellent specialty omelets (perhaps with Boursin and asparagus), fruit pancakes, homemade granola, spicy homefries, broiled flounder and eggs, and a tofu casserole. High-backed booths and small tables fill the lofty second-floor space, bright with skylights and local art. Good strong cappuccino and great signature poppyseed cream Danish. Dishes $5.50–8.50.

✎ **Lobster Pot** (508-487-0842), 321 Commercial Street (between Freeman and Standish Streets). Open daily for lunch and dinner February through November. This venerable waterfront institution has been under the same ownership—Joy McNulty's—since 1979. Over the years, the Lobster Pot's neon red lobster sign has been a symbol of Provincetown. Although the restaurant feels touristy and the service can be hurried, the menu features a wide selection of fresh seafood, shore dinners, and truly great clam chowder. Look for the red neon and then head down the long corridor, past the kitchens, and up the stairs. Lunch $7–13, dinner $13–19, children's dinner specials $8.

❄ **Post Office Café** (508-487-3892), 303 Commercial Street (between Standish and Ryder Streets). Open daily for breakfast, lunch, and dinner (closed mid-January to mid-February). This casual eatery serves less expensive sandwiches, salads, seafood platters, and lots of fried appetizers. Although the menu is a bit disappointing for a year-round establishment, the drag queens who haunt it are fun. Breakfast $4–8; dinner dishes $6–14.

Euro Cafe and Island Grill (508-487-2505), 258 Commercial Street (between Ryder and Gosnold Streets). Open for lunch and dinner, mid-

May through September. For me, the raison d'être is second-floor out-door tables overlooking the street parade. By the looks of the **bar,** though, you'd be hard pressed to believe Euro Cafe serves anything besides tropical drinks. But it does: sandwiches, light entrées, and a New England clambake. A limited menu until 1 AM satisfies late-night munchies. Lunch $7–17.50; dinner entrées $14–25.

🍲 **Cafe Heaven** (508-487-9639), 199 Commercial Street (at Carver Street). Open for breakfast and lunch April through January; dinner June to early September. This excellent storefront eatery with high ceilings is always lively, but sometimes it just feels noisy and cramped. (Look in the window and see for yourself what it's like at the moment.) Deservedly popular for all-day breakfasts, Heaven's specialties include fluffy create-your-own omelets, sweet cornmeal scones, fluffy banana pancakes, garlicky homefries, and excellent granola. An extensive lunchtime selection of cold salads and sandwiches reigns midday, while dinner offers create-your-own pasta dishes: Choose a pasta, maybe penne, then pair it with a sauce and add a topping like zucchini. There are ambitious blackboard specials, too. All dishes are moderately priced, making this a value-oriented place. Homemade desserts, too. Friendly service. Breakfast and lunch $5–8, dinner $10–18. No credit cards.

❋🍲 **Ross' Grill** (508-487-8878), 237 Commercial Street, within Whaler's Wharf. Open lunch and dinner. Overlooking the harbor from a second-floor vantage point, this casual American grill is a happening place, with good music, a structural steel ceiling, and an open kitchen. The menu is simple but very good: perhaps the best burgers in town, pad Thai, jambalaya (the chef-owner is half Cajun), and steak frite with homemade fries. There's also an impressive list of 40 wines by the glass and a dozen international beers. Raw bar, too. Lunch $8–13, dinner entrées kept under $20.

🖉♿ **Bubala's By The Bay** (508-487-0773), 183 Commercial Street (at Court Street). Open for all three meals May through October. Bubala's draws in people because of its streetside tables and indoor bayside views. Breakfast omelets are popular; lunch leans toward burgers (great) and focaccia sandwiches (messy); and dinnertime dishes include spicy fishcakes and baked Cuban cod. Children's menu; **piano bar.** Lunch $7–12; dinner $11–22.

🖉 **Tip For Tops'n Restaurant** (508-487-1811), 31 Bradford Street (at Pleasant Street). Open for all three meals, mid-March to mid-November. Owned by the Carreiros since 1967, this family-style restaurant offers good, simple food at good prices, away from the madding Commercial Street crowds. The name, by the way, is shorthand for "the tip of the Cape for tops in service." Breakfast specials ($5) are served until 3 PM. There are plenty of seafood and Portuguese specialties for lunch and dinner, as well as a few sandwiches ($5) and a children's menu. Early specials ($11); parking on the premises. Dinner $10–16.

🖉 **Silva's Seafood Connection** (508-487-1574), 175 Bradford Street Extension (at West Vine Street). Open daily for lunch and dinner May to mid-October. Housed in a former Dairy Queen, this fry house serves up barely floured and lightly fried seafood platters, lobster rolls, chicken fingers, and scallop dinners ($5–15).

TAKEOUT

Express Deliveries (508-487-4300). Open nightly July to mid-October. For all you house-renters who don't want to leave the comfort of your home, for a charge of $5 ($7 to North Truro), these folks deliver meals from local restaurants. Look for their menu book, which has 15–20 restaurants to choose from—many of the above restaurants participate. They also deliver videos and liquor.

🦃✒ **Mojo's** (508-487-3140), Ryder Street, next to the MacMillan Wharf parking lot. Open daily 11–11 early May to mid-October. Locals and visitors love this clam shack/fry joint, with good reason. There are two important distinctions between it and others of its genre: The selection of dishes is extensive and the fried foods are light and fresh. Try almost anything and you'll not be disappointed: fried mushrooms, baskets of fried shrimp or fish, chicken tenders, subs, french fries, burgers, Mexican dishes, salads, and vegetarian sandwiches. Take your enormous portions to the beach, pier, or, if you're lucky, to one of a few outdoor tables. $3–13.

🦃✒ **Café Crudité** (508-487-6237), 336 Commercial Street (at Center Street). Open for lunch May through October and for dinner in summer. An extensive variety of international vegan and vegetarian dishes plus traditional Japanese macrobiotic fare top the menu of this predominantly take-out place. The veggie burger, which boasts 28 ingredients, comes as a sandwich by day and is dressed up with rice and veggies at dinner. The deck above Commercial Street offers a bird's-eye view of the street scene. Children's menu. Lunch $7–10, dinner under $10.

🦃✒♿**Clem + Ursie's** (508-487-2333, 508-487-2536), 85 Shank Painter Road. Open for lunch and dinner mid-April to late October. This multifaceted, postbeach hangout is dubbed the food ghetto, but if you're not careful you could drop a lot of cash here. In addition to steamed lobster while you wait (to take home or to eat at outdoor picnic tables), you can have fried seafood or raw items from the raw bar. There are lots of Formica tables between the retail and take-out areas. The retail portion (with an excellent bakery) sells fish, homemade seafood cakes, imported cheese, homemade bread, deli sandwiches, and pastries. This very casual roadside joint is always hopping, particularly on lobster nights (Wednesday and Thursday). The hefty barbecue offerings are classic and can feed more people than you'd expect. Children's meals.

Many listings under *Eating Out* have takeout; call to confirm.

CAFÉS AND COFFEE

Spiritus (508-487-2808), 190 Commercial Street (between Carver and Court Streets). Open daily noon–2 AM, April to mid-November (from 8 AM in summer). The place to see and be seen after midnight; it's quite a scene. Most patrons come for great thin-crust pizza, munching it down while socializing out front. But Spiritus also has excellent coffee, espresso shakes, freshly squeezed orange juice, baked goods on summer mornings, and ice cream all day long. There are wooden booths inside for rainy days. Take your coffee across the street to the picnic tables overlooking the bay.

❋ **Joe** (508-487-6656), 148A Commercial Street (between Atlantic and Conant Streets). Absolutely exceptional coffee that's consistently exceptional. (There's nothing worse—well, I'm exaggerating to make a point—than finding a great cup o' joe, only to return the next day and face disappointment.) This tiny shop was so packed the summer it opened in 1998 that it prompted one worker to comment, "It was so busy I thought I was selling drugs." The beans are roasted by two women at Indigo, a small place in the tiny western Massachusetts town of Florence. There are fine pastries, too. Joe has both ends of town covered: look for **Joe** in the East End at 353 Commercial Street (508-487-6868), open mid-April to late November.

& **Flying Cups & Saucers** (508-487-3780), 205 Commercial Street (between Carver and Masonic Streets). Open 8 AM– 9 PM daily May to mid-October. This take-out coffee and pastry bar serves some of the best cappuccino in town. (Seattle's Best is its supplier.) It also blends protein powder drinks and juice combos like Ginger Rogers (carrot, ginger, and apple). The cranberry muffins, lemon poppy muffins, and maple scones are tasty and homemade; low-fat creations are better than you might think. Take your coffee to the deck overlooking the harbor—preferably in the early morning when the town is still quiet.

&& **Café Blasé** (508-487-9465), 328 Commercial Street (between Freeman and Standish Streets). Open daily 9 AM–midnight, late May to mid-September. The food is surprisingly good at this prime people-watching spot, operated by Jeff, Carl, and Kristine Hart since 1990. I can heartily recommend a few dishes: crabmeat salad (with real crabmeat) on dense French bread; smoked turkey, Swiss, and roasted red peppers with oniony potato salad; Caesar salad with grilled tuna. You'll also find inexpensive breakfasts as well as pasta dishes, burgers, and garden burgers. Blue and pink umbrellas and large paper lanterns, all enclosed by a white picket fence and window boxes, set the café apart physically. Get a strong iced coffee (not watered down, like at some places), a streetside table, and stay for a while. Frozen drinks are deservedly popular. Children's menu. Lunch and dinner entrées $10–20.

SNACKS AND DELIS

Provincetown Portuguese Bakery (508-487-1803), 299 Commercial Street (between Standish and Ryder Streets). Open daily April through October. If you haven't tried Portuguese breads and pastries, this is the place to come (short of hopping on a plane to Lisbon): *pasteis de coco*, meat pies, *pasteis de nata* (a custard tart), and *tarte de Amendoa* (almond tart). In summer the ovens are baking 24 hours a day and the fried dough *(mallassadas)* flies out as fast as they can make it.

Pucci's Harborside (508-487-1964), 539 Commercial Street (between Hancock and Kendall Streets). Open mid-April to mid-October. If you find yourself in the East End suffering from hunger pangs and lusting for a water view, stop in here. The atmosphere is informal, bright, and simple, with an enclosed deck over the water and a harborfront bar. At night it's romantic enough to detract from the food. I really recommend only drinks (they make a good margarita) and snacks like Thai seafood salad, spare ribs, and Buffalo wings.

Georgie Porgie's Bagel Factory (508-487-1610), 100 Shank Painter Road, off Route 6. Open mid-March to mid-November. Porgie's makes its own New York–style, kettle-boiled bagels daily. Stop on your way in or out of town (by bike or car, because it's not on the beaten path) for a bagel sandwich made with Boar's Head deli meats.

❉ **Adams' Pharmacy** (508-487-0069), 254 Commercial Street (at Gosnold Street). Open daily. Provincetown's oldest business in continual operation was opened in 1875 by Dr. John Crocker, who was also the first publisher of the *Advocate* newspaper. Adams' still has an old-fashioned soda fountain dispensing coffee and soda.

The deli market is cornered in Provincetown. When you're in the middle of town, head to **Provincetown Cheese Market & Deli** (508-487-3032), 225 Commercial Street (at Masonic Street), purveyors of Starbucks coffee. The West End is catered to by the **Provincetown General Store** (508-487-0300), 147 Commercial Street. In addition to deli sandwiches and salads, they have home-cooked hot meals to take away. In the East End, you'll find **Angel Foods** (508-487-6666), 467 Commercial Street. Owned by the proprietors of the excellent Cafe Heaven, this upscale deli also has gourmet cooking fixings. Too bad they couldn't make a strong cup of cappy, though, on my most recent visit. **Nelson's Market & Deli** (508-487-4335), 43 Race Point Road, can set you up with picnic fixings for your bike ride in the dunes. All are open year-round, except Nelson's.

ENTERTAINMENT

❉ **Provincetown Reservation System** (508-487-2400; 1-800-648-0364; www.ptownres.com), 293 Commercial Street. Open daily (except Sunday off-season). A stone's throw from MacMillan Wharf, this bustling place sells tickets for most of Provincetown's dazzling entertainment scene. What's playing when and where is just a phone call away. Be prepared for theatrical experimentation, innovation, and over-the-top shows.

Provincetown Repertory Theatre (508-487-0600). The Rep was founded in 1995 and has performed to enthusiastic audiences in Town Hall, Pilgrim Monument, and the Provincetown Inn. At press time, the group was looking for a permanent home. Catch them if you can.

Provincetown Theatre Company (508-487-8673), 1 Commercial Street at the Provincetown Inn. New local playwrights and classic drama are featured by this group, founded in 1963 to further the goals of the early-20th-century Provincetown Players.

The Great Music Series (508-487-2400), Universalist Meetinghouse, 236 Commercial Street. The only unfortunate aspect of this absolutely fabulous series is that there aren't more concerts; call for current schedule.

See also the Schoolhouse Center for Art and Design under *Selective Shopping.*

⬆✳MOVIES

New Art Cinema (508-487-9222), 214 Commercial Street. Open mid-June to mid-September. New releases in two small theaters.

Movies at the Best Inn (508-487-1711), Route 6A at Snail Road. Year-round except January. Every night an ever-changing group of about 40 locals get together to watch a free movie and eat unlimited popcorn in the Whaler Lounge. Movies aren't first run, but they haven't made it to video yet, either.

See also Provincetown Tales under *To See.*

NIGHTLIFE

Provincetown's after-dark scene can get rather spicy. There's something for everyone: gay, straight, and in between. When the bars, clubs, and shows close at 1 AM, it seems like everybody ends up in front of the Provincetown Town Hall or Spiritus (see *Where to Eat—Cafés and Coffee*).

Antro (508-487-8800), 258 Commercial Street, upstairs at the Euro Cafe. Open mid-May to mid-September. A wide variety of shows, cabaret, and comedy.

The Boatslip Beach Club (508-487-1669), 161 Commercial Street (between Central and Atlantic Streets), which offers theme dances, is best known for its gay summertime Tea Dances (3:30–6:30 daily) on the poolside, waterfront deck. It's quite the scene for "serious posing." Open late May to mid-October. You can also rent pool chairs for $3 if you're not staying here, as long as you depart by tea time.

✳ **Atlantic House** (508-487-3821), 4 Masonic Place, more commonly referred to as the A-House, has three diverse bars: the so-called Macho Bar (a nationally known men's leather bar); the nautically decorated disco Dance Bar; and the Little Bar (more intimate, with a roaring fireplace in the off-season). No other 18th-century house sees such action. Open 365 days a year. There isn't a gay man in town who doesn't stop into the A-House in the off-season. Some credit the A-House with establishing Provincetown's "off-season" versus "closed for the season."

Pied Piper (508-487-1527), 193A Commercial Street (between Carver and Court Streets). Open May through October. Provincetown's waterfront women's bar hosts popular "after tea" tea dances beginning at 6:30; great

Provincetown dunes are off-limits to four-wheeling unless you take a ride with Art's Dune Tours.

DJs. In 1996, for the first time in Provincetown's collective memory, year-round women outnumbered year-round men.

Vixen (508-487-6424), 336 Commercial Street (between Freeman and Center Streets). Open April through January. This women's bar and dance club opened in 1995 in the newly rebuilt Pilgrim House; check the entertainment schedule for shows.

❄ **Crown & Anchor** (508-487-1430), 247 Commercial Street (between Gosnold and Masonic Streets), which suffered a devastating fire in 1998, has a new leather-and-Levi's bar, piano bar, pool tables, a disco and outdoor pool patio, popular drag shows, and cabaret acts. It draws a gay and mixed crowd. Check it out.

Post Office Cabaret (508-487-3892), 303 Commercial Street (between Standish and Ryder Streets). Open late May to mid-October. Although this long, narrow room has too many seats, it hosts big-name female impersonators like Jimmy Jones along with women comedians. Despite the space limitations, it's a great venue and a great asset.

❄ **Governor Bradford** (508-487-9618), 312 Commercial Street (at Standish Street). To get a different but equally "real" flavor of Provincetown, stop into this townie and straight tourist tavern for a game of chess or backgammon. From the game tables, you can watch people on the streets watching each other.

See also Mews Restaurant and Cafe, Front Street, and Lorraine's under *Dining Out;* Bubala's By The Bay under *Eating Out.*

SELECTIVE SHOPPING

Unlike other chapters, in which shops are arranged according to what type of merchandise they sell, I've listed them here from east to west along Commercial Street. Shops that are not on Commercial Street have been inserted in the text where you would naturally detour to them from Commercial.

Most shops are open mid-April through mid-October, although some galleries keep a shorter season (mid-June to mid-September). Many shops stay open until 11 PM in July and August, and a number of them offer sales in mid-October. Keep in mind that shops designated with "❄" ("open year-round") are usually open in winter on weekends only. Other shops that aren't "supposed" to be open year-round open without notice in winter, depending on the weather.

Provincetown Arts (508-487-3167), 650 Commercial Street, Provincetown 02567. This 150-page annual published in July is Provincetown's bible of visual arts, literature, and theater. Send $10 and they'll mail you one, or you look for it in town.

Galleries hold Friday openings staggered between 5 and 10 PM, so patrons may stroll the street, catching most of the receptions. Artists are often on hand to meet visitors. Most galleries change exhibits every 2 weeks.

For more art galleries, see Provincetown Art Association & Museum under *To See* and Fine Arts Work Center under *To Do—Special Programs.*

DNA Gallery (508-487-7700), 288 Bradford Street, above the Provincetown Tennis Club. Open mid-May to mid-October. DNA opened its spacious gallery in 1994 with innovative work focusing on Provincetown artists, contemporary photography, and art derived from photography. Work is generally forward and bold. In addition, DNA holds video screenings, poetry jams, and, on Sunday evening, a reading series.

East End Gallery (508-487-4745), 491 Commercial Street. Open late May to mid-November and on sunny days in winter. Director Bunny Pearlman has an eye for art; check out what she thinks is worth checking out.

The Schoolhouse Center for Art and Design (508-487-4800), 494 Commercial Street. Open daily, 11–11 in summer, about noon–8 in spring and fall. Located in a mid-19th-century Greek Revival schoolhouse, this new venture opened late in 1998 and has rehearsal and performance space as well as two galleries. The **Driskel Gallery** features photography and fine objects; the **Silas-Kenyon Gallery** showcases contemporary art. Pick up a schedule of exhibitions and events.

Berta Walker Gallery (508-487-6411), 208 Bradford Street (between Howland and Cook Streets). Open late May to late November; otherwise, "often by chance and always by appointment." Walker represents Provincetown-affiliated artists of the past, present, and future. An excellent gallery that would be at home in uptown Manhattan.

KIM GRANT

Commercial Street is lined with more than 20 galleries.

444 Shop (508-487-0444), 444 Commercial Street. Larry Riley's dear little shop carries antiques, vintages items, and collectibles.

William Scott Gallery (508-487-4040), 439 Commercial Street. Open May through December. This venue showcases contemporary work that draws viewers into specific times and places, perhaps with atmospheric pastels. The gallery represents preeminent regional artists like John Dowd and Will Klemm.

❄ **Harvey Dodd Gallery** (508-487-3329), 437 Commercial Street. Dodd has been painting and exhibiting his watercolors, pastels, and oils of Provincetown and other Cape Cod scenes since 1959. His gallery, opened in 1971, is the oldest in town.

❄ **Simie Maryles Gallery** (508-487-7878), 435 Commercial Street. Maryles's vibrant landscapes sold so well in local galleries that the artist decided to open her own shop.

Hilda Neily Gallery (508-487-6300), 432 Commercial Street. Open May through December. Neily's artistic vision of Cape Cod is inspired by the French impressionists, right down to the gilded frames.

CJG Projects (508-487-4479), 432 Commercial Street. Open May through December. Showcasing postwar American and Japanese artists, look to Cortland Jessup for cutting-edge painting, photographs, and sculpture. It's always interesting.

Rice/Polak Gallery (508-487-1052), 430 Commercial Street. Open May through December. Rice/Polak represents more than 100 contemporary artists working in painting, photography, assemblages, graphics, and sculpture. Biweekly exhibitions feature the work of four artists; art consulting, too. I always enjoy this gallery.

Albert Merola Gallery (508-487-4424), 424 Commercial Street. Open mid-April to mid-October. You'll find very fine contemporary art here, as well as notables like Milton Avery and Michael Mazure; it's always worth dropping in.

✻ **Packard Gallery** (508-487-4690), 418 Commercial Street. Gallery director Leslie Packard showcases paintings by her sister Cynthia and her mother, Anne. In fact there are five generations of Packards who have painted in Provincetown. Anne's grandfather was Max Bohm, an early member of the Provincetown Art Association. The gallery is housed in a former Christian Science church, which Anne's grandmother used to attend.

✻ **Giardelli/Antonelli Studio Showroom** (508-487-3016), 417 Commercial Street. Smart and sleek women's clothing by local designers and eye-catching silver jewelry. Don't be deterred by having to ring the buzzer to gain admittance.

Kudu (508-487-0546), 382 Commercial Street. Open mid-April to mid-October, weekends mid-October through December and in March. Two floors of international folk art, Oriental rugs and kilims, and tapestries and ceremonial baskets from major African tribes.

✺✻ **Kidstuff** (508-487-0714), 381 Commercial Street. Clothing for babies, toddlers, and preteens. The owners have another kids shop, **Littlebits** (508-487-3860), at 214 Commercial Street, which is open April through December.

✻ **Turning Point** (508-487-0642), 379 Commercial Street. Chic women's clothing and subtle accessories.

Silk and Feathers (508-487-2057), 377 Commercial Street. Open April through December. Stylish women's clothing and accessories, including cool sunglasses, eyeglass frames, and watches.

✻ **Womencrafts** (508-487-2501), 376 Commercial Street. In addition to books and music, this Provincetown institution features handcrafted items made by and for women.

Wampum Etc. (508-487-0408), 371B Commercial Street. On Pepe's Wharf, this creative gold and silver jewelry is made of colorful quahog (clam) shells.

✻ **Tiffany Lamp Studio** (508-487-1101), 371 Commercial Street. Watch artisan Stephen Donnelly design, produce, and restore fanciful glass lamps.

Northern Lights Hammock Shop (508-487-9376), 361C Commercial Street (on the water). Open March through December. Tired from traipsing up and down the strip? Sample a hammock—in rope, wood, and cotton.

✻ **Mad Hatter** (508-487-4063), 360 Commercial Street. If it fits on your head, you'll find it here. Don't even think of taking photos of yourself in the funny hats. If you try it, disregarding my advice and the numerous posted signs, you'll find out what I mean.

Small Pleasures (508-487-3712), 359 Commercial Street. Every shop has its niche: Here, it's antique jewelry and vintage accessories for men and women.

Song of Myself (508-487-5736; www.songofmyself.com), 349 Commercial Street. Open May through December. Brad Fowler's photographic studio is worth a visit regardless of whether you intend on having a portrait made. The walls are lined with his black-and-white work, showcasing the diversity and pride of town residents and visitors alike. In-studio portrait sitting $245, including one matted and framed print.

❄ **Shop Therapy** (508-487-9387), 346 Commercial Street. It's hard to miss this landmark, psychedelic-swathed building; note the headline atop the building: MONSTERS ATTACK P-TOWN. SHOP THERAPY BLAMED. Merchandise revolves around current alternative lifestyles and the retro look.

❄ **Land's End Marine Supply** (508-487-0784), 337 Commercial Street. It's amazing that this old-fashioned two-story hardware store has survived; beach chairs, umbrellas, coolers, and suntan lotion.

☂ **Puzzle Me This** (1-888-789-9537), 336 Commercial Street. Open April through December. If you're stuck with nothing to do on a rainy day, this shop's brainteasers and mind bogglers should help.

Sunburst Leather (508-487-4624), 331 Commercial Street. Fine leather jackets, bags, wallets, and custom sandals.

Town Camera Shop (508-487-9689), 301 Commercial Street. Overnight processing.

Bodybody Sole (508-487-9472), 301 Commercial Street. Comfortable and hip men's and women's shoes.

❄✍ **Cabot's Candy** (508-487-3550), 276 Commercial Street. The Cicero family has made its own saltwater taffy here since 1969—it's the only shop on the Lower or Outer Cape to do so. Flavors range from peanut butter to piña colada to beach plum.

✍ **Outer Cape Kites** (508-487-6133), Ryder Street Extension (on the beach). Open late April through October. There's no better place to fly a kite than the National Seashore dunes—no pesky telephone wires or tall trees.

❄ **Julie Heller Gallery** (508-487-2169), 2 Gosnold Street. In a little beachfront shack, Heller offers some work by luminaries who established this art colony, including Milton Avery, Ross Moffett, and Charles Hawthorne.

❄ **Provincetown Bookshop** (508-487-0964), 246 Commercial Street. A good selection of children's books, Cape titles, and cookbooks; established in 1932.

Whaler's Wharf, 237 Commercial Street. After having suffered a devastating fire that burned the former building to the ground, Whaler's Wharf is back and it's better than ever. This three-story open arcade is filled with artisans, shops, and a few restaurants. You're bound to find something interesting.

Pixie Dust (508-487-6600), 237 Commercial Street, at the end of Whaler's Wharf, is a veritable museum of American pop culture kitsch. Where else will you find a *Welcome Back Kotter* lunch box or an almost life-size Marie Osmond doll? Furniture, lamps, and vintage toys, too. Closed February.

❋ **Marine Specialties** (508-487-1730), 235 Commercial Street. One of the Cape's most unusual shops stocks an odd jumble of army-navy items in a warehouselike space: parachutes, wool blankets, candles, camel saddles, sand dollars, camping supplies, ships' salvage, and other random military surplus items. You'll undoubtedly walk out with some strange gewgaw you hadn't even thought of buying but you just couldn't pass up for the price.

✎ **Norma Glamp's Rubber Stamps** (508-487-1870), 212 Commercial Street. Open March through December. The name says it all—this shop has thousands of wacky (and not-so-wacky) rubber stamps, as well as an assortment of greeting cards and stationery supplies—on which to use your stamps.

Don't Panic! (508-487-1280), 200 Commercial Street. Open April to late October. Hardly a run-of-the-mill T-shirt shop; this place has attitude: part shocking, part silly, but always amusing.

❋ **WA** (508-487-6355), 184 Commercial Street. This Japanese-inspired oasis carries teapots, ceramics, incense, and fountains as well as offbeat specialty items such as wooden masks from Zaire and antique suitcases covered with Chinese calligraphy.

❋ **Impulse** (508-487-1154), 188 Commercial Street. This contemporary American crafts shop offers a large selection of kaleidoscopes, wind chimes, wood objets d'art, fragile and colorful glass creations, jewelry, and signed celebrity photos and letters.

Bravo! (508-487-4700), 170 Commercial Street. Open mid-May to mid-October. Casual and hip men's fashions.

❋ **Ruby's Fine Jewelry** (508-487-9522), 167 Commercial Street. Closed January. Co-owners Mary DeRocco and Ruby Druss's collection is an art gallery in its own right, featuring elegant and unique silver and gold designs for men and women. Particularly noteworthy are pieces that feature gorgeous Australian opals.

❋ **TJ Walton Gallery** (508-487-0170), 153 Commercial Street. Walton's large, bold canvases are a delight. She also promotes up-and-coming artists.

Tristan Gallery (508-487-3939), 148 Commercial Street. Abstract and impressionistic paintings; some photography.

Santo (508-487-7172), 145 Commercial Street. Open May through October. One of the first commercial establishments in the West End. Santo Garufi offers home furnishings, gifts, accessories, jewelry, and some photography.

Roots (508-487-8807), 142 Commercial Street. Beautiful accessories for the home: stained-glass lamps, kilims, handmade furniture (indoor and outdoor), ceramics, and frames. Another "branch" can be found in the East End at 368 Commercial Street (508-487-2500).

Provincetown Antique Market (508-487-1115), 131 Commercial Street.

Open late May through December. An engaging assortment of this and that: glass, toys, paper, books, tools, and ephemera.

SPECIAL EVENTS

In the off-season, there are dozens of special events on the weekends, geared toward single gay men, cross-dressers, lesbians, or whomever. If you want to be assured of a quieter off-season retreat, call the Chamber of commerce (see *Guidance*) for an up-to-the-minute listing of events.

Early March: **Year-Rounders Festival,** Provincetown Town Hall, 260 Commercial Street. It's not what you know but who you know at this party: dinner, talent show, dancing.

Mid-April: **Whale-watching** begins. Seasonal shops begin to reopen.

Mid- to late May: **Cape Cod Maritime Days** (508-862-0700). Coast Guard–operated lighthouses are open during this festival, including Race Point Light, Wood End, and Long Point. In addition to focusing on the area's lighthouses, the Cape-wide event celebrates the region's fishing heritage, maritime villages, and seafaring way of life.

Late May: **Memorial Day** weekend kicks off the summer season.

Early June: **A Night at the Chef's Table** (508-487-9445). An annual benefit for Provincetown's AIDS Support Group; $70-per-person donation includes a festive, multicourse gala dinner with champagne and wine at many of the town's finest restaurants. More than 70 restaurants from Falmouth to Provincetown participate.

Late June: **Portuguese Festival** and **Blessing of the Fleet,** MacMillan Wharf. This 4-day celebration was developed to coincide with the Blessing of the Fleet (the bishop blesses a parade of fishing boats decked out with flags and families aboard). The festival begins on the Thursday before the last Sunday of the month, when the blessing takes place. Festivities include a swing-band concert, kids' fishing derby, Portuguese menus at various restaurants, a food court and bazaar on Fisherman's Wharf, parade, competitions like lobster-pot pulls and codfish relays, and fireworks.

July 4: **Independence Day.** A spirited parade organized for and by the entire town and a spectacular fireworks display.

Mid-July: **Secret Garden Tour** (508-487-1750). An annual benefit for the Provincetown Art Association; quite popular.

Mid- to late August: **Fine Arts Work Center Annual Benefit Auction** (508-487-9960). Benefit for the nationally recognized fellowship program for artists and writers (see *Even More Things to Do—Special Programs*); since 1969. This is a big Art, with a capital A, event.

Mid- to late August: **Carnival Week** (508-487-2313; 1-800-637-8696). A weeklong gala sponsored by the Provincetown Business Guild (see *Guidance*), capped by a New Orleans Mardi Gras–style parade that's very gay and flashy.

Early September: **AIDS Support Group's Annual Silent Auction** (508-487-9445), at the Town Hall (see *To See*). It seems as if every artist in Provincetown donates work to this auction.

Mid-September: **Harbor Swim for Life** (508-487-3684), an amateur swim from Long Point to the Boatslip Beach Club to raise money for AIDS research. A "paddlers flotilla" escorts 250 swimmers across the bay so they can swim the 1¾ miles back to town. After the swim, the Crown & Anchor holds a "Mermaid Brunch," open to the public for $5 per person. The **Festival of Happiness,** which follows it, takes place on Herring Cove Beach (see *Green Space—Beaches*). In 2000, the event raised over $120,000.

Mid- to late September: **Art Festival,** a 10-day gala featuring gallery openings with artists and craftspeople, demonstrations, and open studios. Also, an ever-growing **consignment auction** of early Provincetown artists sponsored by the Provincetown Art Association & Museum (508-487-1750).

Mid-October: **Women's Week,** perhaps more aptly called Lesbian Week, features women artists and entertainers; there's always a nice political component to the week somewhere.

Mid- to late October: **Fantasia Fair.** This 7-day event brings a few cross-dressers, transgendered persons, transsexuals, and others to town.

Late October: **Halloween,** costume balls and contests; this is a big Provincetown event, as you might imagine. The children's parade ends at the Pilgrim Monument's (see *To See*) "Halloween Haunted Monument."

Early November: **Men's Single Weekend** (508-487-1800; 1-888-887-8696). Workshops, parties, and lots of other organized activities for single gay men.

Late November: **Craft Fairs,** at the Provincetown Art Association & Museum (508-487-1750; see *To See*). Intriguing work may be purchased directly from artists at over 60 booths. Another big fair is held at the Town Hall. The fairs kick off the holiday shopping season when lots of stores have sales.

Late November: **Lighting the Pilgrim Monument** (508-487-3424). Nearly 5,000 white lights (4 miles' worth) illuminate the monument (see *To See*) on Thanksgiving Eve and remain lit until early January.

Early December: **Holly Folly** (www.hollyfolly.com). A annual gay and lesbian festival featuring a concert by the Boston Gay Men's Chorus, seasonally decorated house tours, "The Snow Ball," street caroling, shopping galore (and package wrapping to benefit the AIDS Support Group and Helping Our Women), high tea fireside at the Martin House (see *Dining Out*), special holiday menus, and general gay merriment and revelry.

December 31: **First Night,** ringing in the New Year.

VI. MARTHA'S VINEYARD

Gay Head Cliffs (aka Clay Cliffs of Aquinnah)

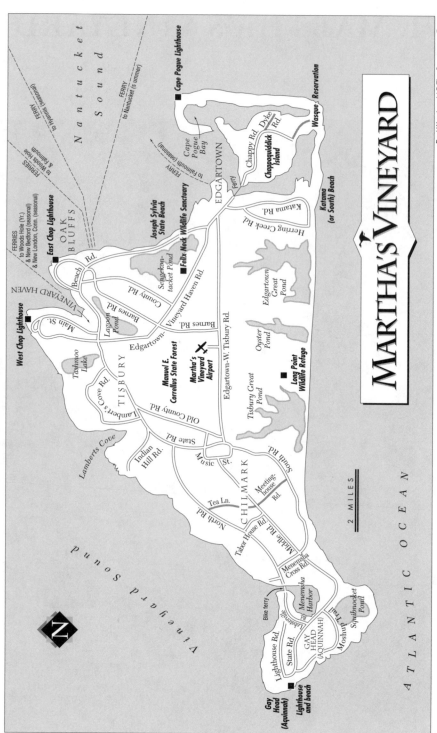

MARTHA'S VINEYARD

Paul Woodward / © The Countryman Press

Nantucket Sound

FERRY to Hyannis (seasonal)

FERRY to Nantucket (summer)

FERRY to Woods Hole & Falmouth (seasonal)

FERRIES to Woods Hole (Yr.) & New Bedford (seasonal) & New London, Conn. (seasonal)

Cape Pogue Lighthouse

Wasque Reservation

Cape Pogue Bay

FERRY to Falmouth (seasonal)

Chappy Rd.

Dyke Rd.

Chappaquiddick Island

Ferry

EDGARTOWN

Katama Rd.

Herring Creek Rd.

Katama (or South) Beach

Edgartown Great Pond

East Chop Lighthouse

OAK BLUFFS

Joseph Sylvia State Beach

Felix Neck Wildlife Sanctuary

Sengekontacket Pond

Beach Rd.

County Rd.

Barnes Rd.

Edgartown-Vineyard Haven Rd.

Vineyard Haven Rd.

Barnes Rd.

VINEYARD HAVEN

Main St.

West Chop Lighthouse

Lagoon Pond

Edgartown-W. Tisbury Rd.

Manuel E. Correllus State Forest

Martha's Vineyard Airport

Oyster Pond

Long Point Wildlife Refuge

Tashmoo Lake

Lambert's Cove Rd.

TISBURY

Old County Rd.

Tisbury Great Pond

Lambert's Cove

State Rd.

Indian Hill Rd.

Music St.

Meetinghouse Rd.

South Rd.

CHILMARK

Tea Ln.

North Rd.

Tabor House Rd.

Middle Rd.

Menemsha Cross Rd.

Vineyard Sound

Bike ferry

Menemsha Harbor

Lobsterville

Scrubnocket Pond

Moshup Trail

Lighthouse Rd.

State Rd.

GAY HEAD (AQUINNAH)

Gay Head (Aquinnah)

Lighthouse and beach

ATLANTIC OCEAN

2 MILES

N

Martha's Vineyard

Intrepid explorer Bartholomew Gosnold was the first European known to have visited Martha's Vineyard (in 1602), although Leif Eriksson may have done so earlier. Gosnold named the island for its bounty of wild grapes, but Martha's identity remains a mystery; she may have been Gosnold's daughter. The island was formally colonized in 1640, when a shipload of English settlers bound for Virginia ran short of supplies. They docked in Edgartown, found the native Wampanoag friendly, and decided to stay.

The settlers converted the Wampanoag to Christianity with startling success, perhaps aided by the imported diseases that were killing Wampanoag by the thousands. A century after Edgartown was founded, the island's Native population had dropped from 3,000 to about 300. During that time, Vineyarders learned (from the surviving Wampanoag) how to catch whales. They also farmed in Chilmark and fished from Edgartown and Vineyard Haven.

During the American Revolution, islanders suffered extreme deprivation after British soldiers sailed into Vineyard Haven Harbor and looted homes and ships. Among their plunder were some 10,000 head of sheep and cattle from island farms. The island didn't fully recover until the 1820s, when the whaling industry took off. The Vineyard enjoyed a heyday from 1820 until the Civil War, with hundreds of whaling vessels sailing in and out of Edgartown. Whaling captains took their enormous profits from whale oil and built large Federal and Greek Revival homes all over the island. Many still stand today as gracious inns, renowned restaurants, and private homes.

After the Civil War, with the whaling industry in decline, tourism became the Vineyard's principal source of income. By 1878 the Methodist Campground of Oak Bluffs had become a popular summer resort, with 12,000 people attending annual meetings. Over the next 30 years, other travelers discovered the island and returned summer after summer to enjoy its pleasant weather, relatively warm water, excellent fishing, and comfortable yet genteel lifestyle. By the turn of the 20th century, there were 2,000 hotels rooms in Oak Bluffs alone—there aren't that many B&B or inn rooms on the entire island today! Summertime traffic was so high that a rail line was built from the Oak

Bluffs ferry terminal to Katama. Daily ferry service ran from the New York Yacht Club to Gay Head (present-day Aquinnah).

Although the whaling industry rapidly declined, other sea-related businesses continued to reap healthy profits. In 1900, Vineyard Sound was one of the busiest sea lanes in the world, second only to the English Channel. Heavy sea traffic continued until the Cape Cod Canal was completed in 1914. Tourism picked up again in the early 1970s. And when President Clinton, Hillary, and Chelsea spent their 1994, 1995, 1997, and 1998 summer vacations here, they created a tidal wave of national and international interest in the island.

Today, the year-round population of 15,000 mushrooms in July and August to about 100,000. Grumpy year-round Vineyarders are fond of saying that the island sinks 3 inches when ferries unload their passengers.

The terms "up-island" and "down-island" are holdovers from the days when the island was populated by seafarers—as you travel west, you move up the scale of longitude. Up-island refers to the less developed, hilly western end, including West Tisbury, Chilmark, Menemsha, and Aquinnah. Edgartown, Oak Bluffs, and Vineyard Haven, which are the most developed towns, are all down-island.

Elegant Edgartown, called Uncle Edgar by some of the old-timers, is chock-full of grand white Greek Revival ship captains' houses, with fanlights and widow's walks. Many of these private homes are clustered on North and South Water Streets, while elsewhere downtown you'll find chic boutiques and shops, galleries, and restaurants.

Although it's less showy than Edgartown, Vineyard Haven maintains a year-round level of activity that Edgartown doesn't. It's the commercial center of the island, where "real" people live and work. The harbor is home to more wooden boats than any other harbor of its size in New England. For an experience straight out of the 19th century, stop in at Gannon and Benjamin Boatbuilders on Beach Road; it's one of the few remaining wooden-boat rebuilding shops in the country. Vineyard Haven is also where literary and journalistic personalities like Bill and Rose Styron, Art Buchwald, Mike Wallace, and Diane Sawyer and husband Mike Nichols vacation.

Oak Bluffs of the 21st century is at once charming, honky-tonk, and a magnet for prominent African Americans, including Spike Lee and Vernon Jordan. Wesleyan Grove began in 1835 as the site of the Methodist congregation's annual summer-camp meetings. The campers' small tents became family tents; then primitive, wooden, tentlike cottages; and finally, brightly painted cottages ornamented with fanciful trim. Cupolas, domes, spires, turrets, and gingerbread cutouts make for an architectural fantasyland. The whimsical, precious, and offbeat cottages are worlds away from Edgartown's traditional white houses. So are Oak Bluff's nightclubs and the baggy-pants-wearing, pierced youth.

West Tisbury is often called the Athens of the Vineyard because of

Rolling, open farmland typifies the up-island landscape.

its fine New England Congregational church, town hall, and Grange Hall. Music Street, where descendants of the island's 19th-century ship captains still live in large houses, was so named because many of these families used whaling profits to purchase pianos. Today's West Tisbury summer residents include *Washington Post* owner and Democratic Party stalwart Katharine Graham, cartoonist Jules Feiffer, and historian David McCullough.

Chilmark is a peaceful place of rolling hills and old stone fences that outline 200-year-old farms. You'll find dozens of working farms up-island, some still run by descendants of the island's original European settlers. Travel down North Road to Menemsha, a small (truly picturesque) village and working harbor that you may recognize as the location of the movie *Jaws*. The surrounding area is crisscrossed by miles and miles of unmarked, interconnected dirt roads, great for exploring. (Alas, many are private.) Until the mid-1980s, Chilmark was sparsely populated, to the tune of 800 or so year-rounders. Today, in order to limit growth, Chilmark issues the island's only 3-acre-minimum building permits. Chilmark has hosted such disparate personalities as *Life* photographer Alfred Eisenstaedt and John Belushi. (Belushi is buried on-island; "Eise's" photos are found in galleries and at his beloved retreat, the Menemsha Inn and Cottages.) Harvard Law School professor and O. J. Simpson attorney Alan Dershowitz is a denizen of Lucy Vincent Beach, one of the island's many residents-only beaches—and a nude one at that.

Aquinnah, a must-see destination, occupies the island's western tip. (If you haven't visited the Vineyard for a while, you may know Aquinnah

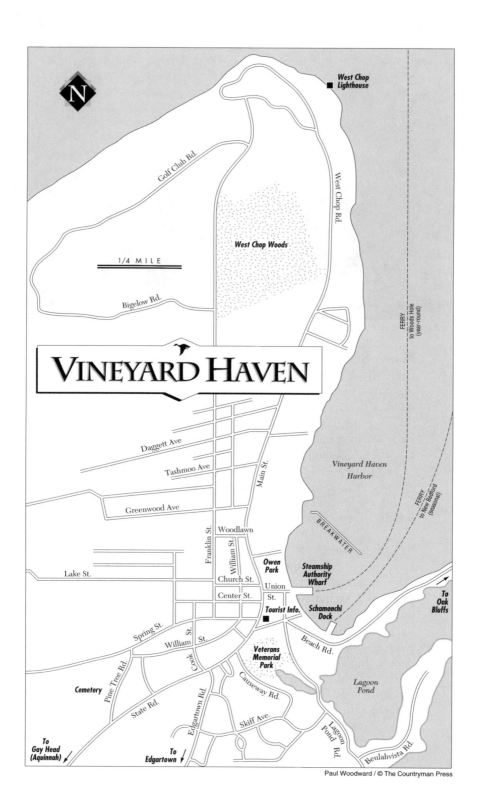

Paul Woodward / © The Countryman Press

as Gay Head. It was renamed Aquinnah, "land under the hill," in mid-1997 by a narrow 79–76 town vote.) Of the 700 members listed on the Wampanoag Indian tribal rolls, approximately 300 still reside on the Vineyard, half in Aquinnah. Tribal legend holds that the giant Moshup created the Vineyard, taught the Wampanoag how to fish and catch whales, and remains a protector. The Wampanoag own the brilliantly colored bluffs and the face of the Clay Cliffs of Aquinnah.

Martha's Vineyard has always attracted celebrity summer visitors. But in recent years many who visited decided they needed to own a piece of it. Beginning in the late 1980s and continuing to this day, a tremendous building boom has changed the face of the Vineyard. While the Vineyard had been a place where the well heeled and well off came to escape notice, today it is as much a retreat where celebrities and power brokers come to see and be seen. Although residents are generally unfazed by their celebrity neighbors—movie stars, authors, journalists, musicians, financial moguls, and a president—many locals and longtime visitors agree that the Vineyard is no longer the quaint, tranquil island it was prior to the mid-1980s.

Martha's Vineyard is unlike most of the rest of America; people tend to get along pretty well with one another. They work hard to maintain a sense of tolerance and community spirit. Most lengthy debates center on land use and preservation rather than on race or religion. Everyone relies, to some extent, on the hectic summer season that brings in most of the island's annual income, though residents do breathe a sigh of relief when the crowds depart after mid-October.

From January to March, the Vineyard is a more sobering place; unemployment can be as high as 16 percent in the off-season. The island is swarming with visitors in July and August. To experience the Vineyard at its best and still have a dependable chance for good weather, plan your visit from May to mid-June or from mid-September to mid-October.

GUIDANCE

❊ **Chamber of Commerce** (508-693-0085; mvcc@vineyard.net; www.mvy.com), Beach Road, P.O. Box 1698, Vineyard Haven 02568. Open 9–5 weekdays year-round, 10–2 Saturday at least from June through December and possibly year-round, 10–2 Sunday mid-June to mid-October. Here you'll find booklets, brochures, maps, and other valuable information.

Information booth (no phone), Steamship Authority terminal, Vineyard Haven. Open Friday through Sunday mid- to late June and early September to mid-October, daily July to early September.

Information booth (508-693-4266), Circuit Avenue at Lake Avenue in Oak Bluffs. This town-sponsored booth is open daily 9–5 from mid-May to mid-October. It's adjacent to the Flying Horses Carousel (see *To See*).

Edgartown Information Center (no phone), Church Street, Edgartown.

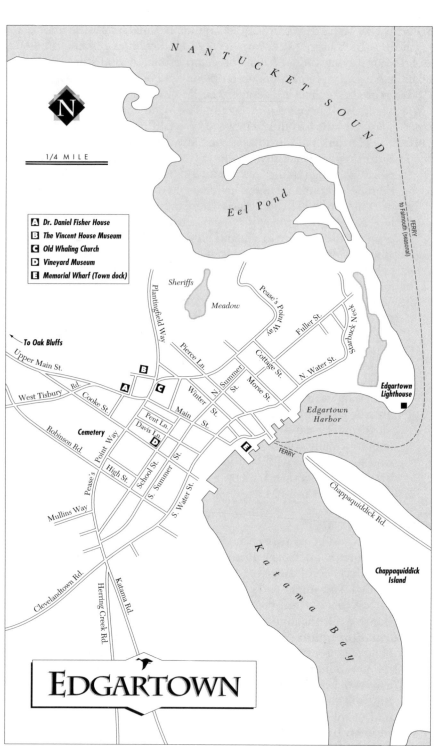

N

1/4 MILE

A Dr. Daniel Fisher House
B The Vincent House Museum
C Old Whaling Church
D Vineyard Museum
E Memorial Wharf (Town dock)

NANTUCKET SOUND

Eel Pond

FERRY
to Falmouth (seasonal)

Sheriffs
Meadow

Plantingfield Way

Pease's Point Way

Fuller St.

Starbuck Neck

Pierce Ln.

Cottage St.

N. Water St.

To Oak Bluffs

Upper Main St.

B

Winter St.

N. Summer St.

Morse St.

Edgartown
Lighthouse

West Tisbury Rd.

Cooke St.

A

C

Main St.

St.

Edgartown
Harbor

Robinson Rd.

Cemetery

Pent Ln.
Davis Ln.

D

Pease's Point Way

High St.

School St.

S. Summer St.

E

FERRY

Mullins Way

S. Water St.

Chappaquiddick Rd.

Clevelandtown Rd.

Herring Creek Rd.

Katama Rd.

Katama Bay

Chappaquiddick
Island

EDGARTOWN

Open year-round. Around the corner from the Old Whaling Church (see *To See*), this minor, town-sponsored center has brochures, souvenirs, rest rooms, postcards, and a post office, and also serves as a shuttle-bus stop (see Getting Around).

ISLAND WEB SITES
www.mvweb.com (an islandwide site)
www.mvgazette.com (the *Vineyard Gazette* newspaper)
www.mvy.com (chamber of commerce)

PUBLIC LIBRARIES
☞🌂❄Most of these libraries have story times; call ahead for opening hours and schedule vagaries: **Aquinnah** (508-645-2314), State Road at Church Street; **Chilmark** (508-645-3360), Chilmark Center; **Edgartown** (508-627-4221), 58 North Water Street; **Oak Bluffs** (508-693-9433), Circuit Avenue at Pennacook Avenue; **Vineyard Haven** (508-696-4210), 200 Main Street; **West Tisbury** (508-693-3366), 1042A State Road.
See also the Martha's Vineyard Historical Society under *To See*.

PUBLIC REST ROOMS AND LAUNDROMAT
Public rest rooms in Vineyard Haven are located at the top of the A&P parking lot and within the Steamship Authority terminal (year-round) off Water Street. In Oak Bluffs they are next to the Steamship Authority terminal on Seaview Avenue (and often atrociously maintained, I might add); on Kennebec Avenue, one block from Circuit Avenue; and next to Our Market on Oak Bluffs Harbor. In Edgartown, they're at the visitors center (year-round) on Church Street. Facilities are also located near the parking lot for the Clay Cliffs of Aquinnah, and at Dutcher's Dock in Menemsha Harbor. In West Tisbury, rest rooms are in Grange Hall next to the Town Hall.

❄ **Airport Laundromat** (508-693-5005), off the Edgartown–West Tisbury Road.

GETTING THERE
❄ *By boat from Woods Hole:* **The Steamship Authority** (508-477-8600 or 508-693-9130 for advance auto reservations; 508-548-3788 for day-of-sailing information from Woods Hole; 508-477-7447 for last-minute day-of-sailing reservations in summer, but don't count on getting lucky; www.islandferry.com), Railroad Avenue, Woods Hole. The Steamship is the only company that provides daily, year-round transport—for people and autos—to Vineyard Haven and Oak Bluffs. The Vineyard is 7 miles from Woods Hole, and the trip takes 45 minutes. About 15 boats ply the waters daily year-round. In 1998, the Steamship carried more than 1.8 million people and 300,000 cars to the Vineyard.

The Steamship begins taking auto reservations by mail and web on February 1. Prior to that, mail your requests with payment to: Reservation Bureau, 509 Falmouth Road, Suite 1C, Mashpee 02649. The Steamship processes tens of thousands of reservations per week in the early part of the year; get your request in as close to February 1 as you

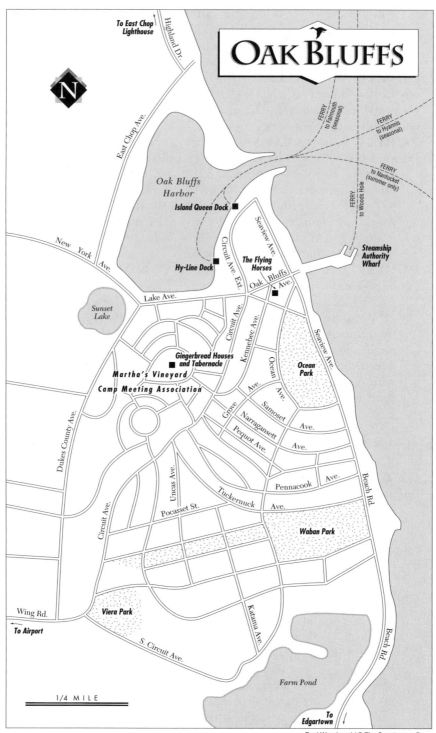

To East Chop
Lighthouse

Highland Dr.

Oak Bluffs

N

FERRY
to Falmouth
(seasonal)

FERRY
to Hyannis
(seasonal)

FERRY
to Nantucket
(summer only)

FERRY
to Woods Hole

East Chop Ave.

*Oak Bluffs
Harbor*

Island Queen Dock ■

Seaview Ave.

Steamship
Authority
Wharf

New York Ave.

Hy-Line Dock ■

The Flying
Horses

Circuit Ave. Ext.

Oak Bluffs Ave.

Lake Ave.

*Sunset
Lake*

Circuit Ave.

Kennebec Ave.

Seaview Ave.

Gingerbread Houses
and Tabernacle ■

Ocean Ave.

*Ocean
Park*

Martha's Vineyard
Camp Meeting Association

Grove Ave.

Samoset Ave.

Dukes County Ave.

Narragansett Ave.

Pequot Ave.

Ave.

Uncas Ave.

Pennacook Ave.

Beach Rd.

Circuit Ave.

Pocasset St.

Tuckernuck Ave.

Waban Park

Wing Rd.

Viera Park

To Airport

S. Circuit Ave.

Katama Ave.

Farm Pond

Beach Rd.

To
Edgartown

1/4 MILE

can. Auto reservations are mandatory on weekends (Friday through Monday) between mid-May and early September. Otherwise, the Steamship has a "guaranteed standby policy" that states if your car is queued up by 2 PM on Tuesday, Wednesday, or Thursday in summer, you are assured of passage that day.

There are lockers at the Steamship terminal for storing luggage.

Round-trip tickets from mid-May to mid-October are: adults $10; children 5–12, $5; bicycles $6; autos $104. In the off-season, auto prices drop to $42–56. If you are not taking your car, the Steamship Authority provides free, frequent buses between the parking lots and the ferry dock. Each bus has a bike rack that holds two bikes. Parking is about $10 per calendar day.

By boat from Falmouth: **Island Queen** (508-548-4800; www.island queen.com), Falmouth Heights Road, Falmouth. This passengers-only service operates late May to mid-October and takes about 35 minutes; departures from Falmouth Inner Harbor to Oak Bluffs. The *Island Queen* is smaller and more comfortable than the Steamship Authority's boat, which also handles freight and delivery trucks. There is plenty of parking near the *Island Queen*'s dock ($10–12 per calendar day). Round-trip fares are adults $10; children age 3–12, $5; bicycles $6.

Falmouth–Edgartown Ferry (508-548-9400), 278 Scranton Avenue, Falmouth. From late May to mid-October, this service plies the waters three times a day between Falmouth and Edgartown. Round trip: adults $24; children 5–12, $18; bicycles $6. Parking is $12 per calendar day.

By boat from Hyannis: **Hy-Line Cruises** (508-778-2600; www. hy-linecruises.com), Ocean Street Dock, Hyannis. Passenger boats to and from Oak Bluffs from May to late October. The trip takes approximately 1¾ hours. In May there is one morning boat per day on weekends. From late May to early June, there are three round trips a day; from early June to mid-September, there are four. If you haven't purchased advance tickets, it's wise to arrive an hour early in July and August. From mid-September through October, the schedule drops back to one trip daily. Round-trip tickets: adults $26, children $13, and bicycles $10.

By boat from New Bedford: **Martha's Vineyard Ferry Schamonchi** (508-997-1688; www.mvferry.com) operates passenger boats to and from Vineyard Haven, mid-May to mid-October. The trip takes about 1½ hours. From mid-May through mid-June and early September to mid-October, there is only one boat per day, at 9 AM. But on weekends during these periods and daily from mid-June to early September, there are three boats. Round-trip fares: adults $19 ($17 same day), children $11 ($8 same day), and bicycles $5. Parking is $8 per calendar day. For visitors coming from the south, New Bedford is a more convenient departure point than Woods Hole. Even those driving from points north may wish to consider taking the New Bedford ferry to avoid bridge

The ferry On-Time *makes the 100-yard dash between Chappaquiddick and Edgartown harbor.*

traffic. From I-195, take exit 15 (Route 18 south) to the third set of lights, turn left, and follow signs to ferry parking.

By boat from New London, Connecticut, and Glen Cove, Long Island, New York: **Fox Navigation** (860-437-6928; 1-888-724-5369; www.fox navigation.com) operates between Long Island and New London and Martha's Vineyard. There are one or two boats that depart Friday through Monday, late May to mid-October. The 2¼-hour trip via high-speed catamaran takes passengers only and saves hordes of time, not to mention traffic headaches. Inquire about the exact departure times. Tickets for New London to Vineyard Haven: Admiral class, offering a higher view and better seats, costs $89 round-trip adults ($44.50 children 5–17). Clipper class, on the enclosed main level, costs $59 adults ($29.50 children). Inquire about ticket prices from Long Island.

By boat from Nantucket: **Hy-Line Cruises** (508-778-2600 in Hyannis; 508-693-0112 in Oak Bluffs; 508-228-3949 on Nantucket; www. hy-linecruises.com) offers inter-island service between Oak Bluffs and Nantucket from early June to mid-September. The trip takes 2¼ hours; three boats make the trip daily. One-way fare: adults $13.50; children age 5–12, $6.75; and bicycles $5.

See also Patriot Party Boats under *Boat Excursions* in "Falmouth and Woods Hole."

By bus: **Bonanza Bus Lines** (1-800-556-3815; www.bonanzabus.com) provides daily year-round service to Woods Hole from Boston, New York, Hartford, and Providence. Buses are scheduled to meet ferries, but ferries won't wait for a late bus.

By air: With a booming increase in jet-setting visitors, it's no wonder a new terminal was built in 1999. Cape Air (1-800-352-0714; www.flycapeair.com) flies to the Vineyard from Boston, Hyannis, Providence, Nantucket, and New Bedford. **Cape Air** has joint ticketing and baggage handling between its flights and most major airlines. It also offers charter services. **USAirways Express** (1-800-428-4322) offers year-round service to and from New York City and Washington, D.C.

Continental Express (1-800-525-0280) has seasonal service between the Vineyard and Newark, New Jersey.

GETTING AROUND

By car: The infamous Five Corners is the trickiest and most dangerous intersection on the island. It's also the first thing you'll encounter as you disembark from the Vineyard Haven ferry terminal. If you're going to Oak Bluffs, Katama, Edgartown, and Chappaquiddick, take the left lane. For West Tisbury, North Tisbury, Lambert's Cove, Menemsha, Chilmark, and Aquinnah, enter the right lane and turn right. A few sample distances: Vineyard Haven to Oak Bluffs, 3 miles; Vineyard Haven to Edgartown, 8 miles; Oak Bluffs to Edgartown, 6 miles; Vineyard Haven to Aquinnah, 18 miles.

Unfortunately, summertime traffic jams are commonplace in down-island towns. Try to park outside of town and take shuttles into town (see below). If you commute into Boston via the Southeast Expressway, why would you want to stop and crawl in a picturesque village on a vacation day?

In-season, expect to pay about $80 daily for the least expensive rental car; $110–160 for a van; $150 for four-wheel drive; and about $45 for a moped. In the off-season, rental companies go as low as $50 daily for a car. Although mopeds are convenient, if Vineyarders had their way, they would be banned. Visitors have too many accidents with them, and they're noisy. Ride with great caution; roads are winding, narrow, and busy in summer.

Car rental companies include **Budget Rent-a-Car** (508-693-1911; 1-800-527-0700), 45 Beach Road, Vineyard Haven; Circuit Avenue Extension (at the ferry dock), Oak Bluffs; 257 Edgartown Road, Edgartown; and Martha's Vineyard Airport. I've always found **Thrifty** (508-693-1959), Five Corners, Vineyard Haven, particularly helpful. **Consumer Rent-a-Car** (508-696-6636) has locations in Vineyard Haven near the ferry, in Edgartown, and at the airport. **All-Island Rent-a-Car** (508-693-6868) is located at the airport. Take the shuttle if you're already in town. For a splurge call **Vineyard Classic Cars** (508-693-5551) in Oak Bluffs and Vineyard Haven. By the way, gas is usually cheapest at the airport.

By moped: If most Vineyarders and emergency room doctors had their way, mopeds would be banned. Once you've seen the face, arms, and legs of a fellow explorer skinned, you'll know why. Sand and mopeds and speed do not mix. Take a look at the mopeds you might be renting; many of their plastic hulls have chunks ripped out from accidents. Having said that and not wanting to seem paternalistic, here goes: Many rental agencies are located near the ferry terminals in Oak Bluffs and Vineyard Haven. **Adventure & Thrifty Rentals** (508-693-1959), in Vineyard Haven, and **Vineyard Bike & Moped** (508-693-4498), in Oak Bluffs, both have mopeds.

By shuttle: **Martha's Vineyard Transit Authority** (VTA) (508-627-7448 recorded information; 508-627-9663; www.vineyardtransit.com) operates an excellent system of white buses. There are 10 different buses traveling between Vineyard Haven, Oak Bluffs, Edgartown, West Tisbury, Chilmark, Menemsha, and Aquinnah year-round. Buses seem to stop everywhere you want to go; you can also flag them down. They even have bike racks. Get a copy of the very helpful VTA map with stops and routes clearly listed. Carry it with you wherever you go. One day passes cost $5, 3 days $10, 7 days $15. Single tickets cost 50¢ per town (if you go from Vineyard Haven to Edgartown, for instance, it costs $1.50 because you have to go through Oak Bluffs).

Edgartown Trolley (508-627-7448 recorded information; 508-627-9663). VTA has an alternative to wrangling for a parking place in Edgartown's car-choked streets. Leave your car at The Triangle (at the corner of Edgartown–Vineyard Haven Road and Oak Bluffs Road) or across from the Edgartown Elementary School (corner of West Tisbury Road and Robinson Road) and ride the shuttle. Parking is free, but the trolley costs 50¢.

Tisbury Park 'n Ride (508-627-7448 recorded information; 508-627-9663), State Road Depot next to Island Cove Mini-Golf. Avoid the parking nightmare in Vineyard Haven and let the VTA shuttle drop you off downtown. The frequent trolleys run from mid-May to mid-October and cost 50¢. Parking is free.

South Beach Trolley (508-627-7448 recorded information; 508-627-9663). Mid-June to early September. The trolley ($1.50) runs from the information building near the corner of Church and Main Streets in Edgartown to three points at South Beach daily.

By bus tour: **Gay Head Sightseeing** (508-693-1555) and M.V. Sightseeing (508-627-8687) are operated by the same company (www.mvtour.com) and offer tours from early May to late October. Buses are clearly marked (they're painted green, pink, and white), and they meet ferries in Vineyard Haven and Oak Bluffs daily. Both tours are approximately 2½ hours. The Gay Head tour makes one stop—at the Clay Cliffs of Aquinnah—where there are small food stands, souvenir shops, public rest rooms, and a wonderful view of the cliffs and the ocean. The M.V. tour only goes to the down-island towns of Vineyard Haven, Oak Bluffs, and Edgartown, but it stops in Edgartown for 90 minutes. Adults $13.50, children $6.

By taxi tour: Most taxis conduct island tours for a price—$100–150 for an all-island trip, depending on the season. But you don't want to go with just anyone. I highly recommend **Jon's Taxi** (508-627-4677). Jon's assistant gives tours around the island for $30 per hour for two people or $40 per hour for four people. If you get lucky, you can arrange a full island tour with Jon himself. It will cost you a bit more, but it will be well worth it. Jon even throws in lunch at Larsen's for free.

    Adam Cab (508-627-4462; 1-800-281-4462) is also very good and offers tours twice daily from Edgartown at 10:30 and 2 from late May to early September. This 2½-hour tour covers the entire island for $20 per person. If you'd prefer to arrange your own itinerary, hire them for $35–50 per hour, depending on the number of people (up to seven).

🐚❋ *By foot:* **Ghosts, Gossip, and Downright Scandals** (508-627-8619) is conducted by very knowledgeable folks from **Vineyard History Tours.** These excellent walking trips depart at various times and from various points in Vineyard Haven, Edgartown, and Oak Bluffs. It's best to call ahead for the current schedule. They will basically take people on walks by appointment any time of the year, except perhaps during a nor'easter. Their special tour focusing on Edgartown's whaling days, "A-Whaling We Will Go," is also very good. All tours are $10 per person.

HERITAGE TRAILS

Aquinnah Cultural Trail (508-645-9265; www.wtgh.vineyard.net). For those interested in something other than beaches and shops, look for the excellent and informative map once you're on-island. It is full of delicious tidbits about the "first people of Noepe," place-name translations, Moshup legends, local government, and a schedule of events.

African-American Heritage Trail (508-693-4361). Tours on request late May to early September. The brainchild of a M.V. Regional High School history teacher and an NAACP archivist, this developing trail currently has 14 sites devoted to telling the story of the island's strong association with African Americans. Every town has sites, including abandoned graveyards; the home of Dorothy West, a wonderful Harlem Renaissance writer who lived on the island and died in 1999; and a decrepit "Gospel Tabernacle" that served as a community church in the late 19th century. Pamphlets are for sale in local bookstores.

MEDICAL EMERGENCY

Martha's Vineyard Hospital (508-693-4400), off Vineyard Haven–Oak Bluffs Road, Oak Bluffs.

Lyme disease. Ticks carry this disease, which has flu-like symptoms and may result in death if left untreated. Immediately and carefully remove any ticks that may have migrated from dune grasses to your body. Better yet, wear long pants, tuck pants into socks, and wear long-sleeved shirts whenever possible when hiking. Avoid hiking in grassy and overgrown areas of dense brush.

West Chop Lighthouse in Vineyard Haven

KIM GRANT

TO SEE

In Vineyard Haven

Compass Bank (508-696-4400), Main Street. Open weekdays. This distinctive 1905 fieldstone building has lovely stained glass and great acoustics. On this site, incidentally, stood the harness shop where the Great Fire of 1883 started. The conflagration destroyed 60 buildings.

William Street. The only street in town that survived the devastating 1883 fire boasts some fine examples of Greek Revival architecture. Carefully preserved sea captains' homes include the **Richard G. Luce House** near the corner of William Street and Spring Street. Captain Luce never lost a whaling ship or a crew member during his 30-year career, and apparently his good fortune at sea extended to life on land.

Jirah Luce House, near the corner of South Main and Main Streets. Built in 1804, this is one of the few buildings to survive the Great Fire of 1883.

Old Schoolhouse, Main Street at Colonial Lane. Built in 1839, the schoolhouse is now home to a youth sailing program, but the Liberty Pole in front of it recounts the story of three courageous girls who defied British troops.

West Chop Lighthouse, at the western end of Main Street. Built in 1817 with wood and replaced with the current brick in 1838, the lighthouse has been moved back from the shore twice, first in 1848 and again in 1891. Today the lighthouse is inhabited by a family from the Menemsha Coast Guard base.

In Oak Bluffs

East Chop Lighthouse (508-627-4441). On Telegraph Hill, off the Vineyard Haven–Oak Bluffs Road. Open Sunday from 90 minutes prior to sunset until 30 minutes after, late June to mid-October; fee $2. The circa-1850 lighthouse was built by Capt. Silas Daggett with the financial help of prosperous fellow seafarers who wanted a better system of relaying signals from the Vineyard to Nantucket and the mainland. Up to that point, they'd used a complex system of raising arms, legs, flags, and lanterns to signal which ships were coming in. In 1875 the government purchased the lighthouse from the consortium of sea captains for $6,000, then constructed the metal structure that stands today. There are nice ocean views from here.

Trinity Park Tabernacle, behind Lake, Circuit, and Dukes County Avenues. The enormous, tentlike tabernacle was built in 1879 to replace the original meeting tent used by the Methodists who met here. The tabernacle is one of the largest wrought-iron structures in the country.

Wesleyan Grove surrounds the tabernacle, which, in turn, is encircled by rows of colorful **"gingerbread" cottages,** built during the late 19th century to replace true tents. Owners painted the tiny houses with bright colors and pastels to accentuate the Carpenter Gothic architecture and woodwork. There are upwards of 330 cottages today, still leased from the Camp Meeting Association. Visitors are free to wander around the community as residents visit with one another and sometimes strike up a conversation with tourists. Although mainly Protestant, the community is ecumenical. No bicycles are allowed in Wesleyan Grove, and quiet time is strictly observed after dark.

Union Chapel (508-693-5350), at the end of Circuit Avenue. This 19th-century octagonal chapel holds interdenominational services as well as hosting performing arts events throughout the summer.

Cottage Museum (508-693-7784), 1 Trinity Park. Open 10–4 Monday through Saturday, mid-June to mid-October. The interior and exterior of this 1867 cottage are typical of the more than 300 tiny cottages in Wesleyan Grove. Memorabilia and photographs span the ages from 1835 to present day. Nominal admission fee.

◊ **Flying Horses Carousel** (508-693-9481), Circuit Avenue at Lake Avenue. Open daily when school is out and weekends otherwise, mid-April to mid-October (10–10 in high season). The oldest operating carousel in the country, carved in New York City in 1876, is marvelously well preserved and lovingly maintained. Adults visit this national historic landmark even without a child in tow to grab for the elusive brass ring. Rides $1, or a book of 10 for $8.

In Edgartown

⬥❊ **Martha's Vineyard Historical Society** (508-627-4441; www.vineyard.net/org/mvhs/), Cooke Street at School Street. Open 10–5 Tuesday through Saturday, mid-June to mid-October; 1–4 Wednesday through Friday and

Dr. Daniel Fisher House in Edgartown

10–4 Saturday the rest of the year. This excellent collection is housed in several buildings. Perhaps the most interesting exhibit is the Oral History Center, which preserves the island's history through more than 250 recorded testaments from the island's older citizens. (The project was begun in 1993.) Other facilities include a fine pre–Revolutionary War house, which has undergone little renovation since the mid–19th century. The Cooke House contains 10 rooms of exhibits focused on various aspects of the island's history, including ethnic groups, architecture, natural history, and agriculture. Other features are a maritime gallery, historical reference library, a tryworks replica, a carriage shed that houses boats and vehicles, and a historic herb garden. The enormous original Fresnel lens from the Aquinnah Lighthouse is here, too, and it's illuminated for a few hours each night. Adults $6; children age 6–15, $4; children under 6 free.

Dr. Daniel Fisher House (508-627-8619), 99 Main Street. The island's best example of Greek Revival architecture, this 1840 house has an enclosed cupola (perhaps more correctly called a "lantern"), roof and porch balustrades, a shallow hipped roof, large windowpanes, and a portico, all exquisitely preserved. Dr. Fisher was a Renaissance man: doctor, whaling magnate, banker (he founded the Martha's Vineyard National Bank), merchant, and miller. He insisted that his house be constructed with the finest materials: Maine pine timbers soaked in lime for two years, and brass and copper nails, for instance. The house is headquarters for the Martha's Vineyard Preservation Trust, which is charged with saving, restoring, and making self-sufficient any important island buildings that might otherwise be sold for commercial purposes or radically remodeled. Combination tours of this house with the Vincent House and Old Whaling Church (see below) are offered late May to mid-October; call for times; $7 per person.

Vincent House Museum (508-627-8619), behind the Old Whaling Church. Open noon–3 Monday through Saturday, late May to mid-October (10:30–3 in summer). Dating to 1672, this is the Vineyard's oldest residence. It was in the same family until 1947, and was eventually given to the Preservation Trust in 1977. Reproduction and antique furniture in three rooms depicts how the residence looked in the 17th, 18th, and 19th centuries. Admission $3; $7 including a tour of the Dr. Fisher House and Old Whaling Church.

Old Whaling Church (508-627-4442 events; 508-627-8619 tours), 89 Main Street, at Church Street. Built in 1843, the thriving parish church also serves as a performing arts center, hosting plays, lectures, concerts, and films. Owned by the Martha's Vineyard Preservation Trust, the building originally housed the Edgartown Methodist Church and was constructed with the same techniques used to build whaling ships. Tours $7, including visits to the Dr. Fisher House and the Vincent House Museum.

North Water Street. Some of these fine Colonial, Federal, and Greek Revival houses may look familiar because many clothing companies, including Talbot's, send crews of models and photographers here to shoot their catalogs. Architectural detailing on these white houses trimmed in black is superb.

Vineyard Gazette (508-627-4311), 34 South Summer Street. Open 9–5 weekdays. It's best to make an appointment if you want to visit the little museum area. The newspaper that first rolled off the press on May 14, 1846, is a beloved island institution. As the masthead declares, it's "A family newspaper—neutral in politics, devoted to general news, literature, morality, agriculture and amusement." Richard Reston is the esteemed publisher. Although its year-round circulation is only 14,000, the paper is mailed to island devotees in all 50 states. There's no single better way for an explorer to get a handle on island life.

Edgartown Lighthouse (508-627-4441), at the end of North Water Street. Open Sunday late June to mid-September; $2. The first lighthouse to direct boats into and around Edgartown Harbor was built in 1828 on a small island. The island became connected to the "mainland" of the Vineyard by a spit of sand soon after a new lighthouse was placed (in 1938) on the site of the old one. Today, the lighthouse is accessible by foot.

Chappaquiddick Island, accessible via the "Chappy ferry," *On-Time III* (508-627-9427), at the corner of Dock and Daggett Streets. The entire journey between the main island and Chappy takes about 5 minutes. The ferry doesn't really have a schedule; it just goes when it's needed, and thus it's always on time. Since it's the only method of transportation between the two islands, and a surprising number of people live on Chappy year-round, the ferry runs daily. Round-trip for car and driver $6; for passenger and bike, $4.

Chappaquiddick contains several lovely beaches and wildlife refuges, including the 500-acre Cape Pogue Wildlife Refuge, the 14-acre Mytoi, and the 200-acre Wasque Reservation (see *Green Space*). Unfortunately, though, the beautiful island is perhaps best known because of Dike Bridge, the scene of the drowning incident involving Sen. Edward Kennedy in July 1969. To reach Dike Bridge, stay on Chappaquiddick Road after you get off the ferry until the road turns into Dike Road. When the road takes a sharp turn to the right (in about a mile), continue straight on the dirt road until you reach the bridge.

The bridge was rebuilt in 1995 and pedestrians once again have direct access to Cape Pogue, a thin ribbon of sand that stretches along the east side of Chappaquiddick and the remote **Cape Pogue Lighthouse.** Four-wheel-drive vehicles can use the bridge when endangered shorebirds like the piping plover are not nesting. Cape Pogue is also accessible by foot or by four-wheel-drive vehicle, over the sand of Wasque Point, several miles south of the beach.

Up-island

Mayhew Chapel and **Indian Burial Ground,** Christiantown Road, off Indian Hill Road, West Tisbury. This tiny chapel, burial ground, and memorial to the Praying Indians (who were converted to Christianity by the Reverend Mayhew Jr. in the mid-1600s) is a quiet place, owned by the Wampanoag tribe of Aquinnah.

❋ **Alley's General Store** (508-693-0088), State Road, West Tisbury. Open daily. Alley's is a beloved Vineyard landmark, recently purchased by the Wampanoag Indian tribe. "Dealers in almost everything" since 1858, Alley's has a wide front porch where locals have gathered over the decades to discuss current events and exchange friendly gossip. But in the early 1990s, economic conditions almost forced Alley's to close. In true island spirit, the Martha's Vineyard Preservation Trust stepped in to renovate the building and ensure its survival. Alley's continues to feel like a country store, selling everything utilitarian: housewares, mismatched saucers, Pendleton blankets, and locally grown produce.

Grange Hall (508-627-4440), State Road, West Tisbury. Open seasonally. The original Agricultural Society Barn now hosts concerts and screens old movies on Thursday night from mid-June to mid-September.

Beetlebung Corner, at the intersection of Middle, South, State, and Menemsha Cross Roads; the center of Chilmark. The intersection was named for the grove of beetlebung trees, the New England name for tupelos, which are unusual in this region. Tupelo wood is very hard and was an excellent material for making mallets (also called beetles) and the plugs (or bungs) that filled the holes in wooden casks and barrels during whale oil days.

The austere interior of the Old Whaling Church in Edgartown

Menemsha Harbor, at Menemsha Cross Road near Beetlebung Corner. This working fishing village has simple, weathered, gray-shingled boat-houses and small, sturdy docks that line the narrow channel. Islanders still earn a living on the large and small boats of Menemsha's fishing fleet. It's a great location from which to watch the setting sun. A few little shacks (shops and fast-food eateries) line the road to Dutcher's Dock.

Quitsa Overlook, off State Road. At Beetlebung Corner, bear left onto State Road, heading toward Aquinnah. After a mile or so, you'll pass over a bridge; Nashaquitsa Pond (also known as Quitsa) is on your right and Stonewall Pond is on your left. Just beyond, a spot overlooks Quitsa and Menemsha Ponds. About half a mile farther locals fill pitchers with water from a fresh, sweet stream that's been siphoned off to run out of a pipe. Local lore attributes various cures to the water—from stress relief, to a flu antidote, to a hangover remedy.

Aquinnah Community Baptist Church (508-693-1539), Aquinnah. Turn left at the small red schoolhouse (now the town library) across the street from the Aquinnah Town Hall, Fire Station, and Police Department. The lovely church is the oldest Indian Baptist church in the country. It may have the prettiest location, too, overlooking windswept grassy dunes, stone walls, and the Atlantic Ocean.

Aquinnah Tribal Center (508-645-9265), 20 Black Brook Road, Aquinnah. Although it's only in the preliminary stages, the Aquinnah Cultural Center expects to have an archive, culturally relevant crafts workshops, and fine and performing arts that preserve, educate, and document the local Wampanoag history, traditions, heritage, and culture.

Clay Cliffs of Aquinnah. The brilliantly colored clay cliffs, a designated national landmark, rise 150 feet above the shore and were formed 100 million years ago by glaciers. For a fine view of the full magnitude of this geological oddity, walk beyond the souvenir shops. In the distance you can see Noman's Land Island and the Elizabeth Islands. A wooden boardwalk leads to the beach, where you can see the towering clay cliffs from sea level. The Wampanoag have lived here for more than 5,000 years and own most of this land (although most of the beach is public); only they may remove clay from the eroding cliffs.

Aquinnah Lighthouse (508-627-4441). The redbrick lighthouse was built in 1844 to replace a wooden lighthouse that had stood there since 1799. In 1856 a powerful Fresnel lens was mounted atop the lighthouse, where it warned ships from the perilous Aquinnah coast; it was used for almost 100 years. From late June to mid-September, on Friday, Saturday, and Sunday evening, you can ascend the lighthouse to enjoy the sunset. It opens 90 minutes prior to sunset and closes 30 minutes after it. Fee $2.

Moshup Beach Overlook, on the northern end of Moshup Trail and south of the parking lot for the lighthouse, off State Road. This scenic coastal road has nice views of wild, low heathlands.

OUTDOOR ACTIVITIES

AIRPLANE RIDES

Classic Aviators (508-627-7677), off Katama Road at the Katama Airfield, Edgartown. Open seasonally. Open-cockpit rides in a biplane or Cessna, solo or with a friend, with or without Snoopy-like leather cap and goggles.

Warbird Flight (1-888-405-6723), Duchess Hanger at the Martha's Vineyard Airport. Open seasonally. Circle the island for 40 minutes ($120 for one to three people) or add on Nantucket or Woods Hole and Cuttyhunk ($200 for 60 minutes).

BERRY PICKING

Thimble Farm (508-693-6396), off State Road, West Tisbury. Open mid-June to mid-October, the farm allows you to pick your own strawberries or raspberries and offers other farm stand goodies as well—homegrown melons, tomatoes, flowers, and other in-season produce. Children are welcome for strawberry picking, but should be over age 12 to pick raspberries because of the dangers of thorns and bees. Call for specific opening hours.

BICYCLING/RENTALS

Several excellent (albeit crowded) bicycle paths connect the main towns: Vineyard Haven to Oak Bluffs, Oak Bluffs to Edgartown, Edgartown to West Tisbury, and Edgartown to South Beach via Katama Road. Because the roads from West Tisbury to Aquinnah are rather hilly, you need to be in pretty good shape to tackle the ride. A less ambitious but rewarding journey would entail taking your bike to Aquinnah and then pedaling the hilly but scenic up-island circular trail that begins at the Aquinnah Lighthouse: Take Lighthouse Road to Lobsterville Road and backtrack up Lobsterville Road to State Road to Moshup Trail. The Manuel E. Correllus State Forest (see *Green Space*), off the Edgartown–West Tisbury Road, also has several bicycle paths.

Rubel Bike Maps (www.bikemaps.com) are simply the best, most detailed maps available for those planning more than cursory cycling between down-island towns. Rubel produces a combination map that covers both the Vineyard and Nantucket ($1.95), as well as another that includes the islands, Cape Cod, and the North Shore ($4.25).

Before heading out, invest $2.95 in the very detailed, gold and orange **Martha's Vineyard Road Map** produced by Edward Thomas (508-693-2059). It's an excellent, accurate resource and even lists mileage between intersections.

The **Martha's Vineyard Commission** also produces a good free map that tells you what to expect on major routes: for instance, narrow roadways, shared with cars, gently rolling terrain, steep rolling terrain, and so on. It does not give estimated times or exact mileage, though.

Bike Ferry (508-645-3511). Weekends 9–5 from late May through June and September; daily (on demand) 8–6 from July to early September. Some people riding out to Menemsha and Aquinnah will be thrilled to know about Hugh Taylor's little ferry, which takes cyclists across Menemsha Creek (it separates the picturesque harbor from Lobsterville Beach and Aquinnah beyond). This 150-yard ferry ride saves cyclists a 7-mile bike ride. $7 round trip, $4 one way.

Dozens of shops rent bikes, including: **Strictly Bikes** (508-693-0782) near the ferry terminal on Union Street in Vineyard Haven; **Anderson Bike Rentals** (508-693-9346) next to the ferry terminal on Circuit Avenue Extension in Oak Bluffs; **R. W. Cutler Bikes** (508-627-4052) on the harborfront at 1 Main Street in Edgartown; and **Wheel Happy** (508-627-5928), 8 South Water Street. If you're staying up-island or you just want to begin pedaling in the center of the island, try **West Tisbury Bikes** (508-693-5495), next to Alley's General Store. Expect to pay $20–25 daily in summer for a mountain or hybrid bike. (There are 3- and 7-day rentals, too.) Most shops are open April through October; ask about delivery and pickup service.

❀ **Cycle Works** (508-693-6966), at 351 State Road in Vineyard Haven, repairs bicycles. John Stevenson and his enthusiastic and helpful crew have the largest selection of cycling equipment (for sale and rental), accessories, and parts on the island. They've been here since 1975.

BOAT EXCURSIONS/RENTALS

Vela **Daysails** (508-627-1963; 207-359-8353 off-season), Memorial Pier next to the Chappy ferry, Edgartown. With a maximum of six people aboard, this 50-foot gaff-headed sloop can feel like a private charter without the hefty price tag. The Hawkins family are your hosts. Snacks are provided but you can bring your own beverages. The 2-hour sail costs $55 per person, $25 for kids under age 12. Four departures daily.

Ayuthia (508-693-7245). This traditional 48-foot, all-teak ketch takes a maximum of eight people on afternoon, daylong, and evening sails from early May through October. BYO food and drink; $60 per person for the afternoon trip. An excellent choice.

Arabella (508-645-3511), Menemsha Harbor. Capt. Hugh Taylor's 50-foot catamaran sails to Cuttyhunk daily at 10 AM in summer. The 6-hour sail includes a 2-hour layover on Cuttyhunk, the only public island in the chain of Elizabeth Islands, and a swim at a remote beach (tide permitting). At 6 PM he offers a sunset excursion with stunning views of the Clay Cliffs of Aquinnah. Taylor, a longtime Aquinnah resident, has sailed these waters since 1970. $60 to Cuttyhunk; $40 for the 2-hour sunset cruise; kids half price for both trips; BYO food and drink.

Mad Max (508-627-7500), in front of the Seafood Shanty restaurant, Edgartown Harbor. This 60-foot catamaran sets sail twice daily (at 2 and 6 PM) from late May through September. Tickets for the 2-hour sail are $45 adults, $35 children under 10.

Edgartown Harbor Tours (508-939-9282), Main Street near the Edgartown Yacht Club. These narrated tours, which depart hourly noon–6 from late May to early September, cost $15 adults, $5 children. On some trips Capt. Bob Blanchard also pulls alongside some aquafarms, where shellfish are grown in "floating nurseries."

Vineyard Water Sports (508-693-8476), Dockside Marina, Oak Bluffs Harbor. Open mid-May to mid-October. One-hour, 4-hour, daily, and weekly rentals of Boston Whalers that seat five or six people.

Wind's Up! (508-693-4252 instruction; 508-693-4340 rentals), at the drawbridge on Beach Road, Vineyard Haven. Rentals and instruction mid-May to late September; retail open March through December. You can rent Sunfish and small catamarans or get beginning, intermediate, and advanced instruction from this full-service outfit, on-island since 1962.

CANOEING/KAYAKING

Martha's Vineyard Kayak (508-627-0151; www.menemsha.com), Vineyard Haven. Late May to mid-October. Eric Carlsen will pick the right pond or protected waterway depending on your skill level, although there really is no experience necessary for paddling on protected, shallow ponds. He delivers kayaks in the mornings and afternoons to about six locations around the island, including Edgartown Harbor ($30 for a 3- to 4-hour paddle), which affords unobstructed views of fine summer homes; Edgartown Great Pond ($30), which features an outer beach and a hidden sanctuary; Menemsha Pond ($40); Tisbury Great Pond ($30); and Squibnocket and Quitsa Ponds ($40), with pristine views. Tandem kayaks have child seats, so you can bring a youngster along, too. All rates are per single kayak.

Wind's Up! (508-693-4252 instruction; 508-693-4340 rentals), at the drawbridge on Beach Road, Vineyard Haven. Rentals and instruction mid-May to late September; retail open March through December. Canoe and kayak rentals by the half and full day. Private and introductory group instruction. If you're in the market to purchase a canoe or kayak, the well-priced fleet is sold at the end of each season.

Kasoon Kayak Company (508-627-2553). Open seasonally. Guided 4-hour tours on Great Pond with instruction as well as kayak rentals. Kasoon caters to the deaf and persons with disabilities.

Poucha Pond (508-627-3599; www.thetrustees.org), Dike Bridge, Chappaquiddick. Early June to mid-September. Members of the Trustees of Reservations may take a self-guided tour of this tidal estuary with a map that comes with the canoe rental: $25 for a half day, $35 daily. Nonmembers can purchase an introductory family membership for $30. Boats are available 9–5 daily. Or take a 2½-hour guided natural history trip offered twice daily from late May to mid-October with the Trustees of Reservations. Call for trip registration.

Long Point Wildlife Refuge Tour (508-693-7392; www.thetrustees.org), led by Trustees of Reservations, is a great way to learn basic paddling techniques and about the local ecology and natural history of Long Point. The guided tours of Tisbury Great Pond, a rich ecosystem that will delight birders, is 2½ hours and costs $30 adults, $15 children 15 and under. With a maximum of 12 people per tour, reservations are recommended. Trips depart twice daily from mid-June to early September.

Chilmark Pond Preserve (508-627-7141), access just before Abel's Hill Cemetery (where, incidentally, John Belushi is buried) on South Road, Chilmark. When you paddle across Chilmark Pond, you'll be rewarded

KIM GRANT

Vineyard Haven's protected harbor

with a small ocean beach on the south shore. Well worth it and a local secret because it is only accessed by canoe or kayak, which you must supply.

See also Cape Pogue Wildlife Refuge under *Green Space.*

FISHING

Fishing is excellent at most of the Vineyard's beaches and bridges; the bridge between Oak Bluffs and Edgartown is perfect for anglers. There's a wide area that hangs over the swiftly running channel between Nantucket Sound and Sengekontacket Pond. You're most likely to catch the island's prized striped bass and bluefish before sunrise. Surf-casting is best from south-facing beaches and the beaches at Aquinnah. On Chappaquiddick, East Beach at Cape Pogue Wildlife Refuge and Wasque Point (see *Green Space* for both) are famed for fishing.

❀ **Fishing Discovery Tour** (508-627-3599; www.thetrustees.org). Late May to mid-October. Operated by the Trustees of Reservations, these 4-hour guided surf-fishing trips (two per day) drift along the legendary Chappaquiddick shores at Wasque Point and Cape Pogue. Adults $50, children 15 and under $25. Limited to eight people per trip. Only members may take this trip, but you can purchase a temporary membership for $20 individual or $30 family.

✳ **Coop's Bait & Tackle** (508-627-3909), 147 West Tisbury Road, Edgartown. Your basic one-stop shopping for those in search of bait, tackle, boat charters, and information on "hot spots" for catching the big ones.

Dick's Bait & Tackle (508-693-7669), New York Avenue in Oak Bluffs; **Larry's Tackle Shop** (508-627-5088), across from the A&P on Upper Main Street in Edgartown; and **Capt. Porky's** (508-627-7117), Dock

Street, Edgartown, rent fishing rods, tackle, and other necessary equipment. Capt. Porky's also arranges charters.

Great Harbor Sport Fishing (508-627-3122; 508-627-2128), Edgartown Harbor. May to late October. Sportfishing with Captain Charlie aboard *Capella,* with light tackle, flies, and by conventional means.

North Shore Charters (508-645-2993), out of Menemsha Harbor. May through October. Capt. Scott McDowell takes anglers in search of bass and blues.

Fly Fishing (508-696-7551), Vineyard Haven. June to mid-November. Ken and Lori Vanderlaske specialize in shoreline, saltwater fly-fishing for stripers. Typically they take out one ($150) or two ($200) people for a 6- to 7-hour trip that usually lasts from sundown until about 1 AM.

☞ FOR FAMILIES

There are so many family- and kid-friendly activities that I've interspersed them throughout this *Outdoor Activities* section. If I'd listed them under *For Families*, the other headings would have been decimated!

⚓ **Dreamland Fun Center/The Game Room** (508-693-5163), Oak Bluffs Avenue across from the Flying Carousel. Open late May to early September. When it rains and the troops are getting restless, head for these arcade games, air hockey, skeeball, and kiddie rides.

GOLF

Farm Neck Golf Course (508-693-3057 reservations), off County Road, Oak Bluffs. Open April through December. Reservations are mandatory at this stately 18-hole course, but they're taken no earlier than 2 days in advance. A challenging course, but not long.

❀ **Mink Meadows** (508-693-0600), off Franklin Street, Vineyard Haven. A fairly long, but very subtle course; more challenging than you might think.

Windfarm Golf (508-693-4842), 203 Edgartown–Vineyard Haven Road, Oak Bluffs. Open April through October and weekends in November. This driving range and practice facility with 38 tees and five target greens will loosen you up before you drop the big bucks on the above courses. Half the tees are covered. Lessons are booked up to 4 weeks in advance.

HORSEBACK RIDING

❀ **Crow Hollow Farm** (508-696-4554), New Lane, West Tisbury. Trail rides, lessons, and summer camp.

❀ **Red Pony Riding** (508-693-3788), 85 Red Pony Road, off the Edgartown–West Tisbury Road, West Tisbury. Private lessons, trails for experienced riders, and packages for B&B and riding.

☞ **Nip-n-Tuck Farm** (508-693-1449), State Road, West Tisbury. Hayrides (call to schedule one) and pony rides (offered during the summer only, daily except Sunday 3–5 PM; $2).

ICE SKATING

Martha's Vineyard Ice Arena (508-693-4438), Edgartown–Vineyard Haven Road, Oak Bluffs. Call for public skating hours. Who brings skates to the Vineyard? No one; you can rent them here, though.

IN-LINE SKATING

Skating is off-limits on Main Street and at the Steamship Authority in Vineyard Haven; on Circuit Avenue in Oak Bluffs; and in downtown Edgartown.

❄ **Sports Haven** (508-696-0456), 5 Beach Street, Vineyard Haven. Half-day ($15), full-day ($20), or weekly rentals ($70) and free skate tours twice weekly in summer. If you're renting, think about the clinics ($15) in how to fall, stop, and start; it could save your skin. If you're buying, the clinic is free.

Island Outfitters (508-693-5003), 27E Circuit Avenue, Oak Bluffs. Open April through October for rentals; $20 for 24 hours and $40 for 3 days.

MINI-GOLF

✎ **Island Cove** (508-693-2611), State Road across from Cronig's Market, Vineyard Haven. Open weekends mid-April to mid-October, 9 AM–11 PM daily in summer.

SAILING LESSONS

✎ **Island Sailing School** (508-627-5720). Basic, intermediate, and advanced instruction and racing techniques (private and group) for adults and children.

See also Wind's Up! under *Boat Excursions/Rentals*.

TENNIS

Public courts are located at the following places: **Church Street** (two clay) near the corner of Franklin Street in Vineyard Haven; **Niantic Avenue** (four hard) in Oak Bluffs; **Robinson Road** (four hard) near Pease's Point Way in Edgartown; **Chilmark Community Center** (508-645-3061) on South Road at Beetlebung Corner in Chilmark (courts are only available when members are not using them); **Old County Road** (two hard) in West Tisbury.

Island Inn Country Club Tennis Courts (508-693-6574), Beach Road in Oak Bluffs. Open mid-April to mid-October. Three clay courts available for $20 per hour.

☂❄ **The Vineyard Fitness Club & Tennis Center** (508-696-8000), 22 Airport Road, off the Edgartown–West Tisbury Road, West Tisbury. When it's raining and you've just got to play, this full-service indoor facility has just what you'd expect: matches arranged, lessons, tennis camps for all ages, and ball machines.

WATERSKIING

MV Parasailing (508-693-2838), Pier 44, Beach Road, Vineyard Haven. Open mid-June to mid-October. If you're over 4 years old, Mark Clarke can teach you how to water-ski, knee-board, tube, wakeboard, and parasail. If you've always wanted to learn but thought you were too klutzy, Mark is the one to teach you. He runs a very safe outfit. Mark also has a shop at the Dockside Marina in Oak Bluffs for parasailing only.

WINDSURFING

Wind's Up! (508-693-4252 for instruction; 508-693-4340 for rentals), at the drawbridge on Beach Road, Vineyard Haven. Rentals and instruction mid-May to late September; retail open March through December. Sheltered Lagoon Pond, where Wind's Up! has a facility, is a great place for beginners to learn windsurfing and sailing. The water is shallow and the instructors patient. Those more experienced can rent equipment, consult the shop's map, and head out on their own. Windsurfing is excellent all over the island, but experienced surfers should head to Menemsha, Aquinnah, and South Beach.

EVEN MORE THINGS TO SEE AND DO

CRAFTS, DO-IT-YOURSELF

✐✳ **The Melting Pot** (508-693-6768), State Road, Vineyard Haven. Use the design catalogs to help design and paint your own pottery. In the off-season, as many adults come here as kids; it's more like meditative therapy or for social interaction at that point.

FITNESS CLUBS

✳ **Muscle Discipline** (508-693-5096), Kennebec Avenue, Oak Bluffs. A full-service aerobics and fitness facility; $15 per visit or $35 per week.

✳ **Triangle Fitness** (508-627-3393), at The Triangle, Vineyard Haven–Edgartown Road, Edgartown. Open daily. Ten-use (can be shared with another person), daily, and weekly passes.

✳ **The Vineyard Fitness Center & Tennis Center** (508-696-8000), off the Edgartown–West Tisbury Road, at the airport; a full-service center.

SPA TREATMENTS

Day "spa treatment" facilities have sprung up out of nowhere since the late 1990s. Believe me, I wish I had personal experience trying them all out for you! Once on-island, ask around for personal recommendations.

SPECIAL PROGRAMS

✳ **Vineyard Conservation Society** (508-693-9588), Wakeman Conservation Center, Lambert's Cove Road, Tisbury. Since it was established in 1965, this nonprofit group has protected thousands of acres from commercial and residential development by engaging in conservation land acquisition and advocacy. The society also sponsors a wide range of public activities, most of them free, including the Winter Walks program, a summer environmental lecture series, educational seminars and workshops on such topics as alternative wastewater treatment and solar building technology, and the annual Earth Day all-island cleanup.

✐✳ **Featherstone Meetinghouse for the Arts** (508-693-1850; www.feather stonearts.org), Vineyard Haven; off Barnes Road, half a mile north of the Edgartown–Vineyard Haven Road, West Tisbury. Arts center open year-round; gallery open daily 2–5 in summer. On 18 acres donated by the Martha's Vineyard Land Bank, this former horse barn and farm has been transformed into a great community art center. A dozen or so artists open their on-site studios once a week so that individuals can use their equipment and gain insight under their creative supervision (for a nominal fee). Classes change with a seasonal schedule but might include woodworking, stained glass, pottery, papermaking, printmaking, weaving, and photography. Weekly summer art camps for kids, too.

Cooking Classes (508-627-5999), Tuscany Inn, 22 North Water Street, Edgartown (see *Lodging—Inns*). Spring and fall weekends. Laura Sabrana operates wonderfully practical and fun Tuscan-style cooking classes that are often booked months in advance. She's a pro and you'll be closer to one yourself after 48 hours under her tutelage. $475 per person for the weekend; $175 for a second student sharing the room; $75 for a student's guest enjoying the meals only.

WINERY

Chicama Vineyards (508-693-0309), Stoney Hill Road off State Road, West Tisbury. Open January to mid-April, Saturday 1–4; mid-April to late May, Monday through Saturday 1–4; late May to mid-October, Monday through Saturday 11–5 and Sunday 1–5; mid-October through December, Monday through Saturday 1–4. Tastings and tours. Despite all these hours, Chicama still counsels that "hours vary, so call ahead." When the Mathiesens planted European wine grapes here in 1971, that hadn't been done commercially in Massachusetts since colonial days. Nestled in the woods of the terminal moraine left by the glaciers that formed the island, Chicama annually makes over 5,000 cases of Chardonnay, Cabernet, Merlot, and other varieties. It also makes herb vinegars, mustards, chutneys, jams, jellies, and salad dressings.

GREEN SPACE

☙ **Martha's Vineyard Land Bank** (508-627-7141), 167 Upper Main Street, Edgartown. The Land Bank was established in 1986 in order to purchase open space with funds raised by a 2 percent tax on real estate transactions. Today, there are more than 42 parcels of land totaling almost 1,500 acres. I highly recommend getting this organization's map prior to your visit for a current look at the Vineyard's open land. Many of the island's conservation areas—ocean beach, moors, meadows, ponds, and woods—are free for all to enjoy.

Manuel E. Correllus State Forest (508-693-2540), off the Edgartown–West Tisbury Road or Barnes Road. Comprising 4,400 acres of woodland and meadows in the center of the island, the forest's trails are used regularly by bikers, joggers, picnickers, and hikers. There's also an exercise trail just north of the headquarters on Barnes Road. Parking near the Barnes Road entrance.

In Oak Bluffs

Ocean Park, along Ocean Avenue. Fringed with some of Oak Bluffs's best-preserved gingerbread cottages, the park's centerpiece is a large white gazebo that serves as a bandstand for summer-evening concerts.

In and near Edgartown

✎ **Felix Neck Wildlife Sanctuary** (508-627-4850), off Edgartown–Vineyard Haven Road, Edgartown. Trails open dawn–7 PM. Visitors center open 8–4 daily June through September, and 8–4 Tuesday through Sunday, October through May. The Vineyard is populated by many species of birds that flock to the island's forests and wildlife sanctuaries. This 350-acre preserve, affiliated with the Audubon Society, has 6 miles of easy trails that traverse thick woods, open meadows of wildflowers, beaches, and salt marshes. The interpretive exhibit center has turtles, aquariums, a gift shop, and a library. There are year-round activities for children and adults, including guided nature walks (almost every day during summer) and bird-watching trips for novices and experts alike. Adults $3, children $2, free to Audubon Society members.

Mytoi (508-693-7662), Dyke Road, Chappaquiddick. Open daily sunrise to sunset. This 14-acre Japanese garden, built by Hugh Jones in 1958, has azaleas, irises, a goldfish pond, and a picturesque little bridge. It is under the auspices of the Trustees of Reservations.

✎ **Cape Pogue Wildlife Refuge** and **Wasque Reservation** (508-693-7662), Chappaquiddick. These adjoining tracts of land on the southeastern corner of Chappaquiddick are relatively isolated, so even on summer weekends you can escape the crowds. This seaside wilderness contains huge tracts of dunes, the long and beautiful East Beach, cedars, salt marshes, ponds, tidal flats, and scrub brush. Overseen by the Massachusetts Trustees of Reservations, Cape Pogue (489 acres) and Wasque (200 acres) are the group's oldest holdings. Half of the state's scallops are harvested each autumn off the coast near the Cape Pogue Lighthouse (on the northern tip of the cape). The lighthouse was built in 1893 and automated in 1964. Parking fee. *Note:* It is dangerous to swim at Wasque Rip because of the forceful tide.

🐾 Three-hour **natural history tours** (508-627-3599; www.thetrustees.org) of the remote **Cape Pogue** are naturalist led, in an open-air four-wheel-drive vehicle, and depart from Mytoi Garden. The fee is $30 for adults, $15 for children under 15. Bring binoculars and water. **Cape Pogue Lighthouse tours** (75 minutes), where you'll learn about the fascinating history of the light and its keepers who lived there, depart from Dike Bridge. Adults $12; children under 15, $6. Both trips are offered twice daily from late May to mid-October. Space is limited on both trips, so reserve early.

In West Tisbury and up-island

Menemsha Hills Reservation (508-693-7662), off North Road, Menemsha. This exceptional Trustees of Reservations property makes for a great 2-hour hike and includes a crestline trail along the island's second highest point. The 3½-mile trail leads down to a rocky beach. This point was used during World War II as a military lookout.

Cedar Tree Neck Sanctuary (508-693-5207), off Indian Hill Road from State Road, West Tisbury. The 300-acre sanctuary, managed by the Sheriff's Meadow Foundation, has trails through bogs, fields, and forests to the bluffs overlooking Vineyard Sound.

Long Point Wildlife Refuge (508-693-7662), off Edgartown–West Tisbury Road, West Tisbury. Open 10–6 daily, mid-June to mid-September. A long, bumpy, dirt road leads to a couple of mile-long trails, Long Cove Pond, and a deserted stretch of South Beach. Parking is limited at this 586-acre preserve, maintained by the Massachusetts Trustees of Reservations, so get there early. Parking $7 per vehicle, plus $3 per person over age 18.

Peaked Hill Reservation, off Tabor House Road from Middle or North Roads, Chilmark. Turn left on the dirt lane opposite (more or less) the town landfill and then keep taking right hand turns until you reach the trail head. This 93-acre Land Bank property is the highest point on the island, at a whopping 311 feet above sea level. Good for hiking, picnicking, and mountain biking, this reservation also offers vistas of Nomans Land Island, Aquinnah peninsula, and Menemsha Bight.

Waskosim's Rock Preservation, North Road, just over the Chilmark town line. At almost 200 acres, this is one of the largest and most diverse of the Land Bank properties, with great hiking, bird-watching, picnicking, and mountain biking. The Waskosim boulder marks the start of a stone wall that ran down to Menemsha Pond, separating the English and Wampanoag lands in the mid–17th century.

Allen Farm Vista, South Road, Chilmark. On the south (or the left side) about 1 mile beyond Bettlebung Corner as you head toward Aquinnah. Practically the entire stretch of South Road in Chilmark once looked like this striking 22-acre field and pastureland, protected as a Land Bank property. Lucy Vincent Beach is just beyond the pond, grazing sheep, and moorlands.

Cranberry Acres, West Tisbury. This cranberry bog, on the south side of Lambert's Cove Road from Vineyard Haven, has walking trails.

Polly Hill Arboretum (508-693-9426), 809 State Road, West Tisbury. Open 7–7 late May to mid-October (otherwise sunrise to sunset), daily except Wednesday. Now totaling 60 acres, this former sheep farm was brought under cultivation in order to preserve it as a native woodland by legendary horticulturist Polly Hill. The arboretum, established in 1996, is a not-for-profit sanctuary devoted to more than 1,600 native plants threatened by extinction. The arboretum is tranquil and beautiful from early spring well into fall. Wandering visitors will discover an extraordinary range of plants. Lecture series, too. Donations gratefully accepted: $5 adults, $3 children under 12.

Fulling Mill Brook, off South Road, about 2 miles beyond the Chilmark Cemetery, Chilmark. Hiking trails pass through 46 acres of forests, fields, and streams.

A wildlife refuge and pristine beaches draw visitors to Chappaquiddick.

See also Featherstone Meetinghouse for the Arts under *Even More Things to See and Do—Special Programs.*

BEACHES

Unlike Nantucket's, many Vineyard beaches are private, open only to homeowners or cottage renters. (By law, though, anyone has the right to fish from any beach between the high- and low-water marks. So if you want to explore where you otherwise aren't allowed, make sure you're carrying a fishing pole!) Many innkeepers, especially those in the up-island establishments, provide walk-on passes to their guests. (A much-coveted Chilmark pass will get you access to **Lucy Vincent Beach** off South Road, the island's prettiest. Even then, you'll still need a photo ID. And just to keep you in the loop, two other private beaches in Chilmark—**Quansoo** and **Hancock**—require a key to gain entry. If you don't summer in Chilmark, *The Improper Bostonian* discovered that you could purchase a key for a mere $120,000 in the late 1990s.) The following are public beaches.

In Vineyard Haven

Lake Tashmoo (or **Herring Creek**), at the end of Herring Creek Road, off Daggett Avenue from Franklin Street. This small beach offers good swimming, surf-fishing, and shellfishing. No facilities; limited parking; lifeguard.

Owen Park Beach, on the harbor just north of the ferry. Good for small children and swimming. Parking.

In Oak Bluffs

Oak Bluffs Town Beach, on both sides of the ferry wharf, Oak Bluffs. This calm, narrow beach is very popular with Oak Bluffs families and seasonal visitors with small children. No facilities, although there are public rest rooms next to the ferry dock.

Joseph Sylvia State Beach, along Beach Road between Edgartown and Oak Bluffs. The Edgartown end of this 2-mile-long barrier beach is also called **Bend-in-the-Road Beach;** this part of the gentle beach has lifeguards but no facilities. Park free along the roadside at the "people's beach." Good shore fishing and crabbing along the jetties, too.

In Edgartown

Fuller Street Beach, at the end of Fuller and North Water Streets, adjoining **Lighthouse Beach.** A favorite among college students, Fuller Street Beach is a short bike ride from town and generally quiet. From Lighthouse Beach you can watch boats going in and out of the harbor. Rarely crowded; gentle waves. No facilities or lifeguards.

Katama (or **South**) **Beach,** off Katama Road. A shuttle runs from Edgartown to this popular, 3-mile-long barrier beach with medium to heavy surf, a strong undertow, and high dunes. Children can swim in the calm and warm salt water of Katama Bay. There are lifeguards, but not along the entire beach. Facilities at the end of Katama Road and Herring Creek Road.

See also Cape Pogue Wildlife Refuge and Wasque Reservation and Long Point Wildlife Refuge, both in *Green Space,* above; see also Joseph Sylvia State Beach, Oak Bluffs, above.

Up-island

Long Point Reservation, off Waldron's Bottom Road from the Edgartown–West Tisbury Road, West Tisbury. Owned by the Trustees of Reservations, this wide beach is isolated and beautiful, with good surf. From here you can also follow nature trails to Tisbury Great Pond. Lifeguard. Limited parking; parking fee.

Menemsha Beach, Menemsha Harbor. This calm, gentle beach is also pebbly. Nearby rest rooms. Sunsets from here can't be beat.

Lobsterville Beach, off State and Lobsterville Roads, Aquinnah. This beach is popular with families because of shallow, warm water and gentle surf. Limited parking along the road. Popular for fishing, too.

Aquinnah Beach, just south of the Clay Cliffs of Aquinnah. Take the boardwalk and path through cranberry and beach plum bushes down to the beach, about a 10-minute walk. Resist the temptation to cover yourself with mud from the cliff's clay baths; the cliffs have eroded irreparably over the past century. (If that doesn't dissuade you, perhaps the law will: It's illegal to remove or use the clay.) Instead, walk along this 5-mile beach (called, from north to south, **Aquinnah Public Beach, Moshup, Philbin,** and **Zack's Cliffs Beaches**). The cliffs are to the north, but the beaches are wider to the south. Philbin and Zack's Cliffs Beaches are reserved for residents, but if you stick close to the waterline, you might not have a problem. Zack's fronts Jacqueline Kennedy Onassis's former estate. The farther south you walk, the fewer people you'll see. But those people you do see, you'll see more of—people come here specifically to sunbathe nude. It's not legal, but generally the authorities look the other way. Swimming is very good here; the surf is usually light to moderate, and the shore doesn't drop off as abruptly as it does along the island's south shore. Facilities include rest rooms and a few small sandwich and chowder shops at the head of the cliff. Parking is plentiful; $15 per day or $5 for one hour.

* **Uncle Seth's Pond,** off Lambert's Cove Road. A tiny (but public), freshwater pond on the side of the road. Good for kids.

* **PICNICS**
  Owen Park, off Main Street, north of the ferry dock, Vineyard Haven. This thin strip of grass runs from Main Street down to the harbor beach. You can usually get a parking space; there are swings for the kids, and it's a great vantage point for watching boats sail in and out of the harbor.
  Mill Pond, West Tisbury. This wonderful place to feed ducks and swans is next to the simple, shingled West Tisbury Police Department.

LODGING

With some exceptions (primarily smaller B&Bs noted by our special value "❀" symbol), it has become extremely expensive to stay on the Vineyard. Between 1998 and 2000 room rates soared well, well, well beyond the rate of inflation. Edgartown lodging is the most expensive by far. Oak Bluffs tends to draw younger visitors. Vineyard Haven and West Tisbury are the most sensibly priced towns.

  Reservations, made well in advance of your visit, are imperative during July and August and on weekends from September to mid-October. The height of high season runs, of course, from late June to early September, but many innkeepers define high season from mid-May to mid-October. In addition, many up-island inns are booked months in advance by hundreds and hundreds of bridal parties, many with no ties to the island, who want meadows, stone walls, and spectacular ocean views as the backdrop for their photographs.

  Most inns require a 2- or 3-night minimum stay in summer and 2 nights on weekends in autumn. Although there are quite a few year-round lodging choices, the island is incredibly quiet from January through March.

INNS
These places serve dinner on the premises.
In West Tisbury 02575

❄ **Lambert's Cove Country Inn** (508-693-2298), Lambert's Cove Road. This secluded country inn, a few miles from Vineyard Haven, is also home to a popular restaurant (see *Dining Out*). The farmhouse estate once belonged to an ardent horticulturist, and the impressive formal gardens are nicely preserved. A tennis court, a lush wisteria arbor surrounded by thick lilacs, an apple orchard, and ancient rock walls also grace the property. Guest rooms are scattered throughout the inn, carriage house, and converted barn. They vary considerably (and some could use freshening, in my opinion, relative to other comparable island properties) but each is positively distinctive; ask for a full description. Some of the 15 rooms (all with private bath) open onto sundecks; one especially comfortable room has a private greenhouse sitting room. Guests receive parking passes to nearby Lambert's Cove, one of the island's prettiest beaches. Full breakfast included. Mid-May to mid-October $185–250; off-season $90–210.

In Edgartown 02539

✳ **Charlotte Inn** (508-627-4751), South Summer Street. Innkeepers Gery and Paula Conover preside over the Vineyard's grande dame. They aren't resting on their laurels, however; they restore and refurbish each room every five years. Ardent Anglophiles, they make frequent trips to the United Kingdom to purchase antiques. Of the inn's 23 rooms and two suites, many have a fireplace, most have TV, and all have telephone. Equestrian prints, elegant armchairs, and collections of beautifully bound classic novels have turned each room a luxuriously inhabitable museum. The Conovers' taste for all things English reveals itself in the inn's grounds, too: ivy-edged brick sidewalks, small croquet-quality lawns, impeccable flower beds. Continental breakfast, but a full breakfast is available for an additional charge. June through October $295–750; November through April $175–550.

Tuscany Inn (508-627-5999; www.mvnet.com/tuscany), 22 North Water Street. Open April through December. Laura Sabrana, a native of Florence, is a designer and it's evident. Her flair for balancing color and space with magnificent antiques, fabrics, and unusual decorative pieces creates an elegant feel. (During my research for this edition, though, I was mystified by the neglected hallway carpeting.) Nonetheless, the eight guest rooms with fine linens have private bath (one is detached), and many have whirlpool bath. Televisions are available on request. The least expensive rooms are quite small, with twin beds tucked under the eaves. Common space includes a library, a plush living room with dramatic orchid sprays, and a flagstone terrace. Laura is a marvelous cook, and her breakfasts are served either on the flagstone terrace or in a tiled dining room with exposed kitchen. (Indoors, you'll swear you're in Italy.) Inquire about Laura's deservedly popular Tuscan-style cooking school offered on off-season weekends (see *Even More Things to See and Do—Special Programs*). June to mid-September $200–395; midseason $150-295; November through April $100–195.

🦋 **Edgartown Inn** (508-627-4794), 56 North Water Street. Open April through October. A hostelry since the early 1800s, the inn has hosted such notables as Daniel Webster, Nathaniel Hawthorne, and then Senator John F. Kennedy. Sandi, the inn's longtime manager, has worked hard at maintaining and upgrading the inn's 20 rooms with firm mattresses and homey antiques. The rooms are simply but nicely decorated and represent perhaps the best value in town. Bathrooms are newly retiled. Two more modern, light and airy rooms in the Garden House have private entrances. Breakfast is additional and served in the old-fashioned, charming period dining room or on the back patio. The inn is appropriate for children 8 and older. June through September $95 for a shared bath, $125–210 for a private bath; off-season $70 and $100–155, respectively. No credit cards.

✻✔ **Daggett House** (508-627-4600; 1-800-946-3400; www.mvweb.com/daggett), 59 North Water Street. This is Edgartown's only waterfront inn, and that remains the principal reason for staying. The original building served as the Vineyard's first tavern in 1660, and since then has been a store, a boardinghouse for sailors, a countinghouse, and a private home. There are 31 guest rooms and suites (each with private bath, cable TV, air-conditioning, and phone) dispersed among four buildings. Each is furnished with antiques and reproductions, lace-canopy beds, and comfortable armchairs. Rooms in the main house are generally preferable to those across the street. The Secret Staircase guest room (one of the inn's best) has a "private" entrance through one of the bookcases in the dining room. Rooms in the harborside cottages have private entrances. Be aware, though, that the clanking of the Chappy ferry, which runs until late at night, bothers some people in these rooms. Breakfast is served to the public (see *Eating Out*) and available to house guests for a fee in the remarkably authentic colonial dining room (or on the waterside patio). It's not often you get to dine in rooms like this; you are usually relegated to seeing them in historic houses at arm's length. Mid-May to mid-October $170–265; mid-October to mid-May $90–125.

Up-island

✺✔ **Inn at Blueberry Hill** (508-645-3322; 1-800-356-3322; www.blueberryinn.com), North Road, Chilmark 02535. Open May through October. This secluded 56-acre retreat has an intentionally exclusive feel to it without being pretentious. It's a personal favorite. Miles from anything but conservation land and stone walls, it's the kind of place you won't want to leave. Completely renovated in 1995, the 25 soothing rooms are scattered throughout six elegantly simple buildings. All rooms have telephones and air-conditioning; cable TV is available on request. Privacy is paramount here: Most rooms have a private deck or balcony. A wide array of spa treatments are available by advance request. A very expanded continental breakfast and use of fitness facilities (heated lap pool, tennis court, aerobic and weight equipment) are included. Box lunches are offered in-season. See Theo's under *Dining Out* for specifics about the inn's excellent dinners. Mid-June to mid-September $230–275 rooms, $405 suites; off-season $161–275 rooms, $220–405 suites; inquire about **cottages** that accommodate a family of six; 10 percent service charge added.

KIM GRANT

Time stands still on vacations, but rocking chairs rarely do.

  ♿ **Beach Plum Inn** (508-645-9454; www.beachpluminn.com), Beach Plum
Lane (off North Road), Menemsha 02552. Open May through December. Secluded amid 8 wooded acres overlooking Menemsha Harbor in
the near distance, the Beach Plum has been blossoming under new
ownership since Craig Arnold and his family took over in 1998. And after
a devastating fire in early 2000, the inn was rebuilt better than ever.
Guest rooms are luxurious, with fine bedding, first-class bathrooms
(many with deep soaking or whirlpool tubs), stylish but unpretentious
furnishings, and high-quality craftsmanship. All have air-conditioning,
cable TV, voice mail, and refrigerators. A few of the inn rooms have small
but private balconies with harbor views, and most rooms have some sort
of water view. Practical in-room amenities like umbrellas, beach chairs,
playing cards, and flashlights are not overlooked, either. The attached
cottages and freestanding **honeymoon cottage** are each decorated
with a simple but fresh style and grace. Facilities include beach access,
a croquet court, and a tennis court. Off-site health club access is also
included. Because this is such a popular place for weddings, you'll find
a large white lawn tent between the inn and the harbor in spring and fall.
The inn also boasts very fine cuisine (see *Dining Out*). Full breakfast
included. Mid-June to mid-September $200–400; off-season $150–300.

Outermost Inn (508-645-3511; www.outermostinn.com), Lighthouse
Road, Aquinnah 02532. Open early May to mid-October. First things
first: It's practically impossible to get a vacancy here. Hugh and Jeanne
Taylor's 20-acre parcel of land has the island's second best ocean view.
(The best view is just up the hill from the Aquinnah Lighthouse, where

Jeanne's great-great-grandfather was born.) The inn's six rooms (one with whirlpool) and one suite feature natural fabrics, wool rugs, and down duvets. Subdued colors and unpainted furniture emphasize the seaside light. Rooms are named after the wood used in each: beech, ash, hickory, and cherry. (Speaking of wood, don't miss the outdoor bar made from one long, impressive hardwood tree.) All guest rooms have TV and telephone. In keeping with the family's musical tradition, guitars, pianos, and other instruments are placed in the common areas. (You might get lucky and wander into an impromptu living room concert given by Hugh's brother James.) The inn's restaurant (see *Dining Out*) is popular. Full breakfast included. Mid-June to mid-September $240–320; off-season $210–280.

BED & BREAKFASTS
In Vineyard Haven 02568

✳❧ **Thorncroft Inn** (508-693-3333; www.thorncroft.com), 460 Main Street. After all these years, the Thorncroft continues to set the service gold standard. Under the care of Lynn and Karl Buder since 1980, this elegant Craftsman-style bungalow on a 3½-acre wooded estate (about a mile out of town) is arguably the island's best-run inn. It's perfect for special getaways. All 14 guest rooms are decorated with Victorian-period antiques and have thick carpeting and private bath. Amenities include plush robes, cable TV, air-conditioning, two telephone lines, and the morning paper delivered to your door. Some rooms have hot tubs or Jacuzzis-for-two; many have working (wood-burning!) fireplaces. A complimentary full breakfast is served in the inn's two intimate dining areas, or you may opt for a continental breakfast in bed. Finally, there's afternoon tea and pastries and evening turndown service. Mid-June to early September $235–500; otherwise $180–400.

✳ **Martha's Place B&B** (508-693-0253; www.marthasplace.com), 114 Main Street. This stately Greek Revival house absolutely glows at night when all the interior lights are turned on. Just two blocks from the center of town, some rooms have a harbor view and all are absolutely elegant. While the house is furnished with chandeliers and Oriental carpets, the place isn't stuffy at all, thanks to down-to-earth innkeepers Richard and Martin. With high ceilings and an open floor plan, the first floor is given over to common space. Amenities include nightly turndown service, breakfast in bed (on request), and morning newspapers. Ultrafine linens, down comforters, plush towels, fancy toiletries, luxe bathrooms, and robes bring a high standard of comfort. Fireplaces (with Duraflame logs) and Jacuzzis warm it year-round. Loaner bicycles and tennis racquets on request. An expanded continental breakfast, with excellent croissants and cinnamon rolls, is included. June through October $175–395; off-season $125–275.

✳❧ **Crocker House Inn** (508-693-1151; 1-800-772-0206; www.crockerhouse inn.com), 12 Crocker Avenue. Although I don't recommend staying only one night, this inn is one of the few that takes one-nighters. And for that fact alone, they get my gratitude on your behalf and a value symbol in my book. In 1998, when innkeepers Jynell and Jeff Kristal purchased this turn-of-the-20th-century B&B on a quiet side street near the center of town, they immediately set about making the rooms lighter and brighter. Each of the eight guest rooms (all with private bath) has a fresh summer charm, and all the bathrooms have been retiled. The third-floor loft is tucked under the eaves and features a gas fireplace, harbor view, and Jacuzzi. Room 5 is one of my favorites, spacious and homey, with good cross breezes and a private feeling. One room (No. 3) is good for three people traveling together and boasts a private entrance. An expanded continental breakfast, served in the small combination living/dining room, is included. But many guests linger over a second cup of coffee and the newspaper on the front wraparound porch set with rockers. All rooms have cable-ready hookups, phones, and computer access. June through October $185–365; off-season $115–265.

Tuckerman House (508-693-0417; www.tuckermanhouse.com), 45 William Street. Open June through October. On the edge of the historic district and a couple of blocks from the center of town, this newly renovated B&B boasts five first-rate guest rooms. Each is outfitted with feather beds, luxurious Ralph Lauren bedding, cable TV, air-conditioning, and telephone. I particularly like the summer porch room and room No. 5 with a private entrance and patio, but even the snug room on the second floor is lovely. The classic 1836 Greek Revival house has a nice side porch overlooking a small garden, too. Innkeepers Donna and Ed Herczeg serve an expanded continental breakfast at individual tables. July through September $185–325; off-season $155–185.

❄☙❀**Kinsman Guest House** (508-693-2311; www.kinsman.vineyard.net), 278 Main Street. Open year-round, ostensibly. Doreen Kinsman's shingled summerhouse is located a 10-minute walk from the center of town and a 20-minute walk to the West Chop Lighthouse. Built in 1880 as the original manse to the church across the street, it boasts high ceilings, an elegant staircase, and a proprietor who goes out of her way to accommodate guests. It has only three guest rooms, two of which share a newly tiled bath with modern fixtures. All rooms are gussied up with Laura Ashley and two have four-poster beds. Although breakfast is not included, many people choose to bring something back from town and eat on the front porch. It's also hard to beat the price: $125 June through August; $100 off-season. Pets accepted on occasion.

❄   **Captain Dexter House** (508-693-6564; www.mvy.com/captdexter), 92 Main Street. This centrally located 1843 B&B, tended by resident managers, has everything you'd expect from a sea captain's house—large rooms (most of them, anyway), wide-plank wood floors, and dormer windows. Seven guest rooms and one suite all have private bathrooms; three have a fireplace, great for those stormy fall and winter days. Decor leans toward Victorian–cum–New England charming. A very extensive continental breakfast, including perhaps five or six baked items, is included. In good weather, grab a tray and head outdoors to the side yard. Common space is limited to a small parlor and small yard. Late May to mid-October $135–235; off-season $80–160.

❊ **Herring Run House** (508-696-7337; www.herringrunhouse.com), 419 Barnes Road. On the edge of Lagoon Pond (which has ocean access) and a few miles from Oak Bluffs and Vineyard Haven, this completely transformed old house has two guest rooms brimming with an updated aesthetic. De rigueur in-room amenities include feather beds, a two-person soaking tub, hardwood floors, thick bathrobes, cable TV and VCR, and a CD player. After a few years of managing Lambert's Cove Country Inn, innkeepers Lewis and Katherine Costabel knew what guests were looking for and opened this B&B in 2000 in response to that. Sunset views over the lagoon from each of the bedrooms and living room doesn't hurt. A full breakfast of quiche or cheese blintzes with mango and blackberry puree is also included. Complimentary kayaks and bicycles, too. At press time, two more rooms with gas fireplaces were in the works. Late May to mid-October $250–285, off-season $150–200.

In West Tisbury 02575

❀ **The Farmhouse** (508-693-5354), State Road. Open May through December. Drive 10 minutes from the ferry to this unpretentious B&B, and you'll be in another world. Dating to 1810, this warm house and its longtime innkeepers—Kathleen and Volker Kaempfert—are a delight. The five guest rooms (four with private bath) are furnished with country antiques and down comforters. Bathrooms are newly renovated. The smallest room has a particularly unique feature: no indoor shower, but rather, its own private outdoor shower! The combination living/dining room, where a decadent continental breakfast is served, features exposed beams and wide floorboards. Additional common space includes a quiet side deck. The Kaempferts are the kind of innkeepers who sit with guests at breakfast time (after they've poured your coffee). My last overnight visit and morning conversation was a pleasure. $110–135 July through October; $85–110 off-season.

❀❊✔**The House at New Lane** (508-696-7331), New Lane. Off the beaten path, this house is appealing to "real B&Bers," according to owners Ann and Bill Fielder. By that they mean the kind of guests who are happy to see family photos above the mantel and who don't need everything to be Martha Stewart perfect. Surrounded by acres of woods and gardens, these five rooms (three of which are quite large) share two baths. One room has a private deck and entrance. Guests have special access to two great beaches, practically worth the cost of the room alone. Children are welcome; futons available for an additional $20 nightly. May through October $85, November through April $65, full breakfast included.

❊ **Pierside** (508-693-5562), off Lambert's Cove Road. Far from the madding crowds, down a dirt road through a small farm, the very secluded Pierside offers two rooms just 100 feet from Lake Tashmoo overlooking the water. Host Phil Fleischman built the house, which features a large guest room with kitchenette, cathedral ceiling, and private deck, and a similar room with private balcony. Swim from the Fleischmans' pier or rent a little boat, sail around the saltwater lake, or fish for blues and stripers just a mile or so from here. Mid-June to mid-September $165; off-season $125; $15 additional person.

The Old Parsonage (508-696-7745), 1005 State Road. Open May through October. Fifth-generation islander Tara Whiting-Watson and her husband, David, operate this family homestead, which sweeps dramatically down to a picturesque pond near the center of West Tisbury. The 1668 house, on the National Register of Historic Places, features period low ceilings and narrow doorways. The house has an incredibly rich history: The first room is said to have been built by Myles Standish's son Josiah. After staying here, you'll surely feel more attached to the island than you did prior to your arrival. Few places like this remain. The nicest accommodation is the East Room, a spacious two-room suite, but there are three other rooms as well. Continental breakfast included. $90–100 shared bath, $145 private bath, $165 suite.

Behind the inn is the **Davis House Gallery,** where Tara's uncle, Allen Whiting, was born, currently resides, and shows his pastoral island landscapes. His historic "barn" studio occupies a building behind the house/gallery.

❄ **The Bayberry** (508-693-1984; 1-800-693-9960; www.mvbayberry.vineyard. net), 49 Old Courthouse Road, North Tisbury. Off the beaten path (if there is such a thing on this island). Host and expert rug hooker Rosalie Powell has been innkeeping here since 1984. Each of the five guest rooms (three with private bath) has its share of cozy, country-style furnishings. I like the first-floor room best, even though it is smaller, and even though a couple of rooms have large picture windows overlooking the yard. There's plenty of common space, including a homey living room with family photos, a grand piano, and a collection of glass bottles in the picture window. A full breakfast (perhaps pancakes, hash browns, and bacon) is served in front of a kitchen fireplace or on the patio. Late May to mid-October $125–175; inquire about off-season rates.

In Oak Bluffs 02557

✐ **Oak Bluffs Inn** (508-693-7171; 1-800-955-6235; www.oakblufffsinn.com), 64 Circuit Avenue at Pequot Avenue. Open Mid-May through October. You can't miss the inn—it's the marvelously detailed pink building with an enormous third-floor cupola. It also has a great location: at the tip of Circuit, on the edge of the "campground," three blocks from a beach, and a 10-minute walk to the ferry. Youthful and fun innkeepers Erik and Rhonda Albert have done a great job freshening the place up. All nine guest rooms have private bath (small but newly redone), air-conditioning, cottage-style bedroom sets, and views of colorful neighboring cottages from every window. An expanded continental buffet breakfast, enjoyed at individual tables, is included; guests may also eat on the wraparound porch. Families are welcome in the carriage house or the first-floor room. Mid-June to mid-September $175–250; off-season $120–180.

Brady's NSEW Bed & Breakfast (508-693-9137; www.sunsol.com/bradys), 10 Canonicus Avenue. A 10-minute walk from the center of town and one block from the water, this house has been in Brady Aikens's family since 1929; he summered here in the 1940s and opened it as a B&B in 1991. Choose your guest room according to direction: north, south, east, or west (hence the "NSEW" in the inn's name). The summery, whitewashed rooms have wood-slat walls and are decorated in soothing colors and designer linens. West (with sunset views) is the largest and nicest room. Two rooms boast a private balcony; one has a private bath; all have a ceiling fan. Start your day with a continental breakfast (homemade bread or bagels and mixed fruit juices) on the wraparound porch with rockers, and and end up back here with Brady as the sun sets. He's here at 5 PM sharp every afternoon. The comfortable living room, decorated with southwestern influences, has a large video and CD collection. May through October $125–162 (including tax); half that off-season. Outdoor shower and hot tub included.

Four Gables (508-696-8384; www.fourgablesmv.com), 14 New York Avenue. On the road leading into town from Vineyard Haven, Four Gables is delightfully unusual and conventional. On one hand, it's a turn-of-the-20th-century shingled house with a wraparound porch and spacious first-floor parlor and dining room. On the other hand, it is filled with eclectic objects and art, and has contemporary porches. The four spare guest rooms (all with private bath) and one suite (perfect for a family or a longer stay, with a complete kitchen) are restful, with natural-fiber bedding, thick towels, and private balcony. Still, this is not your ordinary B&B. There is no innkeeper hovering about, and the chairs on the covered porch look like they're from a fraternity house. An expanded continental breakfast is included. June through September $100–145 rooms, $185 suite; off-season $75–105 rooms, $140 suite; less in winter.

Nashua House (508-693-0043; www.nashuahouse.com), Kennebec Avenue. Open April through November. Owned by the same folks who operate Zapotec Cafe (see *Eating Out*), the 1873 Nashua House has 15 breezy and simple rooms, which all share five bathrooms. The guest house was completely renovated in 2000, and as a result, all its carpeted rooms are looking good. I particularly like the corner rooms (No. 11 included). The guest house is perfectly situated in the thick of the action. Late May to early September $69–99; off-season $69–99.

Narragansett House (508-693-3627), Narragansett Avenue. Open May through October. This 1860s gingerbread cottage, surrounded by whimsical cottages just like it, was originally built as an inn to house visiting

Methodist "campers." Each of 13 very modest guest rooms has a private bath. Some have lime green carpeting; all are quite colorfully painted. Surrounded by a picket fence, perhaps the B&B's best attributes are its porch, set with rockers, and its front yard, teeming with birds and squirrels.

Innkeeper Jane Lofgren has also completely renovated an adjacent period house, the **Iroquois Cottage,** as well as two fully equipped **apartments** that can accommodate six people. Some of the six Iroquois rooms are smallish, but all are tastefully decorated with period antiques and feature fine tongue-and-groove woodwork. All have a modern and tiled bathroom, cable TV, telephone, ceiling fan, and a little private porch. Rooms on the second floor feel more spacious because of higher ceilings. Room 4 overlooks the chapel—perfect when you want to hear a concert—while room 3 boasts an unusual stained-glass door. Late May to mid-September $100–165 at Narragansett, $200–275 at Iroquois; off-season $85–135 and $125–225, respectively.

✿ **Attleboro House** (508-693-4346), 42 Lake Avenue. Open mid-May through September. This authentic gingerbread cottage faces Oak Bluffs Harbor and sits on the outer perimeter of the Methodist Camp Meeting Association. It's been taking in seaside guests since 1874, and it hasn't changed much since then. In Estelle Reagan's family since the 1940s, the guest house has 11 simple but tidy guest rooms that share five bathrooms. (Some rooms have a sink in them.) Most rooms have a porch, but if yours doesn't, there's a wraparound porch on the first floor. One suite on the third floor can accommodate six people. $75–115.

Oak House (508-693-4187; 1-800-245-5979), at Seaview and Pequot Avenues. Open mid-May to mid-October. The shingled, gingerbread Oak House is appropriately named—there's oak everywhere, from the walls to the ceilings. Built in 1872, the inn is itself a finely preserved antique with a lot of Victoriana added. The glassed-in porch overlooking the beach and street is quite sunny and the living room charming, but on a recent visit the guest rooms just felt tired. Nonetheless, most of the 10 rooms (2 of which are suites) have water views; all have private bath and air-conditioning. Even if your room has a private balcony, you may find yourself spending time in a rocking chair or a swing on the large wraparound veranda. Home-baked continental breakfasts and afternoon teas included. Mid-June to early September $180–275; off-season $120–210.

In Edgartown 02539

❋ **Hob Knob Inn** (508-627-9510; 1-800-696-2723; www.hobknob.com), 128 Main Street. More like a small hotel than B&B, the Hob Knob is a first-rate place to stay. Completely renovated from top to bottom in both furnishings and philosophy (in late 1997 by Maggie White), the Hob Knob provides some of the island's most attentive services. Tell the staff what you're interested in and they can arrange almost anything. Just a few minutes' walk from the center of town (request a room off Main Street),

Gingerbread-style houses in Wesleyan Grove, Oak Bluffs

KIM GRANT

this Gothic Revival house has 17 spacious guest rooms with down bedding, king-size beds, fine antiques, and a very soothing and tasteful ambience. Additional amenities include a morning newspaper delivered to your door, cable TV, Bose radios, phones with dataports, and air-conditioning. Afternoon tea and a full country breakfast, served off the menu and at small tables, are included. Or have breakfast in bed. During inclement weather, you'll appreciate the enclosed porch, a private back patio, two sitting rooms, and a front porch with rockers. Exercise hounds will appreciate the fitness room and dry sauna; massages also available. At press time, Maggie was renovating another guest house across the street. Late May through October $200–525 for rooms and suites; off-season $100–300. Inquire about the exceptional **apartment.**

❄️♿🐾✏️**Point Way Inn** (508-627-8633; 1-888-711-6633; www.pointway.com), 104 Main Street at Pease's Point Way. Open year-round except January to mid-February. In 1998 Claudia and John Glendon completely trans-formed this 1850s sea captain's house from a conventional B&B into a stylishly informal yet elegant and contemporary one. It's run very profes-sionally. White walls and recessed living room lighting set off dramatic black-and-white photos, artwork, rattan, leather, and overstuffed fur-nishings. Of the 12 light and airy guest rooms, all have private baths with fresh tiling. One has a private entrance, while two-room suites feature a balcony and a living room with pull-out sofa. The Glendons offer a complimentary guest car available on a "shared-use" basis. A full break-fast of perhaps peach crêpes or burritos is served on handmade dishes. Many guests make it a point to return for high tea, too. The private courtyard is delightfully different for the Vineyard: Tall sea grasses are offset by sculptures, pebbles, flagstone, and mod café-style tables and chairs. One garden room with a private entrance is appropriate for pets and children. Mid-June to mid-October $225–375 rooms; off-season $125–300.

✴︎☙ **Victorian Inn** (508-627-4784; www.thevic.com), 24 South Water Street. This centrally located B&B has been steadily improving since Stephen and Karyn Caliri took over in 1993. There are 14 luxurious guest rooms, some with four-poster canopy bed; all have private bath. Many rooms have a private porch or balcony. While I particularly like No. 10, with a slanting roofline and a steady stream of sunlight, all third-floor rooms are coveted (in my mind) corner chambers with harbor and chimney views. Rooms are furnished with substantial, comfortable armchairs, sofas, loveseats, fresh flowers, and desks. Steve, a gregarious innkeeper, presides over the morning meal, serving three courses on the flower-bordered back patio or indoors at tables for two in the formal breakfast room. Although this B&B accepts children, three people are not permitted in one room. Dogs are welcome off-season. June through September $165–350; off-season $100–195.

✪ **Summer House** (508-627-4857; www.summerhouse.com), 96 South Summer Street. Open mid-May to mid-October. Three blocks from Main Street and a block from Edgartown Harbor, this homey and charming B&B is a welcome relief from many overdone inns. Innkeeper and retired schoolteacher Chloe Nolan offers one charming guest room (with ceiling fan) and one very large suite. Each features a private bath, marvelous quilts, braided rugs, and quiet nights, as well as the benefits of a deep front yard with a tranquil garden. Guests enjoy a continental buffet breakfast of breads, fruit, and granola served in the country kitchen or alfresco, on the brick terrace, both overlooking the yard. The little sunporch with rockers is comfortable, too. $175–200. No credit cards.

✴︎ **Jonathan Munroe House** (508-627-5536; www.menemsha.com), 100 Main Street. This in-town, eight-room B&B is perfect for folks who appreciate the combination of exquisite guest rooms and privacy. What I mean is that while the B&B is small, there is no real sense of an innkeeper presence. Some of the elegant rooms have fireplace and Jacuzzi; all are appointed with extraordinarily good taste. Common space includes a fireplaced living room and a game room. The finest accommodation, though, is the two-story garden **cottage** that rents for $300 nightly or $2,000 weekly from June through October. A full breakfast is served on the sunporch or lovely and lush garden patio, as is afternoon wine and cheese. While I like the tranquil hideaway patio, the small front porch is also set with rockers. January through mid-April $150; off-season $200.

Up-island

Captain Flanders' House (508-645-3123), Box 384 North Road, between Menemsha Cross and Tabor House Roads, Chilmark 02535. Open mid-April to early November. Location, location, location. The 17th-century Captain Flanders' House sits on the crest of a hill overlooking a pond and meadows crisscrossed by stone walls. While there's no real innkeeper presence here, no matter. This is the kind of spot where you want to be left alone to savor the peace and quiet that envelop the place. I don't recommend the main house with five guest rooms (one with a pond view) unless you're taking the whole place with a group of friends and might not notice the lax upkeep. But I can heartily steer you to two adjacent buildings that have been converted into **cottage-style suites.** All rooms are comfortably furnished with country antiques. A continental breakfast is served on the sunporch. The inn provides walk-on passes to Lucy Vincent Beach; a shuttle stops at the inn. Late May to early October $275 suite, off-season $175.

❋❧ **The Duck Inn** (508-645-9018), off State Road, Aquinnah 02535. This is the most unusual place to stay on the island. As long as you can appreciate that it's a work in progress, you'll be happy here. By that I mean that while the window casings may not have trim on them yet, you may be sleeping in a sleigh bed with a silk, hand-painted, feather duvet (my favorite room, and boasting a balcony). Another room has a brass bed, freestanding marble basin, little balcony, and one French door to the water closet. Ask longtime proprietor Elise LeBovit for a complete description of the rooms, especially the cavelike ground-floor room. The whole open first floor is a communal-style gathering space, complete with wax-covered candlesticks on the dining table, a central fireplace and Glenwood stove, and kilims and Native American carpets. There is a well-used game area and special breakfast table for kids. One of its best treats: It's only a 5-minute walk to Philbin Beach. Full breakfast included. $105–215 in summer; $100–125 off-season.

COTTAGES, EFFICIENCIES, AND APARTMENTS
In Oak Bluffs 02557

❧ **East Chop Harborfront Apartments** (508-696-0009), 47 East Chop Drive. Open May through October. These five very well-maintained apartments are right on the harbor, a 5-minute walk from the center of town. The one- and two-bedroom units, with full kitchens, are great for families. Units open onto private, waterfront decks. Call as early as you can; these modern apartments are very nice. July and August $1,350–1,600 weekly Sunday to Sunday; $800–1,000 off-season.

See also Inn at Blueberry Hill under *Inns;* Hob Knob Inn, Jonathan Munroe House, and Narragansett House under *Bed & Breakfasts;* and Island Inn under *Hotels & Motels.*

In Edgartown 02539

❧ **Winnetu Inn and Resort at South Beach** (508-627-4747; 1-978-443-1733 reservations; www.winnetu.com), South Beach, Edgartown. Open May through October. New in 2000, this resort is great for families because of its proximity to South Beach (you can walk along a private path), its heated pool, grocery delivery service, and its variety of upgraded accommodations. Choose from studios with kitchenettes; one-bedroom suites with a kitchenette, combination living/dining area, and a deck or patio (sleeping a family of four); and larger two-bedroom condo units with a full kitchen (sleeping up to four adults and four children). The resort is 3 miles from Edgartown, and there are tennis courts and a restaurant on the premises. An active children's activities center is across the street. July to early September $225–275, $350–455, and $525–850, respectively, for the three different levels of accommodation; early September through October $125–175, $200–300, $325–475, respectively. Inquire about packages at Winnetu and weekly **house rentals** through its associate **Mattakesett Properties** (www.mattakesett.com).

✎ **Edgartown Commons** (508-627-4671; 1-800-439-4671 within Massachusetts), Pease's Point Way. Open May to mid-October. These 35 efficiencies—from studios to two-bedroom apartments—are near the center of town and great for families. Most of the individually owned units are in very good condition; these are rented first. Units in the main building have high ceilings and thus feel more spacious. Many units surround the pool, but all are comfortably furnished and most feature new kitchens. Outside, there are grills, picnic tables, and a nice enclosed play area. Long-time managers Rick and Janet Bayley keep the place humming. Mid-June to early September $150–175 studio or two-room, $225–250 three- to four-room; off-season $90–110 and $140–160, respectively.

Up-island

✎✿ **Menemsha Inn and Cottages** (508-645-2521; www.menemshainn.com), North Road, between Menemsha Cross Road and Menemsha Harbor, Menemsha 02552. Open April through November. This secluded 10-acre parcel of forest has some very special features, not the least of which are the lovely views of Vineyard Sound and friendly atmosphere. Innkeepers Kristin and Jim Travers, longtime associates of the inn, are now managing it with grace and warmth. The inn also boasts a direct wooded path to Menemsha Beach! Over the years (it was actually opened in 1923) the rooms and cottages have been continually upgraded and maintained with pride. An emphasis on peace and quiet, rather than fussy interior decorating, prevails. The complex has six luxurious suites in the carriage house (with a "great room" and fieldstone fireplace), nine smaller but bright motel-style rooms, and 12 tidy housekeeping cottages. Each cottage has a screened-in porch, fully equipped kitchen, outdoor shower, barbecue, and wood-burning fireplace. (Maid service costs an additional $15 daily.) All rooms have cable TV and telephone; suites and cottages have a VCR. An expanded continental breakfast is included with rooms and suites. Walk-on passes to Lucy Vincent and Squibnocket Beaches are provided. Reserve cottages in February if you can; this well-manicured place has a loyal, repeat clientele. Mid-June to mid-September: $215 for rooms and $275 for suites (including continental breakfast), $1,800 weekly for one-bedroom cottages, $2,200 for two-bedroom; off-season: $125 for rooms, $155 for suites, $1,050–1,250 weekly or $170–200 nightly for cottages, with a 2-night minimum. All rates are for two people; $15 per additional person. No credit cards.

HOTELS AND MOTELS

In Oak Bluffs 02557

☀☃♿**Island Inn** (508-693-2002; 1-800-462-0269; www.islandinn.com), Beach Road. Open April through November. This is a fine choice for avoiding in-town crowds, or for having a place for kids to run around, especially since it was renovated in 1997 and 1998. Situated between Oak Bluffs and Edgartown, this 7-acre resort is also within walking distance of two beaches and adjacent to Farm Neck Golf Course. In all there are 51 units with kitchenettes (in the form of studios, one- and two-bedroom suites, town houses, and a **cottage**) in several low-slung buildings. For a quieter stay, choose a room in the one-story buildings. Townhouse units have a fireplace, spiral staircase to the loft bedroom, and a separate bedroom. All rooms have cable TV, telephone, and air-conditioning. Facilities include three well-maintained tennis courts (a tennis pro is available in-season), swimming pool, and plenty of space to picnic and barbecue. Mid-June to early September $165–295, more for the cottage; spring and fall $75–175; $20 each additional person. Pets are accepted off-season. Inquire about the larger **cottage,** which sleeps six.

❄☀♿🐾**Surfside Motel** (508-693-2500; 1-800-537-3007; www.mvsurfside.com), Oak Bluffs Avenue. One of the few places open through the winter, the Surfside has above-average motel-style rooms near the ferry. The area can get a bit boisterous on summer evenings, but room rates reflect that. Each room has either a queen or two double beds, cable TV, and air-conditioning; small refrigerators and cribs are available. Corner rooms are particularly nice and spacious. Pets are welcome for an additional fee of $10 per pet per day. Mid-June to early September $140–180 rooms, $235–285 suites for up to four people; off-season $60–120 and $110–170, respectively; each additional person $20.

🖉 **Wesley Hotel** (508-693-6611; 1-800-638-9027; www.wesleyhotel.vineyard. net), 1 Lake Avenue. Open May to mid-October. Restored in the mid-1980s, this five-story hotel is the last of seven turn-of-the-20th-century oceanfront hotels in Oak Bluffs. While that's its main claim to fame, its next best feature is a wide veranda (with rocking chairs) that wraps around the Carpenter Gothic–style building, across the street from the marina. If you're going to stay, try to reserve a harbor-view room in the main hotel, which has 95 rooms that are fairly large and modestly furnished. Of the dark, air-conditioned, motel-style rooms in the adjacent **Wesley Arms,** I only suggest the rooms with two double beds facing the harbor. Mid-June to mid-September $195–220; off-season $115–130; $20–30 each additional person.

In Edgartown 02539

❄🖉 **Harbor View Hotel** (508-627-7000; 1-800-225-6005; www.harbor-view.com), 131 North Water Street. Overlooking a lighthouse, grass-swept beach, and Chappaquiddick, the grand 1891 Harbor View Hotel is Edgartown's best-situated hostelry. It has 124 rooms and one- and two-bedroom suites with kitchen or kitchenette. There are tranquil harbor views from the hotel's spacious veranda and some guest rooms. Other rooms have porches overlooking the pool. Guest rooms are generally large, and appointed with wicker chairs, pecan-washed armoires, antique prints, and watercolor landscapes by local artists. Facilities include room service, swimming pool, and concierge. Because of its size, the hotel caters to large groups. Children's program in summer. June through September $300–500 for rooms, $450–725 for one- and two-bedroom suites; fall and spring $195–325 for rooms, $260–475 for suites; winter $100–210 for rooms, $260–315 for suites; $20 each additional person.

✑ **Harborside Inn** (508-627-4321; 1-800-627-4009; www.theharborsideinn. com), 3 South Water Street. Open mid-April to mid-November. This seven-building, time-share condominium is one of the few waterfront (harborfront no less!) accommodations on the island. Practically all rooms have some sort of water view; most have a porch or patio. The 90 or so rooms are well appointed with standard hotel-issue furnishings. Facilities include a heated pool overlooking harbor boat slips. June to early September $150 for a few small rooms, $225–280 for other rooms, depending on proximity to the water, $295–325 for two-bedroom suites; $25 each additional person. Children under 12 stay free in parent's room. Rates are about 40 percent less in spring and fall. Sailors: Inquire about transient **boat slips.**

RENTAL HOUSES AND COTTAGES

Dozens of real estate agencies handle thousands of rentals, which vary from tiny cottages to luxe waterfront homes, from dismal and overpriced units to great values. Consequently, there is no way I can recommend any one agency. Your best bet is to find a rental adjacent to the owner's house. That way, you are assured of someone being able to help you if things go awry. Try to get a local newspaper early in the year for these advertisements.

See also Winnetu Inn and Resort at South Beach (Mattakesett Properties) under *Cottages, Efficiencies, and Apartments.*

CAMPGROUND

🏕 **Martha's Vineyard Family Campground** (508-693-3772; www.campmvfc. com), 569 Edgartown Road, Vineyard Haven 02568. Open mid-May to mid-October. As of the 1999 season, this is the only camping facility left on the Vineyard. (Webb's was sold to a golf course developer. Let's keep our fingers crossed that this place won't sell.) In addition to shaded tent and trailer sites, the campground also has rustic one- and two-room **cabins** that sleep five or six people ($90–100). Tents and trailers $32–36. Additional adults $10; children under 18, $2.

YOUTH HOSTEL

🏕 **Manter Memorial AYH Hostel** (508-693-2665; www.hi-travel.org; 1-800-909-4776 for in-season reservations; 617-531-0459 or enecreservations@

juno.com for reservations prior to the start of the season), Edgartown–West Tisbury Road, West Tisbury 02575. Open April to mid-November. This saltbox opened in 1955, and it remains an ideal lodging choice for cycling-oriented visitors. The hostel is at the edge of the Manuel E. Correllus State Forest (which is full of bike paths; see *Green Space*) and next to the path that runs from Edgartown to West Tisbury. Bring your own linens or rent them for the single-sex, dormitory-style bunk beds. The large kitchen is fully equipped, and the common room has a fireplace. Reservations strongly recommended, especially from mid-June to early September, when large groups frequent the hostel. Reserve by phone 2 weeks in advance. $15–17 for AYH members, $18–21 for nonmembers, half price for children under 14.

WHERE TO EAT

Most restaurants are open May to mid-October; some are open through Christmas; a few hearty ones in Vineyard Haven and Oak Bluffs operate year-round. Opening and closing days vary considerably from week to week, largely dependent on the weather and number of visitors, so it is impossible to tell you reliably which days any given restaurant will be open. Always call ahead after September and prior to May.

Vineyard Haven, Tisbury, and up-island towns are "dry," so BYOB wine or beer. (Some restaurants charge a nominal corking fee.) I try to note when there is a chef-owner because generally these places provide the most reliable food. Many Oak Bluffs establishments are family-oriented and casual, though there are a few sophisticated options. The dress code in Edgartown is a bit more conservative, but most places don't warrant a jacket and tie. Dining options are more scarce up-island, and require reservations well ahead of time.

DINING OUT
In Vineyard Haven

Stripers (508-693-8383), 52 Beach Road. Open May through October for dinner; Sunday brunch. Indoor and outdoor harborfront tables are an island rarity, which is reason enough to patronize this restaurant. Fortunately, the eclectic and unconventional South American menu is very good, too. Tired of New American bistro cuisine? Enliven your taste buds with exotic (for the Vineyard) dishes like *croqueta* (crab cakes with charred corn salsa and ancho chili mayo) and *camarones* (shrimp wrapped in crispy potato-scallion polenta with pineapple-mango chutney). Both the Venezuelan flan and passion fruit custard in a guava sauce are terrific. When I last dined here, all the diners around me were audibly raving about their dishes: exciting tastes and a great value relative to other comparable restaurants. Stripers accepts reservations for a waterfront table. BYOB. Children's menu. Entrées $17–26.

Zephrus (508-693-3416), 9 Main Street. Open for lunch and dinner. Chef-owner Joe DaSilva has come up with a winning formula that keeps people coming back: good preparations, good ingredients, and good ambience. The casual bistro is contemporary and warm, with an eclectic menu ranging from crabcakes to a large pot of steamed mussels for starters and heading to free-range roasted chicken and New York strip steak for main dishes. I particularly enjoy Joe's seared salmon with leeks, carrots, red potatoes, and littlenecks in a saffron shellfish broth. Entrée accompaniments change nightly, but the menu always highlights a vegetarian and pasta dish. Reservations recommended. BYOB. Lunch $6–12, dinner entrées $18–32.

Cafe Moxie (508-693-1484), 48 Main Street. Open for dinner March through December. Chef-owner Tina Miller has been serving up eclectic fare from gourmet pizzas, to pan-seared scallops with a leek fondue, to Cornish game hens since 1998. It's a casually hip storefront space, with a friendly staff. Whatever you do, save room for the warm fallen soufflé (aka "the bomb") or crème brûlée. Reservations recommended. BYOB. Entrées $20–32.

❋ **Le Grenier** (508-693-4906), 96 Main Street. Open for dinner. Chef-owner Jean Dupon's place opened in 1979 and is consistently great. Lyons-born, Dupon offers traditional French fare, including bouillabaisse, escargots, frogs' legs Provençal, and calf's brains Grenobloise. The menu is extensive, but each item is expertly prepared. Save room for desserts like crème caramel and banana flambé. Although the food is serious, the decor is relaxed and casual, by candlelight with green-and-white accents and hand-painted florals. Reservations highly recommended. BYOB. Entrées (*plats de résistance*) $21–30.

❋✎ **Black Dog Tavern** (508-693-9223), Beach Road Extension. Open for breakfast, lunch, and dinner daily, as well as Sunday brunch. Longtime Vineyarder Bob Douglas became frustrated when he couldn't find good chowder within walking distance of the harbor, so he opened this place in 1971, naming it for his dog. Now the Black Dog—and the ubiquitous Black Dog T-shirt—is synonymous with a Vineyard vacation. It's a pretty good place to eat, too, although you usually have to wait at least an hour for dinner, since they don't take reservations. (Lunch isn't as much of a problem.) Interior decor is simple, with pine floors, old beams, nautical signs, and shellacked wooden tables packed close together. Best of all, the shingled saltbox is cantilevered over the harbor. Fresh island fish and locally grown vegetables dominate the menu; toothsome desserts are made in the Black Dog Bakery (see *Snacks*). Although the staff are often eager to hustle you out the door, don't be shy about finishing your coffee. BYOB; children's menu. Light dinner meals $7–11; dinner entrées $22–27.

In West Tisbury

❋ **Lambert's Cove Country Inn** (508-693-2298), Lambert's Cove Road. Open for dinner June to mid-September; weekends from mid-September through May (closed January). This traditional country inn, with candlelight and linen table service, serves a limited New American and Continental menu that changes nightly. (The chef changes periodically.) The menu features an even selection of veal, duck, fish, seafood, and vegetarian dishes. If you've never been here before—the inn is located in a pastoral setting about a 10-minute drive from Vineyard Haven—arrive before sunset and walk around a bit. Reservations recommended. BYOB. Entrées $22–32.

In Oak Bluffs

The Sweet Life Cafe (508-696-0200), 168 Circuit Avenue. Open for dinner mid-April through December. If I were allowed to eat only one dinner on the Vineyard, it would be here. Indeed, with its classic gourmet menu of fresh island seafood, Sweet Life rests quite high in my top tier of Vineyard restaurants. Dine with chef-owners Jackson and Mary Kenworth within the restored and airy Victorian house or outside on the garden patio. You won't be disappointed. In fact, if you're anything like me, you'll depart musing about how sweet life is, indeed! My last meal revolved around an oven-roasted halibut with roasted garlic potatoes and spring peas. The wine list is equally exemplary. Entrées $25–36.

Lola's Southern Seafood (508-693-5007), Beach Road. Open for dinner, and an excellent Sunday brunch ($12 per person). Chef-owner Lola Domitrovich's place is a happening, lively, unusual joint with the island's best ethnic food. The atmosphere is a tad unusual, too: leopard-pattern napkins, brown paper tablecloths, cut-glass chandeliers, faux wrought iron, and a large multicultural mural. Come for absolutely huge portions of southern- and New Orleans–style seafood, BBQ ribs, a signature chicken and seafood jambalaya, and ribeye steak. This is one place where a split-plate charge is worth it—unless you want leftovers for days. Or just come for a cosmopolitan at the **bar.** For those more moderate in pocketbook and appetite, there is also a less expensive, early-evening **pub menu** ($11–16). Plenty of parking. Nightly entertainment in summer, Wednesday through Saturday the rest of the year. Children's menu. Entrées (served with buttermilk biscuits and corn bread) $20–28.

Jimmy Sea's Pan Pasta (508-696-8550), 32 Kennebec Avenue. Open for dinner, May to late December. Although it's a bit pricier now than it used to be, locals still enjoy this small, casual place when they're in the mood for enormous portions of delicious pastas, all cooked to order and served in the pan. Chef-owner Jimmy Cipolla's intensely garlic-infused place is an even better value if you have facilities to heat up your leftovers; it's virtually impossible to eat everything you're served. Better yet, if you have facilities, get takeout and split the dishes at home yourself. Try the mussels in white wine sauce. And note the herb garden in front; you know the seasonings are fresh. No reservations. Get there early or be prepared to wait. Children's portions. Dishes $20–28.

Balance (508-696-3000), 57 Circuit Avenue. Open for dinner late May to mid-October. Chef Ben deForest's oh-so-hip restaurant is a feast for

KIM GRANT

Hydrangeas love the Cape and the Islands' sandy soil.

the eyes as well as the palate—with its open kitchen, antique tin ceiling, and handsome bar. But it's not exactly a feast for the ears: It's noisy because the tin ceiling bounces the music and conversations around. Local fish and island produce are featured in Ben's "clean" cooking with European sauces that don't overpower the food. The menu changes weekly. **Bar None** is an equally happening scene, the only island eatery where you can get something to eat until midnight. (Try the pizzettas or fried calamari.) Reservations "absolutely suggested." Entrées $23–35.

In Edgartown

  L'Étoile (508-627-5187), South Summer Street, at the Charlotte Inn. Open nightly June through October; off-season schedule varies; closed January to mid-February. Dine formally in an elegant garden setting: Brick walls and a glass roof surround the conservatory-dining area, filled with plants and flowers. The contemporary French cuisine, meticulously prepared and artistically presented by chef-owner Michael Brisson since 1986, is nothing short of spectacular. On my last visit the roasted pheasant breast with sweet potato, jicama, and celery root gratin exceeded already high expectations. Michael's Dover sole, rack of lamb, and etuvee of native lobster are pretty darn excellent, too. He uses local fish and produce as much as possible and you can taste the difference. Reservations required. Men will feel more comfortable in a jacket here. Prix fixe dinner $68.

  Chesca's (508-627-1234), 38 North Water Street. Open for dinner, early April to late October. Chef-owner Jo Maxwell and her partner, Susan Peltier, offer more than a reliable menu of eclectic Italian-inspired seafood and pasta specials. They feature something few island restaurants do: a diverse menu where you can either eat affordably or drop a bundle. Mix and match a selection of pasta with various types of sauces. Or try a subtly roasted vegetarian risotto, crabcakes, or swordfish with toasted ginger, scallion, and soy. The paella and roasted garlic and cheese ravioli are great choices, too. The atmosphere here is more low-key than at other places serving this high caliber of food. Reservations for six or more only; expect to wait. Entrées $14–32.

  Lattanzi's (508-627-8854), Old Post Office Square, off Main Street behind the brick courthouse. Open for dinner. Chef Albert Lattanzi and his wife, Catherine, offer sophisticated and traditional Italian cuisine in conservative but not stuffy surroundings. Tables are candlelit, covered with bistro paper and linen; the staff are professional. As for the food, it's prepared with flair: from the wonderfully crusty Tuscan bread (with a bottle of olive oil for dipping) to handmade pastas to fresh seafood and hardwood-grilled meats. One very satisfying recent meal included antipasti like grilled portobella mushrooms and a lovely *insalate Toscana* with field greens, pine nuts, Asiago, and sun-dried tomatoes (large enough for two). The red puttanesca sauce was perfect with freshly caught tuna. Of course the *tiramisu* is great, but so is *gianduja* (flourless chocolate hazelnut cake). There is some alfresco dining. Reservations recommended. Entrées $22–38.

  Atria (508-627-5850), 137 Upper Main Street. Open for dinner May through December. New in 2000. Chef-owners and partners Greer Boyle and Christian Thornton specialize in fine, elegant dining with a global flair. The food is simple and straightforward, not overseasoned, allowing natural flavors to come through. It's a classy but casual place, with a rose garden patio raw bar, and a lighter and less expensive bar **menu.** (The burgers with onion rings are great, as are the shellfish spring rolls.) Fish is a big deal here. Signature dishes include rare ahi tuna tempura as a starter and pan-seared Georgees Bank scallops with pancetta and white beans. The menu changes daily, but there is always a vegetarian risotto. Duck lovers will appreciate Boyle's good-size portion. As for dessert, try the gooey chocolate truffle cake or traditional thin pecan tart. Live jazz, folk, and blues in the **bar** many nights. Reservations recommended. Entrées $22-32.

❋ **Alchemy** (508-627-9999), 71 Main Street. Open for lunch and dinner. Chef-owners Scott and Charlotte Caskey, who had been so successful at Savoir Fare for years, have struck again in this larger and more visible space. The open, rotundalike two-story bistro and **bar** is loud and energetic. If you're lucky, you'll get one of a few sidewalk tables. For lunch try the excellent pressed Cuban sandwich or a lobster cake BLT. Fish and seafood specialties at dinner range from seared salmon with creamed lentils, to halibut meunière with lemon, to a traditional lobster clambake for one. The wine list and wine-by-the-glass list is well chosen. Reservations recommended. Lunch $8.50–12, dinner entrées $25–34.

❋❋ **Taylor's** (508-939-8403), Nevin Square, off Winter Street. Open for dinner. This little hidden gem, with an exposed kitchen, paper-covered tables (à la European bistro), and Barry White tunes playing on the stereo, has a 30-something feel to it. The New American menu is limited and well-priced: Perhaps you'll find a tangerine and vidalia mesclun salad to start ($8), an asparagus and squash risotto ($16), and an herb and pepper rack of lamb with creamy mashed potatoes ($20). Chef-owner Brian Teaman has cooked at many island and Boston restaurants, and he and his partner Lindsay Taylor have big plans for this secluded spot. At press time there were plans afoot to serve outdoors and offer coffee and dessert as well. (During the 2000 season, the restaurant was too small for patrons to linger.) Entrées $16–20.

❋ **Square Rigger** (508-627-9968), at The Triangle. Open for dinner. You can tell right away that this place is by and for locals: Patrons and servers are friendly well into September! It's a meat-and-potatoes kind of place; actually, it's a char-grilled meat, seafood, and lobster kind of place. Nothing surprising—just good and casual, with plenty of parking and a publike atmosphere. Entrées $16-23.

Up-island

Beach Plum Inn (508-645-9454), off North Road, Menemsha. Open for breakfast and dinner, May through December. If I were going to drop a wad of cash for one romantic meal, it would be here. Although you may be drawn to the Beach Plum Inn for its panoramic view of Menemsha Harbor (lovely at sunset), the menu features innovative and creatively prepared seafood and locally grown produce. Chef James McDonough's menu changes nightly, but a recent exceptional meal went like this. We started with grilled portobello mushrooms and a seafood sampler with shrimp, tuna, and salmon. For main dishes, the tournedos maison (filet mignon and lobster tips) and pan-roasted halibut were exceptional. And unless you're allergic to chocolate, you'd be crazy not to order the Chambord soufflé for dessert. Service, by the way, is friendly but professional. Order à la carte (entrées $21–39) or a four course prix fixe ($65). BYOB. Reservations only.

Theo's (508-645-3322), North Road, Chilmark, at the Inn at Blueberry Hill. Open for dinner. Chef Robin Ledoux-Forte and her cooking deserve warm accolades. Healthful, artful presentations and hearty portions are served by an accommodating waitstaff. Although the contemporary menu changes daily with an emphasis on organic vegetables from the garden and local seafood, I particularly enjoyed the butternut-squash-filled ravioli and a cornmeal- and herb-crusted yellowtail flounder. Desserts, like a French pear tart and triple chocolate tart, will melt in your mouth. As for the atmosphere, candlelit tables and track lighting glisten off multipaned windows and cobalt glassware in a quiet country setting. BYOB. Entrées $22–38. In the off-season (May and October), it's worth rescheduling your return ferry trip so you can end a holiday with Robin's four-course rustic Sunday supper ($27).

Feast of Chilmark (508-645-3553), State Road at Beetlebung Corner, Chilmark. Open for dinner May through October. Chef-owners David Dubiel and Tony Saccoccia offer consistently fine sophisticated New American selections, which might include a warm pecan-crusted goat cheese salad followed by seafood marinara with lobster, shrimp, scallops, and clams over linguine. This casually upscale fusion restaurant doubles as a **gallery** for local photographer Peter Simon's Vineyard scenes and landscapes. (In case you didn't know, Peter is Carly's brother.) Reservations highly suggested. BYOB. Entrées $21–30.

Outermost Inn (508-645-3511), Lighthouse Road, Aquinnah. Open for dinner early May to mid-October. The set menu is pricey here because of the limited number of tables and the dramatic sunsets over the ocean. A typical New American menu highlighting fresh island ingredients might include a quahog chowder, house salad, grilled free range duck, and scrumptious lemon cheesecake. (There are always six or seven appetizer and entrée choices.) BYOB. Reservations only; two seatings for the four-course, prix fixe dinners, $65 per person.

Home Port (508-645-2679), North Road, Menemsha. Open for dinner, mid-May through September. Sunset views of Menemsha Creek are the big attraction at this local, simple institution. It's an efficient surf-sun-and-turf kind of place, with lobster cooked lots of different ways, thick swordfish, seafood platters, steaks, and a raw bar. The servings are large and the clientele a bit older. Frankly, some prefer to get takeout from the back door and enjoy a harbor view from the harbor. Reservations required. BYOB. Entrées $24–40 for a complete meal.

EATING OUT
In Vineyard Haven

✻🍷🐾**Art Cliff Diner** (508-693-1224), 39 Beach Road. Open for breakfast all day and possibly dinner year-round. This local institution has been here since 1943 but it's had a checkered reputation. Now that chef-owner Gina Stanley (who was the pastry chef at the guest house of the White House) and Ben Eilers have put their heads together, the buzz is great, the dishes stellar, and the spot getting brighter by the minute.

🐾✻ **Louis'** (508-693-3255), 350 State Road, a bit out of town. Open for lunch and dinner. Takeout only: cold pastas sold by the pound (baked orange-ginger chicken, sesame teriyaki noodles, and the like); subs and pizzas; and warm dishes like rotisserie-roasted chicken and lasagna. Dishes $5–12.

✻ **Vineyard Gourmet** (508-693-5181), 71 Main Street. This mouthwatering specialty food store carries picnic baskets and boxed lunches filled with the likes of smoked salmon, spiced asparagus spears, pâtés, and imported cheeses. Who says picnics can't be tasty and easy? Those with cooking facilities will find even more of interest. When the shop isn't too busy, call ahead and ask Helen and Diana what they've got, and have them pull something together so you can saunter right in and then be on your way.

✻ **MV Bagel Authority** (508-693-4152), 82 Main Street. Breakfast bagels with eggs, deli sandwich bagels for lunch, and bagel snacks throughout the day. For the coffee fanatics among us, Seattle's Best is served here.

✻🍷 **The Black Dog Cafe** (508-696-8190), 157 State Road. Open for all three meals, almost daily. The Black Dog began as a cottage industry, but now it's more like an industrial complex (figuratively speaking). About a mile out of town, now you don't have to fight traffic to fork over money to the Black Dog. It's a homey, country-style place, a great place to read one of their newspapers on a Sunday morning—as long as you're not in a hurry. During the 2000 season, I found the service terrible on many, many occasions. Order take-out baked goods from a big display case. If you must sit and eat, the café also serves creative sandwiches, a veggie-stir fry, burgers, soups, pizzas, pastas, and nightly dinner specials. BYOB. Breakfast and lunch $5–12, dinner $15–20.

See also Sandy's Fish & Chips under *Fish Markets.*

In Oak Bluffs

🐾&🍷**Farm Neck Cafe** (508-693-3560), off County Road. Open April through November for lunch and limited breakfasts; June through September for all three meals. When I ask locals for their opinion on a great, inexpensive lunch place, inevitably the Farm Neck Cafe pops up. Yes, the place is crawling with golfers, but the fact of the matter is that the setting is lovely—views of long, manicured fairways. The atmosphere is clubby, but it's public and very comfortable. You can get grilled shrimp and other seafood, soups, Caesar salad, sesame chicken wrapped in a flour tortilla, a burger, or a roast beef sandwich Philly style. Children's menu. Solo and duo jazz in the evenings. Lunch dishes $6–8.

🦞❄️✿**Linda Jean's** (508-693-4093), 25 Circuit Avenue. Open daily for all three meals. Established in 1979, thanks to Lanie and Marc, this pleasant storefront eatery serves old-fashioned meals at old-fashioned prices. It's a classic American diner without the chrome. Breakfast is still the best meal of the day here: Pancakes are thick but light, for instance. But the fish sandwich is quick and good, and the onion rings are crispy. Kids are happy with burgers and PB&J. And the waitstaff are friendly. What more could you ask for? If you haven't tried that famed New England "delicacy," Grape-Nut custard, this is the place to do it. Expect a wait for breakfast even in the dead of winter! Dishes $3–12.

🦞❄️ **Offshore Ale Co**. (508-693-2626), Kennebec Avenue. Open for lunch and dinner. Not only is the food very good—crispy, wood-fired, brick-oven pizzas, hefty burgers, grilled fish, fried calamari, and beer-batter onion rings—but the place is fun, too. Each table is stocked with a mason jar full of peanuts, and patrons toss the shells onto the wood floor already covered in cedar sawdust chips. But freshly fermented beer is reason enough to frequent this dark, two-story barn. Check the blackboard for what's fresh from the shiny copper vats. Frequent entertainment. Dishes $8.50–26.

✿ **Zapotec Cafe** (508-693-6800), 14 Kennebec Avenue. Open for dinner May through October and lunch in summer. This cozy place with twinkling chili pepper lights is festive and fun—as long as you're not old and stuffy. It serves Mexican and southwestern dishes like chicken suiza in a tangy tomatillo sauce, marinated chicken with mole sauce, swordfish fajitas, and Mexican-style paella, as well as old standbys like burritos, chimichangas, and quesadillas. If your grandmother is native-born, you're going to be disappointed here. But for the rest of us: It's a relief from fusion. Flan and Key lime pie are big desserts; sangria is the drink of choice. Children's menu $4–6; crayons, too. Dinner $11–18.

🦞✿ **Giordano's** (508-693-0184), 107 Circuit Avenue, at the corner of Lake Avenue. Open for lunch and dinner May through September. This classic, family-style restaurant is run by fourth-generation Giordanos, who pride themselves on serving value-packed portions. Giordano's serves some of the best fried clams on-island (head to the **take-out window**), along with large portions of chicken cacciatore with spaghetti, veal Parmesan, pizza, sandwiches, and fried seafood. The cocktails are also big. Children's menu; dishes $7.50–15.50.

🦞❄️✿**Papa's Pizza** (508-693-1400), 53 Circuit Avenue. Open daily for lunch and dinner. Papa's serves excellent deep-dish and multigrain pizza from this storefront eatery. Despite its central location, it's not loud or expensive, even though the food is good and the atmosphere friendly. (Call ahead in summer to avoid the wait.) The pleasant interior has lots of long, rustic wooden tables, a tin ceiling, and brass lighting. Calzones and takeout, too. Dishes $6.75–10.

❄️ **Stand By Cafe** (508-696-0220), Lake and Oak Bluffs Avenues. Open for all three meals. It's fun to sit on the swivel bar stools and watch the cook prepare dishes at this casual, tiny, diner-style restaurant. Seating is limited, prices reasonable, and the interior bright thanks to dozens of tiny windows. I didn't get a chance to eat here after the former (renowned) chef left, so ask around. Burgers, sandwiches, and fish-and-chips for lunch ($6–9); roasted turkey and meat loaf for dinner ($12–17).

✿ **Oak Bluffs Harbor Boardwalk** (aka **The Strip**). Among the many eateries that line the boardwalk, the **Coop de Ville** (508-693-3420) is probably the best fry joint and raw bar. You know the menu: seafood by the half pint, pint, and quart; steamed lobster with corn; wings; and fish sandwiches. The small, laid-back eatery offers picnic tables and counters. This is a great location for fast food and people-watching. Open for lunch and dinner, mid-May to mid-October. Dishes $6–21.

❄ **Seasons Eatery & Pub** (508-693-7129), 19 Circuit Avenue. Open for lunch and dinner. Although I've found the staff particularly insolent on recent outings, this is one of the few down-island places for a simple lobster dinner.

In Edgartown

🐾✿ **Among the Flowers** (508-627-3233), Mayhew Lane, off North Water Street. Open for breakfast and lunch, May through October, and dinner in July and August. This small café has been under Susan and George Gamble's stewardship since 1981, many of the staff have been here for years. Perhaps that's why this is one of the friendliest places on-island. As if that weren't enough, prices are the most reasonable in Edgartown ($4–12 for lunch, $15–22 for more upscale dinner entrées like lemon chicken and pasta). There aren't many indoor tables, but there is an outdoor patio, enclosed and heated during inclement weather. A variety of light meals is offered, from excellent omelets and chili, to peanut butter and jelly for the young, crêpes, salads, quiches, corn chowder, and clam chowder.

❄✿ **Lattanzi's Pizzeria** (508-627-9084), Old Post Office Square, off Main Street behind the brick courthouse. Moderately priced wood-fired, stone-oven pizzas, a wood-burning oven, homemade pastas, salads, light appetizers, family fare, and wines by the glass. Main dishes: $10–17.

Daggett House (508-627-4600), 59 North Water Street. Open for breakfast late April through October. Although the people staying at this historic inn might not like having "their" B&B open to the public, the Daggett House serves one of the best breakfasts if you're not staying at a bed & breakfast. Try eggs Benedict, a tomato basil omelet, crabcakes and poached eggs, or steak and eggs. The outdoor waterfront patio and colonial interior can't be beat. Dishes $7.50–11.

🐾❄✿♿**The Newes from America** (508-627-4397), Kelly Street. Open 11:30–11 daily for lunch and dinner. The food is surprisingly good for pub grub—renowned burritos, as well as burgers and sandwiches. Stick to pub mainstays and don't order anything too fancy. At about $8 per person, lunch here is one of the better island values. The atmosphere is cozy, too:

Fishing charters depart from Edgartown Harbor

exposed beams, red brick, and a wood floor. Children's menu. A good selection of microbrews.

✳️🐾**Fernando's** (508-627-8344), Upper Main Street. Open for dinner. This casual, family-friendly Italian restaurant has positioned itself nicely with well-priced dishes made to order. Locals flock here in the off-season. Traditional dishes include everything from linguine with red clam sauce to *zuppa de giorno* shrimp scampi, to a variety of chicken and veal dishes. Children's menu. Entrées $12–19.

🐾✳️🐾&**Main Street Diner** (508-627-9337), 65 Main Street, Old Post Office Square. Open 7 AM–9 PM (8 in the off-season). New in 1995, Nancy and Wayne Talley's nostalgic 1950s-style diner is a fun place for kids because there's plenty to look at—from old signs to a jukebox. As for the actual dining, you've got your basic comfort foods: eggs, pancakes, grilled cheese, meat loaf, PB&J, burgers, and some Italian. Parents won't mind the prices either: Most dishes are $5–8.

See also Morning Glory Farm in Edgartown under *Farm Stands*.

Up-island

🐾🐾 **The Galley** (508-645-9819), Menemsha Harbor. Open mid-May to mid-October. The new owner used to be the chef at the Outermost, so you know this is no ordinary clam shack. In fact, this tiny place has the best chowder on the island and great lobster rolls. Burgers and soft-serve ice cream, too.

🐾🐾 **The Bite** (508-645-9239), Basin Road, Menemsha. Open seasonally. This tiny shack serves arguably the best fried clams on-island. Don't miss the chance to decide for yourself.

🐾✳️ **Back Alley's** (508-693-4432), West Tisbury. Behind Alley's General Store (see *To See—Up-Island*), Back Alley's has sandwiches, salads, great chowder, soups, and baked goods—perfect for hungry bicyclists.

See also Larsen's Fish Market under *Fish Markets*.

LIGHT MEALS, SNACKS, AND ICE CREAM

In Vineyard Haven

❋ **Black Dog Bakery** (508-693-4786), Water Street. Open daily. At the Five Corners intersection near the Steamship Authority parking lot, the Black Dog is well positioned to accommodate the hungry hordes that arrive each day. Indeed, it is many visitors' first stop—for a cup of strong coffee and a sweet pastry, muffin, or other goodies.

❋ **Scottish Bakehouse** (508-693-1873), State Road (between Old County Road and Lambert's Cove Road). Since 1963, this bakery has served some of the best shortbread fingers and rounds west of the Highlands. The Bakehouse also supplies the island with great sandwich breads, especially sourdough and Scottish Crusty loaves. Blueberry pies, scones, spinach quiche, meat pies, steak and kidney pies, too. By all means, stop and see what an old island institution is really like.

In West Tisbury

❋ **Biga** (508-693-6924), 479 State Road. Open for excellent morning pastries and light lunches. The chef here worked at the renowned Beach Plum Inn for years before giving it up for the "simple" life here.

❋ **Vineyard Foodshop & Bakery** (508-693-1079), State Road, North Tisbury. Open mid-April to mid-November. Also known to locals as **Humphrey's,** You can pick up homemade soups and enormous sandwiches made with homemade bread. Save room for their jelly- or cream-filled doughnuts (if you're so inclined), affectionately called belly bombs.

In Oak Bluffs

Juice Caboose (508-693-3825), off Circuit Avenue. Open mid-April through October. It's a small place, just stools and a counter, really. But one hit of sunflower sprouts mixed with some fresh-squeezed juice, and you'll feel larger than life. When you've overdosed on rich desserts and fried seafood, come here to be purged. Smoothie concoctions, too.

In Edgartown

❋ **Soigné** (508-627-8489), 190 Upper Main Street. Open daily except closed for March. A connoisseur's deli just outside Edgartown, Soigné has all the makings for a gourmet picnic: the island's best take-out sandwiches, soups, and myriad cold salads from which to choose. Owners Ron and Diana, who have been at this since 1986, also sell "designer" pastas, pâtés, pastries, mousses, excellent clam chowder, dried fruits, imported cheeses, sauces, and select wines. It's a bit pricey, but worth every penny. By the way, something like "millions and millions" of brownies have been gobbled up here. If you're celebrating a special occasion, they make specialty cakes, too.

See also Espresso Love under *Coffee*.

Around the island

Mad Martha's has irresistible homemade ice cream and many, many locations in all the right places (near the ferries, on Main Streets, at the mini-golf course).

Up-island

Chilmark Store (508-645-3739), State Road, near Beetlebung Corner, Chilmark. Open May through September. This general store offers great pizzas and baked goods (especially the pies) in addition to conventional general store items. (Front-porch rockers are so coveted that, for a moment, I considered listing "people-watching over morning coffee" under *Even More Things to Do*.)

COFFEE

❋ **Mocha Mott's Good Coffee** (508-696-1922), Circuit Avenue, Oak Bluffs. Open daily. This tiny, aromatic basement café is where college students meet on their day off. The rich espresso keeps me going well into the evening, and the newspapers keep me in touch.

Espresso Love (508-627-9211), Old Post Office Square, behind the brick courthouse, Edgartown. Open daily March through December. Tucked back off Main Street, these folks make the strongest cappuccino in town, no question. Their pastries are among the sweetest, too. It's a fun place, with indoor seating and an outdoor patio. A limited selection of soups and sandwiches like Mediterranean eggplant are offered at lunch, but at press time, the owners were planning on staying open at night to serve light dishes with beer and wine. Look for a raw bar, salads, and appetizers. It promises to feel much like a European café.

FISH MARKETS

❀ **Larsen's Fish Market** (508-645-2680), Dutcher's Dock, Menemsha. Open mid-April to late October. Swallow some oysters and cherrystones at the raw bar while you wait for your really fresh lobsters to be boiled. Or pick up some stuffed quahogs and head to the beach.

❋ **Poole's Fish** (508-645-2282), Dutcher's Dock, Menemsha. Open year-round (daily April through November). The Poole family have been selling fish since 1946. They also smoke their own fish and provide a small raw bar while you wait for your lobsters-to-go.

❀ **Sandy's Fish & Chips** (508-693-1220), State Road, Vineyard Haven. Open seasonally. Located next to John's Fish Market, this family-operated no-frills place has great fried fish sandwiches and fried clams. And they've been doing it since the 1960s.

❋ **The Net Result** (508-693-6071; 1-800-394-6071), 79 Beach Road, Vineyard Haven. Lobsters, shellfish, smoked fish, and bay scallops (in-season) purchased on the spot or shipped to you as a nostalgic reminder. Customers attest to the fact that it costs less to have sushi-grade Net Result seafood delivered to their door than it costs to go their local market for lesser quality.

TAKE-OUT DELIVERY SERVICE

❄ **Island Indulgence** (508-693-4130). Open for dinner deliveries nightly. For all you house renters who don't want to leave the comfort of your home, these folks deliver meals from many local restaurants in Vineyard Haven, Oak Bluffs, and Edgartown. The charge is $6–10, depending on how much you order. (Tips are appreciated, too.) If you're staying up-island, they'll meet you at Alley's General Store. Look for their menu book, which has 15 or so restaurants to choose from—many of the above restaurants participate.

FARM STANDS

Despite summer traffic, $40 dinner entrées, chichi boutiques, and a building boom, the Vineyard is an agricultural island at heart. With little effort, you'll find dozens and dozens of farms with produce so fresh you can almost taste the earth. Stop often; it will be one of the things most cherished about a Vineyard holiday.

Morning Glory Farm (508-627-9003), West Tisbury Road, Edgartown. Open late May to late November. Although their business card says ROADSIDE STAND, it's more like a large rustic barnboard building where 75 percent of what the Athearns sell is grown by them. You'll find farm-fresh eggs, a great **salad bar,** home-baked pies and breads, and homemade jellies, including especially tasty white grape jelly.

ENTERTAINMENT

ARTS AND MUSIC

❄☙ **Vineyard Playhouse** (508-693-6450; 508-696-6300 box office; www. vineyardplayhouse.org), 24 Church Street, Vineyard Haven. This small, community-based professional theater produces well-done plays and musicals year-round. The main stage is within a former Methodist meetinghouse. They also host many special events; keep your eyes peeled. Tickets $17.50–27.50; $17.50 for preview tickets on first 2 nights of each show and rush tickets (remaining unsold tickets, 10 minutes prior to curtain). Performances at 8 PM, Tuesday through Sunday in summer. Look for the varied and entertaining lineup (Shakespeare and improv for younger folks) at the troupe's **Tisbury Amphitheater,** Tashmoo Overlook, State Road, Vineyard Haven.

⑤ **The Yard** (508-645-9662; 508-696-6300 box office; www.tiac.net/users/ theyard), Middle Road, near Beetlebung Corner, Chilmark. Mid-June to mid-October. Founded in 1973, this colony of performing artists in residence is always engaging and appreciated. Choreography and dance are spirited. If you have a chance to go to one of their performances, by all means go. The Yard is one of those special organizations that make the Vineyard uniquely the Vineyard.

❄ **Chamber Music Society** (508-696-8055). Year-round performances have been given since 1970. Look for the summer series from mid-July to mid-August. Performances at 8 PM; tickets $15.

Band concerts. The location alternates between Ocean Park in Oak Bluffs and Owen Park in Vineyard Haven, but the time remains constant: Sunday evening at 8 in July and August. If it's raining on the night the concert is in Oak Bluffs, head to the Tabernacle. If it's raining on the night the concert is in Vineyard Haven, you're out of luck.

NIGHTLIFE

Hot Tin Roof (508-693-1137; www.mvhottinroof.com), Martha's Vineyard Airport, Edgartown. Open 8:30 PM–1:30 AM May through October. When Carly Simon co-owned this club years ago, it was the coolest island nightspot. Then its popularity dipped. Now that she's affiliated with it again (as is Miramax's Harvey Weinstein), it's back on the map. In summer, you can reasonably expect to recognize famous faces here. As for the music, there is a diverse lineup of live bands and DJs. National R&B, reggae, and blues acts swing by Friday through Sunday. As for food, the raw bar is absolutely fresh, fresh, fresh. Tickets $8–50.

❄ **The Newes from America** (508-627-4397), 23 Kelly Street, Edgartown. Open daily. This colonial-era basement tavern is atmospheric and cozy, with hand-hewn beams. The Newes features microbrews; try the specialty Rack of Beers, a sampler of five brews from the outstanding and unusual beer menu (see *Eating Out*).

❄ **Atlantic Connection** (508-693-7129), 124 Circuit Avenue, Oak Bluffs. The "AC," another hot nightclub, attracts a younger beer-drinking crowd than does the Hot Tin Roof. Live bands, DJs, comedy, and reggae on alternate nights. It can get a bit rowdy.

❄ **Ritz Cafe** (508-693-9851), 1 Circuit Avenue, Oak Bluffs. Open daily. Locals hang out at this funky blues bar, which, according to *The Improper Bostonian,* has the following adjectives often applied to it: "seedy," "smokin'," "scary," "disgusting," "hilarious," and "a blast."

Lampost/Rare Duck (508-693-9847; 508-696-9352 for current events), Circuit Avenue, Oak Bluffs. On the second floor, the Lampost features dancing from mid-April to mid-October. Rare Duck, open May through September, is a frozen-drink kind of place, a smaller lounge with nightly summer entertainment.

❄ **The Wharf** (508-627-9966), Dock Street, Edgartown. A popular pub by the wharf.

Boathouse Bar (508-627-4320), 2 Main Street, at the Navigator, Edgartown. Open May to mid-October. Sailing types and singles stop here for outdoor cocktails, beers, and margaritas—it's just a few boat-lengths from the harbor. If you must nosh (here), stick to the appetizers. Live entertainment weekends in summer.

See Lola's under *Dining Out* and Offshore Ale Co. and Farm Neck Cafe under *Eating Out,* all in Oak Bluffs, and Atria under *Dining Out* in Edgartown.

☂ **MOVIES**
❄ **Capawock Movie House** (508-696-9200; 508-627-6689 for film information and show times), Main Street, Vineyard Haven. Built in 1912 but
   recently refurbished, the Capawock is the oldest continually operating
   movie theater in Massachusetts. As entertaining as movies can be,
   though, you may be just as entertained by conversations before the film
   begins: In the off-season, this is one of the hot places to hear island gossip,
   real estate prices, and political scoops. You'll also pick up lots of pertinent
   info on where to eat or get a massage, and where not to go.
Strand Theater (508-696-8300; 508-627-6689 for film information and
   show times), Oak Bluffs Avenue, Oak Bluffs.
Island Theater (508-627-6689), Circuit Avenue, Oak Bluffs.
Entertainment Cinema (508-627-8008), 65 Main Street. Edgartown. Two
   screens.
See also Grange Hall, under *To See—Up-Island*.

SELECTIVE SHOPPING

ANTIQUES AND COLLECTIBLES
All Things Oriental (508-693-8375), 123 Beach Road, Vineyard Haven.
   Open May through December, and by appointment. Summering on
   the Vineyard and winter shopping in the Orient sounds like a good deal.
   If you can't afford the time to go yourself, stop in here for a virtual trip
   via furniture, porcelain, jewelry, lamps, and more.
Clock Tower Antiques (508-627-8006), Nevin Square, Winter Street,
   Edgartown. Open June to mid-October. Since the early 1970s, the own-
   ers have collected sterling, glassware, dolls, miniatures, jewelry, ephemera, and objects of virtu.
The Golden Door (508-627-7740), 18 North Summer Street, Edgartown.
   Open March through December, and by appointment. John Chirgwin
   spends half the year in Asia, leading tours and buying art. His Far East
   gallery is delightful; you'll find sculpture, furniture, jewelry, jade, and
   tribal objects.
Jane N. Slater Antiques and Collectibles (508-645-3348), Basin Road,
   Menemsha. Open May to mid-October. The fact that it's small and goes
   by the motto of "Something for Everyone" dictates that the shop be
   crammed with collectibles of pottery, sterling, crystal, and jewelry.
❄ **O.B. Flea Market** (508-696-0700), 8 Uncas Avenue, Oak Bluffs. This
   collective of vendors has every conceivable niche covered: antiques,
   collectibles, furniture, toys, vintage clothing, books, tools. It's quite a
   friendly place, too, offering coffee and pastries while you browse.
See also entries under *Home Furnishings*.

ART GALLERIES
Except for the first two galleries, which are easily the most sophisticated on-
   island, galleries are generally clustered according to town. For a super-

complete listing of artists and galleries, look for the free and excellent ***Arts Directory*** available in many galleries.

❋ **Craven Gallery** (508-693-3535; 212-734-2125 in winter), State Road, West Tisbury. Open May through October, and always by appointment. This contemporary gallery is bursting at the seams with incredible art. Framed pieces are stacked all over the place for you to flip through, and the four little rooms are hung (literally) wall to wall with the likes of nationally acclaimed artists like Milton Avery and Edward Hopper. You'll find landscapes and abstracts, watercolors and mixed media, photography and drawings. What you won't find is any schlock. Check it out; Carol Craven is to be applauded for amassing such a great collection.

❋❀ **Shaw Cramer Gallery** (508-696-7323), 76 Main Street (second floor), Vineyard Haven. Nancy Shaw Cramer's exceptional contemporary crafts gallery features clay, fiber, wood, metal, and mixed media. Believe it or not, the work of about 20–25 islanders and 100 off-islanders is represented here. Nancy is a tapestry weaver herself and is working on a new line of silk pillows. Special exhibits in July and August.

❋ **Etherington Fine Art** (508-693-9696), 52 Beach Road, Vineyard Haven. Open April through December and weekends in winter. Fortunately, Mary Etherington's contemporary gallery has huge picture windows that you can't ignore. Do stop in; the gallery has a very distinctive feeling. Mary represents some 30 island and nonisland artists, some of whom do abstract work.

❀❋ **Craftworks** (508-693-7463), 42 Circuit Avenue, Oak Bluffs. Since 1990 these folks have found a mixed but usually affordable selection of contemporary American crafts that's worth a look and always visually interesting. Clay, metal, glass, paper, and wood.

Firehouse Gallery (508-693-9025), at the old No. 4 Firehouse on Dukes County Avenue (off New York Avenue from the harbor), Oak Bluffs. Shows late May to early September. There's a first-floor gallery and a second floor dedicated to workshops and classes. The Martha's Vineyard Center for the Visual Arts (508-645-9671), which publishes a fine annual arts directory, has its headquarters here.

Argonauta of Martha's Vineyard (508-696-0097), 73 Circuit Avenue, Oak Bluffs. Open April through December. Adrianne Maschit and Catherine Crocket specialize in hand-painted vintage furniture, custom-painted designs, and a permanent exhibition of original artwork by local artists.

Once in a Blue Moon (508-627-9177), 22 Winter Street, Edgartown. Open April through December. A bit tired of serious "art"? This shop revels in fun and funky contemporary ceramics, textiles, mixed media, sculpture, and other objets d'art for the home.

Old Sculpin Gallery (508-627-4881), corner of Dock and Daggett Streets, Edgartown. Open late June to mid-September. Operated by the non-profit Martha's Vineyard Art Association, the building was originally Dr.

Up-island reflection

Daniel Fisher's granary, then a boatbuilder's workshop. Look for the long, wide depression in the main room where boatbuilder Manuel Swartz Roberts's feet wore down the floor as he moved along his workbench during the early 20th century. Paintings and photographs of varying degrees of quality are exhibited.

❋ **Gardner-Colby Gallery** (508-627-6002), 27 North Water Street, Edgartown. Open May through December; winter weekends. Regional and national artists emphasizing Vineyard landscapes, seascapes, maritime scenes, figurative works, and still lifes are represented here.

Granary Gallery at the Red Barn Emporium (508-693-0455), Old County Road, West Tisbury. Open late May through December, and by appointment. In addition to folk art and landscape paintings, this gallery carries old and new photography. There are classic photos by the venerable *Life* magazine photographer Alfred Eisenstaedt (who came to the island on assignment for *Life* in 1937 and vacationed here until his death in 1995), as well as photographer Alison Shaw's island scenes. Most artists represented here have some affiliation with the island.

Field Gallery and Sculpture Garden (508-693-5595), State Road, West Tisbury. Open late May to late December. Tom Maley's field of joyfully dancing white figures, which seem to be celebrating their surrounding beauty, is an icon of the Vineyard's cultural life. Other Vineyard artists are exhibited during summer months; receptions are held 5–7 on many Sundays in July and August.

See also Featherstone Meetinghouse for the Arts under *Even More Things to See and Do—Special Programs.*

ARTISANS

❀ **Larry Hepler, Furniture Maker** (508-645-2578; www.lhepler.vineyard. net), 71 Main Street (upper level), Vineyard Haven. Open daily; it's a self-service kind of gallery. If you see something you like in the showroom, give them a call and talk about it. Larry can and does customize most of his work. The tag line, if you will, on this master craftsman's business card is for furniture that's HANDMADE TO HAND DOWN. He's not kidding. These fine, fine pieces have gentle curves, graceful lines, and remarkable character. He follows his father's advice that "it doesn't matter so much what you do as how you do it." Larry does it quite well indeed. Finishes are smoother than silk. You'll cherish a Hepler purchase.

❀ **Travis Tuck, Metal Sculptor, Studio and Gallery** (508-693-3914), 7 Beach Street, Vineyard Haven. Tuck and his apprentices take weeks and weeks to painstakingly produce one-of-a-kind weather vane commissions (starting at $10,000—and he's booked for the next two years already!). Travis has created a very animated velociraptor for Steven Spielberg, as well as pieces for President and Mrs. Clinton and the former president of Viacom. You can see fine examples of his work around the island, too. Check out the weather vanes atop the new Agricultural Hall in West Tisbury (a Holstein cow); Cronig's Market on State Road (a grasshopper, as a public market symbol); the Tisbury and Edgartown town halls (a whale tail and whaling ship, respectively); and at the Vineyard Gazette building (a quill pen).

Vital Signs (508-693-6057), 67 Circuit Avenue, Oak Bluffs. Open May to mid-October and by appointment year-round. Islander Keren Tonnesen has created a primitive signature style with original block-print garments and artwork.

❀ **Chilmark Pottery** (508-693-6476), off State Road, opposite Nip-n-Tuck Farm, West Tisbury. In 1982 artist Geoffrey Borr established his studio in a weathered shingled barn where he and his staff transform thoughtfully designed, wheel-thrown creations into hand-painted pottery with distinctive seascape hues. You'll find functional mugs and goblets as well as more unusual vases and plates. He also offers classes in wheel throwing and hand building.

Martha's Vineyard Glass Works (508-693-6026), State Road, West Tisbury. Open mid-May through October. Many designers share this dynamic studio, where you can watch the artists and apprentices at work. The shop is a colorfully bold visual feast.

See also Davis House Gallery under The Old Parsonage, *Bed & Breakfasts*, West Tisbury.

BOOKSTORES

✐ **Bickerton and Ripley** (508-627-8463; www.bickertonandripley.com), Main Street at South Summer Street, Edgartown. Open April through December. A charming, well-laid-out shop with everything from travel, to local fiction, to books and activities for children.

❋ **Bunch of Grapes Bookstore** (508-693-2291; www.bunchofgrapes.com), 68 Main Street, Vineyard Haven. A larger general bookstore where browsers are welcome.

❋ **The Book Den East** (508-693-3946), 71 New York Avenue (Vineyard Haven–Oak Bluffs road), Oak Bluffs. Open year-round (Thursday through Sunday off-season). This turn-of-the-20th-century two-story barn—complete with wood shelves, wood floors, and wood crates—is chock-full of used, rare, and out-of-print hardcovers and paperbacks. No haggling allowed. The barn has that great old-book smell, the kind of smell that always tells me that if I look long enough, I'm going to find something I can't live without.

CLOTHING

❋ **The Black Dog General Store** (508-696-8182), behind the eponymous bakery, off Water Street, Vineyard Haven. Open daily. The Black Dog rakes in tens of thousands of dollars per day in merchandise (sweatshirts, towels, caps, and so on). If you get home and regret not buying that must-have T-shirt, you can order it from the **Black Dog Catalog Store** (508-693-1991; 1-800-626-1991), 162 State Road, Vineyard Haven. Open year-round, the shop has the feel of a western company store. It doesn't hurt that it's next to a grain-and-feed store; the island still has its charms. The Black Dog, second largest island employer after the Steamship Authority, has all the bases covered: There is also a seasonal shop in Edgartown (508-627-3360), 11 South Summer Street.

Sola (508-627-7715), 23 Kelly Street, Edgartown. Open May through December. Upscale but affordable, mix-and-match women's linen, wool, and cotton clothing in updated styles and colors.

The Great Put-On (508-627-5495), Dock Street at Mayhew Lane, Edgartown. Open May through October. One of the most fashionable clothing stores on the island stocks an impressive selection of dressy clothing for women, more shoes for women than for men, and unisex accessories like leather backpacks, loose jackets, and sweaters.

❋ **Fleece Dreams** (508-693-6141), 3 Church Street, Tisbury. Betsy Edge makes jackets, capes, swing coats, scarves, and dresses on-site from her own polar fleece and velvet designs. She also works with linen, suede, rayon, and cotton.

Allen's Farm Sheep & Wool Company (508-645-9064), South Road (near Beetlebung Corner), Chilmark. Open late May to mid-October, and by appointment. You'll do your shopping "in the pastures" of one of the most beautiful spots on the island, overlooking sloping meadows crisscrossed with stone walls, with the Atlantic Ocean as a backdrop. A diet of fresh sea air and dense grass makes for thick wool, which the Allens and their friends knit and weave into beautiful scarves, shawls, sweaters, and hats.

Pandora's Box (508-645-9696), Basin Road (off North Road), Menemsha. Open May to mid-October. The emphasis here is on comfortable, contemporary women's clothing.

See also Timeless Treasures under *Home Furnishings.*

HOME FURNISHINGS

❋ **Bramhall & Dunn** (508-693-6437), 23 Main Street, Vineyard Haven. Nesting instincts are satisfied with hand-hooked rugs, picture frames, colorful ceramics, and antique furniture. All have been discovered by owners Emily Bramhall and Tharon Dunn during their annual pilgrimages to England.

Chartreuse (508-696-0500), State Road at Woodland Center, Vineyard Haven. Open May through October. Owners Laura Joseph Haney and Neal Matticks have gathered an extraordinary selection of well-priced antiques, whimsical gifts, and home furnishings from around the world.

❋ **Timeless Treasures** (508-696-7637), Main Street, Vineyard Haven. Gerda O'Rourke offers antique Irish pine furniture in addition to silver and hand-knit items, all of which are from Ireland, to which she returns annually to shop and order handmade sweaters. There are two shops across the street from each other.

❋ **Midnight Farm** (508-693-1997), 18 Water Street at Cronwell Lane, Vineyard Haven. Carly Simon's home furnishing store, located between Main Street and the ferry terminal.

Pik-Nik (508-693-1366), 99 Dukes County Avenue (off New York Avenue), Oak Bluffs. Open seasonally. Unlike any of the other shops in this category, Pik-Nik sells kitschy antiques and vintage housewares, including pottery, dishware, glassware, textiles, jewelry, and artwork from the mid-20th century. You gotta love it.

Mariposa (508-627-9332), 12 North Summer Street, Edgartown. Open April through October, weekends through December. Owner Nancy Antik combines pottery, needlework, and other gifts with carefully selected French country antiques from Provence. Off-season, she escorts clients on antique-buying trips through France.

JEWELRY

❋ **C. B. Stark** (508-693-2284), 53A Main Street, Vineyard Haven. Open daily. Goldsmiths Cheryl Stark and Margery Meltzer have designed gold and silver jewelry with island motifs since 1969. Cheryl also created the original grape design that has become so popular on the island. They're "official jewelers" for the Black Dog. Look for a shop in Edgartown, too.

SPECIAL SHOPS

❋ **Paper Tiger Inc.** (508-693-8970), 29 Main Street, Vineyard Haven. This colorful and fun shop offers a great selection of fine stationery, original cards, and handmade crafts of natural and recycled materials. When other galleries close, Paper Tiger exhibits local art.

Ben & Bill's Chocolate Emporium (508-696-0008), 125 Circuit Avenue, Oak Bluffs. Open May through October. Handmade chocolates, candies, and ice cream.

❋ **Carter Hill Farm** (508-627-3307), West Tisbury. Open year-round; call to arrange a time to stop in, or drop by their booth at the West Tisbury

Farmer's Market (see *Special Events*). At their small farm, Teena and Charlie Parton raise merino sheep for fleece. But now that the demand for their work has grown so much, they must send the fleece off-island to be spun and dyed. If you want to purchase their fiber or yarn, they'll be happy to share knitting and weaving ideas. The Partons ran Alley's General Store for several years, so they're a good source of information about the island's history and people.

Seaside Daylily Farm (508-693-3276), Great Plains Road, off Old County Road, West Tisbury. Open May through September. These lilies are grown without the use of harmful chemicals that disrupt the ecosystem's natural balance. Purchase lilies at the farm or by mail order.

Chilmark Chocolates (508-645-3013), State Road, near Beetlebung Corner, Chilmark. Open irregular hours, days, and months. Good deeds and good products make an unbeatable combination. Not only will you love the rich and creamy truffles and mouthwatering dark and light chocolates, but you'll also appreciate that Chilmark Chocolates is committed to furthering a philosophy that all members of society should be given a chance to be productive. They hire people with disabilities to make and sell the chocolate. Try their Tashmoo Truffles or West Chomps or Squibnuggets.

❋ **Vineyard Photo** (508-627-9537), Dock Street, Edgartown, and **Mosher Photo** (508-693-9430), 25 Main Street, Vineyard Haven, are both open year-round for quickie film processing. **The Wooden Tent** (508-693-2170), 383 State Road, Tisbury, offers custom processing.

SPECIAL EVENTS

There are hundreds and hundreds of charming—great and small—special events throughout the year on this island. What follows is a sampling of the larger, predictable annual events. You'd be well advised to contact the chamber of commerce (508-693-0085) for specific dates, unless an alternative phone number is listed below. For a complete listing, look for the chamber's complete event pamphlet once you get on-island.

Throughout the year: **Mountain bike rides** (508-693-4905), Grange Hall, West Tisbury, every Sunday morning, sponsored by the Vineyard Off Road Bicycle Association.

Throughout the summer: **Vineyard Artisans Summer Festivals.** Don't have time to pop into two dozen galleries? Then check this out. These excellent shows are held indoors and outdoors, rain or shine, weekly and biweekly at the Grange Hall in West Tisbury. Look for furniture, ceramics, book arts, fiber arts, glass, jewelry, mixed media, painting, photography, printmaking, and sculpture. Shows are held 10–2 on most Sundays in June and September and every Sunday and Thursday in July and August.

Mid-June to mid-October: **West Tisbury Farmer's Market** (508-693-

8989), at Grange Hall, 2–5:30 Wednesday, late June to late August; and 9–noon Saturday, mid-June to mid-October.

Mid-June: **Oak Bluffs Harbor Festival** (508-693-3392). Since 1991.

Late June to early September: **Chilmark Flea Market,** Chilmark Community Church Grounds, Menemsha Cross Road, every Saturday and Wednesday 8:30–2.

July and August: **Community Sing** (508-693-0525). Community Sings and more at the Tabernacle, Methodist "campground," Oak Bluffs, every Wednesday at 8 PM.

July and August: **Band concerts** every Sunday evening, alternating between Owen Park in Vineyard Haven and Ocean Park in Oak Bluffs.

Mid-July: **Edgartown Regatta.** Fifteen different classes of boats have been racing since the mid-1920s.

Late July: **Book Sale** (508-693-2592), a benefit since the late '50s for the West Tisbury Library, State Road.

Early August: **Antiques Show & Sale.** Inquire about the current location.

Early August: **Edgartown House Tour** (508-627-5303). This competitive event is limited to six houses each year, and rivalries are fierce. Tea is served in the final house on the tour. Fee.

Early August: **Possible Dreams Auction,** Harborside Inn, Edgartown. Given the celebrity involvement, it's not surprising that national publicity surrounds this event. Celebrities offer "dreams" that vary from predictable to unusual. High bidders in the past have won a tour of the *60 Minutes* studios with Mike Wallace; a sail with Walter Cronkite on his yacht; a seat at a Knicks game with Spike Lee; dinner with Lady Bird Johnson; a tour of Carnegie Hall with violinist Isaac Stern; a walking tour of the Brooklyn Bridge with historian David McCullough; a song and a peanut butter sandwich from Carly Simon; and a lesson in chutzpah at the Five Corners intersection in Vineyard Haven with Alan Dershowitz. Longtime island celebrities see the auction as their chance to give back to the Vineyard—in 1997 the auction raised more than $400,000 for Martha's Vineyard Community Services. Adjusted for inflation, that's a far cry from the $1,000 raised in 1979 when it began and folks bid in $5 increments for helping lobstermen set out their pots. More than 1,000 people usually attend the gavel-to-gavel coverage provided by humorist Art Buchwald. Fee.

Mid-August: **Illumination Night.** The actual date is kept secret until a week prior to the event and varies each year, but the evening always begins with a community sing. Then a selected Oak Bluffs resident (usually the oldest) lights a single Japanese lantern after all the electric lights in town are turned off. Following this signal, the rest of the "camp" residents illuminate their gingerbread cottages with lanterns and candles.

Mid-August: **Agricultural Society Livestock Show & Fair** (508-693-4343). Held at the Ag Hall and Fairgrounds on State Road in West

Tisbury, this is arguably the island's most beloved summer event. It's certainly one of the oldest: It began during the Civil War! Fee.

Mid-September to mid-October: **Striped Bass and Bluefish Derby.** When dozens of surf-casters begin furiously fishing from your favorite beach, you'll know it's derby time. Prizes are awarded for the largest fish caught each day, with a grand prize for the largest fish caught during the monthlong tournament. Weighing is done in Edgartown Harbor, just as it's been done every year since the mid-1950s.

Mid-September: **Tivoli Day** (508-696-7643). A lively street fair on Circuit Avenue in Oak Bluffs.

Mid-October: **Vineyard Craftsmen Art & Craft Fair** (508-693-8989), at the Edgartown School, West Tisbury Road. More than 60 crafters and artists have gathered here since the mid-1960s.

Early to mid-December: **Christmas Events** (508-693-1151). Santa arrives by ferry in Vineyard Haven; there's a chowder contest; horse and carriage rides; and "Christmas in Edgartown."

New Year's Eve: **First Night Martha's Vineyard.** An alcohol-free, family-oriented celebration. Events in Vineyard Haven and Edgartown begin at 1 PM on December 31 and end with Edgartown Harbor fireworks at 10 PM.

VII. NANTUCKET

Rose-covered 'Sconset cottages dating back to the 18th century

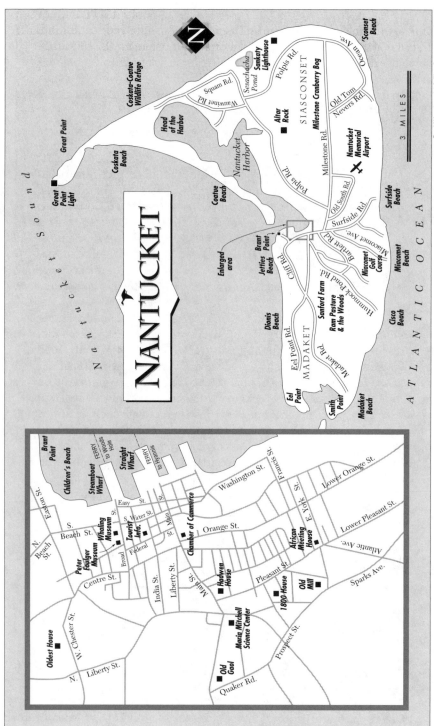

NANTUCKET

Paul Woodward / © The Countryman Press

N

Nantucket Sound

Great Point

Great Point Light

Coskata-Coatue Wildlife Refuge

Coskata Beach

Head of the Harbor

Squam Rd.

Wauwinet Rd.

Sesachacha Pond

Sankaty Lighthouse

Polpis Rd.

'Sconset Beach

Ocean Ave.

SIASCONSET

Milestone Cranberry Bog

Old Tom Nevers Rd.

Altar Rock

Nantucket Harbor

Coatue Beach

Polpis Rd.

Milestone Rd.

Nantucket Memorial Airport

Jetties Beach

Brant Point

Cliff Rd.

Enlarged area

Old South Rd.

Surfside Rd.

Surfside Ave.

Surfside Beach

Bartlett Rd.

Miacomet Golf Course

Miacomet Beach

MADAKET

Eel Point Rd.

Dionis Beach

Sanford Farm

Ram Pasture & the Woods

Hummock Pond Rd.

Cisco Beach

Madaket Rd.

Eel Point

Smith Point

Madaket Beach

ATLANTIC OCEAN

3 MILES

Brant Point

Children's Beach

Easton St.

FERRY to Woods Hole

Steamboat Wharf

Straight Wharf

FERRY to Hyannis

Francis St.

Washington St.

Lower Orange St.

N. Beach St.

S. Beach St.

Whaling Museum

Tourist Info.

Easy St.

S. Water St.

Broad St.

Federal St.

Chamber of Commerce

Orange St.

E. York St.

Lower Pleasant St.

African Meeting House

Atlantic Ave.

Peter Foulger Museum

Centre St.

India St.

Liberty St.

Main St.

Hadwen House

Pleasant St.

1800 House

Old Mill

Sparks Ave.

Oldest House

W. Chester St.

Maria Mitchell Science Center

Old Gaol

Prospect St.

N. Liberty St.

Quaker Rd.

Nantucket

Thirty miles out to sea, Nantucket was called "that far away island" by Native Americans. Just 14 by 3½ miles in area, Nantucket is the only place in America that is simultaneously an island, a county, and a town. In 1659 Thomas Mayhew, who had purchased Nantucket sight unseen (he was more interested in Martha's Vineyard), sold it to Tristram Coffin and eight of his friends for £30 and "two Beaver Hatts." These "original purchasers" quickly sold half shares to craftsmen whose skills they would require to build a community. When Mayhew arrived, there were more than 3,000 Native American residents, who taught the settlers which crops to farm and how to spear whales from shore. By the early 1700s, the number of settlers had grown to more than 300, and the number of Natives had shrunk to less than 800, primarily because of disease. (The last Native descendant died on-island in 1854.)

In 1712, when Captain Hussey's sloop was blown out to sea, he harpooned the first sperm whale islanders had ever seen. For the next 150 years, whaling dominated the island's economy. The ensuing prosperity allowed the island's population to climb to 10,000. In comparison, there are 7,000 year-rounders today.

Nantucket sea captains traveled the world to catch whales and to trade, and they brought back great fortunes. By the late 1700s, trade was booming with England, and in 1791 the *Beaver*, owned by islander William Rotch, rounded Cape Horn and forged an American trade route to the Pacific Ocean. Fortunes were also made in the Indian Ocean—hence, Nantucket's India Street.

In its heyday, Nantucket Harbor overflowed with the smoke and smells from blacksmith shops, cooperages, shipyards, and candle factories. More than 100 whaling ships sailed in and out of Nantucket. But when ships grew larger, to allow for their longer voyages at sea, they couldn't get across the shallow shoals and into Nantucket Harbor. The industry began moving to Martha's Vineyard and New Bedford. At the height of the whaling industry in 1846, the "Great Fire," which began in a hat shop on Main Street, ignited whale oil at the harbor. The catastrophic blaze wiped out the harbor and one-third of the town. Although citizens began to rebuild immediately, other adventurous and energetic souls were enticed to go west in search of gold in 1849. When kerosene

KIM GRANT

The Brant Point Lighthouse guards the entrance to Nantucket Harbor.

replaced whale oil in the 1850s as a less expensive fuel, it leveled the final blow to the island's maritime economy. By 1861 there were only 2,000 people on-island.

Although tourism began soon after the Civil War and picked up with the advent of the railroad to 'Sconset, the island lay more or less in undisturbed isolation until the 1950s. But perhaps it was the sleepiness of those 100 years that ultimately preserved the island's architectural integrity and community spirit, paving the way for its resurrection. In the late 1950s and early 1960s, islander and S&H Green Stamp heir

Walter Beinecke Jr. organized a revitalization of the waterfront area, replacing decrepit wharf buildings with cottages. He also declared the premise that guides tourism to this day: It is preferable to attract one tourist with $100 than 100 tourists with $1 each. In accordance with the maxim, strict zoning laws were adopted, land-conservation groups were launched, and Nantucket's upscale tourism industry began in earnest. At the beginning of the 1998 tourist season, an article in the *New York Times* documented how feverishly the well-to-do set was abandoning the Hamptons and similar enclaves for Nantucket. In contrast to the Vineyard's showy excess and its allure for creative types, Nantucket is a restrained haven for behind-the-scenes power brokers. The big multi-million-dollar trophy houses (and to be fair, some of the more under-stated ones, too) host families like the Gambles of Procter & Gamble, Du Ponts, Jane Fonda and Ted Turner, R. H. Macy, R. J. Reynolds, Bill Blass, author David Halberstam, Pierre Salinger, and architect Graham Gund.

In 1966 Nantucket was declared a national historic landmark: It boasts more than 800 buildings constructed before 1850—the largest concentration of such buildings in the United States. The historic district is picture-perfect: paved cobblestone streets, brick sidewalks, electrified "gas" street lamps. Gray-shingled houses are nestled close together on narrow lanes, which wind as you amble beyond the downtown grid of streets. Sturdy white residences are trimmed with English boxwood hedges, white picket fences, and flower gardens.

With a daily summer population that often swells to 50,000, today's tourist industry is about as well oiled as the whale industry once was. It's difficult to find a grain of sand or a seashell that hasn't been discovered.

Most sites in Nantucket are within a mile of the historic center—you'll probably walk more than you're accustomed to. Although there are little pockets of settlements around the island, the only real "destination" is 'Sconset, an utterly quaint village with rose-covered cottages. But with more than 40 percent of the island's 10,000 acres held by conservation trusts, you'll be able to explore places where most tourists don't venture. In addition to outstanding historic houses (many of which have been turned into bed & breakfasts) and museums, the island boasts excellent bicycle paths and almost limitless public beaches. Nor is it an exaggeration to say that Nantucket prides itself on world-class dining.

Nantucket is a year-round destination. Millions of daffodils blanket the island in yellow as the earth reawakens each April. The weather in May and June is slightly less predictable than in fall, but if you hit a nice stretch, you'll muse that life doesn't get any better. Gardens look best in May and June. Where once there were whaling ships, yachts now fill the harbor in summer. Warm ocean water and beach barbecues beckon, wild roses trail along picket fences, and many special events are staged. Come September (my favorite month on-island), the crowds recede a

Nantucket, often called the little grey lady, is shrouded in fog.

bit. You can swim in the still-temperate ocean by day and not have to wait for a table at your favorite restaurant at night. Skies turn crisp blue, and cranberry bogs, heathlands, and the moors blaze red, russet, and maroon. Many restaurants that close in mid-October (Columbus Day weekend) reopen for the long Thanksgiving weekend. The first three weeks of November are very quiet indeed. Before the monochrome days of winter set in, there is one last burst of activity: Nantucket Noel and Christmas Stroll (see *Special Events*). In January, February, and March you'll discover why whaling captains called the island the little grey lady—she is often shrouded in fog. It's a time of reflection and renewal for year-rounders and visitors alike.

GUIDANCE

❋ **Nantucket Visitor Services & Information Bureau** (508-228-0925), 25 Federal Street. Open 9–5:30 daily, year-round; 8–6 June through August. In addition to information on special events and transportation schedules, the bureau also maintains **seasonal kiosks** at **Steamboat Wharf** and at **Straight Wharf.** Whenever I stop in, I find the staff to be quite overworked. Although the bureau has information on daily guest house vacancies, don't wait until the last minute to locate a place to stay.

❋ **Nantucket Island Chamber of Commerce** (508-228-1700; www. nantucketchamber.org), 48 Main Street. Located on the second floor, the chamber is open 9–5 weekdays year-round. It produces a glossy book, *The Official Guide: Nantucket,* which is free on-island but costs $7 to mail in advance of your visit.

✿ **Nantucket Historical Association** (NHA) (508-228-1894; www.nha. org), 15 Broad Street within the Peter Foulger Museum. The NHA, which celebrated its centennial in 1994 and owns 14 historic properties, is a fabulous source of historical information. NHA properties represent island life from its farming beginnings to its prosperous whaling days. As you walk around Nantucket, notice the small, round plaques—made of different materials—that date the houses: 17TH CENTURY (silver), 1700–1775 (bronze), 1776–1812 (brass), 1813–1846 (green), and 1847–1900 (black). Generally, the NHA properties are open 10–5 daily, mid-June to early September, 11–3 late May to mid-June and from early September to mid-October, and 11–3 weekends in early Spring and late fall. Since the hours change from year to year, it's best to stop in or call ahead. A combination ticket is valid for admission to all properties, all seasons, and includes a very good walking tour: adults $10; children 5–14, $5. Purchase combination tickets at the Nantucket Whaling Museum on Broad Street.

ISLAND WEB SITES

www.nantucket.net

www.nantucketonline.com

www.nantucketvisit.net

PUBLIC LIBRARIES

See Atheneum under *To See*, below.

PUBLIC REST ROOMS

Rest rooms are located at the **Visitor Services & Information Bureau** at 25 Federal Street (open year-round), and at **Children's Beach** (see *Green Space—Beaches*) and **Straight Wharf** (both open seasonally).

INTERNET ACCESS

❋ **InterNet Cafe** (508-228-9165); www.nantucket.net), upstairs at 2 Union Street, behind Nantucket Mills. Hours are variable for public use, so call ahead. If you can't leave the modern world behind, if you want to send or receive e-mail, if you need to check in with the office, this upstairs space with six computers is the place for you. By the way, the savvy publishers of the free weekly *Yesterday's Island* run this useful place. $5 for 30 minutes of computer use.

GETTING THERE

With the inauguration of high-speed ferry service, day-tripping to Nantucket from Hyannis more feasible than ever. Although I still recommend spending a few days on Nantucket (if you can), you are no longer shut out if you can't.

❋ *By boat and high-speed ferry from Hyannis:* **The Steamship Authority** (508-477-8600 for information and advance auto reservations; 508-771-4000 for day-of-sailing information in Hyannis; 508-228-0262 for day-of-sailing information on Nantucket; www.islandferry.com), South Street Dock, Hyannis. The Steamship Authority, established in 1948, carries autos, people, and bikes to Steamship Wharf year-round. Make car reservations in spring for summer if you can; no reservations are needed for passengers. In high season, there are six sailings daily, three off-season. Parking in Hyannis is $8–10 per calendar day, depending on the time of year. The voyage takes 2¼ hours. Round-trip fares: adults $25; children 5–12, $12.50 (free under age 5); bicycles $10. Cars cost a whopping $316 mid-May to mid-October, $194 off-season. There are lockers at the Steamship terminal for storing luggage.

Steamship Authority's *Flying Cloud* High Speed Passenger Boat (508-495-3278; 508-477-8600), South Street Dock, Hyannis. Dock to dock in 1 hour. The boat sails late May through December and makes five to six trips daily; $42 adults, $31.50 children 5–12. Reservations strongly suggested.

❊ **Hy-Line Cruises** (508-778-2600 in Hyannis; 508-228-3949 on Nantucket; 1-888-778-1132 for advance sales; www.hy-linecruises.com), Ocean Street Dock, Hyannis. Passengers and bicycles to Straight Wharf, early May through October. In summer there are five boats daily, one to three daily off-season. There is a first-class lounge aboard the M/V *Great Point* if you don't mind paying $42 round-trip. Otherwise, round trip fares are adults $25; children 5–12, $12.50; bicycles $10. Parking in Hyannis is $8–12 per calendar day.

❊ **Hy-Line's Grey Lady II High Speed Passenger Boat** (508-778-0404; 1-800-492-8082; www.hy-linecruises.com), Ocean Street Dock. This high-speed luxury catamaran costs a bit more but it operates year-round: $55 adults, children 12 and under $40. Reservations are strongly recommended. There are five to six boats daily, with the last one departing at 6 or 8:45 PM, depending on time of year.

By boat from Harwich: **Freedom Cruise Line** (508-432-8999; www.capecod.net/freedom), Saquatucket Harbor in Harwichport, provides daily passenger service to Nantucket, mid-May to mid-October and during the Christmas Stroll (see *Special Events*). During the summer, two of the three trips are scheduled so you can explore Nantucket for about 6 hours and return the same day. In spring and fall, there is only one morning boat daily. Reservations are highly recommended. Round-trip prices: adults $39; children 2–12, $34; bicycles $10. Free parking for day-trippers; $12 per day thereafter. The trip takes 1½ hours each way.

By boat from Martha's Vineyard: **Hy-Line Cruises** (508-778-2600 in Hyannis; 508-228-3949 on Nantucket; 508-693-0112 in Oak Bluffs, Martha's Vineyard; www.hy-linecruises.com). Three daily, inter-island departures from early June to mid-September. The trip takes 2¼ hours. (There is no inter-island car ferry. From the Vineyard, you would take the ferry back to Falmouth or Woods Hole and drive your car to Hyannis—30 to 45 minutes—if you want to take your car to Nantucket.) One way: adults $13.50; children 5–12, $6.75; bicycles $5. No credit cards.

By air: There is a tourist information booth at Nantucket Memorial Airport. **Cape Air** and **Nantucket Airlines** (508-228-7695; 1-800-352-0714; www.flycapeair.com) offer more than 100 daily flights direct from Boston, Hyannis, New Bedford, Providence (T. F. Green), and Martha's Vineyard. Frequent-flier coupon books for 10 one-way trips are available. Round-trip summer fares are $120 from New Bedford, $76 from Hyannis, $180–220 from Boston, $175 from Providence, and $75 from Martha's Vineyard. Don't forget to add the cost of parking. **Island Air** (508-228-7575; 1-800-248-7779) offers daily, year-round flights from Hyannis. Flight time is 20 minutes, and fares are competitive. **Colgan Air** (508-325-5100; 1-800-272-5488) offers year-round service from Nantucket to Hyannis and La Guardia, New York. **Continental Express** (1-800-525-0280) flies out of Newark, New Jersey, and **Business Express/Delta Connection** (1-800-345-3400) from Boston; both are seasonal. **USAir** (1-800-248-7779) also flies to Nantucket.

With the island's growing popularity among a jet-owning crowd and business executives, it's no wonder that Nantucket Memorial Airport logged more landings and takeoffs (1,200) on the 1996 July 4 weekend than anywhere else in the country. If you don't have your own plane, **Ocean Wings/Coastal Air** (508-325-5548; 1-800-253-5039) offers charter flights.

GETTING AROUND

NRTA Shuttle (508-228-7025). Daily 7 AM–11:30 PM late May through September. This is an economical and reliable way to travel to 'Sconset (two routes) and Madaket, but the schedule is fairly complicated to disseminate here. Pick up a route map with all the details on Nantucket. Shuttles have a bike rack, so you can take the bus out to 'Sconset, for instance, and ride back. There are also two routes circling the edges of town (South Loop and Miacomet Loop). The Surfside and Jetties Beach buses run from mid-June to early September. Tickets cost either 50¢ or $1, depending on the route. Three-day ($10) and weekly ($15) passes are a smart idea; purchase them at the Visitor Services & Information Bureau (see *Guidance*), weekdays 9–2.

By car: There isn't a single traffic light in Nantucket, and Nantucketers intend to keep it that way. You don't need a car unless you're here for at least a week or unless you plan to spend most of your time in conservation areas or on outlying beaches. Even then, a four-wheel-drive vehicle is the most useful, as many of the stunning natural areas are off sandy paths. Parking is severely restricted in the historic center. Prices vary considerably; it pays to call around. Rent from **Nantucket Windmill Auto Rental** (508-228-1227; 1-800-228-1227), based at the airport and offering free pickup and delivery of vehicles (if they have an available driver); *Affordable Rentals* (508-228-3501; 1-877-235-3500), South Beach Street; and **Young's** (508-228-1151), Steamboat Wharf. **Budget** (508-228-5666; 1-800-527-0700) and **Hertz** (508-228-9421; 1-800-654-3131) are both based at the airport. The least expensive rental cars cost $90–100 daily in summer, almost half that off-season, and disappear quickly in summer.

By four-wheel drive: Nantucket is ringed by 80 miles of beach, most of which are accessible via four-wheel drive. In addition to the above companies, try **Nantucket Jeep Rental** (508-228-1618), which delivers. Four-wheel drives are rented faster than the speed of light in summer. Make reservations at least a month in advance of summer or as early as June for August. Expect to spend $175–220 daily in-season, $100–125 off-season.

If you get stuck in the sand, as one reader did and confessed to me, call **Harry's Towing** (508-228-3390). Once you do call him, though, wait with your vehicle so he doesn't make the trek out to fetch you, only to find that you've been helped by a friendly local. I'm sure you can appreciate his efforts.

Contact the **Police Department** (508-228-1212), South Water Street, for overland permits required for four-wheel, over-sand driving: $20 yearly for private vehicles. You can purchase them daily mid-May to mid-October.

The Coatue–Coskata–Great Point nature area (see *Green Space*) requires a separate permit, available from the **Nantucket Conservation Foundation** (508-228-2884 for information; 508-228-0006 for the refuge gatehouse, where permits are purchased) mid-May through October ($20 daily, $85 year-round). During the off-season, pay the rangers who patrol the area. Most beaches are open to four-wheel-drive traffic, except when terns are nesting.

By taxi: Taxi fares can add up, but cabs are a useful way to get to the airport or to an outlying restaurant. Taxis usually line up on lower Main Street and at Steamboat Wharf. Flat rates are based on the destination: $15 to 'Sconset, $5 to the airport, and $3 within town, for instance. Rates are for one person; add $1 for each additional passenger.

By bicycle: Bicycling is the best way to get around (see *Outdoor Activities— Bicycling/Rentals*).

By moped: **Nantucket Bike Shop** (508-228-1999), Steamboat Wharf, rents scooters from April through October; daily $50 single and $70 double.

✳ *By van or bus tours:* **Gail's Tours** (508-257-6557), run by seventh-generation Nantucketer Gail Nickerson Johnson, offers 90-minute narrated van tours for up to 13 people. Tours leave at 10 AM, 1 PM, and 3 PM from the Visitor Services & Information Bureau on Federal Street (see *Guidance*). While Gail gives tidbits of trivia, both historic and contemporary, that will bring the island alive, she also spends a lot of time discussing which celebrities and millionaires own which houses. If that happens, and you don't want it to, try asking a few specific questions to get the discussion on the track you want. On my most recent tour, she was on the cell phone quite a bit. Nonetheless, Gail's is a unique perspective; her mother began giving tours in the mid-1950s. $13 per person; reservations advised.

Ara's Tours (508-228-1951), mid-April to mid-December. These late-afternoon, 3-hour barrier beach tours of Great Point (see *Green Space*) attract a lot of photographers and outdoors types; call for prices. Ara also has 90-minute island tours for $12 that make stops for photography.

❄ **Bob Pitman Grimes** (508-228-9382), Lower Main Street, also offers a good van tour for up to eight people, departing three times daily (at 10, 1, and 3).

🎗 **Trustees of Reservations** (508-228-6799) offers excellent 3-hour natural history tours of Great Point from mid-May to mid-October. Tours depart at 9:30 AM and 1:30 PM and culminate with an ascent of the Great Point Lighthouse. Adults $30, children 15 and under $15.

Barrett's Tours (508-228-0174; 1-800-773-0174 in eastern Massachusetts), 20 Federal Street, and **Nantucket Island Tours** (508-228-0334), Straight Wharf, offer 60-minute narrated mini-bus tours May through October. $13 adults, $6 for children.

By foot:

Dirk Gardiner Roggeveen's Nantucket Walking Tours (508-221-0075) are the best on-island. Period. A former Justice Department lawyer and 12th-generation islander, Dirk provides commentary that is delightful, humorous, and rich in anecdotal and island lore. If you thought history was about the past and architecture about bricks, you'll change your mind after his compelling 90-minute strolls. $10 per person.

✐ **Nantucket Ghost Walk** (508-325-8855) departs from in front of the Atheneum (Federal and India Streets) at 7 PM from early September to early December on many Wednesday through Sunday nights. The walk and talk takes 45 minutes and costs $10 adults, $5 children age 6–12. You can always arrange for a private walk.

The Nantucket Historical Association has a self-guided **Walking Tour Map** of its properties. It takes $2^{1}/_{2}$–$3^{1}/_{2}$ hours, without spending too much time in any single house.

MEDICAL EMERGENCY

Nantucket Cottage Hospital (508-228-1200), South Prospect Street. Open 24 hours.

Lyme disease. Ticks carry this disease which has flu-like symptoms and may result in death if left untreated. Immediately and carefully remove any ticks that may have migrated from dune grasses to your body. Better yet, wear long pants, tuck pants into socks, and wear long-sleeved shirts whenever possible when hiking. Avoid hiking in grassy and overgrown areas of dense brush.

TO SEE

ON THE HARBOR

The wharves (from north to south). The Steamship Authority is based at Steamboat Wharf; but from 1881 to 1917, steam trains, which met the early steam-powered ferries and transported passengers to Surfside and 'Sconset, originated here. **Old North Wharf** is home to privately owned summer cottages. **Straight Wharf,** originally built in 1723 by

Richard Macy, is a center of activity. It was completely rebuilt in the 1960s (except for the Thomas Macy Warehouse; see below) as part of a preservation effort. The wharf is home to Hy-Line, a few T-shirt and touristy shops, restaurants, a gallery, a museum, a nice pavilion area, and charter boats and sailboats. Straight Wharf was so named because folks could cart things from here "straight" up Main Street. **Old South Wharf** houses art galleries, crafts shops, and clothing shops in quaint little one-room "shacks" (see *Selective Shopping*). **Commercial Wharf,** also known as **Swain's Wharf,** was built in the early 1800s by Zenas Coffin.

Thomas Macy Warehouse, Straight Wharf. Built after the Great Fire of 1846, when the wharves were completely destroyed and more than 400 houses burned, the warehouse stored supplies to outfit ships. Today, the Nantucket Historical Association leases the warehouse to an excellent private art gallery. (See *Selective Shopping—Art Galleries.*)

MAIN STREET

Main Street. The lower three blocks of Main Street were paved in 1837 with cobblestones, purchased in Gloucester, that proved quite useful— they kept carts laden with whale oil from sinking into the sand and dirt as they were rolled from wharves to factories. After the Great Fire swept through town, Main Street was widened considerably to prevent another fire from jumping from house to house so rapidly. In the mid-1850s Henry and Charles Coffin planted dozens of elm trees along the street, but only a few have survived disease over the years. The former drinking fountain for horses, which today spills over with flowers, has been a landmark on Lower Main since it was moved here in the early 1900s.

Pacific Club, Main Street at South Water Street. This three-story, Georgian brick building was built as a warehouse and countinghouse for shipowner William Rotch, owner of the *Beaver* and *Dartmouth,* two ships that took part in the Boston Tea Party. In 1789 it served as a U.S. Customs House. In 1861 a group of retired whaling captains purchased the building for use as a private social club, where they swapped stories and played cribbage. Descendants of these original founders carry on the tradition of the elite club.

Pacific National Bank (508-228-1917), 61 Main Street at Fair Street. This 1818, two-story, Federal-style brick building is one of only four to survive the Great Fire. It's no coincidence that the two important buildings anchoring Main Street are named "Pacific" for the fortunes reaped from the Pacific Ocean: This bank almost single-handedly financed the wealthy whaling industry. Step inside to see the handsome main room, original teller cages, and murals of the port and street scenes.

Thomas Macy House, 99 Main Street. Many think this is Nantucket's most attractive doorway, with its silver doorplate, porch railing that curves outward, and wooden fan work. This NHA (Nantucket Historical Association) property is open to the public on special occasions.

One of "Two Greeks" (aka Hadwen House) on Main Street

"Three Bricks," 93, 95, and 97 Main Street. These identical Georgian mansions were built in 1836 for the three sons (all under the age of 27) of whaling-ship magnate Joseph Starbuck. Joseph retained the house titles to ensure that his sons would continue the family business. When the sons approached age 40 (firmly entrenched in the business), Joseph deeded the houses to them. One house remains in the Starbuck family; none is open to the public.

Hadwen House (508-228-1894), 96 Main Street. Taken together, 94 Main (privately owned) and 96 Main are referred to architecturally as the Two Greeks. Candle merchant William Hadwen married one of Joseph Starbuck's daughters and built the Greek Revival house (at No. 96).

(Starbuck's two other daughters also ended up living across the street from their brothers—at 92 and 100 Main Street—creating a virtual Starbuck compound.) Docents point out gas chandeliers, a circular staircase, Italian marble fireplaces, silver doorknobs, and period furnishings. Don't overlook the lovely historic garden in back. The "other" Greek (No. 94) was built in the mid–19th century for Mary G. Swain, Starbuck's niece; note the Corinthian capitals supposedly modeled after the Athenian Temple of the Winds. This is another NHA property (see *Guidance* for hours); $4 adults, $3 children.

Henry Coffin House and **Charles Coffin House,** 75 and 78 Main Street. The Coffin brothers inherited their fortunes from their father's candle-making and whaling enterprises and general mercantile business. They built their houses across the street from each other, using the same carpenters and masons. Charles was a Quaker, and his Greek Revival house (No .78) has a simple roof walk and modest brown trim. Henry's late-Federal-style house (No. 75) has fancy marble trim around the front door and a cupola. Neither is open to the public.

John Wendell Barrett House, 72 Main Street. This elegant Greek Revival house features a front porch with Ionic columns and a raised basement. Barrett was the president of the Pacific National Bank and a wealthy whale oil merchant, but the house is best known for another reason. During the Great Fire, Barrett's wife, Lydia, refused to leave the front porch. Firefighters wanted to blow up the house in order to deprive the fire of fuel. Luckily for her, the winds shifted and further confrontation was averted. Not open to the public.

NORTH OF MAIN STREET

✻T✺**Atheneum** (508-228-1110), Lower India Street. Open Monday, Wednesday, Friday, and Saturday 9:30–5; Tuesday and Thursday 9:30–8; closed Monday off-season. This fine Greek Revival building with Ionic columns was designed by Frederick Coleman, who designed the "Two Greeks" (see Hadwen House, above). When the library and all its contents were lost in the Great Fire, donations poured in from around the country and a new building replaced it within six months. The Great Hall on the second floor has hosted such distinguished orators as Frederick Douglass, Daniel Webster, Horace Greeley, Henry David Thoreau, Ralph Waldo Emerson (who gave the inaugural address), and John James Audubon. (The hall seats about 100 people; there are numerous free readings and lectures here.) Maria Mitchell (see Maria Mitchell Association, below) was the first librarian. Since then there have been only five other librarians in its long history. In addition to comfortable reading rooms on both floors, the Atheneum has an excellent children's wing and a nice garden out back. Some of the more than 40,000 volumes include town newspapers dating from 1816, early New England genealogy, and ships' logs. Portraits of whaling captains grace the space, while display cases are filled with scrimshaw and other historical artifacts. This is one of the island's most special places. It's a quiet refuge from the masses in the height of summer, as well as a delightful place to spend a rainy day. Call for information about special events and story hours.

T **Nantucket Whaling Museum** (508-228-1736), Broad Street. Open daily late April through early October, except open only on weekends in early spring and late autumn. This 1846 brick building, now another NHA property (see *Guidance* for hours), began as Richard Mitchell's spermaceti candle factory. (Spermaceti, by the way, is a substance found in the cavity of a sperm whale's head; it was a great source of lamp and machine oil.) Now the building houses an outstanding museum preserving Nantucket's whaling history. It's a must-see on even the shortest itinerary. Exhibits include the lens from the Sankaty Head Lighthouse, a 43-foot skeleton of a finback whale (beached in the 1960s), lightship basket and scrimshaw collections, an around-the-world map tracing the voyages of the whaling ship *Alpha*, and a reproduction tryworks, which was used to boil down whale oil on board ships. You'll also see a fully rigged whale boat, which will help you envision the treacherous "Nantucket sleigh ride": When the small boat harpooned a mammoth whale and remained connected by a rope, the boat was dragged through the waves until the whale tired. Daily lectures are offered by museum staff. Adults $5, children $3.

Peter Foulger Museum (508-228-1894), 15 Broad Street. One of the island's first settlers, Peter Foulger acted as an interpreter when they purchased the island from Native Americans in 1659. Peter's daughter Abiah was Ben Franklin's mother. This NHA property has changing exhibits (see *Guidance* for hours). Adults $5, children $3.

Centre Street. Centre Street was referred to as Petticoat Row during the whaling era, when men were out to sea and women were left to run the shops and businesses. It's still chock-full of fine shops.

First Congregational Church (508-228-0950), 62 Centre Street. Open 10–4 Monday through Saturday, mid-June to mid-October. This church is known for its 120-foot steeple, from which there are 360-degree panoramic views of the island and ocean. On a clear day you can see from Eel Point to Great Point (see *Green Space*), and the moors in between. Photographers shouldn't get too excited, because they'll have to shoot through dirty storm windows. The present steeple was built in 1968; the previous one was dismantled in 1849 when it was deemed too shaky to withstand storms. The church was built with whaling money at the industry's apex in 1834. Note the things money could buy: a 600-pound brass chandelier and trompe l'oeil walls. The rear wing of the church contains the simple vestry, the oldest church building on the island (circa 1720). Since the late 1970s a special concert has been given in early July on Rose Sunday, when the church interior and island are full of blooming wild roses. Donation suggested for climbing the steeple: $2 adult, 50¢ children.

Nantucket's oldest house

KIM GRANT

- **Oldest House** (508-228-1894), Sunset Hill Road. Also known as the Jethro Coffin House, this 1686 home was built as a wedding present for Jethro Coffin and Mary Gardner by their parents. The marriage joined two prominent island families—the Coffins were "original purchasers" while the Gardners were "half-share men." When lightning struck the house in 1987, the NHA (see *Guidance* for hours) decided it was time to restore it. Features include small, diamond-shaped, leaded windows, sparse period furnishings, and a huge central chimney decorated with an upside-down horseshoe. Peter Coffin cut and shipped timbers from his land in Exeter, New Hampshire, for the house. Adults $3, children $2.
- **Brant Point Lighthouse,** off Easton Street. In 1746 the island's first "lighthouse" (and the country's second oldest after Boston Light) guarded the harbor's northern entrance. It was rather primitive, consisting of a lantern hung on rope between two poles. The lighthouse standing today is small in size but large in symbolism. Folklore and tradition suggest that throwing two pennies overboard as you round the point at the lighthouse ensures your return. Many do, and many do.

NEAR OR OFF UPPER MAIN STREET

- **Quaker Meeting House** (508-228-1894), 11 Fair Street. Open mid-June to mid-September. This small, simple building with wooden benches and 12-over-12 windows began as a Friends school in 1838. NHA property (see *Guidance* for hours); free.
- **Fair Street Research Library** (508-228-0722), 11 Fair Street. At press time the Edouard A. Stackpole Library and Research Center (see *Even More Things to See and Do—Special Programs*) was moving its collection of manuscripts, photographs, ships' logs, and other items

here. Look for the possibility of changing exhibits from the NHA's permanent collections. Hours unavailable at press time.

St. Paul's Episcopal Church (508-228-0916), 20 Fair Street. Stop in to admire this granite church's Tiffany windows.

❄ **Unitarian Universalist Church** (508-228-5466), 11 Orange Street. Open July and August 10–4 daily; the office is also open weekday mornings the rest of the year, so you're welcome to stop in. Orange Street was once home to more than 100 whaling captains. This 1809 church, also called South Church, is known for its tall spire (quite visible at sea and a distinct part of the Nantucket "skyline"); a wonderfully illusory trompe l'oeil golden dome; and a mahogany and ivory 1831 Goodrich organ. For years, a town crier watched for ships and fires from the tower.

Macy-Christian House (508-228-1894), 12 Liberty Street. This circa-1740 two-story lean-to was built by Thomas Macy, and it remained in the family until 1827. The upstairs bedrooms are closest to the original colonial home. When the Reverend Mr. Christian purchased the house in 1934, he renovated much of the house in Colonial Revival style. Docents help you sort out what belongs to which period. NHA property (see *Guidance* for hours). Adults $2, children $1.

Lightship Basket Museum (508-228-1177), 49 Union Street. Open late May to mid-October, Wednesday through Sunday, 10–5. New in 2000, this informative little museum has re-created a workshop with simple tools that helps visitors understand the simple techniques artisans employed to make exquisite baskets. It certainly helps promote the craft.

❦ **The Coffin School** (508-228-2505; www.marinehomecenter.com/egan institute), 4 Winter Street, one block off Main Street. Open 1–5 daily from late May to mid-October. The school was founded in 1827 by Adm. Sir Isaac Coffin, English baronet and a descendant of Tristram Coffin, one of the island's first settlers. It was established to provide a "good English education" for Coffin descendants. (In the early 19th century, more than half of Nantucket's children were Coffin descendants.) The impressive brick Greek Revival building now serves as home for the **Egan Institute of Maritime Studies.** It displays changing special exhibits on subjects relating to Nantucket history. A fine collection of 19th-century paintings portraying significant Nantucket events is featured, including works by Elizabeth R. Coffin, a student of Thomas Eakins. Historical lectures on the school and maritime subjects are given year-round. Contact curator and author Margaret Moore Booker about a fine selection of local historical books published by Mill Hill Press. Admission $1.

BEYOND UPPER MAIN STREET

Hose Fire Cart House (508-228-1894), 8 Gardner Street. This small 1886 neighborhood fire station is the only one of its kind remaining on-island. As you can imagine, lots of stations were built after the Great

Fire. On display are leather buckets and an old hand pumper, used more than a century ago. NHA property (see *Guidance* for hours); free.

Old Gaol (508-228-1894), 15R Vestal Street. This 1805 penal institution, built of logs bolted together with iron, was used until 1933. It had only four cells. The first incarcerated felon escaped, but others weren't so lucky. Well, perhaps they were—it's said that most of the prisoners got to sleep at home rather than on the planks that served as beds. NHA property (see *Guidance* for hours); free.

🖉 **Maria Mitchell Association** (508-228-9198; www.mmo.org), 4 Vestal Street. Founded in 1902, the association owns the following five properties that celebrate the life and continue the work of Maria (pronounced mar-EYE-a) Mitchell, born on-island August 1, 1818. At age 13 Maria helped whaling captains set their navigational devices, with the aid of astronomical projections. At 18 she became the librarian at the Atheneum, where she served for the next 20 years. At 29 Mitchell was the first woman to discover a comet (which was dubbed Mitchell's comet)—from atop the Pacific National Bank, where her father (bank president and amateur astronomer) had set up an observatory. Maria was also the first woman to be admitted to the American Academy of Arts and Sciences and the first woman college professor of astronomy. (She taught at Vassar from 1865 until her death in 1888.) The association hosts a number of children's programs that foster an appreciation of the connection between science and "beauty and poetry." Also, look for postings of special lectures and walks sponsored by the group; I've never been to one that was less than excellent. A combination ticket (available at any of the properties) is $7 for adults and $5 for children 6–14, but tickets may also be purchased separately ($3 and $2, respectively).

❋🖉 **Maria Mitchell Science Library** (508-228-9219; www.mmo.org), 4 Vestal Street. Open 10–4 Tuesday through Saturday, mid-June through August; 2–5 Wednesday through Friday and 9–noon Saturday, September to mid-June. The library, which has a children's section, houses 19th-century science books, current scientific periodicals, Maria's own papers, and natural history and astronomy books. Maria's father taught navigation by the stars in this former schoolhouse. Free.

Maria Mitchell Birthplace (508-228-2896; www.mmo.org), 1 Vestal Street. Open 10–4 Tuesday through Saturday, mid-June through August. Built in 1790, Mitchell's birthplace contains family memorabilia and the telescope she used to spot her comet. Tour the house and check out the island's only public roof walk. Adults $3, children $2.

🖉 **Hinchman House** (508-228-0898; www.mmo.org), 7 Milk Street. Open 10–4 Tuesday through Saturday, mid-June through August. This natural science museum has live reptiles and preserved plant and bird specimens from the island. Inquire about excellent nature programs and field trips for children. Adults $3, children $1.

❋ **Loines Observatory** (508-228-8690; www.mmo.org), Milk Street Exten-

KIM GRANT

The Old Mill

sion. The observatory is closed to the public except on clear Monday, Wednesday, and Friday evenings in summer (call to confirm days), when lectures and telescope viewings are held. It's also open year-round on Saturday evening. Admission is $10 adults, $5 children.

🐚 **Aquarium** (508-228-5387; www.mmo.org), 28 Washington Street. Open 10–4 Tuesday through Saturday, mid-June to early August; limited

Nantucket Lifesaving Museum

autumn hours until mid-October. Near the town pier, the small Aquarium has fresh- and saltwater tanks; science interns are on hand to answer questions. Popular marine-life collecting trips are offered Tuesday through Thursday and Saturday; reservations required. Admission $2.

Old Mill (508-228-1894), South Mill and Prospect Streets. Reputed to be made with salvaged wood, this 1746 Dutch-style windmill has canvas sails and a granite stone that still grinds corn in summer. A reminder of when the island's principal activity was farming, this windmill is the only one of the four original that remains. (It's in its original location, too.) NHA property (see *Guidance* for hours). Adults $2, children $1.

African Meeting House (508-228-9833; www.afroammuseum.org), York and Pleasant Streets. Open by appointment. Built as a schoolhouse in the 1820s, when black children were barred from public school, this house is thought to be the second oldest such building in the country. Currently undergoing restoration, it will open as an educational center with interpretive exhibits on the island's African American and Cape Verdean communities. Friends of the African Meeting House publish a very good pamphlet with a walking tour of the island's black heritage sites.

Moor's End, 19 Pleasant Street. This large 1830s Georgian house, the first island house made with brick, belonged to Jared Coffin. Although today it's among the island's finest, Mrs. Coffin was not satisfied with its location. She wanted to be closer to town, and so Jared built another at 29 Broad Street (see Jared Coffin House under *Lodging—Inns*). A beautiful garden lies behind the tall brick wall, but unfortunately for us, like the house, it's private.

AROUND THE ISLAND

Siasconset. More commonly referred to as **'Sconset,** this charming village on the eastern shore is the island's only real "destination," 7 miles from town. (Well, for the adventuresome, Great Point—see *Green Space*—is the other "destination.") The village is renowned for its tiny rose-covered cottages, all a few feet from one another. Some of the oldest are clustered on Broadway, Centre, and Shell Streets. You won't have any problem finding them since the town consists of only a post office, a liquor store, a market, and three restaurants. Of course, 'Sconset has its share of grand summer homes—along Ocean Avenue and Sankaty and Baxter Roads (on the way to Sankaty Head Lighthouse; see below). Recently, the combination of severe winter storms and the absence of offshore shoals to break incoming waves has created extreme beach erosion. Beachfront homes have been moved after several were engulfed by the sea.

Siasconset, which means "land of many bones," was probably named after a right whale was found on the beach. The 17th-century village was settled by and used as a base for fishermen in search of cod and whales. When wives began to join their husbands here in summer, the one-room shanties were expanded with additions called warts. (Perhaps early summer visitors wanted to escape the oil refineries in town, too.) When the narrow-gauge railway was built in 1884, it brought vacationing New York City actors who established a thriving actors' colony. Today there are 150 hardy souls who live here year-round.

A few "sites" in 'Sconset include the 'Sconset Pump, an old wooden water pump dug in 1776, and the 'Sconset Union Chapel, the only place of worship in town. Despite its name, the Siasconset Casino, built in 1899 as a private tennis club, has never been used for gambling. Turn-of-the-20th-century actors used it for summer theater; movies are now shown in summer (see *Entertainment—Movies/Films*).

Sankaty Head Light, 'Sconset. Partially solar powered, this red-and-white-striped light stands on a 90-foot-high bluff at the edge of a rapidly encroaching shoreline. In 1998 it was a mere 100 feet from the ocean's edge. Its light is visible 24 miles out to sea.

Great Point Light, Great Point, is accessible by four-wheel-drive vehicle, by boat, or by a difficult 5-mile (one way) trek through soft sand. A 70-foot stone structure guarded the island's northeastern tip for 166 years, until a ferocious storm destroyed it in 1984. This new one was built to withstand 20-foot waves and 240-mph winds.

Madaket. When Thomas Macy landed here in 1659, he found sandy, poor soil and didn't stay long. Today there is a large summer community, with many rental houses. On the western coast, Madaket is a great place to enjoy a sunset, do some bluefishing, or get a boat repaired in the boatyard. The picturesque creek is best viewed from the little bridge to the right of the main road.

Nantucket Lifesaving Museum (508-228-1885), 158 Polpis Road on

Folger's Marsh. Open 9:30–4 daily, mid-June to mid-October. This building replicates the original 1874 Surfside Lifesaving Service station that survives today as the Nantucket Hostel (see *Lodging—Hostel*). Instead of being at water's edge, however, it's scenically situated on a salt marsh—perfect for a picnic. Dedicated to humanity's dramatic efforts against the relentless sea, this museum houses equipment used in the daring rescues of sailors stranded in their sinking offshore boats. You'll find one of four Massachusetts Humane Society lifesaving surfboats and the only surviving beachcart still used for demonstration drills. You'll also find photographs, accounts of rescues, Nantucket's three Fresnel lighthouse lenses, and artifacts from the *Andrea Doria,* which sank off Nantucket 40 years ago. $4 adults, $2 children 6 and over.

OUTDOOR ACTIVITIES

BICYCLING/RENTALS
Excellent paved, two-way bicycle paths lead to most major "destinations."

Rubel Bike Maps (www.bikemaps.com) are simply the best, most detailed maps available for the Cape and islands. Rubel produces a combination Nantucket and Vineyard map ($1.95), as well as another that includes the islands, Cape Cod, and the North Shore ($4.25). Even though bike rental agencies give you a free map, Rubel's is very good and worthwhile.

Madaket Bike Path begins on Upper Main Street. This 6-mile (one-way) road takes you to the western end of Nantucket in 45 minutes. Although the route is a bit hilly and winding, it's beautiful. There are rest areas along the way and a water fountain at the halfway point. Picnic tables at Long Pond (see *Green Space—Ponds*), and usually elegant swans, too.

'Sconset (or **Milestone**) **Bike Path** begins at the rotary east of the historic district. This 7-mile (one way) route with slight inclines parallels Milestone Road; it takes about an hour to get to 'Sconset. (Visually, the ride is a bit dull.) There's a water fountain at the rotary.

Surfside Bike Path. Take Main Street to Pleasant Street and turn right onto Atlantic Avenue to Surfside Road. There are benches and water fountains along the 3½-mile (one-way) route. This flat path is very popular in summer; it takes about 20 minutes to get to the beach.

Polpis Road Path. After years and years of talking about a bikeway for this road, lined with thousands of daffodils in springtime, this trail was finally finished in 1999. The loop from the 'Sconset Bike Path to Polpis Road and back to town is about 16½ miles. It's definitely worth the detour.

Cliff Road Bike Path begins on Cliff Road from North Water Street. This 2½-mile, slightly hilly road passes large summer houses.

With more than 3,000 rental bikes on-island, companies offer competitive rates. Average prices: $25 per day for adult bikes, $90 per week; $15–20 daily for children's bikes; trailers, zipper strollers, and trail-a-bikes, too. Inquire about discounts for family rentals. The following shops rent bicycles: **Young's Bicycle Shop** (508-228-1151), Steamboat Wharf; **Nantucket Bike Shop** (508-228-1999), Steamboat Wharf; and **Cook's Cycles** (508-228-0800), 6 South Beach. Young's has the longest season, but Cook's is often a bit less expensive.

See also Eco Guides under *Outdoor Adventure.*

BIRD-WATCHING

Maria Mitchell Association (508-228-9198; 508-228-0898), Vestal Street, offers birding walks all over the island, mid-June to mid-September. Adults $10, children $6.

See also Eco Guides under *Outdoor Adventure.*

BOAT EXCURSIONS/RENTALS

❦ **Harbor Cruises *Anna W. II*** (508-228-1444), Slip 11, Straight Wharf. June to mid-October. Since 1961. The very nice and knowledgeable Capt. Bruce Cowan offers lots of good, different trips that leave at different times of the day and on different days; call for current details and prices. Marine Life Discovery tours (hauling traps with crabs, lobsters, eels, and fish), ice cream voyages, shoreline sight-seeing, and sunset cruises for either 60 or 90 minutes. Bring your own food and drink aboard. Seal cruises are offered on weekends in November and December.

Endeavor (508-228-5585), Slip 15, Straight Wharf. May through October. Capt. Jim Genthner and his wife, Sue, operate a 31-foot Friendship sloop that departs on at least three daily harbor tours and a sunset cruise. Adults $22.50–35 for a 90-minute sail; $15 for a 60-minute sail. Custom sails may include pirating for children and an on-board fiddler or story-teller.

Christina (508-325-4000), Slip 1016, Straight Wharf. This 1926 mahogany Catboat departs frequently for $25 harbor sails; $35 per person at sunset. Bring your own beverages.

Nantucket Boat Rentals (508-325-1001), Straight Wharf, Slip 1. Rents runabouts and powerboats by the day or week in-season.

❦ **Nantucket Island Community Sailing** (508-228-6600), Jetties Beach, rents windsurfers, Sunfish, and kayaks. It also holds youth and sailboard and sailing classes, as well as a racing class. Open for business mid- to late June through September (weather permitting).

COOKOUTS

Contact the Fire Department (508-228-2324), 131 Pleasant Street, for the requisite permits for charcoal cookouts and fires on the beach. If you want to make a bonfire, speak to the chief personally.

FISHING/SHELLFISHING

Permits for digging clams, mussels, and quahogs are obtained from the Marine Department and shellfish warden (508-228-7261), 38 Washington Street. Scalloping season opens October 1, after which you'll see fishermen in the harbor and off nearby shoals of Tuckernuck Island; bay scallops harvested from November through March are delicious.

Try your luck at freshwater fishing at **Long Pond** (see *Green Space—*

Ponds). Nantucket blues, which run in schools from May through October, are caught from the southern shore. Fishing isn't as good in July and August when the waters are warmer, but if that's the only time you're here, toss out a line anyway.

Mike Monte (508-228-0529), a year-round island resident, takes people surf-fishing and fly-fishing May through October. His daily trip generally goes out with "first light" at sunrise, and he has folks back in time to have breakfast with their friends and family. He'll take just one person, but no more than four. He also provides all the equipment necessary. Fishing for about 4 hours runs $120 per person.

Whitney Mitchell (508-228-2331) has taken surf-fishers to locations accessible only by four-wheel drives since 1983. Mid-June to mid-October, about $85 per person.

Barry Thurston's Tackle Shop (508-228-9595) at Salem and Candle Streets. Open April through late December. Yes, you need the tangible commodities like bait and tackle, fillet knives, rods, and reels. But even more valuable are fish stories, advice, and fishing gossip that Thurston's has been dishing out since 1976, when the native islander opened his shop. (Barry graduated in Nantucket's 1956 high school class.) He's got the goods on where the fish are running, what time, and what they're biting on. And he's happy to give it out—usually to generations of repeat families. For the casual as well as serious angler.

Bill Fisher Tackle (508-228-2261), 14 New Lane, rents a full line of equipment, supplies daily fishing reports, and provides guide service.

Most charters in search of striped bass and bluefish are located on Straight Wharf, including ***Herbert T*** (508-228-6655), Slip 14, and ***Just Do It Too*** (508-228-7448), Slip 13. You can also call **Sankaty Head Charters** (508-257-9606), which takes up to three people per 4- to 6-hour trip; tackle included. **Hal Herrick** (508-257-9606), highly recommended, is out of Madaket.

FOOTBALL

Nantucket High School (508-228-7280), off Surfside Road. From mid-September to mid-November, after most of the tourists have left, the smallest high school in the state suits up in anticipation of another winning season. If you want to feel like a real insider, check out one of these games with the rest of the 7,000 year-rounders, all of whom seem to show up for home games.

GOLF

Siasconset Golf Club (508-257-6596), Milestone Road. Open late May to mid-October. This nine-hole public course, encircled by conservation land, dates to 1894.

❋ **Miacomet Golf Club** (508-325-0333), off Somerset Road. This flat, nine-hole course is owned by the Nantucket Land Bank and has views of Miacomet Pond, heathland, and the coastline.

Sankaty Head Golf Club (508-257-6655), Sankaty Road, 'Sconset. Although this links-style, 18-hole course is private, the public may play from mid-April to late May and mid-October to early December. There are magnificent lighthouse views.

Nantucket Golf Club (508-257-4494), 250 Milestone Road (there's no sign). One of the most exclusive clubs anywhere. Many members, like gazillionaire Bill Gates, do not own property on-island, but rather jet in, play golf, and jet out. In mid-1998, memberships cost $200,000–300,000, plus annual dues. (The membership list is closely guarded but the *Boston Globe* reports that it has its share from the Forbes 400 Wealthiest Americans list—CEOs and former heads of Chanel, General Electric, Paramount, Corning Glass.) The par-72, links-style course rolls with the naturally undulating landscape, within sight of Sankaty Head Light, on the moors with scrub oak and pitch pine. Generally appreciated by island conservationists, who realize that it could have been developed in less favorable ways, the 250-acre course was designed by Rees Jones.

IN-LINE SKATING
Skating is prohibited in town during the summer. You can skate on the bike paths, though, and at the skateboarding park at Jetties Beach; helmets and pads are required and can be rented at the Parks and Recreation Building tennis office (508-325-5334).

KAYAKING
Sea Nantucket (508-228-7499), at Francis Street Beach, Washington Street Extension. Open May through September for roll-proof kayak and canoe rentals as well as guided tours for children and adults. These folks make deliveries to inland lakes and ponds. Half-day kayak rental: $30 single, $50 double; full day $40 single, $60 double. Canoes: $50 half day, $60 full day. It's usually calm paddling along the 8 miles of scalloped bays at Coatue. When the harbor is choppy, have a kayak delivered to an inland pond.

See also Eco Guides under *Outdoor Adventure* and Nantucket Island Community Sailing under *Boat Excursions/Rentals.*

MINI-GOLF
Nobader Mini Golf (508-228-8977), Nobader Farm and Sun Island Roads, off Milestone Road and the 'Sconset Bike Path. Open daily June to mid-October, until 11 PM in July and August. Families are lured to the island's only mini-golf establishment by the course itself, to be sure: Adults appreciate the lovely gardens, while kids enjoy the golf. Easy access off the 'Sconset Bike Path (see *Bicycling/Rentals*) and nearby NRTA bus stop. Adults $7; kids 4–18, $6. At press time, the mini-golf course was for sale; let's hope it stays a mini-golf course rather than being developed for condos.

OUTDOOR ADVENTURE
Eco Guides (508-228-1769; www.strongwings.com). John Simms offers casual, customized adventure instruction and guided group trips, for

novices and experts, in mountain biking, sea kayaking, snorkeling, and natural history. After settling on a trip, price, and meeting time with John, be absolutely sure that you confirm and reconfirm your trip. I have had reports of missed rendezvous. There is also a large youth organization geared toward year-rounders, but vacationing kids can participate, too.

SCUBA DIVING

❋ **The Sunken Ship** (508-228-9226), Broad and South Water Streets. Perhaps because the *Andrea Doria* sank off Nantucket's treacherous shoals in July 1956, the island is a magnet for Atlantic Ocean divers. If it's underwater and off Nantucket shoals, this full-service dive shop has the market cornered with charters, lessons, rentals, and even fishing referrals.

SEAL CRUISES

❋ **Shearwater Excursions** (508-228-7037) has daily departures, weather permitting, to see lounging seals on the outer island of Muskeget. See also Harbor Cruises *Anna W. II*, under *Boat Excursions/Rentals*.

TENNIS

Free, public courts are located at **Jetties Beach** (see *Green Space— Beaches*). Sign up at the Parks and Recreation Building (508-325-5334; 508-228-7213), North Beach Street, for one of six courts. Clinics and lessons are offered for adults and children.

Brant Point Racquet Club (508-228-3700), 48 North Beach Street. Open May to mid-October. A full-service place, with nine clay courts, a pro shop, round-robins (in summer), and rentals.

Tristram's Landing Tennis Center (508-228-4588), 440 Arkansas Avenue, Madaket.

WHALE-WATCHING

Nantucket Whalewatch (978-283-0313; 1-800-322-0013), Straight Wharf at the Hy-Line dock. Daylong trips depart Tuesday and Friday at 9:30, mid-July to early September. The on-board naturalist simultaneously conducts ongoing whale research. $85 adults, $45 children under 12. Reservations recommended.

WINDSURFING

Indian Summer Sports (508-228-3632), 6 Steamboat Wharf, rents surfboards June through August and skateboards for a bit longer season. **Force 5 Watersports** (508-228-0700), 6 Union Street, a retail surf shop with a knowledgeable staff, is a good source of information, too. Surfing is best on the southern beaches. It's open April to late December.

EVEN MORE THINGS TO SEE AND DO

DAY SPA

❋ **Tresses & The Day Spa** (508-228-0024), 117 Pleasant Street. Choose à la carte treatments—facials and skin therapies, mud or seaweed masks, salt glows, herbal body wraps, and a variety of massages—or packages with mud treatment and aromatherapy. Prices are lower off-season.

FITNESS CLUB

❊ **Nantucket Health Club** (508-228-4750), 10 Young's Way. Open daily. A full array of machines, free weights, and classes, in addition to baby-sitting services and personalized training sessions. $20 day-use fee; $125 for 10 visits.

FOR FAMILIES

Strong Wings Summer Camp (508-228-1769), late June to late August. This weekly action-filled day camp for kids age 5–15 has 3-day and 5-day weekly options that might include sea kayaking, fort building, stunt-kite flying, canoeing, ghost stories, crafts, and nature exploration—depending on the age.

❊ **Nantucket Babysitters Service** (508-228-4970), begun in the mid-1980s, provides parents a respite from the responsibilities of toddlers and youngsters. Ronnie Sullivan-Moran assesses your needs, matches a sitter to your kids (all ages), and then sends the sitter to wherever you're staying. Services are available year-round. She'll also pick-up groceries and provides "lifestyle management" and "new home helper" services.

❊ SPECIAL PROGRAMS

Edouard A. Stackpole Library and Research Center (508-228-1655), 15 Broad Street. At press time the NHA museum was moving its collection of manuscripts, photographs, ships' logs, and other items to the newly renovated Fair Street Research Library (see *To See—Near or Off Upper Main Street*). The center is open only to researchers 10–4 weekdays (plus additional Saturday hours in July and August). $5 per visit.

Nantucket Island School of Design and the Arts (508-228-9248; www.nantucket.net/art/nisda), Wauwinet Road. Founded in 1973, the NISDA presents an extraordinary range of classes and lectures for adults, youths, and kinders, year-round. Summerlong, weeklong, or daylong classes include drawing, design, textile, folk art, floor cloth painting, puppet making, garden tours, yoga, modern dance, clay and sculpture, painting, and photography. Affiliated with the Massachusetts College of Art in Boston, the school offers college graduate and undergraduate summer sessions in a converted dairy barn. Individuals attending classes may rent their studios and one-bedroom cottages on the harbor (see *Lodging—Cottages and Apartments*).

Artist's Association of Nantucket (508-228-0722; 508-325-5251), Gardner Perry Lane. Offering seasonal workshops and classes in a variety of disciplines for adults and children year-round, the association also maintains a fine art library on Gardner Perry Lane and a gallery at 19 Washington Street (see *Selective Shopping—Art Galleries*).

Nantucket Community School (508-228-7257), 10 Surfside Road. Offers adult-education classes and programs and camps for kids.

Lightship Shop (508-228-4164), 20 Miacomet Avenue. Although it takes years to become a pro, Donna Cifranic offers 3-day classes so you can make your own basket (see *Selective Shopping—Special Shops*). Classes

Tuesday through Thursday with a total of 24 hours of instruction for $350. If you want to try making them on your own, you can purchase kits and materials from Peter at the **Lightship Shop Too** (508-228-2267), Pollywog Pond. It's a long walk to the shop; take the South Loop shuttle in summer.

SWIMMING POOL

❄ **Nantucket Community Pool** (508-228-7262), Atlantic and Sparks Avenues. An Olympic-size pool at the Nantucket High School is open daily for swimming; adults $7, children $5 daily; weekly rates also possible. Inquire about swimming lessons, also for a fee.

❄ ## WINERY AND BREWERY

Nantucket Vineyard (508-228-9235), 5 Bartlett Farm Road, about 2½ miles south of town off Hummock Pond Road. Open 11–6 Monday through Saturday, noon–4 Sunday in summer; noon–5 in late spring and early fall. Since vinifera grapes don't grow particularly well on Nantucket, the Vineyard imports other grapes for its wines. Tours and tastings are offered, as are bottles of evocatively named vintages like Nantucket Sleighride and 'Sconset Rose.

Cisco Brewers (508-325-5929), 5 Bartlett Farm Road. Open 10–6 daily except Sunday in summer, Saturday 10–5 the rest of the year. Come for a sample tasting of fresh, traditionally made ales, porters, stouts, and seasonal concoctions like Celebration Libation. Look for the excellent Cisco beer at island restaurants and package stores. It's more satisfying (and cheaper) than most $20 bottles of restaurant wine.

GREEN SPACE

Nantucket is renowned for the amount of open, protected land on the island. In fact, thanks to the efforts of various conservation groups, more than 40 percent of the island is protected from development. Two organizations deserve much of the credit: **Nantucket Conservation Foundation** (508-228-2884; www.nantucketconservation.com), 118 Cliff Road, open 8–4 weekdays; and the **Nantucket Land Bank** (508-228-7240), 22 Broad Street. The Nantucket Conservation Foundation, the country's first land bank, was established in 1963 to manage open land—wetlands, moors, and grasslands. It's a private, nonprofit organization that's supported by membership contributions. Since then, the foundation has purchased or been given more than 8,500 acres on the island. Because the foundation is constantly acquiring land, call for a map of its current properties, published yearly; $5 by mail, $3 in person. The Nantucket Land Bank was created by an act of the state legislature in 1983, granting permission to assess a 2 percent tax for all real estate and land transactions. With the tax receipts, property is purchased and kept as conservation land. In the first 13 years of its existence, the land bank purchased more than 1,600 acres for $45.4 million.

❀ **Maria Mitchell Association** (508-228-9198) leads excellent nature walks around the island (see *To See*) for $10 adults, $5 children.

Coatue–Coskata–Great Point, at the end of Wauwinet Road, accessible only by four-wheel-drive vehicle and by foot. These three adjacent wildlife areas, totaling more than 1,110 acres, are owned by different organizations, but that doesn't matter to visitors. The world's oldest land trust, the Trustees of Reservations, manages part of the land. Ara's Tours and the Trustees of Reservations offer tours of Great Point; see *Getting Around.*

The narrow strip of very soft sand leading to Great Point is about 5 miles long. Note the "haulover," which separates the head of the harbor from the Atlantic Ocean. This stretch of sand is so narrow that fishermen would haul their boats across it instead of going all the way around the tip of Great Point. During severe storms, the ocean breaks through the haulover, effectively creating an island of the refuge. (Sand is eventually redeposited by the currents.) The spit of sand known as Coatue is a series of concave bays that reach all the way to the mouth of Nantucket Harbor. The Nantucket Conservation Foundation owns both Coatue and the haulover.

There's a wealth of things to do in this pristine preserve: birding, surf-casting, shellfishing, sunbathing, picnicking, and walking. Since the riptides are dangerous, especially near the Great Point Lighthouse (see *To See*), swimming is not recommended. For information about four-wheel-drive permits, see *Getting Around.*

Eel Point, off Eel Point Road from the Madaket Bike Path (see *Outdoor Activities—Bicycling/Rentals*), about 6 miles from town. Leave your car or bicycle at the sign that reads 40TH POLE BEACH and walk the last half mile to the beach. There aren't any facilities, just unspoiled nature, good birding, surf-fishing, and a shallow sandbar. Portions of this beach are often closed to protect nesting shorebirds. For in-depth information, pick up a map and self-guided tour from the Maria Mitchell Association (508-228-9198), 4 Vestal Street, or from the Nantucket Conservation Foundation (508-228-2884; www.nantucketconservation.com), 118 Cliff Road, Box 13, Nantucket 02554 ($3 in person, $5 by mail).

Sanford Farm, Ram Pasture, and **the Woods,** off Madaket Road. These 900-plus acres of wetlands, grasslands, and forest are owned and managed by the Nantucket Conservation Foundation and the Nantucket Land Bank. Ram Pasture and the Woods were one of the foundation's first purchases (for $625,000) in 1971. Fourteen years later, Sanford Farm was purchased for $4.4 million from Mrs. Anne Sanford's estate. A 6½-mile (round trip) walking and biking trail goes past Hummock Pond to the ocean, affording great views of heathlands along the way. Interpretive markers identify natural and historic sites. There is also a popular 45-minute (1⅔-mile) loop trail as well as the Barn Trail (1½ hours, 3 miles), which affords beautiful expansive views of the island's southern coastline.

KIM GRANT

Surf-fishing at Great Point

Milestone Bog, off Milestone Road on a dirt road to the north, about 5 miles from town. When cranberries were first harvested here in 1857, there were 330 acres of bogs. Today about two-thirds that many are cultivated by Northland Cranberries, a company that leases the land from the Nantucket Conservation Foundation. (The land was donated to the foundation in 1968.) Berries are shipped off-island for processing, but honey made by bees that pollinate the flowering fruit is sold on-island.

Windswept Cranberry Bog, off Polpis Road to the south. This 40-acre working bog is also part owned by the Nantucket Conservation Foundation. When it's held, the autumnal harvest is a visual feast. First bogs are flooded with water; then a machine shakes and loosens the ripe red berries from the plants. After they float to the top of the water, they're corralled with booms and scooped from the water into waiting trucks. Harvest season generally runs from late September through October, during which time people work in the bogs from dawn to dusk, 7 days a week (see Cranberry Harvest Weekend under *Special Events*). Sadly, the harvest was curtailed in 2000 due to depressed prices and a worldwide glut of berries; it remains to be seen what will happen to the harvest in the future.

BEACHES

Nantucket is ringed by 50 miles of beaches, much of which is publicly accessible. In general, beaches on the south and east have rough surf and undertow; western and northern beaches have warmer, calmer waters. There is limited parking at most beaches; **NRTA** (508-228-7025) provides a special beach bus to Jetties and Surfside Beaches from mid-June to early September, and regular buses to Madaket and 'Sconset beaches.

NORTHERN BEACHES

✐ **Children's Beach,** off South Beach Street on the harbor. A few minutes' walk from Steamboat Wharf, this is a great place for children (hence its name). Amenities include a lifeguard, rest rooms, a bathhouse, a playground, food, picnic tables, game tables, a bandstand, a horseshoe pit, and a grassy play area.

Brant Point, off Easton Street. A 15-minute walk from town, and overlooking the entrance to the harbor, this scenic stretch is great for boatwatching and surf-fishing. A strong current and a beach that drops off suddenly don't create ideal swimming conditions.

✐ **Jetties,** off Bathing Beach Road from North Beach Road. Shuttle buses run to this popular beach—otherwise it's a 20-minute walk. (There is also a fairly large parking lot with lots of bike racks.) A great place for families because of the amenities (rest rooms, lifeguards, showers, changing rooms, snack bar, chairs for rent) and the activities (volleyball, tennis, swings, concerts, a playground, an assortment of sailboats and kayaks). Kids will enjoy the tie-dyeing clinics (508-228-7213) held here noon–1 PM on Friday in July and August. The July 4 fireworks celebration is held here. Also a good beach for walking. Look for the skateboarding park; helmets and pads are required and can be rented at the Parks and Recreation Building tennis office (508-325-5334).

Francis Street Beach, a 5-minute walk from Main Street, at Washington and Francis Streets. This harbor beach is calm. There are kayak rentals, portable rest rooms, and a small playground.

Dionis, off Eel Point Road from the Madaket Bike Path (see *Outdoor Activities—Bicycling/Rentals*). Nantucket's only beach with dunes, Dionis is about 3 miles from town. The beach starts out narrow but becomes more expansive (and less populated) as you walk farther east or west. Amenities include lifeguards and a bathhouse.

SOUTHERN BEACHES

Surfside, off Surfside Road; large parking lot. Three miles from town and accessible by shuttle bus, this wide beach is popular with college students and families with older kids because of its proximity to town and its moderate-to-heavy surf. Rest rooms, lifeguards, showers, and a snack bar. Kite flying, surf-casting, and picnicking are popular.

Nobadeer, east of Surfside, near the airport and about 4 miles from town. There are no facilities at Nobadeer, but there is plenty of surf.

Madaket, at the end of the scenic Madaket Bike Path (see *Outdoor Activities—Bicycling/Rentals*). About 5 miles west of town (served by shuttle bus), Madaket is perhaps the most popular place to watch sunsets. This long beach has heavy surf and strong currents; there are lifeguards and portable rest rooms. Very little parking.

Cisco, off Hummock Pond Road from Milk Street. About 4 miles from town, this long beach is popular with surfers. There are lifeguards, but very little parking.

EASTERN BEACHES

'Sconset (aka Codfish Park), at the end of the 'Sconset Bike Path; turn right at the rotary. About 7 miles from town, accessible by shuttle bus, this narrow, long beach takes a pounding by heavy surf. Lifeguards and a playground. (See Claudette's under *Where to Eat—Light Fare* for informal box lunches.) Seaweed lines the beach when the surf whips up. Very limited parking.

PONDS

Long Pond. Take Madaket Road from town and when you reach the HITHER CREEK sign, turn left onto a dirt road. This 64-acre Nantucket Land Bank property is great for birding. A mile-long path around the pond passes meadows and a cranberry bog.

Miacomet Pond, Miacomet Avenue (which turns into a dirt road), off Surfside Road. This long, narrow, freshwater pond next to the ocean has a sandy shore and is surrounded by grasses and heath. This Nantucket Land Bank property is a pleasant place for a picnic, and the swans and ducks make it more so.

Sesachacha Pond. Take Polpis Road to Quidnet Road. A narrow barrier beach separates the pond and ocean. There is a nice view of the Sankaty Head Lighthouse from here.

WALKS

The Moors and **Altar Rock,** off Polpis Road, to the south, on an unmarked dirt road. When you want to get away from the summertime masses, head to the Moors (preferably at dawn or dusk, when they're most magical). The Moors are crisscrossed with trails and deeply rutted dirt roads. From Altar Rock, the highest island point at 90 feet above sea level, there are expansive views of lowland heath, bogs, and moors. It's stunning in autumn.

Lily Pond Park, North Liberty Street. This 5-acre Nantucket Land Bank property supports lots of wildlife and plant life, but the trail is often muddy. You may find wild blackberries, grapes, or blueberries.

LODGING

Although there are more than 1,200 rooms to rent (not including rental houses), January is not too early to make reservations for July and August. When making reservations, keep in mind that the historic district, while convenient, has its share of foot traffic (and boisterous socializers) late into the evening; houses are also very close together. A 10-minute walk from Straight Wharf will put you in quieter surroundings. Most lodgings require a 2- or 3-night minimum stay in-season; I indicate only minimum-night-stay policies that are extraordinary. Much to my chagrin, many places have higher rates on weekends rather than weekdays and (slightly more understandably) for all special holiday weekends like the Christmas Stroll and the Daffodil Festival (see *Spe-*

cial Events). Lastly, most places are not appropriate for small children. Unless otherwise noted, all lodging is in Nantucket 02554.

RESORTS

Around the island

  � **The Wauwinet** (508-228-0145; 1-800-426-8718; www.wauwinet.com), Wauwinet Road, Nantucket 02584. Open May through October. When privacy and extraordinary service are of utmost concern, the Wauwinet is the place to stay on Nantucket. In fact, for me this Relais & Châteaux property is *the* place to stay in New England. Magnificently restored in 1986 by Newton, Massachusetts, shopping mall developer Stephen Karp, this mid-19th-century hostelry occupies an unparalleled location between oceanside dunes and a beach-rimmed harbor. The 25 guest rooms and five cottages have luxurious bed linens and toiletries, pine armoires, Audubon prints, and soothing and sophisticated decorating touches. **Cottages** have fireplaces and kitchens and can accommodate between two and six guests. Public rooms are awash in chintz, trompe l'oeil, fresh flowers, and bleached woods. Although the inn is 8 miles from town, there's practically no reason to leave the enclave. Facilities include clay tennis courts, a pro shop, boating, mountain bicycles, croquet, a videocassette library (with room-service popcorn), lobstering demonstrations, cranberry bog tours, and four-wheel-drive nature trips out to Great Point. All are included in the room rates. The staff ensure that practically any request is met. Topper's (see *Dining Out*) offers absolutely outstanding dining. Enjoy as much from the breakfast menu as you'd like; it's also included. Mid-June to mid-September $390–900 for rooms, $720–1,400 for cottages (4 nights may be required in July and August). Subtract $120–225 from room rates and $175–200 from cottages off-season.

In town

  ✎ **Cliffside Beach Club** (508-228-0618; 1-800-932-9645; www.cliffsidebeach. com), Jefferson Avenue. Open late May to mid-October. Stylish simplicity, understated elegance, and breezy beachside living are the watchwords here. You can't get a bed closer to the beach than this: Front doors and decks sit right on the beach and a boardwalk over the sand connects the low-slung, weathered-shingle buildings. A private club when it opened in 1924, it has been owned by Robert Currie's family since 1958. The reception area is large and airy, decorated with white wicker furniture, local art, and quilts hanging from the rafters. A continental breakfast is set out here. The 22 contemporary guest rooms (most with ocean views) feature outstanding woodwork, all crafted by islanders. Bathroom renovations during 2000 brought granite vanities and showers. Many rooms have a sofa bed, fine for a young child or two. Five newer suites, with outstanding views of dunes and sunsets, offer the most privacy. There are also a few luxuriously simple three-bedroom **apartments.** The world-class health club is impressive, indeed. Shuffle to the beachside Galley Restaurant (see *Dining Out*) or walk 15 minutes into town. Mid-June to early September $335–535 for rooms and studios, $655–1,310 for suites, apartments, and cottages; off-season $220–395 and $405–990, respectively. Add 5.3 percent service charge.

HOTELS

☙ The Beachside (508-228-2241; 1-800-322-4433; www.thebeachside.com), 30 North Beach Street. Open mid-April to mid-October. Five minutes from Jetties Beach (not beachside as the name implies) and 10 minutes from town, this bilevel motel is distinctly Nantucket—quiet, tasteful, and upscale—with 92 rooms surrounding a heated pool. Newly renovated rooms—some with two double beds, a few connecting—are also freshly decorated with floral wallpapers, fine bedding, and white wicker. Many rooms feature French doors opening onto a small private patio; all have a TV/VCR and air-conditioning. General manager Mary Malavase thankfully runs a professional, tight ship. Mid-June to mid-September $235–275; off-season $125–185 (more for connecting suites). Kids under age 16 free. Continental breakfast included. Shoulder-season air and ferry packages.

White Elephant Hotel (508-228-2500; 1-800-475-2637; www.white elephanthotel.com), Easton Street. Open April through mid-December. After a total renovation in early 2000 that nearly doubled its size with the addition of a new wing, the sedate White Elephant is better than ever. A 10-minute walk from the center of town and on the edge of the harbor, many of the spacious 54 rooms and suites have prime water views framed by shuttered white windows. Most have a balcony or deck; many suites have a fireplace. Decor is a sophisticated blend of leather armchairs and white wicker, of crisp linens and textured, neutral fabrics, of antique prints and contemporary artwork. Bathrooms boast fine toiletries, lots of white tile, and marble counters. Common space includes a handsome library, fitness room, and broad lawns that reach a harborside dock. The harborside Brant Point Grill (see *Eating Out*) is a nice place to lunch. Rates are very expensive and were unavailable at press time.

❄☙ Harbor House (508-228-1500; 1-800-475-2637; www.harborhouse. ack.com), South Beach Street. Under the new ownership of the same folks who run the Wauwinet, this 109-room hotel is a few blocks from the center of town on a quiet lane and consists of traditional Nantucket town houses surrounding a late-19th-century summer hotel. Gas lanterns and brick walkways connect the rooms. Townhouse rooms are spacious and nestled among small gardens or near the heated pool. Open May through October. Rates are expensive and were unavailable at press time.

INNS

In town

Ship's Inn (508-228-0040; www.nantucket.net/lodging/shipsinn), 13 Fair Street. Open May to early December. Beyond the bustle of Main Street, a 10-minute walk from Straight Wharf, the Ship's Inn is a largely un-

KIM GRANT

Stylish harborfront "slounging"

sung and very comfortable choice for lodging as well as fine dining (see *Dining Out*). The three-story 1831 whaling captain's house was completely restored in 1991. Its 10 large guest rooms, named after Capt. Obed Starbuck's ships, all have private bath, refrigerator, telephones with voice mail, and television. Many are bright corner rooms. Like the living room, they're large and airy, sparsely furnished to create a summery feel. Mid-May to mid-October $210 double, $100 single with shared bath; off-season $150 and $50 respectively. Rates include continental breakfast.

Woodbox Inn (508-228-0587; www.woodboxinn.com), 29 Fair Street. Open mid-June through December. Dexter Tutein's atmospheric inn and restaurant (see *Dining Out*) is located in one of the island's oldest houses, which dates to 1709. On a quiet street just beyond the densest concentration of activity and shops, the Woodbox has three rooms and six larger suites (with working fireplaces). All have period antiques and private bath. The two-bedroom suites are a good value at $295, as they can comfortably accommodate four people; they also have a living room. A roll-away cot can be added to the one-bedroom suites ($195) for an additional $10. The renowned breakfasts include wonderful popovers and egg creations. No credit cards. $165–295; 10 percent service charge added.

❄❀**Jared Coffin House** (508-228-2400, 1-800-248-2405; www.jaredcoffin house.com), 29 Broad Street. This brick mansion, topped with a cupola and slate roof, was built in 1845 by a wealthy shipowner for his wife. In fact, it was the island's first three-story house. It was also one of the few buildings to survive the Great Fire of 1846. One year later, after Coffin's wife refused to live here, it was converted to an inn. Guest rooms are located in six adjacent buildings, most with their own common areas. All 60 of the conventional rooms have private bath, telephone, and TV. Rooms outside the main inn are larger, featuring colonial reproduction four-poster canopy beds and in-room refrigerators. (Harrison Grey House rooms are the nicest, although guests are often drawn to the Jared Coffin simply for its history.) A few rooms can accommodate children, but they are reserved quickly. More like a small hotel than an inn, the Jared Coffin employs a concierge and has two restaurants (see Jared's under *Dining Out* and the Tap Room under *Eating Out*). If you're looking for a 1-night reservation, try here. April through October $125–375 ($85–175 single); inquire about a variety of off-season packages; full breakfast included.

BED & BREAKFASTS

In town

Pineapple Inn (508-228-9992; www.pineappleinn.com), 10 Hussey Street. Open late April to late October and Christmas Stroll weekend. The finest B&B on Nantucket, this 1838 whaling captain's house was completely renovated from top to bottom in 1997 by veteran innkeepers Bob and Caroline Taylor. Refined, understated elegance, sincere hospitality, and luscious breakfasts are keys to their early success. Competitors are sure to be nipping at their heels, now that they've set a new in-town industry standard. Historic grace and modern conveniences coexist comfortably here. First-class touches surround you, including white marble bathrooms and custom-made four-poster beds fitted with Ralph Lauren linens and down comforters. There are 12 rooms, all with private bath, air-conditioning, TV, and telephones with voice mail. An extensive three-course breakfast is included (rare on Nantucket), served at one convivial table or on the enclosed back patio, complete with trickling water fountain. I still long for my recent morning meal: strong cappuccino, fruit compote, and a choice of oatmeal or Bircher muesli (organic oats soaked overnight in milk with dried peaches and finished with grated apples and fresh blueberries). Mid-June through September $175–295; off-season $110–195.

Union Street Inn (508-228-9222; 1-800-225-5116; www.union-street-inn.com), 7 Union Street. Open March through December. Innkeepers Ken and Deb Withrow preside over this historic hostelry (circa 1770)—and one of the island's best-run B&Bs—with a sense of understated hospitality. There are a variety of rooms, many with fireplace and all with air-conditioning, television, and private bath. The two-room suite and Captain's Room (with pine-paneled wall and wing chairs in front of the fireplace) are premier, but smaller rooms aren't slighted in any way. After redecorating and renovating in 2000, the 12 rooms are more luxurious than ever, with Frette linens, plush bathrobes, and fluffy duvets. Enjoy a full breakfast (with a hot entrée and meat) on the side patio. The art of providing attentive service remains a strong suit here. June through October $150–325, off-season $80–215.

Corner House (508-228-1530; www.cornerhousenantucket.com), 49 Centre Street. Open early April to mid-December. The Corner House's period restoration is true to its 1723 origins. Refined without being pretentious and comfortable without being casual, this B&B rises to the top of a places-to-stay list. Sandy and John Knox-Johnston, innkeepers since 1981, offer a variety of rooms to suit a variety of budgets. Seventeen rooms and suites, all with private bath and air-conditioning (most with TV), are scattered among three buildings. The main house—with two living rooms, a brick terrace, and an enclosed screened porch where a luscious afternoon tea is served—is filled with period English and American antiques. Even the least expensive rooms on the third floor are charming, with rough plaster walls and exposed beams. There is also a lovely **apartment.** In the off-season, Sandy has begun to offer guests a choice of three evening desserts. It's a very nice way to end your day. Mid-June to mid-September $150–235; off-season about $75–115.

❋ **Anchor Inn** (508-228-0072; www.anchor-inn.net), 66 Centre Street. Open March through mid-December and sometimes through the winter (call first). Adjacent to the Old North Church, from which there is a great view of town, this friendly inn has been innkeeper owned and operated since 1983. Charles and Ann Balas offer 11 guest accommodations in this historic 1806 house, the most spacious of which are corner rooms with a queen canopy bed. All have private bathroom (newly tiled), telephone with voice mail, television, hair dryer, air-conditioning, and comfortable period furnishings. One room has a private porch. The less expensive rooms are snug but inviting, under the eaves in the back of the house. A continental breakfast is served on the enclosed porch or carried to the tranquil side garden. Beach towels and ice packs are available in-season. Mid-June to mid-September $165–195 for rooms; inquire about off-season rates.

❋ **Martin House Inn** (508-228-0678; www.nantucket.net/lodging/martinn), 61 Centre Street. Owner Debbie Wasil presides over this 1803 mariner's house, an elegantly comfortable and relaxed place. The side porch is decked out with white wicker; on cooler days you can curl up in front of the fire or in a window seat in the large living room. Many of the 13 guest rooms (4 with shared baths) have canopy beds, period antiques, fireplaces; all contain a welcoming decanter of sherry. Some bright third-floor singles are tucked under the eaves. A continental buffet breakfast is served at one long table, or you can take a tray table to the porch or your room. Mid-June to mid-September $145–235, $70–80 single, more for the suite; off-season $70–135, $55–65 single.

Centerboard Guest House (508-228-9696; www.nantucket.net/lodging/centerboard), 8 Chester Street. Open April through December. A 10-minute walk from Straight Wharf, Centerboard has a generally light

Victorian sensibility. The six corner rooms are romantic, with feather beds, quilts, robes, luxurious linens, and stripped woodwork. The stunning two-room suite features inlaid floors, dark woodwork, a working fireplace, plum walls, a green marble bathroom, and a pencil-post canopy bed. Two ground-floor rooms are decidedly different. One is reminiscent of a houseboat, with built-in carpentry; it sleeps four. The other has a platform bed suitable for a third person. Modern amenities like a refrigerator, TV/VCR, phone, and private bath haven't been sacrificed, though. Mid-June to mid-October $225 for rooms, $325–395 for the suite; off-season $110 for rooms, $225 for the suite, including an expanded continental breakfast.

Nantucket Landfall (508-228-0500; www.nantucketlandfall.com), 4 Harbor View Way. Open mid-April through October. Overlooking Children's Beach, the Landfall is just a few minutes' walk to downtown, yet far enough to be delightfully quiet. All of longtime innkeepers Gail and David More's eight whitewashed rooms have a breezy summer feel to them, thanks to billowing curtains and colorful quilts. A few have panoramic views of the harbor; one has a screened-in porch with daybed. The nautically inspired living room has a fireplace and library, but you'll probably end up spending most of your time on a front-porch rocker. Inquire about the two-story Snuggery cottage, complete with brick patio, which rents for $2,500 weekly. Mid-June through September $110–210 rooms, $295 suite; off-season $95–160 rooms, $195 suite.

❄❀ **Cliff Lodge** (508-228-9480; www.cliff_lodge.com), 9 Cliff Road. On a little hill in a quiet residential neighborhood, a 10- to 15-minute walk from Straight Wharf, Cliff Lodge is another of the island's beautifully converted sea captains' houses. Dating to 1771, this B&B has 11 English-country-style guest rooms. Glossy, paint-spattered floors and floral wallpapers are offset by white bedding, quilts, and white furniture. Guest rooms have a fresh, light, and airy feel to them. They're also outfitted with telephone, air-conditioning, and TV. Guests have access to a refrigerator, garden patio, wicker-furnished sunporch, and a roof walk with great views. Inquire about the **apartment.** Islander John Bennett and his wife, Debby, purchased the house in 1996. Mid-June through September $155–195 ($110 single) for rooms, $375 for apartment; off-season $90–150, including continental breakfast.

❄ **Nantucket Whaler Guest House** (508-228-6597; 1-800-462-6882; www.nantucketwhaler.com),8 North Water Street. With the exception of a traditional 1850 Greek Revival exterior, nothing about this guest house is conventional. Proprietors Calli Ligelis and Randi Ott have upped the island's already considerable ante with their luxe suites and large studios, each with a private entrance and deck or patio. Furnishings are a blend of country American and English antiques; beds are dressed in linens and down comforters; towels and robes are plush; and the color palettes are soothing. Other amenities include cable TV, VCR, CD player, cordless phone with a private number, refrigerator, microwave, and toaster oven. Mid-June to mid-October $300–375 rooms, $400–575 1- and two-bedroom suites; off season $200–300 and $300–500, respectively.

Lyon Street Inn (508-228-5040), 10 Lyon Street. Open mid-April to early December. Completely rebuilt and renovated in 1986, this B&B has seven romantic and antiques-filled guest rooms (all with private and modernized baths). They are spacious and airy with white walls and light woods. The house is on a quiet street, about a 10-minute walk from Straight Wharf. Although there is little common space, except for the check-in area and a little nook where a continental breakfast is served, guests can relax outside in the front garden. Mid-June to mid-September $190–275; off-season $90–175.

✻❧ **Accommodations et al.** (508-228-9267; 1-800-837-2921; www.robertshouse inn.com). Sara O'Reilly owns a consortium of guest houses—including the **Manor House, Roberts House, Meeting House,** and **Linden House** around Centre Street; the **Periwinkle Guest House and Cottage** at 7 and 9 North Water Street; and a two-bedroom **cottage** on Brant Point. This Is It. Rates, room styles, and furnishings vary; tell them what's important to you and they'll find something that meets your needs, including family suites. The 60 rooms all have phones, TV, and air-conditioning. Among the plethora of options, rooms 10, 11, and 12 at Periwinkle, the first property Sara purchased in 1971, are favorites. They're quaint, with barnboard wainscoting under the eaves. Lots of redecorating was done in 1998, so you might ask about specific units. Early June to late September $175–350 private bath, $125 shared bath; single rates, too. Off-season $60–225 private bath, $50–125 shared bath. Children under 12 free if utilizing existing bedding.

Summer House on Fair Street (508-228-4258; www.thesummerhouse. com), 27 Fair Street. Open late April to early December. Completely renovated by owner and high-powered Boston attorney Danielle DeBenedictis and her husband, Peter Carlson, this 11-room inn combines a nice summery feel with historic touches like wide floorboards and latch doors. Rooms are generally light and breezy, with white walls, hand-painted borders, Laura Ashley fabrics, white eyelet duvets, and English country-pine antiques. Folk art tables line the dining room, where an expanded continental breakfast buffet is laid out, but in good weather guests retreat to the deep lawn and terraced gardens. (At press time, there was talk of a lap pool.) Behind the main inn a garden house has three more private rooms. Guests have access to a 'Sconset shuttle and use of the Summer House pool and beach. Mid-June to mid-September $225–525; off-season $115–400.

Summer House on India Street (508-228-6609; www.thesummerhouse. com), 31 India Street. Open late April to early December. Expanding the Summer House empire, this newly renovated guest house has a much newer feel than its Fair Street counterpart. (During the remodeling, walls were plumbed, for instance, but wide pine floors retained.) The guest rooms are summery, with signature hand-painted borders on the walls, and with modern conveniences like air-conditioning, TV, and telephone. I particularly like Thistle, a large front corner room, and Primrose, under the eaves. The small brick patio boasts a hot tub, and the country-style living room features an overstuffed sectional sofa and woodstove. Expanded continental breakfast included. Guests have access to a 'Sconset shuttle and use of the Summer House pool and beach. Mid-June to mid-September $225–525; off-season $115-400.

❄︎✐ **The Chestnut House** (508-228-0049; www.chestnuthouse.com), 3 Chestnut Street. Not many old-fashioned guest houses remain. This one has been in the Carl family since the early 1980s. Decor is busy and eclectic, with local art taking up almost every inch of wall space. (See Hawthorn House, below, for more about familial contributions to decor.) Two-room suites can sleep four people if they are good friends, or a family with children. Otherwise, for two people, they are nice and roomy. One suite is particularly quiet. There is only one "regular" guest room. All have television, VCR, a small refrigerator, and complimentary sherry. The cottage is more like a suite, with a Murphy bed and separate kitchen. Two additional bathrooms allow for postbeach showering and late departures. The freestanding **cottage** is good for families. Mid-June to mid-October $150 room, $195–235 suites; off-season $85 room, $105–145 suites; includes a breakfast voucher for $8 per person per day valid at three good restaurants; cottage $300 daily for four people.

❄︎ **The Hawthorn House** (508-228-1468; www.hawthorn-house.com), 2 Chestnut Street. A guest house since the mid-1940s, this simple B&B was built in 1849, so the rooms are small. Seven of nine guest rooms are upstairs off a casual common area; two rooms share a bath. Because the B&B is in the historic district, the two ground-floor rooms can be a tad noisy in the evening. Innkeeper Mitchell Carl's family decorated the rooms: His father made the hooked rugs; his wife, Diane, made the needlepoint pillows; and his mother did some of the paintings. Mitchell is responsible for the lovely stained-glass panels. Mid-June to mid-September $145–175; off-season $75–105, including a breakfast voucher for $8 per person per day; valid at three good restaurants.

❀✐ **Nesbitt Inn** (508-228-0156, 508-228-2446), 21 Broad Street. Open mid-March to mid-December. One block from Steamboat Wharf, the Nesbitt Inn exemplifies Nantucket's simpler lodging roots. Built in 1872 as an inn, the house has been in the same family since 1914. The Nesbitt, with in-room sinks and shared showers, is a favorite among Europeans. Ten double and two single rooms (which share only three baths) are Victorian in style; many of the furnishings are original to the house. The living room has a fireplace, games, and TV. Guests can people-watch from the front porch, relax on the back deck, and make use of the outdoor grill, refrigerator, and beach towels. Children are welcome; there's a swing set in the backyard. The inn is located next to the boisterous Brotherhood of Thieves restaurant (see *Eating Out*). Late May to mid-October $85 double, $75 single. Rates include a continental breakfast.

Westmoor Inn (508-228-0877; www.westmoorinn.com), Cliff Road. Open mid-April to early December. About a mile from town, this large yellow 1917 Colonial Revival mansion with a widow's walk was built as a wedding gift for Alice Vanderbilt. It's quiet out here, away from the hustle of town and within a 10-minute walk of a little-used beach. Bikes are complimentary. The spacious living room is decorated with an understated touch, graced with a baby grand piano, game table, and fireplace. (Afternoon wine and cheese are served here.) The 14 guest rooms, each with private bath and telephone, vary greatly in size and view, but all are airy and bright. One king suite has a panoramic view, the other a Jacuzzi. Carpeted third-floor rooms are generally smaller, tucked under the eaves, but they're still summery white. An expanded continental breakfast is served on an indoor flagstone sunporch overlooking a small garden. If you like to be left alone by innkeepers, this is a good choice. Mid-May to mid-October $175–375 rooms; off-season $155–275 rooms.

COTTAGES AND APARTMENTS
In town

❄ **Harbor Cottages** (508-228-4485), 71 Washington Street. These 11 studios and one-bedroom cottages, surrounding a central courtyard and about five blocks from the center of town, are owned by the Nantucket Island School of Design and the Arts (see *Even More Things to See and Do— Special Programs*). On my last visit, they weren't in great shape, but still, lots of artists, writers, and other creative types are drawn here (and have drawn here, for that matter) for the simplicity. The cottages are modest, complete with open rafters, painted floors, and whitewashed walls. The larger one-bedroom units can sleep up to six people snugly; all have complete kitchenette. June through October $750 weekly studio (or $120–145 nightly with 3-night minimum), $850–925 weekly one-bedroom (or $150–185 nightly with 3-night minimum). April, May, November, and December $650 weekly studio ($110–125 nightly), $750–850 weekly one-bedroom ($120–160 nightly). Less in the dead of winter.

Wharf Cottages (508-228-4620; 1-800-475-2637; www.wharfcottages. com), New Whale Street. Open late May to late September. Under the new ownership of the same folks who run the Wauwinet, these 22 snug cottages are fun for a change. Occupying a unique location—jutting out on wharves in the midst of harbor activity—they have private decks, small gardens, water views, fully equipped kitchens, TV/VCRs, and daily maid service. Although the cottages are small, they're efficiently designed and crisply decorated in whites and blues. It can be noisy on the pier, but that's part of the fun of staying here. Open May through October. Rates are very expensive and unavailable at press time.

See also Nantucket Landfall, Corner House, The Chestnut House, Accommodations et al., and Cliff Lodge under *Bed & Breakfasts.*

Around the island

Summer House (508-257-4577; www.thesummerhouse.com), 'Sconset 02564. Open late April to late October. The brochure's photograph is almost too idyllic to believe: Honeysuckle vines and roses cover a shingled cottage with tiny windows; the double Dutch door opens to a white, skylit interior that's cozy and simple. But it's true! Dating to the 1840s, the eight enchanting cottages surround a colorful garden set with Adirondack chairs. The Munchkin-like cottages have been updated with marble Jacuzzi bathtubs, Laura Ashley linens, English-country-pine antiques, and hand-painted borders; some have a fireplace and kitchen. All have off-season heat. Shuffle across the street to the eastern beach or to the inn's pool, nestled in the dunes just below the bluff. (Drinks and lunch are served at the pool.) In addition to a piano bar, the inn (a few minutes' walk from the "center" of 'Sconset) has a restaurant (see *Dining Out*). Early June to mid-September $575–900; off-season $225–525. Continental breakfast included. Add a 10 percent service charge.

✍️♿ **Wade Cottages** (508-257-6308; 212-989-6423 off-season; www.wade cottages.com), 'Sconset 02564. Open late May to mid-October. A portion of this private estate is still used by Wade family members. Its great appeal lies in the fact that there's nothing between the property and the ocean except a broad lawn and an ocean bluff. Parents will appreciate the play area and swings for kids. Four rooms in the main house, where the only common space doubles as a small breakfast room, are quite modestly furnished. The other spare accommodations—a multibedroom suite, six **apartments,** and three **cottages**—are well equipped for the required minimum stays. Ocean views are de rigueur. The best of the cottages (all with large living room) is the newest one closest to the ocean. July and August $600–720 for 3 nights with private bath, $345–410 for 3 nights with shared bath. Apartment and cottage rates drop about half in the off-season.

See also Wauwinet and Cliffside Beach Club under *Resorts.*

RENTAL HOUSES AND COTTAGES

Many islanders are opposed to the residential building boom that began in mid-1990s because the island's infrastructure just can't handle it. One consequence has been the creation of about 2,000 three- and four-bedroom rental houses. According to the Nantucket Association of Real Estate Brokers, the average island home sold for about $1,200,000 in Y2K, but you can bet these owners don't need to rent their houses to ease mortgage payments. The median house price in 1999 was $600,000 and appreciated to $725,000 in Y2K.

Congdon & Coleman (508-325-500; www.congdonandcoleman.com), 57

Main Street. There are hundreds of one- to seven-bedroom houses all over the island. Expect a nice two-bedroom house to rent for an average $2,000 weekly in August. Tell the agents tell them your requirements and they'll fax you a listing sheet with properties that match. **Jordan Associates** (508-228-4449; www.jordanre.com), 8 Federal Street, and **Nantucket Real Estate Co.** (508-228-3131), 17 North Beach Street, offer similar services.

CAMPGROUNDS
Camping is not permitted.

HOSTEL
🐾 **Nantucket Hostel,** of Hostelling International (508-228-0433; www.hi-travel.org), 31 Western Avenue (call 617-531-0459 or enecreservations@juno.com for reservations prior to the opening date). Open mid-April to mid-October. Originally built in 1873 as the island's first lifesaving station, and now on the National Register of Historic Places, the hostel is 3 miles from town on Surfside Beach (see *Green Space—Beaches*) and steps from the NRTA beach shuttle, which operates June through September. Facilities include a kitchen, barbecue and picnic area, and volleyball. Dormitory-style, gender-separated rooms accommodate about 50 people. Reservations are essential in July and August and on all weekends. $15–17 adults for HI members; $18–21 nonmembers; about half price for children under 14.

WHERE TO EAT

Enough Nantucket diners are passionate about food that the island supports one of the densest concentrations of fine dining establishments in the country. And one of the most expensive: $40–50 entrées are becoming more commonplace even as patrons shake their heads in disbelief. Some restaurants offer less expensive, bistro-style fare in addition to their regular menu. Prices aside, many of Nantucket's 60-some restaurants would hold their own in New York or San Francisco, and repeat patrons know it: Some visitors make dinner reservations for an entire stay when they book their lodging. It's rare to be served a "bad meal" in Nantucket, but some restaurants do offer more value (note the symbol for value "🐾" in the margins).

Reservations are highly recommended at the finer establishments; some offer only two seatings. You will be required to reconfirm your reservation on the "day of" or you'll lose it, since many diners make multiple reservations and don't show up.

There are perhaps 10 restaurants (not all are reviewed here) that serve the year-round community. Generally, you may assume places are open daily late June to early September. I have not included shoulder-season hours of operation because they are dependent on weather, number of tourists, and owner's whim. By the way, don't pass up the opportunity to have bay scallops in October. The experience might explain why Nantucketers are so passionate about food.

DINING OUT

Except where noted, reservations are recommended at all *Dining Out* listings.

In town

❊ **Boarding House** (508-228-9622), 12 Federal Street. Open for dinner nightly mid-June to mid-September and Tuesday through Saturday the rest of the year. Chef-owner and executive chef Seth Raynor's innovative and contemporary cuisine stands center stage at one of Nantucket's most consistent and superior restaurants. With brick and plaster arched walls, the main subterranean dining room is cozy. Upstairs, there's a lively **bar** favored by locals and visitors alike; it's a real scene. Hammy, the bartender, mixes a great dry martini and his very own cosmopolitan concoction, dubbed a Hammopolitan. But in good weather, the patio—surrounded by flowers and a white picket fence—is the place you'll want to be. It's common for folks to line up in the summer at 4 PM for one of these seats. An award-winning wine list accompanies signature dishes like grilled lobster tails over mashed potatoes. I'm partial to the rare-grilled yellowfin tuna with wasabi aioli and Thai pesto noodles. There's an extensive appetizer menu. Entrées $24–37.

❧& **American Seasons** (508-228-7111), 80 Centre Street. Open for dinner mid-April to mid-December; closed Wednesday in spring and fall. While inspired by the regional culinary traditions of the four corners of the United States, chef-owner Michael Getter spins decidedly untraditional twists and interpretations. I'm never disappointed here. The ever-changing menu is broken down into: Wild West (perhaps loin of venison with a poblano jam), Pacific Coast (perhaps jumbo sea scallops with Yukon gold potatoes), Down South (perhaps braised lamb shanks with risotto and pecan chutney), and New England (perhaps oven-roasted monkfish with smoked cod whipped potatoes). Absolutely mammoth portions of vertically presented food are balanced with savory and sweet tastes, crunchy and smooth textures. The wine steward is delightful with the award-winning list. If the food weren't so good, I'd suggest simply coming for pastry chef Caren Smallwood's gems: butterscotch crème brûlée (the creamiest I've ever had) and warm banana brioche bread pudding. The candlelit bistro-style dining room features folk art murals and painted tables. Entrées $25–32.

❧ **Ship's Inn Restaurant** (508-228-0040), 13 Fair Street. Open for dinner May through December; closed Tuesday in-season, Tuesday and Wednesday off-season. Longtime chef-owner Mark Gottwald, who graduated from La Varenne in Paris and apprenticed at Le Cirque and Spago, serves California-French cuisine in a romantic, subterranean, bistro-style space. I've always left here very, very satisfied. Many of the dishes are healthful (that is, sans butter or cream) without sacrificing taste or creativity: grilled sea scallops with sorrel risotto, and seared local cod with cider and capers, for instance. The Vidalia onion stuffed with spinach, goat cheese, and Shiitakes was lovely and delicate. Otherwise, there's the signature medallions of lobster with leeks and sauterne. The wine list wins deserved awards. In fall, save room for a cranberry cobbler. Entrées $21–33. In the off-season, the lighter **Dory Bar Grill** menu runs $11–17.

The Pearl (508-228-9701), 12 Federal Street. Open for dinner May through December. Executive chef Seth Raynor (see Boarding House, above) has come up with another winning formula. New in 1999, the Pearl offers coastal cuisine with an Asian flair. The atmosphere and cuisine are sophisticated, relaxing, and dramatic. (Note the onyx **bar,** huge fish tanks filled with brilliant fish and coral, pearl-shaped ceiling, and pale blue lighting. You might just want to get a drink and eat at the bar.) The menu changes all the time, but you can count on creatively prepared and fragrant native seafood and local fish. I particularly enjoyed the sauté of the day: day-boat sea scallops with Thai red coconut curry and noodles. Patrons are particularly fond of tuna martinis (nonalcoholic) and "oyster shooters": six shucked oysters served in crystal-footed shot glasses, served with "three treasures"—sides of basil tomato, ginger, and wasabi. Don't pass up their signature dessert: a decadent flourless chocolate torte with hazelnut inside and caramel sauce. (It's almost like a giant truffle.) Reservations definitely recommended. Entrées $30–45.

❀ **Oran Mor** (508-228-8655), 2 South Beach Street. Open for dinner and Sunday brunch mid-September to mid-May. Chef Peter Wallace, formerly of Topper's fame (see below), has an intimate restaurant inconspicuously located over an antiques shop near the waterfront. Once you find it, you'll come back. Peter's execution never falls short of perfection, whether he's preparing buffalo, elk, scallops, or foie gras. The lobster risotto, a transcendent signature dish, can always be requested even if it's not on the menu. You'd be a fool to bypass it; I almost did, and that's why I'm warning you. The eclectic New American menu ranges from roasted rack and grilled leg of lamb to grilled beef with potato rosti and a chanterelle demiglaze. Specials are always tempting. Entrées $22–32.

🎀 **Le Languedoc Restaurant** (508-228-2552), 24 Broad Street. Open for dinner in summer; lunch and dinner mid-May to mid-December. If you find some Nantucket restaurants intimidating, you'll be happy to know of this friendly place. Sophisticated but not overly pricey relative to the quality, longtime chef-owner Neil Grennan's food is very good and very consistent. The wine list is an award winner, too. During one recent meal, we particularly enjoyed a porcini-dusted rack of veal with potato risotto and truffle oil, as well as a pan-roasted lobster with savory corn pudding. Upstairs dining rooms are intimate, country-French style, while downstairs is less formal, more bistrolike; both are popular. (A lighter, less expensive menu is available downstairs.) The garden patio is a delightful option in warm weather. Reservations recommended for upstairs semi-formal dining. Lunch $10–18, dinner entrées $28–38.

The Galley Restaurant (508-228-9641), at the end of Jefferson Avenue. Open for lunch and dinner, late June through September. At the Cliffside Beach Club beyond the center of town, you'll dine literally beachside, taking in the sunset views. No place on-island beats it for atmosphere. But this isn't a sand-in-your-shoes kind of place—it's elegant yet casual, bistro-style, candlelit dining under an awning facing the sound. The "world-influenced" menu features sea scallops with a creamy polenta; horseradish-crusted rack of lamb; pan-roasted halibut with balsamic-infused lentils. The restaurant has been in the Silva family since 1958. Jazz pianist. Dinner entrées $29–34.

21 Federal (508-228-2121), 21 Federal Street. Open mid-April to mid-December (dinner nightly except Sunday off-season). Loyal patrons return for sophisticated New and traditional American cuisine served in an elegant and reserved dining room. Although the menu highlights seafood, you might also crispy duck breast with cranberry wild rice or roast loin of pork with rosemary pear chutney. The menu changes weekly. The dark-paneled bar is convivial; there is also a lighter bistro menu. Entrées $27–37.

Straight Wharf Restaurant (508-228-4499), Harbor Square. Open for dinner June through September. Steve and Kate Cavagnaro took over the helm of this renowned seafood-only restaurant in 1997 and they didn't miss a beat. Well-prepared and elegantly presented New American dishes might include seafood risotto, lobster chowder, and braised halibut with crayfish and morels. Desserts are decidedly rich. In addition to the deck overlooking the harbor and a lofty main dining room with exposed rafters, there is a pleasant and upbeat **bar.** Entrées $30–39.

Company of the Cauldron (508-228-4016), 7 India Street. Open for dinner late May through October and Stroll weekend (see *Special Events*); closed Monday. Peer through ivy-covered, small-paned windows, and you'll see what looks like an intimate dinner party. Sure enough, since the tables are so close together, you'll probably end up talking to your neighbors before the night is over. With low-beamed ceilings and plaster walls illuminated by candlelight and wall sconces, it's a warm and inviting place. Longtime chef-owner Al Kovalencik's New American prix fixe menu changes nightly and is set a week in advance. It might go something like this: fettuccine carbonara with peas and pancetta; a mesclun salad with caramelized shallot vinaigrette; ginger- and herb-crusted rack of lamb with blackberries and pine nut couscous; and a pear almond tart to top it all off. One or two seatings; reservations highly recommended. $48–50 per person.

DeMarco (508-228-1836), 9 India Street. Open for dinner mid-May to mid-October. Light northern Italian haute cuisine is offered in this restored sea captain's home. Downstairs has a taverny feel with a **bar,**

Nantucket's Main Street is paved with cobblestones.

wood beams, brick, and curtains, while upstairs is more airy. Start with
a rich antipasto, followed by pasta with lobster, chanterelles, sugar snap
peas, chives, and cream, or a braised oxtail risotto. Fresh pasta and
grilled seafood are house specialties. Don DeMarco, who has owned
his namesake restaurant since 1979, has amassed an outstanding wine
cellar. Entrées $28–36.

Cioppino's (508-228-4622), 20 Broad Street. Open for lunch and dinner,
mid-May to mid-October. Continental and New American cuisine, like
rack of lamb, osso buco, and grilled lobster tails with shrimp over a bed
of pesto pasta, is featured, and cioppino is an obvious specialty. Susan and
Tracey Root's dining room is lovely and the **bar** cozy, but in good weather
the garden patio is even more tempting. Cioppino's offers a "twilight
dining" special ($24) and boasts a good wine list. Reservations suggested.
Lunches $9–14, dinners $19–32.

West Creek Cafe (508-228-4943), 11 West Creek Road (between Pleasant
and Orange Streets). Open for dinner year-round (closed Tuesday in-
season, Tuesday and Wednesday off-season). A 10-minute bicycle ride
from the center of town, this charming and casual place is a real treat. It's
a small space, decorated with a New American flair that complements
the eclectic menu. There are three distinct dining rooms, one with a
fireplace that draws patrons throughout winter. Pat Tyler, who has been
on-island for years (at the Boarding House and at Second Story), opened
the café in 1995. Try the pan-seared tuna with roasted veggies and sour
cream mashed potatoes. Entrées $18–32.

Ropewalk (508-228-8886), 1 Straight Wharf. Open for lunch and dinner,
mid-May to mid-October. Night or day, try to get an outdoor patio table
at Nantucket's only harborside (yacht-side might be more appropriate)

restaurant. If you can't, though, don't worry; the interior is open to sea breezes. Although the casual ambience might suggest standard seafood fare, the cuisine is really quite innovative and the menu extensive. Rope-walk also has an excellent raw bar and frozen drinks. Light, eclectic lunch choices include focaccia pizzas, sandwiches, and a little bit of everything really. No reservations taken. Lunch $7–15, dinner entrées $18–28.

Club Car (508-228-1101), 1 Main Street. Open for lunch and dinner mid-May to mid-December. This kitchen has put out fabulous Continental cuisine since 1979, and the menu hasn't really changed since then either. The beef Wellington Sunday-evening specials are classic. Feast on roasted California squab, Wisconsin veal, or Maryland softshell crabs. The elegant and somewhat haughty dining room is set with linen and silver; the lighting is subdued. Or have a simple lunch of hearty soup and salad in the only remaining club car from the narrow-gauge train that used to run between Steamboat Wharf and 'Sconset. Lighter dishes are served in the **bar**/club car to the accompaniment of a nightly pianist. It tends to draw an older crowd. Entrées $30–40.

Woodbox Inn Restaurant (508-228-0587), 29 Fair Street. Open for breakfast, Sunday brunch, and dinner, May through December; closed Monday. Off the beaten path, this 1709 house has three intimate, romantic, and candlelit dining rooms with low ceilings, dark wainscoting and paneling, and wide floorboards. (The rear dining room was used as a colonial kitchen.) Old-fashioned, classical Continental cuisine like beef Wellington and rack of lamb are specialties. Popovers, which accompany all entrées, are classic. If you can't get one of the two dinner seatings, come for an outstanding breakfast in order to enjoy the authentic atmosphere. Wine-tasting dinners off-season. Breakfast and brunch $10–12; dinner entrées $19–32. No credit cards.

India House Restaurant (508-228-9043), 37 India Street. Open for dinner and Sunday brunch July to early September. On the second tier of restaurants, signature dishes here include a pecan-crusted swordfish and roasted rack of lamb with port wine demiglaze. But the eclectic New American and Continental menu feature dishes as varied as lobster-artichoke crêpes, Danish-style bouillabaisse, and a 12-spice salmon sashimi. Dine in one of the three romantic colonial rooms with fireplaces and candlelight, or in the garden café. A la carte brunch is very popular, but reservations are not taken for it. Entrées $19–36.

❊ **Jared's** (508-228-2400), 29 Broad Street at Centre Street. Open for breakfast and dinner May through October; breakfast November through April on weekends. Perhaps Nantucket's most conservative dining room, Jared's features maritime oil paintings, heavy silver table settings, and linen cloths. The all-you-can-eat seafood buffet ($27) is a bargain on Wednesday and Sunday evening from May to mid-October. Otherwise, the traditional American cuisine is occasionally inspired. Entertainment on summer evenings. Breakfast $7–10, dinner entrées $25–35.

See also Centre Street Bistro and Black-Eyed Susans under *Eating Out*.
Around the island

👥♿ **Topper's** (508-228-8768), 120 Wauwinet Road, Wauwinet. Open for lunch,
Sunday brunch, and dinner, May through October. If you're going to
splurge, dinner at Topper's will be the highlight of your trip, worth every
penny. Topper's goes over the top in meeting expectations. The setting
and service are luxurious, indulgent, and sophisticated, yet relaxed.
Regional New American cuisine is matched by outstanding pairings from
a French and California wine list. (Topper's consistently wins the just-
about-impossible-to-win *Wine Spectator* Grand Award. And as I said in
National Geographic Traveler, "Their wine pairing is unrivaled on the
Eastern seaboard.") My most recent food experience included a sublime
tuna tartare; signature lobster and crabcakes; a salad with hydroponic
"micro greens" FedExed from Pennsylvania; and a dramatically presented Nantucket lobster navarin in a light cream sauce (another
signature). Topper's also dishes out a lot of caviar and foie gras. Try hard
to save room for rich desserts, perfect with an after-dinner cordial. A bar
menu offers lighter fare, while the lunch concept is decidedly different:
Choose three, four, or five selections to create your own sampler plate.
Lunch is also served on the bayside porch, a lovely spot for a sunset drink,
too. Topper's offers complimentary van service from town, as well as
transportation aboard the *Wauwinet Lady*, which takes guests from
Straight Wharf to the restaurant's private dock in-season. Jacket requested at dinner. Kudos to chef Christopher Freeman and the whole
staff. Brunch $38, lunch $21–28; dinner entrées $34–56.

The Chanticleer (508-257-6231), 9 New Street, 'Sconset. Open for lunch
and dinner, mid-May to mid-October; closed Monday. The Chanticleer
has won endless accolades since it opened in 1970: Nantucket's premier dining spot; one of the world's top 10 romantic places to dine; one
of the finest wine lists in the world, with more than 40,000 bottles in the
cellar. Chef-owner Jean-Charles Berruet's exquisite classical French
cuisine is served in the courtyard of a rose-covered cottage, in small
dining rooms overlooking the courtyard through small-paned windows,
or in the more formal main dining room with low ceilings. Highlighting
local fish, local produce, and game birds, a meal might go something
like this: an assortment of smoked fish with a horseradish mousse, followed by sautéed Tuckernut lobster and Nantucket bay scallops served
with summer truffles and Madeira wine sauce, garnished with a risotto.
Dessert is equally sublime: fresh figs and raspberries poached in a sweet
white wine with spices and herbs, served with a raspberry sauce. Dining here will live on in your memory for years. Reservations and jacket
required. Lunch entrées $20–25; prix fixe dinner $70 ($25–35 à la
carte).

'Sconset Cafe (508-257-4008), Post Office Square at Main Street, 'Sconset.
Open for all three meals mid-May to mid-October. This tiny place is

known for its blue cheese and bacon burger as well as chowder with herbs, but they also have creative salads and sandwiches at lunch. Chef-owner Rolf Nelson's dinners really shine and tend toward sophisticated New American dishes. The menu changes constantly. Chocolate Volcano Cake is a dessert specialty. No credit cards; BYOB. Reservations accepted for 6 PM seating only. Lunch $8–14; dinner entrées $20–28.

Summer House (508-257-9976), 17 Ocean Boulevard, 'Sconset. Open for lunch June to early September; dinner mid-April to mid-October. Ocean- and poolside light lunches of grilled fish, salads, and sandwiches here are the epitome of a Nantucket summer. Across the street, the dining room is inconsistent, but ask around and see what it's like this year. Just so you know, it's romantic and summery with white wicker, painted furniture, and paintings depicting idyllic Nantucket scenes. The menu is eclectic, ranging from New Zealand lamb to a marinated boneless breast of chicken. Gershwin and Porter melodies waft through the **bar** (where you can get a light menu) and lounge. Lunch $11–25, dinner entrées $32–52 (for a veal chop).

EATING OUT

In town

🌿❆ **Centre Street Bistro** (508-228-8470), 29 Centre Street. Open for brunch on weekends, lunch on weekdays, and dinner nightly. Chef-owners Ruth and Tim Pitts, who have been cooking on-island since 1990, serve exceedingly good food at even better prices. The ever-evolving menu might include a warm goat cheese tart with seasonal accompaniments, or seared salmon with crispy wontons and citrusy soy sauce. Start your day with their "Nantucket Breakfast"—scrambled eggs, bacon, potato pancake, and blueberry pancake. (All dishes are served with potato pancakes rather than the standard homefries.) There are only a couple of dozen seats (and a small **bar**) within this Mediterranean-style space, but that's fine, as people enjoy the front sidewalk patio and the very private back patio. (You must pass through the kitchen to get there, which lends a private-dinner-party feel.) No credit cards. Limited wine and beer list. Brunch and lunch $4–9, dinner $15–22.

Black-Eyed Susans (508-325-0300), 10 India Street. Open mid-April to mid-October. This small, pine-paneled place is part bistro, part diner. The downscale decor belies the stylishly presented plates. The menu changes frequently, but look for dishes like North African spiced chicken with seasonal veggies. Breakfasts run the gamut from bagels and grits to Pennsylvania Dutch pancakes and a veggie scramble with pesto (made with eggs or tofu). Breakfast averages $9, dinner entrées $18–26. No credit cards.

❆🌙 **Espresso Cafe** (508-228-6930), 40 Main Street. Open 7:30–4:30 daily, year-round, until 10 PM in summer. This bustling European-style café with small marble tables is a popular meeting place—everyone ends up here

Storefront restaurants and shops line shady Main Street

sooner or later. Perhaps that's why the staff had such a problem keeping up with things on my repeated visits for this edition. Nonetheless, come early for a bracing morning cappuccino (the best in town) and a breakfast pastry. Come back for black bean chili, clam and corn chowder, hearty sandwiches, and healthy salads. Or come for rich baked goods and desserts any time of day. Linger as long as you like in the large garden patio out back. Takeout, too. Dishes $4–14.

Nantucket Tapas (508-228-2033), 15 Beach Street. Open for lunch and dinner. The concept for Tapas is an old one, but new for Nantucket. Instead of settling for one $25 or $35 entrée at those other restaurants, come here for a selection of small international appetizers that are big on flavor and variety. It's serious food: seared salmon over eggplant, tempura fried calamari, crab- and corncakes, lobster ravioli, Szechuan fried shrimp, sushi, baked goat cheese, and other veggie dishes. Dishes arrive quickly, so order only a few at a time. It's fun for a group of people, or as a way to introduce kids to new tastes, but six plates between two people is fine, too. (Or just come for a Cisco beer and an appetizer.) The simple but stylish storefront-style eatery has both communal and individual tables. Skip dessert. Dishes $6–15.

Sushi by Yoshi (508-228-1801), 2 East Chestnut Street. Open for lunch and dinner daily, mid-April to mid-December. It's the real stuff. When you tire of eating fancy "gourmet" preparations for $25 an entrée, head straight to this small place, which offers fresh sushi and sashimi, "Aloha" rolls using yellowtail tuna from Japan, "dynamite" rolls, noodle dishes, and miso soup. For dessert, don't miss the banana tempura or green tea ice cream. Yoshi won a prize recently for pairing sushi with cranberries; see if this dish is on the menu. Pure and simple. They do a brisk take-out business. Offerings $5–20.

Brotherhood of Thieves (no phone), 23 Broad Street. Open for lunch and dinner. The 1840s former whaling tavern feels like an English pub; it's dark, with brick walls, beamed ceilings, and few windows. It's a convivial place—helped along by an extensive coffee and drinks menu—frequented by locals who chow down on chowder, burgers, cheddar cheese soup, shoestring fries (long and curly), and thick sandwiches. Open until late at night, there is live folk music most evenings in-season; otherwise the music is limited to weekends. Expect a long line in summer. Children's menu. No credit cards. Dishes $9–15.

Arno's 41 Main (508-228-7001), 41 Main Street. Open for breakfast, lunch, Sunday brunch, and dinner, April to mid-December. This two-story storefront eatery is atmospheric, with hurricane lamps on the tables, high ceilings, and large canvas artwork on brick walls. Although it's been around since the early 1960s, Arno's has gained a following recently. Bountiful breakfasts feature frittatas, "bananza" pancakes, and eggs Benedict. Moderately priced lunch fare includes sandwiches, Thai peanut noodles, salads, and a few vegetarian dishes. Dinner is a bit pricier, with specialties including lobster bisque, crabcakes, and scampi Florentine. Large portions of pasta. Children's menu; takeout. Breakfast $7–11, lunch $8–13, dinner $16–23.

Cambridge Street Victuals (508-228-7109), 12 Cambridge Street. Open for dinner, April to mid-December. This jumping place of 20- and 30-somethings, wearing black head to toe, is a dark, barlike joint with a good selection of microbrews and appetizers. But don't be fooled: They serve worthy food, too. Though it's particularly known for monster portions of Dixie-style barbecue, you can also get thin-crust grilled pizzas, schwarma (flame-roasted lamb) sandwiches, burgers, and Tandoori-style chicken. Dishes $9–24.

Brant Point Grill (508-325-1320), at the White Elephant Hotel, Easton Street. Open mid-May to late October. I didn't have a chance to eat here for this edition, but after seeing the harborside terrace, I can think of no more pleasant places to have an alfresco luncheon. Look for grilled chicken sandwiches or a BLT with fish. The handsome grill specializes in steamed and stuffed lobsters and thick, juicy steaks, nothing too fussy or overdone. Raw bar. Lunch $9–15, dinner entrées $24–38.

Tap Room (508-228-2400), 29 Broad Street at Centre Street, in the cellar of the Jared Coffin House (see *Inns*). Open for lunch and dinner. This casual gathering spot has a cozy, publike atmosphere with dark paneling and beamed ceilings. It's best enjoyed at night or with a group of people, as many tables are close together. (The sunny garden patio ringed with flower boxes is lovely in warm weather.) The Tap Room serves traditional New England fare like excellent chowder, burgers, fish-and-chips, lobster rolls, and prime rib. Two surprisingly good specialties are Welsh rarebit and Pride of New England (codcakes and brown bread with molasses baked beans). You can also do some between-meal grazing on freshly shucked oysters or scallops wrapped in bacon. Desserts like mixed berry crisp are very sweet, Key lime pie very tart. Children's menu. Lunch $6–13; dinner $14–20.

❄️✒️ **Atlantic Cafe** (508-228-0570), 15 South Water Street. Open for lunch and dinner. The AC's lively front section is a happening place if you don't mind smoke and the boisterous pitch from the **bar** as the evening progresses. Earlier in the day, though, families enjoy the low-key atmosphere, large portions of pub grub, and good prices. The curly and crispy fries are good, as is the flavorful clam chowder (many say the island's best). Otherwise, stick to burgers, sandwiches, and salads. Lots of grazing dishes like onion rings, zucchini sticks, nachos, and wings. Children's menu $6. Dishes $7–22.

✒️ **Rose & Crown** (508-228-2595), 23 South Water Street. Open for lunch and dinner, mid-April to mid-December. This hopping place with live entertainment serves American fare—sandwiches, pastas, chicken wings, steak, and seafood—in a traditional pub atmosphere. Formerly a carriage livery, the large, barnlike room is decorated with signs from old Nantucket businesses. Early specials (during summer and fall only), children's menu, and kids can draw on the paper-covered tabletops, too. Lunch $6–12, dinner entrées $10–20.

✒️ **Vincent's Restaurant** (508-228-0189), 21 South Water Street. Open for all three meals, mid-April to late October. This casual, moderately priced place is a great choice for families, with plain and fancy pasta dishes, grilled seafood, and take-out pizza. An upstairs lounge; in-season entertainment; children's menu; early dinners; takeout. Breakfast $5–8; lunch specials $7–12; dinner entrées $8–19.

✒️ **Nantucket Lobster Trap** (508-228-4041), 23 Washington Street. Open for dinner May to mid-October. If you've got a hankering for lobster, plain and simple, head to this casual eatery with barnboard walls and booths. (I only recommend the lobster here.) Children's menu; large patio and outdoor bar; delivery and takeout.

✒️♿ **The Tavern** (508-228-1266), Straight Wharf at Harbor Square. Open for lunch and dinner until late at night, mid-May to mid-October. On the edge of the marina, the outdoor tables are well positioned for people-watching, and the American food is above average. If you want a Caesar salad, chowder, a plate of fried calamari, or a drink before hopping on the ferry, this place fits the bill, too. Children's menu. Lunch $8–12, dinner $8–21.

❄️✒️ **Sea Grille** (508-325-5700), 45 Sparks Avenue. Open for lunch and dinner. Located on the edge of town with plenty of parking, this attractive restaurant is often overlooked by nonlocals. Every kind of seafood and fish is prepared practically every way: as bouillabaisse (a specialty), grilled, blackened, steamed, fried, and raw (there's an extensive raw bar). Light meals at the **bar** are a good alternative. Children's menu. Lunch $8–16, dinner $18–29.

Around the island

✿❀🏄♿**Hutch's** (508-228-5550), Nantucket Memorial Airport. Open 6 AM–8 or 9 PM daily. Remember the television show *Wings*, which featured a tiny Nantucket airport restaurant? This is it. The Jamaican line cooks return every spring to prepare simple dishes, and the waitresses hustle like nowhere else. (Wednesday nights are reserved for killer Jamaican specials—it's a real islander thing.) Regularly scheduled dishes include fish-and-chips, meat loaf, chicken fingers, fried scallops, hot turkey sandwiches, seafood omelets. Counter, table, and take-out service; children's menu. The way Hutch figures it, patrons must pass every other restaurant in town to get here, so it has to be good. About 80 percent of his business is local. Children's menu. Breakfast and lunch $2–8; dinner dishes run $6–14.

LIGHT FARE

In town

Provisions (508-228-3258), Straight Wharf at Harbor Square. Open mid-April to early November (8–5:30 in summer, 9–3 in spring and fall). Even in the height of summer, when this place is cranking, they make excellent sandwiches (including one with mildly smoked turkey, stuffing, and cranberries), hearty chowders and soups, and pizza. Sandwiches can often feed two people at this island institution, open since 1978. Hot and cold vegetarian dishes, too.

♿ **Something Natural** (508-228-0504), 50 Cliff Road. Open for breakfast, lunch, early take-out sandwiches for dinner, mid-May to mid-October. Just a short ride from the center as you head toward Madaket, stop here for perhaps the island's best breads and sandwiches (big enough for two to share), as well as salads and bagels. Take-out window and picnic tables. Look for their downtown location at 6 Oak Street (508-228-6616).

🏄 **"The Street."** The first block of Steamboat Wharf is lined with fast-food shops appreciated by families. Take-out eateries are generally open May to mid-October. You'll find a grill with chicken tenders (skip the burritos), burgers, pizza, and the like.

❀🏄♿**Foood for Here and There** (508-228-4291), 149 Lower Orange Street. Open for lunch and dinner (and breakfast in the summer). This fast-food pizza joint on the way to 'Sconset and Surfside Beach offers thin- and thick-crust specialty pizzas (whole and by the slice), calzones, burgers, subs made with Portuguese rolls or pita, and soft-serve ice cream in-season. Video games for the kids. Delivery after 5 PM. As the name implies, eat in or take out.

❀🏄♿**Downy Flake** (508-228-4533), 18 Sparks Avenue. Open 5:30 AM–2 PM. Although the Downy Flake had to relocate twice over a recent five-year period, its loyal clientele followed. Order the justifiably famous doughnuts and pancakes (but not on the same morning, please). Light lunches, too; $3–8.

Nantucket Bake Shop (508-228-2797), 79 Orange Street. Open daily except Sunday, April through November. Its advertisement claims more than 100 different items baked daily, including Portuguese breads, desserts, muffins, croissants, quiches, cakes, and pastries. You can take Jay and Magee Detmer's word for it; they've been baking the goodies since 1976.

The Juice Bar (508-228-5799), 12 Broad Street, one block from the Steamship. Open mid-April to mid-October. Once you find this place, you'll probably stop in a few times before catching your ferry home. Yes, they offer fresh juices like carrot, lemonade, and orange, but they also make their own low-fat ice cream and nonfat yogurts, and breakfast baked goods. In fact, they make everything from scratch.

The Juice Guys (508-228-4464), 4 Easy Street. Open late May to mid-October. A juice bar with fruit smoothies, and carrot and orange juice. In the off-season, look for warming teas and a hot cranberry-ginger concoction. Brought to you by the guys who created Nantucket Nectars.

✳❀ **The Soda Fountain at the Nantucket Pharmacy** (508-228-0180), 45 Main Street. This old-fashioned drugstore soda fountain, complete with swivel stools at Formica counters, offers egg creams, milk shakes, inexpensive soups, hot and cold sandwiches, New York City–style hot dogs, and lobster rolls.

Congdon's Pharmacy (508-228-0020) is similar and right next door—decide for yourself which is better.

See also Espresso Cafe under *Eating Out*.

Around the island

Claudette's (508-257-6622), Post Office Square at Main Street, 'Sconset. Open daily, mid-May to mid-October. Known primarily for catering (in fact, perhaps the best catered clambakes on Nantucket), this tiny shop's raisons d'être are box lunches, clambakes-to-go, and lemon cake. There are a few indoor tables, but most people take their sandwiches to the beach or their ice cream to a bistro table on the front deck.

ENTERTAINMENT

The **Nantucket Arts Alliance** sponsors events across a spectrum of artistic media. The weekly *Nantucket Map & Legend* (www.mapandlegend. com), which bills itself as an events and arts paper, has complete listings, but the island's other free weekly, *Yesterday's Island* (www. yesterdaysisland.com), is also useful. The venerable *Inquirer and Mirror* (published on Thursdays since 1821) also has current listings.

MUSIC

❀ **Band concerts** (508-228-7213) are held at the Children's Beach bandstand (off South Beach Street) Thursday and Sunday 6–7:30 PM in July and August.

Noonday concerts (508-228-5466), 11 Orange Street at the Unitarian Universalist Church (see *To See*), are held Thursday in July and August. Concerts feature ensembles, soloists, and an 1831 Goodrich pipe organ. Donations.

Nantucket Musical Arts Society (508-228-1287), 62 Centre Street at the First Congregational Church (see *To See*), sponsors concerts with world-renowned musicians on most Tuesday evenings 7–8 from July through September. On the night before the concert, there is a meet-the-artist event hosted at the Unitarian Universalist Church, 11 Orange Street. Ticket prices vary.

THEATER/SLIDE SHOW

❄ **Actors Theatre of Nantucket** (508-228-6325), Centre and Main Streets at the Methodist church, has staged evening and family matinees, comedies, plays, drama, and dance concerts since 1985.

❄ **Theatre Workshop of Nantucket** (508-228-4305), Bennett Hall, 62 Centre Street. In existence since 1956, this community-based group stages a variety of plays and musicals.

Nantucket Filmworks/Messages from a Small Island (508-228-3783), Centre and Main Streets at the Methodist church. Cary Hazlegrove, who divides her time between Texas and Nantucket, produces an annual slide show with images culled from her extensive collection. The program is shown Monday through Saturday at 6:30 and 7:30 PM mid-June through mid-September. Adults $5, children 12 and under $3.

☂ MOVIES/FILMS

❄ **Dreamland Theatre** (508-228-5356), 19 South Water Street, which shows seasonal first-run movies, looks from the outside like an old warehouse. This building began as a Quaker meetinghouse, was converted to the Atlantic Straw Company, and was moved to Brant Point to serve as part of a hotel before it was floated back across the harbor in 1905 on a barge.

❄ **Gaslight Theatre** (508-228-4435), 1 North Union Street, shows art films and is connected with the **White Dog Cafe,** where you can have a drink before or after the program.

Siasconset Casino (508-257-6661), New Street, 'Sconset, shows first-run movies in July and August. Tickets $5 per person.

See also Nantucket Film Festival, under *Special Events.*

NIGHTLIFE

See Summer House (live piano in 'Sconset) under *Dining Out;* see Brotherhood of Thieves (live folk), Tap Room (live piano or guitar), and Rose & Crown (dancing or live bands) under *Eating Out.*

SELECTIVE SHOPPING

❄ The principal shopping district is bordered by Main, Broad, and Centre Streets. Straight Wharf shops cater more to the middlebrow tourist market, while Old South Wharf (see below) is more upscale. About 90

Despite Nantucket's rarified prices, some aspects are down-to-earth.

percent of the shops remain open year-round, although many are open
only on weekends in winter. Look for these free brochures: *Nantucket
Guide to Antique Shops* and the *Guideline to Buying a Nantucket
Lightship Basket. Nantucket Arts,* a glossy annual with paid advertisements found in galleries, is useful for its profiles of artists, artisans, and
craftspeople.

ANTIQUES

Currently Nantucket has more than 25 antiques shops. In July and August,
three large annual antiques shows benefit the Nantucket Historical Association and the Nantucket schools.

Rafael Osona (508-228-3942), 21 Washington Street at the American Legion Hall, holds estate auctions on selected weekends from late May to
early December. Osona auctions 18th-, 19th-, and 20th-century antiques from England, the Continent, and the United States. Call for
exact dates.

Tonkin of Nantucket (508-228-9697), 33 Main Street. Purveyors of English and French antiques (both country and formal), brass and silver
items, militaria, and marine objects.

Weeds (508-228-5200), 14 Centre Street. Featuring 19th-century English
country home and garden furnishings, Weeds is also an exclusive dealer
in Wedgwood "Nantucket" fine bone china.

Forager House Collection (508-228-5977), 20 Centre Street. Folk art,
botanical prints, and whirligigs.

Paul La Paglia (508-228-8760), 38 Centre Street. Antique prints of Nantucket, whaling, botanicals, and game fish, as well as La Paglia's own
abstract impressionist oil paintings.

Nina Hellman Antiques (508-228-4677), 48 Centre Street. Nautical items, folk art, Nantucket memorabilia, and work by scrimshander Charles A. Manghis, who gives demonstrations and carves on premises.

J Butler Collection (508-228-8429), 36 Centre Street. Open May to late October. Antiques and reproduction furnishings, collectibles, and dishware in a homey setting.

Antiques Depot (508-228-1287), 14 Easy Street. Open mid-April to mid-December. An interesting collection of furniture and fine decorative arts.

Manor House Antiques Co-operative (508-228-4335), 31½ Centre Street. Open seasonally. This basement-level shop carries porcelain, tea services, glassware, crystal, sterling, and lamps. It's the island's only multidealer shop.

Salt Meadows Antiques (508-228-0230), 78 Union Street. Located on the edge of town in the so-called **Cavendish** neighborhood, this treasure trove of antiques, folk art, and crafts carries a particularly fascinating collection of copper weather vanes. They also specialize in reconditioning 100- and 150-year old trunks.

ART GALLERIES

Sailor's Valentine Gallery (508-228-2011), Lower Main Street at the Thomas Macy Warehouse (see *To See*). Open mid-April to mid-December. My favorite gallery. Eclectic contemporary art and international folk art and, as the name suggests, beautiful valentines made by sailors. Don't miss the sculpture garden out back.

Artist's Association of Nantucket Gallery (508-228-0294; www.nantucketarts.org), 19 Washington Street. This cooperative of 125 artists was founded in 1945 to showcase members' work. Changing AAN member exhibits, juried shows, demonstrations, and special events conspire to make this a vital venue for the local arts scene.

Old South Wharf. Lined with small galleries, clothing stores, artisans, and a marine chandlery, Old South is located in the boat basin just beyond the A&P parking lot. Generally open mid-May to mid-October. Of particular note: **Whitlock Gallery** (No. 13), with sculpture and hand carving by Chad Whitlock; the **Scrimshander Gallery** (No. 19), where you can watch the artist render contemporary scrimshaw and marine art; **Hostetler Sculpture Gallery** (No. 2), with innovative sculpture depicting the artist's quest to understand the nature of woman; and **South Wharf Gallery** (No. 20 and No. 21), showcasing the work of contemporary and traditional painters, photographers, and water-colorists.

(X) Gallery (508-325-4858), 12 Orange Street. Open mid-May to mid-October and by appointment. Displays unusual and imaginative art.

Hoorn-Ashby Gallery (508-228-9557), 10 Federal Street. Open seasonally. Contemporary still lifes and landscapes in oil. Note the prominently posted statement: PLEASE TAKE YOUR CHILDREN BY THE HAND (UNLESS THEY HAVE A VERY LARGE ALLOWANCE).

One-room cottages on Old South Wharf house galleries and shops.

William Welch Gallery (508-228-0687), 14 Easy Street. Open late April to late December. Welch's renderings of idyllic island scenes in watercolors, pastels, and oils.

Art Cabinet (508-325-7202), 2 Union Street. Open May to late October. If you blink as you round the corner of Union and Main Streets, you might miss this little gem of a gallery, so keep your eyes peeled. Owner Dorte Neudert showcases European contemporary artists.

The Artist's House Gallery (508-325-6422), 27 Easy Street. Open seasonally. Frederick Collord's traditional oil paintings of Cape Cod as well as Nantucket town and island scenes; glicee limited editions, too.

Gallery on Centre (508-228-9977), 32 Centre Street. Abstract and modern paintings and sculpture.

Thomas Henry Fine Art (508-228-7679), 19 Centre Street. Open April to early December. Modern marine, seascapes, and landscape paintings at **the Upstairs Gallery**.

BOOKSTORES

Nantucket Bookworks (508-228-4000), 25 Broad Street. A great shop with a helpful staff. Selective travel, literature, children's books, and biographies.

Mitchell's Book Corner (508-228-1080), 54 Main Street. Maritime, whaling, and naturalist books. Sit and browse titles in their small "Nantucket Room," which cover all things Nantucket.

CRAFT SHOPS

Dane Gallery/Nantucket Glass Works (508-228-7779), 28 Centre Street. An outstanding shop, with a dazzling array of glass sculpture by artists like shop owner Robert Dane as well as Richard Newman, Curtiss

Brock, and Richard Royal. You'll also find lighting fixtures and custom-painted and -designed utilitarian glass blocks long favored in hip renovated industrial spaces.

Stephen Swift (508-228-0255), 34 Main Street. Beautifully handcrafted chairs, benches, beds, dressers, and other furnishings.

The Spectrum (508-228-4606), 26 Main Street. Open mid-April through December. Distinctive contemporary objects made from a wide spectrum of materials.

Erica Wilson Needle Works (508-228-9881), 25 Main Street. Featuring namesake designs by Wilson, an islander since 1958. Wilson also has a boutique in Manhattan and has penned many a title on needlepoint.

Nantucket Looms (508-228-1908), 16 Main Street. Features weavers at work on their looms and their creations.

Claire Murray (508-228-1913), 11 South Water Street. Claire Murray came to Nantucket in the late 1970s as an innkeeper and began hooking rugs during the long winter months. She's since given up the B&B business to concentrate on designing and on opening more stores; her staff now make the rugs. She sells finished pieces as well as kits.

Four Winds Craft Guild (508-228-9623), Ray's Courts, of Fair and Main Streets. Baskets, lightship purses, scrimshaw, and marine items.

FARM PRODUCE

Main Street at Federal Street. Local produce is sold from the backs of trucks daily except Sunday, May through October. It doesn't get any fresher than this.

Bartlett's Ocean View Farm & Greenhouse (508-228-9403), off Hummock Pond Road. Bartlett's boasts a 100-acre spread run by an eighth-generation islander family.

Island Herbs (508-228-9450), 2 East York Street. Open May to late October. An organic farm that specializes in fresh herbs and salad greens. Also vegetables, cut flowers, plants, and specialty foods.

SPECIAL SHOPS

Lightship baskets. There are perhaps 20 stores and studios that sell the famed lightship baskets, which retail for hundreds to thousands of dollars and require at least 40 hours of work to produce. Although it is thought that the first baskets were made in the 1820s, they didn't get their name until a bit later. When the first lightship anchored off the Nantucket coast to aid navigation around the treacherous shallow shoals, crew members were stationed on-board for months at a time. In their spare daylight hours sailors created round and oval rattan baskets using lathes and wooden molds. Stiff oak staves were steamed to make them more pliant; the bottoms were wooden. They were made to withstand the test of time. Among the shops that make them and take custom orders: **Michael Kane Lightship Baskets** (508-228-1548), 18A Sparks Avenue; **Bill and Judy Sayle** (508-228-9876), 112 Washington Street Extension; and the **Lightship Shop** (508-228-4164), 20

Miacomet Avenue. (See also Lightship Basket Museum, under *To See—Near or Off Upper Main Street.*)

Best & Co. (508-228-8073), 40 Centre Street. Stop in to see what all the well-heeled toddlers will be wearing next season.

Sweet Inspirations (508-228-5814), 26 Centre Street. Purveyor of Nantucket Clipper Chocolates, displayed in luscious mounds in the glass cases. Of particular note are cranberry-based confections such as cranberry cheesecake truffles and chocolate-covered cranberries.

The Complete Kitchen (508-228-2665), 25 Centre Street. For the recreational cook: glassware, crockery, pots and pans, and gadgets, as well as local and imported cranberry relishes, chutneys, vinegars, pastries, cheeses, and breads.

Beautiful People (508-228-2001), 13 Centre Street. Open April through December. Clothing in styles as diverse as the women who wear them.

The Fragrance Bar (508-325-4740), 5 Centre Street. A treat for the senses, this shop deals in essential oils and perfumes and looks like an old apothecary. Take a seat at the bar and let master perfumer John Harding custom-mix you an original fragrance. Gorgeous handblown glass perfume bottles, too.

L'Ile de France (508-228-3686), 18 Federal Street. Known locally as the French General Store, this charming little shop features the best of France, from crockery to olive oil, from pâté to real French bread. No kidding, owners Joyce and Michel Berruet take orders and fly in fresh-baked loaves from Paris!

Bramhall & Dunn (508-228-4688), 16 Federal Street. Women's clothing, including vests and luxurious, plush scarves, as well as fine objects for the home: quilts and kilims, candlesticks, frames, glass and pottery, and lamps.

Johnstons Cashmere (508-228-5450), 4 Federal Street. Open mid-April to mid-January. Scottish cashmere, with a nice selection of classic women's sweaters, dresses, and scarves.

Pollack's (508-228-9940), 5 South Water Street. Open mid-April through December. The personable proprietor, Bob Pollack, stocks comfortable, fashionable clothing for men and women.

Murray's Toggery Shop (508-228-0437), 62 Main Street. This shop "invented" and practically owns the rights to Nantucket Reds, all-cotton pants that fade to pink after numerous washings—almost as "Nantucket" as lightship baskets. This is the only shop (which, by the way, is featured in *The Preppy Handbook*) that sells the real thing, and has since 1920. They also carry high-end, name-brand sportswear lines.

Peter Beaton Hat Studio (508-228-8456), 16½ Federal Street. Open April through December. Down a little walkway, this fun little shop has finely woven straw hats. Custom fitting and trimming, of course.

Goldsmith Diana Kim England (508-228-3766), 56 Main Street. Elegant and unusual designs and gold lightship baskets.

The Golden Basket (508-228-4344), 44 Main Street. Sells miniature gold versions of the renowned rattan lightship baskets.

The Hub (508-228-3868), at Main and Federal Streets. Get newspapers and magazines here from all over, but more than that, this is a center for island news. Lines form on summer Sunday mornings for the *New York Times.*

The Camera Shop (508-228-0101), 32 Main Street. Film and same-day processing.

Zero Main (508-228-4401), 0 Main Street. A women's store for classic and contemporary clothes and shoes.

David Chase (508-228-4775), 60 Main Street. Open April to mid-December. Elegant yet comfortable women's clothing and accessories.

Vanderbilt Collection (508-325-4454), 18 Federal Street. Open seasonally. An eclectic assemblage of oil paintings, glitzy handbags, sculpture, lightship baskets, and classic custom jewelry. Designer copies.

Hepburn (508-228-1458), 3 Salem Street. Open April through December. A chic boutique with designs for women executed in crushed velvet, satin, silk, and wool.

The Toy Boat (508-228-4552), Straight Wharf. An old-fashioned children's toy store selling a wooden ferryboat and dock system, rocking boats, cradles, handmade toys and puzzles, marbles, and great children's books.

Nantucket Woodcarving (508-325-7010), 110 Orange Street. Open year-round. Once used to identify early sailing ships, "quarterboards" now adorn thousands of island houses. You've seen them: long and narrow carved boards, proclaiming the house's name. The price depends on letter height, number of letters, board length, and whether or not you want 23K gold leaf. A board fitting nicely over a doorway and reading KIM'S HIDEAWAY in $3^{1}/_{2}$-inch painted (not gold leaf) letters, with seashell end posts, would cost about $600.

WREATHS

Nantucket Hydrangea Wreaths (508-228-5608), at the corner of Main and Federal Streets. Islander Joanne Johnson, often aided by her young son Carl, produces lovely wreaths from the back of her pickup truck during summer and well into autumn. When properly displayed and shipped, they are long lasting.

SPECIAL EVENTS

Contact the chamber of commerce (508-228-1700) for specific dates, unless an alternative phone number is listed below. Also, remember that this is just a sampling of the larger, predictable annual events. The Chamber, by the way, produces an excellent *Events Calendar.*

Late April: **Daffodil Festival.** In 1974 an islander donated more than a million daffodil bulbs to be planted along Nantucket's main roads. It is estimated that after years of naturalization, there are now more than 3 million of these beauties. The official kickoff weekend to celebrate spring includes a vintage-car parade to 'Sconset, a tailgate picnic in 'Sconset, house tours, and a garden-club show. This is a very big weekend.

Mid- to late May: **Wine Festival** (508-228-1128). This celebration of wine includes Grand Tastings at the 'Sconset Casino, as well as winery dinners at local restaurants.

Late May: **Figawi Boat Race** (508-771-3333), Memorial Day weekend, from Nantucket to Hyannis since 1972.

Mid-June: **Nantucket Film Festival** (508-325-6274), launched in 1996, has already become an important venue for new independent films. Screenings, Q&A seminars, staged readings, and panel discussions on how screenplays become movies and the art of writing screenplays.

July: **Independence Day** (508-228-7213; 228-0925). Festivities include fireworks from Jetties Beach off Norton Beach Road. Main Street is closed off for pie- and watermelon-eating contests, parades, face painting, fire-hose battles, and more.

Late July/early August: **Billfish Tournament** (508-228-2299), Straight Wharf, a weeklong event since 1969.

Early to mid-August: **House Tour** (508-228-0017), sponsored by the Nantucket Garden Club since 1955. **Sandcastle & Sculpture Day**, on Jetties Beach off Norton Beach Road, since 1974. Pre-registration is required.

Mid-September: **Island Fair** (508-228-7213), at the Tom Nevers Recreation Area, with puppet show, flea market, music, food, pumpkin weighing contest, and more.

Early October: **Nantucket Arts Festival.** This weeklong event, established in 1992, celebrates a variety of island arts, from dance to theater arts, from gallery exhibits to films, from music to literary arts. Highlights include an "organ crawl," with lots of mini recitals, and a "Wet Paint Sale," where artists go out and paint for a day; their works are auctioned that night.

Late November through December: **Nantucket Noel** starts on the day after Thanksgiving with a Christmas-tree-lighting ceremony. Live Christmas trees decorated by island schoolchildren line Main Street; special concerts and theatrical performances heighten the holiday cheer and merriment.

Early December: **Christmas Stroll.** Begun in 1973 and taking place on the first Saturday of December, the Stroll includes vintage-costumed carolers, festive store-window decorations, wreath exhibits, open houses, and a historic house tour. Marking the official "end" of tourist season, like the Daffodil Festival this is a very big event. Make lodging reservations months in advance.

Index

Books from The Countryman Press

EXPLORER'S GUIDES

The alternative to mass-market guides with their homogenized listings, Explorer's Guides focus on independently owned inns, B&Bs, and restaurants, and on family and cultural activities reflecting the character and unique qualities of the area. Explorer's Guides are available for:

Massachusetts: The North Shore, South Coast, Central Massachusetts, and the Berkshires, by Christina Tree & William Davis
Connecticut, by Barnett D. Laschever & Andi Marie Fusco
The Best of the Hudson Valley and Catskill Mountains, by Joanne Michaels & Mary-Margaret Barile
Maine, by Christina Tree & Elizabeth Roundy
New Hampshire, by Christina Tree & Christine Hamm
Rhode Island, by Phyllis Méras & Tom Gannon
Vermont, by Christina Tree & Peter Jennison

A SELECTION OF OUR BOOKS ABOUT CAPE COD, THE ISLANDS, AND THE NORTHEAST

The Architecture of the Shakers
Backroad Bicycling on Cape Cod, Martha's Vineyard, and Nantucket
Backroad Bicycling in Connecticut
Cider, Hard and Sweet: History, Traditions, and Making Your Own
50 Hikes in Massachusetts
In-Line Skate New England
Living with Herbs
King Philip's War: The History and Legacy of America's Forgotten Conflict
The New England Herb Gardener
Paddling Southern New England
Reading the Forested Landscape: A Natural History of New England
Seasoned with Grace: My Generation of Shaker Cooking
The Story of the Shakers
Trout Streams of Southern New England

We offer many more books on hiking, fly-fishing, paddling, travel, nature, and other subjects. Our books are available at bookstores and outdoor stores everywhere. For more information or a free catalog, please call 1-800-245-4151 or write to us at The Countryman Press, P.O. Box 748, Woodstock, VT 05091. You can find us on the Internet at www.countrymanpress.com.